ISBN 978-1-330-21983-6
PIBN 10055913

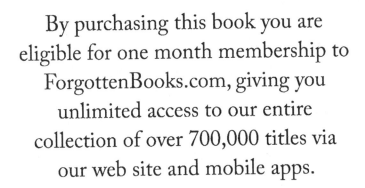

English
Français
Deutsche
Italiano
Español
Português

www.forgottenbooks.com

Mythology Photography **Fiction**
Fishing Christianity **Art** Cooking
Essays Buddhism Freemasonry
Medicine **Biology** Music **Ancient
Egypt** Evolution Carpentry Physics
Dance Geology **Mathematics** Fitness
Shakespeare **Folklore** Yoga Marketing
Confidence Immortality Biographies
Poetry **Psychology** Witchcraft
Electronics Chemistry History **Law**
Accounting **Philosophy** Anthropology
Alchemy Drama Quantum Mechanics
Atheism Sexual Health **Ancient History**
Entrepreneurship Languages Sport
Paleontology Needlework Islam
Metaphysics Investment Archaeology
Parenting Statistics Criminology
Motivational

MASADA—NORTHERN FACE.

The direction of sight is here south-east. A portion of the Dead Sea appears on the left hand, and the distant mountains, therefore, are those of Gebal.

Near to the sharp summit of the hill, as seen in this view, there are traces of what may be regarded as the defences which the desperate company under Eleazar either availed themselves of, or constructed, with the hope of maintaining their position against the Roman legions.

The terrific catastrophe of the Jewish War—or its last awful suicidal slaughter—was transacted, as related by Josephus, upon the summit of a rocky pile, situated on the western shore of the Asphaltic lake. This almost inaccessible height had been rendered, as it was thought, impregnable by Herod: who had not only fortified, but had furnished it also, at a vast cost, as a last retreat for himself, should the turbulence of the Jewish people, or rather his own ferocious treatment of them, drive him, like the hunted tiger, to his lair. Josephus describes this steep with unusual particularity.

This remarkable spot, as thus described and delineated, may now with advantage be thought of as bearing out those statements and those descriptions of Masada which we find in The Jewish War. Confidently it may be affirmed that in few instances where topographical identity is in question, have modern researches better sustained the testimony of an ancient writer than they do in this instance. It is manifest that Josephus must personally, and at leisure, have made himself acquainted with this spot; and in this case, as in others which have come before us, he proves himself to have been conversant with the facts he has to do with—observant of details, and quite as trustworthy in his reports of them as ancient writers generally are.

COMPLETE WORKS

OF

JOSEPHUS

ANTIQUITIES OF THE JEWS
THE WARS OF THE JEWS
AGAINST APION, ETC., ETC.

A NEW AND REVISED EDITION
BASED ON HAVERCAMP'S TRANSLATION

WITH NOTES, COMMENTS AND REFERENCES FROM
WHISTON, Dr. HUDSON, RELAND, Dr. BERNARD, PRIDEAUX,
LE CLERC, DEAN ALDRICH, GROTIUS, PHILO, SPANHEIM,
HERODOTUS AND MANY OTHERS ANCIENT AND MODERN.

IN FOUR VOLUMES

VOLUME THREE

BIGELOW, BROWN & CO., Inc.
NEW YORK

PRINTED BY C. H. SIMONDS COMPANY
BOSTON, MASS., U.S.A.

LIST OF ILLUSTRATIONS.

VOLUME THREE.

ANTIQUITIES OF THE JEWS.

BOOK XVII.

CONTAINING THE INTERVAL OF FOURTEEN YEARS.

[FROM THE DEATH OF ALEXANDER AND ARISTOBULUS, TO THE BANISHMENT OF ARCHELAUS.]

CHAPTER I.

How Antipater was hated by all ·the nation [of the Jews] for the slaughter of his brethren; and how, for that reason, he got into peculiar favour with his friends at Rome, by giving them many presents; as he did also with Saturninus, the president of Syria, and the governors who were under him; and concerning Herod's wives and children.

1. WHEN Antipater had thus taken off his brethren, and had brought his father into the highest degree of impiety, till he was haunted with furies for what he had done, his hopes did not succeed to his mind, as to the rest of his life; for although he was delivered from the fear of his brethren being his rivals as to the government, yet did he find it a very hard thing, and almost impracticable, to come at the kingdom, because the hatred of the nation against him on that account was become very great; and, besides this very disagreeable circumstance, the affair of the soldiery grieved him still more, who were alienated from him,

from which yet these kings derived all the safety which they had, whenever they found the nation desirous of innovation: and all this danger was drawn upon him by his destruction of his brethren. However, he governed the nation jointly with his father, being indeed no other than a king already; and he was for that very reason trusted, and the more firmly depended on, for the affair which he ought himself to have been put to death, as appearing to have betrayed his brethren out of his concern for the preservation of Herod, and not rather out of his ill-will to them, and before them, to his father himself; and this was the accursed state he was in. Now, all Antipater's contrivances tended to make his way to take off Herod, that he might have nobody to accuse him in the vile practices he was devising; and that Herod might have no refuge, nor any to afford him their assistance, since they must thereby have Antipater for their open enemy; insomuch that the very plots he had laid against his brethren, were occasioned by the hatred he bore his father. But at this time he was more than ever set upon the execution of his attempts against Herod, because, if he were once dead, the government would now be firmly secured to him; but, if he were suffered to live any longer, he should be in danger upon a discovery of that wickedness of which he had been the contriver, and his father would of necessity then become his enemy, and on that account it was that he became very bountiful to his father's friends, and bestowed great sums on several of them, in order to surprise men with his good deeds, and take off their hatred against him. And he sent great presents to his friends at Rome particularly, to gain their good-will; and above all to Saturninus, the president of Syria. He also hoped to gain the favour of Saturninus' brother with

the large presents he bestowed on him; as also he used
the same art to (Salome) the king's sister, who had
married one of Herod's chief friends. And, when
he counterfeited friendship to those with whom he
conversed, he was very subtle in gaining their belief,
and very cunning to hide his hatred against any that he
really did hate. But he could not impose upon his
aunt, who understood him of a long time, and was
a woman not easily to be deluded; especially while
she had already used all possible caution in preventing his pernicious designs. Although Antipater's uncle
by the mother's side was married to her daughter, and
this by his own connivance and management, while
she had before been married to Aristobulus, and while
Salome's other daughter by that husband was married
to the son of Calleas, yet that marriage was no obstacle
to her, who knew how wicked he was, in her discovering his designs, as her former kindred to him
could not prevent her hatred of him. Now Herod
had compelled Salome, while she was in love with
Sylleus the Arabian, and had taken a fondness for
him, to marry Alexas; which match was by her submitted to at the instance of Julia, who persuaded
Salome not to refuse it, lest she should .herself be
their open enemy, since Herod had sworn that he
would never be friends with Salome, if she would
not accept of Alexas for her husband; so she submitted to Julia as being Cæsar's wife, and, besides
that, she advised her to nothing but what was very
much for her own advantage. At this time, also,
it was that Herod sent back king Archelaus' daughter,
who had been Alexander's wife, to her father, returning the portion he had with her out of his own
estate, that there might be no dispute between them
about it.

Now Herod brought up his sons' children with

great care; for Alexander had two sons by Glaphyra; and Aristobulus had three sons by Bernice, Salome's daughter, and two daughters; and, as his friends were one with him, he presented the children before them, and deploring the hard fortune of his own sons, he prayed that no such ill fortune would befall these who were their children, but that they might improve in virtue, and obtain what they justly deserved, and might make him amends for his care of their education. He also caused them to be betrothed against they should come to the proper age of marriage: the elder of Alexander's sons to Pheroras' daughter, and Antipater's daughter to Aristobulus' eldest son. He also allotted one of Aristobulus' daughters to Antipater's son, and Aristobulus' other daughter to Herod, a son of his own, who was born to him by the high priest's daughter; for it is the ancient practice among us to have many wives at the same time. Now, the king made these espousals for the children, out of commiseration of them now they were fatherless, as endeavouring to render Antipater kind to them by these intermarriages. But Antipater did not fail to bear the same temper of mind to his brothers' children, which he had borne to his brothers themselves; and his father's concern about them provoked his indignation against them, upon this supposal, that they would become greater than ever his brothers had been; while Archelaus, a king, would support his daughter's sons, and Pheroras, a tetrarch, would accept of one of the daughters as a wife to his son. What provoked him also was this, that all the multitude would so commiserate these fatherless children, and so hate him, [for making them fatherless,] that all would come out, since they were no strangers to his vile disposition towards his brethren. He contrived, therefore, to overturn his father's settlements, as thinking it a terrible thing that they should be so related to him, and be so powerful withal. So Herod yielded to him, and changed his resolution at his entreaty; and the determination now was, that Antipater himself should marry Aristobulus' daughter, and Antipater's son should marry Pheroras' daughter. So the espousals for the marriages were changed after this manner, even without the king's real approbation.

Now Herod [1] the king had at this time nine wives; one of them Antipater's mother, and another, the high priest's daughter, by whom he had a son of his own name: He had also one who was his brother's daughter, and another his sister's daughter, which two had no children. One of his wives also was of the Samaritan nation, whose sons were Antipas and Archelaus, and whose daughter was Olympias; which daughter was afterward married to Joseph, the king's brother's son; but Archelaus and Antipas were brought up with a certain private man at Rome. Herod had also to wife Cleopatra of Jerusalem, and by her he had his sons Herod and Philip; which last was also brought up at Rome; Pallas also was one of his wives, who bore him his son Phasaelus. And besides these, he had for his wives Phedra and Elpis, by whom he had his daughters Roxana and Salome. As for his elder daughters, by the same mother with Alexander and Aristobulus, and whom Pheroras neglected to marry, he gave the one in marriage to Antipater, the king's sister's son, and the other to Phasaelus, his brother's son. And this was the posterity of Herod.

---

[1] Those who have a mind to know all the family and descendents of Antipater the Idumean, and of Herod the Great, his son, and have a memory to preserve them all distinctly, may consult Josephus, Antiq. B. XVIII. ch. v. sect. 4, Vol. III., and Of the War, B. I. ch. xxviii sect. 4, Vol. III., and Noldius in Havercamp's edition, p. 336, and Spanheim, ib. pp. 402-405, and Reland, Palestin. Part I. pp. 175, 176.

CHAPTER II.

Concerning Zamaris, the Babylonian Jew. Concerning the plots laid by Antipater against his father; and somewhat about the Pharisees.

1. AND now it was that Herod, being desirous of securing himself on the side of the Trachonites, resolved to build a village as large as a city for the Jews, in the middle of that country, which might make his own country difficult to be assaulted, and whence he might be at hand to make sallies upon them, and do them a mischief. Accordingly, when he understood that there was a man that was a Jew come out of Babylon, with five hundred horsemen, all of whom could shoot their arrows as they rode on horseback, and with a hundred of his relations, had passed over Euphrates and now abode at Antioch by Daphne of Syria, where Saturninus, who was then president, had given them a place for habitation, called *Valatha,* he sent for this man, with the multitude that followed him, and promised to give him land in the toparchy called *Batanea,* which country is bounded with Trachonitis, as desirous to make that his habitation a guard to himself. He also engaged to let him hold the country free from tribute, and that they should dwell entirely without paying such customs as used to be paid, and gave it him tax free.

2. The Babylonian was induced by these offers to come hither; so he took possession of the land, and built in it fortresses and a village, and named it *Bathyra.* Whereby this man became a safeguard to the inhabitants against the Trachonites, and preserved those Jews who came out of Babylon, to offer

their sacrifices at Jerusalem, from being hurt by the
Trachonite robberies; so that a great number came
to him from all those parts where the ancient Jewish
laws were observed, and the country became full of
people, by reason of their universal freedom from
taxes. This continued during the life of Herod; but
when Philip, who was [tetrarch] after him, took the
government, he made them pay some small taxes,
and that for a little while only; and Agrippa the
Great, and his son of the same name, although they
harassed them greatly, yet would they not take their
liberty away. From whom, when the Romans have
now taken the government into their own hands, they
still give them the privilege of their freedom, but
oppress them entirely with the imposition of taxes.
Of which matter I shall treat more accurately in the
progress·of this history.[1]

3. At length Zamaris the Babylonian, to whom
Herod had given that country for a possession, died;
having lived virtuously, and left children of a good
character behind him; one of whom was Jacimus, who
was famous for his valour, and taught his Babylonians
how to ride their horses; and a troop of them were
guards to the forementioned kings. And when
Jacimus was dead in his old age, he left a son whose
name was Philip, one of great strength in his hands,
and in other respects also more eminent for his valour
than any of his contemporaries; on which account
there was a confidence and firm friendship between
him and king Agrippa. He had also an army which
he maintained, as great as that of a king; which he exercised and led wheresoever he had occasion to march.

4. When the affairs of Herod were in the condition
I have described, all the public affairs depended upon
Antipater; and his power was such, that he could

---

[1] This is now wanting.

do good turns to as many as he pleased, and this by his father's concession, in hopes of his good-will and fidelity to him; and this till he ventured to use his powers still farther, because his wicked designs were concealed from his father, and he made him believe every thing he said. He was also formidable to all, not so much on account of the power and authority he had, as for the shrewdness of his vile attempts beforehand: but he who principally cultivated a friendship with him was Pheroras, who received the like marks of his friendship; while Antipater had cunningly encompassed him about by a company of women, whom he placed as guards about him: for Pheroras was greatly enslaved to his wife, and to her mother, and to her sister; and this notwithstanding the hatred he bore them, for the indignities they had offered to his virgin daughters. Yet did he bear them, and nothing was to be done without the women, who had got this man into their circle, and continued still to assist each other in all things, insomuch that Antipater was entirely addicted to them, both by himself and by his mother; for these four women [1] said all one and the same thing; but the opinions of Pheroras and Antipater were different in some points of no consequence. But the king's sister [Salome] was their antagonist, who for a good while had looked about all their affairs, and was apprized that this their friendship was made in order to do Herod some mischief, and was disposed to inform the king of it. And since these people knew that their friendship was very disagreeable to Herod, as tending to do him a mischief, they contrived that their meetings should not be discovered; so they pretended to hate one another, and to abuse one another when time

---

[1] Pheroras' wife, and her mother and sister, and Doris, Antipater's mother.

served, and especially when Herod was present, or
when any one was there that would tell him; but still
their intimacy was firmer than ever, when they were
in private. And this was the course they took; but
they could not conceal from Salome neither their
first contrivance, when they set about these their
intentions, nor when they had made some progress in
them; but she searched out every thing; and, ag-
gravating the relations to her brother, declared to
him, "As well their secret assemblies and compota-
tions, as their counsels taken in a clandestine manner,
which, if they were not in order to destroy him, they
might well enough have been open and public. But,
to appearance, they are at variance, and speak about
one another as if they intended one another a mischief, but agree so well together when they are out
of the sight of the multitude; for when they are alone
by themselves, they act in concert, and profess that
they will never leave off their friendship, but will
fight against those from whom they conceal their
designs." And thus did she search out these things,
and get a perfect knowledge of them, and then told
her brother of them, who understood also of himself a great deal of what she said, but still durst
not depend upon it, because of the suspicions he had
of his sister's calumnies. For there was a certain sect
of men that were Jews, who valued themselves highly
upon the exact skill they had in the law of their
fathers, and made men believe they were highly
favoured by God, by whom this set of women were
inveigled. These are those that are called the sect
of the *Pharisees,* who were in a capacity of greatly
opposing kings. A cunning sect they were, and soon
elevated to a pitch of open fighting, and doing mischief. Accordingly, when all the people of the Jews
gave assurance of their good-will to Cæsar, and to

the king's government, these very men did not swear, being above six thousand; and when the king imposed a fine upon them, Pheroras' wife paid their fine for them. In order to requite which kindness of hers, since they were believed to have the foreknowledge of things to come by divine inspiration, they foretold how God had decreed, that Herod's government should cease, and his posterity should be deprived of it; but that the kingdom should come to her and Pheroras, and to their children. These predictions were not concealed from Salome, but were told the king; as also how they had perverted some persons about the palace itself: so the king slew such of the Pharisees as were principally accused, and Bagoas the eunuch, and one Carus, who exceeded all men of that time in comeliness, and one that was his catamite. He slew also all those of his own family who had consented to what the Pharisees foretold; and for Bagoas, he had been puffed up by them, as though he should be named the father and the benefactor of him who, by the prediction, was foretold to be their appointed king; for that this king would have all things in his power, and would enable Bagoas to marry, and to have children of his own body begotten.

CHAPTER III.

Concerning the enmity between Herod and Pheroras; how Herod sent Antipater to Cæsar; and of the death of Pheroras.

1. WHEN Herod had punished those Pharisees who had been convicted of the foregoing crimes, he gathered an assembly together of his friends, and

accused Pheroras' wife; and ascribing the abuses of
the virgins to the impudence of that woman, brought
an accusation against her for the dishonour she had
brought upon them; That "she had studiously introduced a quarrel between him and his brother, and,
by her ill temper, had brought them into a state
of war, both by her words and actions; that the fines
which he had laid had not been paid, and the offenders
had escaped punishment by her means; and that
nothing which had of late been done had been done
without her: for which reason Pheroras would do well,
if he would, of his own accord, and by his own command, and not at my entreaty, or as following my
opinion, put this his wife away, as one that will still
be the occasion of war between thee and me. And
now, Pheroras, if thou valuest thy relation to me,
put this wife of thine away; for by this means thou
wilt continue to be a brother to me, and wilt abide
in thy love to me." Then said Pheroras, (although
he were pressed hard by the former words,) that "as
he would not do so unjust a thing as to renounce
his brotherly relation to him, so would he not leave
off his affection for his wife; that he would rather
choose to die than to live and be deprived of a wife
that was so dear unto him." Hereupon Herod put
off his anger against Pheroras on these accounts,
although he himself thereby underwent a very uneasy
punishment. However, he forbade Antipater and his
mother to have any conversation with Pheroras, and
bid them to take care to avoid the assemblies of the
women: which they promised to do; but still got
together when occasion served, and both Pheroras
and Antipater had their own merry meetings. The
report went also, that Antipater had criminal conversation with Pheroras' wife, and that they were
brought together by Antipater's mother.

2. But Antipater had now a suspicion of his father, and was afraid that the effects of his hatred to him might increase: so he wrote to his friends at Rome, and bid them to send to Herod, that he would immediately send Antipater to Cæsar; which, when it was done, Herod sent Antipater thither, and sent most noble presents along with him; as also his testament, wherein Antipater was appointed to be his successor; and that if Antipater should die first, his son [Herod Philip] by the high priest's daughter should succeed. And, together with Antipater, there went to Rome, Sylleus the Arabian, although he had done nothing of all that Cæsar had enjoined. Antipater also accused him of the same crimes of which he had been formerly accused by Herod. Sylleus was also accused by Aretas, that without his consent he had slain many of the chief of the Arabians at Petra; and particularly Sohemus, a man that deserved to be honoured by all men, and that he had slain Fabatus, a servant of Cæsar's. These were the things of which Sylleus was accused, and that on the occasion following: There was one Corinthus, belonging to Herod, of the guards of the king's body, and one who was greatly trusted by him. Sylleus had persuaded this man with the offer of a great sum of money, to kill Herod; and he had promised to do it. When Fabatus had been acquainted with this, for Sylleus had himself told him of it, he informed the king of it; who caught Corinthus, and put him to the torture, and thereby got out of him the whole conspiracy. He also caught two other Arabians, who were discovered by Corinthus; the one the head of a tribe, and the other a friend to Sylleus, who both were by the king brought to the torture, and confessed, that they were come to encourage Corinthus not to fail of doing what he had undertaken to do; and to assist him with

their own hands in the murder, if need should require their assistance. So Saturninus, upon Herod's discovering the whole to him, sent them to Rome.

3. At this time, Herod commanded Pheroras, that since he was so obstinate in his affection for his wife, he should retire into his own tetrarchy; which he did very willingly, and swore many oaths that he would not come again, till he heard that Herod was dead. And indeed, when, upon a sickness of the king's, he was desired to come to him before he died, that he might intrust him with some of his injunctions, he had such a regard to his oath, that he would not come to him; yet did not Herod so retain his hatred to Pheroras, but remitted of his purpose [not to see him,] which he before had, and that for such great causes as have been already mentioned; but as soon as he began to be ill, he came to him, and this without being sent for: and when he was dead, he took care of his funeral, and had his body brought to Jerusalem, and buried there, and appointed a solemn mourning for him. This [death of Pheroras] became the origin of Antipater's misfortunes, although he were already sailed for Rome, God now being about to punish him for the murder of his brethren. I will explain the history of this matter very distinctly, that it may be for a warning to mankind, that they take care of conducting their whole lives by the rules of virtue.

CHAPTER IV.

Pheroras' wife is accused by his freed men, as guilty
of poisoning him; and how Herod, upon examining
of the matter by torture, found the poison; but so
that it had been prepared for himself by his son
Antipater; and, upon an inquiry by torture, he
discovered the dangerous designs of Antipater.

1. As soon as Pheroras was dead, and his funeral
was over, two of Pheroras' freed men, who were much
esteemed by him, came to Herod, and entreated him
not to leave the murder of his brother without avenging it, but to examine into such an unreasonable and
unhappy death. When he was moved with these
words, for they seemed to him to be true, they said,
That "Pheroras supped with his wife the day before
he fell sick, and that a certain potion was brought
him in such a sort of food as he was not used to
eat, but that when he had eaten he died of it, that
this potion was brought out of Arabia by a woman,
under pretence indeed as a love potion, for that was
its name, but in reality to kill Pheroras; for that
the Arabian women are skilful in making such poisons:
and the woman to whom they ascribe this, was con-
fessedly a most intimate friend of one of Sylleus'
mistresses, and that both the mother and the sister
of Pheroras' wife had been at the places where she
lived, and had persuaded her to sell them this potion,
and had come back and brought it with them the day
before that his supper." Hereupon the king was
provoked, and put the women slaves to the torture,
and some that were free with them: and as the fact
did not yet appear, because none of them would

confess it, at length one of them under the utmost agonies, said no more but this, that "she prayed that God would send the like agonies upon Antipater's mother, who had been the occasion of these miseries to all of them." This prayer induced Herod to increase the women's tortures, till thereby all was discovered: "Their merry meetings, their secret assemblies, and the disclosing of what he had said to his son alone unto Pheroras' ¹ women." (Now what Herod had charged Antipater to conceal, was the gift of a hundred talents to him not to have any conversation with Pheroras.) "And what hatred he bore to his father; and that he complained to his mother how very long his father lived; and that he was himself almost an old man, insomuch, that if the kingdom should come to him, it would not afford him any great pleasure; and that there were a great many of his brothers, or brothers' children, bringing up, that might have hopes of the kingdom as well as himself, all which made his own hopes of it uncertain; for that even now, if he should himself not live, Herod had ordained that the government should be conferred, not on his son, but rather on a brother. He also had accused the king of great barbarity, and of the slaughter of his sons; and that it was out of the fear he was under, lest he should do the like to him, that made him contrive this his journey to Rome, and Pheroras contrive to go to his own tetrarchy."

2. These confessions agreed with what his sister

¹ His wife, her mother, and sister.
It seems by this whole story put together, that Pheroras was not himself poisoned, as is commonly supposed; for Antipater had persuaded him to poison Herod, ch. v. sect. 1, which would fall to the ground, if he were himself poisoned; nor could the poisoning of Pheroras serve any design that appears now going forward; it was only the supposal of two of his freed men, that this love potion, or poison, which they knew was brought to Pheroras' wife, was made use of for poisoning him; whereas it appears to have been brought for her husband to poison Herod withal, as the future examinations demonstrate.

had told him, and tended greatly to corroborate her testimony, and to free her from the suspicion of her unfaithfulness to him. So the king having satisfied himself of the spite which Doris, Antipater's mother, as well as himself, bore to him, took away from her all her fine ornaments, which were worth many talents, and then sent her away, and entered into friendship with Pheroras' women. But he who most of all irritated the king against his son, was one Antipater, the procurator of Antipater the king's son, who, when he was tortured, among other things said, That Antipater had prepared a deadly potion, and given it to Pheroras, with his desire that he would give it to his father during his absence, and when he was too remote to have the least suspicion cast upon him thereto relating: that Antiphilus, one of Antipater's friends, brought that potion out of Egypt, and that it was sent to Pheroras by Theudion, the brother of the mother of Antipater the king's son, and by that means came to Pheroras' wife, her husband having given it her to keep. And when the king asked her about it, she confessed it; and as she was running to fetch it, she threw herself down from the house-top, yet did she not kill herself, because she fell upon her feet: by which means, when the king had comforted her, and had promised her and her domestics pardon, upon condition of their concealing nothing of the truth from him, but had threatened her with the utmost miseries if she proved ungrateful, [and concealed any thing;] so she promised and swore that she would speak out every thing, and tell after what manner every thing was done; and said, what many took to be entirely true, that "the poison was brought out of Egypt by Antiphilus; and that his brother, who was a physician, had procured it; and that when Theudion brought it us, she kept it upon Pheroras'

committing it to her; and that it was prepared by
Antipater for thee. When, therefore, Pheroras was
fallen sick, and thou came to him and took care of
him, and when he saw the kindness thou hadst for
him, his mind was overborne thereby. So he called
me to him, and said to me, 'O woman! Antipater
had circumvented me in this affair of his father and
my brother, by persuading me to have a murderous
intention to him, and procuring a potion to be subservient thereto; do thou, therefore, go and fetch my
potion, (since my brother appears to have still the
same virtuous disposition towards me which he had
formerly, and I do not expect to live long myself,
and that I may not defile my forefathers by the
murder of a brother,) and burn it before my face:'
that accordingly she immediately brought it, and did
as her husband bade her; and that she burnt the
greatest part of the potion; but that a little of it
was left, that if the king, after Pheroras' death, should
treat her ill, she might poison herself, and thereby get
clear of her miseries." Upon her saying thus, she
brought out the potion, and the box in which it was,
before them all. Nay, there was another brother of
Antiphilus', and his mother also, who, by the extreme
of pain and torture, confessed the same things, and
owned the box [to be that which had been brought
out of Egypt.] The high priest's daughter also, who
was the king's wife, was accused to have been conscious of all this, and had resolved to conceal it; for
which reason Herod divorced her, and blotted her
son out of his testament, wherein he had been mentioned as one that was to reign after him; and he
took the high priesthood away from his father-in-law,
Simeon the son of Boethus, and appointed Matthias
the son of Theophilus, who was born at Jerusalem,
to be high priest in his room.

3. While this was doing, Bathyllus, also Antipater's freed man, came from Rome, and, upon the torture, was found to have brought another potion, to give it into the hands of Antipater's mother, and of Pheroras, that if the former potion did not operate upon the king, this at least might carry him off. There came also letters from Herod's friends at Rome, by the approbation, and at the suggestion of Antipater, to accuse Archelaus and Philip, as if they calumniated their father on account of the slaughter of Alexander and Aristobulus, and as if they commiserated their deaths; and as if, because they were sent for home, (for their father had already recalled them,) they concluded they were themselves also to be destroyed. These letters had been procured by great rewards, by Antipater's friends; but Antipater himself wrote to his father about them, and laid the heaviest things to their charge; yet did he entirely excuse them of any guilt, and said, they were but young men, and so imputed their words to their youth. But he said, that he had himself been very busy in the affair relating to Sylleus, and in getting interest among the great men; and on that account had brought splendid ornaments to present them withal, which cost him two hundred talents. Now, one may wonder how it came about, that while so many accusations were laid against him in Judea during seven months before this time, he was not made acquainted with any of them. The causes of which were, that the roads were exactly guarded, and that men hated Antipater; for there was nobody who would run any hazard himself, to gain him any advantages.

CHAPTER V.

*Antipater's navigation from Rome to his father; and
how he was accused by Nicolaus of Damascus, and
condemned to die by his father, and by Quintilius
Varus, who was then president of Syria; and how
he was then bound till Cæsar should be informed
of his cause.*

1. Now Antipater, upon Herod's writing to him,
that having done all that he was to do, and this in
the manner he was to do it, he would suddenly come
to him, and bid him not delay his journey, lest any
harm should befall himself in his absence. At the
same time also he made some little complaint about
his mother, but promised that he would lay those
complaints aside when he should return. He withal
expressed his entire affection for him, as fearing lest
he should have some suspicion of him, and defer his
journey to him, and lest, while he lived at Rome, he
should lay plots for the kingdom, and, moreover, do
somewhat against himself. This letter Antipater
met with in Celicia; but had received an account of
Pheroras' death before at Tarentum. This last news
affected him deeply; not out of any affection for
Pheroras, but because he was dead without having
murdered his father, which he had promised him to
do. And when he was at Celenderis in Celicia, he
began to deliberate with himself about his sailing
home, as being much grieved with the ejection of
his mother. Now, some of his friends advised him
that he should tarry a while somewhere, in expectation of farther information. But others advised him
to sail home without delay; for that if he were once

come thither, he would soon put an end to all accusations, and that nothing afforded any weight to his accusers at present but his absence. He was persuaded by these last, and sailed on, and landed at the haven called Sebastus, which Herod had built at vast expenses in honour of Cæsar, and called Sebastus. And now was Antipater evidently in a miserable condition, while nobody came to him nor saluted him, as they did at his going away, with good wishes or joyful acclamations; nor was there now any thing to hinder them from entertaining him, on the contrary, with bitter curses, while they supposed he was come to receive his punishment for the murder of his brethren.

2. Now, Quintilius Varus was at this time at Jerusalem, being sent to succeed Saturninus as president of Syria, and was come as an assessor to Herod, who had desired his advice in his present affairs; and as they were sitting together, Antipater came upon them, without knowing any thing of the matter; so he came into the palace clothed in purple. The porters indeed received him in, but excluded his friends. And now he was in great disorder, and presently understood the condition he was in, while upon his going to salute his father, he was repulsed by him, who called him a murderer of his brethren, and a plotter of destruction against himself, and told him that Varus should be his auditor and his judge the very next day; so he found, that what misfortune he now heard of was already upon him, with the greatness of which he went away in confusion; upon which his mother and his wife met him, (which wife was the daughter of Antigonus, who was king of the Jews before Herod,) from whom he learned all circumstances which concerned him, and then prepared himself for his trial.

3. On the next day Varus and the king sat to-

gether in judgment, and both their friends were also
called in, as also the king's relations, with his sister
Salome, and as many as could discover any thing,
and such as had been tortured; and besides these,
some slaves of Antipater's mother, who were taken
up a little before Antipater's coming, and brought
with them a written letter, the sum of which was
this, that "he should not come back, because all was
come to his father's knowledge; and that Cæsar was
the only refuge he had left to prevent both his and
her delivery into his father's hands." Then did Antipater fall down at his father's feet, and besought
him "not to prejudge his cause, but that he might be
first heard by his father, and that his father would
keep him still unprejudiced." So Herod ordered him
to be brought into the midst, and then "lamented
himself about his children, from whom he had suffered such great misfortunes; and because Antipater
fell upon him in his old age. He also reckoned up
what maintenance, and what education he had given
them; and what seasonable supplies of wealth he had
afforded them, according to their own desires, none
of which favours had hindered them from contriving
against him, and from bringing his very life into
danger, in order to gain his kingdom, after an impious
manner, by taking away his life before the course
of nature, their father's wishes, or justice, required
that that kingdom should come to them; and that
he wondered what hopes could elevate Antipater to
such a pass as to be hardy enough to attempt such
things; that he had. by his testament in writing
declared him his successor in the government: and
while he was alive, he was in no respect inferior to
him, either in his illustrious dignity, or in power and
authority, he having no less than fifty talents for his
yearly income, and had received for his journey to

Rome no fewer than thirty talents. He also objected to him the case of his brethren whom he had accused; and if they were guilty, he had imitated their example; and if not, he had brought him groundless accusations against his near relations; for that he had been acquainted with all those things by him, and by nobody else, and had done what was done by his approbation, and whom he now absolved from all that was criminal, by becoming the inheritor of the guilt of such their parricide."

4. When Herod had thus spoken, he fell a-weeping, and was not able to say any more; but at his desire Nicolaus of Damascus, being the king's friend, and always conversant with him, and acquainted with whatsoever he did, and with the circumstances of his affairs, proceeded to what remained, and explained all that concerned the demonstrations and evidences of the facts. Upon which Antipater, in order to make his legal defence, turned himself to his father, and "enlarged upon the many indications he had given of his good-will to him; and instanced in the honours that had been done him, which yet had not been done, had he not deserved them by his virtuous concern about him; for that he had made provision for every thing that was fit to be foreseen beforehand, as to giving him his wisest advice; and whenever there was occasion for the labour of his own hands, he had not grudged any such pains for him. And that it was almost impossible that he who had delivered his father from so many treacherous contrivances laid against him, should be himself in a plot against him, and so lose all the reputation he had gained for his virtue, by his wickedness which succeeded it, and this while he had nothing to prohibit him, who was already appointed his successor, to enjoy the royal honour with his father also at present; and that there was no

likelihood that a person who had the one half of
that authority without any danger, and with a good
character, should hunt after the whole with infamy
and danger, and this when it was doubtful whether
he could obtain it or not; and when he saw the sad
example of his brethren before him, and was both
the informer and the accuser against them, at a time
when they might not otherwise have been discovered;
nay, was the author of the punishment inflicted upon
them, when it appeared evidently that they were
guilty of a wicked attempt against their father; and
that even the contentions there were in the king's
family, were indications that he had ever managed
affairs out of the sincerest affection to his father.
And as to what he had done at Rome, Cæsar was
a witness thereto; who yet was no more to be imposed upon than God himself: of whose opinions his
letters sent hither are sufficient evidence, and that it
was not reasonable to prefer the calumnies of such
as proposed to raise disturbances, before these letters;
the greatest part of which calumnies had been raised
during his absence, which gave scope to his enemies
to forge them, which they had not been able to do if
he had been there." Moreover, he showed the weakness of the evidence obtained by torture, which was
commonly false; because the distress men are in under
such tortures naturally obliges them to say many
things in order to please those that govern them.
He also offered himself to the torture.

5. Hereupon there was a change observed in the
assembly while they greatly pitied Antipater, who
by weeping and putting on a countenance suitable
to his sad case, made them commiserate the same;
insomuch that his very enemies were moved to compassion; and it appeared plainly that Herod himself
was affected in his own mind, although he was not

willing it should be taken notice of. Then did Nicolaus begin to prosecute what the king had begun, and that with great bitterness; and summed up all the evidence which arose from the tortures, or from the testimonies. "He principally and largely cried up the king's virtues, which he had exhibited in the maintenance and education of his sons, while he never could gain any advantage thereby, but still fell from one misfortune to another. Although he owned that he was not so much surprised with that thoughtless behaviour of his former sons, who were but young, and were besides corrupted by wicked counsellors, who were the occasion of their wiping out of their minds the righteous dictates of nature, and this out of a desire of coming to the government sooner than they ought to do; yet that he could not but justly stand amazed at the horrid wickedness of Antipater, who, although he had not only had great benefits bestowed on him by his father, enough to tame his reason, yet could not be more tamed than the most envenomed serpents; whereas even those creatures admit of some mitigation, and will not bite their benefactors, while Antipater hath not let the misfortunes of his brethren be any hinderance to him, but he hath gone on to imitate their barbarity notwithstanding. Yet wast thou, O Antipater! (as thou hast thyself confessed,) the informer as to what wicked actions they had done, and the searcher out of the evidence against them, and the author of the punishment they underwent upon their detection. Nor do we say this as accusing thee for being so zealous in thy anger against them, but are astonished at thy endeavours to imitate their profligate behaviour; and we discover thereby, that thou didst not act thus for the safety of thy father, but for the destruction of thy brethren, that by such outside hatred of their

impiety, thou mightest be believed a lover of thy
father, and mightest thereby get thee power enough
to do mischief with the greatest impunity; which design thy actions indeed demonstrate. It is true, thou
tookest thy brethren off, because thou didst convict
them of their wicked designs; but thou didst not yield
up to justice those who were their partners; and
thereby didst make it evident to all men, that thou
madest a covenant with them against thy father,
when thou chosest to be the accuser of thy brethren,
as desirous to gain to thyself alone this advantage
of laying plots to kill thy father, and so to enjoy
double pleasure, which is truly worthy of thy evil
disposition, which thou hast openly showed against
thy brethren; on which account thou didst rejoice,
as having done a most famous exploit, nor was that
behaviour unworthy of thee. But if thy intention
were otherwise, thou art worse than they; while thou
didst contrive to hide thy treachery against thy father,
thou didst hate them, not as plotters against thy
father, for in that case thou hadst not thyself fallen
upon the like crime, but as successors of his dominions,
and more worthy of that succession than thyself.
Thou wouldest kill thy father after thy brethren,
lest thy lies raised against them might be detected;
and lest thou shouldst suffer what punishment thou
hadst deserved, thou hadst a mind to exact that punishment of thy unhappy father, and didst devise such
a sort of uncommon parricide as the world never yet
saw. For thou who art his son didst not only lay a
treacherous design against thy father, and didst it
while he loved thee, and had been thy benefactor, had
made thee in reality his partner in the kingdom, and
had openly declared thee his successor, while thou
wast not forbidden to taste the sweetness of authority
already, and hadst the firm hope of what was future

by thy father's determination, and the security of
a written testament. But for certain thou didst not
measure these things according to thy father's various
dispositions, but according to thy own thoughts and
inclinations; and wast desirous to take the part that
remained away from thy too indulgent father, and
soughtest to destroy him with thy deeds, whom thou
in words pretendedst to preserve. Nor wast thou
content to be wicked thyself, but thou filledst thy
mother's head with thy devices, and raised disturbances
among thy brethren, and hadst the boldness to call
thy father a wild beast; while thou hadst thyself a
mind more cruel than any serpent, whence thou
sendest out that poison among thy nearest kindred
and greatest benefactors, and invitedst them to assist
thee and guard thee, and didst hedge thyself in on
all sides by the artifices of both men and women,
against an old man; as though that mind of thine
was not sufficient of itself to support so great a hatred
as thou baredst to him. And here thou appearest
after the tortures of freemen, of domestics, of men
and women, which have been examined on thy account,
and after the informations of thy fellow-conspirators,
as making haste to contradict the truth; and hast
thought on ways not only how to take thy father out
of the world, but to disannul that written law which
is against thee, and the virtue of Varus, and the
nature of justice; nay such is that impudence of
thine on which thou confidest, that thou desirest to
be put to the torture thyself, while thou allegest, that
the tortures of those already examined thereby have
made them tell lies; that those that have been the
deliverers of thy father may not be allowed to have
spoken the truth; but that thy tortures may be
esteemed the discoverers of truth. Wilt not thou, O
Varus! deliver the king from the injuries of his

kindred? Wilt not thou destroy this wicked wild beast, which hath pretended kindness to his father, in order to destroy his brethren; while yet he is himself alone ready to carry off the kingdom immediately, and appears to be the most bloody butcher to him of them all? For thou art sensible, that parricide is a general injury both to nature and to common life, and that the intention of parricide is not inferior to its perpetration: and he who does not punish it, is injurious to nature itself."

6. Nicolaus added farther what belonged to Antipater's mother, and whatsoever she had prattled like a woman; as also about the predictions and the sacrifices relating to the king; and whatsoever Antipater had done lasciviously in his cups and his amours among Pheroras' women; the examination upon torture; and whatsoever concerned the testimonies of the witnesses, which were many, and of various kinds; some prepared beforehand, and others were sudden answers, which farther declared and confirmed the foregoing evidence. For those men who were now acquainted with Antipater's practices, but had concealed them out of fear, when they saw that he was exposed to the accusations of the former witnesses, and that his great good fortune, which had supported him hitherto, had now evidently betrayed him into the hands of his enemies, who were now insatiable in their hatred to him, told all they knew of him. And his ruin was now hastened, not so much by the enmity of those that were his accusers, as by his gross, and impudent, and wicked contrivances, and by his ill-will to his father and his brethren; while he had filled their house with disturbance, and caused them to murder one another; and was neither fair in his hatred, nor kind in his friendship, but just so far as served his own turn. Now, there were a great num-

ber who for a long time beforehand had seen all this,
and especially such as were naturally disposed to
judge of matters by the rules of virtue, because they
were used to determine about affairs without passion,
but had been restrained from making any open complaints before; these, upon the leave now given them,
produced all that they knew before the public. The
demonstration also of these wicked facts could no
way be disproved: because the many witnesses there
were did neither speak out of favour to Herod, nor
were they obliged to keep what they had to say silent,
out of suspicion of any danger they were in; but
they spoke what they knew; because they thought
such actions very wicked, and that Antipater deserved
the greatest punishment; and indeed not so much
for Herod's safety, as on account of the man's own
wickedness. Many things were also said, and those
by a great number of persons, who were no way
obliged to say them; insomuch, that Antipater, who
used generally to be very shrewd in his lies and impudence, was not able to say one word to the contrary. When Nicolaus had left off speaking, and
had produced the evidence, Varus bid Antipater to
betake himself to the making his defence, if he had
prepared any thing whereby it might appear that he
was not guilty of the crimes he was accused of; for
that, as he was himself desirous, so did he know that
his father was in like manner desirous also, to have
him found entirely innocent. But Antipater fell down
on his face, and appealed to God, and to all men,
for testimonials of his innocency, desiring that God
would declare, by some evident signals, that he had
not laid any plot against his father. This being the
usual method of all men destitute of virtue, that,
when they set about any wicked undertakings, they
fall to work according to their own inclinations, as

if they believed that God was unconcerned in human affairs; but when once they are found out, and are in danger of undergoing the punishment due to their crimes, they endeavour to overthrow all the evidence against them, by appealing to God; which was the very thing which Antipater now did; for whereas he had done every thing as if there were no God in the world, when he was on all sides distressed by justice, and when he had no other advantage to expect from any legal proofs by which he might disprove the accusations laid against him, he impudently abused the majesty of God, and ascribed it to his power, that he had been preserved hitherto; and produced before them all what difficulties he had ever undergone in his bold acting for his father's preservation.

7. So when Varus, upon asking Antipater what he had to say for himself, found that he had nothing to say besides his appeal to God, and saw that there was no end of that, he bid them bring the potion before the court, that he might see what virtue still remained in it; and when it was brought, and one that was condemned to die had drunk it, by Varus' command, he died presently. Then Varus got up, and departed out of the court, and went away the day following to Antioch, where his usual residence was, because that was the .palace of the Syrians; upon which Herod laid his son in bonds. But what were Varus' discourses to Herod, was not known to the generality, and upon what words it was that he went away; though it was also generally supposed, that whatsoever Herod did afterward about his son, was done with his approbation. But when Herod had bound his son, he sent letters to Rome to Cæsar about him, and such messengers withal as should, by word of mouth, inform Cæsar of Antipater's wickedness. Now, at this very time there was seized a

letter of Antiphilus, written to Antipater out of
Egypt, (for he lived there;) and, when it was opened
by the king, it was found to contain what follows:
"I have sent thee Acme's letter, and hazarded my
own life; for thou knowest that I am in danger from
two families, if I be discovered. I wish thee good
success in thy affair." These were the contents of
this letter: but the king made enquiry about the other
letter also, for it did not appear, and Antiphilus'
slave, who brought that letter which had been read,
denied that he had received the other. But, while
the king was in doubt about it, one of Herod's friends
seeing a seam upon the inner coat of the slave, and
a doubling of the cloth, (for he had two coats on,)
he guessed that the letter might be within that doubling, which accordingly proved to be true. So they
took out the letter, and its contents were these: "Acme
to Antipater. I have written such a letter to thy
father as thou desirest me. I have also taken a
copy and sent it, as if it came from Salome to my
lady [Livia;] which, when thou readest, I know that
Herod will punish Salome, as plotting against him."
Now, this pretended letter of Salome's to her lady
was composed by Antipater, in the name of Salome,
as to its real meaning, but in the words of Acme.
The letter was this: "Acme to king Herod. I have
done my endeavour that nothing that is done against
thee should be concealed from thee. So upon my
finding a letter of Salome written to my lady against
thee, I have written out a copy, and sent it to thee,
with hazard to myself, but for thy advantage. The
reason why she wrote it was this, that she had a mind
to be married to Sylleus. Do thou therefore tear this
letter in pieces, that I may not come into danger of
my life." Now Acme had written to Antipater himself, and informed him, that, in compliance with his

command, she had both herself written to Herod, as if Salome had laid a sudden plot entirely against him, and had herself sent a copy of an epistle, as coming from Salome to her lady. Now, Acme was a Jew by birth, and a servant to Julia, Cæsar's wife; and did this out of her friendship for Antipater, as having been corrupted by him with a large present of money, to assist in his pernicious designs against his father and his aunt.

8. Hereupon Herod was so amazed at the prodigious wickedness of Antipater, that he was ready to have ordered him to be slain immediately, as a turbulent person in the most important concerns, and as one that had laid a plot not only against himself, but against his sister also, and even corrupted Cæsar's own domestics. Salome also provoked him to it, beating her breast, and bidding him kill her, if he could produce any credible testimony that she had acted in that manner. Herod also sent for his son, and asked him about this matter, and bid him contradict it if he could, and not suppress any thing he had to say for himself; and, when he had not one word to say, he asked him, since he was every way caught in his villainy, that he would make no farther delay, but discover his associates in these his wicked designs. So he laid all upon Antiphilus; but discovered nobody else. Hereupon Herod was in such great grief, that he was ready to send his son to Rome to Cæsar, there to give an account of these his wicked contrivances. But he soon became afraid, lest he might there, by the assistance of his friends, escape the danger he was in: so he kept him bound as before, and sent more ambassadors and letters [to Rome] to accuse his son, and an account of what assistance Acme had given him in his wicked designs, with copies of the epistles before mentioned.

CHAPTER VI.

Concerning the disease that Herod fell into, and the sedition which the Jews raised thereupon; with the punishment of the seditious.

1. Now Herod's ambassadors made haste to Rome; but sent as instructed beforehand what answers they were to make to the questions put to them. They also carried the epistles with them. But Herod now fell into a distemper, and made his will, and bequeathed his kingdom to [Antipas] his youngest son; and this out of that hatred to Archelaus and Philip, which the calumnies of Antipater had raised against them. He also bequeathed a thousand talents to Cæsar, and five hundred to Julia, Cæsar's wife, to Cæsar's children, and friends, and freed men. He also distributed among his sons and their sons his money, his revenues, and his lands. He also made Salome his sister very rich, because she had continued faithful to him in all his circumstances, and was never so rash as to do him any harm: and as he despaired of recovering, for he was about the seventieth year of his age, he grew fierce, and indulged the bitterest anger upon all occasions; the cause whereof was this, that he thought himself despised, and that the nation was pleased with his misfortunes; besides which, he resented a sedition which some of the lower sort of men excited against him, the occasion of which was as follows:

2. There was one Judas, the son of Sariphæus, and Matthias, the son of Margalothus, two of the most eloquent men among the Jews, and the most celebrated interpreters of the Jewish laws, and men

well beloved by the people, because of their education
of their youth; for all those that were studious of
virtue frequented their lectures every day. These
men, when they found that the king's distemper was
incurable, excited the young men that they would
pull down all those works which the king had erected
contrary to the law of their fathers, and thereby
obtain the rewards which the law will confer on them
for such actions of piety, for that it was truly on
account of Herod's rashness in making such things
as the law had forbidden, that his other misfortunes,
and this distemper also, which was so unusual among
mankind, and with which he was now afflicted, came
upon him; for Herod had caused such things to be
made, which were contrary to the law, of which he
was accused by Judas and Matthias; for the king
had erected over the great gate of the temple a large
golden eagle, of great value, and had dedicated it
to the temple. Now, the law forbids those that propose to live according to it, to erect images [1] or rep-
resentations of any living creature. So these wise
men persuaded [their scholars] to pull down the
golden eagle; alleging that "although they should
incur any danger, which might bring them to their
deaths, the virtue of the action now proposed to them
would appear much more advantageous to them than
the pleasures of life; since they would die for the
preservation and observation of the law of their
fathers; since they would also acquire an everlasting
fame and commendation; since they would be both
commended by the present generation, and leave an
example of life that would never be forgotten to
posterity; since that common calamity of dying can-

---

[1] That the making of images, without an intention to worship them,
was not unlawful to the Jews, see the note on Antiq. B. VIII. ch. vii.
sect. 5.

not be avoided by our living so as to escape any
such dangers; that therefore it is a right thing for
those who are in love with a virtuous conduct, to
wait for that fatal hour by such a behaviour as may
carry them out of the world with praise and honour;
and that this will alleviate death to a great degree,
thus to come at it by the performance of brave actions, which bring us into danger of it; and, at the
same time, to leave that reputation behind them to
their children, and to all their relations, whether they
be men or women, which will be of great advantage
to them afterward."

3. And with such discourses as this, did these
men excite the young men to this action; and a report
being come to them that the king was dead, this
was an addition to the wise men's persuasions; so,
in the very middle of the day, they got upon the
place, they pulled down the eagle, and cut it into
pieces with axes, while a great number of the people
were in the temple. And now the king's captain,
upon hearing what the undertaking was, and supposing it was a thing of a higher nature than it
proved to be, came up thither, having a great band
of soldiers with him, such as was sufficient to put a
stop to the multitude of those who pulled down what
was dedicated to God: so he fell upon them unexpectedly, and as they were upon this bold attempt,
in a foolish presumption rather than a cautious circumspection, as is usual with the multitude, and
while they were in disorder, and incautious of what
was for their advantage; so he caught no fewer than
forty of the young men, who had the courage to
stay behind when the rest ran away, together with
the authors of this bold attempt, Judas and Matthias,
who thought it an ignominious thing to retire upon
his approach, and led them to the king. And when

they were come to the king, and he had asked them
if they had been so bold as to pull down what he had
dedicated to God? "Yes, (said they,) what was
contrived, we contrived, and what hath been performed, we performed it, and that with such a virtuous courage as becomes men; for we have given
our assistance to those things which are dedicated to
the majesty of God, and we have provided for what
we have learned by hearing the law; and it ought
not to be wondered at, if we esteem those laws which
Moses had suggested to him, and were taught him
by God, and which he wrote and left behind him,
more worthy of observation than the commands.
Accordingly, we will undergo death, and all sorts
of punishment which thou canst inflict upon us, with
pleasure, since we are conscious to ourselves that we
shall die, not for any uprighteous actions, but for
our love to religion." And thus they all said, and
their courage was still equal to their profession, and
equal to that with which they readily set about this
undertaking. And when the king had ordered them
to be bound, he sent them to Jericho, and called
together the principal men among the Jews; and when
they were come, he made them assemble in the theatre,
and because he could not himself stand, he lay upon
a couch, and "enumerated the many labours that he
had long endured on their account, and his building
of the temple, and what a vast charge that was to
him, while the Asamoneans, during the hundred and
twenty-five years of their government, had not been
able to perform any so great a work for the honour
of God as that was: that he had also adorned it with
very valuable donations, on which account he hoped
that he had left himself a memorial, and procured
himself a reputation after his death. He then cried
out, that these men had not abstained from affronting

him, even in his lifetime, but that, in the very day time, and in the sight of the multitude, they had abused him to that degree, as to fall upon what he had dedicated, and in that way of abuse had pulled it down to the ground. They pretended, indeed, that they did it to affront him; but if any one considered the thing truly, they will find that they were guilty of sacrilege against God therein."

4. But the people on account of Herod's barbarous temper, and for fear he should be so cruel as to inflict punishment on them, said, "What was done, was done without their approbation, and that it seemed to them that the actors might well be punished for what they had done " But as for Herod, he dealt more mildly with others [of the assembly;] but he deprived Matthias of the high priesthood, as in part on occasion of this action, and made Joazer, who was Matthias' wife's brother, high priest in his stead. Now it happened, that during the time of the high priesthood of this Matthias, there was another person made high priest for a single day, that very day which the Jews observed as a fast. The occasion was this: This Matthias the high priest, on the night before that day, when the fast was to be celebrated, seemed in a dream,[1] to have conversation with his wife; and because he could not officiate himself on

---

[1] This fact, that one Joseph was made high priest for a single day, on occasion of the action here specified, that befell Matthias, the real high priest, in his sleep, the night before the great day of expiation, is attested to both in the Mishna and Talmud, as Dr. Hudson here informs us. And indeed, from this fact, thus fully attested, we may confute the pretended rule in the Talmud here mentioned, and endeavoured to be excused by Reland, that the high priest was not suffered to sleep the night before that great day of expiation; which watching would surely rather unfit him for the many important duties he was to perform on that solemn day, than dispose him duly to perform them. Nor do such Talmudical rules, when unsupported by better evidence, much less when contradicted thereby, seem to me of weight enough to deserve that so great a man as Reland should spend his time in endeavours at their vindication.

that account, Joseph, the son of Ellemus, his kinsman, assisted him in that sacred office. But Herod
deprived this Matthias of the high priesthood, and
burnt the other Matthias, who had raised the sedition,
with his companions, alive. And that very night
there was an eclipse of the moon.[1]

5. But now Herod's distemper greatly increased
upon him after a severe manner, and this by God's
judgment upon him for his sins; for a fire glowed
in him slowly, which did not so much appear to the
touch outwardly, as it augmented his pains inwardly;
for it brought upon him a vehement appetite to eating,
which he could not avoid to supply with one sort of
food or other. His entrails were also exulcerated,
and the chief violence of his pain lay on his colon;
an aqueous and transparent liquor also had settled
itself about his feet, and a like matter afflicted him
at the bottom of his belly. Nay, farther, his privy-
member was putrified, and produced worms; and
when he sat upright, he had a difficulty of breathing,
which was very loathsome, on account of the stench
of his breath, and the quickness of its returns; he
had also convulsions in all parts of his body, which
increased his strength to an unsufferable degree. It
was said by those who pretended to divine, and who
were endued with wisdom to foretell such things,
that God inflicted this punishment on the king on
account of his great impiety; yet was he still in hopes
of recovering, though his afflictions seemed greater
than any one could bear. He also sent for physi-

[1] This eclipse of the moon (which is the only eclipse of either of the
luminaries mentioned by our Josephus in any of his writings,) is of the
greatest consequence for the determination of the time for the death of
Herod and Antipater, and for the birth and entire chronology of Jesus
Christ. It happened March 13th in the year of the Julian period 4710,
and the 4th year before the Christian era. See its calculation by the
rules of astronomy, at the end of the Astronological Lectures, edit. Lat.
pp. 451, 452.

cians, and did not refuse to follow what they prescribed for his assistance, and went beyond the river Jordan, and bathed himself in the warm baths that were at Callirrhoe, which, besides their other general virtues, were also fit to drink; which water runs into the lake called *Asphaltitis.* And when the physicians once thought fit to have him bathed in a vessel full of oil, it was supposed that he was just dying; but upon the lamentable cries of his domestics, he revived; and having no longer the least hopes of recovering, he gave order that every soldier should be paid fifty drachmæ; and he also gave a great deal to their commanders, and to his friends, and came again to Jericho, where he grew so choleric, that it brought him to do all things like a madman, and though he were near his death, he contrived the following wicked designs. He commanded that all the principal men of the entire Jewish nation, wheresoever they lived, should be called to him. Accordingly, they were a great number that came, because the whole nation was called, and all men heard of this call, and death was the penalty of such as should despise the epistles that were sent to call them. And now the king was in a wild rage against them all, the innocent as well as those that had afforded ground for accusations; and when they were come, he ordered them to be all shut up in the hippodrome, and sent for his sister Salome, and her husband Alexis, and spoke thus to them: "I shall die in a little time, so great are my pains; which death ought to be cheerfully borne, and to be welcomed by all men; but what principally troubles me is this, that I shall die without being lamented, and without such mourning as men usually expect at a king's death. For that he was not unacquainted with the temper of the Jews, that his death would be a thing very desirable, and exceedingly acceptable to them; because during his lifetime they were ready to revolt from him, and to abuse the donations he had dedicated to God; that it therefore was their business to resolve to afford him some alleviation of his great sorrows on this occasion; for that, if they do not refuse him their consent in what he desires, he shall have a great mourning at his funeral, and such as never any king had before him; for then the whole nation would mourn from their very soul, which otherwise would be done in sport and mockery only. He desired therefore that as soon as they see he hath given up the ghost, they shall place soldiers round the hippodrome, while they do not know that he is dead; and that they shall not declare his death to the multitude till this is done, but that they shall give orders to have those that are in custody shot with their darts; and that this slaughter of them all will cause that he shall not miss to rejoice on a double account; that as he is dying, they will make him secure that his will shall be executed in what he charges them to do; and that he shall have the honour of a memorable mourning at his funeral. So he deplored his condition, with tears in his eyes, and obtested them by the kindness due from them, as of his kindred and by the faith they owed to God, and begged of them that they would not hinder him of this honourable mourning at his funeral." So they promised him not to transgress his commands.

6. Now, any one may easily discover the temper of this man's mind, which not only took pleasure in doing what he had done formerly against his relations, out of the love of life, but by those commands of his which savoured of no humanity, since he took care when he was departing out of this life, that the whole nation should be put into mourning, and in-

deed made desolate of their dearest kindred, when
he gave order that one out of every family should
be slain, although they had done nothing that was
unjust, or that was against him, nor were they accused
of any other crimes; while it is usual for those who
have any regard to virtue, to lay aside their hatred
at such a time, even with respect to those they justly
esteemed their enemies.

CHAPTER VII.

*Herod has thoughts of killing himself with his own
hand; and a little afterwards he orders Antipater
to be slain.*

1. As he was giving these commands to his relations, there came letters from his ambassadors, who
had been sent to Rome unto Cæsar, which, when they
were read, their purport was this: That "Acme was
slain by Cæsar, out of his indignation at what hand
she had in Antipater's wicked practices; and that as
to Antipater himself, Cæsar left it to Herod to act
as became a father and a king, and either to banish
him or take away his life, which he pleased." When
Herod heard this, he was somewhat better, out of the
pleasure he had from the contents of the letters, and
was elevated at the death of Acme, and at the power
that was given him over his son; but, as his pains were
become very great, he was now ready to faint for
want of somewhat to eat; so he called for an apple,
and a knife; for it was his custom formerly to pare
the apple himself, and soon afterwards to cut it, and
eat it. When he had got the knife, he looked about,
and had a mind to stab himself with it; and he had

done it, had not his first cousin, Achiabus, prevented him, and held his hand, and cried out loudly. Whereupon a woful lamentation echoed through the palace, and a great tumult was made, as if the king was dead. Upon which, Antipater, who verily believed his father was deceased, grew bold in his discourse, as hoping to be immediately and entirely released from his bonds, and to take the kingdom into his hands, without any more ado; so he discoursed with the jailor about letting him go, and in that case promised him great things, both now and hereafter, as if that were the only thing now in question. But the jailor did not only refuse to do what Antipater would have him, but informed the king of his intentions, and how many solicitations he had had from him [of that nature.] Hereupon Herod, who had formerly no affection nor good-will towards his son to restrain him, when he heard what the jailor said, he cried out, and beat his head, although he was at death's door, and raised himself upon his elbow, and sent for some of his guards, and commanded them to kill Antipater without any farther delay, and to do it presently, and to bury him in an ignoble manner* at Hyrcania.

CHAPTER VIII.

Concerning Herod's death, and testament and burial.

1. AND now Herod altered his testament upon the alteration of his mind; for he appointed Antipas, to whom he had before left the kingdom, to be tetrarch of Galilee and Perea, and granted the kingdom to Archelaus. He also gave Gaulonitis, and Trachonitis, and Paneas, to Philip, who was his son, but own

brother [1] to Archelaus, by the name of tetrarchy; and bequeathed Jamnia, and Ashdod, and Phasaelis, to Salome his sister, with five hundred thousand [drachmæ] of silver that was coined. He also made provision for all the rest of his kindred, by giving them sums of money and annual revenues, and so left them all in a wealthy condition. He bequeathed also to Cæsar ten millions of [drachmæ] of coined money, besides both vessels of gold and silver, and garments exceedingly costly, to Julia, Cæsar's wife; and to certain others, five millions. When he had done these things, he died, the fifth day, after he had caused Antipater to be slain; having reigned, since he had procured Antigonus [2] to be slain, thirty-four years; but since he had been declared king by the Romans, thirty-seven. A man he was of great barbarity towards all men equally, and a slave to his passion; but above the consideration of what was right: yet was he favoured by fortune as much as any man ever was, for from a private man he became a king; and though he were encompassed with ten thousand dangers, he got clear of them all, and continued his life till a very old age. But then, as to the affairs of his family and children, in which indeed, according to his own opinion, he was also very fortunate, because he was able to conquer his

---

[1] When it is here said, that Philip the tetrarch, and Archelaus the king, or ethnarch, were αδελφοι γνηιοι, or *genuine brothers*, if those words mean *own brothers*, or born of the same father and mother, there must be here some mistake; because they had indeed the same father, Herod, but different mothers; the former Cleopatra, and Archelaus, Malthace. They were indeed brought up altogether at Rome, like own brothers; and Philip was Archelaus' deputy when he went to have his kingdom confirmed to him at Rome, ch. ix. sect. 5, Of the War, B. II. ch. ii. sect. 1, which intimacy is perhaps all that Josephus intended by the words before us.

[2] These numbers of years for Herod's reign, 34, and 37, are the very same with those Of the War, B. I. ch. xxxiii. sect. 8, and are among the principal chronological characters belonging to the reign or death of Herod. See Harm. of the Evang. pp. 150-155.

enemies, yet, in my opinion, he was herein very unfortunate.

2. But then Salome and Alexis, before the king's death was made known, dismissed those that were shut up in the hippodrome, and told them that the king ordered them to go away to their own lands, and take care of their own affairs, which was esteemed by the nation a great benefit. And now the king's death was made public, when Salome and Alexis gathered the soldiery together in the amphitheatre at Jericho; and the first thing they did was, they read Herod's letter, written to the soldiery, thanking them for their fidelity and good-will to him, and exhorting them to afford his son Archelaus, whom he had appointed for their king, like fidelity and good-will. After which Ptolemy, who had the king's seal entrusted to him, read the king's testament, which was to be of force no otherwise than as it should stand when Cæsar had inspected it; so there was presently an acclamation made to Archelaus, as king, and the soldiers came by bands, and their commanders with them, and promised the same good-will to him, and readiness to serve him, which they had exhibited to Herod; and they prayed God to be assistant to him.

3. After this was over, they prepared for his funeral, it being Archelaus' care that the procession to his father's sepulchre should be very sumptuous. Accordingly he brought out all his ornaments to adorn the pomp of the funeral. The body was carried upon a golden bier, embroidered with very precious stones of great variety, and it was covered over with purple, as well as the body itself: he had a diadem upon his head, and above it a crown of gold; he also had a sceptre in his right hand. About the bier were his sons and his numerous relations; next to these was the soldiery, distinguished according to their several

countries and denominations; and they were put into
the following order: First of all went his guards;
then the band of Thracians; and after them the Germans; and next the band of Galatians; every one in
their habiliments of war; and behind these marched
the whole army in the same manner as they used to
go out to war, and as they used to be put in array
by their muster-masters and centurions; these were
followed by five hundred of his domestics carrying
spices. So they went eight furlongs,[1] to Herodium;
for there by his own command he was to be buried.
And thus did Herod end his life.

4. Now Archelaus paid him so much respect, as
to continue his mourning till the seventh day; for
so many days are appointed for it by the law of our
fathers. And when he had given a treat to the multitude, and left off his mourning, he went up into
the temple; he had also acclamations and praises given
him, which way soever he went, every one striving
with the rest who should appear to use the loudest
acclamations. So he ascended a high elevation made
for him, and took his seat, in a throne made of gold,
and spoke kindly to the multitude, and declared,
"with what joy he received their acclamations, and
the marks of the good-will they showed to him; and
returned them thanks that they did not remember the
injuries his father had done them, to his disadvantage;
and promised them he would endeavour not to be
behindhand with them in rewarding their alacrity in
his service, after a suitable manner; but that he should
abstain at present from the name of king, and that
he should have the honour of that dignity, if Cæsar
should confirm and settle that testament which his

---

[1] At eight *stadia* or furlongs a day, as here, Herod's funeral, conducted to Herodium, (which lay at the distance from Jericho, where he
died, of 200 *stadia* or furlongs, Of the War, B. I. ch. xxxiii. sect. 9,)
must have taken up no less than twenty-five days.

father had made; and that it was on this account,
that when the army would have put the diadem on
him at Jericho, he would not accept of that honour,
which is usually so much desired, because it was not
yet evident that he who was to be principally concerned in bestowing it, would give it him; although,
by his acceptance of the government, he should not
want the ability of rewarding their kindness to him;
and that it should be his endeavour, as to all things
wherein they were concerned, to prove in every respect
better than his father." Whereupon the multitude,
as it is usual with them, supposed that the first days
of those that enter upon such governments, declare
the intentions of those that accept them; and so by
how much Archelaus spoke the more gently and civilly
to them, by so much did they more highly commend
him, and made application to him for the grant of
what they desired. Some made a clamour that he
would ease them of some of their annual payments;
but others desired him to release those that were put
into prison by Herod, who were many, and had been
put there at several times; others of them required
that he would take away those taxes which had been
severely laid upon what was publicly sold and bought.
So Archelaus contradicted them in nothing, since
he pretended to do all things so as to get the good-
will of the multitude to him, as looking upon that
good-will to be a great step towards the preservation
of his government. Hereupon he went and offered
sacrifice to God, and then betook himself to feast
with his friends.

CHAPTER IX.

How the people raised a sedition against Archelaus, and how he sailed to Rome.

1. At this time also it was, that some of the Jews got together out of a desire of innovation. They lamented Matthias, and those that were slain with him by Herod, who had not any respect paid them by a funeral mourning, out of the fear men were in of that man; they were those who had been condemned for pulling down the golden eagle. The people made a great clamour and lamentation hereupon, and cast out some reproaches against the king also, as if that tended to alleviate the miseries of the deceased. . The people assembled together, and desired of Archelaus, that, in way of revenge on their account, he would inflict punishment on those who had been honoured by Herod: and that, in the first and principal place, he would deprive that high priest whom Herod had made, and would choose one more agreeable to the law, and of greater purity, to officiate as high priest. This was granted by Archelaus, although he was mightily offended at their importunity, because he proposed to himself to go to Rome immediately, to look after Cæsar's determination about him. However, he sent the general of his forces to use persuasions, and to tell them that the death which was inflicted on their friends, was according to the law; and to represent to them, that their petitions about these things were carried to a great height of injury to him; that the time was not now proper for such petitions, but required their unanimity until such time as he should be established in the government

by the consent of Cæsar, and should then be come
back to them; for that he would then consult with
them in common concerning the purport of their
petitions, but that they ought at present to be quiet,
lest they should seem seditious persons.

2. So when the king had suggested these things,
and instructed his general in what he was to say, he
sent him away to the people; but they made a clamour,
and would not give him leave to speak, and put him
in danger of his life, and as many more as were
desirous to venture upon saying openly any thing
which might reduce them to a sober mind, and prevent their going on in their present courses; because
they had more concern to have all their own wills
performed, than to yield obedience to their governors;
thinking it to be a thing insufferable, that, while
Herod was alive, they should lose those that were
the most dear to them, and that when he was dead,
they could not get the actors to be punished. So
they went on with their designs after a violent
manner; and thought all to be lawful and right which
tended to please them, and being unskilful in foreseeing what dangers they incurred; and when they
had suspicion of such a thing, yet did the present
pleasure they took in the punishment of those they
deemed their enemies, overweigh all such considerations; and although Archelaus sent many to speak
to them, yet they treated them not as messengers
sent by him, but as persons that came of their own
accord to mitigate their anger, and would not let
one of them speak. The sedition, also, was made
by such as were in a great passion; and it was evident
that they were proceeding farther in seditious prae-
tices, by the multitude's running so fast upon them.

3. Now, upon the approach of that feast of unleavened bread, which the law of their fathers had

appointed for the Jews at this time, which feast is
called the Passover,[1] and is a memorial of their deliverance out of Egypt, (when they offer sacrifices
with great alacrity; and when they are required to
slay more sacrifices in number than at any other
festival, and when an innumerable multitude came
thither out of the country, nay, from beyond its limits
also, in order to worship God;) the seditious lamented
Judas and Matthias, those teachers of the laws, and
kept together in the temple, and had plenty of food,
because these seditious persons were not ashamed to
beg it. And as Archelaus was afraid lest some terrible thing should spring up by means of these
men's madness, he sent a regiment of armed men,
and with them a captain of a thousand, to suppress
the violent efforts of the seditious, before the whole
multitude should be infected with the like madness;
and gave them this charge, that if they found any
much more openly seditious than others, and more
busy in tumultuous practices, they should bring them
to him. But those that were seditious on account
of those teachers of the law, irritated the people by
the noise and clamours they used to encourage the
people in their designs; so they made an assault upon
the soldiers, and came up to them, and stoned the
greatest part of them, although some of them ran
away wounded, and their captain among them; and
when they had thus done, they returned to the sacrifices which were already in their hands. Now Archelaus thought there was no way to preserve the
entire government, but by cutting off those who
made this attempt upon it; so he sent out the whole
army upon them, and sent the horsemen to prevent

---

[1] This Passover, when the sedition here mentioned was moved against
Archelaus, was not one, but thirteen months after the eclipse of the moon
already mentioned.

those that had their tents without the temple, from
assisting those that were within the temple, and to
kill such as ran away from the footmen when they
thought themselves out of danger, which horsemen
slew three thousand men, while the rest went to the
neighbouring mountains. Then did Archelaus order
proclamation to be made to them all, that they should
retire to their own homes; so they went away, and
left the festival out of fear of somewhat worse which
would follow, although they had been so bold by
reason of their want of instruction. So Archelaus
went down to the sea with his mother, and took with
him Nicolaus and Ptolemy, and many others of his
friends, and left Philip, his brother, as governor of
all things belonging both to his own family, and to
the public. There went out also with him Salome,
Herod's sister, who took with her her children, and
many of her kindred were with her; which kindred
of hers went, as they pretended, to assist Archelaus
in gaining the kingdom, but in reality to oppose
him, and chiefly to make loud complaints of what
he had done in the temple. But Sabinus, Cæsar's
steward for Syrian affairs, as he was making haste
into Judea, to preserve Herod's effects, met with
Archelaus at Cæsarea; but Varus (president of Syria)
came at that time and restrained him from meddling
with them, for he was there as sent for by Archelaus,
by the means of Ptolemy. And Sabinus, out of regard to Varus, did neither seize upon any of the
castles that were among the Jews, nor did he seal
up the treasures in them, but permitted Archelaus
to have them, until Cæsar should declare his resolution about them; so that, upon this his promise, he
tarried still at Cæsarea. But after Archelaus was
sailed for Rome, and Varus was removed to Antioch,
Sabinus went to Jerusalem, and seized on the king's

palace. He also sent for the keepers of the garrisons, and for all those that had the charge of Herod's effects, and declared publicly, that he should require them to give an account of what they had: and he disposed of the castles in the manner he pleased; but those who kept them did not neglect what Archelaus had given them in command, but continued to keep all things in the manner that had been enjoined them; and their pretence was, that they kept them all for Cæsar.

4. At the same time, also, did Antipas, another of Herod's sons, sail to Rome, in order to gain the government; being buoyed up by Salome with promises, that he should take that government; and that he was a much honester and fitter man than Archelaus for that authority; since Herod had, in his former testament, deemed him the worthiest to be made king, which ought to be esteemed more valid than his latter testament. Antipas also brought with him his mother, and Ptolemy the brother of Nicolaus, one that had been Herod's most honoured friend, and was now zealous for Antipas: but it was Ireneus the orator, and one who, on account of his reputation for sagacity, was entrusted with the affairs of the kingdom, who most of all encouraged him to attempt to gain the kingdom; by whose means it was, that when some advised him to yield to Archelaus, as to his elder brother, and who had been declared king by their father's last will, he would not submit so to do. And when he was come to Rome, all his relations revolted to him: not out of their good-will to him, but out of their hatred to Archelaus; though indeed they were most of all desirous of gaining their liberty, and to be put under a Roman governor; but if there were too great an opposition made to that, they thought Antipas preferable to Archelaus, and

so joined with him, in order to procure the kingdom
for him. Sabinus also, by letters, accused Archelaus
to Cæsar.

5. Now, when Archelaus had sent in his papers
to Cæsar, wherein he pleaded his right to the kingdom, and his father's testament, with the accounts
of Herod's money, and with Ptolemy, who brought
Herod's seal, he so expected the event; but when
Cæsar had read these papers, and Varus' and Sabinus'
letters, with the account of the money, and what
were the annual incomes of the kingdom, and understood that Antipas had also sent letters to lay claim
to the kingdom, he summoned his friends together,
to know their opinions, and with them Caius, the
son of Agrippa, and of Julia his daughter, whom
he had adopted, and took him and made him sit first
of all, and desired such as pleased to speak their
minds about the affairs now before them. Now
Antipater, Salome's son, a very subtle orator, and
a bitter enemy to Archelaus, spoke first to this purpose: That "it was ridiculous in Archelaus to plead
now to have the kingdom given him, since he had
in reality taken already the power over it to himself,
before Cæsar had granted it to him: and appealed
to those bold actions of his, in destroying so many
at the Jewish festival, and, if the men have acted unjustly, it was but fit the punishing of them should
have been reserved to those that were out of the
country, but had the power to punish them, and
not been executed by a man that, if he pretended
to be a king, he.did an injury to Cæsar, by usurping
that authority before it was determined for him by
Cæsar, but, if he owned himself to be a private
person, his case was much worse, since he who was
putting in for the kingdom, could by no means expect
to have that power granted him, of which he had

already deprived Cæsar [by taking it to himself.] He also touched sharply upon him, and appealed to his changing the commanders in the army, and his sitting in the royal throne beforehand, and his determination of law suits; all done as if he were no other than a king. He appealed also to his concessions to those that petitioned him on a public account, and indeed doing such things, than which he could devise no greater if he had been already settled in the kingdom by Cæsar. He also ascribed to him the releasing of the prisoners that were in the Hippodrome, and many other things, that either had been certainly done by him, or were believed to be done, and easily might be believed to have been done, because they were of such a nature, as to be usually done by young men, and by such as, out of a desire of ruling, seize upon the government too soon. He also charged him with the neglect of the funeral mourning for his father, and with having merry meetings the very night in which he died; and that it was thence the multitude took the handle of raising a tumult; and if Archelaus could thus requite his dead father, who had bestowed such benefits upon him, and bequeathed such great things to him, by pretending to shed tears for him in the daytime, like an actor on the stage, but every night making mirth for having gotten the government, he would appear to be the same Archelaus with regard to Cæsar, if he granted him the kingdom, which he hath been to his father: since he had then dancing and singing, as though an enemy of his were fallen, and not as though a man were carried to his funeral, that was so nearly related, and had been so great a benefactor to him. But he said that the greatest crime of all was this, that he came now before Cæsar to obtain the government by his grant, while he had before acted in all things as he could have acted if Cæsar himself, who ruled all, had fixed him firmly in the government. And what he most aggravated in his pleading, was the slaughter of those about the temple, and the impiety of it, as done at the festival; and how they were slain like sacrifices themselves, some of whom were foreigners, and others of their own country, till the temple was full of dead bodies: and all this was done, not by an alien, but by one who pretended to the lawful title of a king, that he might complete the wicked tyranny which his nature prompted him to, and which is hated by all men. On which account his father never so much as dreamed of making him his successor in the kingdom, when he was of a sound mind, because he knew his disposition; and in his former and more authentic testament, he appointed his antagonist Antipas to succeed; but that Archelaus was called by his father to that dignity, when he was in a dying condition, both of body and mind, while Antipas was called when he was ripest in his judgment, and of such strength of body as made him capable of managing his own affairs, and if his father had the like notion of him formerly that he hath now showed, yet hath he given a sufficient specimen what a king he is likely to be, when he hath [in effect] deprived Cæsar of that power of disposing of the kingdom, which he justly hath, and hath not abstained from making a terrible slaughter of his fellow-citizens in the temple, while he was but a private person."

6. So when Antipater had made this speech, and had confirmed what he had said by producing many witnesses from among Archelaus' own relations, he made an end of his pleading. Upon which Nicolaus arose up to plead for Archelaus, and said, "That what had been done at the temple was rather to be

attributed to the mind of those that had been killed,
than to the authority of Archelaus; for that those
who were the authors of such things, are not only
wicked in the injuries they do of themselves, but in
forcing sober persons to avenge themselves upon them.
Now, it is evident, that what these did in way of
opposition was done under pretence, indeed, against
Archelaus, but in reality against Cæsar himself, for
they, after an injurious manner, attacked and slew
those who were sent by Archelaus, and who came
only to put a stop to their doings. They had no
regard, either to God or to the festival, whom Antipater yet is not ashamed to patronize, whether it be
out of his indulgence of an enmity to Archelaus, or
out of his hatred of virtue and justice. For as to
those who begin such tumults, and first set about
such unrighteous actions, they are the men who force
those that punish them, to betake themselves to arms
even against their will. So that Antipater in effect
ascribes the rest of what was done to all those who
were of counsel to the accusers, for nothing which
is here accused of injustice has been done, but what
was derived from them as its authors; nor are those
things evil in themselves, but so represented only in
order to do harm to Archelaus. Such are these
men's inclinations to do an injury to a man that is
of their kindred, their father's benefactor, and famil-
iarly acquainted with them, and that hath ever lived
in friendship with them; for that, as to this testament, it was made by the king when he was of a
sound mind, and so ought to be of more authority
than his former testament; and that for this reason,
because Cæsar is therein left to be the judge and
disposer of all therein contained; and for Cæsar he
will not, to be sure, at all imitate the unjust proceedings of those men, who during Herod's whole life,

had on all occasions been joint partakers of power
with him, and yet do zealously endeavour to injure
his determination; while they have not themselves
had the same regard to their kinsmen, [which Archelaus had.] Cæsar will not therefore disannul the
testament of a man whom he had entirely supported,
of his friend and confederate, and that which is committed to him in trust to ratify: nor will Cæsar's
virtuous and upright disposition, which is known and
uncontested through all the habitable world, imitate
the wickedness of these men in condemning a king
as a madman, and as having lost his reason, while
he hath bequeathed the succession to a good son of
his, and to one who flies to Cæsar's upright determination for refuge. Nor can Herod at any time have
been mistaken in his judgment about a successor,
while he showed so much prudence as to submit all
to Cæsar's determination."

7. Now when Nicolaus had laid these things
before Cæsar, he ended his plea; whereupon Cæsar
was so obliging to Archelaus, that he raised him up
when he had cast himself down at his feet, and said,
that "he well deserved the kingdom;" and he soon
let them know, that he was so far moved in his favour,
that he would not act otherwise than his father's
testament directed, and than was for the advantage
of Archelaus. However, while he gave this encouragement to Archelaus to depend on him securely,
he made no full determination about him; and, when
the assembly was broken up, he considered by himself, whether he should confirm the kingdom to Archelaus, or whether he should part it among all
Herod's posterity; and this because they all stood
in need of much assistance to support them.

CHAPTER X.

A sedition of the Jews against Sabinus; and how Varus brought the authors of it to punishment.

1. BUT before these things could be brought to a settlement, Malthace, Archelaus' mother, fell into a distemper, and died of it; and letters came from Varus, the president of Syria, which informed Cæsar of the revolt of the Jews; for, after Archelaus was sailed, the whole nation was in a tumult. So Varus, since he was there himself, brought the authors of the disturbance to punishment; and when he had restrained them for the most part from this sedition, which was a great one, he took his journey to Antioch, leaving one legion of his army at Jerusalem to keep the Jews quiet, who were now very fond of innovation. Yet did not this at all avail to put an end to that their sedition; for after Varus was gone away, Sabinus, Cæsar's procurator, stayed behind, and greatly distressed the Jews, relying on the forces that were left there, that they would by their multitude protect him: for he made use of them, and armed them as his guards, thereby so oppressing the Jews, and giving them so great disturbance, that at length they rebelled; for he used force in seizing the citadels, and zealously pressed on the search after the king's money, in order to seize upon it by force, on account of his love of gain, and his extraordinary covetousness.

2. But on the approach of Pentecost, which is a festival of ours, so called from the days of our forefathers, a great many ten thousands of men got together; nor did they come only to celebrate the festival, but out of their indignation at the madness

of Sabinus, and at the injuries he offered them. A great number there was of Galileans, and Idumeans, and many men from Jericho, and others who had passed over the river Jordan, and inhabited those parts. This whole multitude joined themselves to all the rest, and were more zealous than the others in making an assault on Sabinus, in order to be avenged on him; so they parted themselves into three bands, and encamped themselves in the places following: some of them seized upon the Hippodrome, and of the other two bands, one pitched themselves from the northern part of the temple to the southern, on the east quarter; but the third band held the western part of the city, where the king's palace was. Their work tended entirely to besiege the Romans, and to inclose them on all sides. Now, Sabinus was afraid of these men's number, and of their resolution, who had little regard to their lives, but were very desirous not to be overcome, while they thought it a point of puissance to overcome their enemies; so he sent immediately a letter to Varus, and, as he used to do, was very pressing with him, and entreated him to come quickly to his assistance; because the forces he had left were in imminent danger, and would probably, in no long time, be seized upon, and cut to pieces; while he did himself get up to the highest tower of the fortress Phasaelus, which had been built in honour of Phasaelus, king Herod's brother, and called so when the [1] Parthians had brought him to his death. So Sabinus gave thence a signal to the Romans to fall upon the Jews, although he did not himself venture so much as to come down to his friends, and thought he might expect that the others should expose themselves first to die on account of his avarice. How-

[1] See Antiq. B. XVI. ch. xiii. sect. 10, and Of the War, B. II. ch. xii. sect. 9.

ever, the Romans ventured to make a sally out of the place, and a terrible battle ensued: wherein, though it is true the Romans beat their adversaries, yet were not the Jews daunted in their resolutions, even when they had the sight of that terrible slaughter that was made of them, but they went round about, and got upon those cloisters, which encompassed the outer court of the temple, where a great fight was still continued, and they cast stones at the Romans, partly with their hands and partly with slings, as being much used to those exercises. All the archers also in array did the Romans a great deal of mischief; because they used their hands dexterously from a place superior to the others, and because the others were at an utter loss what to do; for when they tried to shoot their arrows against the Jews upwards, these arrows could not reach them, insomuch that the Jews were easily too hard for their enemies. And this sort of fight lasted a great while, till at last the Romans, who were greatly distressed by what was done, set fire to the cloisters so privately, that those who were gotten upon them did not perceive it. This fire [1] being fed by a great deal of combustible matter, caught hold immediately on the roof of the cloisters; so the wood, which was full of pitch and wax, and whose gold was laid on it with wax, yielded to the flame presently, and those vast works which were of the highest value and esteem, were destroyed utterly, while those that were on the roof unexpectedly perished at the same time; for, as the roof tumbled down, some of these men tumbled down with it, and others of them were killed by their enemies who encompassed them. There

---

[1] These great devastations made about the temple here, and Of the War, B. II. ch. iii. sect. 3, seem not to have been fully re-edified in the days of Nero; till whose time there were 18,000 workmen continually employed in rebuilding and repairing that temple, as Josephus informs us, Antiq. B. XX. ch. ix. sect. 7. See the note on that place,

was a great number more, who, out of despair of
saving their lives, and out of astonishment at the
misery that surrounded them, did either cast them
selves into the ·fire, or threw themselves upon their
own swords, and so got out of their misery. But
as to those that retired behind the same way by which
they ascended, and thereby escaped, they were all
killed by the Romans, as being unarmed men, and
their courage failing them; their wild fury being now
not able to help them, because they were destitute of
armour; insomuch that, of those that went up to
the top of the roof, not one escaped. The Romans
also rushed through the fire, where it gave them room
so to do, and seized on that treasure where the sacred
money was reposited; a great part of which was stolen
by the soldiers, and Sabinus got openly four hundred
talents.

3. But this calamity of the Jews' friends, who
fell in this battle, grieved them, as did also this
plundering of the money dedicated to God in the
temple. Accordingly, that body of them which continued best together, and was the most warlike, encompassed the palace, and threatened to set fire to
it, and kill all that were in it. Yet still they commanded them to go out presently, and promised, that
if they would do so, they would not hurt them, nor
Sabinus neither; at which time the greatest part of
the king's troops deserted to them, while Rufus and
Gratus, who had three thousand of the most warlike
of Herod's army with them, who were men of active
bodies, went over to the Romans. There was also
a band of horsemen under the command of Rufus,
which itself went over to the Romans also. However, the Jews went on with the siege, and dug mines
under the palace walls, and besought those that were
gone over to the other side, not to be their hinderance.

now they had such a proper opportunity for the recovery of their country's ancient liberty; and for Sabinus, truly he was desirous of going away with his soldiers, but was not able to trust himself with the enemy, on account of what mischief he had already done them; and he took this great [pretended] lenity of theirs for an argument why he should not comply with them: and so, because he expected that Varus was coming, he still bore the siege.

4. Now, at this time there were ten thousand other disorders in Judea, which were like tumults; because a great number put themselves into a warlike posture, either out of hopes of gain to themselves, or out of enmity to the Jews. In particular, two thousand of Herod's old soldiers, who had been already disbanded, got together in Judea itself and fought against the king's troops; although Achiabus, Herod's first cousin, opposed them; but as he was driven out of the plains into the mountainous parts, by the military skill of those men; he kept himself in the fastnesses that were there, and saved what he could.

5. There was also Judas, [1] the son of that Ezekias who had been head of the robbers; which Ezekias was a very strong man, and had with great difficulty been caught by Herod. This Judas having gotten together a multitude of men of a profligate character

[1] Unless this Judas, the son of Ezekias, be the same with that Theudas mentioned, Acts v. 36, Josephus must have omitted him; for that other Theudas, whom he afterwards mentioned under Fadus, the Roman governor, B. XX. ch. v. sect. l, is much too late to correspond to him that is mentioned in the Acts. The names *Theudas, Thadeus,* and *Judas,* differ but little. See Abp. Usher's Annals at A. M. 4001. However, since Josephus does not pretend to reckon up the heads of all those *ten thousand* disorders in Judea, which he tells us were then abroad, see sect. 4, and 8, the Theudas of the Acts might be at the head of one of those seditions, though not particularly named by him. Thus he informs us here, sect. 6, and Of the War, B. II. ch. iv. sect. 2, that certain of the seditious came and burnt the royal palace at Amathus, or Bethramphta, upon the river Jordan. Perhaps their leader, who is not named by Josephus, might be this Theudas.

about Sepphoris in Galilee, made an assault upon
the palace [there,] and seized upon all the weapons
that were laid up in it, and with them armed every
one of those that were with him, and carried away
what money was left there: and he became terrible
to all men, by tearing and rending those that came
near him; and all this in order to raise himself, and
out of an ambitious desire of the royal dignity; and
he hoped to obtain that as the reward not of his
virtuous skill in war, but of his extravagance in doing
injuries.

6. There was also Simon, who had been a slave
of Herod the king, but in other respects a comely
person, of a tall and robust body; he was one that
was much superior to others of his order, and had
had great things committed to his care. This man
was elevated at the disorderly state of things, and
was so bold as to put a diadem on his head, while a
certain number of the people stood by him, and by
them he was declared to be a king, and thought
himself more worthy of that dignity than any one
else. He burnt down the royal palace at Jericho,
and plundered what was left in it. He also set fire
to many other of the king's houses in several places
of the country, and utterly destroyed them, and permitted those that were with him to take what was
left in them for a prey; and he would have done
greater things, unless care had been taken to repress
him immediately; for Gratus, when he had joined himself to some Roman soldiers, took the forces he had
with him, and met Simon, and after a great and a
long fight, no small part of those that came from
Perea, who were a disordered body of men, and
fought rather in a bold than in a skilful manner,
were destroyed; and although Simon had saved himself by flying away through a certain valley, yet

Gratus overtook him, and cut off his head. The royal palace also, at Amathus, by the river Jordan, was burnt down by a party of men that were got together, as were those belonging to Simon. And thus did a great and wild fury spread itself over the nation, because they had no king to keep the multitude in good order, and because those foreigners, who came to reduce the seditious to sobriety, did, on the contrary, set them more in a flame, because of the injuries they offered them, and the avaricious management of their affairs.

7. At this time also Athronges, a person neither eminent by the dignity of his progenitors, nor for any great wealth he was possessed of, but one that had in all respects been a shepherd only, and was not known by any body; yet because he was a tall man, and excelled others in the strength of his hands, he was so bold as. to set up for king. This man thought it so sweet a thing to do more than ordinary injuries to others, that although he should be killed, he did not much care if he lost his life in so great a design. He had also four brethren, who were tall men themselves, and were believed to be superior to others in the strength of their hands, and thereby were encouraged to aim at great things, and thought that strength of theirs would support them in retaining the kingdom. Each of these ruled over a band of men of their own: for those that got together to them were very numerous. They were every one of them also commanders; but, when they came to fight, they were subordinate to him, and fought for him, while he put a diadem about his head, and assembled a council to debate about what things should be done, and all things were done according to his pleasure. And this man retained his power a great while; he was also called king, and had nothing to hinder him

from doing what he pleased. He also, as well as his brethren, slew a great many both of the Romans and of the king's forces, and managed matters with the like hatred to each of them. The king's forces they fell upon, because of the licentious conduct they had been allowed under Herod's government, and they fell upon the Romans, because of the injuries they had so lately received from them. But in process of time, they grew more cruel to all sorts of men, nor could any one escape from one or other of those seditions, since they slew some out of the hopes of gain, and others from a mere custom of slaying men. They once attacked a company of Romans at Emmaus, who were bringing corn and weapons to the army, and fell upon Arius, the centurion, who commanded the company, and shot forty of the best of his foot-soldiers; but the rest of them were affrighted at their slaughter, and left their dead behind them, but saved themselves by the means of Gratus, who came with the king's troops that were about him to their assistance. Now, these four brethren continued the war a long while by such sort of expeditions, and much grieved the Romans; but did their own nation also a great deal of mischief. Yet were they afterwards subdued; one of them in a fight with Gratus, another with Ptolemy; Archelaus also took the eldest of them prisoner, while the last of them was so dejected, at the others' misfortune, and saw so plainly that he had no way now left to save himself, his army being worn away with sickness and continual labours, that he also delivered himself up to Archelaus, upon his promise and oath to God [to preserve his life.] But these things came to pass a good while afterward.

8. And now Judea was full of robberies: and, as the several companies of the seditious light upon any one to head them, he was created a king immediately,

in order to do mischief to the public. They were in small measure indeed, and in small matters, hurtful to the Romans but the murders they committed upon their own people lasted a long while.

9. As soon as Varus was once informed of the state of Judea by Sabinus' writing to him, he was afraid for the legion he had left there; so he took the two other legions, (for there were three legions in all belonging to Syria,) and four troops of horsemen, with the several auxiliary forces which either the kings or certain of the tetrarchs afforded him, and made what haste he could to assist those that were then besieged in Judea. He also gave order, that all that were sent out for this expedition, should make haste to Ptolemais. The citizens of Berytus also gave him 1500 auxiliaries, as he passed through their city. Aretas also, the king of Arabia Petrea, out of his hatred to Herod, and in order to purchase the favour of the Romans, sent him no small assistance, besides their footmen and horsemen; and, when he had now collected all his forces together, he committed part of them to his son, and to a friend of his, and sent them upon an expedition into Galilee, which lies in the neighbourhood of Ptolemais; who made an attack upon the enemy, and put them to flight, and took Sepphoris, and made its inhabitants slaves, and burnt the city. But Varus himself pursued his march for Samaria with his whole army: yet did not he meddle with the city of that name, because it had not at all joined with the seditious; but pitched his camp at a certain village that belonged to Ptolemy, whose name was Arus, which the Arabians burnt, out of their hatred to Herod, and out of the enmity they bore to his friends; whence they marched to another village, whose name was Sampho, which the Arabians plundered and burnt, although it was a

fortified and a strong place; and all along this march nothing escaped them, but all places were full of fire and of slaughter. Emmaus was also burnt by Varus' order, after its inhabitants had deserted it, that he might avenge those that had there been destroyed. From thence he now marched to Jerusalem; whereupon those Jews whose camp lay there, and who had besieged the Roman legion, now hearing the coming of this army, left the siege imperfect; but as to the Jerusalem Jews, when Varus reproached them bitterly for what had been done, they cleared themselves of the accusation, and alleged, that the conflux of the people was occasioned by the feast; that the war was not made with their approbation, but the rashness of the strangers, while they were on the side of the Romans, and besieged together with them, rather than having any inclination to besiege them. There also came beforehand to meet Varus, Joseph, the cousin-german of king Herod, as also Gratus and Rufus, who brought their soldiers along with them, together with those Romans who had been besieged: but Sabinus did not come into Varus' presence, but stole out of the city privately, and went to the seaside.

10. Upon this Varus sent a part of his army into the country, to seek out those that had been the authors of the revolt; and when they were discovered, he punished some of them that were most guilty, and some he dismissed: now the number of those that were crucified on this account was two thousand. After which he disbanded his army, which he found nowise useful to him in the affairs he came about; for they behaved themselves very disorderly, and disobeyed his orders, and what Varus desired them to do, and this out of regard to that gain which they made by the mischief they did. As for himself,

when he was informed that ten thousand Jews had
gotten together, he made haste to catch them;. but
they did not proceed so far as to fight him, but, by
the advice of Achiabus, they came together, and
delivered themselves up to him: hereupon Varus forgave the crime of revolting to the multitude, but sent
their several commanders to Cæsar; many of them
Cæsar dismissed: but for the several relations of
Herod who had been among these men in this war,
they were the only persons whom he punished, who,
without the least regard to justice, fought against
their own kindred.

CHAPTER XI.

*An embassage of the Jews to Cæsar, and how Cæsar
confirmed Herod's testament.*

1. So when Varus had settled these affairs, and
had placed the former legion at Jerusalem, he returned
back to Antioch: but as for Archelaus, he had new
sources of trouble come upon him at Rome, on the
occasions following: for an embassage of the Jews
was come to Rome, Varus having permitted the nation
to send it, that they might petition for the liberty
of living by their own laws.[1] Now, the number of
the ambassadors that were sent by the authority of
the nation was fifty, to which they joined above eight
thousand of the Jews that were at Rome already.
Hereupon Cæsar assembled his friends, and the chief
men among the Romans, in the temple of Apollo,[2]
which he had built at a vast charge; whither the
ambassadors came, and a multitude of the Jews that

---

[1] See Of the War, B. II. ch. ii. sect. 3.
[2] See the note Of the War, B. II. ch. vi. sect. 1.

were there already, came with them, as did also
Archelaus and his friends; but as for the several
kinsmen which Archelaus had, they would not join
themselves with him out of their hatred to him; and
yet they thought it too gross a thing for them to assist
the ambassadors [against him,] as supposing it would
be a disgrace to them in Cæsar's opinion to think of
thus acting in opposition to a man of their own
kindred.[1] Philip also was come hither out of Syria,
by the persuasion of Varus, with this principal intention to assist his brother [Archelaus;] for Varus
was his great friend: but still so, that if there should
any change happen in the form of government (which
Varus suspected there would,) and if any distribution should be made on account of the number that
desired the liberty of living by their own laws, that
he might not be disappointed, but might have his
share in it.

2. Now upon the liberty that was given to the
Jewish ambassadors to speak, they who hoped to
obtain a dissolution of kingly government betook
themselves to accuse Herod of his iniquities; and
they declared, "That he was indeed in name a king,
but that he had taken to himself that uncontrollable
authority which tyrants exercise over their subjects,
and had made use of that authority for the destruction of the Jews, and did not abstain from making
many innovations among them, besides, according to
his own inclinations; and that whereas there were a
great many who perished by that destruction he
brought upon them, so many indeed as no other
history relates, they that survived were far more
miserable than those that suffered under him: not
only by the anxiety they were in from his looks
and disposition towards them, but from the danger

[1] He was tetrarch afterward.

their estates were in of being taken away by him.
That he did never leave off adorning these cities
that lay in their neighbourhood, but were inhabited
by foreigners; but so that the cities belonging to his
own government were ruined, and utterly destroyed:
that whereas, when he took the kingdom, it was in
an extraordinary flourishing condition, he had filled
the nation with the utmost degree of poverty; and
when, upon unjust pretences, he had slain any of
the nobility, he took away their estates; and when he
permitted any of them to live, he condemned them to
the forfeiture of what they possessed. And, besides
the annual impositions which he laid upon every one
of them, they were to make liberal presents to himself, to his domestics and friends, and to such of his
slaves as were vouchsafed the favour of being his
tax-gatherers; because there was no way of obtaining
a freedom from unjust violence, without giving either
gold or silver for it. That they would say nothing
of the corruption of the chastity of their virgins, and
the reproach laid on their wives for incontinency, and
those things acted after an insolent and inhuman
manner; because it was not a smaller pleasure to the
sufferers to have such things concealed than it would
have been to have suffered them. That Herod had
put such abuses upon them as a wild beast would
not have put on them, if he had power given him
to rule over us; and that although their nation had
passed through many subversions and alterations of
government, their history gave no account of any
calamity they had ever been under, that could be
compared with this which Herod had brought upon
their nation; that it was for this reason, that they
thought they might justly and gladly salute Archelaus
as king, upon this supposition, that whosoever should
be set over their kingdom, he would appear more

mild to them than Herod had been; and that they
had joined with him in the mourning for his father,
in order to gratify him, and were ready to oblige him
in other points also, if they could meet with any
degree of moderation from him: but that he seemed
to be afraid lest he should not be deemed Herod's
own son; and so, without any delay, he immediately
let the nation understand his meaning, and this before
his dominion was well established, since the power
of disposing of it belonged to Cæsar, who could either
give it to him or not, as he pleased. That he had
given a specimen of his future virtue to his subjects,
and with what kind of moderation and good administration he would govern them, by that his first
action which concerned them, his own citizens, and
God himself also, when he made the slaughter of
three thousand of his own countrymen at the temple.
How, then, could they avoid the just hatred of him,
who to the rest of his barbarity, had added this as
one of our crimes, that we have opposed and contradicted him in the exercise of his authority?" Now,
the main thing they desired was this, "That they
might be delivered from kingly [1] and the like forms
of government, and might be added to Syria, and be
put under the authority of such presidents of theirs

---

[1] If any one compare that divine prediction concerning the tyrannical
power which Jewish kings would exercise over them, if they would be so
foolish as to prefer it before their ancient theocracy or aristocracy, 1
Sam. viii. 1-22, Antiq. B. I. ch. iv. sect. 4, he will soon find that it was
super-abundantly fulfilled in the days of Herod, and that to such a
degree, that the nation now at last seem sorely to repent of such their
ancient choice, in opposition to God's better choice for them, and had
much rather be subject to even a Pagan Roman government, and their
deputies, than to be longer under the oppression of the family of Herod;
which request of theirs Augustus did not now grant them, but did it
for the one-half of that nation, in a few years afterward, upon fresh
complaints made by the Jews against Archelaus, who, under the more
humble name of an ethnarch, which Augustus only would now allow
him, soon took upon him the insolence and tyranny of his father, king
Herod, as the remaining part of this book will inform us, and particularly
ch. xiii. sect. 2.

as should be sent to them; for that it would thereby be made evident, whether they be really a seditious people, and generally fond of innovations, or whether they would live in an orderly manner, if they might have governors of any sort of moderation set over them."

3. Now, when the Jews had said this, Nicolaus vindicated the kings from those accusations, and said, "That, as for Herod, since he had never been thus accused [1] all the time of his life, it was not fit for those that might have accused them of lesser crimes than those now mentioned, and might have procured him to be punished during his life time, to bring an accusation against him now he is dead. He also attributed the actions of Archelaus to the Jews' injuries to him, who affecting to govern contrary to the laws, and going about to kill those that would have hindered them from acting unjustly, when they were by him punished for what they had done, made their complaints against him; so he accused them of their attempts for innovations, and of the pleasure they took in sedition, by reason of their not having learned to submit to justice, and to the laws, but still desiring to be superior in all things." This was the substance of what Nicolaus said.

4. When Cæsar had heard these pleadings, he dissolved the assembly; but a few days afterwards he appointed Archelaus, not indeed to be king of the whole country, but ethnarch of the one-half of that which had been subject to Herod, and promised to give him the royal dignity hereafter, if he governed his part virtuously. But as for the other half, he divided it into two parts, and gave it to two other of

[1] This is not true. See Antiq. B. XIV. ch. ix. sect. 3, 4, and ch. xii. sect. 2, and ch. xiii. sect. 1, 2, Antiq. B. XV. ch. iii. sect. 5, and ch. x. sect. 2, 3, Antiq. B. XVI. ch. ix. sect. 3.

Herod's sons, to Philip and to Antipas, that Antipas who disputed with Archelaus for the whole kingdom. Now, to him it was that Perea and Galilee paid their tribute, which amounted [1] annually to two hundred talents, while Batanea, with Trachonitis, as well as Auranitis, with a certain [2] part of what was called the *house of Zenodorus,* paid the tribute of one hundred talents to Philip; but Idumea, and Judea, and the country of Samaria, paid tribute to Archelaus,

[1] Since Josephus here informs us that Archelaus had one-half of the kingdom of Herod, and presently informs us farther that Archelaus' annual income, after an abatement of one-quarter for the present, was 600 talents, we may therefore gather pretty nearly what was Herod the Great's yearly income, I mean about 1600 talents, which at the known value of 3000 shekels to a talent, and about 2s. 10d. to a shekel, in the days of Josephus, see the note on Antiq. B. III. ch. viii. sect. 2, amounts to £680,000 sterling *per annum;* which income, though great in itself, bearing no proportion to his vast expenses every where visible in Josephus, and to the vast sums he left behind him in his will, ch. viii. sect. 1, and ch. xii. sect. 1, the rest must have arisen, either from his confiscation of those great men's estates whom he put to death, or made to pay a fine for the saving of their lives, or from some other heavy methods of oppression which such savage tyrants usually exercise upon their miserable subjects; or rather from these several methods put together, all which yet seem very much too small for his expenses, being drawn from no larger a nation than that of the Jews, which was very populous, but without the advantage of trade, to bring them riches; so that I cannot but strongly suspect that no small part of this his wealth arose from another source; I mean from some vast sums he took out of David's sepulchre, but concealed from the people. See the note on Antiq. B. VIII. ch. xv. sect. 3.

[2] Take here a very useful note of Grotius, on Luke, B. III. ch. i. here quoted by Dr. Hudson: "When Josephus says that some part of the house (or possession) of Zenodorus (i. e. Abilene,) was allotted to Philip, he thereby declares that the larger part of it belonged to another; this other was Lysanias, whom Luke mentions of the posterity of that Lysanias who was possessed of the same country called *Abilene,* from the city Abila, and by others *Chalcedene,* from the city Chalcis, when the government of the east was under Antonius, and this after Ptolemy, the son of Mennius: from which Lysanias, this country came to be commonly called the *Country of Lysanias;* and as, after the death of the former Lysanias, it was called the *tetrarchy of Zenodorus,* so after the death of Zenodorus, or when the time for which he had hired it was ended, when another Lysanias, of the same name with the former, was possessed of the same country, it began to be called the *tetrarchy of Lysanias.*" However, since Josephus elsewhere, Antiq. B. XX. ch. vii. sect. 1, clearly distinguishes Abilene from Chalcidene, Grotius must be here so far mistaken.

but had now a fourth part of that tribute taken off by the order of Cæsar, who decreed them that mitigation, because they did not join in this revolt with the rest of the multitude. There were also certain of the cities which paid tribute to Archelaus, Strato's Tower, and Sebaste, with Joppa and Jerusalem; for as to Gaza and Gadara, and Hippos, they were Grecian cities, which Cæsar separated from his government, and added them to the province of Syria. Now the tribute-money that came to Archelaus every year from his own dominions, amounted to six hundred talents.

5. And so much came to Herod's sons from their father's inheritance. But Salome, besides what her brother left her by his testament, which were Jamnia, and Ashdod, and Phasaelis, and five hundred thousand [drachmæ] of coined silver, Cæsar made her a present of a royal habitation at Askelon; in all, her revenues amounted to sixty talents by the year, and her dwelling-house was within Archelaus' government. The rest, also, of the king's relations received what his testament allotted them. Moreover, Cæsar made a present to each of Herod's two virgin daughters, besides what their father left them, of two hundred and fifty thousand [drachmæ] of silver, and married them to Pheroras' sons; he also granted all that was bequeathed to himself to the king's sons, which was one thousand five hundred talents, excepting a few of the vessels, which he reserved for himself; and they were acceptable to him, not so much for the great value they were of, as because they were memorials of the king to him.

CHAPTER XII.

Concerning a Spurious Alexander.

1. W HEN these affairs had been thus settled by
Cæsar, a certain young man, by birth a Jew, but
brought up a Roman freed man in the city Sidon,
ingrafted himself into the kindred of Herod, by
the resemblance of his ·countenance, which those that
saw him attested to be that of Alexander the son
of Herod, whom he had slain; and this was an incitement to him to endeavour to obtain the government; so he took to him as an assistant, a man of
his own country, (one that was well acquainted with
the affairs of the palace, but on other accounts, an
ill man, and one whose nature made him capable of
causing great disturbances to the public, and one
that became a teacher of such a mischievous contrivance to the other,) and declared himself to be
Alexander, and the son of Herod, but stolen away
by one of those that were sent to slay him, who, in
reality, slew other men in order to deceive the spectators, but saved both him and his brother Aristobulus. Thus was this man elated, and able to impose
on those that came to him; and when he was come
to Crete, he made all the Jews that came to discourse
with him believe him [to be Alexander.] And when
he had gotten much money which had been presented
to him there, he passed over to Melos, where he got
much more money than he had before, out of their
belief they had that he was of the royal family, and
their hopes that he would recover his father's principality, and reward his benefactors: so he made
haste to Rome, and was conducted thither by those

strangers who entertained him. He was also so fortunate, as, upon his landing at Dicearchia, to bring the Jews that were there into the same delusion; and not only other people, but also all those that had been great with Herod, or had a kindness for him, joined themselves to this man as to their king. The cause of it was this, that men were glad of his pretences, which were seconded by the likeness of his countenance, which made those that had been acquainted with Alexander strongly to believe that he was no other but the very same person, which they also confirmed to others by oath; insomuch that when the report went about him that he was coming to Rome, the whole multitude of the Jews that were there went out to meet him, ascribing it to divine Providence that he had so unexpectedly escaped, and being very joyful on account of his mother's family. And when he was come, he was carried in a royal litter through the streets, and all the ornaments about him were such as kings are adorned withal; and this was at the expense of those that entertained him. The multitude also flocked about him greatly, and made mighty acclamations to him, and nothing was omitted which could be thought suitable to such as had been so unexpectedly preserved.

2. When this thing was told Cæsar he did not believe it, because Herod was not easily to be imposed upon in such affairs as were of great concern to him; yet, having some suspicion it might be so, he sent one Celadus, a freed man of his, and one that had conversed with the young men themselves, and bade him bring Alexander into his presence: so he brought him, being no more accurate in judging about him than the rest of the multitude. Yet did not he deceive Cæsar; for although there were a resemblance between him and Alexander, yet was it

not so exact as to impose on such as were prudent
in discerning; for this spurious Alexander had his
hands rough, by the labours he had been put to, and
instead of that softness of body which the other had,
and this as derived from his delicate and generous
education, this man, for the contrary reason, had
a rugged body. When, therefore, Cæsar saw how
the master and the scholar agreed in this lying story,
and in a bold way of talking, he inquired about
Aristobulus, and asked what became of him, who
(it seems) was stolen away together with him, and
for what reason it was that he did not come along
with him, and endeavour to recover that dominion
which was due to his high birth also? And when
he said, That "he had been left in the isle of Crete,
for fear of the dangers of the sea, that, in case any
accident should come to himself, the posterity of
Mariamne might not utterly perish, but that Aristobulus might survive, and punish those that laid
such treacherous designs against them." And when
he persevered in his affirmations, and the author of
the imposture agreed in supporting it, Cæsar took
the young man by himself, and said to him, "If thou
wilt not impose upon me, thou shalt have this for
thy reward, that thou shalt escape with thy life; tell
me, then, who thou art, and who it was that had
boldness enough to contrive such a cheat as this. For
this contrivance is too considerable a piece of villainy
to be undertaken by one of thy age." Accordingly,
because he had no other way to take, he told Cæsar
the contrivance, and after what manner, and by
whom it was laid together. So Cæsar, upon observing the spurious Alexander to be a strong active
man, and fit to work with his hands, that he might
not break his promise to him, put him among those
that were to row among the mariners; but slew him

that induced him to do what he had done; for as for
the people of Melos, he thought them sufficiently
punished, in having thrown away so much of their
money upon this spurious Alexander. And such was
the ignominious conclusion of this bold contrivance
about the spurious Alexander.

CHAPTER XIII.

*How Archelaus, upon a second accusation, was ban-
ished to Vienna.*

1. When Archelaus was entered on his ethnarchy,
and was come into Judea, he accused Joazer, the
son of Boethus, of assisting the seditious, and took
away the high priesthood from him, and put Eleazar
his brother in his place. He also magnificently rebuilt the royal palace that had been at Jericho, and
he diverted half the water with which the village
of Neara used to be watered, and drew off that water
into the plain, to water those palm-trees which he
had there planted: he also built a village, and put
his own name upon it, and called it *Archeleis.* Moreover, he [1] transgressed the law of our fathers, and
married Glaphyra, the daughter of Archelaus, who
had been the wife of his brother Alexander, which
Alexander had three children by her, while it was
a thing detestable among the Jews, to marry the
brother's wife; nor did this Eleazar abide long in
the high priesthood, Jesus, the son of Sie, being
put in his room while he was still living.

2. But in the tenth year of Archelaus' govern-

[1] Spanheim seasonably observes here, that it was forbidden the Jews
to marry their brother's wife, when she had children by her first husband,
and that Zenora (cites, or) interprets the clause before us accordingly.

ment, both his brethren, and the principal men of
Judea and Samaria, not being able to bear his barbarous and tyrannical usage of them, accused him
before Cæsar, and that especially because they knew
he had broken the commands of Cæsar, which obliged
him to behave himself with moderation among them.
Whereupon Cæsar, when he heard it, was very angry,
and called for Archelaus' steward, who took care of
his affairs at Rome, and whose name was Archelaus '
also, and thinking it beneath him to write to Archelaus, he bid him sail away as soon as possible,
and bring him to us: so the man made haste in his
voyage, and when he came into Judea he found
Archelaus feasting with his friends; so he told him
what Cæsar had sent him about, and hastened him
away. And when he was come [to Rome,] Cæsar,
upon hearing what certain accusers of his had to
say, and what reply he could make, both banished
him, and appointed Vienna, a city of Gaul, to be
the place of his habitation, and took his money away
from him.

3. Now, before Archelaus was gone up to Rome
upon this message, he related this dream to his friends,
that "he saw ears of corn, in number ten, full of
wheat, perfectly ripe, which ears, as it seemed to
him, were devoured by oxen." And when he was
awake and gotten up, because the vision appeared
to be of great importance to him, he sent for the
diviners, whose study was employed about dreams.
And while some were of one opinion, and some of
another, (for all their interpretations did not agree,)
Simon, a man of the sect of the Essens, desired leave
to speak his mind freely, and said, that "the vision
denoted a change in the affairs of Archelaus, and
that not for the better; that oxen, because that animal
takes uneasy pains in his labours, denoted afflictions,

and indeed denoted, farther, a change of affairs;
because that land which is ploughed by oxen cannot
remain in its former state: and that the ears of corn
being ten, determined the like number of years, because an ear of corn grows in one year; and that
the time of Archelaus' government was over." And
thus did this man expound the dream. Now, on the
fifth day after this dream came first to Archelaus,
the other Archelaus, that was sent to Judea by Cæsar
to call him away, came hither also.

4. The like accident befell Glaphyra his wife, who
was the daughter of king Archelaus, who, as I said
before, was married, while she was a virgin, to Alexander, the son of Herod, and brother of Archelaus;
but since it fell out so that Alexander was slain by
his father, she was married to Juba, the king of
Lydia, and when he was dead, and she lived in
widowhood in Cappadocia with her father, Archelaus
divorced his former wife Mariamne, and married her,
so great was his affection for this Glaphyra; who,
during her marriage to him, saw the following dream.
She thought "she saw Alexander standing by her,
at which she rejoiced, and embraced him with great
affection; but that he complained of her, and said,
O Glaphyra! thou provest that saying to be true,
which assures us, that women are not to be trusted.
Didst not thou pledge thy faith to me? and wast
not thou married to me when thou wast a virgin?
and had we not children between us? Yet thou
hast forgotten the affection I bore to thee, out of
the desire of a second husband. Nor hast thou been
satisfied with that injury thou didst me, but thou
hast been so bold as to procure thee a third husband
to lie by thee, and in an indecent and imprudent
manner hast entered into my house, and hast been
married to Archelaus, thy husband, and my brother.

However, I will not forget thy former kind affection for me, but will set thee free from every such reproachful action, and cause thee to be mine again, as thou once wast." When she had related this to her female companions, in a few days' time she departed this life.

5. Now, I do not think these histories improper for the present discourse, both because my discourse now is concerning kings, and otherwise also on account of the advantage hence to be drawn, as well as for the confirmation of the immortality of the soul, as of the providence of God over human affairs, I thought them fit to be set down; but if any one does not believe such relations, let him indeed enjoy his own opinion, but let him not hinder another, that would thereby encourage himself in virtue. So Archelaus' country was laid to the province of Syria; and Cyrenius, one that had been consul, was sent by Cæsar to take account of people's effects in Syria, and to sell the house of Archelaus.

BOOK XVIII.

CONTAINING THE INTERVAL OF THIRTY-TWO YEARS.

[FROM THE BANISHMENT OF ARCHELAUS TO THE DEPAR-
TURE OF THE JEWS FROM BABYLON.]

CHAPTER I.

*How Cyrenius was sent by Cæsar to make a taxation
of Syria and Judea; and how Coponius was sent
to be procurator of Judea: concerning Judas of
Galilee, and concerning the sects that were among
the Jews.*

1. Now Cyrenius, a Roman senator, and one who
had gone through other magistracies, and had passed
through them till he had been consul, and one who,
on other accounts, was of great dignity, came at
this time into Syria, with a few others, being sent
by Cæsar to be a judge of that nation, and to take
an account of their substance: Coponius also, a man
of the equestrian order, was sent together with him,
to have the supreme power over the Jews. More
over, Cyrenius came himself into Judea, which was
now added to the province of Syria, to take an account of their substance, and to dispose of Archelaus'
money: but the Jews, although at the beginning they
took the report of a taxation heinously, yet did they

leave off any farther opposition to it, by the persuasion of Joazer, who was the son of Boethus, and high priest; so they being over persuaded by Joazer's words, gave an account of their estates, without any dispute about it. Yet was there one Judas,[1] a Gaulonite, of a city whose name was *Gamala,* who taking with him Saddouk,[2] a Pharisee, became zealous to draw them to a revolt, who both said, that this taxation was no better than an introduction to slavery, and exhorted the nation to assert their liberty, as if they could procure them happiness and security for what they possessed, and assured enjoyment of a still greater good, which was that of the honour and glory they would thereby acquire for magnanimity. They also said, that God would not otherwise be assisting to them, than upon their joining with one another in such councils as might be suc-

---

[1] Since St. Luke once, Acts v. 37, and Josephus four several times, once here, sect. 6, and B. XX. ch. v. sect. 2, Of the War, B. II. ch. viii. sect. 1, and ch. xvii. sect. 8, calls this Judas, who was the pestilent author of that seditious doctrine and temper which brought the Jewish nation to utter destruction, a *Galilean,* but here, sect. 1, Josephus calls him a *Gaulonite,* of the city Gamala. It is a great question where this Judas was born, whether in Galilee on the west side, or in Gaulonitis, on the east side of the river Jordan; while in the place just now cited out of the Antiquities, B. XX. ch. v. sect. 2, he is not only called a Galilean, but it is added to his story, *as I have signified in the books that go before these,* as if he had still called him a *Galilean* in those Antiquities before, as well as in that particular place, as Dean Aldrich observes, On the War, B. II. ch. viii. sect. 1. Nor can one well imagine why he should here call him a *Gaulonite,* when in the 6th sect. following here, as well as twice of the war, he still calls him a *Galilean.* As for the city of Gamala, whence this Judas was derived, it determines nothing, since there were two of that name, the one in Gaulonitis, the other in Galilee. See Reland on the city or town of that name.

[2] It seems not very improbable to me, that this Sadduc, the Pharisee, was the very same man of whom the Rabbins speak, as the unhappy, but undesigning occasion of the impiety or infidelity of the Sadducees: nor perhaps had the men this name of Sadducees till this very time, though they were a distinct sect long before. See the note on B. XIII. ch. x. sect. 3, and Dean Prideaux, as there quoted; nor do we, that I know of, find the least footsteps of such impiety or infidelity of these Sadducees before this time, the Recognitions assuring us, that they began about the days of John the Baptist, B. I. ch. liv.

cessful, and for their own advantage; and this especially, if they would set about great exploits, and not grow weary in executing the same; so men received what they said with pleasure, and this bold attempt proceeded to a great height. All sorts of misfortunes also sprang from these men, and the nation was infected with this doctrine to an incredible degree: one violent war came upon us after another, and we lost our friends who used to alleviate our pains; there were also very great robberies and murders of our principal men. This was done in pretence indeed for the public welfare, but in reality from the hopes of gain to themselves; whence arose seditions, and from them murders of men, which sometimes fell on those of their own people, (by the madness of these men towards one another, while their desire was that none of the adverse party might be left,) and sometimes on their enemies; a famine also coming upon us reduced us to the last degree of despair, as did also the taking and demolishing of cities; nay, the sedition at last increased so big, that the very temple of God was burnt down by their enemies' fire. Such were the consequences of this, that the customs of our fathers were altered, and such a change was made, as added a mighty weight toward bringing all to destruction, which these men occasioned by their thus conspiring together, for Judas and Sadducus,[1] who excited a fourth philosophic sect among us, and had a great many followers therein, filled our civil government with tumults at present, and laid the foundations of our future miseries by this system of philosophy, which we were before unacquainted withal, concerning which I will discourse a little, and this the rather, because the infection which spread thence among the younger

---

[1] See the preceding note.

sort, who were zealous for it, brought the public to destruction.

2. The Jews had for a great while had three sects of philosophy peculiar to themselves, the sect of the Essens, and the sect of the Sadducees, and the third sort of opinions was that of those called Pharisees; of which sects, although I have already spoken in the second book of the Jewish war, yet will I a little touch upon them now.

3. Now, for the Pharisees, they live meanly, and despise delicacies in diet, and they follow the contract of reason; and what that prescribes to them as good for them, they do; and they think they ought earnestly to strive to observe reason's dictates for practice. They also pay a respect to such as are in years; nor are they so bold as to contradict them in any thing which they have introduced; and when they determine that all things are done by fate, they do not take away the freedom from men of acting as they think fit; since their notion is, that it hath pleased God to make a temperament, whereby what he wills is done, but so that the will of man can act virtuously or·viciously. They also believe, that souls have an immortal vigour in them, and that under the earth there will be rewards or punishments, according as they have lived virtuously or viciously in this life; and the latter are to be detained in an everlasting prison, but that the former shall have power to revive and live again; on account of which doctrines, they are able greatly to persuade the body of the people, and whatsoever they do about divine worship, prayers, and sacrifices, they perform them according to their direction; insomuch that the cities give great attestations to them on account of their entire virtuous conduct, both in the actions of their lives, and their discourses also.

4. But the doctrine of the Sadducees is this, That
souls die with the bodies; nor do they regard the observation of any thing besides what the law enjoins
them; for they think it an instance of virtue to dispute with those teachers of philosophy whom they
frequent; but this doctrine is received but by a few,
yet by those still of the greatest dignity. But they
are able to do almost nothing of themselves; for
when they become magistrates, as they are unwillingly and by force sometimes obliged to be, they
addict themselves to the notions of the Pharisees,
because the multitude would not otherwise bear them.

5. The doctrine of the Essens is this, That all
things are best ascribed to God. They teach the
immortality of souls, and esteem that the rewards
of righteousness are to be earnestly striven for; and
when they send what they have dedicated to God
into the temple, they do not offer sacrifices, because
they have more pure lustrations of their own; [1] on
which account they are excluded from the common
court of the temple, but offer their sacrifices themselves; yet is their course of life better than that of
other men: and they entirely addict themselves to
husbandry. It also deserves our admiration, how
much they exceed all other men that addict themselves
to virtue, and this in righteousness: and indeed to
such a degree, that as it hath never appeared among
any other men, neither Greeks nor Barbarians, no
not for a little time, so hath it endured for a long
while among them. This is demonstrated by that

---

[1] It seems by what Josephus says here, and Philo himself elsewhere,
Op. p. 679, that these Essens did not use to go to the Jewish festivals
at Jerusalem, or to offer sacrifices there, which may be one great occasion why they are never mentioned in the ordinary books of the New
Testament; though in the Apostolical Constitutions, they are mentioned
as those that *observed the customs of their forefathers,* and that without
any such ill character laid upon them, as is there laid upon the other
sects among that people.

institution of theirs, which will not suffer any thing
to hinder them from having all things in common;
so that a rich man enjoys no more of his own wealth
than he who hath nothing at all. There are about
four thousand men that live in this way; and neither
marry wives, nor are desirous to keep servants; as
thinking the latter tempts men to be unjust, and
the former gives the handle to domestic quarrels;
but as they live by themselves, they minister one to
another. They also appoint certain stewards to receive the incomes of their revenues, and of the fruits
of the ground; such as are good men and priests; who
are to get their corn and their food ready for them.
They none of them differ from others of the Essens,
in their way of living, but do the most resemble those
Dacæ, who are called *Polistæ,* [dwellers in cities.]

6. But of the fourth sect of Jewish philosophy,
Judas the Galilean was the author. These men agree
in all other things with the Pharisaic notions; but
they have an inviolable attachment to liberty, and
say, that God is to be their only Ruler and Lord.
They also do not value dying any kinds of death,
nor indeed do they heed the deaths of their relations
and friends, nor can any such fear make them call
any man lord. And since this immovable resolution of theirs is well known to a great many, I shall
speak no farther about that matter; nor am I afraid
that anything I have said of them should be disbelieved, but rather fear, that what I have said is
beneath the resolution they show when they undergo
pain. And it was in Gessius Florus' time that the
nation began to grow mad with this distemper, who
was our procurator, and who occasioned the Jews
to go wild with it by the abuse of his authority, and
to make them revolt from the Romans. And these
are the sects of Jewish philosophy.

CHAPTER II.

How Herod and Philip built several cities in honour of Cæsar. Concerning the succession of priests and procurators; as also what befell Phraates and the Parthians.

1. WHEN Cyrenius had now disposed of Archelaus' money, and when the taxings were come to a conclusion, which were made in the thirty-seventh of Cæsar's victory over Antony at Actium, he deprived Joazer of the high priesthood, which dignity had been conferred on him by the multitude, and he appointed Ananus, the son of Seth, to be high priest; while Herod and Philip had each of them received their own tetrarchy, and settled the affairs thereof. Herod also built a wall about Sepphoris, (which is the security of all Galilee,) and made it the metropolis of the country. He also built a wall round Betharamphtha, which was itself a city also, and called it *Julias,* from the name of the emperor's wife. When Philip, also, had built Paneas, a city at the fountains of Jordan, he named it *Cæsarea.* He also advanced the village Bethsaida, situate at the lake of Gennesareth, unto the dignity of a city, both by the number of inhabitants it contained, and its other grandeur, and called it by the name of *Julias,* the same name with Cæsar's daughter.

2. As Coponius, who we told you was sent along with Cyrenius, was exercising his office of procurator, and governing Judea, the following accidents happened. As the Jews were celebrating the feast of unleavened bread, which we call the *Passover,* it was customary for the priests to open the temple gates

just after midnight. When, therefore, those gates were first opened, some of the Samaritans came privately into Jerusalem, and threw about dead men's bodies in the cloisters; on which account the Jews afterward excluded them out of the temple, which they had not used to do at such festivals; and on other accounts also they watched the temple more carefully than they had formerly done. A little after which accident, Coponius returned to Rome, and Marcus Ambivius came to be his successor in that government; under whom Salome, the sister of king Herod, died, and left to Julia [Cæsar's wife,] Jamnia, all its toparchy, and Phasaelis in the plain, and Archelais, where is a great plantation of palm-trees, and their fruit is excellent in its kind. After him came Annius Rufus, under whom died Cæsar, the second emperor of the Romans, the duration of whose reign was fifty-seven years, besides six months and two days, (of which time Antonius ruled together with him fourteen years; but the duration of his life was seventy-seven years;) upon whose death Tiberius Nero, his wife Julia's son, succeeded. He was now the third emperor; and he sent Valerius Gratus to be procurator of Judea, and to succeed Annius Rufus. This man deprived Ananus of the high priesthood, and appointed Ishmael, the son of Phabi, to be high priest. He also deprived him in a little time, and ordained Eleazar, the son of Ananus, who had been high priest before, to be high priest; which office, when he had held for a year, Gratus deprived him of it, and gave the high priesthood to Simon, the son of Camithus, and, when he had possessed that dignity no longer than a year, Joseph Caiaphas was made his successor. When Gratus had done those things, he went back to Rome, after he had tarried in Judea eleven years, when Pontius Pilate came as his successor.

3. And now Herod the tetrarch, who was in great favour with Tiberius, built a city of the same name with him, and called it *Tiberias*. He built it in the best part of Galilee, at the lake of Gennesareth. There are warm baths at a little distance from it, in a village named *Emmaus*. Strangers came and inhabited this city; a great number of the inhabitants were Galileans also; and many were necessitated by Herod to come thither out of the country belonging to him, and were by force compelled to be its inhabitants; some of them were persons of condition. He also admitted poor people, such as those that were collected from all parts to dwell in it. Nay, some of them were not quite freemen, and these he was benefactor to, and made them free in great numbers; but obliged them not to forsake the city, by building them very good houses at his own expenses, and by giving them land also; for he was sensible, that to make this place a habitation was to transgress the Jewish ancient laws, because many sepulchres were to be here taken away, in order to make room for the city Tiberias;[1] whereas our laws pronounce, that such inhabitants are unclean for seven days.[2]

4. About this time died Phraates, king of the Parthians, by the treachery of Phraataces his son, upon the occasion following: When Phraates had had legitimate sons of his own, he had also an Italian maid-servant, whose name was *Thermusa,* who had been formerly sent to him by Julius Cæsar, among other presents. He first made her his concubine,

[1] We may here take notice, as well as in the parallel parts of the books Of the War, B. II. ch. ix. sect. 1, that after the death of Herod the Great, and the succession of Archelaus, Josephus is very brief in his accounts of Judea, till near his own time. I suppose the reason is, that after the large history of Nicolaus of Damascus, including the life of Herod, and probably the succession and first actions of his sons, he had but few good histories of those times before him.

[2] Numb. xix. 11-14.

but, he being a great admirer of her beauty, in
process of time having a son by her, whose name
was *Phraataces,* he made her his legitimate wife, and
had a great respect for her. Now, she was able to
persuade him to do any thing that she said, and
was earnest in procuring the government of Parthia
for her son; but still she saw that her endeavours
would not succeed, unless she could contrive how
to remove Phraates' legitimate sons [out of the
kingdom;] so she persuaded him to send those his
sons as pledges of his fidelity to Rome; and they
were sent to Rome accordingly, because it was not
easy for him to contradict her commands. Now,
while Phraataces was alone brought up in order to
succeed in the government, he thought it very tedious
to expect that government by his father's donation
[as his successor;] he therefore formed a treacherous
design against his father, by his mother's assistance,
with whom, as the report went, he had criminal conversation also. So he was hated for both these vices,
while his subjects esteemed this [wicked] love of his
mother to be no way inferior to his parricide; and
he was by them, in a sedition, expelled out of the
country before he grew too great, and died. But,
as the best sort of Parthians agreed together, that
it was impossible they should be governed without
a king, while also it was their constant practice to
choose one of the family of Arsaces, [nor did their
law allow of any others; and they thought this kingdom had been sufficiently injured already by the
marriage with an Italian concubine, and by her
issue,] they sent ambassadors, and called Orodes [to
take the crown;] for the multitude would not otherwise have borne them; and though he were accused
of very great cruelty, and was of an untractable
temper, and prone to wrath, yet still he was one

of the family of Arsaces. However, they made a
conspiracy against him, and slew him, and that, as
some say, at a festival, and among their sacrifices;
(for it is the universal custom there to carry their
swords with them;) but, as the more general report
is, they slew him when they had drawn him out a
hunting. So they sent ambassadors to Rome, and
desired they would send one of those that were there
as pledges, to be their king. Accordingly, Vonones
was preferred before the rest, and sent to them; (for
he seemed capable of such great fortune, which two
of the greatest kingdoms under the sun now offered
him, his own, and a foreign one.) However, the
barbarians soon changed their minds, they being
naturally of a mutable disposition, upon the supposal, that this man was not worthy to be their governor; for they could not think of obeying the commands of one that had been a slave, (for so they
called those that had been hostages,) nor could they
bear the ignominy of that name; and this was the
more intolerable, because then the Parthians must
have such a king set over them, not by right of war,
but in time of peace. So they presently invited
Artabanus, king of Media, to be their king, he being
also of the race of Arsaces. Artabanus complied with
the offer that was made him, and came to them with
an army. So Vonones met him; and at first the
multitude of the Parthians stood on his side, and he
put his army in array; but Artabanus was beaten,
and fled to the mountains of Media. Yet did he
a little after gather a great army together, and fought
with Vonones, and beat him; whereupon Vonones
fled away on horseback, with a few of his attendants
about him to Seleucia, [upon Tigris.] So when Artabanus had slain a great number, and this after he
had gotten the victory, by reason of the very great

dismay the barbarians were in, he retired to Ctesiphon
with a great number of his people; and so he now
reigned over the Parthians. But Vonones fled away
to Armenia: and as soon as he came thither, he had
an inclination to have the government of the country
given him, and sent ambassadors to Rome [for that
purpose.] But because Tiberius refused it him, and
because he wanted courage, and because the Parthian
king threatened him and sent ambassadors to him
to denounce war against him if he proceeded, and
because he had no way to take to regain any other
kingdom, (for the people of authority among the
Armenians about Niphates joined themselves to
Artabanus,) he delivered up himself to Silanus, the
president of Syria, who out of regard to his educa
tion at Rome, kept him in Syria, while Artabanus
gave Armenia to Orodes, one of his own sons.

5. At this time died Antiochus, the king of Com-
magene, whereupon the multitude contended with the
nobility, and both sent ambassadors to [Rome;] for
the men of power were desirous that their form of
government might be changed into that of a [Roman]
province; as were the multitude desirous to be under
kings, as their fathers had been. So the senate made
a decree, that Germanicus should be sent to settle
the affairs of the east, fortune hereby taking a proper
opportunity for depriving him of his life; for when
he had been in the east, and settled all affairs there,
his life was taken away by the poison which Piso
gave him, as hath been related elsewhere.[1]

----

[1] This citation is now wanting.

CHAPTER III.

A sedition of the Jews against Pontius Pilate. Concerning Christ, and what befell Paulina and the Jews at Rome.

1. BUT now Pilate, the procurator of Judea, removed the army from Cæsarea to Jerusalem, to take their winter quarters there, in order to abolish the Jewish laws. So he introduced Cæsar's effigies, which were upon the ensigns, and brought them into the city; whereas our law forbids us the very making of images; on which account the former procurators were wont to make their entry into the city with such ensigns as' had not those ornaments. Pilate was the first who brought those images to Jerusalem, and set them up there; which was done without the knowledge of the people, because it was done in the night time; but as soon as they knew it, they came in multitudes to Cæsarea, and interceded with Pilate many days that he would remove the images; and when he would not grant their requests, because it would tend to the injury of Cæsar, while yet they persevered in their request, on the sixth day he ordered his soldiers to have their weapons privately, while he came and sat upon his judgment-seat, which seat was so prepared in the open place of the city, that it concealed the army that lay ready to oppress them; and when the Jews petitioned him again, he gave a signal to the soldiers to encompass them round, and threatened that their punishments should be no less than immediate death, unless they would leave off disturbing him, and go their ways home. But they threw themselves upon the ground, and laid their

necks bare, and said they would take their death very
willingly rat^l er than the wisdom of their laws should
be transgressed; upon which Pilate was deeply affected with their firm resolution to keep their laws
inviolable, and presently commanded the images to
be carried back from Jerusalem to Cæsarea.

2. But Pilate undertook to bring a current of
water to Jerusalem, and did it with the sacred money,
and derived the origin of the stream from the distance
of two hundred furlongs. However, the Jews [1] were
not pleased with what had been done about this
water; and many ten thousands of the people got
together and made a clamour against him, and insisted that he should leave off that design. Some
of them also used reproaches, and abused the man,
as crowds of such people usually do. So he habited
a great number of his soldiers in their habit, who
carried daggers under their garments, and sent them
to a place where they might surround them. So he
bid the Jews himself go away; but they boldly casting reproaches upon him, he gave the soldiers that
signal which had been beforehand agreed on; who

---

[1] These Jews, as they are here called, whose blood Pilate shed on this
occasion, may very well be those very Galilean Jews *whose blood Pilate
had mingled with their sacrifices,* Luke xiii. 1, 2, these tumults being
usually excited at some of the Jews' great festivals, when they slew
abundance of sacrifices, and the Galileans being commonly much more
busy in such tumults than those of Judea and Jerusalem, as we learn
from the history of Archelaus, Antiq. B. XVII. ch. ix. sect. 3, and ch. x.
sect. 2, 9, though, indeed, Josephus' present copies say not one word of
those eighteen upon whom the tower in Siloam fell and slew them, which
the 4th verse of the same 13th chapter of St. Luke informs us of. Luke
xxiii. 6, 7, teaches us that, "when Pilate heard of Galilee, he asked whether
Jesus were a Galilean? And as soon as he knew that he belonged to
Herod's jurisdiction, he sent him to Herod." And ver. 12, "The same
day Pilate and Herod were made friends together; for before they had
been at enmity between themselves." Take the very probable key of this
matter, in the words of the learned Noldius de Herod. No. 249. "The
cause of the enmity between Herod and Pilate (says he) seems to have
been this, that Pilate had intermeddled with the tetrarch's jurisdiction,
and had slain some of his Galilean subjects, Luke xiii. 1, and, as he was
willing to correct that error, he sent Christ to Herod at this time."

laid upon them with much greater blows than Pilate had commanded them, and equally punished those that were tumultuous, and those that were not; nor did they spare them in the least: and since the people were unarmed, and were caught by men prepared for what they were about, there were a great number of them slain by this means, and others of them ran away wounded. And thus an end was put to this sedition.

3. Now, there was about this time Jesus, a wise man, if it be lawful to call him a man, for he was a doer of wonderful works, a teacher of such men as receive the truth with pleasure. He drew over to him both many of the Jews, and many of the Gentiles. He was Christ. And when Pilate, at the suggestion of the principal men amongst us, had condemned him to the cross,[1] those that loved him at the first did not forsake him; for he appeared to them alive again at the third day;[2] as the divine prophets had foretold these and ten thousand other wonderful things concerning him. And the tribe of Christians, so named from him, are not extinct at this day. .

4. About the same time, also, another sad calamity put the Jews into disorder, and certain shameful practices happened about the temple of Isis that was at Rome. I will now first take notice of the wicked attempt about the temple of Isis, and will then give an account of the Jewish affairs. There was at Rome a woman whose name was Paulina; one who, on account of the dignity of her ancestors, and by the regular conduct of a virtuous life, had a great reputation; she was also very rich, and although she were of a beautiful countenance, and in that flower of her age wherein women are the most gay, yet did she lead a life of great modesty. She was married

[1] A. D. 33, April 3.   [2] April 5.

to Saturninus, one that was every way answerable
to her in an excellent character.   Decius Mundus fell
in love with this woman, who was a man very high
in the equestrian order; and as she was of too great
dignity to be caught by presents, and had already
rejected them, though they had been sent in great
abundance, he was still more inflamed with love to
her, insomuch that he promised to give her two
hundred thousand Attic drachmæ for one night's
lodging; and when this would not prevail upon her,
and he was not able to bear this misfortune in his
amours, he thought it the best way to famish himself to death for want of food, on account of Paulina's
sad refusal; and he determined with himself to die
after such a manner, and he went on with his
purpose accordingly.   Now, Mundus had a free woman, who had been made free by his father, whose
name was Ide, one skilful in all sorts of mischief.
This woman was very much grieved at the young
man's resolution to kill himself, (for he did not
conceal his intentions to destroy himself from others,)
and came to him, and encouraged him by her discourse; and made him to hope, by some promises
she gave him, that he might obtain a night's lodging
with Paulina; and when he joyfully hearkened to
her entreaty, she said she wanted no more than fifty
thousand drachmæ for the entrapping of the woman.
So when she had encouraged the young man, and
gotten as much money as she required, she did not
take the same methods as had been taken before,
because she perceived that the woman was by no
means to be tempted by money, but as she knew
that she was very much given to the worship of the
goddess Isis, she devised the following stratagem:
She went to some of Isis' priests, and upon the
strongest assurances [of concealment,] she persuaded

them by words, but chiefly by the offer of money,
of 25,000 drachmæ in hand, and as much more when
the thing had taken effect, and told them the passion
of•the young man, and persuaded them to use all
means possible to beguile the woman. So they were
drawn in to promise so to do, by that large sum
of gold they were to have. Accordingly, the oldest
of them went immediately to Paulina, and upon his
admittance, he desired to speak with her by herself.
When that was granted him, he told her, that "he
was sent by the god Anubis, who was fallen in love
with her, and enjoined her to come to him." Upon
this she took the message very kindly, and valued
herself greatly upon this condescension of Anubis,
and told her husband, that she had a message sent
her, and was to sup and lie with Anubis; so he agreed
to her acceptance of the offer, as fully satisfied with
the chastity of his wife. Accordingly, she went to
the temple, and after she had supped there, and it
was the hour to go to sleep, the priest shut the doors
of the temple, when in the holy part of it, the lights
were also put out. Then did Mundus leap out, (for
he was hidden therein,) and did not fail of enjoying
her, who was at his service all the night long, as
supposing he was the god; and when he was gone
away, which was before those priests who knew nothing of this stratagem were stirring, Paulina came
early to her husband, and told him how the god
Anubis had appeared to her. Among her friends,
also, she declared how great a value she put upon
this favour, who partly disbelieved the thing, when
they reflected on its nature, and partly were amazed
at it, as having no pretence for not believing it, when
they considered the modesty and the dignity of the
person. But now, on the third day after what had
been done, Mundus met Paulina, and said, "Nay,

Paulina, thou hast saved me two hundred thousand drachmæ, which sum thou mightest have added to thy own family; yet hast thou not failed to be at my service in the manner I invited thee. As for the reproaches thou hast laid upon Mundus, I value not the business of names; but I rejoice in the pleasure I reaped by what I did, while I took to myself the name of Anubis." When he said this, he went his way. But now she began to come to the sense of the grossness of what she had done, and rent her garments, and told her husband of the horrid nature of this wicked contrivance, and prayed him not to neglect to assist her in this case. So he discovered the fact to the emperor; whereupon Tiberius inquired into the matter thoroughly by examining the priests about it, and ordered them to be crucified, as well as Ide, who was the occasion of their perdition, and who had contrived the whole matter, which was so injurious to the woman. He also demolished the temple of Isis, and gave order that her statue should be thrown into the river Tiber; while he only banished Mundus, but did no more to him, because he supposed that what crime he had committed was done out of the passion of love. And these were the circumstances which concerned the temple of Isis, and the injuries occasioned by her priests. I now return to the relation of what happened about this time to the Jews at Rome, as I formerly told you I would.

5.   There was a man who was a Jew, but had been driven away from his own country by an accusation laid against him for transgressing their laws, and by the fear he was under of punishment for the same; but in all respects a wicked man. He, then living at Rome, professed to instruct men in the wisdom of the laws of Moses. He procured also three other men, entirely of the same character with himself to

be his partners. These men persuaded Fulvia, a woman of great dignity, and one that had embraced the Jewish religion, to send purple and gold to the temple at Jerusalem, and, when they had gotten them, they employed them for their own uses, and spent the money themselves, on which account it was that they at first required it of her. Whereupon Tiberius, who had been informed of the thing by Saturninus, the husband of Fulvia, who desired inquiry might be made about it, ordered all the Jews to be banished out of Rome; at which time the consuls listed 4000 men out of them, and sent them to the island Sardinia; but punished a great number of them, who were unwilling to become soldiers, on account of keeping the laws of their forefathers.[1] Thus were these Jews banished out of the city by the wickedness of four men.

CHAPTER IV.

How the Samaritans made a tumult, and Pilate destroyed many of them: how Pilate was accused, and what things were done by Vitellius relating to the Jews and the Parthians.

1. BUT the nation of the Samaritans did not escape without tumults. The man who excited them

---

[1] Of the banishment of these 4000 Jews into Sardinia by Tiberius, see Suetonius in Tiber. sect. 36. But as for Mr. Reland's note here, which supposes that Jews could not, consistently with their laws, be soldiers, it is contradicted by one branch of the history before us, and contrary to innumerable instances of their fighting, and proving excellent soldiers in war; and indeed many of the best of them, and even under heathen kings themselves, did so, those, I mean, who allowed them their rest on the Sabbath day, and other solemn festivals, and let them live according to their own laws, as Alexander the Great and the Ptolemies of Egypt did. It is true, they could not always obtain those privileges, and then they got excused as well as they could, or sometimes absolutely refused

to it, was one who thought lying a thing of little consequence, and who contrived every thing so that the multitude might be pleased: so he bid them to get together upon Mount Gerizzim, which is by them looked upon as the most holy of all mountains, and assured them, that when they were come thither, he would show them those sacred vessels which were laid under that place, because Moses [1] put them there. So they came thither armed, and thought the discourse of the man probable; and as they abode at a certain village, which was called Tirathaba, they got the rest together to them and desired to go up the mountain in a great multitude together: but Pilate prevented their going up, by seizing upon the roads with a great band of horsemen and footmen, who fell upon those that were gotten together in the village; and when it came to an action, some of them they slew, and others of them they put to flight, and took a great many alive, the principal of whom, and also the most potent of those that fled away, Pilate ordered to be slain.

2. But when this tumult was appeased, the Samaritan senate sent an embassy to Vitellius, a man that had been consul, and who was now president of Syria, and accused Pilate of the murder of those that were killed, for that they did not go to Tirathaba in order to revolt from the Romans, but to escape the violence of Pilate. So Vitellius sent Marcellus,

to fight, which seems to have been the case here, as to the major part of the Jews now banished, but nothing more. See several of the Roman decrees in their favour as to such matters, B. XIV. ch. x.

[1] Since Moses never came himself beyond Jordan, nor particularly to Mount Gerizzim, and since these Samaritans have a tradition among them, related here by Dr. Hudson, from Reland, who was very skilful in Jewish and Samaritan learning, that in the days of Uzzi or Ozzi the high priest, 1 Chron. vi. 6, the ark and other sacred vessels were, by God's command, laid up or hidden in Mount Gerizzim, it is highly probable that this was the foolish foundation the present Samaritans went upon, in the sedition here described.

a friend of his, to take care of the affairs of Judea, and ordered Pilate to go to Rome, to answer before the emperor to the accusations of the Jews. So Pilate, when he had tarried ten years in Judea, made haste to Rome, and this in obedience to the orders of Vitellius, which he durst not contradict; but before he could get to Rome, Tiberius was dead.

3. But Vitellius came into Judea, and went up to Jerusalem: it was at the time of that festival which is called the *Passover*. Vitellius was there magnificently received, and released the inhabitants of Jerusalem from all the taxes upon the fruits that were bought and sold, and gave them leave to have the care of the high priest's vestments, with all their ornaments, and to have them under the custody of the priests in the temple, which power they used to have formerly, although at this time they were laid up in the tower of Antonia, the citadel so called, and that on the occasion following: There was one of the [high] priests, named Hyrcanus, and as there were many of that name, he was the first of them; this man built a tower near the temple, and when he had so done, he generally dwelt in it, and had these vestments with him; because it was lawful for him alone to put them on, and he had them there reposited when he went down into the city, and took his ordinary garments; the same things were continued to be done by his sons, and by their sons after them. But when Herod came to be king, he rebuilt this tower, which was very conveniently situated, in a magnificent manner; and because he was a friend to Antonius, he called it by the name of *Antonia*. And as he found these vestments lying there, he retained them in the same place, as believing that while he had them in his custody, the people would make no innovations against him. The like to what

Herod did was done by his son Archelaus, who was
made king after him; after whom the Romans, when
they entered on the government, took possession of
these vestments of the high priest, and had them
reposited in a stone chamber, under seal of the priests,
and of the keepers of the temple, the captain of the
guard lighting a lamp there every day; and [1] seven
days before a festival they were delivered to them
by the captain of the guard, when the high priest
having purified them, and made use of them, laid
them up again in the same chamber where they had
been laid up before, and this the very next day after
the feast was over. This was the practice at the
three yearly festivals, and on the fast day; but Vitellius put these garments into our own power, as
in the days of our forefathers, and ordered the captain of the guard not to trouble himself to inquire
where they were laid, or when they were to be used:
and this he did as an act of kindness, to oblige the
nation to him. Besides which, he also deprived
Joseph, who was also called *Caiaphas*, of the high
priesthood, and appointed Jonathan, the son of
Ananus, the former high priest, to succeed him.
After which, he took his journey back to Antioch.

4. Moreover, Tiberius sent a letter to Vitellius,
and commanded him to make a league of friendship
with Artabanus, the king of Parthia; for, while he
was his enemy, he terrified him, because he had taken
Armenia away from him, lest he should proceed
farther, and told him he should no otherwise trust

[1] This mention of the high priest's sacred garments received seven
days before a festival, and purified in those days against a festival, as
having been polluted by being in the custody of heathens, in Josephus,
agrees well with the traditions of the Talmudists, as Reland here observes. Nor is there any question but the three feasts here mentioned,
were the Passover, Pentecost, and Feast of Tabernacles; and the Fast,
so called by way of distinction, as Acts xxvii. 9, was the great day of
expiation.

him than upon his giving him hostages, and especially
his son Artabanus. . Upon Tiberius' writing thus to
Vitellius, by the offer of great presents of money,
he persuaded both the king of Iberia, and the king
of Albania, to make no delay, but to fight against
Artabanus; and although they would not do it themselves, yet did they give the Scythians a passage
through their country, and opened the Caspian gates
to them, and brought them upon Artabanus. So
Armenia was again taken from the Parthians, and
the country of Parthia was filled with war, and the
principal of their men were slain, and all these things
were in disorder among them: the king's son also
himself fell in these wars, together with many ten
thousands of his army. Vitellius had also sent such
great sums of money to Artabanus' father's kinsmen
and friends, that he had almost procured him to be
slain by the means of those bribes which they had
taken. And when Artabanus perceived that the plot
laid against him was not to be avoided, because it
was laid by the principal men, and those a great
many in number, and that it would certainly take
effect; when he had estimated the number of those
that were truly faithful to him, as also of those who
were already corrupted, but were deceitful in the
kindness they professed to him, and were likely, upon
trial, to go over to his enemies, he made his escape
to the upper provinces, where he afterwards raised
a great army out of the Dabæ and Sacæ, and fought
with his enemies, and retained his principality.

5. When Tiberius had heard of these things, he
desired to have a league of friendship made between
him and Artabanus; and, when, upon this invitation,
he received the proposal kindly, Artabanus and Vi-
tellins went to Euphrates, and as a bridge was laid
over the river, they each of them came with their

guards about them, and met one another on the midst of the bridge. And when they had agreed upon the terms of peace, Herod the tetrarch erected a rich tent in the midst of the passage, and made them a feast there; Artabanus also, not long afterwards, sent his son Darius, as a hostage, with many presents, among which there was a man seven cubits tall, a Jew he was by birth, and his name was *Eleazar*, who, for his tallness, was called a giant. After which Vitellius went to Antioch, and Artabanus to Babylon; but Herod [the tetrarch] being desirous to give Cæsar the first information that they had obtained hostages, sent posts with letters, wherein he had accurately described all the particulars, and had left nothing for the consular Vitellius to inform him of. But when Vitellius' letters were sent, and Cæsar had let him know that he was acquainted with the affairs already, because Herod had given him an account of them before, Vitellius was very much troubled at it; and supposing that he had been thereby a greater sufferer than he really was, he kept up a secret anger upon this occasion, till he could be revenged on him, which was after Caius had taken the government.

6. About this time it was that Philip, Herod's brother, departed this life, in the twentieth year [1] of the reign of Tiberius, after he had been tetrarch of Trachonitis, and Gaulonitis, and of the nation of the Bataneans also, thirty-seven years. He had showed himself a person of moderation and quietness

[1] This calculation from all Josephus' Greek copies, is exactly right: for since Herod died about September, in the fourth year before the Christian era, and Tiberius began, it is well known, Aug. 19, A.D. 14, it is evident that the 37th year of Philip, reckoned from his father's death, was the 20th of Tiberius, or near the end of A.D. 33, or, however, in the beginning of the next year, A.D. 34. This Philip the tetrarch seems to have been the best of all the posterity of Herod, for his love of peace, and his love of justice.

in the conduct of his life and government; he constantly lived in that country which was subject to him; [1] he used to make his progress with a few chosen friends; his tribunal also, on which he sat in judgment, followed him in his progress; and when any one met him who wanted his assistance, he made no delay, but had his tribunal set down immediately, wheresoever he happened to be, and sat down upon it, and heard his complaint: he there ordered the guilty that were convicted to be punished, and absolved those that had been accused unjustly. He died at Julias; and when he was carried to that monument which he had already erected for himself beforehand, he was buried with great pomp. His principality Tiberius took, for he left no sons behind him, and added it to the province of Syria, but gave order that the tributes which arose from it should be collected, and laid up in his tetrarchy.

CHAPTER V.

Herod the tetrarch makes war with Aretas, the king of Arabia, and is beaten by him; as also concerning the death of John the Baptist; how Vitellius went up to Jerusalem; together with some account of Agrippa, and of the posterity of Herod the Great.

1. ABOUT this time, Aretas, the king of Arabia Petrea, and Herod, had a quarrel on the account following: Herod the tetrarch had married the daughter of Aretas, and had lived with her a great while, but when he was once at Rome, he lodged with

---

[1] An excellent example this.

Herod,[1] who was his brother indeed, but not by the same mother; for this Herod was the son of the high priest Simon's daughter. However, he fell in love with Herodias, this last Herod's wife, who was the daughter of Aristobulus their brother, and the sister of Agrippa the Great; this man ventured to talk to her about a marriage between them, which address when she admitted, an agreement was made for her to change her habitation, and come to him as soon as he should return from Rome: one article of this marriage also was this, that he should divorce Aretas' daughter. So Antipas, when he had made this agreement, sailed to Rome; but when he had done there the business he went about, and was returned again, his wife having discovered the agreement he had made with Herodias, and having learned it before he had notice of her knowledge of the whole design, she desired him to send her to Macherus, which is a place in the borders of the dominions of Aretas and Herod, without informing him of any of her intentions. Accordingly Herod sent her thither, as thinking his wife had not perceived any thing. Now, she had sent a good while before to Macherus, who was subject to her father, and so all things necessary for her journey were made ready for her by the general of Aretas' army; and by that means she soon came into Arabia, under the conduct of the several

[1] This Herod seems to have had the additional name of *Philip,* as Antipas was named *Herod Antipas,* and as Antipas and Antipater seem to be in a manner the very same name, yet were the names of two sons óf Herod the Great; so might Philip the tetrarch and this Herod Philip be two different sons of the same father, all which Grotius observes on Matt. xiv. 3. Nor was it, as I agree with Grotius and others of the learned, Philip the tetrarch, but this Herod Philip, whose wife Herod the tetrarch had married, and that in her first husband's lifetime, and when her first husband had issue by her; for which adulterous and incestuous marriage, John the Baptist justly reproved Herod the tetrarch, and for which reproof Salome, the daughter of Herodias, by her first husband Herod Philip, who was still alive, occasioned him to be unjustly beheaded.

generals, who carried her from one to another successively, and she soon came to her father, and told him of Herod's intentions. So Aretas made this the first occasion of his enmity between him and Herod, who had also some quarrel with him about their limits at the country of Gemalitis. So they raised armies on both sides, and prepared for war, and sent their generals to fight instead of themselves, and, when they had joined battle, all Herod's army was destroyed by the treachery of some fugitives, who, though they were of the tetrarchy of Philip, joined with Herod's army. So Herod wrote about these affairs to Tiberius, who being very angry at the attempt made by Aretas, wrote to Vitellius, to make war upon him, and either to take him alive, and bring him to him in bonds, or to kill him, and send him his head. This was the charge that Tiberius gave to the president of Syria.

2. Now, some of the Jews thought that the destruction of Herod's army came from God, and that very justly, as a punishment of what he did against John, that was called the Baptist, for Herod slew him, who was a good man, and commanded the Jews to exercise virtue, both as to righteousness towards one another, and piety towards God, and so to come to baptism; for that the washing [with water] would be acceptable to him, if they made use of it, not in order to the putting away [or the remission] of some sins [only,] but for the purification of the body; supposing still that the soul was thoroughly purified beforehand by righteousness. Now, when [many] others came in crowds about him; for they were greatly moved [or pleased] by hearing his words; Herod, who feared lest the great influence John had over the people might put it into his power and inclination to raise rebellion, (for they seemed to do

any thing he should advise,) thought it best, by putting him to death, to prevent any mischief he might
cause, and not bring himself into difficulties, by
sparing a man who might make him repent of it
when it should be too late. Accordingly he was
sent a prisoner, out of Herod's suspicious temper,
to Macherus, the castle I before mentioned, and was
there put to death. Now, the Jews had an opinion
that the destruction of this army was sent as a punishment to Herod, and a mark of God's displeasure to him.

3. So Vitellius prepared to make war with Aretas,
having with him two legions of armed men: he also
took with him all those of light armature, and of
the horsemen which belonged to them, and were
drawn out of those kingdoms which were under the
Romans, and made haste for Petra, and came to
Ptolemais. But as he was marching very busily, and
leading his army through Judea, the principal men
met him, and desired that he would not thus march
through their land: for that the laws of their country
would not permit them to overlook those images
which were brought into it, of which there were a
great many in their ensigns; so he was persuaded
by what they said, and changed that resolution of
his, which he had before taken in this matter. Whereupon he ordered the army to march along the great
plain, while he himself, with Herod the tetrarch,
and his friends, went up to Jerusalem to offer sacrifice to God, an ancient festival of the Jews being
then just approaching; and when he had been there,
and been honourably entertained by the multitude
of the Jews, he made a stay there for three days,
within which time he deprived Jonathan of the high
priesthood, and gave it to his brother Theophilus.
But when on the fourth day letters came to him,
which informed him of the death of Tiberius, he

obliged the multitude to take an oath of fidelity to Caius; he also recalled his army, and made them every one go home, and take their winter quarters there, since upon the devolution of the empire upon Caius, he had not the like authority of making this war which he had before. It was also reported, that when Aretas heard of the coming of Vitellius to fight him, he said, upon his consulting the diviners, that it was impossible that this army of Vitellius' could enter Petra; for that one of the rulers would die, either he that gave the orders for the war, or he that was marching at the other's desire, in order to be subservient to his will, or else he against whom this army is prepared. So Vitellius truly retired to Antioch: but Agrippa, the son of Aristobulus, went up to Rome, a year before the death of Tiberius, in order to treat of some affairs with the emperor, if he might be permitted so to do. I have now a mind to describe Herod and his family, how it fared with them, partly because it is suitable to this history, to speak of that matter, and partly because this thing is a demonstration of the interposition of Providence, how a multitude of children is of no advantage, no more than any other strength that mankind set their hearts upon, besides those acts of piety which are done towards God: for it happened, that, within the revolution of a hundred years, the posterity of Herod, which were a great many in number, were, excepting a few, utterly destroyed.[1] One may well apply this for the instruction of mankind, and learn thence how unhappy they were; it will also show

---

[1] Whether this sudden extinction of almost the entire lineage of Herod the Great, which was very numerous, as we are both ·here and in the next section informed, was not in part as a punishment for the gross incests they were frequently guilty of, in marrying their own nephews and nieces, well deserves to be considered. See Levit. xviii. 6, 7, xxi. 10, and Noldius de Herod. No. 269, 270.

us the history of Agrippa, who, as he was a person
most worthy of admiration, so was he from a private
man, beyond all the expectation of those that knew
him, advanced to great power and authority. I have
said something of them formerly, but I shall now
also speak accurately about them.

4. Herod the Great had two daughters by Mariamne, the [gränd] daughter of Hyrcanus; the one
was Salampsio, who was married to Phasaelus, her
first cousin, who was himself the son of Phasaelus,
Herod's brother, her father making the match; the
other was Cypros, who was herself married also to
her first cousin Antipater, the son of Salome, Herod's
sister. Phasaelus had five children by Salampsio,
Antipater, Herod, and Alexander; and two daughters,
Alexandra and Cypros; which last, Agrippa, the son
of Aristobulus, married, and Timius of Cyprus
married Alexandra; he was a man of note, but had
by her no children. Agrippa had by Cypros two
sons, and three daughters, which daughters were
named Bernice, Mariamne, and Drusilla; but the
names of the sons were Agrippa, and Drusus, of
which Drusus died before he came to the years of
puberty; but their father, Agrippa, was brought up
with his other brethren, Herod and Aristobulus, for
these were also the sons of the son of Herod the
Great, by Bernice; but Bernice was the daughter
of Costobarus and of Salome, who was Herod's sister.
Aristobulus left these infants, when he was slain by
his father, together with his brother Alexander, as
we have already related. But when they were arrived at years of puberty, this Herod, the brother
of Agrippa, married Mariamne, the daughter of
Olympias, who was the daughter of Herod the king,
and of Joseph, the son of Joseph, who was brother
to Herod the king, and had by her a son, Aristobulus;

but Aristobulus, the third brother of Agrippa, married Jotape, the daughter of Sampsigeramus, king of Emesa;[1] they had a daughter who was deaf, whose name also was Jotape: and these hitherto were the children of the male line. But Herodias, their sister, was married to Herod [Philip,] the son of Herod the Great, who was born of Mariamne, the daughter of Simon the high priest, who had a daughter, Salome; after whose birth Herodias took upon her to confound the laws of our country, and divorced herself from her husband while he was alive, and was married to Herod [Antipas,] her husband's brother by the father's side; he was tetrarch of Galilee: but her daughter Salome was married to Philip, the son of Herod, and tetrarch of Trachonitis, and, as he died childless, Aristobulus, the son of Herod, the brother of Agrippa, married her; they had three sons, Herod, Agrippa, and Aristobulus, and this was the posterity of Phasaelus and Salampsio. But the daughter of Antipater by Cypros, was Cypros, whom Alexis Selcias, the son of Alexas, married; they had a daughter, Cypros; but Herod and Alexander, who, as we told you, were the brothers of Antipater, died childless. As to Alexander, the son of Herod the king, who was slain by his father, he had two sons, Alexander and Tigranes, by the daughter of Archelaus, king of Cappadocia; Tigranes, who was king of Armenia, was accused at Rome, and died childless; Alexander had a son of the same name with his brother Tigranes, and was sent to take possession of the kingdom of Armenia by Nero; he had a son, Alexander, who married Jotape,[2] the daughter of Antiochus, the king of Commagena; Vespasian made

---

[1] There are coins still extant of this Emesa, as Spanheim informs us
[2] Spanheim also informs us of a coin still extant of this Jotape, daughter of the king of Commagena.

him king of an island in Cicilia. But these descendants of Alexander, soon after their birth, deserted the Jewish religion, and went over to that of the Greeks; but for the rest of the daughters of Herod the king, it happened that they died childless. And as these descendants of Herod, whom we have enumerated, were in being at the same time that Agrippa the Great took the kingdom, and I have now given an account of them, it now remains that I relate the several hard fortunes which befell Agrippa, and how he got clear of them, and was advanced to the greatest height of dignity and power.

CHAPTER VI.

Of the navigation of king Agrippa to Rome, to Tiberius Cæsar; and how, upon his being accused by his own freed man, he was bound: how also he was set at liberty by Caius, after Tiberius' death, and was made king of the tetrarchy of Philip.

1. A LITTLE before the death of Herod the king, Agrippa lived at Rome, and was generally brought up and conversed with Drusus, the Emperor, Tiberius' son, and contracted a friendship with Antonio, the wife of Drusus the Great, who had his mother Bernice in great esteem, and was very desirous of advancing her son. Now, as Agrippa was by nature magnanimous and generous in the presents he made, while his mother was alive, this inclination of his mind did not appear, that he might be able to avoid her anger for such his extravagance; but when Bernice was dead, and he was left to his own conduct, he spent a great deal extravagantly in his daily way

of living, and a great deal in the immoderate presents
he made, and those chiefly among Cæsar's freed men,
·in order to gain their assistance, insomuch that he
was in a little time, reduced to poverty, and could
not live at Rome any longer. Tiberius also forbade
the friends of his deceased son to come into his sight,
because on seeing them he should be put in mind of
his son, and his grief would thereby be revived.

2. For these reasons he went away from Rome,
and sailed to Judea, but in evil circumstances, being
dejected with the loss of that money, which he once
had, and because he had not wherewithal to pay his
creditors, who were many in number, and such as
gave him no room for escaping them. Whereupon
he knew not what to do; so, for shame of his present
condition, he retired to a certain tower, at Malatha,
in Idumea, and had thoughts of killing himself; but
his wife Cypros perceived his intentions, and tried
all sorts of methods to divert him from his taking
such a course: so she sent a letter to his sister
Herodias, who was now the wife of Herod the
tetrarch, and let her know Agrippa's present design,
and what necessity it was which drove him thereto,
and desired her, as a kinswoman of his, to give him
her help, and to engage her husband to do the same,
since she saw how she alleviated these her husband's
troubles all she could, although she had not the like
wealth to do it withal. So they sent him, and allotted him Tiberias for his habitation, and appointed
him some income of money for his maintenance, and
made him a magistrate of that city, by way of honour
to him. Yet did not Herod long continue in that
resolution of supporting him, though even that support was not sufficient for him; for, as once they
were at a feast at Tyre, and in their cups, and reproaches were cast upon one another, Agrippa thought

that was not to be borne, while Herod hit him in the
teeth with his poverty, and with his owing his necessary food to him. So he went to Flaccus, one that
had been consul, and had been a very great friend
to him at Rome formerly, and was now president of
Syria.

3. Hereupon Flaccus received him kindly, and he
lived with him. Flaccus had also with him there
Aristobulus, who was indeed Agrippa's brother, but
was at variance with him; yet did not their enmity
to one another hinder the friendship of Flaccus to
them both, but still they were honourably treated by
him. However, Aristobulus did not abate of his ill-
will to Agrippa, till at length he brought him into
ill terms with Flaccus: the occasion of bringing on
which estrangement was this: The Damascens were
at difference with the Sidonians about their limits,
and when Flaccus was about to hear the cause between them, they understood that Agrippa had a
mighty influence upon him; so they desired that he
would be of their side and for that favour promised
him a great deal of money; so he was zealous in
assisting the Damascens as far as he was able. Now,
Aristobulus had gotten intelligence of this promise
of money to him, and accused him to Flaccus of
the same; and when, upon a thorough examination
of the matter, it appeared plainly so to be, he rejected Agrippa out of the number of his friends.
So he was reduced to the utmost necessity, and came
to Ptolemais; and because he knew not where else
to get a livelihood, he thought to sail to Italy; but
as he was restrained from so doing by want of money,
he desired Marsyas, who was his freed man, to find
some method for procuring him so much as he wanted
for that purpose, by borrowing such a sum of some
person or other. So Marsyas desired of Peter, who

was the freed man of Bernice, Agrippa's mother, and by the right of her testament was bequeathed to Antonia, to lend so much upon Agrippa's own bond and security; but he accused Agrippa of having defrauded him of certain sums of money, and so obliged Marsyas, when he made the bond of 20,000 Attic drachmæ, to accept of 2,500 drachmæ[1] less than what he desired, which the other allowed of, because he could not help it. Upon the receipt of this money, Agrippa came to Anthedon, and took shipping, and was going to set sail; but Herennius Capito, who was the procurator of Jamnia, sent a band of soldiers to demand of him 300,000 drachmæ of silver which were by him owing to Cæsar's treasury while he was at Rome, and so forced him to stay He then pretended that he would do as he bid him: but when night came on, he cut his cables, and went off, and sailed to Alexandria, where he desired Alex ander the Alabarch[2] to send him 200,000 drachmæ; but he said he would not lend it to him, but would not refuse it to Cypros, as greatly astonished at her affection to her husband, and at the other instances of her virtue, so she undertook to repay it. Accordingly, Alexander paid them five talents at Alexandria, and promised to pay them the rest of that sum at Dicearchia [Puteoli;] and this he did out of the fear he was in that Agrippa would soon spend it. So this Cypros set her husband free, and dismissed him to go on with his navigation to Italy, while she and her children departed for Judea.

4.   And now Agrippa was come to Puteoli, whence he wrote a letter to Tiberius Cæsar, who then lived at Capreæ, and told him, that he was come so far

---

[1] Spanheim observes, that we have here an instance of the Attic quantity of use-money, which was the eighth part of the original sum, or 12 *per cent,* for such is the proportion of 2,500 to 20,000,
[2] The governor of the Jews there,

in order to wait on him, and to pay him a visit; and
desired that he would give him leave to come over
to Capreæ: so Tiberius made no difficulty, but wrote
to him in an obliging way in other respects, and
withal told him, he was glad of his safe return, and
desired him to come to Capreæ, and when he was
come, he did not fail to treat him as kindly as he
had promised him in his letter to do. But the next
day came a letter to Cæsar from Herenius Capito,
to inform him, that Agrippa had borrowed 300,000
drachmæ, and not paid it at the time appointed; but,
when it was demanded of him, he ran away like a
fugitive, out of the places under his government, and
put it out of his power to get the money of him.
When Cæsar had read this letter, he was much
troubled at it, and gave order that Agrippa should
be excluded from his presence, until he had paid
that debt: upon which he was no way daunted at
Cæsar's anger, but entreated Antonia, the mother
of Germanicus, and of Claudius, who was afterwards
Cæsar himself, to lend him those 300,000 drachmæ,
that he might not be deprived of Tiberius' friendship;
so, out of regard to the memory of Bernice his mother,
(for these two women were very familiar with one
another,) and out of regard to his and Claudius'
education together, she lent him the money; and,
upon the payment of this debt, there was nothing
to hinder Tiberius' friendship to him. After this,
Tiberius Cæsar recommended to him his grandson,[1]
and ordered that he should always accompany him
when he went abroad. But, upon Agrippa's kind
reception by Antonia, he betook himself to pay his
respects to Caius, who was her grandson, and in
very high reputation by reason of the good-will they
bore his father.[2] Now there was one Thallus, a freed

---

[1] Tiberius junior.   [2] Germanicus.

man of Cæsar, of whom he borrowed a million of drachmæ, and thence repaid Antonia the debt he owed her; and by spending the overplus in paying his court to Caius, became a person of great authority with him.

5. Now as the friendship which Agrippa had for Caius was come to a great height, there happened some words to pass between them, as they once were in a chariot together, concerning Tiberius; Agrippa praying [to God,] (for they two sat by themselves,) that "Tiberius might soon go off the stage, and leave the government to Caius, who was in every respect more worthy of it." Now, Eutychus, who was Agrippa's freed man, and drove his chariot, heard these words, and at that time said nothing of them: but when Agrippa accused him of stealing some garments of his, (which was certainly true,) he ran away from him; but when he was caught, and brought before Piso, who was governor of the city, and the man was asked why he ran away? he replied, that he had somewhat to say to Cæsar, that tended to his security and preservation: so Piso bound him, and sent him to Capreæ. But Tiberius, according to his usual custom, kept him still in bonds, being a delayer of affairs, if ever there was any other king or tyrant that was so; for he did not admit ambassadors quickly, and no successors were despatched away to governors or procurators of the provinces, that had been formerly sent, unless they were dead; whence it was, that he was so negligent in hearing the causes of prisoners; insomuch, that when he was asked by his friends, what was the reason of his delay in such cases? he said, That "he delayed to hear ambassadors, lest, upon their quick dismission, other ambassadors should be appointed, and return upon him; and so he should bring trouble upon him-

self in their public reception and dismission: that he
permitted those governors, who had been sent once
to their government [to stay there a great while,]
out of regard to the subjects that were under them;
for that all governors are naturally disposed to get
as much as they can, and that those who are not to
fix there, but to stay a short time, and that an uncertainty, when they shall be turned out, do the more
severely hurry themselves on to fleece the people;
but that, if their government be long continued to
them, they are at last satiated with the spoils, as
having gotten a vast deal, and so become at length
less sharp in their pillaging; but that, if successors
are sent quickly, the poor subjects, who are exposed
to them as a prey, will not be able to bear the new
ones, while they shall not have the same time allowed
them, wherein their predecessors had filled themselves, and so grew more unconcerned about getting
more; and this because they are removed before they
have had time [for their oppressions.]   He gave them
an example to show his meaning: A great number
of flies came about the sore places of a man that
had been wounded; upon which one of the standers
by pitied the man's misfortune, and thinking he was
not able to drive those flies away himself, was going
to drive them away for him; but he prayed him to
let them alone: the other, by way of reply, asked
him the reason of such preposterous proceeding, in
preventing relief from his present misery; to which
he answered, If thou drivest these flies away, thou
wilt hurt me worse; for, as these are already full of
my blood, they do not crowd about me, nor pain me
so much as before, but are sometimes more remiss,
while the fresh ones that come almost famished, and
find me quite tired down already, will be my destruction.   For this cause, therefore, it is, that I am

myself careful not to send such new governors perpetually to those my subjects, who are already sufficiently harassed by many oppressions, as many, like these flies, farther distress them; and so, besides their natural desire of gain, may have this additional incitement to it, that they expect to be suddenly deprived of that pleasure which they take in it." And, as a farther attestation to what I say of the dilatory nature of Tiberius, I appeal to this his practice itself; for, although he were emperor twenty-two years, he sent in all but two procurators to govern the nation of the Jews, Gratus, and his successor in the government, Pilate. Nor was he in one way of acting with respect to the Jews, and in another with respect to the rest of his subjects. He farther informed them, that even in the hearing of the causes of prisoners, he made such delays, "because immediate death to those that must be condemned to die, would be an alleviation of their present miseries, while those wicked wretches have not deserved any such favour; but I do it, that, by being harassed with the present calamity, they may undergo greater misery."

6. On this account it was that Eutychus could not obtain a hearing, but was kept still in prison. However, some time afterward, Tiberius came from Capreæ to Tusculanum, which is about a hundred furlongs from Rome. Agrippa then desired of Antonia, that she would procure a hearing for Eutychus, let the matter whereof he accused him prove what it would. Now, Antonia was greatly esteemed by Tiberius on all accounts, from the dignity of her relation to him, who had been his brother Drusus' wife, and from her eminent chastity; [1] for though she

---

[1] This high commendation of Antonia for marrying but once, given here, and supposed elsewhere, Antiq. B. XVII. ch. xiii. sect. 4, and this, notwithstanding the strongest temptations, shows how honourable single marriages were both among the Jews and Romans, in the days of Jo-

were still a young woman, she continued in her widowhood, and refused all other matches, although Augustus had enjoined her to be married to somebody else;
yet did she all along preserve her reputation free
from reproach. She had also been the greatest bene-
factress to Tiberius, when there was a very dangerous plot laid against him by Sejanus, a man who
had been her husband's friend, and who had the
greatest authority, because he was general of the
army, and when many members of the senate, and
many of the freed men joined with him, and the
soldiery was corrupted, and the plot was come to
a great height. Now Sejanus had certainly gained
his point, had not Antonia's boldness been more
wisely conducted than Sejanus' malice; for, when she
had discovered his designs against Tiberius, she wrote
him an exact account of the whole, and gave the
letter to Pallus, the most faithful of her servants,
and sent him to Capreæ to Tiberius, who, when he
understood it, slew Sejanus and his confederates; so
that Tiberius, who had her in great esteem before,
now looked upon her with still greater respect, and
depended upon her in all things. So, when Tiberius
was desired by this Antonia to examine Eutychus,
he answered, "If indeed Eutychus hath falsely accused
Agrippa in what he hath said of him, he hath had
sufficient punishment by what I have done to him
already; but if, upon examination, the accusation appears to be true, let Agrippa have a care, lest out
of desire of punishing his freed man, he do not rather
bring a punishment upon himself." Now when An-

sephus and of the apostles, and takes away much of that surprise which
the modern Protestants have at those laws of the apostles, where no
widows, but those who had been the wives of *one husband* only, are
taken into the church-list, and no bishops, priests, or deacons, are
allowed to marry more than once, without leaving off to officiate as
clergymen any longer.

tonia told Agrippa of this, he was still much more
pressing that the matter might be examined into;
so Antonia, upon Agrippa's lying hard at her continually to beg his favour, took the following opportunity: As Tiberius lay once at his ease upon his
sedan, and was carried about, and Caius, her grandson, and Agrippa, were before him after dinner, she
walked by the sedan, and desired him to call Eutychus,
and have him examined; to which he replied, "O
Antonia! the gods are my witnesses, that I am induced to do what I am going to do, not by my own
inclination, but because I am forced to it by thy
prayers." When he had said this, he ordered Macro,
who succeeded Sejanus, to bring Eutychus to him;
accordingly, without any delay, he was brought.
Then Tiberius asked him, what he had to say against
a man who had given him his liberty? Upon which
he said, "O my lord! this Caius and Agrippa with
him, were once riding in a chariot, when I sat at
their feet, and among other discourses that passed,
Agrippa said to Caius, O that the day would once
come, when this old fellow will die, and name thee
for the governor of the habitable earth! for then
this Tiberius, his grandson, would be no hinderance,
but would be taken off by thee, and that earth would
be happy, and I happy also." Now, Tiberius took
these to be truly Agrippa's words, and bearing a
grudge withal at Agrippa, because, when he had
commanded him to pay his respects to Tiberius his
grandson, and the son of Drusus, Agrippa had not
paid him that respect, but had disobeyed his commands, and transferred all their regard to Caius;
he said to Macro, "Bind this man." But Macro,
not distinctly knowing which of them it was whom
he bid him bind, and not expecting that he would
have any such thing done to Agrippa, he forbore,

and came to ask more distinctly what it was that he
said? But, when Cæsar had gone round the hippodrome, he found Agrippa standing; "For certain,"
said he, "Macro, this is the man I meant to have
bound;" and when he still asked, "Which of these
is to be bound?" he said, "Agrippa." Upon which
Agrippa betook himself to make supplication for
himself, putting him in mind of his son, with whom
he was brought up, and of Tiberius [his grandson]
whom he had educated: but all to no purpose, for
they led him about bound even in his purple garments.
It was also very hot weather, and they had but little
wine to their meal, so that he was very thirsty; he
was also in a sort of agony, and took this treatment
of him heinously; as he therefore saw one of Caius'
slaves, whose name was *Thaumastus,* carrying some
water in a vessel, he desired that he would let him
drink; so the servant gave him some water to drink,
and he drank heartily, and said, "O thou boy! this
service of thine to me will be for thy advantage;
for, if I once get clear of these my bonds, I will
soon procure thee thy freedom of Caius, who has
not been wanting to minister to me, now I am in
bonds, in the same manner as when I was in my
former state and dignity." Nor did he deceive him
in what he promised him, but made him amends for
what he had now done; for, when afterward Agrippa
was come to the kingdom, he took particular care
of Thaumastus, and got him his liberty from Caius,
and made him the steward over his own estate; and
when he died, he left him to Agrippa his son, and
to Bernice his daughter, to minister to them in the
same capacity. The man also grew old in that honourable post, and therein died. But all this happened
a good while later.

7. Now Agrippa stood in his bonds before the

royal palace, and leaned on a certain tree for grief,
with many others, who were in bonds also; and as
a certain bird sat upon the tree on which Agrippa
leaned, (the Romans call this bird *bubo,*) [an owl,]
one of those that were bound, a German by nation,
saw him, and asked a soldier what that man in purple
was? and when he was informed that his name was
Agrippa, and that he was by nation a Jew, and one
of the principal men of that nation, he asked leave
of the soldier to whom he was bound,[1] to let him
come nearer to him, to speak with him; for that he
had a mind to inquire of him about some things
relating to his country; which liberty when he had
obtained, and as he stood near him, he said thus to
him by an interpreter, That "this sudden change of
thy condition, O young man! is grievous to thee, as
bringing on thee a manifold and very great adversity;
nor wilt thou believe me, when I foretell how thou
wilt get clear of this misery which thou art now
under, and how divine Providence will provide for
thee. Know therefore (and I appeal to my own
country gods, as well as to the gods of this place,
who have awarded these bonds to us,) that all I
am going to say about thy concerns, shall neither be
said for favour nor bribery, nor out of an endeavour
to make thee cheerful without cause, for such predictions, when they come to fail, make the grief at
last, and in earnest, more bitter than if the party
had never heard of any such thing. However, though
I run the hazard of my ownself, I think it fit to
declare to thee the prediction of the gods. It cannot
be that thou shouldest long continue in these bonds;
but thou wilt soon be delivered from them, and wilt

[1] Dr. Hudson here takes notice, out of Sabeca, Epistle V. that this
was the custom of Tiberius, to couple the prisoner and the soldier that
guarded him together in the same chain.

be promoted to the highest dignity and power, and
thou wilt be envied by all those who now pity thy
hard fortune; and thou wilt be happy till thy death,
and wilt leave thine happiness to the children whom
thou shalt have. But, do thou remember, when thou
seest this bird again, that thou wilt then live but
five days longer. This event will be brought to pass
by that God who hath sent this bird hither to be
a sign unto thee. And I cannot but think it unjust
to conceal from thee what I foreknow concerning
thee, that, by thy knowing beforehand what happiness is coming upon thee, thou mayest not regard
thy present misfortunes. But when this happiness
shall actually befall thee, do not forget what misery
I am in myself, but endeavour to deliver me." So,
when the German had said this he made Agrippa
laugh at him as much as he afterwards appeared
worthy of admiration. But now Antonia took
Agrippa's misfortune to heart; however, to speak to
Tiberius on his behalf, she took to be a very difficult
thing, and indeed quite impracticable, as to any hope
of success; yet did she procure of Macro, that the
soldiers that kept him, should be of a gentle nature,
and that the centurion who was over them, and was
to diet with him, should be of the same disposition,
and that he might have leave to bathe himself every
day, and that his freed men and friends might come
to him, and that other things that tended to ease
him might be indulged him. So his friend Silas
came in to him, and two of his freed men, Marsyras
and Stechus, brought him such sorts of food as he
was fond of, and indeed took great care of him; they
also brought him garments, under pretence of selling
them, and, when the night came on, they laid them
under him; and the soldiers assisted them, as Macro
had given them order to do beforehand. And this

was Agrippa's condition for six months' time, and in this case were his affairs.

8. But for Tiberius, upon his return to Capreæ, he fell sick. At first his distemper was but gentle; but as that distemper increased upon him, he had small or no hopes of recovery. Hereupon he bid Euodus, who was that freed man whom he most of all respected, to bring the children [1] to him; for that he wanted to talk to them before he died. Now he had at present no sons of his own alive; for Drusus, who was his only son, was dead; but Drusus' son Tiberius was still living, whose additional name was *Gemellus:* there was also living Caius, the son of Germanicus, who was the son [2] of his brother [Drusus.] He was now grown up, and had a liberal education, and was well improved by it, and was in esteem and favour with the people, on account of the excellent character of his father Germanicus, who had attained the highest honour among the multitude, by the firmness of his virtuous behaviour, by the easiness and agreeableness of his conversing with the multitude, and because the dignity he was in did not hinder his familiarity with them all, as if they were his equals; by which behaviour he was not only greatly esteemed by the people and the senate, but by every one of those nations that were subject to the Romans; some of which were affected, when they came to him, with the gracefulness of their reception by him, and others were affected in the same manner by the report of the others that had been with him: and upon his death there was a lamentation made by all men; not such a one as was to be made in way of flattery to their rulers, while they

---

[1] Tiberius his own grandson, and Caius his brother Drusus' grandson.

[2] So I correct Josephus' copy, which calls Germanicus his brother, who was his brother's son.

did but counterfeit sorrow, but such as was real; while every body grieved at his death, as if they had lost one that was near to them. And truly such had been his easy conversation with men, that it turned greatly to the advantage of his son among all; and, among others, the soldiery were so peculiarly affected to him, that they reckoned it an eligible thing, if need were, to die themselves, if he might but attain to the government.

9. But when Tiberius had given order to Euodus to bring the children to him the next day in the morning, he prayed to his country gods to show him a manifest signal, which of those children should come to the government; being very desirous to leave it to his son's son, but still depending upon what God should foreshow concerning them, more than upon his own opinion and inclination; so he made this to be the omen, that the government should be left to him who should come to him first the next day. When he had thus resolved within himself, he sent to his grandson's tutor, and ordered him to bring the child to him early in the morning, as supposing that God would permit him to be made emperor. But God proved opposite to his designation; for, while Tiberius was thus contriving matters, and as soon as it was at all day, he bid Euodus to call in that child which should be there ready. So he went out, and found Caius before the door, for Tiberius was not yet come, but stayed waiting for his breakfast; for Euodus knew nothing of what his lord intended; so he said to Caius, "Thy father calls thee," and then brought him in. As soon as Tiberius saw Caius, and not before, he reflected on the power of God, and how the ability of bestowing the government on whom he would, was entirely taken from him; and thence he was not able to establish what

he had intended. So he greatly lamented that his power of establishing what he had before contrived was taken from him, and that his grandson Tiberius was not only to lose the Roman empire by his fatality, but his own safety also, because his preservation would now depend upon such as would be more potent than himself, who would think it a thing not to be borne, that a kinsman should live with them, and so his relation would not be able to protect him: but he would be feared and hated by him who had the supreme authority, partly on account of his being next to the empire, and partly on account of his perpetually contriving to get the government, both in order to preserve himself, and to be at the head of affairs also. Now Tiberius had been very much given to astrology,[1] and the calculation of nativities, and had spent his life in the esteem of what predictions had proved true, more than those whose profession it was. Accordingly, when he once saw Galba coming in to him, he said to his most intimate friends, that "there came in a man that would one day have the dignity of the Roman empire." So that this Tiberius was more addicted to all such sorts of diviners than any other of the Roman emperors, because he had found them to have told him truth in his own affairs. And indeed he was now in great distress upon this incident that had befallen him, and was very much grieved at the destruction of his son's son, which he foresaw, and complained of himself, that he should have made use of such a method of divination beforehand, while it was in his power to have died without grief by his knowledge of futurity; whereas, he was now tormented by his foreknowledge of the misfortune of such as were

---

[1] This is a known thing among the Roman historians and poets, that Tiberius was greatly addicted to astrology and divination.

dearest to him, and must die under that torment.
Now, although he were disordered at this unexpected
revolution of the government to those for whom he
did not intend it, he spoke thus to Caius, though
unwillingly, and against his own inclination: "O child!
though Tiberius be nearer related to me than thou
art, I, by my own determination, and the conspiring
suffrage of the gods, do give, and put into thy hand,
the Roman empire; and I desire thee never to be
unmindful when thou comest to it, either of my kindness to thee, who set thee in so high a dignity, or of
thy relation to Tiberius. But as thou knowest that
I am, together with and after the gods, the procurer
of so great happiness to thee, so I desire that thou
wilt make me a return for my readiness to assist
thee, and wilt take care of Tiberius because of his
near relation to thee. Besides which, thou art to
know, that, while Tiberius is alive, he will be a security to thee, both as to empire and as to thy own
preservation; but, if he die, that will be but a prelude to thy own misfortunes; for, to be alone, under
the weight of such vast affairs, is very dangerous;
nor will the gods suffer those actions which are unjustly done, contrary to that law which directs men
to act otherwise, to go off unpunished." This was
the speech which Tiberius made, which did not persuade Caius to act accordingly, although he promised
so to do; but, when he was settled in the government,
he took off this Tiberius, as was predicted by the
other Tiberius; as he was also himself, in no long
time afterward, slain by a secret plot laid against him.

10. So when Tiberius had at this time appointed
Caius to be his successor, he outlived but a few days,
and then died, after he had held the government
twenty-two years five months and three days: now
Caius was the fourth emperor. But, when the Ro-

mans understood that Tiberius was dead, they rejoiced at the good news, but had not courage to believe it; not because they were unwilling it should be true, for they would have given large sums of money that it might be so, but because they were afraid, that if they had showed their joy, when the news proved false, their joy should be openly known, and they should be accused for it, and be thereby undone. For this Tiberius had brought a vast number of miseries on the best families of the Romans, since he was easily inflamed with passion in all cases, and was of such a temper as rendered his anger irrevocable, till he had executed the same, although he had taken a hatred against men without reason; for he was by nature fierce in all the sentences he gave, and made death the penalty for the lightest offences; insomuch that when the Romans heard the rumour about his death gladly, they were restrained from the enjoyment of that pleasure by the dread of such miseries as they foresaw would follow, if their hopes proved ill grounded. Now, Marsyas, Agrippa's freed man, as soon as he heard of Tiberius' death, came running to tell Agrippa the news; and finding him going out to the bath, he gave him a nod, and said, in the Hebrew tongue, "The lion [1] is dead:" who understanding his meaning, and being overjoyed at the news, "Nay, said he, but all sorts of thanks and happiness attend thee for this news of thine: only I wish that what thou sayest may prove true." Now the centurion, who was set to keep Agrippa, when he saw with what haste Marsyas came, and what joy Agrippa had from what he said, he had a suspicion that his

---

[1] The name of a *lion* is often given to tyrants, especially by the Jews, such as Agrippa, and probably his freed man Marsyas, in effect were, Ezek. xix. 1, 9, Esth. xiv. 13, 2 Tim. iv. 17. They are also sometimes compared to or represented by wild beasts, of which the lion is the principal, Dan. vii. 3, 8, Apoc. xiii. 1, 2.

words implied some great innovation of affairs, and he asked them about what was said. They at first diverted the discourse; but upon his farther pressing, Agrippa, without more ado, told him, for he was already become his friend; so he joined with him in that pleasure which this news occasioned, because it would be fortunate to Agrippa, and made him a supper. But, as they were feasting, and the cups went about, there came one who said, That "Tiberius was still alive, and would return to the city in a few days." At which news the centurion was exceedingly troubled, because he had done what might cost him his life, to have treated so joyfully a prisoner, and this upon the news of the death of Cæsar; so he thrust Agrippa from the couch whereon he lay, and said, "Dost thou think to cheat me by a lie about the emperor without punishment? and shalt not thou pay for this thy malicious report at the price of thine head?" When he had so said, he ordered Agrippa to be bound again, (for he had loosed him before,) and kept a severer guard over him than formerly, and in that evil condition was Agrippa that night; but the next day the rumour increased in the city, and confirmed the news that Tiberius was certainly dead; insomuch that men durst now openly and freely talk about it; nay, some offered sacrifices on that account. Several letters also came from Caius, one of them to the senate, which informd them of the death of Tiberius, and of his own entrance on the government; another to Piso, the governor of the city, who told him the same thing. He also gave order that Agrippa should be removed out of the camp, and go to that house where he lived before he was put in prison; so that he was now out of fear as to his own affairs; for, although he were still in custody, yet it was now

with ease as to his own affairs. Now, as soon as
Caius was come to Rome, and had brought Tiberius'
dead body with him, and had made a sumptuous
funeral for him, according to the laws of his country,
he was much disposed to set Agrippa at liberty that
very day, but Antonia hindered him, not out of any
ill will to the prisoner, but out of regard to decency
in Caius, lest that should make men believe that he
received the death of Tiberius with pleasure, when
he loosed one whom he had bound immediately. However, there did not many days pass ere he sent for
him to his house, and had him shaved, and made him
change his raiment, after which he put his diadem
upon his head, and appointed him to be king of the
tetrarchy of Philip. He also gave him the tetrarchy
of Lysanias,[1] and changed his iron chain for a golden
one of equal weight. He also sent Marullus to be
procurator of Judea.

11. Now, in the second year of the reign of
Caius Cæsar, Agrippa desired leave to be given him
to sail home, and settle the affairs of his government, and he promised to return again, when he had
put the rest in order, as it ought to be put. So,
upon the emperor's permission, he came into his own
country, and appeared to them all unexpectedly as
a king, and thereby demonstrated to the men that
saw him the power of fortune, when they compared
his former poverty with his present happy affluence;
so some called him a happy man, and others could
not well believe that things were so much changed
with him for the better.

[1] Although Caius now promised to give Agrippa the tetrarchy of
Lysanias, yet was it not actually conferred upon him till the reign of
Claudius, as we learn, Antiq. B. XIX. ch. v. sect. 1.

CHAPTER VII.

How Herod the Tetrarch was banished.

1. BUT Herodias, Agrippa's sister, who now lived as wife to that Herod who was tetrarch of Galilee and Perea, took this authority of her brother in an envious manner, particularly when she saw that he had a greater dignity bestowed on him than her husband had; since when he ran away, it was because he was in a way of dignity, and of great good fortune. She was therefore grieved, and much displeased at so great a mutation of his affairs, and chiefly when she saw him marching among the multitude with the usual ensigns of royal authority, she was not able to conceal how miserable she was, by reason of the envy she had towards him; but she excited her husband, and desired him that he would sail to Rome, to court honours equal to his: for she said, that "she could not bear to live any longer, while Agrippa, the son of that Aristobulus who was condemned to die by his father, one that came to her husband in such extreme poverty, that the necessaries of life were forced to be entirely supplied him day by day; and when he fled away from his creditors by sea, he now returned a king; while he was himself the son of a king, and while the near relation he bore to royal authority, called upon him to gain the like dignity: he sat still, and was contented with a privater life. But then, Herod, although thou wast formerly not concerned to be in a lower condition than thy father, from whom thou wast derived, had been; yet do thou now seek after the dignity which thy kinsman hath attained to; and do not thou bear this contempt, that a man who admired thy riches should be in a greater honour than

thyself, nor suffer his poverty to show itself able to purchase greater things than our abundance; nor do thou esteem it other than a shameful thing to be inferior to one, who, the other day, lived upon thy charity. But, let us go to Rome, and let us spare no pains nor expenses, either of silver or gold, since they cannot be kept for any better use, than for the obtaining of a kingdom."

2. But, for Herod, he opposed her request at this time, out of the love of ease, and having a suspicion of the trouble he should have at Rome; so he tried to instruct her better. But the more she saw him draw back, the more she pressed him to it, and desired him to leave no stone unturned in order to be king: and at last she left not off till she engaged him, whether he would or not, to be of her sentiments, because he could no otherwise avoid her importunity. So he got all things ready, after as sumptuous a manner as he was able, and spared for nothing, and went up to Rome, and took Herodias along with him. But Agrippa, when he was made sensible of their intentions and preparations, he also prepared to go thither; and as soon as he heard they set sail, he sent Fortunatus, one of his freed men, to Rome, to carry presents to the emperor, and letters against Herod, and to give Caius a particular account of those matters, if he should have any opportunity. This man followed Herod so quick, and had so prosperous a voyage, and came so little after Herod, that while Herod was with Caius, he came himself, and delivered his letters; for they both sailed to Dicearchia, and found Caius at Balæ, which is itself a little city of Campania, at the distance of about five furlongs from Dicearchia. There are in that place royal palaces, with sumptuous apartments, every emperor still endeavouring to outdo his predecessor's magnif-

icence; the place also affords warm baths, that spring
out of the ground of their own accord, which are of
advantage for the recovery of the health of those
that make use of them, and, besides, they minister
to men's luxury also. Now Caius saluted Herod,
for he first met with him, and then looked upon the
letters which Agrippa had sent him, and which were
written in order to accuse Herod; wherein he accused him, that he had been in confederacy with
Sejanus, against Tiberius' government, and that he
was now confederate with Artabanus, the king of
Parthia, in opposition to the government of Caius;
as a demonstration of which he alleged, that he had
armour sufficient for seventy thousand men ready
in his armoury. Caius was moved at this information, and asked Herod, whether what was said about
the armour was true? and when he confessed there
was such armour there, for he could not deny the
same, the truth of it being too notorious, Caius took
that to be a sufficient proof of the accusation, that
he intended to revolt. So he took away from him his
tetrarchy, and gave it by way of addition to Agrippa's
kingdom; he also gave Herod's money to Agrippa,
and by way of punishment, awarded him a perpetual
banishment, and appointed Lyons, a city of Gaul,
to be his place of habitation. But when he was informed that Herodias was Agrippa's sister, he made
her a present of what money was her own; and told
her, that "it was her brother who prevented her
being put under the same calamity with her husband."
But she made this reply: "Thou, indeed, O emperor!
actest after a magnificent manner, and as becomes
thyself in what thou offerest me; but the kindness
which I have for my husband, hinders me from partaking of the favour of thy gift; for it is not just,
that I, who have been made a partner in his prosperity,

should forsake him in his misfortunes." Hereupon
Caius was angry at her, and sent her with Herod
into banishment, and gave her estate to Agrippa.
And thus did God punish Herodias for her envy
at her brother, and Herod also for giving ear to the
vain discourses of a woman. Now, Caius managed
public affairs with great magnanimity, during the
first and second year of his reign, and behaved himself with such moderation, that he gained the good-
will of the Romans themselves, and of his other
subjects. But, in process of time, he went beyond
the bounds of human nature, in his conceit of himself,
and by reason of the vastness of his dominions, made
himself a god, and took upon himself to act in all
things to the reproach of the Deity itself.

CHAPTER VIII.

Concerning [1] *the embassage of the Jews to Caius and
how Caius sent Petronius into Syria to make war
against the Jews, unless they would receive his
statue.*

1. THERE was now a tumult arisen at Alexandria,
between the Jewish inhabitants and the Greeks; and
three [2] ambassadors were chosen out of each party

[1] This is a most remarkable chapter, as containing such instances of
the interposition of Providence, as have been always very rare among
the other idolatrous nations, but of old very many among the posterity
of Abraham, the worshippers of the true God; nor do these seem much
inferior to those in the Old Testament, which are the more remarkable,
because among all other follies and vices, the Jews were not at this
time idolaters; and the deliverances here mentioned, were done in order
to prevent their relapse into that idolatry.

[2] Josephus here assures us, that the ambassadors from Alexandria to
Caius were on each part no more than three in number, for the Jews,
and for the Gentiles, which are but six in all: whereas Philo, who was

that were at variance, who came to Caius. Now,
one of these ambassadors from the people of Alexandria, was Apion, who uttered many blasphemies
against the Jews; and, among other things that he
said, he charged them with neglecting the honours
that belonged to Cæsar; for that while all who were
subject to the Roman empire, built altars and temples'
to Caius, and in other regards universally received
him as they received the gods, these Jews alone
thought it a dishonourable thing for them to erect
statues, in honour of him, as well as to swear by his
name. Many of these severe things were said by
Apion, by which he hoped to provoke Caius to
anger at the Jews, as he was likely to be; but Philo,
the principal of the Jewish ambassage, a man eminent
on all accounts, brother to Alexander[1] the alabarch,
and one not unskilful in philosophy, was ready to
betake himself to make his defence against those
accusations: but Caius prohibited him and bid him
be gone; he was also in such a rage, that it openly
appeared he was about to do them some very great
mischief. So Philo being thus affronted, went out,
and said to those Jews who were about him, that
"they should be of good courage, since Caius' words
indeed showed anger at them, but in reality had
already set God against himself."

2. Hereupon Caius, taking it very heinously that
he should be thus despised by the Jews alone, sent
Petronius to be president of Syria, and successor in

the principal ambassador from the Jews, as Josephus here confesses (as
was Apion for the Gentiles,) says, the Jews' ambassadors were themselves no fewer than five, towards the end of his legation to Caius;
which, if there be no mistake in the copies, must be supposed the truth:
nor, in that case, would Josephus have contradicted so authentic a witness, had he seen that account of Philo's: which, that he ever did, does
not appear.

[1] This Alexander the alabarch, or governor of the Jews at Alexandria,
and brother to Philo, is the same Alexander who is mentioned by St.
Luke, as of the kindred of the high priests, Acts iv. 6,

the government to Vitellius, and gave him order to make an invasion into Judea, with a great body of troops; and, if they would admit of his statue willingly, to erect it in the temple of God; but, if they were obstinate, to conquer them by war, and then to do it. Accordingly Petronius took the government of Syria, and made haste to obey Cæsar's epistle. He got together as great a number of auxiliaries as he possibly could, and took with him two legions of the Roman army, and came to Ptolemais, and there wintered, as intending to set about the war in the spring. He also wrote word to Caius what he had resolved to do, who commended him for his alacrity, and ordered him to go on, and to make war with them, in case they would not obey his commands. But there came many ten thousands of the Jews to Petronius, to Ptolemais, to offer their petitions to him, that "he would not compel them to transgress and violate the law of their forefathers; but if, said they, thou art entirely resolved to bring this statue, and erect it, do thou first kill us, and then do what thou hast resolved on; for, while we are alive, we cannot permit such things as are forbidden us to be done by the authority of our legislator, and by our forefathers' determination, that such prohibitions are instances of virtue." But Petronius was angry at them, and said, "If indeed I were myself emperor, and were at liberty to follow my own inclination, and then had designed to act thus, these your words would be justly spoken to me; but now Cæsar hath sent to me, I am under the necessity of being sub-servient to his decrees, because a disobedience to them will bring upon me inevitable destruction." Then the Jews replied, "Since, therefore, thou art so disposed, O Petronius! that thou wilt not disobey Caius' epistles, neither will we transgress the commands of our *law*;

and as we depend upon the excellency of our laws, and by the labours of our ancestors have continued hitherto without suffering them to be transgressed, we dare not by any means suffer ourselves to be so timorous as to transgress those laws out of the fear of death, which God hath determined are for our advantage; and, if we fall into misfortunes, we will bear them in order to preserve our laws, as knowing, that those who expose themselves to dangers, have good hope of escaping them, because God will stand on our side, when out of regard to him, we undergo afflictions, and sustain the uncertain turns of fortune. But, if we should submit to thee, we should be greatly reproached for our cowardice, as thereby showing ourselves ready to transgress our law; and we should incur the great anger of God also, who, even thyself being judge, is superior to Caius."

3.   When Petronius saw by their words that their determination was hard to be removed, and that, without a war, he should not be able to be subservient to Caius in the dedication of his statue, and that there must be a great deal of bloodshed, he took his friends, and the servants that were about him, and hasted to Tiberius, as wanting to know in what posture the affairs of the Jews were; and many ten thousands of the Jews met Petronius again, when he was come to Tiberius. These thought they must run a mighty hazard if they should have a war with the Romans, but judged that the transgression of the law was of much greater consequence, and made supplication to him, that he would by no means reduce them to such distresses, nor defile their city with the dedication of the statue. Then Petronius said to them, "Will you then make war with Cæsar, without considering his great preparations for war, and your own weakness?" They replied, "We will not by any means make war

with him, but still we will die before we see our laws transgressed." So they threw themselves down upon their faces, and stretched out their throats, and said they were ready to be slain; and this they did for forty days together, and in the meantime left off the tilling of their ground, and that while the season [1] of the year required them to sow it. Thus they continued firm in their resolution, and proposed to themselves to die willingly, rather than to see the dedication of the statue.

4. When matters were in this state, Aristobulus, king Agrippa's brother, and Helcias the Great, and the other principal men of that family with them, went in unto Petronius, and besought him, that "since he saw the resolution of the multitude, he would not make any alteration, and thereby drive them to despair; but would write to Caius, that the Jews had an insuperable aversion to the reception of the statue, and how they continued with him, and left off the tillage of their ground: that they were not willing to go to war with him, because they were not able to do it, but were ready to die with pleasure, rather than suffer their laws to be transgressed: and how, upon the lands continuing unsown, robberies would grow up, on the inability they would be under of paying their tributes; and that perhaps Caius might be thereby moved to pity, and not order any barbarous action to be done to them, nor think of destroying the nation; that if he continues inflexible in his former opinion to bring a war upon them, he may then set about it himself." And thus did Aristobulus, and the

---

[1] What Josephus here, and sect. 6, relates as done by the Jews, *before seedtime*, is in Philo not far off the time *when the corn was ripe*, who, as Le Clerc notes, differ here one from the other. This is another indication, that Josephus, when he wrote this account, had not seen Philo's Legat. ad Caium, otherwise he would hardly have herein differed from him.

rest with him, supplicate Petronius. So Petronius,[1] partly on account of the pressing instances which Aristobulus and the rest with him made, and because of the great consequence of what they desired, and the earnestness wherewith they made their supplication; partly on account of the firmness of the opposition made by the Jews, which he saw, while he thought it an horrible thing for him to be such a slave to the madness of Caius, as to slay so many ten thousand men: only because of their religious disposition towards God, and after that to pass his life in expectation of punishment: Petronius, I say, thought it much better to send to Caius, and to let him know how intolerable it was to him to bear the anger he might have against him for not serving him sooner, in obedience to his epistle, for that perhaps he might persuade him: and that if this mad resolution continued, he might then begin the war against them; nay, that in case he should turn his hatred against himself, it was fit for virtuous persons even to die for the sake of such vast multitudes of men. Accordingly he determined to hearken to the petitioners in this matter.

5. He then called the Jews together to Tiberias, who came, many ten thousands in number; he also placed that army he now had with him opposite to them; but did not discover his own meaning, but the commands of the emperor, and told them, That "his wrath would, without delay, be executed on such as had the courage to disobey what he had commanded, and this immediately; and that it was fit for him,

[1] This Publius Petronius was after this still president of Syria, under Claudius, and, at the desire of Agrippa, published a severe decree against the inhabitants of Dora, who, in a sort of imitation of Caius, had set up a statue of Claudius in a Jewish synagogue there. This decree is extant, B. XIX. ch. vi. sect. 3, and greatly confirms the present accounts of Josephus, as do the other accounts of Claudius, relating to the like Jewish affairs, B. XIX. ch. v. sect. 2, 3.

who had obtained so great a dignity by his grant,
not to contradict him in any thing; yet," said he,
"I do not think it just to have such a regard to
my own safety and honour, as to refuse to sacrifice
them for your preservation, who are so many in
number, and endeavour to preserve the regard that
is due to your law, which as it hath come down to
you from your forefathers, so do you esteem it worthy
of your utmost contention to preserve it; nor, with
the supreme assistance and power of God, will I be
so hardy as to suffer your temple to fall into contempt
by the means of the imperial authority. I will, therefore, send to Caius, and let him know what your
resolutions are, and will assist your suit as far as I
am able; that you may not be exposed to suffer on
account of the honest designs you have proposed to
yourselves; and may God be our assistant, for his
authority is beyond all the contrivance and power of
men; and may he procure you the preservation of your
ancient laws, and may not he be deprived, though
without your consent, of his accustomed honours.
But, if Caius be irritated, and turn the violence of
his rage upon me, I will rather undergo all that
danger and that affliction that may come either on
my body or my soul, than see so many of you to
perish, while you are acting in so excellent a manner.
Do you, therefore, every one of you, go your way
about your own occupations, and fall to the cultiva-
tion of your ground; I will myself send to Rome,
and will not refuse to serve you in all things, both
by myself and by my friends."

6. When Petronius had said this, and had dismissed the assembly of the Jews, he desired the
principal of them to take care of their husbandry,
and to speak kindly to the people, and encourage
them to have good hope of their affairs. Thus did

he readily bring the multitude to be cheerful again. And now did God show his presence [1] to Petronius, and signify to him, that he would afford him his assistance in his whole design; for he had no sooner finished the speech that he made to the Jews, but God sent down great showers of rain, contrary to human expectation, for that day was a clear day, and gave no sign, by the appearance of the sky, of any rain; nay, the whole year had been subject to a great drought, and made men despair of any water from above, even when at any time they saw the heavens overcast with clouds; insomuch, that when such a great quantity of rain came, and that in an unusual manner, and without any other expectation of it, the Jews hoped that Petronius would by no means fail in his petition for them. But as to Petronius, he was mightily surprised when he perceived that God evidently took care of the Jews, and gave very plain signs of his appearance, [2] and this to such a degree, that those that were in earnest much inclined to the contrary, had no power left to contradict it. This was also among those other particulars which he wrote to Caius, which all tended to dissuade him, and by all means to entreat him not to make so many ten thousands of these men go distracted, whom if he should slay, (for without war they would by no means suffer the laws of their worship to be set aside,) he would lose the revenue they paid him, and would be publicly cursed by them

---

[1] Josephus here uses the solemn New Testament words παρουσεα and επιωνφεικ, the *presence* and *appearance* of God, for the extraordinary manifestation of his power and providence to Petronius, by sending rain in a time of distress, immediately upon the resolution he had taken to preserve the temple unpolluted, at the hazard of his own life, without any other miraculous appearance at all in that case, which well deserves to be taken notice of here, and greatly illustrates several texts, both in the Old and New Testament.

[2] See the preceding note.

for all future ages. Moreover, that God, who was their governor, had shown his power most evidently on their account, and that such a power of his as left no room for doubt about it. And this was the business that Petronius was now engaged in.

7. But king Agrippa, who now lived at Rome, was more and more in the favour of Caius; and when he had once made him a supper, and was careful to exceed all others, both in expenses and in such preparation as might contribute most to his pleasure; nay, it was so far from the ability of others, that Caius himself could never equal, much less exceed it, (such care had he taken beforehand to exceed all men, and particularly to make all agreeable to Cæsar:) hereupon Caius admired his understanding and magnificence, that he should force himself to do all to please him, even beyond such expenses as he could bear, and was desirous not to be behind Agrippa in that generosity, which he exerted in order to please him. So Caius, when he had drunk wine plentifully, and was merrier than ordinary, said thus during the feast, when Agrippa had drunk to him: "I knew before now [1] how great a respect thou hast had for me, and how great kindness thou hast shown me, though with those hazards to thyself, which thou underwentest under Tiberius on that account; nor hast thou omitted any thing to show thy good-will towards us, even beyond thy ability; whence it would be a base thing for me to be conquered by thy affection. I am therefore desirous to make thee amends for every thing in which I have been formerly deficient, for all that I have bestowed on thee, that may be called my gifts, is but little. Every thing that may contribute to

---

[1] This behaviour of Caius to Agrippa, is very like that of Herod Antipas, his uncle, to Herodias, Agrippa's sister, about John the Baptist, Matt. xiv. 6-11.

thy happiness shall be at thy service, and that cheerfully, and so far as my ability will reach." And
this was what Caius said to Agrippa, thinking he
would ask for some large country, or the revenues
of certain cities. But, although he had prepared
beforehand what he would ask, yet had he not discovered his intentions, but made this answer to Caius
immediately, That "it was not out of any expectation
of gain that he formerly paid his respects to him,
contrary to the commands of Tiberius, nor did he
now do any thing relating to him out of regard to
his own advantage, and in order to receive any thing
from him: that the gifts he had already bestowed upon
him were great, and beyond the hopes of even a
craving man; for, although they may be beneath thy
power, [who art the donor,] yet are they greater
than my inclination and dignity, who am the receiver."
And, as Caius was astonished at Agrippa's inclinations, and still the more pressed him to make his
request for somewhat which he might gratify him
with, Agrippa replied, "Since thou, O my lord!
declarest such is thy readiness to grant, that I am
worthy of thy gifts, I will ask nothing relating to
my own felicity; for what thou hast already bestowed
on me has made me excel therein; but I desire somewhat which may make thee glorious for piety, and
render the Divinity assistant to thy designs, and may
be for an honour to me among those that inquire
about it, as showing that I never once fail of obtaining what I desire of thee; for my petition is this,
That thou wilt no longer think of the dedication of
that statue which thou hast ordered to be set up in
the Jewish temple by Petronius."

8. And thus did Agrippa venture to cast the die
upon this occasion, so great was the affair in his
opinion, and in reality though he knew how dangerous

a thing it was so to speak; for, had not Caius approved of it, it had tended to no less than the loss of his life. So Caius, who was mightily taken with Agrippa's obliging behaviour, and on other accounts thinking it a dishonourable thing to be guilty of falsehood before so many witnesses, in points wherein he had with such alacrity forced Agrippa to become a petitioner, and that it would look as if he had already repented of what he had said, and because he greatly admired Agrippa's virtue, in not desiring him at all to augment his own dominions, either with large revenues, or other authority, but took care of the public tranquillity, of the laws, and of the Divinity itself, he granted him what he had requested. He also wrote thus to Petronius, "commending him for his assembling his army, and then consulting him about these affairs. If, therefore, said he, thou hast already erected my statue, let it stand; but, if thou hast not yet dedicated it, do not trouble thyself farther about it, but dismiss thy army, go back, and take care of those affairs which I sent thee about at first, for I have now no occasion for the erection of that statue. This I have granted as a favour to Agrippa, a man whom I honour so very greatly, that I am not able to contradict what he would have, or what he desired me to do for him." And this was what Caius wrote to Petronius, which was before he received his letter, informing him that the Jews were very ready to revolt about the statue, and that they seemed resolved to threaten war against the Romans, and nothing else. When therefore Caius was much displeased that any attempt should be made against his government, as he was a slave to base and vicious actions on all occasions, and had no regard to what was virtuous and honourable, and against whomsoever he resolved to show his anger, and that for any cause whatsoever, he suffered not himself to be restrained by any admonition, but thought the indulging his anger to be a real pleasure, he wrote thus to Petronius: "Seeing thou esteemest the presents made thee by the Jews to be of greater value than my commands, and art grown insolent enough to be subservient to their pleasure, I charge thee to become thy own judge, and to consider what thou art to do, now thou art under my displeasure; for I will make thee an example to the present and to all future ages, that they may not dare to contradict the commands of their emperor."

9. That was the epistle which Caius wrote to Petronius, but Petronius did not receive it while Caius was alive, that ship which carried it sailed so slow, that other letters came to Petronius before this, by which he understood that Caius was dead; for God would not forget the dangers Petronius had undertaken on account of the Jews, and of his own honour. But when he had taken Caius away, out of his indignation of what he had so insolently attempted in assuming to himself divine worship, both Rome and all that dominion conspired with Petronius, especially those that were of the senatorian order, to give Caius his due reward, because he had been unmercifully severe to them; for he died not long after he had written to Petronius that epistle which threatened him with death. But as for the occasion of his death, and the nature of the plot against him, I shall relate them in the progress of this narration. Now, that epistle which informed Petronius of Caius' death came first, and a little afterward came that which commanded him to kill himself with his own hands. Whereupon he rejoiced at this coincidence as to the death of Caius, and admired God's providence, who without the least delay, and immediately, gave

him a reward for the regard he had to the temple,
and the assistance he afforded the Jews for avoiding
the dangers they were in. And by this means Petronius escaped that danger of death which he could not
foresee.

CHAPTER IX.

*What befell the Jews that were in Babylon, on oc-
casion of Asineus and Anileus, two brethren.*

1. A VERY sad calamity now befell the Jews that
were in Mesopotamia, and especially those that dwelt
in Babylonia. Inferior it was to none of the calamities which had gone before, and came together with
a great slaughter of them, and that greater than any
upon record before; concerning all which I shall
speak accurately, and shall explain the occasions
whence those miseries came upon them. There was
a city in Babylonia called Neerda; not only a very
populous one, but one that had a good and a large
territory about it, and, besides its other advantages,
full of men also. It was, besides, not easily to be
assaulted by enemies, from the river Euphrates encompassing it all round, and from the walls that were
built about it. There was also the city Nisibis,
situate on the same current of the river. For which
reason, the Jews, depending on the natural strength
of these places, deposited in them that half shekel
which every one, by the custom of our country, offers
unto God, as well as they did other things devoted
to him, for they made use of these cities as a treasury,
whence, at a proper time, they were transmitted to
Jerusalem; and many ten thousand men undertook
the carriage of those donations, out of fear of the

ravages of the Parthians, to whom the Babylonians were then subject. Now, there were two men, Asineus and Anileus, of the city Neerda by birth, and brethren to one another. They were destitute of a father, and their mother put them to learn the art of weaving curtains, it not being esteemed a disgrace among them for men to be weavers of cloth. Now, he that taught them that art, and was set over them, complained that they came too late to their work, and punished them with stripes: but they took this just punishment as an affront, and carried off all the weapons which were kept in that house, which were not a few, and went into a certain place where was a partition of the rivers, and was a place naturally very fit for the feeding of cattle, and for preserving such fruits as were usually laid up against winter. The poorest sort of the young men also resorted to them, whom they armed with the weapons they had gotten, and became their captains; and nothing hindered them from being their leaders into mischief; for, as soon as they were become invincible, and had built them a citadel, they sent to such as fed cattle, and ordered them to pay so much tribute out of them as might be sufficient for their maintenance, proposing also that they would be their friends, if they would submit to them, and that they would defend them from all their other enemies on every side, but that they would kill all the cattle of those that refused to obey them. So they hearkened to their proposals (for they could do nothing else,) and sent them as many sheep as were required of them; whereby their forces grew greater, and they became lords over all they pleased, because they marched suddenly, and did them a mischief, insomuch that every body who had to do with them, chose to pay them respect, and they became formidable to such

as came to assault them, till the report about them
came to the ears of the king of Parthia himself.

2. But when the governor of Babylonia understood this, and had a mind to put a stop to them
before they grew greater, and before greater mischiefs
should arise from them, he got together so great an
army as he could, both of Parthians and Babylonians,
and marched against them, thinking to attack them,
and destroy them before any one should carry them
the news that he had got an army together. He then
encamped at a lake, and lay still; but, on the next
day, (it was the Sabbath, which is among the Jews
a day of rest from all sorts of work,) he supposed
that the enemy would not dare to fight him thereon,
but that he would take them and carry them away
prisoners, without fighting. He therefore proceeded
gradually, and thought to fall upon them on the
sudden. Now Asineus was sitting with the rest, and
their weapons lay by them; upon which he said, "Sirs,
I hear a neighing of horses; not of such as are feeding, but such as have men on their backs; I also hear
such a noise of their bridles, that I am afraid that
some enemies are coming upon us to encompass us
round. However, let somebody go to look about,
and make report of what reality there is in the present
state of things; and may what I have said prove a
false alarm." And when he said this, some of them
went out to spy out what was the matter, and they
came again immediately and said to him, that "neither
hast thou been mistaken in telling us what our
enemies were doing, nor will those enemies be injurious to people any longer. We are caught by
their intrigues like brute beasts, and there is a large
body of cavalry marching upon us, while we are
destitute of hands to defend ourselves withal, because
we are restrained from doing it by the prohibition

of our law, which obliges us to rest [on this day."]
But Asineus did not by any means agree with the
opinion of his spy as to what was to be done, but
thought it more agreeable to the law to pluck up
their spirits in this necessity they were fallen into,
and break their law by avenging themselves, although
they should die in the action, than by doing nothing,
to please their enemies in submitting to be slain by
them. Accordingly he took up his weapons, and infused courage into those that were with him to act
as courageously as himself. So they fell upon their
enemies, and slew a great many of them, because
they despised them, and came as to a certain victory
and put the rest to flight.

3. But when the news of this fight came to the
king of Parthia, he was surprised at the boldness of
these brethren, and was desirous to see them, and
speak with them. He therefore sent the most trusty
of all his guards to say thus to them, "That king
Artabanus, although he hath been unjustly treated
by you, who have made an attempt against his
government, yet hath he more regard to your courageous behaviour than to the anger he bears to
you, and hath sent me to give you his right hand,[1]
and security, and he permits you to come to him
safely, and without any violence upon the road, and
he wants to have you address yourselves to him as
friends, without meaning any guile or deceit to you.
He also promises to make you presents, and to pay
you those respects which will make an addition of his
power to your courage, and thereby be of advantage
to you." Yet did Asineus himself put off his journey

---

[1] The joining of the right hands was esteemed among the Persians
[and Parthians] in particular, a most inviolable obligation to fidelity, as
Dr. Hudson here observes, and refers to the commentary on Justin, B. XI.
ch. xv. for its confirmation. We often meet with the like use of it in
Josephus.

thither, but sent his brother Anileus with all such presents as he could procure. So he went, and was admitted to the king's presence; and when Artabanus saw Anileus coming alone, he inquired into the reason why Asineus avoided to come along with him; and when he understood that he was afraid, and stayed by the lake, he took an oath by the gods of his country, that he would do them no harm, if they came to him upon the assurances he gave them, and gave them his right hand. This is of the greatest force there with all these barbarians, and affords a firm security to those who converse with them; for none of them will deceive you, when once they have given you their right hands, nor will any one doubt of their fidelity, when that is once given, even though they were before suspected of injustice. When Artabanus had done this, he sent away Anileus to persuade his brother to come to him. Now this the king did, because he wanted to curb his own governors of provinces by the courage of these Jewish brethren, lest they should make a league with them; for they were ready for a revolt, and were disposed to rebel, had they been sent on an expedition against them. He was also afraid, lest, when he was engaged in a war in order to subdue those governors of provinces that had revolted, the party of Asineus, and those in Babylonia, should be augmented, and either make war upon him, when they should hear of that revolt, or, if they should be disappointed in that case, they would not fail of doing farther mischief to him.

4. When the king had these intentions, he sent away Anileus, and Anileus prevailed on his brother [to come to the king,] when he had related to him the king's good-will, and the oath that he had taken. Accordingly they made haste to go to Artabanus, who received them, when they were come, with pleas-

ure, and admired Asineus' courage in the actions
he had done, and this because he was a little man
to see ·to, and at first sight appeared contemptible
also, and such as one might deem a person of no
value at all. He also said to his friends, how, upon
the comparison, he showed his soul to be, in all
respects, superior to his body; and when, as they
were drinking together, he once showed Asineus to
Abdagases, one of the generals of his army, and told
him his name, and described the great courage he
was of in war, and Abdagases had desired leave to
kill him, and thereby to inflict on him a punishment
for those injuries he had done to the Parthian government, the king replied, "I will never give thee leave
to kill a man who hath depended on my faith,
especially not after I have sent him my right hand,
and endeavoured to gain his belief by oaths made by
the gods. But if thou beest a truly warlike man,
thou standest not in need of my perjury. Go thou
then and avenge the Parthian government; attack
this man, when he is returned back, and conquer him
by the forces that are under thy command, without my privity." Hereupon the king called for
Asineus, and said to him, "It is time for thee, O
thou young man! to return home, and not provoke
the indignation of my generals in this place any
farther, lest they attempt to murder thee, and that
without my approbation. I commit to thee the
country of Babylonia in trust, that it may, by thy
care, be preserved free from robbers, and from other
mischiefs. I have kept my faith inviolable to thee,
and that not in trifling affairs, but in those that
concerned thy safety, and do therefore deserve thou
shouldest be kind to me " When he had said this,
and given Asineus some presents, he sent him away
immediately; who, when he was come home, built

fortresses, and became great in a little time, and managed things with such courage and success, as no other person, that had no higher a beginning, ever did before him. Those Parthian governors also, who were sent that way, paid him great respect; and the honour that was paid him by the Babylonians seemed to them too small, and beneath his deserts, although he were in no small dignity and power there; nay, indeed, all the affairs of Mesopotamia depended on him, and he more and more flourished in this happy condition of his for fifteen years.

5. But as their affairs were in so flourishing a state, there sprang up a calamity among them on the following occasion. When once they had deviated from that course of virtue whereby they had gained so great power, they affronted and transgressed the laws of their forefathers, and fell under the dominion of their lusts and pleasures. A certain Parthian, who came as general of an army into those parts, had a wife following him, who had a vast reputation for other accomplishments, and particularly was admired above all other women for her beauty; Anileus, the brother of Asineus, either heard of that her beauty from others, or perhaps saw her himself also, and so became at once her lover and her enemy; partly because he could not hope to enjoy this woman but by obtaining power over her as a captive, and partly because he thought he could not conquer his inclinations for her; as soon therefore as her husband had been declared an enemy to them, and was fallen in the battle, the widow of the deceased was married to this her lover. However, this woman did not come into their house without producing great misfortunes both to Anileus himself, and to Asineus also, but brought great mischiefs upon them on the occasion following. Since she was led away captive, upon

the death of her husband, she concealed the images
of those gods which were their country gods, common
to her husband and to herself: now it is the custom [1]
of that country for all to have the idols they worship
in their own houses, and to carry them along with
them when they go into a foreign land, agreeable
to which custom of theirs she carried her idols with
her. Now at first she performed her worship to them
privately, but when she was become Anileus' married
wife, she worshipped them in her accustomed manner,
and with the same appointed ceremonies which she
used in her former husband's days; upon which their
most esteemed friends blamed him at first that he
did not act after the manner of the Hebrews, nor
perform what was agreeable to their laws, in marrying a foreign wife, and one that transgressed the
accurate appointments of their sacrifices and religious
ceremonies; that he ought to consider, lest by allowing
himself in many pleasures of the body, he might
lose his principality, on account of the beauty of a
wife, and that high authority which, by God's blessing,
he had arrived at. But, when they prevailed not at
all upon him, he slew one of them for whom he had
the greatest respect, because of the liberty he took
with him; who, when he was dying out of regard
to the laws, imprecated a punishment upon his
murderer, Anileus, and upon Asineus also, and that
all their companions might come to a like end from
their enemies; upon the two first as the principal
actors of this wickedness, and upon the rest as
those that would not assist him when he suffered

---

[1] This custom of the Mesopotamians to carry their household gods
along with them wherever they travelled, is as old as the days of Jacob,
when Rachel his wife did the same, Gen. xxxi. 19, 30-35, nor is it to
pass here unobserved, what great miseries came on these Jews, because
they suffered one of their leaders to marry an idolatrous wife, contrary
to the law of Moses. Of which matter see the note on B. XIX. ch. v.
sect. 3.

in the defence of their laws. Now these latter were sorely grieved, yet did they tolerate these doings, because they remembered that they had arrived at their present happy state by no other means than their fortitude. But when they also heard of the worship of those gods whom the Parthians adore, they thought the injury that Anileus offered to their laws was to be borne no longer; and a great number of them came to Asineus, and loudly complained of Anileus, and told him, that "it had been well that he had of himself seen what was advantageous to them, but that however it was now high time to correct what had been done amiss, before the crime that had been committed proved the ruin of himself and all the rest of them. They added, that the marriage of this woman was made without their consent, and without a regard to their old laws; and that the worship which this woman [paid to their gods] was a reproach to the God whom they worshipped." Now, Asineus was sensible of his brother's offence that it had been already the cause of great mischiefs, and would be so for the time to come; yet did he tolerate the same from the good-will he had to so near a relation, and forgiving it to him, on account that his brother was quite over-borne by his wicked inclinations. But as more and more still came about him every day, and the clamours about it became greater, he at length spoke to Anileus about these clamours, reproving him for his former actions, and desiring him for the future to leave them off, and send the woman back to her relations. But nothing was gained by these reproofs; for, as the woman perceived what a tumult was made among the people on her account, and was afraid for Anileus, lest he should come to any harm for his love to her, she infused poison into Asineus' food, and thereby

took him off, and was now secure of prevailing, when
her lover was to be judge of what should be done
about her.

6. So Anileus took the government upon himself alone, and led his army against the villages of
Mithridates, who was a man of principal authority in
Parthia, and had married king Artabanus' daughter;
he also plundered them, and among that prey was
found much money, and many slaves, as also a great
number of sheep and many other things, which, when
gained, make men's condition happy. Now, when
Mithridates, who was there at this time, heard that
his villages were taken, he was very much displeased
to find that Anileus had first began to injure him,
and to affront him in his present dignity, when he
had not offered any injury to him beforehand; and
he got together the greatest body of horsemen he
was able, and those out of that number which were
of an age fit for war, and came to fight Anileus;
and when he was arrived at a certain village of his
own, he lay still there, as intending to fight him on
the day following, because it was the sabbath, the
day on which the Jews rest. And when Anileus
was informed of this by a Syrian stranger of another
village, who not only gave him an exact account of
other circumstances, but told him where Mithridates
would have a feast, he took his supper at a proper
time, and marched by night, with an intent of falling
upon the Parthians while they were unapprized what
they should do; so he fell upon them about the fourth
watch of the night, and some of them he slew while
they were asleep, and others he put to flight, and
took Mithridates alive, and set him naked upon an
ass, which, among the Parthians, is esteemed the
greatest reproach possible. And when he had
brought him into a wood with such a resolution, and

his friends desired him to kill Mithridates; he soon told them his own mind to the contrary, and said, that "it was not right to kill a man who was one of the principal families among the Parthians, and greatly honoured with matching into the royal family; that so far as they had hitherto gone was tolerable; for although they had injured Mithridates, yet if they preserved his life, this benefit would be remembered by him to the advantage of those that gave it him, but that if he were once put to death, the king would not be at rest till he had made a great slaughter of the Jews that dwelt at Babylon; to whose safety we ought to have a regard, both on account of our relation to them, and because if any misfortune befall us, we have no other place to retire to, since he hath gotten the flower of their youth under him." By this thought, and this speech of his made in council, he persuaded them to act accordingly, so Mithridates was let go. But, when he was got away, his wife reproached him, that although he was son-in-law to the king, he neglected to avenge himself on those that had injured him, while he took no care about it, but was contented to have been made a captive by the Jews, and to have escaped them, and she bid him "either to go back like a man of courage, or else she swore by the gods of their royal family, that she would certainly dissolve her marriage with him." Upon which, partly because he could not bear the daily trouble of her taunts, and partly because he was afraid of her insolence, lest she should in earnest dissolve her marriage, he unwillingly, and against his inclinations, got together again as great an army as he could, and marched along with them, as himself thinking it a thing not to be borne any longer, that he, a Parthian, should owe his preservation to the Jews, when they had been too hard for him in the war.

7. But as soon as Anileus understood that Mithridates was marching with a great army against him, he thought it too ignominious a thing to tarry about the lakes, and not to take the first opportunity of meeting his enemies, and he hoped to have the same success, and to beat their enemies as they did before; as also he ventured boldly upon the like attempts. Accordingly he led out his army,. and a great many more joined themselves to that army, in order to betake themselves to plunder the people, and in order to terrify the enemy again by their numbers. But when they had marched ninety furlongs, while the road had been through dry [and sandy] places, and about the midst of the day, they were become very thirsty; and Mithridates appeared, and fell upon them, as they were in distress for want of water, on which account, and on account of the time of the day, they were not able to bear their weapons. So Anileus and his men were put to an ignominious rout, while men in despair were to attack those that were fresh and in good plight; so great slaughter was made, and many ten thousand men fell. Now Anileus, and all that stood firm about him, ran away as fast as they were able, into a wood, and afforded Mithridates the pleasure of having gained a great victory over them. But there now came unto Anileus a conflux of bad men, who regarded their own lives very little, if they might but gain some present ease, insomuch that they, by thus coming to him, compensated the multitude of those that perished in the fight. Yet were not these men like to those that fell, because they were rash, and unexercised in war; however, with these he came upon the villages of the Babylonians, and a mighty devastation of all things was made there by the injuries that Anileus did them. So the Babylonians, and those that had already been

in the war, sent to Neerda to the Jews there, and demanded Anileus. But, although they did not agree to their demands, (for if they had been willing to deliver him up, it was not in their power so to do,) yet did they desire to make peace with them. To which the other replied, that they also wanted to settle conditions of peace with them, and sent men together with the Babylonians, who discoursed with Anileus about them. But the Babylonians, upon taking a view of his situation, and having learned where Anileus and his men lay, fell secretly upon them as they were drunk, and fallen asleep, and slew all that they caught of them, without any fear, and killed Anileus himself also.

8. The Babylonians were now freed from Anileus' heavy incursions, which had been a great restraint to the effects of that hatred they bore to the Jews, for they were almost always at variance, by reason of the contrariety of their laws; and which party soever grew boldest before the other, they assaulted the other; and at this time in particular it was, that upon the ruin of Anileus' party, the Babylonians attacked the Jews, which made those Jews so vehemently to resent the injuries they received from the Babylonians, that being neither able to fight them, nor bearing to live with them, they went to Seleucia, the principal city of those parts, which was built by Seleucus Nicator. It was inhabited by many of the Macedonians, but by more of the Grecians; not a few of the Syrians also dwelt there; and thither did the Jews fly, and lived there five years, without any misfortunes. But on the sixth year, a pestilence came upon these at Babylon, which occasioned new removals of men's habitations out of that city: and because they came to Seleucia, it happened that a still heavier calamity came upon them on

that account, which I am going to relate immediately.

9. Now the way of living of the people of
Seleucia, who were Greeks and Syrians, was commonly quarrelsome, and full of discords, though the
Greeks were too hard for the Syrians. When therefore, the Jews were come thither and dwelt among
them, there arose a sedition, and the Syrians were
too hard for the other, by the assistance of the Jews,
who are men that despise dangers, and very ready to
fight upon any occasion. Now, when the Greeks
had the worst in this sedition, and saw that they had
but one way of recovering their former authority,
and that was, if they could prevent the agreement
between the Jews and the Syrians, they every one
discoursed with such of the Syrians as were formerly
their acquaintance, and promised they would be at
peace and friendship with them. Accordingly they
gladly agreed so to do; and when this was done by
the principal men of both nations, they soon agreed
to a reconciliation, and when they were so agreed,
they both knew that the great design of such their
union, would be their common hatred to the Jews.
Accordingly they fell upon them, and slew about
fifty thousand of them; nay, the Jews were all
destroyed, excepting a few who escaped, by the compassion which their friends or neighbours afforded
them, in order to let them fly away. These retired
to Ctesiphon, a Grecian city, and situate near to
Seleucia, where the king [of Parthia] lives in winter
every year, and where the greatest part of his riches
are reposited, but the Jews had here no certain
settlement, those of Seleucia having little concern
for the king's honour. Now the whole nation of the
Jews were in fear both of the Babylonians, and of
the Seleucians, because all the Syrians that lived in
those places agreed with the Seleucians in the war

against the Jews: so the most of them gathered themselves together, and went to Neerda, and Nisibis, and obtained security there by the strength of those cities; besides which their inhabitants, who were a great many, were all warlike men. And this was the state of the Jews at this time in Babylonia.

BOOK XIX.

CONTAINING THE INTERVAL OF THREE YEARS AND A HALF.

[FROM THE DEPARTURE OF THE JEWS OUT OF BABYLON
TO FADUS, THE ROMAN PROCURATOR.]

CHAPTER I.

How Caius was [1] slain by Cherea.

1. Now this Caius [2] did not demonstrate his madness in offering injuries only to the Jews at Jerusalem, or to those that dwelt in the neighbourhood, but suffered it to extend itself through all the earth and sea, so far as was in subjection to the Romans, and filled it with ten thousand mischiefs, so many indeed in number as no former history relates. But Rome itself felt the most dismal effects of what he did, while he deemed that not to be any way more honourable than the rest of the cities; but he pulled and hauled its other citizens, but especially

---

[1] In this and the three next chapters, we have a larger and more distinct account of the slaughter of Caius, and the succession of Claudius, than we have of any such ancient facts whatsoever elsewhere. Some of the occasions of which probably were, Josephus' bitter hatred against tyranny, and the pleasure he took in giving the history of the slaughter of such a barbarous tyrant as was this Caius Caligula, as also the deliverance his own nation had by that slaughter, of which he speaks, sect. 2, together with the great intimacy he had with Agrippa junior, whose father was deeply concerned in the advancement of Claudius upon the death of Caius; from which Agrippa junior, Josephus might be fully informed of his history.

[2] Called *Caligula* by the Romans.

161

the senate, and particularly the nobility, and such as had been dignified by illustrious ancestors; he also had ten thousand devices against such of the equestrian order, as it was styled, who were esteemed by the citizens equal in dignity and wealth with the senators, because out of them the senators were themselves chosen; these he treated after an ignominious manner, and removed them out of his way, while they were at once slain, and their wealth plundered; because he slew men generally in order to seize on their riches. He also asserted his own divinity, and insisted on greater honours to be paid him by his subjects, than are due to mankind. He also frequented that temple of Jupiter which they style the Capitol, which is with them the most holy of all their temples, and had boldness enough to call himself the brother of Jupiter. And other pranks he did like a madman; as when he laid a bridge from the city Dicearchia, which belongs to Campania, to Misenum, another city upon the seaside, from one promontory to another, of the length of thirty furlongs, as measured over the sea. And this was done, because he esteemed it to be a most tedious thing to row over it in a small ship, and thought withal, that it became him to make that bridge, since he was lord of the sea, and might oblige it to give marks of obedience as well as the earth; so he inclosed the whole bay within his bridge, and drove his chariot over it, and thought that, as he was a god, it was fit for him to travel over such roads as this was. Nor did he abstain from the plunder of any of the Grecian temples, and gave order that all the engravings and sculptures, and the rest of the ornaments of the statues and donations therein dedicated, should be brought to him, saying, that "the best things ought to be set nowhere but in the best place, and that the city of Rome was that best

place." He also adorned his own house and his
gardens with the curiosities brought from those
temples, together with the houses he lay at when he
travelled all over Italy; whence he did not scruple
to give a command, that the statue of Jupiter
Olympius, so called because he was honoured at the
Olympian games by the Greeks, which was the work
of Phidias the Athenian, should be brought to Rome.
Yet did not he compass his end, because the architects
told Memmius Regulus, who was commanded to
remove that statue of Jupiter, that the workmanship
was such as would be spoiled, and would not bear
the removal. It was also reported that Memmius,
both on that account, and on account of some such
mighty prodigies as are of an incredible nature, put
off the taking it down, and wrote to Caius those
accounts, as his apology for not having done what
his epistle required of him; and that when he was
thence in danger of perishing, he was saved by Caius
being dead himself, before he had put him to death.

2. Nay, Caius' madness came to this height, that
when he had a daughter born, he carried her into
the capitol, and put her upon the knees of the statue,
and said, that the child was common to him and to
Jupiter, and determined that she had two fathers,
but which of these fathers was the greatest, he left
undetermined; and yet mankind bore him in such
his pranks! He also gave leave to slaves to accuse
their masters of any crimes whatsoever they pleased;
for all such accusations were terrible, because they
were in great part made to please him, and at his
suggestion, insomuch that Pallux, Claudius' slave,
had the boldness to lay an accusation against Claudius
himself, and Caius was not ashamed to be present
at his trial of life and death, to hear that trial of
his own uncle, in hopes of being able to take him off,

although he did not succeed to his mind. But when
he had filled the whole habitable world, which he
governed, with false accusations and miseries, and
had occasioned the greatest insult of slaves against
their masters, who, indeed, in a great measure ruled
them, there were many secret plots now laid against
him; some in anger, and in order for men to revenge
themselves, on account of the miseries they had
already undergone from him, and others made attempts upon him, in order to take him off before
they should fall into such great miseries, while his
death came very fortunately for the preservation of
the laws of all men, and had a great influence upon
the public welfare; and this happened most happily
for our nation in particular, which had almost utterly
perished if he had not been suddenly slain. And
I confess I have a mind to give a full account of
this matter, particularly because it will afford great
assurance of the power of God, and great comfort
to those that are under afflictions, and wise caution
to those who think their happiness will never end,
nor bring them at length to the most lasting miseries,
if they do not conduct their lives by the principles
of virtue.

3.   Now there were three several conspiracies made
in order to take off Caius, and each of these three
was conducted by excellent persons. Emilius Regulus, born at Corduba in Spain, got some men
together, and was desirous to take Caius off either
by them, or by himself. Another conspiracy there
was laid by them, under the conduct of Cherea Cassius, the tribune [of the Petronian band;] Minucianus
Annius was also one of great consequence among
those that were prepared to oppose his tyranny. Now
the several occasions of these men's several hatred
and conspiracy against Caius were these: Regulus

had indignation and hatred against all injustice, for
he had a mind naturally angry, and bold, and free,
which made him not conceal his counsels; so he communicated them to many of his friends, and to others,
who seemed to him persons of activity and vigour;
Minucianus entered into this conspiracy, because of
the injustice done to Lepidus his particular friend,
and one of the best character of all the citizens, whom
Caius had slain, as also because he was afraid of
himself, since Caius' wrath tended to the slaughter
of all alike: and for Cherea, he came in, because he
thought it a deed worthy of a free ingenuous man
to kill Caius, and was ashamed of the reproaches he
lay under from Caius, as though he were a coward;
as also because he was himself in danger every day
from his friendship with him, and the observance he
paid him. These men proposed this attempt to all
the rest that were concerned, who saw the injuries
that were offered them, and were desirous that Caius'
slaughter might succeed by their mutual assistance
of one another, and they might themselves escape
being killed by the taking off Caius: that perhaps
they should gain their point, and that it would be
a happy thing if they should gain it, to approve
themselves to so many excellent persons as earnestly
wished to be partakers with them in their design,
for the delivery of the city and of the government,
even at the hazard of their own lives. But still
Cherea was the most zealous of them all, both out
of a desire of getting himself the greatest name, and
also by reason of his access to Caius' presence, with
less danger, because he was tribune, and could therefore the more easily kill him.

4. Now at this time came on the horse-races
[Circensian games,] the view of which games was
eagerly desired by the people of Rome, for they

come with great alacrity into the hippodrome [circus] at such times, and petition their emperors, in great multitudes for what they stand in need of; who usually did not think fit to deny them their requests, but readily and gratefully granted them. Accordingly they most importunately desired, that Caius would now ease them in their tributes, and abate somewhat of the rigour of the taxes imposed upon them; but he would not hear their petition; and, when their clamours increased, he sent soldiers, some one way, and some another, and gave order that they should lay hold on those that made the clamours, and without any more ado, bring them out, and put them to death. These were Caius' commands, and those who were commanded executed the same; and the number of those who were slain on this occasion was very great. Now the people saw this, and bore it so far, that they left off clamouring, because they saw with their own eyes, that this petition to be relieved, as to the payment of their money, brought immediate death upon them. These things made Cherea more resolute to go on with his plot, in order to put an end to this barbarity of Caius against men. He then, at several times, thought to fall upon Caius even as he was feasting: yet did he restrain himself by some considerations; not that he had any doubt on him about killing him, but as watching for a proper season, that the attempt might not be frustrated, but that he might give the blow so as might certainly gain his purpose.

5. Cherea had been in the army a long time, yet was he not pleased with conversing so much with Caius. But Caius had set him to require the tributes, and other dues, which, when not paid in due time, were forfeited to Cæsar's treasury; and he had made some delays in requiring them, because those burdens

had been doubled, and had rather indulged his own mild disposition, than performed Caius' command, nay, indeed, he provoked Caius to anger by his sparing men, and pitying the hard fortunes of those from whom he demanded the taxes, and Caius upbraided him with his sloth and effeminacy in being so long about collecting the taxes. And indeed he did not only affront him in other respects, but when he gave him the watch-word of the day, to whom it was to be given by his place, he gave him feminine words, and those of a nature very reproachful; and these watch-words he gave out, as having been initiated in the secrets of certain mysteries, which he had been himself the author of. Now, although he had sometimes put on woman's clothes, and had been wrapt in some embroidered garments to them belonging, and done a great many other things, in order to make the company mistake him for a woman; yet did he, by way of reproach, object the like womanish behaviour to Cherea. But when Cherea received the watch-word from him, he had indignation at it, but had greater indignation at the delivery of it to others, as being laughed at by those that received it; insomuch that his fellow-tribunes made him the subject of their drollery; for they would foretell that he would bring them some of his useful watchwords when he was about to take the watch-word from Cæsar, and would thereby make him ridiculous; on which accounts he took the courage of assuming certain partners to him, as having just reasons for his indignation against Caius. Now there was one Pompedius, a senator, and one who had gone through almost all posts in the government, but otherwise an epicurean, and for that reason loved to lead an inactive life. Now Timidius, an enemy of his, had informed Caius that he had used indecent reproaches against him, and he made use of Quintilia, for a witness to them; a woman she was, much beloved by many that frequented the theatre, and particularly by Pompedius, on account of her great beauty. Now this woman thought it a horrible thing to attest to an accusation that touched the life of her lover, which was also a lie. Timidius, however, wanted to have her brought to the torture. Caius was irritated at this reproach upon him, and commanded Cherea, without any delay, to torture Quintilia, as he used to employ Cherea in such bloody matters, and those that required the torture, because he thought he would do it the more barbarously, in order to avoid that imputation of effeminacy which he had laid upon him. But Quintilia, when she was brought to the rack, trod upon the foot of one of her associates, and let him know, that he might be of good courage, and not be afraid of the consequence of her tortures; for that she would bear them with magnanimity. Cherea tortured this woman after a cruel manner: unwillingly indeed, but because he could not help it. He then brought her, without being in the least moved at what she had suffered, into the presence of Caius, and that in such a state as was sad to behold; and Caius, being somewhat affected with the sight of Quintilia, who had her body miserably disordered by the pains she had undergone, freed both her and Pompedius of the crime laid to their charge. He also gave her money to make her an honourable amends, and comfort her for that maiming of her body which she had suffered; and for her glorious patience under such unsufferable torments.

6. This matter sorely grieved Cherea, as having been the cause, as far as he could, or the instrument of those miseries to men, which seemed worthy of consolation to Caius himself; on which account he

said to Clement and to Papinius (of whom Clement
was general of the army, and Papinius was a tribute,)
"To be sure, Clement, we have no way failed in our
guarding the emperor; for as to those that have made
conspiracies against his government, some have been
slain by our care and pains, and some have been by
us tortured, and this to such a degree, that he hath
limself pitied them. How great then is our virtue
in submitting to conduct his armies!" Clement held
his peace, but showed the shame he was under in
obeying Caius' orders, both by his eyes and his blush-
ing countenance, while he thought it by no means
right to accuse the emperor in express words, lest
their own safety should be endangered thereby.
Upon which Cherea took courage, and spoke to him
without fear of the dangers that were before him,
and discoursed largely of the sore calamities under
which the city and the government then laboured,
and said, "We may indeed pretend in words, that
Caius is the person unto whom the cause of such
miseries ought to be imputed; but, in the opinion
of such as are able to judge uprightly, is it not I,
O Clement! and this Papinius, and before us thou
thyself who bring these tortures upon the Romans,
and upon all mankind? It is not done by our being
subservient to the commands of Caius, but it is done
by our own consent; for whereas it is in our power
to put an end to the life of this man, who hath so
terribly injured the citizens and his subjects, we are
his guard in mischief, and his executioners instead
of his soldiers, and are the instruments of his cruelty.
We bear these weapons, not for our liberty, not for
the Roman government, but only for his preservation,
who hath enslaved both their bodies and their minds;
and we are every day polluted with the blood that
we shed; and the torments we inflict upon others;

and this we do, till somebody becomes Caius' instrument in bringing the like miseries upon ourselves. Nor does he thus employ us, because he hath a kindness for us, but rather because he hath a suspicion of us, as also because when abundance more have been killed (for Caius will set no bounds to his wrath, since he aims to do all, not out of regard to justice but to his own pleasure,) we shall also ourselves be exposed to his cruelty; whereas we ought to be the means of confirming the security and liberty of all, and at the same time to resolve to free ourselves from dangers."

7. Hereupon Clement openly commended Cherea's intentions; but bid him "hold his tongue; for that in case his words should get out among many, and such things should be spread abroad as were fit to be concealed, the plot would come to be discovered before it was executed, and they should be brought to punishment: but that they should leave all to futurity, and the hope which thence arose, that some fortunate event would come to their assistance: that, as for himself, his age would not permit him to make any attempt in that case. However, although perhaps I could suggest what may be safer than what thou, Cherea, hast contrived and said, yet how is it possible for any one to suggest what is more for thy reputation?" So Clement went his way home, with deep reflections on what he had heard, and what he had himself said. Cherea also was under a concern, and went quickly to Cornelius Sabinus, who was himself one of the tribunes, and whom he otherwise knew to be a worthy man, and a lover of liberty, and on that account very uneasy at the present management of public affairs, he being desirous to come immediately to the execution of what had been determined, and thinking it right for him to propose

it to the other, and afraid lest Clement should discover them, and besides looking upon delays and
puttings off to be the next to desisting from the
enterprise.
8. But as all was agreeable to Sabinus, who had
himself, equally without Cherea, the same design,
but had been silent for want of a person to whom
he could safely communicate that design, so having
now met with one, who not only promised to conceal
what he heard, but who had already opened his mind
to him, he was much more encouraged, and desired
of Cherea, that no delay might be made therein. Accordingly they went to Minucianus, who was as virtuous
a man, and as zealous to do glorious actions as themselves, and suspected by Caius on occasion of the
slaughter of Lepidus; for Minucianus and Lepidus
were intimate friends, and both in fear of the dangers
that they were under; for Caius was terrible to all
the great men, as appearing ready to act a mad
part towards each of them in particular, and towards
all of them in general; and these men were afraid
of one another, while they were yet uneasy at the
posture of affairs, but avoided to declare their mind
and their hatred against Caius to one another, out
of fear of the dangers they might be in thereby,
although they perceived by other means their mutual
hatred against Caius, and on that account were not
averse to mutual kindness one towards another.
9. When Minucianus and Cherea had met together, and saluted one another, (as they had been
used on former conversations to give the upper hand
to Minucianus, both on account of his eminent dignity,
for he was the noblest of all the citizens, and highly
commended by all men, especially when he made
speeches to them,) Minucianus began first, and asked
Cherea, What was the watch-word he had received

that day from Caius? for the affront, which was
offered Cherea in giving the watch-words was famous
over the city. But Cherea made no delay, so long
as to reply to that question out of the joy he had
that Minucianus would have such confidence in him
as to discourse with him. "But do thou," said he,
"give me the watch-word of liberty. And I return
thee my thanks, that thou hast so greatly encouraged
me to exert myself after an extraordinary manner;
nor do I stand in need of many words to encourage
me, since both thou and I are of the same mind,
and partakers of the same resolutions, and this before
we have conferred together. I have indeed but one
sword girt on, but this one will serve us both. Come
on, therefore, let us set about the work. Do thou
go first, if thou hast a mind, and bid me follow thee;
or else I will go first, and thou shalt assist me, and
we will assist one another, and trust one another.
Nor is there a necessity for even one sword to such
as have a mind disposed to such works, by which mind
the sword uses to be successful. I am zealous about
this action, nor am I solicitous what I may myself
undergo; for I am not at leisure to consider the
dangers that may come upon myself, so deeply am
I troubled at the slavery our once free country is
now under, and at the contempt cast upon our
excellent laws, and at the destruction which hangs
over all men, by the means of Caius. I wish that I
may be judged by thee, and that thou mayest esteem
me worthy of credit in these matters, seeing we are
both of the same opinion, and there is herein no
difference between us."

10. When Minucianus saw the vehemency with
which Cherea delivered himself, he gladly embraced
him, and encouraged him in his bold attempt, commending him, and embracing him; so he let him go

with his good wishes; and some affirm, that he thereby
confirmed Minucianus in the prosecution of what had
been agreed among them; for, as Cherea entered
into the court, the report runs, that a voice came from
among the multitude to encourage him, which bid
him finish what he was about, and take the opportunity that providence afforded; and that Cherea
at first suspected that some one of the conspirators
had betrayed him, and he was caught, but at length
perceived that it was by way of exhortation.
Whether somebody, that was conscious of what he
was about, gave a signal for his encouragement, or
whether it were God himself, who looks upon the
actions of men, that encouraged him to go on boldly
in his design is uncertain. The plot was now communicated to a great many, and they were all in
their armour; some of the conspirators being senators,
and some of the equestrian order, and as many of
the soldiery as were made acquainted with it, for
there was not one of them who would not reckon it
a part of his happiness to kill Caius, and on that
account they were all very zealous in the affair by
what means soever any one could come at it, that he
might not be behindhand in these virtuous designs,
but might be ready with all his alacrity or power,
both by words and actions, to complete this slaughter
of a tyrant. And besides these Callistus also, who
was a freed man of Caius, and was the only man that
had arrived at the greatest degree of power under
him; such a power, indeed, as was in a manner equal
to the power of the tyrant himself, by the dread
that all men had of him, and by the great riches he
had acquired; for he took bribes most plenteously,
and committed injuries without bounds, and was
more extravagant in the use of his power in unjust
proceedings than any other; he also knew the dis-

position of Caius to be implacable, and never to be turned from what he had resolved on. He had withal many other reasons why he thought himself in danger, and the vastness of his wealth was not one of the least of them: on which account he privately ingratiated himself with Claudius, and transferred his courtship to him out of this hope, that in case, upon the removal of Caius, the government should come to him, his interest in such changes should lay a foundation for his preserving his dignity under him, since he laid in beforehand a stock of merit, and did Claudius good offices in his promotion. He had also the boldness to pretend, that he had been persuaded to make away Claudius, by poisoning him, but had still invented ten thousand excuses for delaying to do it. But it seems probable to me, that Callistus only counterfeited this, in order to ingratiate himself with Claudius, for if Caius had been in earnest resolved to take off Claudius, he would not have admitted of Callistus' excuses, nor would Callistus, if he had been enjoined to do such an act as was desired by Caius, have put it off, nor, if he had disobeyed those injunctions of his master, had he escaped immediate punishment: while Claudius was preserved from the madness of Caius by a certain divine providence, and Callistus pretended to such a piece of merit as he no way deserved.

11. However, the execution of Cherea's designs was put off from day to day, by the sloth of many therein concerned; for as to Cherea himself, he would not willingly make any delay in that execution, thinking every time, a fit time for it; for frequent opportunities offered themselves; as when Caius went up to the capitol to sacrifice for his daughter, or when he stood upon his royal palace, and threw gold and silver pieces of money among the people, he

might be pushed down headlong, because the top of
the palace, that looks towards the market-place, was
very high; and also when he celebrated the mysteries,
which he had appointed at that time; for he was then
no way secluded from the people, but solicitous to
do every thing carefully and decently, and was free
from all suspicion that he should be then assaulted
by any body; and although the gods should afford
him no divine assistance to enable him to take away
his life, yet had he strength himself sufficient to
despatch Caius, even without a sword: Thus was
Cherea angry at his fellow-conspirators, for fear they
should suffer a proper opportunity to pass by; and
they were themselves sensible that he had just cause
to be angry at them, and that his eagerness was for
his advantage; yet did they desire he would have a
little longer patience, lest, upon any disappointment
they might meet with, they should put the city into
disorder, and an inquisition should be made after
the conspiracy, and should render the courage of
those that were to attack Caius without success, while
he would then secure himself more carefully than
ever against them; that it would therefore be the
best to set about the work when the shows were
exhibited in the palace. These shows were acted in
honour of that Cæsar [1] who first of all changed the
popular government, and transferred it to himself;
galleries being fixed before the palace, where the
Romans that were Patricians became spectators, together with their children and their wives, and Cæsar
himself was to be also a spectator; and they reckoned,
among those many ten thousands, who would there
be crowded into a narrow compass, they should have

---

[1] Here Josephus supposes that it was Augustus, and Julius Cæsar,
who first changed the Roman commonwealth into a monarchy; for these
shows were in honour of Augustus, as we shall learn in the next section
but one.

a favourable opportunity to make their attempt upon
him as he came in; because his guards that should
protect him, if any of them should have a mind to
do it, would not here be able to give him any assistance.

12. Cherea consented to this delay, and when the
shows were exhibited, it was resolved to do the work
the first day. But fortune, which allowed a farther
delay to his slaughter, was too hard for their foregoing resolutions, and, as three days of the regular
times for these shows were now over they had much
ado to get the business done on the last day. Then
Cherea called the conspirators together, and spoke
thus to them: "So much time passed away without
effect is a reproach to us, as delaying to go through
such a virtuous design as we are engaged in; but
more fatal will this delay prove, if we be discovered
and the design be frustrated; for Caius will then
become more cruel in his unjust proceedings. Do
not we see how long we deprive all our friends of
their liberty, and give Caius leave still to tyrannize
over them! while we ought to have procured them
security for the future, and by laying a foundation
for the happiness of others, gain to ourselves great
admiration and honour for all time to come." Now,
while the conspirators had nothing tolerable to say
by way of contradiction, and yet did not quite relish
what they were doing, but stood silent and astonished,
he said farther, "O my brave comrades! why do we
make such delays? Do not you see that this is the
last day of these shows, and that Caius is about to
go to sea? for he is preparing to sail to Alexandria,
in order to see Egypt. Is it therefore for your
honour to let a man go out of your hands who is a
reproach to mankind, and to permit him to go after
a pompous manner, triumphing both at land and

sea? shall not we be justly ashamed of ourselves, if we give leave to some Egyptian or other, who shall think his injuries insufferable to freemen, to kill him? As for myself, I will no longer bear your slow proceedings, but will expose myself to the dangers of the enterprise this very day, and bear cheerfully whatsoever shall be the consequence of the attempt; nor, let them be ever so great will I put them off any longer; for, to a wise and courageous man, what can be more miserable than that, while I am alive, any one else should kill Caius, and deprive me of the honour of so virtuous an action."

13. When Cherea had spoken thus, he zealously set about the work, and inspired courage into the rest to go on with it, and they were all eager to fall to it without farther delay. So he was at the palace in the morning, with his equestrian sword girt on him; for it was the custom that the tribunes should ask for the watch-word with their swords on, and this was the day on which Cherea was, by custom, to. receive the watch-word; and the multitude were already come to the palace, to be soon enough for seeing the shows, and that in great crowds, and one tumultuously crushing another, while Caius was delighted with this eagerness of the multitude; for which reason there was no order observed in the seating men, nor was any peculiar place appointed for the senators, or for the equestrian order; but they sat at random, men and women together, and free men were mixed with the slaves. So Caius came out in a solemn manner, and offered sacrifice to Augustus Cæsar, in whose honour indeed these shows were celebrated. Now it happened, upon the fall of a certain priest, that the garment of Asprenas, a senator, was filled with blood, which made Caius laugh, although this was an evident omen to Asprenas, for

he was slain at the same time with Caius. It is also related, that Caius was that day, contrary to his usual custom, so very affable and good-natured in his conversation, that every one of those that were present were astonished at it. After the sacrifice was over, Caius betook himself to see the shows, and sat down for that purpose, as did also the principal of his friends sit near him. Now the parts of the theatre were so fastened together, as it used to be every year, in the manner following: It had two doors, the one door led to the open air, the other was for going into, or going out of the cloisters, that those within the theatre might not be thereby disturbed; but out of one gallery there was an inward passage, partly into partitions also, which led into another gallery, to give room to the combatants, and to the musician to go out as occasion served. When the multitude were set down, and Cherea, with the other tribunes were set down also, and the right corner of the theatre was allotted to Cæsar, one Vatinius, a senator, commander of the pretorian band, asked of Cluvius, one that sat by him, and was of consular dignity also, "Whether he had heard any thing of news or not?" but took care that nobody should hear what he said; and when Cluvius replied, That "he had heard no news," "Know then," said Vatinius, "that the game of the slaughter of tyrants is to be played this day." But Cluvius replied, "O brave comrade! hold thy peace, lest some other of the Achians hear thy tale." And, as there was abundance of autumnal fruit thrown among the spectators, and a great number of birds, that were of great value to such as possessed them, on account of their rareness, Caius was pleased with the birds fighting for the fruits, and with the violence wherewith the spectators seized upon them; and here he perceived two prodigies

that happened there; for an actor was introduced, by
whom a leader of robbers was crucified, and the
pantomime brought in a play called Cinyras, wherein
he himself was to be slain, as well as his daughter
Myrrha, and wherein a great deal of fictitious blood
was shed, both about him that was crucified, and also
about Cinyras. It is also confessed, that this was the
same day wherein Pausanias, a friend of Philip, the
son of Amyntus, who was king of Macedonia, slew
him, as he was entering into the theatre. And now
Caius was in a doubt whether he should tarry to the
end of the shows, because it was the last day, or
whether he should not go first to the bath, and to
dinner, and then return and sit down as before.
Hereupon Minucianus, who sat over Caius, and was
afraid that the opportunity should fail them, got
up, because he saw Cherea was already gone out,
and made haste out, to confirm him in his resolution;
but Caius took hold of his garment, in an obliging
way, and said to him, "O brave man! whither art
thou going?" Whereupon, out of reverence to Cæsar
as it seemed, he sat down again; but his fear prevailed
over him, and in a little time he got up again, and
then Caius did no way oppose his going out, as
thinking that he went out to perform some necessities
of nature. And Asprenas, who was one of the confederates, persuaded Caius to go out to the bath,
and to dinner, and then to come again, as desirous
that what had been resolved on might be brought
to a conclusion immediately.

14. So Cherea's associates placed themselves in
order, as the time would permit them, and they were
obliged to labour hard, that the place which was appointed them should not be left by them; but they
had an indignation at the tediousness of the delays,
and that what they were about should be put off any

longer, for it was already about the ninth [1] hour of
the day, and Cherea, upon Caius' tarrying so long,
had a great mind to go in, and fall upon him in
his seat, although he foresaw that this could not be
done without much bloodshed, both of the senators,
and of those of the equestrian order that were present;
and although he knew this must happen, yet had he
a great mind to do so, as thinking it a right thing
to procure security and freedom to all, at the expense
of such as might perish at the same time. And as
they were just going back into the entrance to the
theatre, word was brought them that Caius was
arisen, whereby a tumult was made; hereupon the
conspirators thrust away the crowd, under pretence
as if Caius was angry at them, but in reality as
desirous to have a quiet place, that should have none
in it to defend him, while they set about Caius'
slaughter. Now Claudius, his uncle, was gone out
before, and Marcus Vinitius, his sister's husband,
as also Valerius of Asia; whom, though they had
such a mind to put out of their places, the reverence
to their dignity hindered them so to do; then followed Caius, with Paulus Arruntius; and because
Caius was now gotten within the palace, he left the
direct road, along which those his servants stood that
were in waiting, and by which road Claudius had
gone out before, Caius turned aside into a private
narrow passage, in order to go to the place for
bathing, as also in order to take a view of the boys
that came out of Asia, who were sent thence, partly
to sing hymns in these mysteries, which were now
celebrated, and partly to dance in the pyric way of
dancing upon the theatre. So Cherea met him, and
asked him for the watch-word; upon Caius' giving

[1] Suetonius says Caius was slain about the seventh hour of the day,
Josephus about the ninth. The series of the narration favours Josephus.

him one of his ridiculous words, he immediately reproached him, and drew his sword, and gave him
a terrible stroke with it, yet was not this stroke
mortal. And although there be those that say, it
was so contrived on purpose by Cherea, that Caius
should not be killed at one blow, but should be
punished more severely by a multitude of wounds,
yet does this story appear to me incredible; because
the fear men are under in such actions does not
allow them to use their reason. And if Cherea was
of that mind, I esteem him the greatest of all fools,
in pleasing himself in his spite against Caius, rather
than immediately procuring safety to himself and to
his confederates from the dangers they were in;
because there might many things still happen for
helping Caius' escape, if he had not already given
up the ghost; for certainly Cherea would have regard,
not so much to the punishment of Caius, as to the
affliction himself and his friends were in, while it was
in his power, after such success, to keep silent, and
to escape the wrath of Caius' defenders, and not to
leave it to uncertainty whether he should gain the
end he aimed at or not, and after an unreasonable
manner to act as if he had a mind to ruin himself, and lose the opportunity that lay before him;
but every body may guess as he pleases about this
matter. However, Caius was staggered with the pain
that blow gave him; for the stroke of the sword
falling in the middle, between the shoulder and the
neck, was hindered by the first bone of the breast
from proceeding any farther. Nor did he either cry
out, in such astonishment was he, nor did he call
out for any of his friends; whether it were that he
had no confidence in them, or that his mind was
otherwise disordered, but he groaned under the pain
he endured, and presently went forward and fled;

when Cornelius Sabinus, who was already prepared
in mind so to do, thrust him down upon his knee,
where many of them stood round about him, and
struck him with their swords, and they cried out,
and encouraged one another all at once to strike him
again; but all agree that Aquila gave him the finishing stroke, which directly killed him. But one may
justly ascribe this act to Cherea, for although many
concurred in this act itself, yet was he the first
contriver of it, and began long before all the rest to
prepare for it, and was the first man that boldly
spoke of it to the rest; and upon their admission of
what he said about it; he got the dispersed conspirators
together; he prepared every thing after a prudent
manner, and by suggesting good advice, showed himself far superior to the rest, and made obliging
speeches to them, insomuch that he even compelled
them all to go on, who otherwise had not courage
enough for that purpose; and when opportunity served
to use his sword in hand, he appeared first of all ready
so to do, and gave the first blow in this virtuous
slaughter; he also brought Caius easily into the power
of the rest, and almost killed him himself, insomuch
that it is but just to ascribe all that the rest did
to the advice, and bravery, and labours, of the hands
of Cherea.

15. Thus did Caius come to his end, and lay dead,
by the many wounds which had been given him.
Now Cherea and his associates, upon Caius' slaughter,
saw that it was impossible for them to save themselves, if they should all go the same way, partly on
account of the astonishment they were under: for
it was no small danger they had incurred by killing
an emperor, who was honoured and loved by the
madness of the people, especially when the soldiers were
likely to make a bloody inquiry after his murderers.

The passages also were narrow wherein the work was done, which were also crowded with a great multitude of Caius' attendants, and of such of the soldiers as were of the emperor's guard that day: whence it was that they went by other ways, and came to the house of Germanicus, the father of Caius, whom they had now killed, (which house adjoined to the palace; for while the edifice was one, it was built in its several parts by those particular persons who had been emperors, and those parts bore the names of those that built them, or the name of him who had begun to build any of its parts.) So they got away from the insults of the multitude, and then were for the present out of danger, that is, so long as the misfortune which had overtaken the emperor was not known. The Germans were the first that perceived that Caius was slain. These Germans were Caius' guard, and carried the name of the country whence they were chosen, and composed the Celtic legion. The men of that country are naturally passionate, which is commonly the temper of some other of the barbarous nations also, as not being used to consider much about what they do; they are of robust bodies, and fall upon their enemies as soon as ever they are attacked by them; and which way soever they go, they perform great exploits. When, therefore, these German guards understood that Caius was slain, they were very sorry for it, because they did not use their reason in judging about public affairs, but measured all by the advantages themselves received, Caius being beloved by them, because of the money he gave them, by which he had purchased their kindness to him: so they drew their swords, and Sabinus led them on. He was one of the tribunes, not by the means of the virtuous actions of his progenitors, for he had been a gladiator, but he had

obtained that post in the army by his having a
robust body. So these Germans marched along the
houses in quest of Cæsar's murderers, and cut
Asprenas to pieces, because he was the first man
they fell upon, and whose garment it was that the
blood of the sacrifice stained, as I have said already,
and which foretold that this his meeting the soldiers
would not be for his good. Then did Norbanus meet
them, who was one of the principal nobility of the
city, and could show many generals of armies among
his ancestors, but they paid no regard to his dignity;
yet was he of such great strength, that he wrested
the sword of the first of those that assaulted him
out of his hands, and appeared plainly not to be
willing to die without a struggle for his life, until
he was surrounded by a great number of assailants,
and died by the multitude of the wounds which they
gave him. The third man was Anteius, a senator,
and a few others with him. He did not meet with
these Germans by chance, as the rest did before,
but came to show his hatred to Caius, and because
he loved to see Caius lie dead with his own eyes,
and took a pleasure in that sight, for Caius had
banished Anteius' father who was of the same name
with himself, and, being not satisfied with that, he
sent out his soldiers, and slew him: so he was come
to rejoice at the sight of him, now he was dead.
But as the house was now all in a tumult, when he
was aiming to hide himself, he could not escape
that accurate search which the Germans made, while
they barbarously slew those that were guilty, and
those that were not guilty, and this equally also.
And thus were these [three] persons slain.

16. But when the rumour that Caius was slain
reached the theatre, they were astonished at it, and
could not believe it: even some that entertained his

destruction with great pleasure, and were more desirous of its happening than almost any other satisfaction that could come to them, were under such
a fear, that they could not believe it. There were
also those who greatly distrusted it, because they
were unwilling that any such thing should come to
Caius, nor could believe it, though it were ever so
true, because they thought no man could possibly
have so much power as to kill Caius. These were
the women, and the children, and the slaves, and
some of the soldiery. This last sort had taken his
pay, and in a manner tyrannized with him, and had
abused the best of his citizens, in being subservient
to his unjust commands, in order to gain honours
and advantages to themselves; but for the women,
and the youth, they had been inveigled with shows,
and the fightings of the gladiators, and certain dis-
tributions of flesh meat among them, which things
in pretence were designed for the pleasing of the
multitude, but in reality to satiate the barbarous
cruelty and madness of Caius. The slaves also were
sorry, because they were by Caius allowed to accuse,
and to despise their masters, and they could have
recourse to his assistance, when they had unjustly
affronted them; for he was very easy in believing
them against their masters, even when they accused
them falsely; and, if they would discover what money
their masters had, they might soon obtain both riches
and liberty, as the rewards of their accusations,
because the reward of these informers was the eighth
[1] part of the criminal's substance. As to the nobles,
although the report appeared credible to some of
them, either because they knew of the plot before-

---

[1] The reward proposed by the Roman laws to informers, was sometimes an eighth part of a criminal's goods, as here, and sometimes a
fourth part, as Spanheim assures us, from Suetonius and Tacitus.

hand, or because they wished it might be true: however, they concealed not only the joy they had at the relation of it, but that they had heard any thing at all about it. These last acted so out of the fear they had, that if the report proved false, they should be punished for having so soon let men know their minds. But those that knew Caius was dead, because they were partners with the conspirators they concealed all still more cautiously, as not knowing one another's minds; and fearing lest they should speak of it to some of those to whom the continuance of tyranny was advantageous; and, if Caius should prove to be alive, they might be informed against, and punished. And another report went about, that although Caius had been wounded indeed, yet was not he dead, but alive still, and under the physician's hands. Nor was any one looked upon by another, as faithful enough to be trusted, and to whom any one would open his mind; for he was either a friend to Caius, and therefore suspected to favour his tyranny, or he was one that hated him, who therefore might be suspected to deserve the less credit, because of his ill-will to him. Nay, it was said by some, (and this indeed it was that deprived the nobility of their hopes, and made them sad,) that Caius was in a condition to despise the dangers he had been in, and took no care of healing his wounds, but was gotten away into the market-place, and, bloody as he was, was making a harangue to the people. And these were the conjectural reports of those that were so unreasonable as to endeavour to raise tumults, which they turned different ways, according to the opinions of the hearers. Yet did they not leave their seats, for fear of being accused, if they should go out before the rest, for they should not be sentenced according to the real intention with which they went out, but according to the supposals of the accusers, and of the judges

17. But now a multitude of Germans had surrounded the theatre, with their swords drawn; all the spectators looked for nothing but death, and at every one's coming in a fear seized upon them, as if they were to be cut in pieces immediately; and in great distress they were, as neither having courage enough to go out of the theatre, nor believing themselves safe from dangers if they tarried there. And when the Germans came upon them, the cry was so great, that the theatre rang again with the entreaties of the spectators to the soldiers: pleading that they were entirely ignorant of every thing that related to such seditious contrivances, and that if there were any sedition raised, they knew nothing of it; they therefore begged that they would spare them, and not punish those that had not the least hand in such bold crimes as belonged to other persons, while they neglected to search after such as had really done whatsoever it be that hath been done. Thus did these people appeal to God, and deplore their infelicity with shedding of tears, and beating their faces, and said every thing that the most imminent danger, and the utmost concern for their lives, could dictate to them. This broke the fury of the soldiers, and made them repent of what they minded to do to the spectators, which would have been the greatest instance of cruelty. And so it appeared to even these savages, when they had once fixed the heads of those that were slain with Asprenas upon the altar; at which sight the spectators were sorely afflicted, both upon the consideration of the dignity of the persons, and out of a commiseration of their sufferings; nay, indeed, they were almost in as great disorder at the prospect of the danger themselves were in, seeing

it was still uncertain whether they should entirely escape the like calamity. Whence it was, that such as thoroughly and justly hated Caius, could yet no way enjoy the pleasure of his death, because they were themselves in jeopardy of perishing together with him, nor had they hitherto any firm assurance of surviving.

18. There was at this time, one Euaristus Arruntius, a public crier in the market, and therefore of a strong and audible voice, who vied in wealth with the richest of the Romans, and was able to do what he pleased in the city, both then and afterward. This man put himself into the most mournful habit he could, although he had a greater hatred against Caius than any one else, his fear and his wise contrivance to gain his safety taught him so to do, and prevailed over his present pleasure; so he put on such a mournful dress as he would have done had he lost his dearest friends in the world; this man came into the theatre, and informed them of the death of Caius, and by this means put an end to that state of ignorance the men had been in. Arruntius also went round about the pillars, and called out to the Germans, as did the tribunes with him, bidding them put up their swords, and telling them that Caius was dead. And this proclamation it was, plainly, which saved those that were collected together in the theatre, and all the rest who any way met the Germans; for, while they had hopes that Caius had still any breath in him, they abstained from no sort of mischief; and such an abundant kindness they still had for Caius, that they would willingly have prevented the plot against him, and procured his escape from so sad a misfortune, at the expense of their own lives. But they now left off the warm zeal they had to punish his enemies, now

they were fully satisfied that Caius was dead, because it was now in vain for them to show their zeal and kindness to him, when he that should reward them was perished. They were also afraid that they should be punished by the senate, if they should go on in doing such injuries, that is, in case the authority of the supreme governor should revert to them. And thus at length a stop was put, though not without difficulty, to that rage which possessed the˙ Germans on account of Caius' death.

19. But Cherea was so much afraid for Minucianus lest he should light upon the Germans, now they were in their fury, that he went and spoke to every one of the soldiers, and prayed them to take care of his preservation, and made himself great inquiry about him, lest he should have been slain. And for Clement, he let Minucianus go when he was brought to him, and, with many other ˙of the senators, affirmed the action was right, and commended the virtue of those that contrived, and had courage enough to execute it; and said that "tyrants do indeed please themselves and look big for a while, upon having the power to act unjustly; but do not however go happily out of the world, because they are hated by the virtuous; and that Caius, together with all his unhappiness, was become a conspirator against himself, before these other men who attacked him did so; and by becoming intolerable, in setting aside the wise provision the laws had made, taught his dearest friends to treat him as an enemy; insomuch, that although in common discourse these conspirators were those that slew Caius, yet that, in reality, he lies now dead, as perishing by his own self."

20. Now by this time the people in the theatre were arisen from their seats, and those that were within made a very great disturbance; the cause of which

was this, that the spectators were too hasty in getting away. There was also one Alcyon, a physician, who hurried away, as if to cure those that were wounded, and, under that pretence, he sent those that were with him to fetch what things were necessary for the healing of those wounded persons, but in reality to get them clear of the present dangers they were in. Now the senate, during this interval, had met, and the people also assembled together in the accustomed form, and were both employed in searching after the murderers of Caius. The people did it very zealously, but the senate in appearance only: for there was present Valerius of Asia, one that had been consul; this man went to the people, as they were in disorder, and very uneasy that they could not yet discover who they were that murdered the emperor: he was then earnestly asked by them all, "Who it was that had done it?" He replied, "I wish I had been the man." The consuls [1] also published an edict wherein they accused Caius, and gave order to the people then got together, and to the soldiers, to go home; and gave the people hopes of the abatement of the oppressions they lay under; and promised the soldiers, if they lay quiet as they used to do, and would not go abroad to do mischief unjustly, that they would bestow rewards upon them; for there was reason to fear lest the city might suffer harm by their wild and ungovernable behaviour, if they should once betake themselves to spoil the citizens, or plunder the temples. And now the whole multitude of the senators were assembled together, and especially those that had conspired to take away the life of Caius, who put on at this time an air of great assurance, and

---

[1] These consuls are named in the Wars of the Jews, B. II. ch. xi. sect. 1, Sentius Saturninus and Pomponius Secundus, as Spanheim notes here. The speech of the former of them is set down in the next chapter, sect. 2.

appeared with great magnanimity, as if the administration of the public affairs were already devolved upon them.

CHAPTER II.

How the senators determined to restore the democracy; but the soldiers were for preserving the monarchy. Concerning the slaughter of Caius' wife and daughter. A character of Caius' morals.

1. W HEN the public affairs were in this posture, Claudius was on the sudden hurried away out of his house: for the soldiers had a meeting together, and when they had debated about what was to be don.², they saw that a democracy was incapable of managing such a vast weight of public affairs; and that if it should be set up, it would not be for their advantage: and in case any one of those already in the government should obtain the supreme power, it would in all respects be to their grief, if they were not assisting to him in this advancement: that it would therefore be right for them, while the public affairs were unsettled, to choose Claudius emperor, who was uncle to the deceased Caius, and of a superior dignity and worth to every one of those that were assembled together in the senate, both on account of the virtues of his ancestors, and of the learning he had acquired by his education, and who, if once settled in the empire, would reward them according to their deserts, and bestow largesses upon them. These were their consultations, and they executed the same immediately. Claudius was therefore seized upon suddenly by the soldiery. But Cneas Sentius Saturninus, although he understood that Claudius was seized, and that he

intended to claim the government, unwillingly indeed in appearance, but in reality by his own free consent, stood up in the senate, and without being dismayed, made an exhortatory oration to them, and such a one indeed as was fit for men of freedom and generosity, and spoke thus:

2. "Although it be a thing incredible, O Romans! because of the great length of time, that so unexpected an event hath happened, yet are we now in possession of liberty. How long indeed this will last is uncertain, and lies at the disposal of the gods, whose grant it is; yet such it is as is sufficient to make us rejoice, and be happy for the present, although we may soon be deprived of it; for one hour is sufficient to those that are exercised in virtue, wherein we may live with a mind accountable to ourselves, in our own country, now free, and governed by such laws as this country once flourished under. As for myself, I cannot remember our former time of liberty, as being born after it was gone; but I am beyond measure filled with joy at the thoughts of our present freedom. I also esteem those that were born and bred up in that our former liberty, happy men, and that those men are worthy of no less esteem than the gods themselves, who have given us a taste of it in this age; and I heartily wish, that this quiet enjoyment of it, which we have at present, might continue to all ages. However, this single day may suffice for our youth, as well as for us that are in years. It will seem an age to our old men, if they might die during its happy duration; it may also be for the instruction of the younger sort, what kind of virtue those men, from whose loins we are derived, were exercised in. As for ourselves, our business is, during the space of time, to live virtuously, than which nothing can be more to our advantage; which

course of virtue it is alone that can preserve our liberty; for, as to our ancient state, I have heard of it by the relation of others, but as to our later state, during my lifetime, I have known it by experience, and learned thereby what mischiefs tyrannies have brought upon this commonwealth, discouraging all virtue, and depriving persons of magnanimity of their liberty, and proving the teachers of flattery and slavish fear, because it leaves the public administration not to be governed by wise laws, but by the humour of those that govern. For since Julius Cæsar took it into his head to dissolve our democracy, and, by overbearing the regular system of our laws, to bring disorders into our administration, and to get above right and justice, and to be a slave to his own inclinations, there is no kind of misery but what hath tended to the subversion of this city; while all those that have succeeded him have striven one with another to overthrow the ancient laws of their country, and have left it destitute of such citizens as were of generous principles; because they thought it tended to their safety to have vicious men to converse withal, and not only to break the spirits of those that were best esteemed for their virtue, but to resolve upon their utter destruction. Of all which emperors, who have been many in number, and who laid upon us insufferable hardships during the times of their government, this Caius, who hath been slain to-day, hath brought more terrible calamities upon us than did all the rest, not only by exercising his ungoverned rage upon his fellow-citizens, but also upon his kindred and friends, and alike upon all others, and by inflicting still greater miseries upon them, as punishments, which they never deserved, he being equally furious against men, and against the gods. For tyrants are not content to gain their sweet pleasure,

and this by acting injuriously, and in the vexation
they bring both upon men's estates and their wives;
but they look upon that to be their principal advantage, when they can utterly overthrow the entire
families of their enemies; while all lovers of liberty
are the enemies of tyranny. Nor can those that patiently endure what miseries they bring on them,
gain their friendship; for as they are conscious of the
abundant mischiefs they have brought on these men,
and how magnanimously they have borne their hard
fortunes, they cannot but be sensible what evils they
have done, and thence only depend on security from
what they are suspicious of, if it may be in their
power to take them quite out of the world. Since,
then, we are now gotten clear of such great misfortunes, and are only accountable to one another,
(which form of government affords us the best assurance of our present concord, and promises us
the best security from evil designs, and will be most
for our own glory in settling the city in good order,)
you ought every one of you in particular, to make
provision for his own, and in general for the public
utility; or, on the contrary, they may declare their
dissent to such things as have been proposed, and
this without any hazard of danger to come upon
them; because they have now no lord set over them,
who, without fear of punishment, could do mischief
to the city, and had an uncontrollable power to take
off those that freely declare their opinions. Nor has
any thing so much contributed to this increase of
tyranny of late as sloth, and a timorous forbearance
of contradicting the emperor's will; while men had
an overgreat inclination to the sweetness of peace,
and had learned to live like slaves; and as many of
us as either heard of intolerable calamities that happened at a distance from us, or saw the miseries that

were near us, out of the dread of dying virtuously,
endured a death joined with the utmost infamy.
We ought, then, in the first place, to decree the
greatest honours we are able to those that have taken
off the tyrant, especially to Cherea Cassius; for this
one man, with the assistance of the gods, hath by
his counsel, and by his actions, been the procurer
of our liberty. Nor ought we to forget him now
we have recovered our liberty, who, under the foregoing tyranny, took counsel beforehand, and beforehand hazarded himself for our liberties, but ought
to decree him proper honours, and thereby freely
declare, that he from the beginning acted with our
approbation. And certainly it is a very excellent
thing, and what becomes freemen, to requite their
benefactor, as this man hath been a benefactor to
us all, though not at all like Cassius and Brutus;
who slew Caius Julius [Cæsar;] for those men laid
the foundations of sedition and civil war in our
city, but this man, together with his slaughter of the
tyrant, hath set our city free from all those sad miseries which arose from the tyranny." [1]

3. And this was the purport of Sentius' oration,
which was received with pleasure by the senators, and
by as many of the equestrian order as were present.
And now one Trebellius Maximus rose up hastily,
and took off Sentius' finger a ring, which had a stone,
with the image of Caius engraven upon it, and which,
in his zeal in speaking, and his earnestness in doing
what he was about, as it was supposed, he had forgotten to take off himself. This sculpture was broken

---

[1] In this oration of Sentius Saturninus, we may see the great value
virtuous men put upon public liberty, and the sad misery they underwent,
while they were tyrannized over by such emperors as Caius. See Josephus'
own short but pithy reflection at the end of the chapter: "So difficult,"
says he, "it is for those to obtain the virtue that is necessary to a wise
man, who have the absolute power to do what they please, without control."

immediately. But, as it was now far in the night, Cherea demanded of the consuls the watch-word, who gave him this word, *Liberty*. These facts were the subjects of admiration to themselves, and almost incredible; for it was a hundred years[1] since the democracy had been laid aside, when this giving the watch-word returned to the consuls; for, before the city was subject to tyrants, they were the commanders of the soldiers. But, when Cherea had received that watch-word, he delivered it to those who were on the senate's side, which were four regiments, who esteemed the government without emperors to be preferable to tyranny. So these went away with their tribunes. The people also now departed very joyful, full of hope and of courage, as having recovered their former democracy, and were no longer under an emperor; and Cherea was in very great esteem with them.

4. And now Cherea was very uneasy that Caius' daughter and wife were still alive, and that all his family did not perish with him, since whosoever was left of them must be left for the ruin of the city and of the laws. Moreover, in order to finish this matter with the utmost zeal, and in order to satisfy his hatred of Caius, he sent Julius Lupus, one of the tribunes, to kill Caius' wife and daughter. They proposed this office to Lupus as to a kinsman of Clement, that he might be so far a partaker of this murder of the tyrant, and might rejoice in the virtue of having assisted his fellow-citizens, and that he might appear to have been a partaker with those that were first in their designs against him. Yet did this action appear to some of the conspirators

---

[1] Hence we learn that, in the opinion of Saturninus, the sovereign authority of the consuls and senate had been taken away just 100 years before the death of Caius, A. D. 41, or in the 60th year before the Christian era; when the first triumvirate began under Cæsar, Pompey, and Crassus.

to be too cruel, as to this using such severity to a woman, because Caius did more indulge his own ill nature, than use her advice in all that he did; from which ill nature it was that the city was in so desperate a condition with the miseries that were brought on it, and the flower of the city was destroyed. But others accused her of giving her consent to these things: nay, they ascribed all that Caius had done to her as the cause of it, and said, she had given a potion to Caius, which had made him obnoxious to her, and had tied him down to love her by such evil methods; insomuch that she, having rendered him distracted, was become the author of all the mischiefs that had befallen the Romans, and that habitable world which was subject to them. So that at length it was determined that she must die; nor could those of the contrary opinion at all prevail to have her saved; and Lupus was sent accordingly. Nor was there any delay made in executing what he went about, but he was subservient to those that sent him on the first opportunity, as desirous to be no way blamable in what might be done for the advantage of the people. So, when he was come into the palace, he found Cesonia, who was Caius' wife, lying by her husband's dead body, which also lay down on the ground, and destitute of all such things as the law allows to the dead, and all over herself besmeared with the blood of her husband's wounds, and bewailing the great affliction she was under, her daughter lying by her also: and nothing else was heard in these her circumstances, but her complaint of Caius, as if he had not regarded what she had often told him of beforehand; which words of hers were taken in a different sense even at that time, and are now esteemed equally ambiguous by these that hear of them, and are still interpreted according to the dif-

ferent inclinations of people. Now some said that
the words denoted, that she had advised him to leave
off his mad behaviour and his barbarous cruelty to
the citizens, and to govern the public with moderation and virtue, lest he should perish by the same
way, upon their using him as he had used them. But
some said, that, as certain words had passed concerning the conspirators, she desired Caius to make no
delay, but immediately to put them all to death, and
this whether they were guilty or not, and that
thereby he would be out of the fear of any danger;
and that this was what she reproached him for, when
she advised him so to do; but he was too slow and
tender in the matter. And this was what Cesonia
said, and what the opinions of men were about it.
But, when she saw Lupus approach, she showed him
Caius' dead body, and persuaded him to come nearer,
with lamentation and tears: and as she perceived that
Lupus was in disorder, and approached her in order
to execute some design disagreeable to himself, she
was well aware for what purpose he came, and
stretched out her naked throat, and that very cheerfully to him, bewailing her case, like one utterly
despairing of her life, and bidding him not to boggle
at finishing the tragedy they had resolved upon relating to her. So she boldly received her death's
wound at the hand of Lupus, as did the daughter
after her. So Lupus made haste to inform Cherea
of what he had done.

5.   Thus was the end of Caius, after he had reigned
four years within four months. He was, even before
he came to be emperor, ill natured, and one that
had arrived at the utmost pitch of wickedness; a
slave to his pleasures, and a lover of calumny; greatly
affected by every terrible accident, and on that account of a very murderous disposition, where he

durst show it. He enjoyed his exorbitant power to this only purpose, to injure those who least deserved it, with unreasonable insolence, and got his wealth by murder and injustice. He laboured to appear above regarding either what was divine or agreeable to the laws, but was a slave to the commendations of the populace; and whatsoever the laws determined to be shameful, and punished, that he esteemed more honourable than what was virtuous. He was unmindful of his friends, how intimate soever, and though they were persons of the highest character; and, if he was once angry at any of them, he would inflict punishment upon them on the smallest occasions, and esteemed every man that endeavoured to lead a virtuous life his enemy. And whatsoever he commanded, he would not admit of any contradiction to his inclinations: whence it was that he had criminal conversation with his own sister;[1] from which occasion chiefly it was also, that a bitter hatred first sprang up against him among the citizens, that sort of incest not having been known of a long time; and so this provoked men to distrust him, and to hate him that was guilty of it. And for any great or royal work that he ever did, which might be for the present and for future ages, nobody can name any such, but only the haven that he made about Rhegium and Sicily, for the reception of the ships that brought corn from Egypt; which was indeed a work without dispute very great in itself, and of very great advantage to the navigation. Yet was not this work brought to perfection by him, but was

[1] Spanheim here notes from *Suetonius,* that the name of Caius' sister, with whom he was guilty of incest, was *Drusilla;* and that Suetonius adds, he was guilty of the same crime with all his sisters also. He notes farther, that Suetonius omits the mention of the haven for ships, which our author esteems the only public work for the good of the present and future ages which Caius left behind him, though in an imperfect condition.

the one half of it left imperfect, by reason of his want of application to it; the cause of which was this, that he employed his studies about useless matters, and that by spending his money upon such pleasures as concerned no one's benefit but his own, he could not exert his liberality in things that were undeniably of great consequence. Otherwise he was an excellent orator, and thoroughly acquainted with the Greek tongue, as well as with his own country or Roman language. He was also able, off hand and readily, to give answers to compositions made by others, of considerable length and accuracy. He was also more skilful in persuading others to very great things than any one else, and this from a natural affability of temper, which had been improved by much exercise and painstaking: for as he was the grandson [1] of the brother of Tiberius, whose successor he was, this was a strong inducement to his acquiring of learning, because Tiberius aspired after the highest pitch of that sort of reputation; and Caius aspired after the like glory for eloquence, being induced thereto by the letters of his kinsman and his emperor. He was also among the first rank of his own citizens. But the advantages he received from his learning did not countervail the mischief he brought upon himself in the exercise of his authority; so difficult it is for those to obtain the virtue that is necessary for a wise man, who have the absolute power to do what they please without control. At the first he got himself such friends as were in all respects the most worthy, and was greatly beloved by them, while he imitated their zealous application to the learning and to the glorious actions of the best men; but when he became insolent towards them, they laid aside the kindness they had

---

[1] This Caius was the son of that excellent person Germanicus; who was the son of Drusus, the brother of Tiberius the emperor.

for him, and began to hate him; from which hatred
came that plot which they raised against him, and
wherein he perished.

CHAPTER III.

*How Claudius was seized upon, and brought out of
his house, and brought to the camp, and how the
senate sent an embassage to him.*

1. Now Claudius, as I said above, went out of
that way along which Caius was gone; and, as the
family was in a mighty disorder upon the sad accident
of the murder of Caius, he was in great distress how
to save himself, and was found to have hidden himself, in a certain narrow place,[1] though he had no
other occasion for suspicion of any dangers, besides
the dignity of his birth; for, while he was a private
man, he behaved himself with moderation, and was
contented with his present fortune, applying himself
to learning, and especially to that of the Greeks, and
keeping himself entirely clear from every thing that
might bring on any disturbance. But as at this time
the multitude were under a consternation, and the
whole palace was full of the soldiers' madness, and
the very emperor's guards, seemed under the like
fear and disorder with private persons, the band
called *pretorian,* which was the purest part of the
army, was in consultation what was to be done at
this juncture. Now all those that were at this consultation, had little regard to the punishment Caius
had suffered, because he justly deserved such his

---

[1] The first place Claudius came to was inhabited, and called *Hormæum,*
as Spanheim here informs us from Suetonius, in Claud. ch. x.

fortune; but they were rather considering their own circumstances, how they might take the best care of themselves, especially while the Germans were busy in punishing the murderers of Caius; which yet was rather done to gratify their own savage temper, than for the good of the public: all which things disturbed Claudius, who was afraid of his own safety, and this particularly because he saw the heads of Asprenas and his partners carried about. His station had been on a certain elevated place, whither a few steps led him, and whither he had retired in the dark by himself. But when Gratus, who was one of the soldiers that belonged to the palace, saw him, but did not well know by his countenance who he was, because it was dark, though he could well judge that it was a man who was privately there on some design, he came nearer to him, and when Claudius desired that he would retire, he discovered who he was, and owned him to be Claudius. So he said to his followers: "This is a Germanicus;[1] come on, let us choose him for our emperor." But when Claudius saw they were making preparations for taking him away by force, and was afraid they would kill him, as they had killed Caius, he besought them to spare him, putting them in mind how quietly he had demeaned himself, and that he was unacquainted with what had been done. Hereupon Gratus smiled upon him, and took him by the right hand, and said, "Leave off, Sir, these low thoughts of saving yourself, while you ought to have greater thoughts, even of obtaining the empire, which the gods, out of their concern for the habitable world, by taking Caius

---

[1] How Claudius, another son of Drusus, which Drusus was the father of Germanicus, could be here himself called *Germanicus*, Suetonius informs us, when he assures us, that, by a decree of the senate, the sirname of *Germanicus* was bestowed upon Drusus, and his posterity also. In Claud. ch. i.

out of the way, commit to thy virtuous conduct. Go to, therefore, and accept of the throne of thy ancestors." So they took him up and carried him, because he was not then able to go on foot, such was his dread and his joy at what was told him.

2. Now there was already gathered together about Gratus a great number of the guards; and when they saw Claudius carried off, they looked with a sad countenance, as supposing that he was carried to execution for the mischiefs that had been lately done; while yet they thought him a man who never meddled with public affairs all his life long, and one that had met with no contemptible dangers under the reign of Caius; and some of them thought it reasonable, that the consuls should take cognizance of these matters; and, as still more and more of the soldiery got together, the crowd about him ran away, and Claudius could hardly go on, his body was then so weak; and those who carried his sedan, upon an inquiry that was made about his being carried off, ran away and saved themselves, as despairing of their lord's preservation. But when they were come into the large court of the palace, (which, as the report goes about it, was inhabited first of all the parts of the city of Rome,) and had just reached the public treasury, many more soldiers came about him as glad to see Claudius' face, and thought it exceeding right to make him emperor, on account of their kindness for Germanicus, who was his brother, and had left behind him a vast reputation among all that were acquainted with him. They reflected also on the covetous temper of the leading men of the senate, and what great errors they had been guilty of, when the senate had the government formerly: they also considered the impossibility of such an undertaking, as also what dangers they should be in,

if the government should come to a single person, and that such a one should possess it, as they had no hand in advancing, and not to Claudius, who would take it as their grant, and as gained by their goodwill to him, and would remember the favours they had done him, and would make them a sufficient recompense for the same.

3. These were the discourses the soldiers had one with another by themselves, and they communicated them to all such as came unto them. Now, those that inquired about this matter, willingly embraced the invitation that was made to them to join with the rest: so they carried Claudius into the camp, crowding about him as his guard, and encompassing him about, one chairman still succeeding another, that their vehement endeavours might not be hindered. But as to the populace and senators, they disagreed in their opinions. The latter were very desirous to recover their former dignity, and were zealous to get clear of the slavery that had been brought on them by the injurious treatment of the tyrants, which the present opportunity afforded them; but for the people, who were envious against them, and knew that the emperors were capable of curbing their covetous temper, and were a refuge from them, they were very glad that Claudius had been seized upon, and brought to them, and thought, that if Claudius were made emperor, he would prevent a civil war, such as there was in the days of Pompey. But, when the senate knew that Claudius was brought into the camp by the soldiers, they sent to him those of their body which had the best character for their virtues, that they might inform him, "that he ought to do nothing by violence, in order to gain the government: that he who was a single person, one either already, or hereafter to be a member of their body,

ought to yield to the senate, which consisted of so great a number: that he ought to let the law take place in the disposal of all that related to the public order, and to remember how greatly the former tyrants had afflicted their city; and what dangers both he and they had escaped under Caius, and that he ought not to hate the heavy burden of tyranny, when the injury is done by others, while he did himself wilfully treat his country after a mad and insolent manner; that if he would comply with them, and demonstrate that his firm resolution was to live quietly and virtuously, he would have the greatest honours decreed to him that a free people could bestow, and by subjecting himself to the law, would obtain this branch of commendation, that he acted like a man of virtue, both as a ruler and a subject; but that if he would act foolishly, and learn no wisdom by Caius' death, they would not permit him to go on; that a great part of the army was got together for them, with plenty of weapons, and a great number of slaves, which they could make use of: that good hope was a great matter in such cases, as was also good fortune, and that the gods would never assist any others but those that undertook to act with virtue and goodness, who can be no other than such as fight for the liberty of their country."

4. Now these ambassadors, Veranius and Brocchus, who were both of them tribunes of the people, made this speech to Claudius, and falling down upon their knees, they begged of him, that he would not throw the city into wars and misfortunes; but when they saw what a multitude of soldiers encompassed and guarded Claudius, and that the forces that were with the consuls were, in comparison of them, perfectly inconsiderable, they added, that "if he did desire the government, he should accept of it as given by the

senate; that he would prosper better, and be happier, if he came to it, not by the injustice, but by the goodwill of those that would bestow it upon him."

CHAPTER IV.

What things king Agrippa did for Claudius, and how Claudius when he had taken the government, commanded the murderers of Caius to be slain.

1. Now Claudius, though he was sensible after what an insolent manner the senate had sent to him, yet did he according to their advice, behave himself for the present with moderation; but not so far that he could not recover himself out of his fright: so he was encouraged [to claim the government] partly by the boldness of the soldiers, and partly by the persuasion of king Agrippa, who exhorted him not to let such a dominion slip out of his hands, when it came thus to him of its own accord. Now, this Agrippa, with relation to Caius, did what became one that had been so much honoured by him; for he embraced Caius' body after he was dead, and laid it upon a bed, and covered it as well as he could, and went out to the guards, and told them that Caius was still alive; but he said that they should call for physicians, since he was very ill of his wounds. But when he had learned that Claudius was carried away violently by the soldiers, he rushed through the crowd to him, and when he found that he was in disorder, and ready to resign up the government to the senate, he encouraged him; and desired him to keep the government; but when he had said this to Claudius, he retired home. And, upon the senate's sending for

him, he anointed his head with ointment, as if he
had lately accompanied with his wife, and had dismissed her, and then came to them: he also asked
of the senators what Claudius did; who told him the
present state of affairs, and then asked his opinion
about the settlement of the public. He told them
in words, that he was ready to lose his life for the
honour of the senate, but desired them to consider
what was for their advantage, without any regard
to what was most agreeable to them; for that those
who grasp at government, will stand in need of
weapons, and soldiers to guard them, unless they
will set up without any preparation for it, and so
fall into danger. And when the senate replied, That
"they would bring in weapons in abundance, and
money, and that as to an army, a part of it was
already collected together for them, and they would
raise a larger one by giving the slaves their liberty."
Agrippa made answer, "O senators! may you be
able to compass what you have a mind to; yet will
I immediately tell you my thoughts, because they
tend to your preservation: take notice, then, that
the army which will fight for Claudius hath been
long exercised in warlike affairs: but our army will
be no better than a rude multitude of raw men, and
those such as have been unexpectedly made free
from slavery, and ungovernable; we must then fight
against those that are skilful in war, with men who
know not so much as how to draw their swords. So
that my opinion is, that we should send some persons to Claudius, to persuade him to lay down the
government, and I am ready to be one of your ambassadors."

2. Upon this speech of Agrippa, the senate complied with him, and he was sent among others, and
privately informed Claudius of the disorder the

senate was in, and gave instructions to answer them in a somewhat commanding strain, and as one invested with dignity and authority. Accordingly, Claudius said to the ambassadors, That "he did not wonder the senate had no mind to have an emperor over them, because they had been harassed by the barbarity of those that had formerly been at the head of their affairs; but that they should taste of an equitable government under him, and moderate times, while he should only be their ruler in name, but the authority should be equally common to them all; and since he had passed through many and various scenes of life before their eyes, it would be good for them not to distrust him." So the ambassadors, upon their hearing this his answer, were dismissed. But Claudius discoursed with the army which was there gathered together, who took oaths that they would persist in their fidelity to him; upon which he gave the guards every man five thousand[1] drachmæ a-piece, and a proportionable quantity to their captains, and promised to give the same to the rest of the armies wheresoever they were.

3. And now the consuls called the senate together into the temple of Jupiter the Conqueror, while it was still night; but some of those senators concealed themselves in the city, being uncertain what to do, upon the hearing of this summons, and some of them went out of the city to their own farms, as foreseeing whither the public affairs were going, and despairing of liberty; nay, these supposed it much better for them to be slaves without danger to themselves, and

[1] This number of drachmæ to be distributed to each private soldier, 5,000 drachmæ, equal to 20,000 sesterces, or £161 sterling, seems much too large, and directly contradicts Suetonius, ch. x. who makes them in all but 15 sesterces, or 2s. 4d. Yet might Josephus have this number from Agrippa junior, though I doubt the thousands, or at least the hundreds have been added by the transcribers, of which we have had several examples already in Josephus.

to live a lazy and inactive life, than, by claiming the
dignity of their forefathers, to run the hazard of
their own safety. However, a hundred and no more,
were gotten together; and as they were in consultation about the present posture of affairs, a sudden
clamour was made by the soldiers that were on their
side, "desiring that the senate would choose them
an emperor, and not bring the government into ruin
by setting up a multitude of rulers." So they fully
declared themselves to be for the giving the government not to all, but to one; but they gave the senate
leave to look out for a person worthy to be set over
them, insomuch, that now the affairs of the senate
were much worse than before; because they had not
only failed in the recovery of their liberty, which
they boasted themselves of, but were in dread of
Claudius also. Yet were there those that hankered
after the government, both on account of the dignity
of their families, and that accruing to them by their
marriages; for Marcus Minucianus was illustrious,
both by his own nobility, and by his having married
Julia, the sister of Caius, who accordingly was very
ready to claim the government, although the consuls
discouraged him and made one delay after another
in proposing it: that Minucianus also, who was one
of Caius' murderers, restrained Valerius of Asia from
thinking of such things; and a prodigious slaughter
there had been, if leave had been given to these men
to set up for themselves, and oppose Claudius. There
were also a considerable number of gladiators besides, and of those soldiers who kept watch by night
in the city, and rowers of ships, who all ran into
the camp; insomuch, that of those who put in for
the government, some left off their pretensions in
order to spare the city, and others out of fear for
their own persons.

4. But as soon as ever it was day, Cherea, and those that were with him, came into the senate, and attempted to make speeches to the soldiers. However, the multitude of those soldiers, when they saw that they were making signals for silence with their hands, and were ready to begin to speak to them, grew tumultuous, and would not let them speak at all, because they were all zealous to be under a monarchy: and they demanded of the senate one for their ruler, as not enduring any longer delays; but the senate hesitated about either their own governing, or how they should themselves be governed, while the soldiers would not admit them to govern, and the murderers of Caius would not permit the soldiers to dictate to them. When they were in these circumstances, Cherea was not able to contain the anger he had, and promised, that if they desired an emperor, he would give them one, if any one would bring him the watch-word from Eutychus. Now, this Eutychus was charioteer of the green-band faction, styled Prasine, and a great friend of Caius, who used to harass the soldiery with building stables for the horses, and spent his time in ignominious labours, which occasioned Cherea to reproach them with him, and to abuse them with much other scurrilous language; and told them, "he would bring them the head of Claudius; and that it was an amazing thing, that after their former madness, they should commit their government to a fool." Yet were not they moved with his words, but drew their swords, and took up their ensigns, and went to Claudius, to join in taking the oath of fidelity to him. So the senate were left without any body to defend them, and the very consuls differed nothing from private persons. They were also under consternation and sorrow, men not knowing what would become of them, be-

cause Claudius was very angry at them; so they
fell a-reproaching one another, and repented of
what they had done. At which juncture Sabinus,
one of Caius' murderers, threatened that he would
sooner come into the midst of them and kill himself,
than consent to make Claudius emperor, and see
slavery returning upon them; he also abused Cherea
for loving his life too well, while he who was the
first in his contempt of Caius, could think it a good
thing to live, when, even by all that they had done
for the recovery of their liberty, they found it impossible to do it. But Cherea said, he had no manner of doubt upon him about killing himself; that
yet he would first sound the intention of Claudius
before he did it.

5. These were the debates [about the senate:]
but in the camp every body was crowding on all
sides to pay their court to Claudius, and the other
consul, Quintus Pompenius, was reproached by the
soldiery, as having rather exhorted the senate to
recover their liberty; whereupon they drew their
swords, and were going to assault him, and they had
done it, if Claudius had not hindered them, who
snatched the consul out of the danger he was in,
and set him by him. But he did not receive that
part of the senate which was with Quintus, in the
like honourable manner; nay, some of them received
blows, and were thrust away as they came to salute
Claudius; nay, Aponius went away wounded, and
they were all in danger. However, king Agrippa
went up to Claudius, and desired he would treat
the senators more gently; for if any mischief should
come to the senate, he would have no others over
whom to rule. Claudius complied with him, and
called the senate together into the palace, and was
carried thither himself through the city, while the

soldiery conducted him, though this was to the great vexation of the multitude; for Cherea and Sabinus, two of Caius' murderers, went in the fore-front of them, in an open manner, while Pollio, whom Claudius, a little before, had made captain of his guards, had sent them an epistolary edict, to forbid them to appear in public. Then did Claudius, upon his coming to the palace, get his friends together, and desired their suffrages about Cherea. They said, that the work he had done was a glorious one, but they accused him that he did it of perfidiousness, and thought it just to inflict the punishment [of death] upon him, to discountenance such actions for the time to come. So Cherea was led to his execution, and Lupus, and many other Romans with him; now it is reported, that Cherea bore this calamity courageously, and this, not only by the firmness of his own behaviour under it, but by the reproaches he laid upon Lupus, who fell into tears; for when Lupus laid his garment aside and complained of the cold,[1] he said, that cold was never hurtful to Lupus, [i. e. a wolf.] And as a great many men went along with them to see the sight, when Cherea came to the place, he asked the soldier who was to be their executioner whether this office was what he was used to? or whether this was the first time of his using his sword in that manner, and desired him to bring him that very sword with which he himself slew Caius. So he was happily killed at one stroke. But Lupus did not meet with such good fortune in going out of the world, since he was timorous, and had many blows levelled at his neck, because he did

---

[1] This piercing cold here complained of by Lupus, agrees well to the time of the year when Claudius began his reign: it being for certain about the months of November, December, or January, and most probably a few days after January 24th, and a few days before the Roman Parentalia.

not stretch it out boldly, [as he ought to have done.]

6. Now, a few days after this, as the parental solemnities were just at hand, the Roman multitude made their usual oblations to their several ghosts, and put portions into the fire, in honour of Cherea, and besought him to be merciful to them, and not continue his anger against them for their ingratitude. And this was the end of the life that Cherea came to. But for Sabinus, although Claudius not only set him at liberty, but gave him leave to retain his former command in the army, yet did he think it would be unjust in him to fail of performing his obligations to his fellow-confederates; so he fell upon his sword, and killed himself, the wound reaching up to the very hilt of the sword.

CHAPTER V.

How Claudius restored to Agrippa his grandfather's kingdoms, and augmented his dominions: and how he published an edict in behalf of the Jews.

1. Now, when Claudius had taken out of the way all those soldiers whom he suspected, which he did immediately, he published an edict, and therein confirmed that kingdom to Agrippa, which Caius had given him, and therein commended the king highly. He also made an addition to it, of all that country over which Herod, who was his grandfather, had reigned, that is, Judea and Samaria: and this he restored to him as due to his family. But for Abila [1] of Lysanias, and all that lay at mount

---

[1] Here St. Luke is in some measure confirmed, when he informs us, ch. iii. 1, that Lysanias was some time before tetrarch of Abilene, whose

Libanus, he bestowed them upon him, as out of his own territories. He also made a league with this Agrippa, confirmed by oaths, in the middle of the forum, in the city of Rome: he also took away from Antiochus that kingdom which he was possessed of, but gave him a certain part of Cilicia and Commagena: he also set Alexander Lysimachus, the alabarch, at liberty, who had been his old friend, and steward to his mother Antonia, but had been imprisoned by Caius, whose son [Marcus] married Bernice, the daughter of Agrippa. But when Marcus, Alexander's son, was dead, who had married her when she was a virgin, Agrippa gave her in marriage to his brother Herod, and begged for him of Claudius the kingdom of Chalcis.

2. Now, about this time, there was a sedition between the Jews and the Greeks, at the city of Alexandria; for, when Caius was dead, the nation of the Jews, which had been very much mortified under the reign of Caius, and reduced to very great distress by the people of Alexandria, recovered itself, and immediately took up their arms to fight for themselves. So Claudius sent an order to the president of Egypt, to quiet that tumult; he also sent an edict, at the requests of king Agrippa and king Herod, both to Alexandria and to Syria, whose contents were as follows: "Tiberius Claudius Cæsar Augustus Germanicus, high priest, and tribune of the people, ordains thus. Since I am assured that the Jews of Alexandria, called *Alexandrians,* have been joint inhabitants in the earliest times with the

capital was Abila; as he is farther confirmed by Ptolemy, the great geographer, which Spanheim here observes, when he calls that city *Abila of Lysanias.* See the note on B. XVII. ch. xi. sect. 4, and Frid. at the years 36 and 22. I esteem this principality to have belonged to the land of Canaan originally, to have been the burying place of Abel, and referred to as such, Matt. xxiii. 35, Luke xi. 51. See Authent. Rec. Part II. pp. 883-885.

Alexandrians, and have obtained from their kings equal privileges with them, as is evident by the public records that are in their possession, and the edicts themselves; and that after Alexandria had been subjected to our empire by Augustus, their rights and privileges have been preserved by those presidents who have at divers times been sent thither; and that no dispute had been raised about those rights and privileges, even when Aquila was governor of Alexandria; and that when the Jewish ethnarch was dead, Augustus did not prohibit the making such ethnarchs, as willing that all men should be so subject to the Romans, as to continue in the observation of their own customs, and not be forced to transgress the ancient rules of their own country religion; but that in the time of Caius, the Alexandrians became insolent towards the Jews that were among them, which Caius, out of his great madness and want of understanding, reduced the nation of the Jews very low, because they would not transgress the religious worship of their country, and call him a god. I will, therefore, that the nation of the Jews be not deprived of their rights and privileges, on account of the madness of Caius; but that those rights and privileges, which they formerly enjoyed be preserved to them, and that they may continue in their own customs. And I charge both parties to take very great care that no troubles may arise after the promulgation of this edict."

3. And such were the contents of this edict on behalf of the Jews that were sent to Alexandria. But the edict that was sent into the other parts of the habitable earth was this which follows: "Tiberius Claudius Cæsar Augustus Germanicus, high priest, tribune of the people, chosen consul the second time, ordains thus. Upon the petition of king Agrippa

and king Herod, who are persons very dear to me, that I would grant the same rights and privileges should be preserved to the Jews which are in all the Roman empire, which I have granted to those of Alexandria, I very willingly comply therewith; and this grant I make not only for the sake of the petitioners, but as judging those Jews for whom I have been petitioned worthy of such a favour, on account of their fidelity and friendship to the Romans. I think it also very just that no Grecian city should be deprived of such rights and privileges, since they were preserved to them under the great Augustus. It will therefore be fit to permit the Jews, who are in all the world under us,˙ to keep their ancient customs without being hindered so to do. And I do charge them also to use this my kindness to them with moderation, and not to show a contempt of the superstitious observances of other nations, but to keep their own laws only. And I will that this decree of mine be engraved on tables by the magistrates of the cities and colonies, and municipal places, both those within Italy, and those without it, both kings and governors, by the means of the ambassadors, and to have them exposed to the public for full thirty days, in such a place,[1] whence it may plainly be read from the ground."

---

[1] This form was so known and frequent among the Romans, as Dr. Hudson here tells us, from the great Selden, that it used to be thus represented at the bottom of their edicts by the initial letters only *U. D. P. R. L. Unde De Plano Recte Legi Possit.* "Whence it may be plainly read from the ground."

CHAPTER VI.

*What things were done by Agrippa at Jerusalem,
when he was returned back into Judea: and what
it was that Petronius wrote to the inhabitants of
Doris, in behalf of the Jews.*

1. Now Claudius Cæsar, by these decrees of his
which were sent to Alexandria, and to all the hab
itable earth, made known what opinion he had of the
Jews. So he soon sent Agrippa away to take his
kingdom, now he was advanced to a more illustrious
dignity than before, and sent letters to the presidents and procurators of the provinces, that they
should treat him very kindly. Accordingly, he returned in haste, as was likely he would, now he returned in much greater prosperity than he had before.
He also came to Jerusalem, and offered all the sacrifices that belonged to him, and omitted nothing [1]
which the law required; on which account he ordained that many of the Nazarites should have their
heads shorn. And for the golden chain which had
been given him by Caius, of equal weight with that
iron chain wherewith his royal hands had been bound,
he hung it up within the limits of the temple, over
the treasury, that it might be a memorial of the
severe fate he had lain under, and a testimony of
his change for the better; that it might be a demon-

---

[1] Josephus shows both here and ch. vii. sect. 3, that he had a much
greater opinion of king Agrippa I. than Simon the learned Rabbi, than
the people of Cæsarea and Sebaste, ch. vii. sect. 4, and ch. ix. sect. 1, and
indeed than his double dealing between the senate and Claudius, ch. iv.
sect. 2, than his slaughter of James, the brother of John, and his imprisonment of Peter, or his vainglorious behaviour before he died, both
in Acts xii. 1, 2, 3, and here, ch. iv. sect. 1, will justify or allow. Josephus'
character was probably taken from his son, Agrippa junior.

stration how the greatest prosperity may have a fall, and that God sometimes raises up what is fallen down: for this chain thus dedicated afforded a document to all men, that king Agrippa had been once bound in a chain for a small cause, but recovered his former dignity again; and a little while afterward got out of his bonds, and was advanced to be a more illustrious king than he was before. Whence men may understand, that all that partake of human nature, how great soever they are, may fall; and that those that fall may gain their former illustrious dignity again.

2. And when Agrippa had entirely finished all the duties of the divine worship, he removed Theophilus, the son of Ananus, from the high priesthood, and bestowed that honour of his on Simon the son of Botheus, whose name was also Cantheras, whose daughter king Herod married, as I have related above. Simon, therefore, had the [high] priesthood with his brethren, and with his father, in like manner as the sons of Simon, the son of Onias, who were three, had it formerly under the government of the Macedonians, as we have related in a former book.

3. When the king had settled the high priesthood after this manner, he returned the kindness which the inhabitants of Jerusalem had showed him; for he released them from the tax upon houses, every one of which paid it before, thinking it a good thing to requite the tender affections of those that loved him. He also made Silas the general of his forces, as a man who had partaken with him in many of his troubles. But after a very little while, the young men of Doris, preferring a rash attempt before piety, and being naturally bold and insolent, carried a statue of Cæsar into a synagogue of the Jews, and erected it there. This procedure of theirs greatly

provoked Agrippa; for it plainly tended to the dissolution of the laws of his country. So he came without delay to Publius Petronius, who was then president of Syria, and accused the people of Doris. Nor did he less resent what was done than did Agrippa; for he judged it a piece of impiety to transgress the laws that regulate the actions of men. So he wrote the following letter to the people of Doris in an angry strain: "Publius Petronius, the president under Tiberius Claudius Cæsar Augustus Germanicus, to the magistrates of Doris, ordains as follows: Since some of you have had the boldness, or madness rather, after the edict of Claudius Cæsar Augustus Germanicus was published, for permitting the Jews to observe the laws of their country, not to obey the same, have acted in entire opposition thereto, as forbidding the Jews to assemble together in the synagogue, by removing Cæsar's statue, and setting it up therein, and thereby have offended not only the Jews, but the emperor himself, whose statue is more commodiously placed in his own temple, than in a foreign one, where is the place of assembling together; while it is but a part of natural justice, that every one should have the power over the place belonging peculiarly to themselves, according to the determination of Cæsar; to say nothing of my own determination, which it would be ridiculous to mention after the emperor's edict, which gives the Jews leave to make use of their own customs, as also gives order, that they enjoy equally the rights of citizens with the Greeks themselves. I therefore ordain, that Proculus Vitelius, the centurion, bring those men to me, who, contrary to Augustus' edict, have been so insolent as to do this thing, at which those very men, who appear to be of principal reputation among them, have an indig-

nation also, and allege for themselves, that it was
not done with their consent, but by the violence of
the multitude, that they might give an account of
what hath been done. I also exhort the principal
magistrates among them, unless they have a mind
to have this action esteemed to be done with their
consent, to inform the centurion of those that were
guilty of it, and take care that no handle be hence
taken for raising a sedition or quarrel among them;
which those seem to me to hunt after, who encourage
such doings; while both I myself, and king Agrippa,
for whom I have the highest honour, have nothing
more under our care, than that the nation of the
Jews may have no occasion given them of getting
together under the pretence of avenging themselves,
and become tumultuous. And that it may be more
publicly known what Augustus hath resolved about
this whole matter, I have subjoined those edicts
which he hath lately caused to be published at Alexandria, and which, although they may be well known
to all, yet did king Agrippa, for whom I have the
highest honour, read them at that time before my
tribunal, and pleaded that the Jews ought not to
be deprived of those rights which Augustus had
granted them. I therefore charge you, that you
do not, for the time to come, seek for any occasion
of sedition or disturbance, but that every one be
allowed to follow their own religious customs."

4. Thus did Petronius take care of this matter
that such a breach of the law might be corrected,
and that no such thing might be attempted afterwards against the Jews. And now king Agrippa
took the [high] priesthood away from Simon Cantheras, and put Jonathan, the son of Ananus, into
it again, and owned that he was more worthy of
that dignity than the other. But this was not a

thing acceptable to him, to recover that his former dignity. So he refused it, and said, "O king! I rejoice in the honour that thou hast for me, and take it kindly that thou wouldst give me such a dignity of thy own inclinations, although God hath judged that I am not at all worthy of the high priesthood. I am satisfied with having once put on the sacred garments; for I then put them on after a more holy manner, than I should now receive them again. But, if thou desirest that a person more worthy than myself should have this honourable employment, give me leave to name thee such a one. I have a brother that is pure from all sin against God, and of all offences against thyself; I recommend him to thee, as one that is fit for this dignity." So the king was pleased with these words of his, and passed by Jonathan, and, according to his brother's desire, bestowed the high priesthood upon Matthias. Nor was it long before Marcus succeeded Petronius, as president of Syria.

CHAPTER VII.

Concerning Silas, and on what account it was that king Agrippa was angry at him. How Agrippa began to encompass Jerusalem with a wall; and what benefits he bestowed on the inhabitants of Berytus.

1. Now Silas, the general of the king's horse, because he had been faithful to him under all his misfortunes, and had never refused to be a partaker with him in any of his dangers, but had oftentimes undergone the most hazardous dangers for him, was full of assurance, and thought he might expect a

sort of equality with the king, on account of the firmness of the friendship he had showed to him. Accordingly, he would nowhere let the king sit as his superior, and took the like liberty in speaking to him upon all occasions; till he became troublesome to the king, when they were merry together, extolling himself beyond measure, and oft putting the king in mind of the severity he had undergone, that he might, by way of ostentation, demonstrate what zeal he had showed in his service; and was continually harping upon this string, what pains he had taken for him, and much enlarged still upon that subject. The repetition of this so frequently seemed to reproach the king, insomuch that he took the ungovernable liberty of talking very ill at his hands. For the commemoration of times, when men have been under ignominy, is by no means agreeable to them; and he is a very silly man, who is perpetually relating to a person what kindness he had done him. At last, therefore, Silas had so thoroughly provoked the king's indignation, that he acted rather out of passion than good consideration, and did not only turn Silas out of his place, as general of his horse, but sent him in bonds into his own country. But the edge of his anger wore off by length of time, and made room for more just reasonings as to his judgment about this man, and he considered how many labours he had undergone for his sake. So when Agrippa was solemnizing his birthday, and he gave festival entertainments to all his subjects, he sent for Silas on the sudden to be his guest. But, as he was a very frank man, he thought he had now a just handle given him to be angry; which he could not conceal from those that came for him, but said to them, "What honour is this the king invites me to, which I conclude will soon be over? For the king hath not let me keep those original marks of the good-will I bore him, which I once had from him; but he hath plundered me, and that unjustly also. Does he think, that I leave off that liberty of speech, which, upon the consciousness of my deserts, I shall use more loudly than before, and shall relate how many misfortunes I have delivered him from; how many labours I have undergone for him, whereby I procured him deliverance and respect; as a reward for which I have borne the hardships of bonds, and a dark prison. I shall never forget this usage. Nay, perhaps, my very soul, when it is departed out of the body, will not forget the glorious actions I did on his account." This was the clamour he made, and he ordered the messengers to tell it to the king. So he perceived that Silas was incurable in his folly, and still suffered him to lie in prison.

2. As for the walls of Jerusalem, that were adjoining to the new city [Bezetha,] he repaired them at the expense of the public, and built them wider in breadth, and higher in altitude; and he had made them too strong for all human power to demolish, unless Marcus, the then president of Syria, had by letter informed Claudius Cæsar of what he was doing. And, when Claudius had some suspicion of attempts for innovation, he sent to Agrippa to leave off the building of those walls presently. So he obeyed; as not thinking it proper to contradict Claudius.

3. Now, this king was by nature very beneficent, and liberal in his gifts, and very ambitious to oblige people with such large donations; and he made himself very illustrious by the many chargeable presents he made them. He took delight in giving, and rejoiced in living with good reputation. He was not at all like that Herod who reigned before him; for that Herod was *ill*-natured, and severe in his

punishments, and had no mercy on them that he hated; and every one perceived that he was more friendly to the Greeks than to the Jews; for he adorned foreign cities with large presents in money; with building them baths and theatres besides; nay, in some of those places, he erected temples, and porticoes in others; but he did not vouchsafe to raise one of the least edifices in any Jewish city, or make them any donation that was worth mentioning. But Agrippa's temper was mild, and equally liberal to all men. He was humane to foreigners, and made them sensible of his liberality. He was in like manner rather of a gentle and compassionate temper. Accordingly, he loved to live continually at Jerusalem, and was exactly careful in the observance of the laws of his country. He therefore kept himself entirely pure; nor did any day pass over his head without its appointed sacrifice.

4. However, there was a certain man of the Jewish nation at Jerusalem, who appeared to be very accurate in the knowledge of the law. His name was *Simon*. This man got together an assembly, while the king was absent at Cæsarea, and had the insolence to accuse him as not living holily, and that he might justly be excluded out of the temple, since it belonged only to native Jews. But the general of Agrippa's army informed him, that Simon had made such a speech to the people. So the king sent for him; and, as he was sitting in the theatre, he bid him sit down by him, and said to him with a low and gentle voice, "What is there done in this place that is contrary to the law?" But he had nothing to say for himself, but begged his pardon. So the king was more easily reconciled to him than one could have imagined, as esteeming mildness a better quality in a king than anger, and knowing

that moderation is more becoming in great men than passion. So he made Simon a small present, and dismissed him.

5. Now, as Agrippa was a great builder in many places, he paid a peculiar regard to the people of Berytus; for he erected a theatre for them, superior to many other of that sort, both in sumptuousness and elegance, as also an amphitheatre, built at vast expense; and besides these he built them baths and porticoes, and spared for no cost in any of his edifices to render them both handsome and large. He also spent a great deal upon their dedication, and exhibited shows upon them, and brought thither musicians of all sorts and such as made the most delightful music of the greatest variety. He also showed his magnificence upon the theatre, in his great number of gladiators; and there it was that he exhibited the several antagonists, in order to please the spectators; no fewer indeed than seven hundred men to fight with seven hundred other men,[1] and allotted all the malefactors he had for this exercise, that both the malefactors might receive their punishment, and that this operation of war might be a recreation in peace. And thus were these criminals all destroyed at once.

CHAPTER VIII.

What other acts were done by Agrippa until his death: and after what manner he died.

1. When Agrippa had finished what I have above related at Berytus, he removed to Tiberius, a city of

---

[1] A strange number of condemned criminals to be under the sentence of death at once, no fewer, it seems, than 1400!

Galilee. Now he was in great esteem among other kings. Accordingly there came to him Antiochus, king of Commagena, Sampsigeramus, king of Emesa, and Cotys, who was king of the lesser Armenia, and Polemo, who was king of Pontus, as also Herod his brother, who was king of Chalcis. All these he treated with agreeable entertainments, and after an obliging manner, and so to exhibit the greatness of his mind, and so as to appear worthy of those respects which the king paid to him, by coming thus to see him. However, while these kings stayed with him, Marcus, the president of Syria, came thither. So the king in order to preserve that respect that was due to the Romans, went out of the city to meet him, as far as seven furlongs. But this proved to be the beginning of a difference between him and Marcus; for he took with him in his chariot those other kings as his assessors. But Marcus had a suspicion what the meaning could be of so great a friendship of these kings one with another, and did not think so close an agreement of so many potentates to be for the interest of the Romans. He therefore sent some of his domestics to every one of them, and enjoined them to go their ways home without farther delay. This was very ill taken by Agrippa, who after that became his enemy. And now he took the high priesthood away from Matthias, and made Elioneus, the son of Cantheras, high priest in his stead.

2. Now, when Agrippa had reigned three years all over Judea, he came to the city Cæsarea, which was formerly called Strato's Tower; and there he exhibited shows in honour of Cæsar, upon his being informed that there was a certain festival celebrated to make vows for his safety. At which festival, a great multitude was gotten together of the principal persons, and such as were of dignity through his

province. On the second day of which shows he put on a garment made wholly of silver, and of a contexture truly wonderful, and came into the theatre early in the morning; at which time the silver of his garment being illuminated by the fresh reflection of the sun's rays upon it, shone out after a surprising manner, and was so resplendent as to spread a horror over those that looked intently upon him; and presently his flatterers cried out, one from one place, and another from another, (though not for his good,) that "he was a god;" and they added, "Be thou merciful to us; for although we have hitherto reverenced thee only as a man, yet shall we henceforth own thee as superior to mortal nature." Upon this the king did neither rebuke them, nor reject their impious flattery. But as he presently afterwards looked up, he saw an owl sitting on a certain rope over his head, and immediately understood that this bird was the messenger of ill tidings, as it had once been the messenger of good tidings to him; and fell into the deepest sorrow. A severe pain also arose in his belly, and began in a most violent manner. He therefore looked upon his friends, and said, "I, whom ye call a *god,* am commanded presently to depart this life; while Providence thus reproves the lying words you just now said to me; and I, who was by you called *immortal,* am immediately to be hurried away by death. But I am bound to accept of what Providence allots, as it pleases God; for we have by no means lived ill, but in a splendid and happy manner." When he said this, his pain was become violent. Accordingly he was carried into the palace, and the rumour went abroad every where, that he would certainly die in a little time. But the multitude presently sat in sackcloth, with their wives and children after the law of their country, and besought God for the king's recovery. All places were also full of mourning and lamentation. Now the king rested in a high chamber, as he saw them below lying prostrate on the ground, he could not himself forbear weeping. And when he had been quite worn out by the pain in his belly for five days, he departed this life, being in the fifty-fourth year of his age, and in the seventh year of his reign; for he reigned four years under Caius Cæsar, three of them were over Philip's tetrarchy only, and on the fourth he had that of Herod added to it, and he reigned, beside those, three years under the reign of Claudius Cæsar. In which time he reigned over the forementioned countries, and also had Judea added to them, as well as Samaria and Cæsarea. The revenues that he received out of them were very great, no less than twelve [1] millions of drachmæ. Yet did he borrow great sums from others; for he was so very liberal that his expenses exceeded his incomes, and his generosity was boundless. [2]

3. But before the multitude were made acquainted with Agrippa's being expired, Herod the king of Chalcis, and Helcias the master of his horse, and the king's friend, sent Asisto, one of the king's most faithful servants, and slew Silas, who had been their enemy, as if it had been done by the king's own command.

[1] This sum of 12,000,000 drachmæ, which is equal to 3,000,000 shekels, i. e. at 2s. 10d. a shekel, equal to £425,000 sterling, was Agrippa the Great's yearly income, or about three-quarters of his grandfather Herod's income; he having abated the tax upon houses at Jerusalem, ch. vi. sect. 3, and was not so tyrannical as Herod had been to the Jews. See the note on Antiq. B. XVII. ch. xi. sect. 4. A large sum this! but not, it seems, sufficient for his extravagant expenses.

[2] Reland takes notice here, not improperly, that Josephus omits the reconciliation of this Herod Agrippa to the Tyrians and Sidonians, by the means of Blastus the king's chamberlain, mentioned Acts xii. 20. Nor is there any history in the world so complete, as to omit nothing that other historians take notice of, unless the one be taken out of the other, and accommodated to it.

CHAPTER IX.

What things were done after the death of Agrippa;
and how Claudius, on account of the youth and
unskilfulness of Agrippa junior, sent Cuspius
Fadus to be procurator of Judea and of the entire
kingdom.

1. AND thus did king Agrippa depart this life.
But he left behind him a son, Agrippa by name, a
youth in the seventeenth year of his age, and three
daughters; one of whom, Bernice, was married to
Herod his father's brother, and was sixteen years
old; the other two, Mariamne and Drusilla, were still
virgins; the former was ten years old, and Drusilla
six. Now these his daughters were thus espoused
by their father, Mariamne to Julias Archelaus
Epiphanes, the son of Antiochus, the son of Chelcias,
and Drusilla to the king of Commagena. But when
it was known that Agrippa was departed this life,
the inhabitants of Cæsarea and of Sebaste forgot the
kindnesses he had bestowed on them, and acted the
part of the bitterest enemies: for they cast such reproaches upon the deceased as are not fit to be spoken
of; and so many of them as were then soldiers, which
were a great number, went to his house, and hastily
carried off the statues [1] of this king's daughters, and
all at once carried them into the brothel houses, and,
when they had set them on the tops of those houses,
they abused them to the utmost of their power, and
did such things to them as are too indecent to be

---

[1] Photius, who made an extract out of this section, says, they were
not the statues or images, but the ladies themselves, who were thus basely
abused by the soldiers. Cod. CCXXXVIIı.

related. They also laid themselves down in public places and celebrated general feastings, with garlands on their heads, and with ointments and libations to Charon, and drinking to one another for joy that the king was expired. Nay, they were not only unmindful of Agrippa, who had extended his liberality to them in abundance, but of his grandfather Herod also, who had himself rebuilt their cities, and had raised them havens and temples at vast expense.

2. Now Agrippa the son of the deceased, was at Rome, and brought up with Claudius Cæsar. And when Cæsar was informed that Agrippa was dead, and that the inhabitants of Sebaste and Cæsarea had abused him, he was sorry for the first news, and was displeased with the ingratitude of those cities. He was therefore disposed to send Agrippa junior away presently to succeed his father in the kingdom, and was willing to confirm him in it by his oath. But those freed men and friends of his, who had the greatest authority with him, dissuaded him from it, and said, that "it was a dangerous experiment to permit so large a kingdom to come under the government of so very young a man, and one hardly yet arrived at years of discretion, who would not be able to take sufficient care of its administration; while the weight of a kingdom is heavy enough to a grown man." So Cæsar thought what they said to be reasonable. Accordingly he sent Cuspius Fadus to be procurator of Judea, and of the entire kingdom; and paid that respect to the deceased, as not to introduce Marcus, who had been at variance with him, into his kingdom. But he determined, in the first place, to send orders to Fadus, that he should chastise the inhabitants of Cæsarea and Sebaste for those abuses they had offered to him that was deceased,

and their madness towards his daughters that were still alive; and that he should remove that body of soldiers that were at Cæsarea and Sebaste, with the five regiments, into Pontus, that they might do their military duty there, and that he should choose an equal number of soldiers out of the Roman legions, that were in Syria, to supply their place. Yet were not those that had such orders actually removed; for by sending ambassadors to Claudius, they mollified him, and got leave to abide in Judea still; and these were the very men that became the source of very great calamities to the Jews in after times, and sowed the seeds of that war which began under Florus; whence it was, that when Vespasian had subdued the country, he removed them out of his province as we shall relate hereafter.[1]

[1] This history is now wanting.

BOOK XX.

CHAPTER I.

A sedition of the Philadelphians against the Jews, and also concerning the vestments of the high priest.

1. Upon the death of king Agrippa, which we have related in the foregoing book, Claudius Cæsar sent Cassius Longinus, as successor to Marcus out of regard to the memory of king Agrippa, who had often desired of him by letters, while he was alive, that he would not suffer Marcus to be any longer president of Syria. But Fadus, as soon as he was come procurator into Judea, found quarrelsome doings between the Jews that dwelt in Perea, and the people of Philadelphia, about their borders, at a village called Mia, that was filled with men of a warlike temper; for the Jews of Perea had taken up arms without the consent of their principal men, and had destroyed many of the Philadelphians. When Fadus was informed of this procedure, it provoked him very much that they had not left the determination of the matter to him, if they thought that the Philadelphians had done them any wrong, but had rashly

taken up arms against them. So he seized upon three of their principal men, who were also the causes of this sedition, and ordered them to be bound, and afterward had one of them slain, whose name was Hannibal, and he banished the other two, Amram and Eleazar. Tholomy also, the arch robber, was, after some time, brought to him bound, and slain, but not till he had done a world of mischief to Idumea and the Arabians. And indeed, from that time, Judea was cleared of robberies by the care and providence of Fadus. He also at this time sent for the high priests and the principal citizens of Jerusalem, and this at the command of the emperor, and admonished them, that they should lay up the long garment, and the sacred vestment, which it is customary for nobody but the high priest to wear, in the tower of Antonia, that it might be under the power of the Romans, as it had been formerly. Now the Jews durst not contradict what he had said, but desired Fadus, however, and Longinus, (which last was come to Jerusalem, and had brought a great army with him, out of a fear that the [rigid] injunctions of Fadus should force the Jews to rebel, that they might, in the first place, have leave to send ambassadors to Cæsar, to petition him that they may have the holy vestments under their own power, and that in the next place, they would tarry till they knew what answer Claudius would give to that their request. So they replied, that they would give them leave to send their ambassadors, provided they would give them their sons as pledges [for their peaceable behaviour.] And when they had agreed so to do, and had given them the pledges they desired, the ambassadors were sent accordingly. But when, upon their coming to Rome, Agrippa junior, the son of the deceased, understood the reason why they came, (for he dwelt with Claudius Cæsar, as we said before,) he besought Cæsar to grant the Jews their request about the holy vestments, and to send a message to Fadus accordingly.

2. Hereupon Claudius called for the ambassadors, and told them, that "he granted their request;" and bade them to return their thanks to Agrippa for this favour which had been bestowed on them upon this entreaty. And, besides these answers of his he sent the following letter by them: "Claudius Cæsar Germanicus, tribune of the people the fifth time, and designed consul the fourth time, and imperator the tenth time, the father of his country, to the magistrates, senate, and people, and the whole nation of the Jews, sendeth greeting. Upon the presentation of your ambassadors to me by Agrippa, my friend, whom I have brought up, and have now with me, and who is a person of very great piety, who are come to give me thanks for the care I have taken of your nation, and to entreat me, in an earnest and obliging manner, that they may have the holy vestments, with the crown belonging to them, under their power; I grant their request, as that excellent person Vitellius, who is very dear to me, had done before me. And I have complied with your desire, in the first place, out of regard to that piety which I profess, and because I would have every one worship God according to the laws of their own country; and this I do also because I shall hereby highly gratify king Herod and Agrippa junior, whose sacred regards to me, and earnest good-will to you, I am well acquainted with, and with whom I have the greatest friendship, and whom I highly esteem, and look on as persons of the best character. Now I have written about these affairs to Cuspius Fadus, my procurator. The names of those that brought me your letter are,

Cornelius, the son of Cero, Trypho, the son of Theudio, Dorotheus, the son of Nathaniel, and John, the son of John. This was dated before the fourth of the kalends of July, when Rufus and Pompeius Sylvanus were consuls."

3. Herod also, the brother of the deceased Agrippa, who was then possessed of the royal authority over Chalcis, petitioned Claudius Cæsar for the authority over the temple, and the money of the sacred treasure, and the choice of the high priests, and obtained all that he petitioned for. So that after that time this authority continued [1] among all his descendants till the end of the war. Accordingly Herod removed the last high priest, called *Cantheras,* and bestowed that dignity on his successor Joseph, the son of Camus.

CHAPTER II.

How Helena, the queen of Adiabene, and her son Izates, embraced the Jewish religion; and how Helena supplied the poor with corn, when there was a great famine at Jerusalem.

1. About this time it was that Helena, queen of Adiabene, and her son Izates, changed their course of life, and embraced the Jewish customs, and this on the occasion following: Monobazus, the king of Adiabene, who had also the name of Bazeus, fell in love with his sister Helena, and took her to be his wife, and begat her with child. But as he was in

---

[1] Here is some error in the copies, or mistake in Josephus; for the power of appointing high priests, after Herod king of Chalcis was dead, and Agrippa, junior, was made king of Chalcis in his room, belonged to him, and he exercised the same all along till Jerusalem was destroyed, as Josephus elsewhere informs us, ch. viii. sect. 8, 11, ch. ix. sect. 1, 4, 6, 7.

bed with her one night, he laid his hand upon his wife's belly, and fell asleep, and seemed to hear a voice, which bade him take his hand off his wife's belly, and not hurt the infant that was therein, which, by God's providence, would be safely born, and have a happy end. This voice put him into disorder; so he awaked immediately, and told the story to his wife; and when his son was born, he called him *Izates*. He had indeed Monobazus, his elder brother, by Helena also, as he had other sons by other wives besides. Yet did he openly place all his affections on this his only begotten [1] son Izates, which was the origin of that envy, which on this account they hated him more and more, and were all under great affliction that their father should prefer Izates before all them. Now although their father was very sensible of these their passions, yet did he forgive them, as not indulging those passions out of an ill disposition, but out of a desire each of them had to be beloved by their father. However, he sent Izates with many presents, to Abennerig, the king of Charax-Spasini, and that out of the· great dread he was in about him, lest he should come to some misfortune by the hatred his brethren bore him; and he committed his son's preservation to him. Upon which Abennerig gladly received the young man, and had a great affection for him, and married him to his own daughter, whose name was *Samacha:* he also bestowed a country upon him, from which he received large revenues.

2. But when Monobazus was grown old, and saw that he had but a little time to live, he had a mind to come to the sight of his son before he died. So he sent for him, and embraced him after the most

---

[1] Josephus here uses the word μονογενη, an *only begotten son*, for no other than one *best beloved*, as does both the Old and New Testament, I mean where there were one or more sons besides, Gen. xxii. 2, Heb. xi. 17. See the note on B. I. ch. xiii. sect. 1.

affectionate manner, and bestowed on him the country called *Carræ;* it was a soil that bare ammomum in great plenty: there are also in it the remains of that ark, wherein it is related that Noah escaped the deluge, and where they are still shown to such as are desirous to see them.[1] Accordingly Izates abode in that country until his father's death. But the very day that Monobazus died, queen Helena sent for all the grandees, and governors of the kingdom, and for those that had the armies committed to their command: and when they were come, she made the following speech to them: "I believe you are not unacquainted that my husband was desirous Izates should succeed him in the government, and thought him worthy so to do. However, I wait your determination; for happy is he who receives a kingdom not from a single person only, but from the willing suffrages of a great many." This she said in order to try those that were invited, and to discover their sentiments. Upon the hearing of which, they first of all paid their homage to the queen, as their custom was, and then they said, That, "they confirmed the king's determination, and would submit to it; and they rejoiced that Izates' father had preferred him before the rest of his brethren, as being agreeable to all their wishes: but that they were desirous first of all to slay his brethren and kinsmen, that so the government might come securely to Izates; because if they were once destroyed, all that fear would be over which might arise from their hatred and envy to him." Helena replied to this, That "she returned them her thanks for their kindness to herself, and to Izates; but desired that they would however defer

---

[1] It is here very remarkable, that the remains of Noah's ark were believed to be still in being in the days of Josephus. See the note on B. I. ch. 3, sect. 5.

the execution of this slaughter of Izates' brethren till he should be there himself, and give his approbation to it." So, since these men had not prevailed with her, when they advised her to slay them, they exhorted her at least to keep them in bonds till he should come, and that for their own security; they also gave her counsel to set up some one whom she should put the greatest trust in, as a governor of the kingdom in the mean time. So queen Helena complied with this counsel of theirs, and set up Monobazus, the eldest son, to be king, and put the diadem upon his head, and gave him his father's ring, with its signet; as also the ornament which they call *Sampser,* and exhorted him to administer the affairs of the kingdom till his brother should come; who came suddenly upon hearing that his father was dead, and succeeded his brother Monobazus, who resigned up the government to him.

3. Now, during the time Izates abode at Charax-Spasini, a certain Jewish merchant, whose name was Ananias, got among the women that belonged to the king, and taught them to worship God according to the Jewish religion. He, moreover, by their means, became known to Izates, and persuaded him, in like manner to embrace that religion; he also, at the earnest entreaty of Izates, accompanied him when he was sent for by his father to come to Adiabene; it also happened that Helena, about the same time, was instructed by a certain other Jew, and went over to them. But, when Izates had taken the kingdom, and was come to Adiabene, and there saw his brethren, and other kinsmen in bonds, he was displeased at it; and as he thought it an instance of impiety either to slay or imprison them, but still thought it a hazardous thing for to let them have their liberty with the remembrance of the injuries

that had been offered them, he sent some of them and
their children for hostages to Rome, to Claudius
Cæsar, and sent the others to Artabanus, the king
of Parthia, with the like intentions.

4. And when he perceived that his mother was
highly pleased with the Jewish customs, he made
haste to change, and to embrace them entirely; and,
as he supposed that he could not be thoroughly a
Jew unless he were circumcised, he was ready to have
it done. But, when his mother understood what he
was about, she endeavoured to hinder him from doing
it, and said to him, that "this thing would bring him
into danger, and that, as he was a king, he would
thereby bring himself into great odium among his
subjects, when they should understand that he was
so fond of rites that were to them strange and foreign;
and that they would never bear to be ruled over by
a Jew." This it was that she said to him, and for
the present persuaded him to forbear. And when
he had related what she had said to Ananias, he confirmed what his mother had said, and when he had
also threatened to leave him, unless he complied with
him, he went away from him, and said, that "he was
afraid lest such an action being once made public
to all, he should himself be in danger of punishment,
for having been the occasion of it, and having been
the king's instructor in actions that were of ill reputation; and he said, that he might worship God
without being circumcised, even though he did resolve
to follow the Jewish law entirely, which worship of
God was of a superior nature to circumcision. He
added, that God would forgive him, though he did
not perform the operation, while it was omitted out
of necessity, and for fear of his subjects." So the
king at that time complied with these persuasions of
Ananias. But afterwards, as he had not quite left

off his desire of doing this thing, a certain other Jew that come out of Galilee, whose name was Eleazar, and who was esteemed very skilful in the learning of his country, persuaded him to do the thing; for as he entered into his palace to salute him, and found him reading the law of Moses, he said to him, "Thou dost not consider, O king! that thou unjustly breakest the principal of those laws, and art injurious to God himself, [by omitting to be circumcised;] for thou oughtest not only to read them, but chiefly to practise what they enjoin thee. How long wilt thou continue uncircumcised? But, if thou hast not yet read the law about circumcision, and dost not know how great impiety thou art guilty of by neglecting it, read it now." When the king had heard what he said, he delayed the thing no longer, but retired to another room, and sent for a surgeon, and did what he was commanded to do. He then sent for his mother, and Ananias his tutor, and informed them that he had done the thing, upon which they were presently struck with astonishment and fear, and that to a great degree, lest the thing should be openly discovered and censured, and the king should hazard the loss of his kingdom, while his subjects would not bear to be governed by a man who was so zealous in another religion; and lest they should themselves run some hazard, because they would be supposed the occasion of his so doing. But it was God [1] himself who hindered what they feared from taking effect; for he preserved both Izates himself, and his sons when they fell into many dangers, and procured their deliverance when it seemed to be impossible, and demonstrated thereby, that the fruit of

[1] Josephus is very full and express in these three chapters, iii., iv. and v. in observing how carefully Divine Providence preserved this Izates, king of Adiabene, and his sons, while he did what he thought was his bounden duty, notwithstanding the strongest political motives to the contrary.

piety does not perish as to those that have regard to him, and fix their faith upon him only. But these events we shall relate hereafter.

5. But as to Helena, the king's mother, when she saw that the affairs of Izates' kingdom were in peace, and that her son was a happy man, and admired among all men, and even among foreigners by the means of God's providence over him, she had a mind to go to the city Jerusalem, in order to worship at that temple of God which was so very famous among all men, and to offer her thank-offerings there. So she desired her son to give her leave to go thither: upon which he gave his consent to what she desired very willingly, and made great preparations for her dismission, and gave her a great deal of money, and she went down to the city Jerusalem, her son conducting her on her journey a great way. Now her coming was of very great advantage to the people of Jerusalem, for whereas a famine did oppress them at that time, and many people died for want of what was necessary to procure food withal, queen Helena sent some of her servants to Alexandria with money to buy a great quantity of corn, and others of them to Cyprus, to bring a cargo of dried figs. And as soon as they were come back, and had brought those provisions, which was done very quickly, she distributed food to those that were in want of it, and left a most excellent memorial behind her of this benefaction, which she bestowed on our whole nation. And when her son Izates was informed of this famine, he sent great sums of money to the principal men in Jerusalem. However, what favours this king and ꞏueen conferred upon our city Jerusalem, shall be farther related hereafter.[1]

[1] This farther account of the benefactions of Izates and Helena to the Jerusalem Jews, which Josephus here promises, is, I think, nowhere

CHAPTER III.

How Artabanus, the king of Parthia, out of fear of the secret contrivances of his subjects against him, went to Izates, and was by him reinstated in his government; as also how Bardanes, his son, denounced war against Izates.

1. BUT now Artabanus, king of the Parthians, perceiving that the governors of the provinces had framed a plot against him, did not think it safe for him to continue among them, but resolved to go to Izates, but Izates did not know him. When Artaervation by his means, and if possible, for his return to his own dominions. So he came to Izates, and brought a thousand of his kindred and servants with him, and met him upon the road, while he well knew Izates, but Izates did not know him. When Artabanus stood near him, and, in the first place, worshipped him, according to the custom, he then said to him, "O king! do not thou overlook me thy servant, nor do thou proudly reject the suit I make thee: for,

performed by him in his present works. But of this terrible famine itself in Judea, take Dr. Hudson's note here: "This is that famine foretold by Agabus, Acts xi. 28, which happened when Claudius was consul the fourth time; and not that other which happened when Claudius was consul the second time, and Cæsina was his colleague, as Scaliger says upon Eusebius, p. 174." Now, when Josephus had said a little afterward, ch. v. sect. 2, that "Tiberius Alexander succeeded Cuspius Fadus as procurator," he immediately subjoins, that "under these procurators there happened a great famine in Judea." Whence it is plain that this famine continued for many years on account of its duration under these two procurators. Now Fadus was not sent into Judea till after the death of king Agrippa, i. e. towards the latter end of the 4th year of Claudius; so that this famine foretold by Agabus, happened upon the 5th, 6th, and 7th years of Claudius, as says Valerius on Euseb. II. 12. Of this famine also, and queen Helena's supplies, and her monument, see Moses Chorenensis, pp. 144, 145, where it is observed in the notes, that Pausanias mentions her monument also.

as I am reduced to a low estate, by the change of fortune, and of a king am become a private man, I stand in need of thy assistance. Have regard, therefore, unto the uncertainty of fortune, and esteem the care thou shalt take of me to be taken of thyself also; for if I be neglected, and my subjects go off unpunished, many other subjects will become the more insolent towards other kings also." And this speech Artabanus made with tears in his eyes, and with a dejected countenance. Now as soon as Izates heard Artabanus' name, and saw him stand as a supplicant before him, he leaped down from his horse immediately, and said to him, "Take courage, O king! nor be disturbed at thy present calamity, as if it were incurable; for the change of thy sad condition shall be sudden, for thou shalt find me to be more thy friend and thy assistant than thy hopes can promise thee; for I will either re-establish thee in the kingdom of Parthia, or lose my own."

2. When he had said this, he set Artabanus upon his horse, and followed him on foot, in honour of a king whom he owned as greater than himself; which, when Artabanus saw, he was very uneasy at it, and swore by his present fortune and honour, -that he would get down from his horse, unless Izates would get upon his horse again, and go before him. So he complied with his desire, and leaped upon his horse: and when he had brought him to his royal palace, he showed him all sorts of respect, when they sat together, and he gave him the upper place at festivals also, as regarding not his present fortune, but his former dignity, and that upon this consideration also, that the changes of fortune are common to all men. He also wrote to the Parthians, to persuade them to receive Artabanus again; and gave them his right hand and his faith, that he should

forget what was past and done, and that he would undertake for this as a mediator between them. Now the Parthians did not themselves refuse to receive him again, but pleaded that it was not now in their power so to do: because they had committed the government to another person, who had accepted of it, and whose name was Cinnamus, and that they were afraid lest a civil war should arise on this account. When Cinnamus understood their intentions, he wrote to Artabanus, himself, for he had been brought up by him, and was of a nature good and gentle also, and desired him to put confidence in him, and to come and take his own dominions again. Accordingly Artabanus trusted him, and returned home; when Cinnamus met him, worshipped him, and saluted him as a king, and took the diadem off his own head, and put it on the head of Artabanus.

3. And thus was Artabanus restored to his kingdom again by the means of Izates, when he had lost it by the means of the grandees of the kingdom. Nor was he unmindful of the benefits he had conferred upon him, but rewarded him with such honours as were of greatest esteem among them; for he gave him leave to wear his tiara upright, and to sleep upon a golden bed, which are privileges and marks of honour peculiar to the kings of Parthia. He also cut off a large and fruitful country from the king of Armenia, and bestowed it upon him. The name of the country is Nisibis, wherein the Macedonians had formerly built that city which they called Antioch of Mygdonia. And these were the honours that were paid Izates by the king of the Parthians.

4. But in no long time, Artabanus died, and left his kingdom to his son Bardanes. Now this Bardanes came to Izates, and would have persuaded him to join him with his army, and to assist him in the war

he was preparing to make with the Romans, but he could not prevail with him. For Izates so well knew the strength and good fortune of the Romans, that he took Bardanes to attempt what was impossible to be done; and having besides sent his sons, five in number, and they but young also, to learn accurately the language of our nation, together with our learning, as well as he had sent his mother to worship at our temple, as I have said already, was the more backward to a compliance; and restrained Bardanes, telling him perpetually of the great armies and famous actions of the Romans, and thought thereby to terrify him, and desired thereby to hinder him from that expedition. But the Parthian king was provoked at this his behaviour, and denounced war immediately against Izates. Yet did he gain no advantage by this war, because God cut off all his hopes therein; for the Parthians, perceiving Bardanes' intentions, and how he had determined to make war with the Romans, slew him, and gave his kingdom to his brother Gotarzes. He also, in no long time, perished by a plot made against him, and Vologases, his brother, succeeded him, who committed two of his provinces to two of his brothers, by the same father; that of the Medes to the elder, Pacorus, and Armenia to the younger, Tiridates.

CHAPTER IV.

*How Izates was betrayed by his own subjects, and
fought against by the Arabians: and how Izates,
by the providence of God, was delivered out of
their hands.*

1. Now when the king's brother, Monobazus, and
his other kindred, saw how Izates, by his piety to
God, was become greatly esteemed by all men, they
also had a desire to leave the religion of their country,
and to embrace the customs of the Jews; but that
act of theirs was discovered by Izates' subjects.
Whereupon the grandees were much displeased, and
could not contain their anger at them: but had an
intention, when they should find a proper opportunity, to inflict a punishment upon them. Accordingly, they wrote to Abia, king of the Arabians, and
promised him great sums of money, if he would
make an expedition against their king: and they
farther promised him, that on the first onset they
would desert their king, because they were desirous
to punish him, by reason of the hatred he had to
their religious worship; then they obliged themselves,
by oaths, to be faithful to each other, and desired
that he would make haste in this design. The king
of Arabia complied with their desires, and brought
a great army into the field, and marched against
Izates; and, in the beginning of the first onset, and
before they came to close fight, those grandees, as
if they had a panic terror upon them, all deserted
Izates, as they had agreed to do, and, turning their
backs upon their enemies, ran away. Yet was not
Izates dismayed at this: but when he understood that

the grandees had betrayed him, he also retired into his camp, and made inquiry into the matter; and as soon as he knew who they were that made this conspiracy with the king of Arabia, he cut off those that were found guilty; and renewing the fight on the next day, he slew the greatest part of his enemies, and forced all the rest to betake themselves to flight. He also pursued their king, and drove him into a fortress called *Arsamus,* and, following on the siege vigorously, he took that fortress. And, when he had plundered it of all the prey that was in it, which was not small, he returned to Adiabene; yet did not he take Abia alive; because, when he found himself encompassed on every side, he slew himself.

2. But although the grandees of Adiabene had failed in their first attempt, as being delivered up by God into their king's hands, yet would they not even then be quiet, but wrote again to Vologases, who was then king of Parthia, and desired that he would kill Izates, and set over them some other potentate, who should be of a Parthian family; for they said, That "they hated their own king for abrogating the laws of their forefathers, and embracing foreign customs." When the king of Parthia heard this, he boldly made war upon Izates; and he had just pretence for this war: he sent to him, and demanded back these honourable privileges, which had been bestowed on him by his father, and threatened on his refusal, to make war upon him. Upon hearing of this, Izates was under no small trouble of mind, as thinking it would be a reproach upon him to appear to resign those privileges that had been bestowed upon him, out of cowardice; yet, because he knew, that though the king of Parthia should receive back those honours, yet would he not be quiet, he resolved to commit himself to God, his protector,· in the present danger he was

in of his life: and as he esteemed him to be his principal assistant, he intrusted his children and his wives to a very strong fortress, and laid up his corn in his citadels, and set the hay and the grass on fire. And when he had thus put things in order, as well as he could, he awaited the coming of the enemy. And when the king of Parthia was come with a grəat army of footmen and horsemen, which he did sooner than was expected, (for he marched in great haste,) and had cast up a bank at the river that parted Adiabene from Media; Izates also pitched his camp not far off, having with him six thousand horsemen. But there came a messenger to Izates, sent by the king of Parthia, who told him, "How large his dominions were, as reaching from the river Euphrates to Bactria, and enumerated that king's subjects: he also threatened him, that he should be punished, as a person ungrateful to his lords; and said, that the God whom he worshipped could not deliver him of the king's hands." When the messenger had delivered this his message, Izates replied, That "he knew the king of Parthia's power was much greater than his own; but that he knew also that God was much more powerful than all men." And when he had returned him this answer, he betook himself to make supplication [1] to God, and threw himself upon the ground, and put ashes upon his head, in testimony of his confusion, and fasted, together with his wives and children. When he called upon God, and said, "O Lord and Governor, if I have not in vain committed myself to thy goodness, but have justly determined

---

[1] This mourning, and fasting, and praying, used by Izates, with prostration of his body, and ashes upon his head, are plain signs that he was become either a Jew, or an Ebionite Christian, who indeed differed not much from proper Jews, see ch. vi. sect. 1. However, his supplications were heard, and he was providentially delivered from that imminent danger he was in.

that thou only art the Lord and principal of all beings, come now to my assistance, and defend me from my enemies, not only on my own account, but on account of their insolent behaviour with regard to thy power, while they have not feared to lift up their proud and arrogant tongue against thee." Thus did he lament and bemoan himself, with tears in his eyes; whereupon God heard his prayer. And immediately, that very night, Vologases received letters, the contents of which were these, that a great band of Dahæ and Sahæ, despising him, now he was gone so long a journey from home, had made an expedition, and laid Parthia waste, so that he [was forced to] retire back, without doing any thing. And thus it was that Izates escaped the threatenings of the Parthians, by the providence of God.

3. It was not long ere Izates died, when he had completed fifty-five years of his life, and had ruled his kingdom twenty-four years. He left behind him twenty-four sons and twenty-four daughters. However, he gave order that his brother Monobazus should succeed in the government, thereby requiting him, because, while he was himself absent after their father's death, he had faithfully preserved the government for him. But when Helena, his mother, heard of her son's death, she was in great heaviness, as was but natural upon her loss of such a most dutiful son; yet was it a comfort to her, that she heard the succession came to her eldest son. Accordingly she went to him in haste, and when she was come into Adiabene, she did not long outlive her son Izates. But Monobazus sent her bones, as well as those of Izates, his brother, to Jerusalem, and gave order that they should be buried at the pyramids [1]

---

[1] These pyramids or pillars, erected by Helena, queen of Adiabene, near Jerusalem, three in number, are mentioned by Eusebius, in his

which their mother had erected; they were three in number, and distant more than three furlongs from the city Jerusalem. But for the actions of Monobazus the king, which he had during the rest of his life, we will relate them hereafter.[1]

CHAPTER V.

Concerning Theudas, and the sons of Judas the Galilean; as also what calamity fell upon the Jews on the day of the Passover.

1. Now it came to pass, while Fadus was procurator of Judea, that a certain magician, whose name was Theudas,[2] persuaded a great part of the people to take their effects with them, and follow him to the river Jordan; for he told them he was a prophet, and that he would, by his own command, divide the river, and afford them an easy passage over it: and many were deluded by his words. However, Fadus did not permit them to make any advantage of his wild attempt, but sent a troop of horsemen out against them: who, falling upon them unexpectedly, slew many of them, and took many of them alive. They also took Theudas alive, and cut off his head, and carried it to Jerusalem. This was what befell the Jews in the time of Cuspius Fadus' government.

Eccles. Hist. B. I. ch. xii., for which Dr. Hudson refers us to Valesius' notes upon that place. They are also mentioned by Pausanias, as hath been already noted, ch. ii. sect. 6. Reland guesses that that now called *Absalom's pillar* may be one of them.

[1] This account is now wanting.
[2] This Theudas, who arose under Fadus the procurator, about A. D. 45, or 46, could not be that Theudas who arose in the days of the taxing, under Cyrenius; or about A. D. 7, Acts v. 36, 37. Who that earlier Theudas was, see the note on B. XVII, ch. x, sect. 5.

2. Then came Tiberius Alexander as successor to Fadus; he was the son of Alexander the alabarch of Alexandria, which Alexander was a principal person among all his contemporaries, both for his family and wealth: he was also more eminent for his piety than this his son Alexander, for he did not continue in the religion of his country. Under these procurators that great famine happened in Judea, in which queen Helena bought corn in Egypt at a great expense, and distributed it to those that were in want, as I have related already. And besides this, the sons of Judas of Galilee were now slain, I mean of that Judas who caused the people to revolt, when Cyrenius came to take an account of the estates of the Jews, as we have showed in a foregoing book. The names of those sons were James and Simon, whom Alexander commanded to be crucified. But now Herod, king of Chalcis, removed Joseph, the son of Camydus, from the high priesthood, and made Ananias, the son of Nebedus, his successor. And now it was that Cumanus came as successor to Tiberius Alexander; as also that Herod, brother of Agrippa the great king, departed this life, in the eighth year of the reign of Claudius Cæsar. He left behind him three sons, Aristobulus, whom he had by his first wife, with Bernictanus, and Hircanus, both whom he had by Bernice his brother's daughter. But Claudius Cæsar bestowed his dominions on Agrippa junior.

3. Now, while the Jewish affairs were under the administration of Cumanus, there happened a great tumult at the city of Jerusalem, and many of the Jews perished therein. But I shall first explain the occasion whence it was derived. When that feast which is called the Passover, was at hand, at which time our custom is to use unleavened bread, and a

great multitude was gathered together from all parts to that feast, Cumanus was afraid lest some attempt of innovation should then be made by them; so he ordered that one regiment of the army should take their arms, and stand in the temple cloisters, to repress any attempts of innovation, if perchance any such should begin: and this was no more than what the former procurators of Judea did at such festivals. But on the fourth day of the feast, a certain soldier let down his breeches, and exposed his privy members to the multitude, which put those that saw him into a furious rage, and made them cry out, that this impious action was not done to reproach them, but God himself; nay, some of them reproached Cumanus, and pretended that the soldier was set on by him, which, when Cumanus heard, he was also himself not a little provoked at such reproaches laid upon him; yet did he exhort them to leave off such seditious attempts, and not to raise a tumult at the festival. But when he could not induce them to be quiet, for they still went on in their reproaches to him, he gave order that the whole army should take their entire armour, and come to Antonia, which was a fortress, as we have said already, which overlooked the temple; but when the multitude saw the soldiers there, they were affrighted at them, and ran away hastily: but as the passages out were but narrow, and as they thought their enemies followed them, they were crowded together in their flight, and a great number were pressed to death in these narrow passages; nor indeed was the number fewer than twenty thousand that perished in this tumult. So, instead of a festival, they had at last a mournful day of it; and they all of them forgot their prayers and sacrifices, and betook themselves to lamentation and weeping; so great an affliction did the impudent obsceneness of a single soldier bring upon them.[1]

4. Now before this their first mourning was over, another mischief befell them also; for some of those that raised the foregoing tumult, when they were travelling along the public road, about a hundred furlongs from the city, robbed Stephanus, a servant of Cæsar, as he was journeying, and plundered him of all that he had with him. Which things when Cumanus heard of, he sent soldiers immediately, and ordered them to plunder the neighbouring villages, and to bring the most eminent persons among them in bonds to him. Now, as this devastation was making, one of the soldiers seized the laws of Moses that lay in one of those villages, and brought them out before the eyes of all present, and tore them to pieces; and this was done with reproachful language, and much scurrility. Which things when the Jews heard of, they ran together, and that in great numbers, and came down to Cæsarea, where Cumanus then was, and besought him that he would avenge, not themselves, but God himself, whose laws had been affronted; for that they could not bear to live any longer, if the laws of their forefathers must be affronted after this manner. Accordingly Cumanus, out of fear lest the multitude should go into a sedition, and by the advice of his friends also, took care that the soldier who had offered the affront to the laws should be beheaded and thereby put a stop to the sedition which was ready to be kindled a second time.

---

[1] This, and many more tumults and seditions, which arose at the Jewish festivals, in Josephus, illustrate the cautious procedure of the Jewish governors, when they said, Matt. xxvi. 5, "Let us not take Jesus on the feast-day lest there be an uproar among the people;" as Reland well observes on this place. Josephus also takes notice of the same thing. Of the War. B. I. ch. iv. sect. 3.

CHAPTER VI.

How there happened a quarrel between the Jews and the Samaritans, and how Claudius put an end to their differences.

1. Now there arose a quarrel between the Samaritans and the Jews, on the occasion following: It was the custom of the Galileans, when they came to the holy city at the festivals, to take their journeys through the country of the Samaritans;[1] and at this time there lay, in the road they took, a village that was called *Ginoa,* which was situated in the limits of Samaria and the great plain, where certain persons thereto belonging fought with the Galileans, and killed a great many of them. But, when the principal of the Galileans were informed of what had been done, they came to Cumanus, and desired him to avenge the murder of those that were killed: but he was induced by the Samaritans, with money, to do nothing in the matter: upon which the Galileans were much displeased, and persuaded the multitude of the Jews to betake themselves to arms, and to regain their liberty, saying, That "slavery was in itself a bitter thing, but that, when it was joined with direct in juries, it was perfectly intolerable." And when their principal men endeavoured to pacify them, and promised to endeavour to persuade Cumanus to avenge those that were killed, they would not hearken to

---

[1] This constant passage of the Galileans through the country of Samaria, as they went to Judea and Jerusalem, illustrates several passages in the gospels, to the same purpose, as Dr. Hudson rightly observes. See Luke xvii. 1, John iv. 4. See also Josephus in his own life, sect. 52, where that journey is determined to three days.

them, but took their weapons, and entreated the assistance of Eleazar, the son of Dineus, a robber, who had many years made his abode in the mountains, with which assistance they plundered many villages of the Samaritans. When Cumanus heard of this action of theirs, he took the band of Sebaste, with four regiments of footmen, and armed the Samaritans, and marched out against the Jews, and caught them, and slew many of them, and took a great number of them alive; whereupon those that were the most eminent persons at Jerusalem, and that both in regard to the respect that was paid them, and the families they were of, as soon as they saw to what a height things were gone, put on sackcloth, and heaped ashes upon their heads, and by all possible means besought the seditious, and persuaded them that they would set before their eyes the utter subversion of their country, the conflagration of their temple, and the slavery of themselves, their wives and children, which would be the consequences of what they were doing, and would alter their minds, would cast away their weapons, and for the future be quiet, and return to their own homes. These persuasions of theirs prevailed upon them. So the people dispersed themselves, and the robbers went away again to their places of strength; and after this time all Judea was overrun with robberies.

2. But 'the principal of the Samaritans went to Ummidius Quadratus, the president of Syria, who at that time was at Tyre, and accused the Jews of setting their villages on fire, and plundering them; and said withal, That "they were not so much displeased at what they had suffered, as they were at the contempt thereby showed the Romans; while, if they had received any injury, they ought to have made them the judges of what had been done, and

not presently to make such devastation, as if they
had not the Romans for their governors; on which
account they came to him, in order to obtain the
vengeance they wanted." This was the accusation
which the Samaritans brought against the Jews. But
the Jews affirmed, that the Samaritans were the
authors of this tumult and fighting, and that, in the
first place, Cumanus had been corrupted by their
gifts, and passed over the murder of those that were
slain in silence. Which allegations when Quadratus
heard, he put off the hearing of the cause, and
promised that he would give sentence when he should
come into Judea, and should have a more exact
knowledge of the truth of that matter. So these
men went away without success. Yet was it not
long ere Quadratus came to Samaria, where, upon
hearing the cause, he supposed that the Samaritans
were the authors of that disturbance. But, when he
was informed that certain of the Jews were making
innovations, he ordered those to be crucified whom
Cumanus had taken captives. From whence he came
to a certain village called *Lydda,* which was not less
than a city in largeness, and there heard the Samaritan
cause a second time before his tribunal, and there
learned from a certain Samaritan, that one of the
chief of the Jews, whose name was *Dortus,* and some
other innovators with him, four in number, persuaded
the multitude to a revolt from the Romans, whom
Quadratus ordered to be put to death; but still he
sent away Ananias the high priest, and Ananus the
commander [of the temple,] in bonds to Rome, to
give an account of what they had done to Claudius
Cæsar. He also ordered the principal men, both of
the Samaritans and of the Jews, as also Cumanus
the procurator, and Celer the tribune, to go to Italy
to the emperor, that he might hear their cause, and

determine their differences one with another. But he
came again to the city of Jerusalem, out of his fear
that the multitude of the Jews should attempt some
innovations: but he found the city in a peaceable state,
and celebrating one of the usual festivals of their
country to God. So he believed that they would not
attempt any innovations, and left them at the celebra-
tion of the festival, and returned to Antioch.

3. Now Cumanus, and the principal of the Samaritans, who were sent to Rome, had a day appointed
them by the emperor, whereon they were to have
pleaded their cause about the quarrels they had one
with another. But now Cæsar's freed men, and his
friends, were very zealous on the behalf of Cumanus
and the Samaritans; and they had prevailed over the
Jews, unless Agrippa junior, who was then at Rome,
had seen the principal of the Jews hard set, and had
earnestly entreated Agrippina, the emperor's wife, to
persuade her husband to hear the cause, as was agreeable to his justice, and to condemn those to be
punished who were really the authors of this revolt
from the Roman government. Whereupon Claudius
was so well disposed beforehand, that when he had
heard the cause, and found that the Samaritans had
been the ringleaders in those mischievous doings, he
gave order, that those who came up to him should
be slain, and that Cumanus should be banished. He
also gave order, that Celer the tribune should be
carried back to Jerusalem, and should be drawn
through the city in the sight of all the people, and
then should be slain.

CHAPTER VII.

Felix is made procurator of Judea; as also concerning Agrippa junior and his sisters.

1. So Claudius sent Felix, the brother of Pallans, to take care of the affairs of Judea; and when he had already completed the twelfth year of his reign, he had bestowed upon Agrippa, the tetrarchy of Philip and Batanea, and added thereto Trachonitis, with Abila; which last had been the tetrarchy of Lysanias; but he took from him Chalcis, when he had been governor thereof four years. And when Agrippa had received these countries as the gift of Cæsar, he gave his sister Drusilla in marriage to Azizus, king of Emesa, upon his consent to be circumcised; for Epiphanes, the son of king Antiochus, had refused to marry her, because, after he had promised her father formerly to come over to the Jewish religion, he would not now perform that promise. He also gave Mariamne in marriage to Archelaus, the son of Helcias, to whom she had formerly been betrothed by Agrippa her father; from which marriage was derived a daughter, whose name was *Bernice.*

2. But for the marriage of Drusilla with Azizus, it was in no long time afterward dissolved upon the following occasion: While Felix was procurator of Judea, he saw this Drusilla, and fell in love with her; for she did indeed exceed all other women in beauty; and he sent to her a person whose name was *Simon,*[1] one of his friends; a Jew he was, and by

---

[1] This Simon, a friend of Felix, a Jew, born in Cyprus, though he pretended to be a magician, and seems to have been wicked enough, could hardly be that famous Simon the magician, in the Acts of the Apostles,

birth a Cypriot, and one who pretended to be a
magician, and endeavoured to persuade her to forsake her present husband, and marry him; and
promised, that if she would not refuse him, he would
make her a happy woman. Accordingly she acted
ill, and because she was desirous to avoid her sister
Bernice's envy, for she was very ill treated by her
on account of her beauty, was prevailed upon to
transgress the laws of her forefathers, and to marry
Felix; and, when he had had a son by her, he named
him *Agrippa*. But after what manner that young
man, with his wife, perished at the conflagration of
the mountain Vesuvius, in the days of Titus Cæsar,
shall be related hereafter.[1]

3. But as for Bernice, she lived a widow a good
while after the death of Herod [king of Chalcis,]
who was both her husband and her uncle; but when

viii. 9, etc., as some are ready to suppose. This Simon mentioned in the
Acts was not properly a Jew, but a Samaritan of the town of Gittæ in
the country of Samaria, as the Apostolical Constitutions, VI. 7, the
Recognitions of Clement, II. 6, and Justin Martyr, himself, born in the
country of Samaria, Apology, I. 34, inform us. He was also the author,
not of any ancient Jewish, but of the first Gentile heresies, as the forementioned authors assure us. So I suppose him a different person from
the other. I mean this only upon the hypothesis, that Josephus was not
misinformed as to his being a Cypriot Jew; for otherwise the time, the
name, the profession, and the wickedness of them both, would strongly
incline one to believe them the very same. As to that Drusilla, the sister
of Agrippa junior, as Josephus informs us here, and a Jewess, as St.
Luke informs us, Acts xxiv. 24, whom this Simon mentioned by Josephus,
persuaded to leave her former husband, Azizus, king of Emesa, a proselyte
of justice, and to marry Felix, the heathen procurator of Judea, Tacitus'
Hist. V. 9, supposes her to be a heathen, and the granddaughter of
Antonius and Cleopatra, contrary both to St. Luke and Josephus. Now
Tacitus lived somewhat too remote, both as to time and place, to be compared with either of those Jewish writers, in a matter concerning the Jews
in Judea in their own days, and concerning a sister of Agrippa junior, with
which Agrippa, Josephus was himself so well acquainted. It is probable
that Tacitus may say true, when he informs us, that this Felix (who
had in all three wives, or queens, as Suetonius in Claudius, sect. 28,
assures us) did once marry such a grandchild of Antonius and Cleopatra:
and, finding the name of one of them to have been Drusilla, he mistook
her for that other wife, whose name he did not know.

[1] This is now wanting.

the report went that she had criminal conversation
with her brother, [Agrippa junior,] she persuaded
Polemo, who was king of Cilicia, to be circumcised,
and to marry her, as supposing, that by this means
she should prove those calumnies upon her to be
false; and Polemo was prevailed upon, and that chiefly
on account of her riches. Yet did not this matrimony
endure long; but Bernice left Polemo, and, as was
said, with impure intentions. So he forsook at once
this matrimony, and the Jewish religion: and, at the
same time, Mariamne put away Archelaus, and was
married to Demetrius, the principal man among the
Alexandrian Jews, both for his family and his wealth;
and indeed he was then their alabarch. So she named
her son whom she had by him *Agrippinus*. But of
all those particulars we shall hereafter treat more
exactly.[1]

CHAPTER VIII.

After what manner, upon the death of Claudius, Nero
succeeded in the government; as also what barbarous
things he did. Concerning the robbers, murderers,
and impostors, that arose, while Felix and Festus
were procurators of Judea.

1. Now Claudius Cæsar died when he had reigned
thirteen years, eight months, and twenty days;[2] and
a report went about that he was poisoned by his wife
Agrippina. Her father was Germanicus, the brother

---

[1] This also is now wanting.
[2] This duration of the reign of Claudius agrees with Dio, as Dr. Hudson here remarks; as he also remarks, that Nero's name, which was at first *L. Domitius Ænobarbus*, after Claudius had adopted him, was *Nero Claudius Cæsar Drusus Germanicus*.

of Cæsar. Her husband was Domitius Ænobarbus, one of the most illustrious persons that was in the city of Rome; after whose death, and her long continuance in widowhood, Claudius took her to wife: she brought along with her a son, Domitius, of the same name with his father. He had before this slain his wife Messalina, out of jealousy, by whom he had his children Britannicus and Octavia; their eldest sister was Antonia, whom he had by Pelina his first wife. He also married Octavia to *Nero;* for that was the name that Cæsar gave him afterward, upon adopting him for his son.

2. But now Agrippina was afraid, lest, when Britannicus should come to man's estate, he should succeed his father in the government, and desired to seize upon the principality beforehand for her own son [Nero;] upon which the report went, that she thence compassed the death of Claudius. Accordingly she sent Burrhus, the general of the army, immediately, and with him the tribunes, and such also of the freed men, as were of the greatest authority, to bring Nero away into the camp and to salute him emperor. And when Nero had thus obtained the government, he got Britannicus to be so poisoned, that the multitude should not perceive it; although he publicly put his own mother to death not long afterward, making her thus requital, not only for being born of her, but by bringing it so about by her contrivances that he obtained the Roman empire. He also slew Octavia his own wife, and many other illustrious persons, under this pretence that they plotted against him.

3. But I omit any farther discourse about these affairs, for there have been a great many who have composed the history of Nero; some of whom have departed from the truth of facts out of favour, as

having received benefits from him; while others, out of hatred to him, and the great ill-will which they bore him, have so impudently raved against him with their lies, that they justly deserve to be condemned: nor do I wonder at such as have told lies of Nero, since they have not in their writings preserved the truth of history as to those facts that were earlier than his time, even when the actors could have no way incurred their hatred, since those writers lived a long time after them. But as to those that have no regard to truth, they may write as they please; for in that they take delight: but as to ourselves, who have made truth our direct aim, we shall briefly touch upon what only belongs remotely to this under-taking, but shall relate what hath happened to us Jews with great accuracy, and shall not grudge our pains in giving an account both of the calamities we have suffered, and of the crimes we have been guilty of. I will now therefore return to the relation of our own affairs.

4. For in the first year of the reign of Nero, upon the death of Azizus, king of Emesa, Soemus,[1] his brother, succeeded in his kingdom, and Aristobulus, the son of Herod, king of Chalcis, was intrusted by Nero, with the government of Lesser Armenia. Cæsar also bestowed on Agrippa a certain part of Galilee, Tiberias,[2] and Taricheæ, and ordered them to submit to his jurisdiction. He gave him also Julias, a city of Perea, with fourteen villages that lay about it.

5. Now, as for the affairs of the Jews, they grew worse and worse continually; for the country was

---

[1] This Soemus is elsewhere mentioned [by Josephus in his own Life, sect. 11, as also] by Dio Cassius and Tacitus.

[2] This agrees with Josephus' frequent accounts elsewhere in his own Life, that Tiberias, and Taricheæ, and Gamala, were under this Agrippa junior, till Justus, the son of Pistus, seized upon them for the Jews upon the breaking out of the war.

again filled with robbers and impostors, who deluded the multitude. Yet did Felix catch, and put to death, many of those impostors every day, together with the robbers. He also caught Eleazar, the son of Dineas, who had gotten together a company of robbers; and this he did by treachery; for he gave him assurance, that he should suffer no harm, and thereby persuaded him to come to him; but when he came he bound him, and sent him to Rome. Felix also bore an ill-will to Jonathan, the high priest, because he frequently gave him admonitions about governing the Jewish affairs better than he did, lest he should himself have complaints made of him by the multitude, since he it was who had desired Cæsar to send him as procurator of Judea. So Felix contrived a method whereby he might get rid of him, now he was become so continually troublesome to him; for such continual admonitions are grievous to those who are disposed to act unjustly. Wherefore Felix persuaded one of Jonathan's most faithful friends, a citizen of Jerusalem, whose name was Doras, to bring the robbers upon Jonathan, in order to kill him; and this he did by promising to give him a great deal of money for so doing. Doras complied with the proposal, and contrived matters so, that the robbers might murder him after the following manner: Certain of those robbers went up to the city, as if they were going to worship God, while they had daggers under their garments, and, by thus mingling themselves among the multitude, they slew Jonathan,[1]

[1] This treacherous and barbarous murder of the good high priest, Jonathan, by the contrivance of this wicked procurator, Felix, was the immediate occasion of the ensuing murders by the Sicarii or ruffians, and one great cause of the following horrid cruelties and miseries of the Jewish nation, as Josephus here supposes; whose excellent reflection on the gross wickedness of that nation, as the direct cause of their terrible destruction, is well worthy the attention of every Jewish, and of every Christian reader. And, since we are soon coming to the catalogue of

and as this murder was never avenged, the robbers
went up with the greatest security at the festivals
after this time, and having weapons concealed in like
manner as before, and mingling themselves among
the multitude, they slew certain of their own enemies,
and were subservient to other men for money, and
slew others, not only in remote parts of the city, but
in the temple itself also; for they had the boldness
to murder men there, without thinking of the impiety
of which they were guilty. And this seems to me
to have been the reasons why God, out of his hatred
of these men's wickedness, rejected our city, and as
for the temple, he no longer esteemed it sufficiently
pure for him to inhabit therein, but brought the
Romans upon us, and threw a fire upon the city to
purge it, and brought upon us, our wives and children,
slavery, as desirous to make us wiser by our calamities.

the Jewish high priests, it may not be amiss, with Reland, to insert this
Jonathan among them, and to transcribe his particular catalogue of the
last twenty-eight high priests, taken out of Josephus, and begin with
Ananelus, who was made by Herod the Great. See Antiq. B. XV. ch. ii.
sect. 4, and the note there.

1. Ananelus.
2. Aristobulus.
3. Jesus, the son of Fabus.
4. Simon, the son of Boethus.
5. Matthias, the son of Theophilus.
6. Joazer, the son of Boethus.
7. Eleazer, the son of Boethus.
8 Jesus, the son of Sie.
9. [Annas, or] Ananns, the son of Seth.
10. Ishmael, the son of Fabus.
11. Eleazar, the son of Ananus.
12. Simon, the son of Camithus.
13. Josephus Caiaphas, the son-in-law to Ananus.
14. Jonathan, the son of Ananus.
15. Theophilus, his brother, and son of Ananus.
16. Simon, the son of Boethus.
17. Matthias, the brother of Jonathan, and son of Ananus.
18. Aljoneus.
19. Josephus, the son of Camydus.
20. Ananias, the son of Nebedeus.
21. Jonathan.
22. Ishmael, the son of Fabi.
23. Joseph Cabi, the son of Simon.
24. Ananus, the son of Ananns.
25. Jesus, the son of Damneus.
26. Jesus, the son of Gamaliel.
27. Matthias, the son of Theophilus.
28. Phannias, the son of Samuel.

As for Ananus, and Josephus Caiaphas, here mentioned about the
middle of this catalogue, these are no other than the Ananus and Caiaphas,
so often mentioned in the four gospels; and that Ananias, the son of
Nebedeus, was that high priest before whom St. Paul pleaded his own
cause, Acts xxiv.

6. These works, that were done by the robbers, filled the city with all sorts of impiety. And now these impostors and deceivers persuaded the multitude to follow them into the wilderness, and pretended that they would exhibit manifest wonders and signs, that should be performed by the providence of God. And many that were prevailed on by them suffered the punishment of their folly: for Felix brought them back, and then punished them. Moreover, there came out of Egypt[1] about this time to Jerusalem, one that said he was a prophet, and advised the multitude of the common people to go along with him to the Mount of Olives, as it was called, which lay over against the city, and at the distance of five furlongs. He said farther, that he would show them from hence, how, at his command, the walls of Jerusalem would fall down; and he promised them, that he would procure them an entrance into the city through those walls, when they were fallen down. Now, when Felix was informed of these things, he ordered his soldiers to take their weapons, and came against them with a great number of horsemen and footmen, from Jerusalem, and attacked the Egyptian and the people that were with him. He also slew four hundred of them, and took two hundred alive. But the Egyptian himself escaped out of the fight, but did not appear any more. And again the robbers stirred up· the people to make war with the Romans, and said, they ought not to obey them at all; and when any person would not comply with them, they set fire to their villages, and plundered them.

7. And now it was that a great sedition arose between the Jews that inhabited Cæsarea, and the Syrians who dwelt there also, concerning their equal

---

[1] Of this Egyptian impostor, and the number of his followers, in Josephus, see Acts xxi. 38.

right to the privileges belonging to citizens, for the
Jews claimed the pre-eminence, because Herod their
king was the builder of Cæsarea, and because he was
by birth a Jew. Now, the Syrians did not deny what
was alleged about Herod; but they said, that Cæsarea
was formerly called Strato's Tower, and that then
there was not one Jewish inhabitant. When the
presidents of that country heard of these disorders,
they caught the authors of them on both sides, and
tormented them with stripes, and by that means put
a stop to the disturbance for a time. But the Jewish
citizens, depending on their wealth, and on that account despising the Syrians, reproached them again,
and hoped to provoke them by such reproaches.
However, the Syrians, though they were inferior in
wealth, yet valuing themselves highly on this account,
that the greatest part of Roman soldiers that were
there, were either of Cæsarea or Sebaste, they also
for some time used reproachful language to the Jews
also; and thus it was, till at length they came to
throwing stones at one another, and several were
wounded, and fell on both sides, though still the Jews
were the conquerors. But when Felix saw that this
quarrel was become a kind of war, he came upon
them on the sudden, and desired the Jews to desist,
and when they refused so to do, he armed his soldiers,
and sent them out upon them, and slew many of
them, and took more of them alive, and permitted
his soldiers to plunder some of the houses of the
citizens, which were full of riches. Now those Jews
that were more moderate, and of principal dignity
among them, were afraid of themselves, and desired
of Felix that he would sound a retreat to his soldiers,
and spare them for the future, and afford them room
for repentance for what they had done; and Felix
was prevailed upon to do so.

8. About this time king Agrippa gave the high priesthood to Ishmael, who was the son of Fabi. And now arose a sedition between the high priests and the principal men of the multitude of Jerusalem, each of which got them a company of the boldest sort of men, and of those that loved innovations, about them, and became leaders to them; and when they struggled together, they did it by casting reproachful words against one another, and by throwing stones also. And there was nobody to reprove them; but these disorders were done after a licentious manner in the city, as if it had no government over it. And such was the impudence [1] and boldness that had seized on the high priests, that they had the hardiness to send their servants into the threshing-floors, to take away those tithes that were due to the priests; insomuch that it so fell out that the poorest sort of the priests died for want. To this degree did the violence of the seditious prevail over all right and justice!

9. Now, when Porcius Festus was sent as successor to Felix by Nero, the principal of the Jewish inhabitants of Cæsarea went up to Rome to accuse Felix; and he had certainly been brought to punishment, unless Nero had yielded to the importunate solicitations of his brother Pallas, who was at that time had in the greatest honour by him. Two of the principal Syrians in Cæsarea persuaded Burrhus, who was Nero's tutor, and secretary for his Greek epistles, by giving him a great sum of money, to disannul that equality of the Jewish privileges of citizens which they hitherto enjoyed. So Burrhus, by his solicitations, obtained leave of the emperor,

---

[1] The wickedness here was very peculiar and extraordinary, that the high priests should so oppress their brethren the priests, as to starve the poorest of them to death. See the like presently, ch. ix. sect. 2. Such fatal crimes are covetousness and tyranny in the clergy, as well as in the laity, in all ages,

that an epistle should be written to that purpose. This epistle became the occasion of the following miseries that befell our nation; for, when the Jews of Cæsarea were informed of the contents of this epistle to the Syrians, they were more disorderly than before, till a war was kindled.

10. Upon Festus' coming into Judea, it happened that Judea was afflicted by the robbers, while all the villages were set on fire, and plundered by them. And then it was that the Sicarii, as they were called, who were robbers, grew numerous. They made use of small swords, not much different in length from the Persian *acinacæ,* but somewhat crooked, and like the Roman *sicæ* [or sickles,] as they were called: and from these weapons these robbers got their denomination, and with those weapons they slew a great many; for they mingled themselves among the multitude at their festivals, when they were come up in crowds from all parts to the city to worship God, as we said before, and easily slew those ·that they had a mind to slay. They also came frequently upon the villages belonging to their enemies, with their weapons, and plundered them, and set them on fire. So Festus sent forces, both horsemen and footmen, to fall upon those that had been seduced by a certain impostor, who promised them deliverance and freedom from the miseries they were under, if they would but follow him as far as the wilderness. Accordingly those forces that were sent destroyed both him that had deluded them, and those that were his followers also.

11. About the same time king Agrippa built himself a very large dining-room in the royal palace at Jerusalem, near to the portico. Now this palace had been erected of old by the children of Asamoneus, and was situate upon an elevation, and afforded a

most delightful prospect to those that had a mind to
take a view of the city, which prospect was desired
by the king; and there he could lie down, and eat,
and thence observe what was done in the temple:
which thing, when the chief men of Jerusalem saw,
they were very much displeased at it; for it was not
agreeable to the institutions of our country or law,
that what was done in the temple should be viewed
by others, especially what belonged to the sacrifices.
They therefore erected a wall upon the uppermost
building which belonged to the inner court of the
temple towards the west, which wall, when it was
built, did not only intercept the prospect of the dining-
room in the palace, but also of the western cloisters
that belonged to the outer court of the temple also,
where it was that the Romans kept guards for the
temple at the festivals. At these doings both king
Agrippa, and principally Festus the procurator, were
much displeased; and Festus ordered them to pull
the wall down again; but the Jews petitioned him to
give them leave to send an embassage about this
matter to Nero; for they said they could not endure
to live, if any part of the temple should be demolished;
and when Festus had given them leave so to do, they
sent ten of their principal men to Nero, as also
Ishmael the high priest, and Helcias, the keeper of
the sacred treasure. And when Nero had heard what
they had to say, he not only forgave [1] them what they
had already done, but also gave them leave to let
the wall they had built stand. This was granted them

---

[1] We have here one eminent example of Nero's mildness and goodness in his government towards the Jews, during the five first years of
his reign, so famous in antiquity; we have perhaps another in Josephus'
own Life, sect. 3, and a third, though of a very different nature here,
in sect. 9, just before. However, both the generous acts of kindness
were obtained of Nero by his queen Poppea, who was a religious lady,
and perhaps privately a Jewish proselyte, and so were not owing entirely
to Nero's own goodness.

in order to gratify Poppea, Nero's wife, who was a religious woman, and had requested these favours of Nero, and who gave order to the ten ambassadors to go their way home; but retained Helcias and Ishmael as hostages with herself. As soon as the king heard this news, he gave the high priesthood to Joseph, who was called *Cabi,* the son of Simon, formerly high priest.

CHAPTER. IX.

Concerning Abbinus, under whose procuratorship James was slain; as also what edifices were built by Agrippa.

1. AND now Cæsar, upon hearing of the death of Festus, sent Albinus into Judea, as procurator. But the king deprived Joseph of the high priesthood, and bestowed the succession to that dignity on the son of Ananus, who was also himself called *Ananus.* Now the report goes, that this eldest Ananus proved a most fortunate man; for he had five sons, who had all performed the office of a high priest to God, and who had himself enjoyed that dignity a long time formerly, which had never happened to any other of our high priests. But this younger Ananus, who, as we have told you already, took the high priesthood, was a bold man-in his temper, and very insolent; he was also of the sect of the Sadducees,[1] who are very

---

[1] It hence evidently appears, that Sadducees might be high priests in the days of Josephus, and that these Sadducees were usually very severe and inexorable judges, while the Pharisees were much milder, and more merciful, as appears by Reland's instances in his note on this place, and on Josephus' Life, sect. 34, and those taken from the New Testament, from Josephus himself, and from the Rabbins; nor do we meet with any Sadducees later than this high priest in all Josephus.

rigid in judging offenders above all the rest of the Jews, as we have already observed: when, therefore, Ananus was of this disposition, he thought he had now a proper opportunity [to exercise his authority.] Festus was now dead, and Albinus was but upon the road; so he assembled the Sanhedrim of judges, and brought before them the brother of Jesus, who was called *Christ*, whose name was *James*, and some others, [or, some of his companions.] And when he had formed an accusation against them as breakers of the law, he delivered them to be stoned; but as for those who seemed the most equitable of the citizens, and such as were the most uneasy at the breach of the laws, they disliked what was done; they also sent to the king, [Agrippa,] desiring him to send to Ananus that he should act so no more, for that what he had already done was not to be justified: nay,[1] some of them went also to meet Albinus, as he was upon his journey from Alexandria, and informed him that it was not lawful for Ananus to assemble a Sanhedrim without his consent. Whereupon Albinus complied with what they said, and wrote in anger to Ananus and threatened that he would bring him to punishment for what he had done; on which king Agrippa took the high priesthood from him, when he had ruled but three months, and made Jesus the son of Damneus high priest.

2. Now as soon as Albinus was come to the city of Jerusalem, he used all his endeavours and care that the country might be kept in peace, and this by destroying many of the Sicarii. But as for the high

---

[1] Of this condemnation of James the Just, and its causes, as also that he did not die till long afterwards, see Prim. Christ. Revived, Vol. III. ch. 43-46. The sanhedrim condemned Jesus, but could not put him to death without the approbation of the Roman procurator; nor could therefore Ananias and his sanhedrim do more here, since they never had Albinus' approbation for the putting this James to death.

priest Ananias,[1] he increased in glory every day,
and this to a great degree, and had obtained the
favour and esteem of the citizens in a signal manner,
for he was a great hoarder up of money; he therefore cultivated the friendship of Albinus, and of the
high priest [Jesus,] by making them presents, he also
had servants who were very wicked, who joined themselves to the boldest sort of the people, and went to
the threshing-floors, and took away the tithes that
belonged to the priests by violence, and did not refrain
from beating such as would not give these tithes to
them. So the other high priests acted in the like
manner, as did those his servants, without any one's
being able to prohibit them; so that [some of the]
priests that of old were wont to be supported with
those tithes died for want of food.

3. But now the Sicarii went into the city by night
just before the festival, which was now at hand, and
took the scribe belonging to the governor of the
temple, whose name was *Eleazer,* who was the son of
Ananus [Ananias] the high priest, and bound him,
and carried him away with them; after which they sent
to Ananias, and said that they would send the scribe
to him, if he would persuade Albinus to release ten
of those prisoners which he had caught of their party;

---

[1] This Ananias was not the son of Nebedeus, as I take it, but he
who was called Annas or Ananus the elder, the 9th in the catalogue,
and who had been esteemed high priest for a long time; and besides,
Caiaphas his son-in-law had five of his own sons high priests after him,
which were those numbers, 11, 14, 15, 17, 24, in the foregoing catalogue.
Nor ought we to pass slightly over what Josephus here says of Annas
or Ananias, that he was high priest a long time before his children were
so; he was the son of Seth, and is set down first for high priest in the
foregoing catalogue, under number 9. He was made by Quirinus, and
continued till Ishmael, the 10th in number, for about 23 years, which
long duration of his high priesthood, joined to the succession of his son-
in-law, and five children of his own, made him a sort of perpetual
high priest, and was perhaps the occasion that former high priests kept
their titles ever afterwards; for I believe it is hardly met with before
him.

so Ananias was plainly forced to persuade Albinus, and gained his request of him. This was the beginning of greater calamities; for the robbers perpetually contrived to catch some of Ananias' servants, and when they had taken them alive, they would not let them go, till they thereby recovered some of their own Sicarii. And as they were again become no small number, they grew bold, and were a great affliction to the whole country.

4. About this time it was that king Agrippa built Cæsarea Philippi larger than it was before, and, in honour of Nero, named it *Neronias*. And when he had built a theatre at Berytus, with vast expense, he bestowed on them shows, to be exhibited every year, and spent therein many ten thousand [drachmæ;] he also gave the people a largess of corn, and distributed oil among them, and adorned the entire city with statues of his own donation, and with original images made by ancient hands; nay, he almost transferred all that was most ornamental in his own kingdom thither. This made him more than ordinarily hated by his subjects; because he took those things away that belonged to them, to adorn a foreign city. And now Jesus, the son of Gamaliel, became the successor of Jesus, the son of Damneus, in the high priesthood, which the king had taken from the other; on which account a sedition arose between the high priests, with regard to one another; for they got together bodies of the boldest sort of the people, and frequently came, from reproaches to throwing of stones at each other. But Ananias was too hard for the rest by his riches, which enabled him to gain those that were most ready to receive. Costobarus also, and Saulus, did themselves get together a multitude of wicked wretches, and this because they were of the royal family; and so they obtained favour

among them, because of their kindred to Agrippa; but still they used violence with people, and were very ready to plunder those that were weaker than themselves. And from that it principally came to pass, that our city was greatly disordered, and that all things grew worse and worse among us.

5. But when Albinus heard that Gessius Florus was coming to succeed him, he was desirous to appear to do somewhat that might be grateful to the people of Jerusalem; so he brought out all those prisoners who seemed to him to be the most plainly worthy of death, and ordered them to be put to death accordingly. But as to those who had been put into prison on some trifling occasions, he took money of them, and dismissed them; by which means the prisons were emptied, but the country was filled with robbers.

6. Now, as many of the Levites,[1] which is a tribe of ours, as were singers of hymns, persuaded the king to assemble a Sanhedrim, and to give them leave to wear linen garments, as well as the priests; for they said, that this would be a work worthy the times of his government, that he might have a memorial of such a novelty, as being his doing. Nor did they fail of obtaining their desire; for the king, with the suffrages of those that came into the Sanhedrim, granted the singers of hymns this privilege, that they may lay aside their former garments, and wear such a linen one as they desired; and as a part of this tribe ministered in the temple, he also permitted them to learn those hymns as they had besought him for. Now all this was contrary to the laws of our

[1] This insolent petition of some of the Levites, to wear the sacerdotal garments, when they sung hymns to God in the temple, was very probably owing to the great depression and contempt the haughty high priests had now brought their brethren the priests into; of which see ch. viii. sect. 8, and ch. ix. sect. 2.

country, which, whenever they have been transgressed, we have never been able to avoid the punishment of such transgressions.

7. And now it was that the temple[1] .was finished. So, when the people saw that the workmen were unemployed, who were above eighteen thousand, and that they, receiving no wages, were in want, because they had earned their bread by their labours about the temple, and while they were unwilling to keep them by the treasures that were there deposited, out of fear of [their being carried away by] the Romans: and while they had a regard to the making provision for the workmen, they had a mind to expend those treasures upon them; for if any one of them did but labour for a single hour, he received his pay immediately; so they persuaded him to rebuild the eastern cloisters. These cloisters belonged to the outer court, and were situated in a deep valley, and had walls that reached four hundred cubits [in length,] and were built of square and very white stones, the length of each of which stones was twenty cubits, and their height six cubits. This was the work of king Solomon,[2] who first of all built the entire temple. But king Agrippa, who had the care of the temple committed to him by Claudius Cæsar, considering that it is easy to demolish any building, but hard to build it up again, and that it was particularly hard to do it to these cloisters, which would require a considerable time, and great sums of money, he denied the petitioners their request, about that matter; but he did not obstruct them when they desired the city might be paved with white stone. He

---

[1] Of this finishing, not of the *holy house,* but of the courts about it, called in general the *temple.* see the note on B. XVII. ch. x. sect. 2.

[2] Of these cloisters of Solomon, see the description of the temple, ch. xiii. They seem, by Josephus' words, to have been built from the bottom of the valley.

also deprived Jesus the son of Gamaliel, of the high priesthood, and gave it to Matthias, the son of Theophilus, under whom the Jews' war with the Romans took its beginning.

CHAPTER X.

An enumeration of the high priests.

1. AND now I think it proper and agreeable to this history, to give an account of our high priests; how they began, who those are which are capable of that dignity, and how many of them there had been at the end of the war. In the first place, therefore, history informs us, that Aaron, the brother of Moses, officiated to God as a high priest, and that, after his death, his sons succeeded him immediately; and that, this dignity hath been continued down from them all to their posterity. Whence it is a custom of our country, that no one should take the high priesthood of God, but he who is of the blood of Aaron, while every one that is of another stock, though he were king, can never obtain that high priesthood. Accordingly, the number of all the high priests from Aaron, of whom we have spoken already, as of the first of them, until Phanas, who was made high priest during the war by the seditious, was eighty-three; of whom thirteen, officiated as high priests in the wilderness, from the days of Moses, while the tabernacle was standing, until the people came into Judea, when king Solomon erected the temple to God: for at the first they held the high priesthood till the end of their life, although afterward they had successors while they were alive. Now these thirteen, who were the descendants of two of the sons of Aaron, received

this dignity by succession, one after another; for their form of government was an aristocracy, and after that a monarchy, and in the third place the government was regal. Now, the number of years during the rule of these thirteen, from the day when our fathers departed out of Egypt, under Moses their leader, until the building of that temple which king Solomon erected at Jerusalem, were six hundred and twelve. After those thirteen high priests, eighteen took the high priesthood at Jerusalem, one in succession to another, from the days of king Solomon, until Nebuchadnezzar, king of Babylon, made an expedition against that city, and burnt the temple, and removed our nation into Babylon, and then took Josadek, the high priest, captive; the times of these high priests were four hundred sixty-six years, six months, and ten days, while the Jews were still under the regal government. But after the term of seventy years' captivity under the Babylonians, Cyrus, king of Persia, sent the Jews from Babylon to their own land again, and gave them leave to rebuild their temple; at which time, Jesus, the son of Josadek, took the high priesthood over the captives when they were returned home. Now he and his posterity, who were in all fifteen, until king Antiochus Eupator, were under a democratical government for four hundred and fourteen years; and then the forementioned Antiochus, and Lysia the general of his army, deprived Onias, who was also called Menelaus, of the high priesthood, and slew him at Berea, and driving away the son [of Onias the third,] put Jacimus into the place of the high priest, one that was indeed of the stock of Aaron, but not of that family of Onias. On which account, Onias, who was the nephew of Onias that was dead, and bore the same name with his father, came into Egypt, and got into the friendship of Ptolemy Philometer, and Cleopatra his wife, and persuaded them to make him the high priest of that temple which he built to God in the præfecture of Heliopolis, and this in imitation of that at Jerusalem; but as for that temple which was built in Egypt, we have spoken of it frequently already. Now, when Jacimus had retained the priesthood three years, he died, and there was no one that succeeded him, so that the city continued seven years without a high priest; but then the posterity of the sons of Asamoneus, who had the government of the nation conferred upon them, when they had beaten the Macedonians in war, appointed Jonathan to be their high priest, who ruled over them seven years. And when he had been slain by the treacherous contrivance of Trypho, as we have related somewhere, Simon his brother took the high priesthood; and when he was destroyed at a feast by the treachery of his son-in-law, his own son, whose name was Hyrcanus, succeeded him, after he had held the high priesthood one year longer than his brother. This Hyrcanus enjoyed that dignity thirty years, and died an old man, leaving the succession to Judas, who was also called Aristobulus, whose brother Alexander was his heir; which Judas died of a sore distemper, after he had kept the priesthood, together with the royal authority, for this Judas was the first that put on his head a diadem, for one year. And when Alexander had been both king and high priest twenty-seven years, he departed this life, and permitted his wife Alexandra to appoint him that should be high priest; so she gave the high priesthood to Hyrcanus, but retained the kingdom herself nine years, and then departed this life. The like duration [and no longer] did her son Hyrcanus enjoy the high priesthood; for after her death his brother Aristobulus fought against him, and beat him, and deprived him of his principality; and he did himself both reign, and perform the office of high priest to God. But when he had reigned three years and as many months, Pompey came upon him, and not only took the city of Jerusalem by force, but put him and his children in bonds, and sent them to Rome. He also restored the high priesthood to Hyrcanus, and made him governor of the nation, but forbade him to wear a diadem. This Hyrcanus ruled, besides his first nine years, twenty-four years more, when Barzapharnes and Pacorus, the generals of the Parthians, passed over Euphrates, and fought with Hyrcanus, and took him alive, and made Antigonus, the son of Aristobulus, king; and when he had reigned three years and three months, Sosius and Herod besieged him, and took him, when Antony had him brought to Antioch, and slain there. Herod was then made king by the Romans, but did no longer appoint high priests out of the family of Asamoneus; but made certain men to be so that were of no eminent families, but barely of those that were priests, excepting that he gave that dignity to Aristobulus; for when he had made this Aristobulus, the grandson of that Hyrcanus who was then taken by the Parthians, and had taken his sister Mariamne to wife, he thereby aimed to win the good-will of the people, who had a kind remembrance of Hyrcanus [his grandfather.] Yet did he afterward, out of his fear lest they should all bend their inclinations to Aristobulus, put him to death, and that by contriving how to have him suffocated as he was swimming at Jericho, as we have already related that matter; but after this man he never intrusted the high priesthood to the posterity of the sons of Asamoneus. Archelaus also, Herod's son, did like his father in the appointment of the high priests, as did the Romans also who took the government over the Jews into their hands afterward. Accordingly the number of the high priests, from the days of Herod until the day when Titus took the temple and the city, and burnt them, were in all twenty-eight; the time also that belonged to them was a hundred and seven years. Some of these were the political governors of the people under the reign of Herod, and under the reign of Archelaus his son, although, after their death, the government became an aristocracy, and the high priests were intrusted with a dominion over the nation. And thus much may suffice to be said concerning our high priests.

CHAPTER XI.

Concerning Florus the procurator, who necessitated the Jews to take up arms against the Romans. The conclusion.

1. Now Gessius Florus, who was sent as successor to Albinus by Nero, filled Judea with abundance of miseries. He was by birth of the city of Clazomenæ, and brought along with him his wife Cleopatra, (by whose friendship with Poppea, Nero's wife, he obtained this government,) who was no way different from him in wickedness. This Florus was so wicked, and so violent in the use of his authority, that the Jews took Albinus to have been [comparatively] their benefactor; so excessive were the mischiefs that he brought upon them. For Albinus concealed his wickedness, and was careful that it might not be discovered to all men; but Gessius Florus, as though he had been sent on purpose to show his crimes to everybody, made a pompous ostentation of them to

our nation, as never omitting any sort of violence,
nor any unjust sort of punishment; for he was not
to be moved by pity, and never was satisfied with
any degree of gain that came in his way; nor had he
any more regard to great than to small acquisitions,
but became a partner with the robbers themselves.
For a great many fell then into that practice without
fear, as having him for their security, and depending
on him, that he would save them harmless in their
particular robberies; so that there were no bounds
set to the nation's miseries; but the unhappy Jews,
when they were not able to bear the devastations
which the robbers made among them, were all under
a necessity of leaving their own habitations, and of
flying away, as hoping to dwell more easily any where
else in the world among foreigners, [than in their own
country.] And what need I say any more upon this
head? since it was this Florus who necessitated us to
take up arms against the Romans, while we thought
it better to be destroyed at once, than by little and
little. Now this war began in the second year of
the government of Florus, and the twelfth year of
the reign of Nero. But then what actions we were
forced to do, or what miseries we were enabled to
suffer, may be accurately known by such as will peruse
those books which I have written about the Jewish
war.

2. I shall now, therefore, make an end here of
my Antiquities; after the conclusion of which events,
I begin to write that account of the war; and these
Antiquities contain what hath been delivered down
to us from the original creation of man, until the
twelfth year of the reign of Nero, as to what hath
befallen the Jews, as well in Egypt as in Syria, and
in Palestine, and what we have suffered from the
Assyrians and Babylonians, and what afflictions the

Persians and Macedonians, and after them the Romans have brought upon us; for I think I may say that I have composed this history with sufficient accuracy in all things. I have attempted to enumerate those high priests that we have had during the interval of two thousand years: I have also carried down the successions of our kings, and related their actions, and political administration; without [considerable] errors, as also the power of our monarchs; and all according to what is written in our sacred books; for this it was that I promised to do in the beginning of this history. And I am so bold as to say, now I have so completely perfected the work I proposed to myself to do, that no other person, whether he were a Jew or a foreigner, had he ever so great an inclination to it, could so accurately deliver these accounts to the Greeks as is done in these books. For those of my own nation freely acknowl edge, that I far exceed them in the learning belonging to Jews; I have also taken a great deal of pains to obtain the learning of the Greeks, and understand the elements of the Greek language, although I have so long accustomed myself to speak our own tongue, that I cannot pronounce Greek with sufficient exactness; for our own nation does not encourage those that learn the languages of many nations, and so adorn their discourses with the smoothness of their periods; because they look upon this sort of accomplishment as common, not only to all sorts of free men, but to as many of the servants as please to learn them. But they give him the testimony of being a wise man, who is fully acquainted with our laws, and is able to interpret their meaning; on which account, as there have been many who have done their endeavours with great patience to obtain this learning, there have yet hardly been so many as two or three that have succeeded therein, who were immediately well rewarded for their pains.

And now it will not be perhaps an invidious thing, if I treat briefly of my own family, and of the actions of my own life, while there is still living such as can either prove what I say to be false, or can attest that it is true; with which accounts I shall put an end to these Antiquities, which are contained in twenty books and sixty thousand verses. And if God [1] permit me, I will briefly run over this war again, with what befell us therein to this very day, which is the thirteenth year of the reign of Cæsar Domitian, and the fifty-sixth year of my own life. I have also an

---

[1] What Josephus here declares his *intention* to do, *if God permitted,* to give the public *again an abridgment of the Jewish War* and to add *what befell them farther to that very day,* the 13th of Domitian, or A. D. 93, is not, that I have observed, taken distinct notice of by any one; nor do we ever hear of it, elsewhere, whether he performed what he now intended or not. Some of the reasons of this design of his might possibly be, his observation of the many errors he had been guilty of in the two first of those seven books of the War, which were written when he was comparatively young, and less acquainted with the Jewish Antiquities than he now was, and in which abridgment we might have hoped to find those many passages which he mentions himself, as well as those several passages which others refer to, as written by him, but which are not extant in his present works. However, since many of his own references to what he had written elsewhere, as well as most of his own errors, belong to such early times as could not well come into this abridgment of the Jewish war; and since none of those that quote things not now extant in his works, including himself as well as others, ever cite any such abridgment, I am forced rather to suppose that he never did publish any such work at all; I mean, as distinct from his own life, written by himself, for an appendix to these Antiquities, and this at least seven years after these Antiquities were finished. Nor indeed does it appear to me that Josephus ever published that other work here mentioned, as intended by him for the public also; I mean the three or four books, *concerning God and his essence,* and concerning *the Jewish laws; why, according to them, some things were permitted the Jews and others prohibited;* which last seems to be the same work which Josephus had also promised, *if God permitted,* as the conclusion of his preface to these Antiquities; nor do I suppose that he ever published any of them. The death of all his friends at court, Vespasian, Titus, and Domitian, and the coming of those he had no acquaintance with to the crown, I mean Nerva and Trajan, together with his removal from Rome to Judea, with what followed it, might easily interrupt such his intentions, and prevent his publication of those works.

intention to write three books concerning our Jewish opinions about God and his essence, and about our laws; why, according to them, some things are permitted us to do, and others are prohibited.

THE LIFE
OF
FLAVIUS JOSEPHUS.

1. The family from which I am derived is not an ignoble one, but hath descended all along from the priests; and as nobility among several people is of a different origin, so with us to be of a sacerdotal dignity, is an indication of the splendour of a family. Now, I am not only sprung from a sacerdotal family in general, but from the first of the twenty-four [1] courses; and as among us there is not only a considerable difference between one family of each course and another, I am of the chief family of that first course also; nay, farther, by my mother I am of the royal blood; for the children of Asamoneus, from whom that family was derived, had both the office of the high priesthood, and the dignity of a king, for a long time together. I will accordingly

---

[1] We may hence correct the error of the Latin copy of the second book against Apion, sect. 7, 8, (for the Greek is there lost,) which says, there were then only four tribes or courses of the priests instead of twenty-four. Nor is this testimony to be disregarded, as if Josephus there contradicted what he had affirmed here; because even the account there given better agrees to twenty-four than to four courses, while he says that each of those courses contained above 5,000 men, which multiplied by only four, will make not more than 20,000 priests; whereas the number 120,000, as multiplied by 24, seems much the most probable, they being one-tenth of the whole people, even after the captivity. See Ezra ii. 36-39, Neh. vii. 39-42, 1 Esd. v. 24, 25, with Ezra ii. 54, Neh. vii. 66, 1 Esd. v. 41. Nor will this common reading or notion of but four courses of priests, agree with Josephus' own farther assertion elsewhere, Antiq. B. VII. ch. xiv. sect. 7, that David's partition of the priests into twenty-four courses had continued to that day.

set down my progenitors in order. My grandfather's father was named Simon, with the addition of Psellus he lived at the same time with that son of Simon the high priest, who, first of all the high priests, was named Hyrcanus. This Simon Psellus had nine sons, one of which was Matthias, called Ephlias; he married the daughter of Jonathan the high priest, which Jonathan was the first of the sons of Asamoneus, who was high priest, and was the brother of Simon the high priest also. This Matthias had a son called Matthias Curtus, and that in the first year of the government of Hyrcanus; his son's name was Joseph, born in the ninth year of the reign of Alexandra; his son Matthias was born in the tenth year of the reign of Archelaus, as was I born to Matthias on the first year of the reign of Caius Cæsar. I have three sons: Hyrcanus, the eldest, was born on the fourth year of the reign of Vespasian; as was Justus born on the seventh, and Agrippa on the ninth. Thus have I set down the genealogy of my family as I have found it described [1] in the public records, and so bid adieu to those who calumniate me, [as of a lower original.]

2. Now my father Matthias was not only eminent on account of his nobility, but had a higher commendation on account of his righteousness, and was in great reputation in Jerusalem, the greatest city we have. I was myself brought up with my brother, whose name was Matthias, for he was my own brother, by both father and mother; and I made mighty proficiency in the improvements of my learning, and appeared to have both a great memory and understanding. Moreover, when I was a child, and about fourteen years of age, I was commended by all for

---

[1] An eminent example of the care of the Jews about their genealogies, especially as to the priests. See Contr. Ap. B. I. ch. 7.

the love I had to learning; on which account the high priests and principal men of the city came then frequently to me together, in order to know my opinion about the accurate understanding of points of the law. And when I was about sixteen years old, I had a mind to make trial of the several sects that were among us. These sects are three: the first is that of the Pharisees, the second that of the Sadducees, and the third that of the Essens, as we have frequently told you; for I thought that by this means I might choose the best, if I were once acquainted with them all; so I contented myself with hard fare, and underwent great difficulties, and went through them all. Nor did . I content myself with these trials only; but when I was informed that one whose name was Banus, lived in the desert, and used no other clothing than grew upon trees, and had no other food than what grew of its own accord, and bathed himself in cold water frequently, both by night and by day, in order to preserve his chastity, I imitated him in those things, and continued with him three years.[1] So when I had accomplished my desires, I returned back to the city, being now nineteen years old, and began to conduct myself according to the rules of the sect of the Pharisees, which is of kin to the sect of the Stoics, as the Greeks call them.

3. But when I was in the twenty-sixth year of my age, it happened that I took a voyage to Rome, and this on the occasion which I shall now describe. At the time when Felix was procurator of Judea,

---

[1] When Josephus here says, that from sixteen to nineteen, or for three years, he made trial of the three Jewish sects, the Pharisees, the Sadducees, and the Essens, and yet says presently, in all our copies, that he stayed besides with one particular ascetic, called *Banus, παρ αυτω with him,* and this still before he was nineteen, there is little room left for his trial of the three other sects. I suppose, therefore, that for *παρ αυτω, with him,* the old reading might be *παρ αυτυις, with them:* which is a very small emendation, and takes away the difficulty before us.

there were certain priests of my acquaintance, and very excellent persons they were, whom on a small and trifling occasion he had put into bonds, and sent to Rome to plead their cause before Cæsar. These I was desirous to procure deliverance for, and that especially because I was informed that they were not unmindful of piety towards God even under their afflictions, but supported themselves with figs and nuts.[1] Accordingly I came to Rome, though it were through a great number of hazards by sea; for, as our ship was drowned in the Adriatic sea, we that were in it, being about six hundred in number,[2] swam for our lives all the night; when, upon the first appearance of the day, and upon our sight of a ship of Cyrene, I and some others, eighty in all, by God's providence, prevented the rest, and were taken up into the other ship. And when I had thus escaped, and was come to Dicearchia, which the Italians call Puteoli, I became acquainted with Aliturius, an actor of plays, and much beloved by Nero, but a Jew by birth; through his interest became known to Poppea, Cæsar's wife, and took care, as soon as possible, to entreat her to procure, that the priests might be set at liberty. And when, besides this favour, I had obtained many presents from Poppea, I returned home again.

4. And now I perceived innovations ·were already begun, and that there were a great many very much elevated in hopes of a revolt from the Romans. I therefore endeavoured to put a stop to these tumultuous persons, and persuaded them to change

---

[1] We may note here, that religious men among the Jews, or at least those that were priests, were sometimes ascetics also, and, like Daniel and his companions in Babylon, Dan. i. 8-16, ate no flesh, but *figs and nuts*, etc. only.

* [2] It hath been thought the number of Paul and his companions on ship hoard, Acts xxvii. 37, which are 276 in our copies, are too many; whereas we find here that Josephus and his companions, a very few years after the other, were about 600.

their minds; and laid before their eyes against whom it was that they were going to fight, and told them that they were inferior to the Romans not only in martial skill, but also in good fortune; and desired them not rashly, and after the most foolish manner, to bring on the dangers of the most terrible mischiefs upon their country, upon their families, and upon themselves. And this I said with a vehement exhortation, because I foresaw that the end of such a war would be most unfortunate to us. But I could not persuade them; for the madness of desperate men was quite too hard for me.

5. I was then afraid, lest by inculcating these things so often, I should incur their hatred and their suspicions, as if I were of our enemies' party, and should run into the danger of being seized by them, and slain; since they were already possessed of Antonia, which was the citadel; so I retired into the inner court of the temple. Yet did I go out of the temple again, after Manahem and the principal of the band of robbers were put to death, when I abode among the high priests and the chief of the Pharisees. But no small fear seized upon us when we saw the people in arms, while we ourselves knew not what we should do, and were not able to restrain their seditions. However, as the danger was directly upon us, we pretended that we were of the same opinion with them, but only advised them to be quiet for the present, and to let the enemy go away, still hoping, that Gessius [Florus] would not be long ere he came, and that with great forces, and so put an end to these seditious proceedings.

6. But, upon his coming and fighting, he was beaten, and a great many of those that were with him fell. And this disgrace [which Gessius with Cestius] received, became the calamity of our whole

nation; for those that were fond of the war were so far elevated with this success, that they had hopes of finally conquering the Romans. Of which war another occasion was ministered, which was this: Those that dwelt in the neighbouring cities of Syria seized upon such Jews as dwelt among them, with their wives and children, and slew them, when they had not the least occasion of complaint against them: for they did neither attempt any innovation or revolt from the Romans, nor had they given any marks of hatred or treacherous designs towards the Syrians. But what was done by the inhabitants of Scythopolis was the most impious and most highly criminal of all; [1] for, when the Jews, their enemies, came upon them from without, they forced the Jews that were among them to bear arms against their own countrymen, which it is unlawful for us to do: [2] and when by their assistance, they had joined battle with those that attacked them, and had beaten them, after that victory they forgot the assurances they had given these their fellow-citizens and confederates, and slew them all, being in number many ten thousand [13,000.] The like miseries were undergone by those Jews that were the inhabitants of Damascus. But we have given a more accurate account of these things in the books of the Jewish war. I only mention them now, because I would demonstrate to my readers, that the Jews' war with the Romans was not voluntary, but that, for the main, they were forced by necessity to enter into it.

[1] See Of the War, B. II. ch. xviii. sect. 3.

[2] The Jews might collect the unlawfulness of fighting against their brethren from that law of Moses, Lev. xix. 16, "Thou shalt not stand against the blood of thy neighbour;" and that, ver. 17, "Thou shalt not avenge, nor bear any grudge against the children of thy people; but thou shalt love thy neighbour as thyself;" as well as from many other places in the Pentateuch and Prophets. See Antiq. B. VIII. ch. viii. sect. 3.

7. So when Gessius had been beaten, as we have said already, the principal men of Jerusalem, seeing that the robbers and innovators had arms in great plenty, and fearing lest they, while they were unprovided with arms, should be in subjection to their enemies, which also came to be the case afterward; and, being informed that all Galilee had not yet revolted from the Romans, but that some part of it was still quiet, they sent me and two others of the priests, who were men of excellent characters, Jozar and Judas, in order to persuade the ill men there to lay down their arms, and to teach them this lesson, that it were better to have those arms reserved for the most courageous men that the nation had, [than to be kept there;] for that it had been resolved, that those our best men should always have their arms ready against futurity, but still so, that they should wait to see what the Romans would do.

8. When I had therefore received these instructions, I came into Galilee, and found the people of Sepphoris in no small agony about their country, by reason that the Galileans had resolved to plunder it, on account of the friendship they had with the Romans, and because they had given their right hand, and made a league with Cestius Gallus, the president of Syria. But I delivered them all out of the fear they were in, and persuaded the multitude to deal kindly with them, and permitted them to send to those that were their own hostages with Gessius to Dora, which is a city of Phenicia, as often as they pleased; though I still found the inhabitants of Tiberias ready to take arms, and that on the occasion following:

9. There were three factions in this city. The first was composed of men of worth and gravity; of these Julius Capellus was the head. Now he, as well

as all his companions, Herod the son of Miarus, and
Herod the son of Gamalus, and Compsus the son
of Compsus, (for as to Compsus' brother Crispus,
who had once been governor of the city under the
great king [1] [Agrippa,] he was beyond Jordan in
his own possessions;) all these persons before named
gave their advice, that the city should then continue
in their allegiance to the Romans, and to the king.
But Pistus, who was guided by his son Justus, did
not acquiesce in that resolution; otherwise he was
himself naturally of a good and virtuous character.
But the second faction was composed of the most
ignoble persons, and was determined for war. But
as for Justus, the son of Pistus, who was the head
of the third faction, although he pretended to be
doubtful about going to war, yet was he really
desirous of innovation, as supposing that he should
gain power to himself by the change of affairs. He
therefore came into the midst of them, and endeavoured to inform the multitude, That "the city
Tiberias had ever been a city of Galilee, and that in
the days of Herod the tetrarch, who had built it,
it had obtained the principal place, and that he had
ordered that the city Sepphoris should be subordinate
to the city Tiberias; that they had not lost this pre-
eminence even under Agrippa the father, but had
retained it until Felix was procurator of Judea. But
he told them, that now they had been so unfortunate
as to be made a present by Nero to Agrippa junior;
and that, upon Sepphoris' submission of itself to the
Romans, that was become the capital city of Galilee,
and that the royal treasury, and the archives were
now removed from them." When he had spoken

---

[1] That this Herod Agrippa, the father, was of old called a *Great
King*, as here appears by his coins still remaining; to which Havercamp
refers us.

these things, and a great many more against Agrippa, in order to provoke the people to a revolt, he added, That "this was the time for them to take arms, and join with the Galileans as their confederates, (whom they might command, and who would now willingly assist them out of the hatred they bore to the people of Sepphoris, because they preserved their fidelity to the Romans), and to gather a great number of forces in order to punish them." And, as he said this, he exhorted the multitude [to go to war;] for his abilities lay in making harangues to the people, and in being too hard in his speeches for such as opposed him, though they advised what was more to their advantage, and this by his craftiness and his fallacies, for he was not unskilful in the learning of the Greeks, and in dependance on that skill it was, that he undertook to write a history of these affairs, as aiming by his way of haranguing to disguise the truth. But as to this man, and how ill were his character and conduct of life, and how he and his brother were, in a great measure, the authors of our destruction, I shall give the reader an account in the progress of my narration. So when Justus had, by his persuasions, prevailed with the citizens of Tiberias to take arms, nay, and had forced a great many so to do against their will, he went out, and set the villages that belonged to Gadara and Hippos on fire; which villages were situated on the borders of Tiberias, and of the region of Scythopolis.

10. And this was the state Tiberias was now in. But as for Gischala, its affairs were thus: When John, the son of Levi, saw some of his citizens much elevated upon their revolt from the Romans, he laboured to restrain them, and entreated them, that they would keep their allegiance to them. But he could not gain his purpose, although he did his en-

deavours to the utmost; for the neighbouring people of Gadara, and Gabara, and Sogana, with the Tyrians, got together a great army, and fell upon Gischala, and took Gischala by force, and set it on fire; and when they had entirely demolished it, they returned -home. Upon which John was so enraged, that he armed all his men; and joined battle with the people forementioned, and rebuilt Gischala after a manner better than before, and fortified it with walls for its future security.

11. But Gamala persevered in its allegiance to the Romans, for the reason following: Philip the son of Jacimus, who was their governor under king Agrippa, had been unexpectedly preserved when the royal palace at Jerusalem had been besieged; but as he fled away, had fallen into another danger, and that was of being killed by Manahem, and the robbers that were with him, but certain Babylonians, who were of his kindred, and were then in Jerusalem, hindered the robbers from executing their design. So Philip stayed there four days, and fled away on the fifth, having disguised himself with fictitious hair, that he might not be discovered; and when he was come to one of the villages to him belonging, but one that was situated at the borders of the citadel of Gamala, he sent to some of those that were under him, and commanded them to come to him. But God himself hindered that his intention, and this for his own advantage also; for had it not so happened, he had certainly perished. For a fever having seized upon him immediately, he wrote to Agrippa and Bernice, and gave them to one of his freed men to carry them to Varus, who at this time was procurator of the kingdom, which the king and his sister had intrusted him withal, while they were gone to Berytus with an intention of meeting Gessius. When Varus

had received these letters of Philip, and had learned that he was preserved, he was very uneasy at it, as supposing that he should appear useless to the king and his sister, now Philip was come. He therefore produced the carrier of the letters before the multitude, and accused him of forging the same; and said, that he spoke falsely when he related that Philip was not at Jerusalem, fighting among the Jews against the Romans. So he slew him. And when this freed man of Philip did not return again, Philip was doubtful what should be the occasion of his stay, and sent a second messenger with letters, that he might upon his return, inform him what had befallen the other that had been sent before, and why he tarried so long. Varus accused this messenger also, when he came, of telling a falsehood, and slew him. For he was puffed up by the Syrians that were at Cæsarea, and had great expectations; for they said that Agrippa would be slain by the Romans for the crimes which the Jews had committed, and that he should himself take the government, as derived from their kings; for Varus was, by the confession of all, of the royal family, as being a descendent of Sohemus, who had enjoyed a tetrarchy about Libanus; for which reason it was that he was puffed up, and kept the letters to himself. He contrived, also, that the king should not meet with those writings, by guarding all the passes, lest any one should escape, and inform the king what had been done. He moreover slew many of the Jews, in order to gratify the Syrians of Cæsarea. He had a mind also to join with the Trachonites in Batanea, and to take up arms and make an assault upon the Babylonian Jews that were at Ecbatana; for that was the name they went by. He therefore called to him twelve of the Jews of Cæsarea, of the best character, and ordered them to go to

Ecbatana, and inform their countrymen who dwelt there, that Varus hath heard, that "you intend to march against the king; but, not believing that report, he hath sent us to persuade you to lay down your arms, and that this compliance will be a sign: that he did well not to give credit to those that raised the report concerning you." He also enjoined them to send seventy of their principal men to make a defence for them as to the accusation laid against them. So when the twelve messengers came to their countrymen at Ecbatana, and found that they had no designs of innovation at all, they persuaded them to send the seventy men also; who not at all suspecting what would come, sent them accordingly. So these seventy[1] went down to Cæsarea, together with the twelve ambassadors, where Varus met them with the king's forces, and slew them all, together with the [twelve] ambassadors, and made an expedition against the Jews of Ecbatana. But there was one of the seventy who escaped, and made haste to inform the Jews of their coming; upon which they took their arms, with their wives and children, and retired to the citadel at Gamala, leaving their own villages full of all sorts of good things, and having many ten thousands of cattle therein. When Philip was informed of these things, he also came to the citadel of Gamala; and when he was come, the multitude cried aloud, and desired him to resume the government, and to make an expedition against Varus, and the Syrians of Cæsarea; for it was reported that they had slain the king. But Philip restrained their zeal, and put them in mind of the benefits the king had bestowed upon them; and told them how powerful the Romans were, and said it was not for their advantage to make war

---

[1] The famous Jewish numbers of twelve and seventy are here remarkable.

with them; and at length he prevailed with them. But now, when the king was acquainted with Varus' design, which was to cut off the Jews of Cæsarea, being many ten thousands, with their wives and children, and all in one day, he called to him Equiculus Modius, and sent him to be Varus' successor, as we have elsewhere related. But still Philip kept possession of the citadel of Gamala, and of the country adjoining to it, which thereby continued in their allegiance to the Romans.

12. Now, as soon as I was come into Galilee, and had learned this state of things by the information of such as told me of them, I wrote to the Sanhedrim at Jerusalem about them, and required their direction what I should do. Their direction was, that I should continue there, and that, if my fellow-legates were willing, I should join with them in the care of Galilee. But those my fellow-legates, having gotten great riches from those tithes which as priests were their dues, and were given to them, determined to return to their own country. Yet when I desired them to stay so long, that we might first settle the public affairs, they complied with me. So I removed, together with them, from the city of Sepphoris, and came to a certain village called Bethmaus, four furlongs distant from Tiberias; and thence I sent messengers to the senate of Tiberias, and desired that the principal men of the city would come to me: and when they were come, Justus himself being also with them, I told them, that I was sent to them by the people of Jerusalem as a legate, together with these other priests, in order to persuade them to demolish that house which Herod the tetrarch had built there, and which had the figures of living creatures in it, although our laws had forbidden us to make any such figures; and I desired, that they would give us

leave so to do immediately. But for a good while Capellus and the principal men belonging to the city would not give us leave, but were at length entirely overcome by us, and were induced to be of our opinion. So Jesus the son of Sapphias, one of those whom we have already mentioned as the leader of a seditious tumult of mariners and poor people, prevented us, and took with him certain Galileans, and set the entire palace on fire, and thought he should get a great deal of money thereby, because he saw some of the roofs gilt with gold. They also plundered a great deal of the furniture, which was done without our approbation; for, after we had discoursed Capellus and the principal men of the city, we departed from Bethmaus and went into the upper Galilee. But Jesus and his party slew all the Greeks that were inhabitants of Tiberias, and as many others as were their enemies before the war began.

13. When I understood this state of things, I was greatly provoked, and went down to Tiberias, and took all the care I could of the royal furniture, to recover all that could be recovered from such as had plundered it. They consisted of candlesticks made of Corinthian brass; and of royal tables, and of a great quantity of uncoined silver; and I resolved to preserve whatsoever came to my hand for the king. So I sent for ten of the principal men of the senate, and for Capellus the son of Antyllus, and committed the furniture to them, with this charge, that they should part with it to nobody else but to myself. From thence I and my fellow-legates went to Gischala to John, as desirous to know his intentions, and soon saw that he was for innovations, and had a mind to the principality; for he desired me to give him authority to carry off that corn which belonged to Cæsar, and lay in the villages of Upper

Galilee; and he pretended that he would expend what it came to in building the walls of his own city. But when I perceived what he endeavoured at, and what he had in his mind, I said I would not permit him so to do; for that I thought either to keep it for the Romans, or for myself, now I was intrusted with the public affairs there by the people of Jerusalem. But when he was not able to prevail with me, he betook himself to my fellow-legates; for they had no sagacity in providing for futurity, and were very ready to take bribes. So he corrupted them with money to decree, that all that corn which was within his province should be delivered to him; while I, who was but one, was outvoted by two, and held my tongue. Then did John introduce another cunning contrivance of his; for he said, that those Jews who inhabited Cæsarea Philippi, and were shut up by the order of the king's deputy there, had sent to him to desire him, that, since they had no oil that was pure for their use, he would provide a sufficient quantity of such oil that came from the Greeks, and thereby transgress their own laws. Now this was said by John, not out of his regard to religion, but out of his most flagrant desire of gain; for he knew, that two sextaries were sold with them at Cæsarea for one drachma, but that at Gischala fourscore sextaries were sold for four drachma. So he gave ·order, that all the oil which was there should be carried away, as having my permission for so doing; which yet I did not grant him voluntarily, but only out of fear of the multitude, since, if I had forbidden him, I should have been stoned by them. When I had therefore permitted this to be done by John, he gained vast sums of money by this his knavery.

14. But when I had dismissed my fellow-legates, and sent them back to Jerusalem, I took care to have

arms provided, and the cities fortified. And, when I had sent for the most hardy among the robbers, I saw that it was not in my power to take their arms from them; but I persuaded the multitude to allow them money as pay, and told them it was better for them to give them a little willingly, rather than to [be forced to] overlook them when they plundered their goods from them. And when I had obliged them to take an oath not to come into that country, unless they were invited to come, or else when they had not their pay given them, I dismissed them, and charged them neither to make an expedition against the Romans, nor against those their neighbours that lay round about them; for my first care was to keep Galilee in peace. So I was willing to have the principal of the Galileans, in all seventy, as hostages for their fidelity, but still under the notion of friendship. Accordingly I made them my friends and companions as I journeyed, and sent them to judge causes; and with their approbation it was that I gave my sentences, while I endeavoured not to mistake what justice required, and to keep my hands clear of all bribery in these determinations.

15. I was now about the thirtieth year of my age; in which time of life it is a hard thing for any one to escape the calumnies of the envious, although he restrain himself from fulfilling any unlawful desires, especially where a person is-in great authority. Yet did I preserve every woman free from injuries; and, as to what presents were offered me, I despised them, as not standing in need of them. Nor indeed would I take those tithes, which were due to me as a priest, from those that brought them. Yet do I confess, that I took part of the spoils of those Syrians who inhabited the cities that adjoined to us, when I had conquered them, and that I sent them to my

THE HOT BATHS OF TIBERIAS.

A deep depression runs nearly due south, and at a sharp descent, from the foot of the Lebanon range, including the waters of Merom, the Sea of Galilee, and the bed of the Jordan, to the Dead Sea; and in this sea also terminates a corresponding valley or ravine, which, commencing at the head of the eastern arm of the Red Sea, Bahr Akabah, and running north-east by north, constitutes the torrent course, called Wady el Arabah. Throughout this rugged valley the indications of intense volcanic action, in a remote age, may everywhere be seen, and especially so on the western borders of the Lake of Tiberias (Sea of Galilee) where the perennial and copious rise of several strongly impregnated springs, at a high temperature, sufficiently prove that those interior fires which once convulsed the surface, and found vent in the two craters that are now lakes, are not extinct. Nor does it seem—if we take the testimony of the earliest writers who mention these hot springs—and they are mentioned by a series of writers during two thousand years, either that the subterranean heat has been diminished in the course of ages, or that the waters have lost their medicative properties.

The structures exhibited in the engraving were erected by Ibrahim Pasha, during the period of his occupation of the Syrian provinces (1833). The view here given is taken in a direction nearly north-west by north. The remains of Tiberias—the modern Tubariyeh, are seen skirting the margin of the lake on a gently rising ground at the distance of less than two miles.

kindred at Jerusalem; although, when I twice took Sepphoris by force, and Tiberias four times, and Gadara once, and when I had subdued and taken John, who often laid treacherous snares for me, I did not punish [with death] either him or any of the people forenamed, as the progress of this discourse will show. And on this account, I suppose, it was that God,[1] who is never unacquainted with those that do as they ought to do, delivered me still out of the hands of these my enemies, and afterward preserved me when I fell into those many dangers which I shall relate hereafter.

16. Now the multitude of the Galileans had that great kindness for me, and fidelity to me, that when their cities were taken by force, and their wives and children carried into slavery, they did not so deeply lament for their own calamities, as they were solicitous for my preservation. But when John saw this, he envied me, and wrote to me, desiring that I would give him leave to come down, and make use of the hot baths of Tiberias for the recovery of the health of his body. Accordingly, I did not hinder him, as having no suspicion of any wicked designs of his; and I wrote to those to whom I had committed the administration of the affairs of Tiberias by name, that they should provide a lodging for John; and for such as should come with him, and should procure him what necessaries soever he should stand in need of. Now at this time my abode was in a village of Galilee, which is named *Cana*.

17. But when John was come to the city of Ti-

---

[1] Our Josephus shows, both here and every where, that he was a most religious person, and one that had a deep sense of God and his providence upon his mind, and ascribed all his numerous and wonderful escapes and preservations, in times of danger, to God's blessing him, and taking care of him, and this on account of his acts of piety, justice, humanity, and charity, to the Jews his brethren.

berias, he persuaded the men to revolt from their
fidelity to me, and to adhere to him; and many of
them gladly received that invitation of his, as ever
fond of innovations, and by nature disposed to
changes, and delighting in seditions: but they were
chiefly Justus and his father Pistus, that were earnest
in their revolt from me, and their adherence to John.
But I came upon them, and prevented them: for a
messenger had come to me from Silas, whom I had
made governor of Tiberias, as I have said already,
and had told me of the inclinations of the people of
Tiberias, and advised me to make haste thither; for
that, if I made any delay, the city would come under
another's jurisdiction. Upon the receipt of this letter
of Silas', I took two hundred men along with me,
and travelled all night, having sent before a messenger to let the people of Tiberias know that I was
coming to them. When I came near to the city,
which was early in the morning, the multitude came
out to meet me: and John came with them, and
saluted me, but in a most disturbed manner, as being
afraid that my coming was to call him to an account
for what I was now sensible he was doing. So he
in great haste went to his lodging. But when I was
in the open place of the city, having dismissed the
guards I had about me, excepting one, and ten armed
men that were with him, I attempted to make a
speech to the multitude of the people of Tiberias:
and, standing on a certain elevated place, I entreated
them not to be so hasty in their revolt; for that such
a change in their behaviour would be to their reproach,
and that they would then justly be suspected by
those that should be their governors hereafter, as if
they were not likely to be faithful to them neither.

18. But, before I had spoken all I designed, I
heard one of my own domestics bidding me come

down; for that it was not a proper time to take care of retaining the good-will of the people of Tiberias, but to provide for my own safety, and escape my enemies there; for John had chosen the most trusty of those armed men that were about him out of those thousand that he had with him, and had given them orders, when he sent them to kill me, having learned that I was alone, excepting some of my domestics. So those that were sent came as they were ordered, and they had executed what they came about, had I not leaped down from the elevation I stood on, and with one of my guards, whose name was James, been carried [out of the crowd] upon the back of one Herod of Tiberias, and guided by him down to the lake, where I seized a ship, and got into it, and escaped my enemies unexpectedly, and came to Taricheæ.

19. Now, as soon as the inhabitants of the city understood the perfidiousness of the people of Tiberias, they were greatly provoked at them. So they snatched up their arms, and desired me to be their leader against them; for they said they would avenge their commander's cause upon them. They also carried the report of what had been done to me to all the Galileans, and eagerly endeavoured to irritate them against the people of Tiberias and desired that vast numbers of them would get together, and come to them, that they might act in concert with their commander, what should be determined as fit to be done. Accordingly, the Galileans came to me in great numbers, from all parts, with their weapons, and besought me to assault Tiberias, to take it by force, and to demolish it, till it lay even with the ground, and then to make slaves of its inhabitants, with their wives and children. Those that were Josephus' friends also, and had escaped out of Ti-

berias, gave him the same advice. But I did not comply with them; thinking it a terrible thing to begin a civil war among them; for I thought that this contention ought not to proceed farther than words, nay, I told them that it was not for their own advantage to do what they would have me to do, while the Romans expected no other than that we should destroy one another by our mutual seditions. And by saying this, I put a stop to the anger of the Galileans.

20. But now John was afraid for himself, since his treachery had proved unsuccessful. So he took the armed men that were about him, and removed from Tiberias to Gischala, and wrote to me to apologize for himself concerning what had been done, as if it had been done without his approbation, and desired me to have no suspicion of him to his disadvantage. He also added oaths and certain horrible curses upon himself, and supposed he should be thereby believed in the points he wrote about to me.

21. But now another great number of the Galileans came together again with their weapons, as knowing the man how wicked and how sadly perjured he was, and desired me to lead them against him, and promised me that they would utterly destroy both him and Gischala. Hereupon I professed, that I was obliged to them for their readiness to serve me, and that I would more than requite that their good-will to me. However, I entreated them to restrain themselves, and begged of them to give me leave to do what I intended, which was to put an end to these troubles without bloodshed; and when I had prevailed with the multitude of the Galileans to let me do so, I came to Sepphor's

22 But the inhabitants of this city having determined to continue in their allegiance to the Romans,

were afraid of my coming to them, and tried, by putting me upon another action, to divert me, that they might be freed from the terror they were in. Accordingly they sent to Jesus, the captain of those robbers who were in the confines of Ptolemais, and promised to give him a great deal of money, if he would come with those forces he had with him, which were in number eight hundred, and fight with us. Accordingly he complied with what they desired, upon the promises they had made him, and was desirous to fall upon us when we were unprepared for him, and knew nothing of his coming beforehand. So he sent to me, and desired that I would give him leave to come and salute me. When I had given him that leave, which I did without the least knowledge of his treacherous intentions beforehand, he took his band of robbers, and made haste to come to me. Yet did not this his knavery succeed well at last; for, as he was already nearly approaching, one of those with him deserted him, and came to me, and told me what he had undertaken to do. When I was informed of this, I went into the market-place, and pretended to know nothing of his treacherous purpose. I took with me many Galileans that were armed, as also some of those of Tiberias: and, when I had given orders that all the roads should be carefully guarded, I charged the keepers of the gates to give admittance to none but Jesus, when he came with the principal of his men, and to exclude the rest; and in case they aimed to force themselves in, to use stripes, [in order to repel them.] Accordingly, those that had received such a charge did as they were bidden, and Jesus came in with a few others; and when I had ordered him to throw down his arms immediately, and told him, that if he refused so to do, he was a dead man, he seeing armed men standing all round about him, was terrified, and complied; and as for those of his followers that were excluded, when they were informed that he was seized, they ran away. I then called Jesus to me by himself, and told him, that "I was not a stranger to that treacherous design he had against me, nor was I ignorant by whom he was sent for; that however, I would forgive what he had done already; if he would repent of it, and be faithful to me hereafter." And thus upon his promise to do all that I desired, I let him go, and gave him leave to get those whom he had formerly had with him together again. But I threatened the inhabitants of Sepphoris, that if they would not leave off their ungrateful treatment of me, I would punish them sufficiently.

23. At this time it was that two great men, who were under the jurisdiction of the king [Agrippa,] came to me out of the region of Trachonitis, bringing their horses and their arms, and carrying with them their money also; and when the Jews would force them to be circumcised, if they would stay among them, I would not permit them to have any force put upon them,[1] but said to them, "Every one ought to worship God according to his own inclinations, and not to be constrained by force; and that these men, who had fled to us for protection, ought not to be so treated as to repent of their coming hither." And when I had pacified the multitude, I provided for the men that were come to us whatsoever it was they wanted, according to their usual way of living, and that in great plenty also.

---

[1] Josephus' opinion is here well worth noting, that every one is to be permitted to worship God according to his own conscience, and is not to be compelled in matters of religion: as one may here observe on the contrary, that the rest of the Jews were still for obliging all those who married Jews to be circumcised, and become Jews, and were ready to destroy all that would not submit to do so. See sect. 31, and Luke ix. 54.

24. Now king Agrippa sent an army to make themselves masters of the citadel of Gamala, and over it Equiculus Modius: but the forces that were sent were not enow tô encompass the citadel quite round, but lay before it in the open places, and besieged it. But when Ebutius the decurion, who was intrusted with the government of the great plain, heard that I was at Simonias, a village situated in the confines of Galilee, and was distant from him sixty furlongs, he took a hundred horsemen that were with him by night and a certain number of footmen, about two hundred, and brought the inhabitants of the city Gibea along with him as auxiliaries, and marched in the night, and came to the village where I abode. Upon this I pitched my camp over against him, which had a great number of forces in it; but Ebutius tried to draw us down into the plain, as greatly depending on his horsemen; but we would not come down; for when I was satisfied of the advantage that his horse would have if we came down into the plain, while we were all footmen, I resolved to join battle with the enemy where I was. Now Ebutius and his party made a courageous opposition for some time; but when he saw that his horse were useless to him in that place, he retired back to the city Gibea, having lost three of his men in the fight. So I followed him directly with two thousand armed men; and when I was at the city Besara, that lay in the confines of Ptolemais, but twenty furlongs from Gibea, where Ebutius abode, I placed my armed men on the outside of the village, and gave orders that they should guard the passes with great care, that the enemy should not disturb us, until we should have carried off the corn, a great quantity of which lay there; it belonged to Bernice the queen and had been gathered together

out of the neighbouring villages into Besara; so I loaded my camels and asses, a great number of which I had brought along with me, and sent the corn into Galilee. When I had done this, I offered Ebutius battle; but when he would not accept of the offer, for he was terrified at our readiness and courage, I altered my route, and marched towards Neopolitanus, because I had heard that the country about Tiberias was laid waste by him. This Neopolitanus was captain of a troop of horse, and had the custody of Scythopolis intrusted to his care by the enemy: and when I had hindered him from doing any farther mischief to Tiberias, I set myself to make provision for the affairs of Galilee.

24. But when John, the son of Levi, who, as we before told you, abode at Gischala, was informed how all things had succeeded to my mind, and that I was much in favour with those that were under me, as also that the enemy were greatly afraid of me, he was not pleased with it, as thinking my prosperity tended to his ruin. So he took up a bitter envy and enmity against me; and hoping, that if he could inflame those that were under me to hate me, he should put an end to the prosperity I was in, he tried to persuade the inhabitants of Tiberias, and of Sepphoris, (and for those of Gabara he supposed they would be also of the same mind with the others,) which were the greatest cities of Galilee, to revolt from their subjection to me, and to be of his party; and told them, that he would command them better than I did. As for the people of Sepphoris, who belonged to neither of us, because they had chosen to be in subjection to the Romans, they did not comply with his proposal: and for those of Tiberias, they did not indeed so far comply as to make a revolt from under me, but they agreed to be his

friends, while the inhabitants of Gabara did go over to John: and it was Simon that persuaded them so to do, one who was both the principal man in the city, and a particular friend and companion of John. It is true, these did not openly own the making a revolt, because they were in great fear of the Galileans, and had frequent experience of the good-will they bore to me; yet did they privately watch for a proper opportunity to lay snares for me, and indeed I thereby came into the greatest danger, on the occasion following.

25. There were some bold young men of the village Dabaritta, who observed that the wife of Ptolemy, the king's procurator, was to make a progress over the great plain with a mighty attendance, and with some horsemen that followed, as a guard to them, and this out of a country that was subject to the king and queen, into the jurisdiction of the Romans; and fell upon them on the sudden, and obliged the wife of Ptolemy to fly away, and plundered all the carriages. They also came to me to Taricheæ, with four mules' lading of garments, and other furniture; and the weight of the silver they brought was not small, and there were five hundred pieces of gold also. Now I had a mind to preserve these spoils for Ptolemy, who was my countryman; and it is prohibited us by our laws even to spoil our enemies; so I said to those that brought these spoils, that they ought to be kept in order to rebuild the walls of Jerusalem with them, when they came to be sold. But the young men took it very ill that they did not receive a part of these spoils for themselves, as they expected to have done; so they went among the villages in the neighbourhood of Tiberias, and told the people, that I was going to betray their country to the Romans, and that I used deceitful

language to them, when I said that what had been thus gotten by rapine should be kept for the rebuilding of the walls of the city of Jerusalem; although I had resolved to restore these spoils again to their former owner. And indeed they were herein not mistaken as to my intentions; for when I had gotten clear of them, I sent for two of the principal men, Dassion, and Janneus the son of Levi, persons that were among the chief friends of the king, and commanded them to take the furniture that had been plundered, and to send it to him; and I threatened that I would order them to be put to death, by way of punishment, if they discovered this my command to any other person.

26. Now, when all Galilee was filled with this rumour, that their country was about to be betrayed by me to the Romans, and when all men were exasperated against me, and ready to bring me to punishment, the inhabitants of Taricheæ did also themselves suppose that what the young men said was true, and persuaded my guards and armed men to leave me when I was asleep, and to come presently to the hippodrome, in order there to take counsel against me their commander. And, when they had prevailed with them, and they were gotten together, they found there a great company assembled already, who all joined in one clamour, to bring the man who was so wicked to them as to betray them, to his due punishment; and it was Jesus, the son of Sapphias, who principally set them on. He was ruler in Tiberias, a wicked man, and naturally disposed to make disturbances in matters of consequence; a seditious person he was indeed, and an innovator beyond every body else. He then took the laws of Moses into his hands, and came into the midst of the people, and said, "O my fellow citizens! if you are not disposed

to hate Josephus on your own account, have regard, however, to these laws of your country, which your commander-in-chief is going to betray; hate him therefore on both these accounts, and bring the man who hath acted thus insolently, to his deserved punishment."

27. When he had said this, and the multitude had openly applauded him for what he had said, he took some of the armed men, and made haste away to the house in which I lodged, as if he would kill me immediately, while I was wholly insensible of all till this disturbance happened; and by reason of the pains I had been taking, was fallen fast asleep. But Simon, who was intrusted with the care of my body, and was the only person that stayed with me, and saw the violent incursion the citizens made upon me, he awaked me, and told me of the danger I was in, and desired me to let him kill me, that I might die bravely, and like a general, before my enemies came in, and forced me (to kill myself,) or kill me themselves. Thus did he discourse to me; but I committed the care of my life to God, and made haste to go out to the multitude. Accordingly, I put on a black garment, and hung my sword at my neck, and went by such a different way to the hippodrome, wherein I thought none of my adversaries would meet me; so I appeared among them on the sudden, and fell down flat on the earth, and bedewed the ground with my tears: then I seemed to them all an object of compassion. And when I perceived the change that was made on the multitude, I tried to divide their opinions, before the armed men should return from my house; so I granted them, that I had been as wicked as they supposed me to be; but still I entreated them to let me first inform them for what use I had kept that money which arose from the

plunder, and that they might then kill me if they pleased; and, upon the multitude's ordering me to speak, the armed men came upon me, and when they saw me, they ran to kill me; but when the multitude bid them hold their hands, they complied, and expected that as soon as I should own to them that I kept the money for the king, it would be looked on as a confession of my treason, and they should then be allowed to kill me.

28. When, therefore, silence was made by the whole multitude, I spoke thus to them: "O my countrymen! I refuse not to die, if justice so require. However, I am desirous to tell you the truth of this matter before I die: for as I know that this city of yours [Taricheæ] was a city of great hospitality, and filled with abundance of such men as have left their own countries, and are come hither to be partakers of your fortune whatever it be, I had a mind to build walls about it, out of this money, for which you are so angry with me, while yet it was to be expended in building your own walls." Upon my saying this, the people of Taricheæ and the strangers cried out, That "they gave me thanks, and desired me to be of good courage." Although the Galileans and the people of Tiberias continued in their wrath against me, insomuch that there arose a tumult among them, while some threatened to kill me, and some bid me not to regard them; but when I promised them that I would build them walls at Tiberias, and at other cities that wanted them, they gave credit to what I promised, and returned every one to his own home. So I escaped the forementioned danger, beyond all my hopes, and returned to my own house, accompanied with my friends, and twenty armed men also.

29. However, these robbers and other authors of this tumult, who were afraid on their own account, lest

I should punish them for what they had done, took six hundred armed men, and came to the house where I abode, in order to set it on fire. When this their insult was told me, I thought it indecent for me to run away, and I resolved to expose myself to danger, and to act with some boldness; so I gave orders to shut the doors, and went up into an inner room, and desired that they would send some of their men in to receive the money [from the spoils;] for I told them they would then have no occasion to be angry with me; and when they had sent in one of the boldest of them all, I had him whipped severely, and I commanded that one of his hands should be cut off, and hung about his neck; and in this case was he put out to those that sent him. At which procedure of mine they were greatly affrighted and in no small consternation, and were afraid that they should themselves be served in like manner, if they stayed there; for they supposed that I had in the house more armed men than they had themselves; so they ran away immediately, while I, by the use of this stratagem, escaped this their second treacherous design against me.

30. But there were still some that irritated the multitude against me, and said that those great men that belonged to the·king, ought not to be suffered to live, if they would not change their religion to the religion of those to whom they fled for safety: they spoke reproachfully of them also, and said, that they were wizards,[1] and such as called in the Romans upon them. So the multitude were soon deluded by such plausible pretences as were agreeable to their own inclinations, and were prevailed on by them. But when I was informed of this, I instructed the multi-

---

[1] Here we may observe the common Jewish notions of witchcraft; but that our Josephus was too wise to give any countenance to.

tude again, that those who fled to them for refuge ought not to be persecuted; I also laughed at the allegation about witchcraft,[1] and told them that the Romans would not maintain so many ten thousand soldiers, if they could overcome their enemies by wizards. Upon my saying this, the people assented for a while; but they returned afterward, as irritated by some ill people, against the great men; nay, they once made an assault upon the house in which they dwelt at Taricheæ, in order to kill them; which, when I was informed of, I was afraid lest so horrid a crime should take effect, and nobody else would make that city their refuge any more. I therefore came myself, and some others with me, to the house where these great men lived, and locked their doors, and had a trench drawn from their house leading to the lake, and sent for a ship, and embarked therein with them, and sailed to the confines of Hippos: I also paid them the value of their horses, nor in such a flight could I have their horses brought to them. I then dismissed them, and begged of them earnestly that they would courageously bear this distress which befell them. I was also myself greatly displeased that I was compelled to expose those that had fled to me to go again into an enemy's country; yet did I think it more eligible that they should perish among the Romans, if it should so happen, than in the country that was under my jurisdiction. However, they escaped at length, and king Agrippa forgave them their offences. And this was the conclusion of what concerned these men.

31. But as for the inhabitants of the city of Tiberias, they wrote to the king, and desired him to send them forces sufficient to be guard to their country; for that they were desirous to come over to him:

_____
[1] See the preceding note.

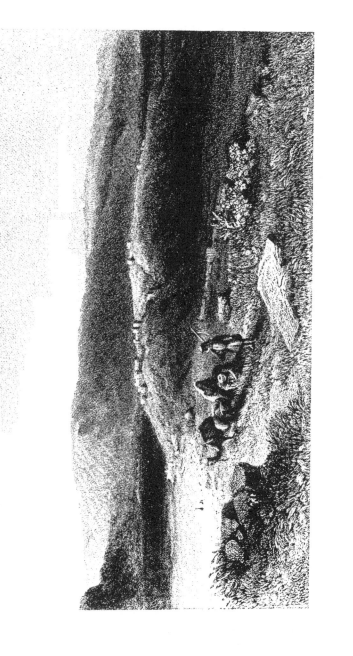

TARICHÆA.

The two towns, or cities, if they could claim to be so
designated—Tiberias and Tarichæa, the feuds and rivalries
of which occupy so considerable a space in the personal nar-
rative of Josephus, are situated at the distance of about four-
and-a-half miles, on the western margin of the lake; and
the latter place, near its southern extremity; Tiberias being
close upon the water's edge, and on a slope, which rises but
little above the level of the lake, while Tarichæa stands on
the brow of a hill, overlooking it, throughout its extent.

No difficulty can be thought to attach to the identification
of these sites, indicated as they are by the remains of the
two towns, with their fortifications, as well as by their mutual
bearing, and the relation of each to the Hot Springs. Besides
the traditional preservation of the Greek name of the one,
vouches for both; Tiberias having become the Arabic, Tubariyeh. Tarichæa has been less often visited and described
than its rival.

this was what they wrote to him. But when I came to them they desired me to build their walls, as I had promised them to do; for they had heard that the walls of Tariche æ were already built. I agreed to the proposal accordingly; and when I had made preparation for the entire building, I gave order to the architects to go to work; but on the third day, when I was gone to Tariche æ, which was thirty furlongs distant from Tiberias, it fell out, that some Roman horsemen were discovered on their march not far from the city, which made it be supposed that the forces were come from the king; upon which they shouted, and lifted up their voices in commendations of the king, and in reproaches against me. Hereupon one came running to me, and told me what their dispositions were, and that they had resolved to revolt from me; upon hearing which news, I was very much alarmed: for I had already sent away my armed men from Tariche æ, to their own homes, because the next day was our sabbath; for I would not have the people of Tariche æ disturbed [on that day] by a multitude of soldiers; and indeed, whenever I sojourned at that city, I never took any particular care for a guard about my own body, because I had had frequent instances of the fidelity its inhabitants bore to me. I had now about me no more than seven armed men besides some friends, and was doubtful what to do; for to send to recall my cwn forces I did not think proper, because the present day was almost over; and had those forces been with me, I could not take up arms on the next day, because our laws forbade us so to do; even though our necessity should be very great; and if I should permit the people of Tariche æ, and the strangers with them to guard the city, I saw that they would not be sufficient for that purpose, and I perceived

that I should be obliged to delay my assistance a
great while; for I thought with myself that the
forces that came from the king would prevent me,
and that I should be driven out of the city. I considered, therefore, how to get clear of these forces
by a stratagem; so I immediately placed those my
friends of Taricheæ, on whom I could best confide,
at the gates, to watch those very carefully who went
out at those gates; I also called to me the heads of
families, and bid every one of them to seize upon
a ship, to go on board it, and to take a master with
them, and follow him to the city of Tiberias. I also
myself went on board one of those ships, with my
friends, and the seven armed men already mentioned,
and sailed for Tiberias.

32. But now, when the people of Tiberias perceived that there were no forces come from the king,
and yet saw the whole lake full of ships, they were
in fear what would become of their city, and were
greatly terrified, as supposing that the ships were
full of men on board; so then they changed their
minds, and threw down their weapons, and met me
with their wives and children, and made acclamations
to me with great commendations; for they imagined
that I did not know their former inclinations [to
have been against me;] so they persuaded me to
spare the city. But when I was come near enough,
I gave order to the masters of the ships to cast anchor
a good way off the land, that the people of Tiberias
might not perceive that the ships had no men on
board; but I went nearer to the people in óne of
the ships, and rebuked them for their folly, and that
they were so fickle as, without any just occasion in
the world, to revolt from their fidelity to me. However, I assured them, that I would entirely forgive
them for the time to come, if they would send ten

of the ringleaders of the multitude to me; and when they complied readily with this proposal, and sent me the men forementioned, I put them on board a ship, and sent them away to Taricheæ, and ordered them to be kept in prison.

33. And by this stratagem it was, that I gradually got all the senate of Tiberias into my power, and sent them to the city forementioned, with many of the principal men among the populace, and those not fewer in number than the other. But, when the multitude saw into what great miseries they had brought themselves, they desired me to punish the author of this sedition: his name was *Clitus,* a young man, bold and rash in his undertakings. Now, since I thought it not agreeable to piety to put one of my own people to death, and yet found it necessary to punish him, I ordered Levi, one of my own guards, to go to him, and cut off one of Clitus' hands; but as he that was ordered to do this, was afraid to go out of the ship alone, among so great a multitude, I was not willing that the timorousness of the soldier should appear to the people of Tiberias. So I called to Clitus himself, and said to him, "Since thou deservest to lose both thine hands for thy ingratitude to me, be thou thine own executioner, lest, if thou refusest so to be, thou undergo a worse punishment." And, when he earnestly begged of me to spare him one of his hands, it was with difficulty that I granted it. So, in order to prevent the loss of both his hands, he willingly took his sword, and cut off his own left hand; and this put an end to the sedition.

34. Now the men of Tiberias, after I was gone to Taricheæ, perceived what stratagem I had used against them, and they admired how I had put an end to their foolish sedition, without shedding of blood. But now, when I had sent for some of those

multitudes of the people of Tiberias out of prison, among whom were Justus and his father Pistus, I made them to sup with me; and during our supper-time, I said to them, that I knew the power of the Romans was superior to all others, but did not say so [publicly] because of the robbers. So I advised them to do as I did, and to wait for a proper opportunity, and not to be uneasy at my being their commander; for that they could not expect to have another who would use the like moderation that I had done. I also put Justus in mind how the Galileans had cut off his brother's hands, before ever I came from Jerusalem, upon an accusation laid against him, as if he had been a rogue, and had forged some letters; as also how the people of Gamala, in a sedition they raised against the Babylonians, after the departure of Philip, slew Chares, who was a kinsman of Philip, and withal how they had wisely punished Jesus, his brother Justus' sister's husband, [with death.] When I had said this to them during supper-time, I in the morning ordered Justus, and all the rest that were in prison, to be loosed out of it, and sent away.

35. But before this, it happened that Philip, the son of Jacimus, went out of the citadel of Gamala upon the following occasion: When Philip had been informed that Varus was put out of his government by king Agrippa; and that Modius Equiculus, a man that was of old his friend and companion, was come to succeed him, he wrote to him, and related what turns of fortune he had had, and desired him to forward the letters he sent to the king and queen. Now, when Modius had received these letters, he was exceedingly glad, and sent the letters to the king and queen, who were then about Berytus. But when king Agrippa knew that the story about Philip was false, (for it had been given out, that the Jews had

begun a war with the Romans, and that this Philip
had been their commander in that war,) he sent some
horsemen to conduct Philip to him, and, when he
was come, he saluted him very obligingly, and showed
him to the Roman commanders, and told them that
this was the man of whom the report had gone about
as if he had revolted from the Romans. He also
bid him to take some horsemen with him, and to go
quickly to the citadel of Gamala, and to bring out
thence all his domestics, and to restore the Babylonians to Batanea again. He also gave it him in
charge to take all possible care that none of his subjects should be guilty of making any innovation.
Accordingly, upon these directions from the king,
he made haste to do what he was commanded.

36. Now there was one Joseph, the son of a
female physician, who excited a great many young
men to join with him. He also insolently addressed
himself to the principal persons at Gamala, and persuaded them to revolt from the king, and take up
arms, and gave them hopes that they should, by his
means, recover their liberty. And some they forced
into the service; and those that would not acquiesce
in what they had resolved on, they slew. They also
slew Chares, and with him Jesus, one of his kinsmen, and a brother of Justus of Tiberias, as we have
already said. Those of Gamala also wrote to me,
desiring me to send them an armed force, and workmen to raise up the walls of their city; nor did I
reject either of their requests. The region of Gaulonitis did also revolt from the king, as far as the village Solyma. I also built a wall about Seleucia and
Soganni, which are villages naturally of very great
strength. Moreover, I, in like manner, walled several villages of Upper Galilee, though they were
very rocky of themselves. Their names are, Jamnia,

and Meroth, and Achabare. I also fortified, in the Lower Galilee, the cities Tarichee, Tiberias, Sepphoris, and the villages, the Cave of Arbela, Bersobe, Selamin, Jotapata, Caphareccho, and Siggo, and Japha, and Mount Tabor. I also laid up a great quantity of corn in these places, and arms withal, that might be for their security afterward.

37. But the hatred that John, the son of Levi, bore to me, grew now more violent, while he could not bear my prosperity with patience. So he proposed to himself, by all means possible, to make away with me, and built the walls of Gischala, which was the place of his nativity. He then sent his brother Simon, and Jonathan the son of Sisenna, and about a hundred armed men to Jerusalem, to Simon the son of Gamaliel,[1] in order to persuade him to induce the commonality of Jerusalem to take from me the government over the Galileans, and to give their suffrages for conferring that authority upon him. This Simon was of the city Jerusalem, and of a very noble family of the sect of the Pharisees, which are supposed to excel others in the accurate knowledge of the laws of their country. He was a man of great wisdom and reason, and capable of restoring public affairs by his prudence, when they were in an ill posture. He was also an old friend and companion of John's; but at that time he had a difference with me. When therefore he had received such an exhortation, he persuaded the high priests, Ananus, and Jesus the son of Gamala, and some others of the same seditious faction, to cut me down, now I was growing so great, and not to overlook me while

---

[1] This Gamaliel may be the very same that is mentioned by the rabbins in the Mishna in Juchasin and in Porto Mosis, as is observed in the Latin notes. He might be also that Gamaliel II. whose grandfather was Gamaliel I. who is mentioned Acts v. 34, and at whose feet St. Paul was brought up, Acts xxii. 2. See Frid. at the year 449.

I was aggrandizing myself to the height of glory; and he said, that it would be for the advantage of the Galileans, if I were deprived of my government there. Ananus also, and his friends, desired them to make no delay about the matter, lest I should get the knowledge of what was doing too soon, and should come and make an assault upon the city with a great army. This was the counsel of Simon; but Ananus the high priest demonstrated to them, that this was not an easy thing to be done, because many of the high priests and of the rulers of the people bore witness that I had acted like an excellent general, and that it was the work of ill men to accuse one against whom they had nothing to say.

38. When Simon heard Ananus say this, he desired that the messengers would conceal the thing, and not let it come among many; for that he would take care to have Josephus removed out of Galilee very quickly. So he called for John's brother, [Simon] and charged him, that they should send presents to Ananus and his friends; for, as he said, they might probably by that means persuade them to change their minds. And indeed Simon did at length thus compass what he aimed at; for Ananus, and those with him, being corrupted by bribes, agreed to expel me out of Galilee, without making the rest of the citizens acquainted with what they were doing. Accordingly they resolved to send men of distinction as to their families, and of distinction as to their learning also. Two of these were of the populace, Jonathan [1] and Ananias, by sect of the Pharisees; while the third, Jozar, was of the stock of the priests, and a Pharisee also; and Simon, the last of them, was of the youngest of the high priests. These had

---

[1] This Jonathan is also taken notice of in the Latin note, as the same that is mentioned by the rabbins in Porto Mosis.

it given them in charge, that, when they were come to the multitude of the Galileans, they should ask them, what was the reason of their love to me? and if they said, that it was because I was born in Jerusalem, that they should reply, that they four were all born at the same place; and if they should say, it was because I was well versed in their law, they should reply, that neither were they unacquainted with the practices of their country; but if, besides these, they should say, they loved me because I was a priest, they should reply, that two of these were priests also.

39. Now, when they had given Jonathan and his companions these instructions, they gave them forty thousand [drachmæ] out of the public money: but when they heard that there was a certain Galilean that then sojourned at Jerusalem, whose name was Jesus, who had about him a band of six hundred armed men, they sent for him, and gave him three months' pay, and gave him orders to follow Jonathan and his companions, and be obedient to them. They also gave money to three hundred men that were citizens of Jerusalem, to maintain them all, and ordered them also to follow the ambassadors; and when they had complied, and were gotten ready for the march, Jonathan and his companions went out with them, having along with them John's brother, and a hundred armed men. The charge that was given them by those that sent them was this, that if I would voluntarily lay down my arms, they should send me alive to the city Jerusalem, but that, in case I opposed them, they should kill me and fear nothing; for that it was their command for them so to do. They also wrote to John to make all ready for fighting me, and gave order to the inhabitants of Sepphoris and Gabara, and Tiberias, to send auxiliaries to John.

40. Now, as my father wrote me an account of this, (for Jesus the son of Gamala, who was present in that council, a friend and companion of mine, told him of it,) I was very much troubled, as discovering thereby, that my fellow-citizens proved so ungrateful to me, as, out of envy, to give order that I should be slain; my father earnestly pressed me also in his letter to come to him, for that he longed to see his son before he died. I informed my friends of these things, and that in three days time I should leave the country, and go home. Upon hearing this, they were all very sorry, and desired me, with tears in their eyes, not to leave them to be destroyed; for so they thought they should be, if I were deprived of the command over them: but as I did not grant their request, but was taking care of my own safety, the Galileans, out of their dread of the consequence of my departure, that they should then be at the mercy of the robbers, sent messengers over all Galilee to inform them of my resolution to leave them. Whereupon as soon as they heard it, they got together in great numbers, from all parts, with their wives and children; and this they did, as it appeared to me, not more out of their affection to me, than out of their fear on their own account; for, while I stayed with them, they supposed that they should suffer no harm. So they all came into the great plain wherein I lived, the name of which was *Asochis*.

41. But wonderful it was what a dream I saw that very night; for when I had betaken myself to my bed, as grieved and disturbed at the news that had been written to me, it seemed to me, that a certain person stood by me,[1] and said; "O Josephus! leave

---

[1] This I take to be the first of Josephus' remarkable or divine dreams which were predictive of the great things that afterward came to pass; of which see more in the note on Antiq. B. III. ch. viii. sect. 9. The other is in the War, B. III. ch. viii. sect. 3, 9.

off to afflict thy soul, and put away all fear; for what now grieves thee will render thee very considerable, and in all respects most happy; for thou shalt get over not only these difficulties, but many others, with great success. However, be not cast down, but remember that thou art to fight with the Romans." When I had seen this dream, I got up with an intention of going down to the plain. Now, when the whole multitude of the Galileans, among whom were the women and children, saw me, they threw themselves down upon their faces, and, with tears in their eyes, besought me not to leave them exposed to their enemies, nor to go away and permit their country to be injured by them. But, when I did not comply with their entreaties, they compelled me to take an oath, that I would stay with them: they also cast abundance of reproaches upon the people of Jerusalem, that they would not let their country enjoy peace.

42. When I heard this, and saw what sorrow the people were in, I was moved with compassion to them, and thought it became me to undergo the most manifest hazards for the sake of so great a multitude; so I let them know I would stay with them. And when I had given order that five thousand of them should come to me armed, and with provisions for their maintenance, I sent the rest away to their own homes; and, when those five thousand were come, I took them, together with three thousand of the soldiers that were with me before, and eighty horsemen, and marched to the village of Chabolo, situated in the confines of Ptolemais, and there kept my forces together, pretending to get ready to fight with Placidus, who was come with two cohorts of footmen, and one troop of horsemen, and was sent thither by Cestius Gallus to burn those villages of

Galilee that were near Ptolemais. Upon whose casting up a bank before the city Ptolemais, I also pitched my camp at about the distance of sixty furlongs from that village. And now we frequently brought out our forces as if we would fight, but proceeded no farther than a skirmish at a distance; for, when Placidus perceived that I was earnest to come to battle, he was afraid, and avoided it. Yet did he not remove from the neighbourhood of Ptolemais.

43. About this time it was that Jonathan and his fellow-legates came. They were sent, as we have said already, by Simon and Ananus the high priest. And Jonathan contrived how he might catch me by treachery; for he durst not make any attempt upon me openly. So he wrote me the following epistle: "Jonathan and those that are with him, and are sent by the people of Jerusalem, to Josephus, send greeting. We are sent by the principal men of Jerusalem, who have heard that John of Gischala hath laid many snares for thee, to rebuke him, and to exhort him to be subject to thee hereafter. We are also desirous to consult with thee about our common concerns, and what is fit to be done. We therefore desire thee to come to us quickly, and to bring only a few men with thee; for this village will not contain a great number of soldiers." Thus it was that they wrote, as expecting one of these two things, either that I should come without armed men; and then they should have me under their power; or, if I came with a great number, they should judge me to be a public enemy. Now it was a horseman who brought the letter, a man at other times bold, and one that had served in the army under the king. It was the second hour of the night that he came, when I was feasting with my friends, and the principal of the Galileans. This man, upon my servant's

telling me that a certain horseman of the Jewish nation was come, was called in at my command, but did not so much as salute me at all, but held out a letter, and said, "This letter is sent thee by those that are come from Jerusalem; do thou write an answer to it quickly, for I am obliged to return to them very soon." Now my guests could not but wonder at the boldness of the soldier. But I desired him to sit down and sup with us; but when he refused so to do, I held the letter in my hands as I received it, and fell a talking with my guests about other matters. But a few hours afterwards, I got up, and, when I had dismissed the rest to go to their beds, I bid only four of my intimate friends to stay, and ordered my servant to get some wine ready. I also opened the letter so that nobody could perceive it; and understanding thereby presently the purport of the writing, I sealed it up again, and appeared as if I had not yet read it, but only held it in my hands. I ordered twenty drachmæ should be given the soldier for the charges of his journey; and when he took the money, and said he thanked me for it, I perceived that he loved money, and that he was to be caught chiefly by that means, and I said to him, "If thou wilt but drink with us, thou shalt have a drachmæ for every glass thou drinkest." So he gladly embraced the proposal, and drank a great deal of wine, in order to get the more money, and was so drunk, that at last he could not keep the secrets he was intrusted with, but discovered them, without my putting questions to him, viz. that a treacherous design was contrived against me, and that I was doomed to die by those that sent him. When I heard this, I wrote back this answer: "Josephus, to Jonathan and those that are with him, sendeth greeting. Upon the information that you are come in health into Galilee, I rejoice, and this especially because I can now resign the care of public affairs here into your hands, and return into my native country; which is what I have desired to do a great while; and I confess I ought not only to come to you as far as Xaloth, but farther, and this without your commands. But I desire you to excuse me, because I cannot do it now, since I watch the motions of Placidus, who hath a mind to go up into Galilee; and this I do here at Chabolo. Do you, therefore, on the receipt of this epistle, come hither to me: Fare you well."

44. When I had written thus, and given the letter to be carried by the soldier, I sent along with him thirty of the Galileans of the best characters, and gave them instructions to salute those ambassadors, but to say nothing else to them. I also gave orders to as many of those armed men, whom I esteemed most faithful to me, to go along with the others, every one with him whom he was to guard, lest some conversation might pass between those whom I sent and those that were with Jonathan. So these men went [to Jonathan.] But, when Jonathan and his partners had failed in this their first attempt, they sent me another letter, the contents whereof were as follows: "Jonathan and those with him, to Josephus, send greeting. We require thee to come to us to the village Gabaroth, on the third day, without any armed men, that we may hear what thou hast to lay to the charge of John [of Gischala."] When they had written this letter, they saluted the Galileans whom I sent, and came to Japha, which was the largest village of all Galilee, and encompassed with very strong walls, and had a great number of inhabitants in it. There the multitude of men, with their wives and children, met them, and exclaimed

loudly against them, and desired them to be gone, and not to envy them the advantage of an excellent commander. With these clamours Jonathan and his partners were greatly provoked, although they durst not show their anger openly; so they made them no answer, but went to other villages. But still the same clamours met them from all the people, who said, "Nobody should persuade them to have any other commander besides Josephus." So Jonathan and his partners went away from them without success, and came to Sepphoris, the greatest city of all Galilee. Now the men of that city who inclined to the Romans in their sentiments, met them indeed, but neither praised nor reproached me; and when they were gone down from Sepphoris to Asochis, the people of that place made a clamour against them, as those of Japha had done. Whereupon they were able to contain themselves no longer, but ordered the armed men that were with them to beat those that made the clamour with their clubs. And when they came to Gabara, John met them with three thousand armed men; but, as I understood by their letter, that they had resolved to fight against me, I arose from Chabolo, with three thousand armed men also; but left in my camp one of my fastest friends and came to Jotapata, as desirous to be near them, the distance being no more than forty furlongs. Whence I wrote thus to them: "If you are very desirous that I should come to you, you know there are two hundred and forty cities and villages in Galilee, I will come to any of them which you please, excepting Gabara and Gischala; the one of which is John's native city, and the other in confederacy and friendship with him."

45. When Jonathan and his partners had received this letter, they wrote to me no more answers, but

called a council of their friends together, and taking John into their consultation, they took counsel together by what means they might attack me. John's opinion was, that they should write to all the cities and villages that were in Galilee; for that there must be certainly one or two persons in every one of them that were at variance with me, and that they be invited to come to oppose me as an enemy. He would also have them send this resolution of theirs to the city Jerusalem, that its citizens upon the knowledge of my being adjudged to be an enemy by the Galileans, might themselves also confirm that determination. He said also, that when this was done, even those Galileans who were affected to me, would desert me out of fear. When John had given them this counsel, what he had said was very agreeable to the rest of them. I was also made acquainted with these affairs about the third hour of the night, by the means of one Saccheus, who had belonged to them, but now deserted them and came over to me, and told me what they were about; so I perceived that no time was to be lost. Accordingly I gave command to Jacob, an armed man of my guard, whom I esteemed faithful to me, to take two hundred men and to guard the passages that led from Gabara to Galilee, and to seize upon the passengers, and send them to me, especially such as were caught with letters about them: I also sent Jeremias himself, one of my friends, with six hundred armed men, to the borders of Galilee, in order to watch the roads that led from the country to the city Jerusalem, and gave him charge to lay hold of such as travelled with letters about them, to keep the men in bonds upon the place, but to send me the letters.

46. When I had laid these commands upon them, I gave them orders, and bid them to take their arms

and bring three days' provisions with them, and be with me the next day. I also parted those that were about me into four parts, and ordained those of them that were most faithful to me to be a guard to my body. I also set over them centurions, and commanded them to take care that not a soldier which they did not know should mingle himself among them. Now, on the fifth day following, when I was at Gabaroth, I found the entire plain that was before the village full of armed men, who were come out of Galilee to assist me: many others of the multitude, also, out of the village, ran along with me. But as soon as I had taken my place, and began to speak to them, they all made an acclamation, and called me the benefactor and saviour of the country. And when I had made them my acknowledgments, and thanked them [for their affection to me,] I also advised them to fight [1] with nobody, nor to spoil the country, but to pitch their tents in the plain, and be content with their sustenance they had brought with them: for I told them I had a mind to compose these troubles without shedding any blood. Now it came to pass, that, on the very same day, those who were sent by John with letters fell among the guards whom I appointed to watch the roads, so the men were themselves kept upon the place, as my orders were, but I got the letters, which were full of reproaches and lies; and I intended to fall upon these men, without saying a word of these matters to anybody.

47. Now, as soon as Jonathan and his companions heard of my coming, they took all their own friends, and John with them, and retired to the house of Jesus, which indeed was a large castle, and no way unlike

---

[1] Josephus' directions to his soldiers here are much the same that John the Baptist gave, Luke iii. 14, "Do violence to no man, neither accuse any falsely, and be content with your wages."

a citadel; so they privately laid a band of armed men therein, and shut all the doors but one, which they kept open, and they expected that I should come out of the road to them, to salute them. And indeed they had given orders to the armed men, that when I came they should let nobody besides me come in, but should exclude others; as supposing that by this means they should easily get me under their power: but they were deceived in their expectation; for I perceived what snares they had laid for me. Now, as soon as I was got off my journey, I took up my lodgings over against them, and pretended to be asleep; so Jonathan and his party thinking that I was really asleep, and at rest, made haste to go down into the plain, to persuade the people that I was an ill governor. But the matter proved otherwise; for upon their appearance there was a cry made by the Galileans immediately, declaring their good opinion of me as their governor; and they made a clamour against Jonathan and his partners, for coming to them when they had suffered no harm, and as though they would overturn their happy settlement; and desired them by all means to go back again, for that they would never be persuaded to have any other to rule over them but myself. When I heard of this, I did not fear to go down into the midst of them; I went, therefore, myself down presently to hear what Jonathan and his companions said. As soon as I appeared, there was immediately an acclamation made to me by the whole multitude, and a cry in my commendation by them, who confessed their thanks was owing to me for my good government of them.

48. When Jonathan and his companions heard this, they were in fear of their own lives, and in danger lest they should be assaulted by the Galileans

on my account; so they contrived how they might run away. But as they were not able to get off, for I desired them to stay, they looked down with concern at my words to them. I ordered, therefore, the multitude to restrain entirely their acclamations, and placed the most faithful of my armed men upon the avenues, to be a guard to us, lest John should unexpectedly fall upon us: and I encouraged the Galileans to take their weapons, lest they should be disturbed at their enemies, if any sudden assault should be made upon them. And then, in the first place, I put Jonathan and his partners in mind of their [former] letter, and after what manner they had written to me, and declared they were sent by the common consent of the people of Jerusalem, to make up the differences I had with John, and how they had desired me to come to them; and as I spoke thus, I publicly showed that letter they had written, till they could not at all deny what they had done, the letter itself convicting them. I then said, "O Jonathan! and you that are sent with him as his colleagues, if I were to be judged as to my behaviour, compared with that of John's, and had brought no more than two [1] or three witnesses, good men and true, it is plain you had been forced, upon the examination of their characters beforehand, to discharge the accusations; that therefore you may be informed that I have acted well in the affairs of Galilee, I think three witnesses too few to be brought by a man that hath done as he ought to do; so I give you all these for witnesses. Inquire of them [2] how I

---

[1] We here learn the practice of the Jews, in the days of Josephus, to inquire into the character of witnesses, before they were admitted, and that their number ought to be three, or two at the least, also exactly as in the law of Moses, and in the Apostolical Constitutions, B. II. ch. 37. See Horeb Covenant Revived, pp. 97, 98.

[2] This appeal to the whole body of the Galileans by Josephus, and the testimony they gave him of integrity in his conduct as their governor,

have lived, and whether I have not behaved myself with all decency, and after a virtuous manner, among them. And I farther conjure you, O Galileans! to hide no part of the truth, but to speak before these men as before judges, whether I have in any thing acted otherwise than well."

49. While I was thus speaking, the united voices of all the people joined together, and called me their benefactor and saviour, and attested to my former behaviour, and exhorted me to continue so to do hereafter; and they all said, upon their oaths, that their wives had been preserved free from injuries, and that no one had ever been aggrieved by me. After this, I read to the Galileans two of those epistles which had been sent by Jonathan and his colleagues, and which those whom I had appointed to guard the road had taken, and sent to me. These were full of reproaches, and of lies, as if I had acted more like a tyrant than a governor against them, with many other things besides therein contained, which were no better indeed than impudent falsities. I also informed the multitude how I came by these letters, and that those who carried them delivered them up voluntarily; for I was not willing that my enemies should know any thing of the guards I had set, lest they should be afraid, and leave off writing hereafter.

50. When the multitude heard those things, they were greatly provoked at Jonathan, and his colleagues that were with him, and were going to attack them, and kill them; and this they had certainly done, unless I had restrained the anger of the Galileans, and said, That "I forgave Jonathan and his colleagues what was past, if they would repent, and go to their own country, and tell those who sent them

is very like that appeal and testimony in the case of the prophet Samuel, 1 Sam. xii. 1-5, and perhaps was done by Josephus in imitation of him.

the truth, as to my conduct." When I had said this, I let them go, although I knew they would do nothing of what they had promised. But the multitude were very much enraged against them, and entreated me to give them leave to punish them for their insolence; yet did I try all methods to persuade them to spare the men; for I knew that every instance of sedition was pernicious to the public welfare. But the multitude was too angry with them to be dissuaded, and all of them went immediately to the house in which Jonathan and his colleagues abode. However, when I perceived that their rage could not be restrained, I got on horseback, and ordered the multitude to follow me to the village Sogane, which was twenty furlongs off Gabara; and by using this stratagem, I so managed myself, as not to appear to begin a civil war amongst them.

51. But when I was come near Sogane, I caused the multitude to make a halt, and exhorted them not to be so easily provoked to anger, and to the inflicting such punishments as could not be afterwards recalled: I also gave order, that a hundred men, who were already in years, and were principal men among them, should get themselves ready to go to the city Jerusalem, and should make a complaint before the people of such as raised seditions in the country. And I said to them, that "in case they be moved with what you say, you shall desire the community to write to me, and to enjoin me to continue in Galilee, and to order Jonathan and his colleagues to depart out of it." When I had suggested these instructions to them, and while they were getting themselves ready as fast as they could, I sent them on this errand the third day after they had been assembled: I also sent five hundred armed men with them [as a guard.] I then wrote to my friends in Samaria, to take care

that they might safely pass through the country: for Samaria was already under the Romans, and it was absolutely necessary for those that go quickly [to Jerusalem,] to pass through that country; for in that road you may, in three days' time, go from Galilee to Jerusalem. I also went myself, and conducted the old men as far as the bounds of Galilee, and set guards in the roads, that it might not be easily known by any one that these men were gone. And when I had thus done, I went and abode at Japha.

52. Now Jonathan and his colleagues having failed of accomplishing what they would have done against me, they sent John back to Gischala, but went themselves to the city Tiberias, expecting it would submit itself to them; and this was founded on a letter which Jesus, their then governor, had written them, promising, that if they came, the multitude would receive them, and choose to be under their government; so they went their ways with this expectation. But Silas, who, as I said, had been left curator of Tiberias by me, informed me of this, and desired me to make haste thither. Accordingly, I complied with his advice immediately, and came thither; but found myself in danger of my life, from the following occasion: Jonathan and his colleagues had been at Tiberias, and had persuaded a great many of such as had a quarrel with me to desert me; but when they heard of my coming they were in fear for themselves, and came to me, and when they had saluted me, they said, that I was a happy man in having behaved myself so well in the government of Galilee; and they congratulated me upon the honours that were paid me: for they said that my glory was a credit to them, since they had been my teachers and fellow-citizens: and they said farther, that it was but just that they should prefer my friendship to them rather

than John's, and that they would have immediately
gone home, but that they stayed that they might deliver up John into my power: and when they said
this they took their oaths of it, and those such as
are most tremendous amongst us, and such as I did
not think fit to disbelieve. However, they desired
me to lodge somewhere else; because the next day
was the sabbath, and that it was not fit the city of
Tiberias should be disturbed [on that day.]

53. So I suspected nothing, and went away to
Taricheæ; yet did I withal leave some to make inquiry in the city how matters went, and whether any
thing was said about me: I also set many persons
all the way that led from Taricheæ to Tiberias, that
they might communicate from one to another, if they
learned any news from those that were left in the
city. On the next day therefore, they all came into
the Proseucha;[1] it was a large edifice and capable
of receiving a great number of people; thither Jonathan went in, and though he durst not openly speak
of a revolt, yet did he say that their city stood in
need of a better governor than it then had. But
Jesus, who was the ruler, made no scruple to speak
out, and said openly, "O fellow-citizens! it is better
for you to be in subjection to four than to one; and
those such as are of high birth, and not without reputation for their wisdom;" and pointed to Jonathan
and his colleagues. Upon his saying this, Justus
came in and commended him for what he had said,
and persuaded some of the people to be of his mind
also. But the multitude were not pleased with what

---

[1] It is worth noting here, that there was now a great Proseucha, or
place of prayer, in the city Tiberias itself, though such Proseucha used
to be out of cities, as the synagogues were within them: of them see Le
Moyne on Polycarp's epistle, p. 76. It is also worth our remark, that
the Jews, in the days of Josephus used to dine at the sixth hour, or
noon; and that in obedience to their notions of the law of Moses also.

was said, and had certainly gone into tumult, unless the sixth hour, which was now come, had dissolved the assembly, at which hour our laws require us to go to dinner on sabbath-days; so Jonathan and his colleagues put off their council till the next day, and went off without success. When I was informed of these affairs, I determined to go to the city of Tiberias in the morning. Accordingly, on the next day, about the first hour of the day, I came to Tiberias, and found the multitude ready assembled in the Proseucha; but on what account they were gotten together, those that were assembled did not know. But, when Jonathan and his colleagues saw them there unexpectedly, they were in disorder; after which they raised a report of their own contrivance, that Roman horsemen were seen at a place called Union, in the borders of Galilee; thirty furlongs distant from the city. Upon which report, Jonathan and his colleagues cunningly exhorted me not to neglect this matter, nor to suffer the land to be spoiled by the enemy. And this they said with a design to remove me out of the city: under the pretence of the want of extraordinary assistance, while they might dispose of the city to my enemy.

54. As for myself, although I knew of their design, yet did I comply with what they proposed, lest the people of Tiberias should have occasion to suppose, that I was not careful of their security. I therefore went out; but when I was at the place, I found not the least footsteps of any enemy, so I returned as fast as ever I could, and found the whole council assembled, and the body of the people gotten together, and Jonathan and his colleagues bringing vehement accusations against me, as one that had no concern to ease them of the burdens of war, and as one that lived luxuriously. And as they were

discoursing thus, they produced four letters as written to them, from some people that lived at the borders of Galilee; imploring that they would come to their assistance, for that there was an army of Romans, both horsemen and footmen, who would come and lay waste the country on the third day; they desired them also to make haste, and not to overlook them. When the people of Tiberias heard this, they thought they spoke truth, and made a clamour against me, and said, I ought not to sit still, but to go away to the assistance of their countrymen. Hereupon I said, (for I understood the meaning of Jonathan and his colleagues,) that I was ready to comply with what they proposed, and without delay to march to the war which they spoke of, yet did I advise them, at the same time, that since these letters declared that the Romans would make their assault in four several places, they should part their forces into five bodies, and make Jonathan and his colleagues generals of each body of them, because it was fit for brave men, not only to give counsel, but to take the place of leaders, and assist their countrymen when such a necessity pressed them; for, said I, it is not possible for me to lead more than one party. This advice of mine greatly pleased the multitude; so they compelled them to go forth to war. But their designs were put into very much disorder, because they had not done what they designed to do, on account of my stratagem, which was opposite to their undertakings.

55. Now there was one whose name was Ananias, a wicked man he was, and very mischievous; he proposed that a general religious fast [1] should be appointed the next day for all the people, and gave

---

[1] One may observe here, that this lay-Pharisee Ananias, as we have seen he was, sect. 39, took upon him to appoint a fast at Tiberias, and was obeyed; though indeed it was not out of religion, but knavish policy.

order that at the same hour they should come before God, that while they obtained his assistance, they thought all these weapons useless. This he said, not out of piety, but that they might catch me and my friends unarmed. Now, I was hereupon forced to comply, lest I should appear to despise a proposal. that tended to piety. As soon, therefore, as we were gone home, Jonathan and his colleagues wrote to John, to come to them in the morning, and desiring him to come with as many soldiers as he possibly could, for that they should then be able easily to get me into their hands, and to do all that they desired to do. When John had received this letter, he resolved to comply with it. As for myself, on the next day, I ordered two of the guards of my body, whom I esteemed the most courageous and most faithful, to hide daggers under their garments, and to go along with me, that we might defend ourselves, if any attack should be made upon us by our enemies. I also myself took my breastplate, and girt on my sword, so that it might be, as far as was possible, concealed, and came into the Proseucha.

56. Now Jesus, who was the ruler, commanded that they should exclude all that came with me, for he kept the door himself, and suffered none but his friends to go in. And while we were engaged in the duties of the day, and had betaken ourselves to our prayers, Jesus got up, and inquired of me what was become of the vessels that were taken out of the king's palace, when it was burnt down [and] of that uncoined silver: and in whose possession they now were? This he said, in order to drive away time till John should come. I said that Capellus and the ten principal men of Tiberias had them all; and I told him that they might ask them whether I told a lie or not. And when they said they had them,

he asked me, what is become of those twenty pieces of gold which thou didst receive upon the sale of a certain weight of uncoined money? I replied, that I had given them to those ambassadors of theirs, as a maintenance for them, when they were sent by them to Jerusalem. So Jonathan and his colleagues said, that I had not done well to pay the ambassadors out of the public money. And, when the multitude were very angry at them for this, for they perceived the wickedness of the men, I understood that a tumult was going to arise; and being desirous not to provoke the public to great rage against the men, I said, "But if I have not done well in paying our ambassadors out of the public stock, leave off your anger at me, for I will repay the twenty pieces of gold myself."

57. When I had said this, Jonathan and his colleagues held their peace; but the people were still more irritated against them, upon their openly showing their unjust ill-will to me. When Jesus saw this change in the people, he ordered them to depart, but desired the senate to stay; for that they could not examine things of such a nature in tumult: and, as the people were crying out that they would not leave me alone, there came one and told Jesus and his friends privately, that John and his armed men were at hand: whereupon Jonathan and his colleagues being able to contain themselves no longer, (and perhaps the providence of God hereby procuring my deliverance, for, had not this been so, I had certainly been destroyed by John,) said, "O you people of Tiberias! leave off this inquiry about the twenty pieces of gold; for Josephus hath not deserved to die for them; but he hath deserved it by his desire of tyrannizing, and by cheating the multitude of the Galileans with his speeches, in order to gain the dominion over

them." When he had said this, they presently laid hands upon me, and endeavoured to kill me: but, as soon as those that were with me saw what they did, they drew their swords, and threatened to smite them, if they offered any violence to me. The people also took up stones and were about to throw them at Jonathan; and so they snatched me from the violence of my enemies.

58. But, as I was going out a little way, I was just upon meeting John, who was marching with his armed men. So I was afraid of him, and turned aside, and escaped by a narrow passage to the lake, and seized on a ship, and embarked in it, and sailed over to Taricheæ. So, beyond my expectation, I escaped this danger. Whereupon I presently sent for the chief of the Galileans, and told them after what manner, against all faith given, I had been very near to destruction from Jonathan and his colleagues, and the people of Tiberias. Upon which the multitude of the Galileans were very angry, and encouraged me to delay no longer to make war upon them, but to permit them to go against John, and utterly to destroy him, as well as Jonathan and his colleagues. However, I restrained them, though they were in such a rage, and desired them to tarry a while, till we should be informed what orders those ambassadors, that were sent by them to the city of Jerusalem, should bring thence; for I told them, that it was best for them to act according to their determination: whereupon they were prevailed on. At which time also, John, when the snares he had laid did not take effect, returned back to Gischala.

59. Now in a few days those ambassadors whom he had sent, came back again and informed us, that the people were greatly provoked at Ananus, and Simon, the son of Gamaliel, and their friends; that,

without any public determination, they had sent to
Galilee, and had done their endeavours that I might
be turned out of the government. The ambassadors
said farther, that the people were ready to burn their
houses. They also brought letters, whereby the chief
men of Jerusalem, at the earnest petition of the
people, confirmed me in the government of Galilee,
and enjoined Jonathan and his colleagues to return
home quickly. When I had gotten these letters, I
came to the village Arbella, where I procured an
assembly of the Galileans to meet, and bid the ambassadors declare to them the anger of the people of
Jerusalem at what had been done by Jonathan and
his colleagues, and how much they hated their wicked
doings, and how they had confirmed me in the government of their country, as also what related to the
order they had in writing for Jonathan and his colleagues to return home. So I immediately sent them
the letter, and bid him that carried it to inquire, as
well as he could, how they intended to act [on this
occasion.]

60. Now, when they had received that letter, and
were thereby greatly disturbed, they sent for John,
and for the senators of Tiberias, and for the principal men of the Gabarens, and proposed to hold a
council, and desired them to consider what was to
be done by them. However the governors of Tiberias were greatly disposed to keep the government
to themselves; for they said it was not fit to desert
the city, now it was committed to their trust, and
that otherwise I should not delay to fall upon them;
for they pretended falsely that so I had threatened
to do. Now John was not only of their opinion, but
advised them, that two of them should go to accuse
me before the multitude [at Jerusalem,] that I did
not manage the affairs of Galilee as I ought to do;

and that they would easily persuade the people, because of their dignity, and because the whole multitude are very mutable. When, therefore, it appeared that John had suggested the wisest advice to them, they resolved that two of them, Jonathan and Ananias, should go to the people of Jerusalem, and the other two [Simon and Joazer] should be left behind to tarry at Tiberias. They also took along with them a hundred soldiers for their guard.

61. However, the governors of Tiberias took care to have their city secured with walls, and commanded their inhabitants to take their arms. They also sent for a great many soldiers from John to assist them against me, if there should be occasion for them. Now John was at Gischala; Jonathan, therefore, and those that were with him, when they were departed from Tiberias, and as soon as they were come to Dabaritta, a village that lay in the utmost parts of Galilee, in the great plain, they, about midnight, fell among the guards I had set, who both commanded them to lay aside their weapons, and kept them in bonds upon the place, as I had charged them to do. This news was written to me by Levi, who had command of that guard committed to him by me. Hereupon I said nothing of it for two days; and pretending to know nothing about it, I sent a message to the people of Tiberias, and advised them to lay their arms aside, and to dismiss their men, that they might go home. But supposing that Jonathan, and those that were with him, were already arrived at Jerusalem, they made reproachful answers to me; yet was •I not terrified thereby, but contrived another stratagem against them, for I did not think it agreeable with piety to kindle the fire of war against the citizens. As I was desirous to draw those men away from Tiberias, I chose out ten thousand of the best

of my armed men, and divided them into three bodies, and ordered them to go privately, and lie still as an ambush, in the villages. I also led a thousand into another village, which lay indeed in the mountains, as did the others, but only four furlongs distant from Tiberias, and gave order, that when they saw my signal, they should come down immediately: while I myself lay with my soldiers in the sight of everybody. Hereupon the people of Tiberias, at the sight of me, came running out of the city perpetually, and abused me greatly. Nay, their madness was come to that height, that they made a decent bier for me, and, standing about it, they mourned over me in the way of jest and sport: and I could not but be myself in a pleasant humour upon the sight of this madness of theirs.

62. And now being desirous to catch Simon by a wile, and Joazer with him, I sent a message to them, and desired them to come a little way out of the city, with many of their friends to guard them; for I said I would come down to them, and make a league with them, and divide the government of Galilee with them. Accordingly, Simon was deluded on account of his imprudence, and out of the hopes of gain, and did not delay to come; but Joazer, suspecting snares were laid for him, stayed behind. So, when Simon was come out, and his friends with him for his guard, I met him, and saluted him with great civility, and professed that I was obliged to him for his coming up to me; but a little while afterward I walked along with him, as though I would say something to him by myself, and, when I had drawn him a good way from his friends, I took him about the middle, and gave him to my friends that were with me, to carry him into a village: and, commanding my armed men to come down, I with them

made an assault upon Tiberias. Now, as the fight grew hot on both sides, and the soldiers belonging to Tiberias were in a fair way to conquer me, (for my armed men were already fled away,) I saw the posture of my affairs; and encouraging those that were with me, I pursued those of Tiberias, even when they were already conquerors, into the city. I also sent another band of soldiers into the city by the lake, and gave them orders to set on fire the first house they could seize upon. When this was done, the people of Tiberias thought that their city was taken by force, and so threw down their arms for fear, and implored, they, their wives and children, that I would spare their city. So I was over-persuaded by their entreaties, and restrained the soldiers from the vehemency with which they pursued them; while I myself, upon the coming on of the evening, returned back with my soldiers; and went to refresh myself. I also invited Simon to sup with me, and comforted him on occasion of what had happened; and I promised that I would send him safe and secure to Jerusalem, and withal would give him provision for his journey thither.

63. But on the next day, I brought ten thousand men with me, and came to Tiberias. I then sent for the principal men of the multitude into the public place, and enjoined them to tell me who were the authors of the revolt; and when they had told me who the men were, I sent them bound to the city Jotapata. But, as to Jonathan and Ananias, I freed them from their bonds, and gave them provisions for their journey, together with Simon and Joazer, and five hundred armed men who should guard them, and so I sent them to Jerusalem. The people of Tiberias also came to me again, and desired that I would forgive them for what they had done, and they

said they would amend what they had done amiss
with regard to me, by their fidelity for the time to
come; and they besought me to preserve what spoils
remained upon the plunder of the city, for those that
had lost them. Accordingly, I enjoined those that
had got them, to bring them all before us; and when
they did not comply for a great while, and I saw
one of the soldiers that were about me with a garment on that was more splendid than ordinary, I
asked him whence he had it, and he replied that he
had it out of the plunder of the city; I had him
punished with stripes, and I threatened all the rest
to inflict a severer punishment upon them, unless they
produced before us whatsoever they had plundered;
and when a great many spoils were brought together,
I restored to every one of Tiberias what they claimed
to be their own.

64. And now I am come to this part of my narration, I have a mind to say a few things to Justus,
who hath himself written a history concerning these
affairs, as also to others who profess to write history,
but have little regard to truth, and are not afraid,
either out of ill-will or good-will to some persons, to
relate falsehoods. These men do, like those who compose forged deeds and conveyances; and because they
are not brought to the like punishment with them,
they have no regard to truth. When, therefore, Justus undertook to write about these facts, and about
the Jewish war, that he might appear to have been
an industrious man, he falsified in what he related
about me, and could not speak truth even about his
own country; whence it is, that being belied by him,
I am under a necessity to make my defence; and so
I shall say what I have concealed till now. And let
no one wonder that I have not told the world these
things a great while ago. For although it be neces-

sary for a historian to write the truth, yet is such a one not bound severely to animadvert on the wickedness of certain men, not out of any favour to them, but out of an author's own moderation. How, then, comes it to pass, O Justus! thou most sagacious of writers, (that I may address myself to him as if he were here present,) for so thou boastest of thyself, that I and the Galileans have been the authors of that sedition which thy country engaged in both against the Romans and against the king [Agrippa junior?] For before ever I was appointed governor of Galilee by the community of Jerusalem, both thou and all the people of Tiberias had not only taken up arms, but had made war with Decapolis of Syria. Accordingly, thou hadst ordered their villages to be burnt, and a domestic servant of thine fell in the battle. Nor is it I only who say this; but so it is written in the commentaries of Vespasian the emperor, as also how the inhabitants of Decapolis came clamouring to Vespasian at Ptolemais, and desired that thou, who wast the author [of that war,] mightest be brought to punishment. And thou hadst certainly been punished at the command of Vespasian, had not king Agrippa, who had power given him to have thee put to death, at the earnest entreaty of his sister Bernice, changed the punishment from death into a long imprisonment. Thy political administration of affairs afterward doth also clearly discover both thy other behaviour in life, and that thou wast the occasion of thy country's revolt from the Romans; plain signs of which I shall produce presently. I have also a mind to say a few things to the rest of the people of Tiberias on thy account, and to demonstrate to those that light upon this history, that you bore no good-will, neither to the Romans, nor to the king. To be sure, the greatest cities of Galilee, O

Justus! were Sepphoris, and thy country Tiberias.
But Sepphoris, situated in the very midst of Galilee,
and having many villages about it, and able with
ease to have been bold and troublesome to the Romans,
if they had so pleased, yet did it resolve to continue
faithful to those their masters, and at the same time
excluded me out of their city, and prohibited all their
citizens from joining with the Jews in the war, and
that they might be out of danger from me, they by
a wile got leave of me to fortify their city with walls;
they also of their own accord, admitted of a garrison
of Roman legions, sent them by Cestius Gallus, who
was then president of Syria, and so had me in contempt, though I was then very powerful, and all
were greatly afraid of me; and at the same time
that the greatest of our cities, Jerusalem, was besieged, and that temple of ours, which belonged to
us all, was in danger of falling under the enemy's
power, they sent no assistance thither, as not willing
to have it thought they would bear arms against the
Romans. But as for thy country, O Justus! situated upon the lake of Gennesareth, and distant from
Hippos thirty furlongs, from Gadara sixty, and from
Scythopolis, which was under the king's jurisdiction,
a hundred and twenty, when there was no Jewish
city near, it might easily have preserved its fidelity
[to the Romans,] if it had so pleased them to do;
for the city and its people had plenty of weapons.
But as thou sayest, I was *then* the author [of their
revolt.] And I pray, O Justus! who was that author
afterwards? For thou knowest that I was in the
power of the Romans before Jerusalem was besieged,
and before the same time Jotapata was taken by
force, as well as many other fortresses, and a great
many of the Galileans fell in the war. It was therefore then a proper time, when you were certainly

freed from any fear on my account, to throw away your weapons, and to demonstrate to the king and to the Romans, that it was not of choice, but as forced by necessity, that you fell into the war against them; but you stayed till Vespasian came himself as far as your walls, with his whole army; and then you did indeed lay aside your weapons out of fear, and your city had for certain been taken by force, unless Vespasian had complied with the king's supplication for you, and had excused your madness. It was not I, therefore, who was the author of this, but your own inclinations to war. Do not you remember how often I got you under my power, and yet put none of you to death? nay, you once fell into a tumult one against another, and slew one hundred and eighty-five of your citizens, not on account of your good-will to the king and to the Romans, but on account of your own wickedness, and this while I was besieged by the Romans in Jotapata. Nay, indeed, were there not reckoned up two thousand of the people of Tiberias during the siege of Jerusalem, some of which were slain, and the rest caught and carried captives? But thou wilt pretend that thou didst not engage in the war, since thou didst flee to the king. Yes, indeed, thou didst flee to him; but I say it was out of fear of me. Thou sayest, indeed, that it is I who am a wicked man. But then, for what reason was it that king Agrippa, who procured thee thy life when thou wast condemned to die by Vespasian, and who bestowed so much riches upon thee, did twice afterward put thee into bonds, and as often obliged thee to run away from thy country, and, when he had once ordered thee to be put to death, he granted thee a pardon at the earnest request of Bernice? and when (after so many of thy wicked pranks) he had made thee his secre-

tary, he caught thee falsifying his epistles, and drove
thee away from his sight. But I shall not inquire
accurately into these matters of scandal against thee.
Yet cannot I but wonder at thy impudence, when
thou hast the assurance to say, that thou hast better
related these [affairs of the war] than have all the
others that have written about them, whilst thou didst
not know what was done in Galilee; for thou wast
then at Berytus with the king; nor didst thou know
how much the Romans suffered at the siege of Jotapata, or what miseries they brought upon us; nor
couldest thou learn by inquiry what I did during that
siege myself; for all those that might afford such
information were quite destroyed in that siege. But
perhaps thou wilt say, thou hast written of what was
done against the people of Jerusalem exactly. But
how should that be? for neither wast thou concerned
in that war, nor hast thou read the commentaries of
Cæsar; of which we have evident proof, because thou
hast contradicted those commentaries of Cæsar in
thy history. But if thou art so hardy as to affirm,
that thou hast written that history better than all
the rest, why didst thou not publish thy history while
the emperors Vespasian and Titus, the generals in
that war, as well as king Agrippa and his family,
who were men very well skilled in the learning of
the Greeks, were all alive? for thou hast had it written
these twenty years, and then mightest thou have had
the testimony of thy accuracy. But now when these
men are no longer with us, and thou thinkest thou
canst not be contradicted, thou venturest to publish
it. But then I was not in like manner afraid of
mine own writing, but I offered my books to the
emperors themselves, when the facts were almost
under men's eyes; for I was conscious to myself, that
I had observed the truth of the facts; and as I ex-

pected to have their attestation to them, so I was not deceived in such expectation. Moreover I immediately presented my history to many other persons, some of whom were concerned in the war, as was king Agrippa and some of his kindred. Now the emperor Titus was so desirous that the knowledge of these affairs should be taken from these books alone, that he subscribed his own hand to them, and ordered that they should be published; and for Agrippa, he wrote me sixty-two letters, and attested to the truth of what I had therein delivered; two of which letters I have here subjoined, and thou mayest know thereby their contents. "King Agrippa to Josephus, his dear friend, sendeth greeting. I have read over thy book with great pleasure, and it appears to me, that thou hast done it much more accurately, and with greater care, than have the other writers. Send me the rest of these books. Farewell, my dear friend." "King Agrippa to Josephus, his dear friend, sendeth greeting. It seems by what thou hast written, that thou standest in need of no instruction, in order to our information from the beginning. However, when thou comest to me, I will inform thee of a great many things which thou dost not know." So when this history was perfected, Agrippa, neither by way of flattery, which was not agreeable to him, nor by way of irony, as thou wilt say, (for he was entirely a stranger to such an evil disposition of mind,) but he wrote this by way of attestation to what was true, as all that read histories may do. And so much shall be said concerning Justus,[1] which I am obliged to add by way of digression.

---

[1] The character of this history of Justus of Tiberias, the rival of our Josephus, which is now lost, with its only remaining fragment, are given us by a very able critic, Photius, who read that history. It is in the 33d code of his Bibliotheca, and runs thus: "I have read (says Photius) the chronology of Justus of Tiberias, whose title is this. [*The chronology of*] *the Kings of Judah which succeeded one another.* This [Justus] came out of the city Tiberias in Galilee. He begins his history from

65. Now, when I had settled the affairs of Tiberias, and had assembled my friends as a Sanhedrim, I consulted what I should do as to John. Whereupon it appeared to be the opinion of all the Galileans, that I should arm them all, ànd march against John, and punish him as the author of all the disorders that had happened. Yet was I not pleased with their determination; as purposing to compose these troubles without bloodshed. Upon this I exhorted them to use the utmost care to learn the names of all that were under John; which when they had done, and I thereby was apprised who the men were, I published an edict, wherein I offered security and my right-hand to such of John's party as had a mind to repent; and I allowed twenty days' time to such as would take this most advantageous course for themselves. I also threatened, that unless they threw down their arms, I would burn their houses, and expose their goods to public sale. When the men heard of this, they were in no small disorder, and deserted John; and to the number of four thousand threw down their arms and came to me. So that no others stayed with John but his own citizens, and about fifteen hundred strangers that came from the metropolis of Tyre; and when John saw that he had been outwitted by my stratagem, he continued afterward in his own country, and was in great fear of me.

Moses, and ends it not till the death of Agrippa the seventh [ruler] of the family of Herod, and the last king of the Jews; who took the government under Claudius, had it augmented under Nero, and still more augmented by Vespasian. He died in the third year of Trajan, where also his history ends. He was a man, as he is described by Josephus, of a most profligate character; a slave both to money and to pleasures. In public affairs he was opposite to Josephus; and it is related, that he laid many plots against him, but that Josephus, though he had this his enemy frequently under his power, did only reproach him in words, and so let him go without farther punishment. He says also, that the history which this man wrote is, for the main, fabulous, and chiefly as to those parts where he describes the Roman war with the Jews, and the taking of Jerusalem."

SEPPHORIS.

Sepphoris was the principal city of this part of Galilee. It is easy to understand that its commanding position—easily fortified, and on the skirts of a very fertile plain, would give it a decided advantage, as compared with most other spots. This advantage had in fact secured to it, notwithstanding frequent assaults and overthrows, a sort of metropolitan supremacy, from an early period of Jewish history, and down to the period of the Crusades.

In the LIFE, Sepphoris is frequently mentioned. In Sect. ix. its having been constituted by the Romans the metropolitan city of Galilee, in the place of Tiberias, which, with Tarichæa, had been appended to the domains of Agrippa, is mentioned. In consequence of this arrangement the people of Sepphoris, feeling themselves to be in a position which would enable them to maintain their allegiance, and to repel the assaults of the brigand bands, and of the revolted Galilean cities, declared their determination to adhere to "Cæsar," in which wise purpose they persevered, Sect. xxii.; and WAR, ii. 18, 11; nevertheless availing themselves of the aid of Josephus to fortify still further their city, Sect. xxxvii. WAR, ii. 20, 6, he says he left them to fortify their city, wealthy as they were. In the Section lxvii., we are told that the Sepphorites, confiding in the strength of their walls attempted to make good their resistance to the Galilean insurrectionists. Josephus, however, carried the (lower) town, compelling the people to take refuge in "the citadel"—no doubt the capacious fort on the summit of the hill, where the modern castle now stands. On a second occasion (Sect. lxxi.) he made himself master of a part of the town by a nocturnal assault, from which, however, he was forced to retire; and in his retreat was encountered, in the plain (which in the view is seen stretching beyond the town) by a body of Roman cavalry, where he was defeated.

66. But about this time it was that the people of
Sepphoris grew insolent, and took up arms, out of
a confidence they had in the strength of their walls,
and because they saw me engaged in other affairs
also. So they sent to Cestius Gallus, who was president of Syria, and desired that he would either come
quickly to them, and take their city under his protection, or send them a garrison. Accordingly Gallus
promised them to come, but did not send word when
he would come; and, when I had learned so much,
I took the soldiers that were with me, and made an
assault upon the people of Sepphoris, and took the
city by force. The Galileans took this opportunity,
as thinking they had now a proper time for showing
their hatred to them, since they bore ill-will to that
city also. Then they exerted themselves, as if they
would destroy them all utterly, with those that sojourned there also. So they ran upon them, and
set their houses on fire, as finding them without inhabitants; for the men out of fear ran together to
the citadel. So the Galileans carried off every thing,
and omitted no kind of desolation which they could
bring upon their countrymen. When I saw this, I
was exceedingly troubled at it, and commanded them
to leave off, and put them in mind that it was not
agreeable to piety to do such things to their countrymen; but since they neither would hearken to what
I exhorted, nor to what I commanded them to do,
(for the hatred they bore to the people there was too
hard for my exhortations to them,) I bid those my
friends, who were most faithful to me, and were
about me, to give out reports, as if the Romans were
falling upon the other part of the city with a great
army; and this I did, that, by such a report's being
spread abroad, I might restrain the violence of the
Galileans, and preserve the city of Sepphoris. And

at length this stratagem had its effect; for, upon hearing this report, they were in fear for themselves, and so they left off plundering and ran away; and this more especially, because they saw me, their general, do the same also, for, that I might cause this report to be believed, I pretended to be in fear as well as they. Thus were the inhabitants of Sepphoris unexpectedly preserved by this contrivance of mine.

67. Nay, indeed, Tiberias had like to have been plundered by the Galileans also, upon the following occasion: The chief men of the senate wrote to the king, and desired that he would come to them, and take possession of their city. The king promised to come, and wrote a letter in answer to theirs, and gave it to one of his bed-chamber, whose name was *Crispus,* and who was by birth a Jew, to carry it to Tiberias. When the Galileans knew that this man carried such a letter, they caught him, and brought him to me; but as soon as the whole multitude heard of it, they were enraged, and betook themselves to their arms. So a great many of them got together from all quarters the next day and came to the city of Asochis, where I then lodged, and made heavy clamours, and called the city of Tiberias a traitor to them, and a friend to the king; and desired leave of me to go down, and utterly destroy it; for they bore the like ill-will to the people of Tiberias, as they did to those of Sepphoris.

68. When I heard this, I was in doubt what to do, and hesitated by what means I might deliver Tiberias, from the rage of the Galileans; for I could not deny that those of Tiberias had written to the king, and invited him to come to them; for his letters to them, in answer thereto, would fully prove the truth of that. So I sat a long while musing with myself, and then said to them, "I know well enough

that the people of Tiberias have offended; nor shall I forbid you to plunder the city. However, such things ought to be done with discretion; for they of Tiberias have not been the only betrayers of our liberty, but many of the most eminent patriots of the Galileans, as they pretended to be, have done the same. Tarry therefore till I shall thoroughly find out those authors of our danger, and then you shall have them all at once under your power, with all such as you shall yourselves bring in also." Upon my saying this, I pacified the multitude, and they left off their anger, and went their ways; and I gave orders that he who brought the king's letters should be put into bonds; but in a few days I pretended that I was obliged, by a necessary affair of my own, to go out of the kingdom. I then called Crispus privately, and ordered him to make the soldier that kept him drunk, and to run away to the king. So, when Tiberias was in danger of being utterly destroyed a second time, it escaped the danger by my skilful management, and the care that I had for its preservation.

69. About this time it was that Justus, the son of Pistus, without my knowledge, ran away to the king; the occasion of which I will here relate. Upon the beginning of the war between the Jews and the Romans, the people of Tiberias resolved to submit to the king, and not to revolt from the Romans; while Justus tried to persuade them to betake themselves to their arms, as being himself desirous of innovations, and having hopes of obtaining the government of Galilee, as well as of his own country [Tiberias] also. Yet did he not obtain what he hoped for; because the Galileans bore ill-will to those of Tiberias, and this on account of their anger at what miseries they had suffered from them before

the war; thence it was that they would not endure that Justus should be their governor; I myself also, who had been intrusted by the community of Jerusalem with the government of Galilee, did frequently come to that degree of rage at Justus, that I had almost resolved to kill him, as not able to bear his mischievous disposition. He was therefore much afraid of me, lest at length my passion should come to extremity; so he went to the king, as supposing that he should dwell better and more safely with him.

70. Now, when the people of Sepphoris had, in so surprising a manner, escaped their first danger, they sent to Cestius Gallus, and desired him to come to them immediately, and take possession of their city, or else to send forces sufficient to repress all their enemies' incursions upon them; and at the last they did prevail with Gallus to send them a considerable army, both of horse and foot, which came in the night-time, and which they admitted into the city. But when the country round about it was harassed by the Roman army, I took those soldiers that were about me, and came to Garisme, where I cast up a bank, a good way off the city Sepphoris; and when I was at twenty furlongs distance, I came upon it by night, and made an assault upon its walls with my forces; and when I had ordered a considerable number of my soldiers to scale them with ladders, I became master of the greatest part of the city. But soon after, our unacquaintedness with the places forced us to retire, after we had killed twelve of the Roman footmen, and two horsemen, and a few of the people of Sepphoris, with the loss of only a single man of our own. And when it afterward came to a battle in the plain against the horsemen, and we had undergone the dangers of it courageously for a long time, we were beaten; for upon the Romans

encompassing me about, my soldiers were afraid, and fled back. There fell in that battle one of those that had been intrusted to guard my body, his name was *Justus,* who at this time had the same post with the king. At the same time also there came forces, both horsemen and footmen, from the king, and Sylla their commander, who was the captain of this guard; this Sylla pitched his camp at five furlongs distance from Julias, and set a guard upon the roads, both that which led to Cana, and that which led to the fortress Gamala, that he might hinder their inhabitants from getting provisions out of Galilee.

71. As soon as I had gotten intelligence of this, I sent two thousand armed men, and a captain over them, whose name was *Jeremiah,* who raised a bank a furlong off Julias, near to the river Jordan, and did no more than skirmish with the enemy; till I took three thousand soldiers myself, and came to them. But on the next day, when I had laid an ambush in a certain valley, not far from the banks, I provoked those that belonged to the king to come to a battle, and gave orders to my own soldiers to turn their backs upon them, until they should have drawn the enemy away from their camp, and brought them out into the field, which was done accordingly; for Sylla, supposing that our party did really run away, was ready to pursue them, when our soldiers that lay in ambush took them on their backs, and put them all into great disorder. I also immediately made a sudden turn with my own forces, and met those of the king's party, and put them to flight. And I had performed great things that day, if a certain fate had not been my hinderance; for the horse on which I rode, and upon whose back I fought, fell into a quagmire, and threw me on the ground, and I was bruised on my wrist, and carried into a

village named *Cepharnome* or *Capernaum.* When
my soldiers heard of this, they were afraid I had
been worse hurt than I was; and so they did not go
on with their pursuit any further, but returned in
very great concern for me. I therefore sent for
the physicians, and while I was under their hand, I
continued feverish all that day; and as the physicians
directed, I was that night removed to Taricheæ.

72. When Sylla and his party were informed
what happened to me, they took courage again; and
understanding that the watch was negligently kept
in our camp, they by night placed a body of horsemen in ambush beyond Jordan, and when it was
day they provoked us to fight; and as we did not
refuse it, but came into the plain, their horsemen
appeared out of that ambush in which they had lain,
and put our men into disorder, and made them run
away; so they slew six men of our side. Yet did
they not go off with the victory at last; for when
they heard that some armed men were sailed from
Tariche æ to Julias, they were afraid, and retired.

73. It was not now long before Vespasian came
to Tyre, and king Agrippa with him; but the Tyrians
began to speak reproachfully of the king, and called
him an enemy to the Romans. For they said, that
Philip, the general of his army, had betrayed the
royal palace, and the Roman forces that were in
Jerusalem, and that it was done by his command.
When Vespasian heard of this report, he rebuked the
Tyrians, for abusing a man who was both a king,
and a friend to the Romans; but he exhorted the king
to send Philip to Rome, to answer for what he had
done before Nero. But, when Philip was sent thither,
he did not come into the sight of Nero, for he found
him very near death, on account of the troubles that
then happened, and a civil war; and so he returned

to the king. But, when Vespasian was come to Ptolemais, the chief men of Decapolis of Syria made a clamour against Justus of Tiberias, because he had set their villages on fire: so Vespasian delivered him to the king, to be put to death by those under the king's jurisdiction: yet did the king [only] put him into bonds, and concealed what he had done from Vespasian, as I have before related. But the people of Sepphoris met Vespasian, and saluted him, and had forces sent him, with Placidus their commander: he also went up with them, as I also followed them, till Vespasian came into Galilee. As to which coming of his, and after what manner it was ordered, and how he fought his first battle with me near the village Taricheæ, and how from thence they went to Jotapata, and how I was taken alive, and bound, and how I was afterward loosed, with all that was done by me in the Jewish war, and during the siege of Jerusalem, I have accurately related them in the books concerning the War of the Jews. However, it will, I think, be fit for me to add now an account of those actions of my life, which I have not related in that book of the Jewish War.

74. For when the siege of Jotapata was over, and I was among the ·Romans, I was kept with much care, by means of the great respect that Vespasian showed me. Moreover, at his command, I married a virgin,[1] who was from among the captives of that country; yet did she not live with me long, but was divorced, upon my being freed from my bonds, and my going to Alexandria. However, I married an-

[1] Here Josephus, a priest, honestly confesses that he did that at the command of Vespasian, which he had before told us was not lawful for a priest to do by the law of Moses, Antiq. B. III. ch. xii. sect. 2. I mean the taking a captive woman to wife. See also against Appion, B. I. ch. vii. But he seems to have been quickly sensible that his compliance with the commands of an emperor would not excuse him, for he soon put her away, as Reland justly observes here.

other wife at Alexandria, and was thence sent, together with Titus, to the siege of Jerusalem, and was frequently in danger of being put to death; while both the Jews were very desirous to get me under their power, in order to have me punished, and the Romans also, whenever they were beaten, supposed that it was occasioned by my treachery, and made continual clamours to the emperors, and desired that they would bring me to that punishment, as a traitor to them: but Titus Cæsar was well acquainted with the uncertain fortune of war, and returned no answer to the soldiers' vehement solicitations against me. Moreover, when the city Jerusalem was taken by force, Titus Cæsar persuaded me frequently to take whatsoever I would of the ruins of my country; and said that he gave me leave so to do. But when my country was destroyed, I thought nothing else to be of any value, which I could take and keep as a comfort under my calamities; so I made this request to Titus, that my family might have their liberty: I had also the holy books [1] by Titus' concession. Nor was it long after that I asked of him the life of my brother, and of fifty friends with him, and was not denied. When I also went once to the temple, by the permission of Titus, where there were a great multitude of captive women and children, I got all those that I remembered as among my own friends and acquaintances to be set free, being in number about one hundred and ninety; and so I delivered them without their paying any price of redemption, and restored them to their former fortune. And when I was sent by Titus Cæsar with Cerealius, and a thousand horsemen, to a certain village called Thecoa, in order to know whether it

---

[1] Of this most remarkable clause, and its most important consequences, see Essay on the Old Testament, pp. 193-195.

were a place fit for a camp, as I came back, I saw many captives crucified, and remembered three of them as my former acquaintance. I was very sorry at this in my mind, and went with tears in my eyes to Titus, and told him of them; so he immediately commanded them to be taken down, and to have the greatest care taken of them, in order to their recovery; yet two of them died under the physician's hands, while the third recovered.

75. But when Titus had composed the troubles in Judea, and conjectured that the lands which I had in Judea would bring me in no profit, because a garrison to guard the country was afterward to pitch there, he gave me another country in the plain. And, when he was going away to Rome, he made choice of me to sail along with him, and paid me great respect: and, when we were come to Rome, I had great care taken of me by Vespasian; for he gave me an apartment in his own house, which he lived in before he came to the empire. He also honoured me with the privilege of a Roman citizen, and gave me an annual pension; and continued to respect me to the end of his life, without any abatement of his kindness to me; which very thing made me envied, and brought me into danger; for a certain Jew whose name was Jonathan, who had raised a tumult in Cyrene, and had persuaded two thousand men of that country to join with him, was the occasion of their ruin. But, when he was bound by the governor of that country, and sent to the emperor, he told him, that I had sent him both weapons and money. However, he could not conceal his being a liar from Vespasian, who condemned him to die; according to which sentence he was put to death. Nay, after that, when those that envied my good fortune did frequently bring accusations against me,

by God's providence I escaped them all. I also received from Vespasian no small quantity of land, as free gift in Judea; about which time I divorced my wife also, as not pleased with her behaviour, though not till she had been the mother of three children, two of which are dead, and one, whom I named *Hyrcanus,* is alive. After this I married a wife who had lived at Crete, but a Jew by birth: a woman she was of eminent parents, and such as were the most illustrious in all the country, and whose character was beyond that of most other women, as her future life did demonstrate. By her I had two sons, the elder's name was Justus, and the next *Simonides,* who was also named *Agrippa.* And these were the circumstances of my domestic affairs. However, the kindness of the emperor to me continued still the same; for when Vespasian was dead, Titus, who succeeded him in the government, kept up the same respect for me which I had from his father: and, when I had frequent accusations laid against me, he would not believe them. And Domitian, who succeeded, still augmented his respects to me; for he punished those Jews that were my accusers, and gave command that a servant of mine, who was a eunuch, and my accuser, should be punished. He also made that country I had in Judea, tax-free, which is a mark of the greatest honour to him who hath it; nay, Domitia, the wife of Cæsar, continued to do me kindnesses. And this is the account of the actions of my whole life; and let others judge of my character by them as they please. But to thee, O Epaphroditus![1] thou most excellent of men, do I dedicate all this treatise of our Antiquities; and so, for the present, I here conclude the whole.

[1] Of this Epaphroditus, see the note on the Preface to the Antiquities.

THE WARS OF THE JEWS,

OR,

THE HISTORY OF THE DESTRUCTION
OF JERUSALEM.

PREFACE.

1. [1] W HEREAS the war which the Jews made with
the Romans hath been the greatest of all those, not
only that have been in our times, but, in a manner,
of those that ever were heard of; both of those wherein
cities have fought against cities, or nations against
nations; while some men who were not concerned
in the affairs themselves, have gotten together vain
and contradictory stories by hearsay, and have written
them down after a sophistical manner; and while
those that were there present have given false accounts
of things, and this either out of humour of flattery

---

[1] I have already observed more than once, that this history of the
Jewish war was Josephus' first work, and published about A. D. 75, when
he was but 38 years of age; and that when he wrote it, he was not
thoroughly acquainted with several circumstances of history from the
days of Antiochus Epiphanes, with which it begins, till near his own
times, contained in the first and former part of the second book, and
so committed many involuntary errors therein. That he published his
Antiquities 18 years afterward, perused those most authentic histories,
the first book of Maccabees, in the 13th year of Domitian, A D. 93, when
he was much more completely acquainted with those ancient times, and
after he had written the Chronicles of the priesthood of John Hyrcanus,
etc. That accordingly he then reviewed those parts of this work, and
gave the public a more faithful, complete, and accurate account of the
facts therein related; and honestly corrected the errors he had before
run into.

to the Romans, or of hatred towards the Jews; and while their writings contain sometimes accusations, and sometimes encomiums, but nowhere the accurate truth of the facts; I have proposed to myself, for the sake of such as live under the government of the Romans, to translate those books into the Greek tongue, which I formerly composed in the language of our country, and sent to the Upper Barbarians;[1] I Joseph, the son of Matthias, by birth a Hebrew, a priest also, and one who at first fought against the Romans myself, and was forced to be present at what was done afterwards, [am the author of this work.]

2. Now at the time when this great concussion of affairs happened, the affairs of the Romans were themselves in great disorder. Those Jews also, who were for innovations, then arose when the times were disturbed; they were also in a flourishing condition for strength and riches, insomuch that the affairs of the east were then exceeding tumultuous, while some hoped for gain, and others were afraid of loss in such troubles; for the Jews hoped that all of their nation who were beyond Euphrates would have raised an insurrection together with them. The Gauls also, in the neighbourhood of the Romans, were in motion, and the Celtæ were not quiet; but all was in disorder after the death of Nero. And the opportunity now offered induced many to aim at the royal power; and the soldiery affected change, out of the hopes of getting money. I thought it therefore an absurd

[1] Who these Upper Barbarians, remote from the sea, were, Josephus himself will inform us, sect. 2, viz.: The Parthians and Babylonians, and remotest Arabians [or the Jews among them;] besides the Jews beyond Euphrates, and the Adiabeni, or Assyrians. When we also learn, that these Parthians, Babylonians, the remotest Arabians [or at least the Jews among them,] as also the Jews beyond Euphrates, and the Adiabeni, or Assyrians, understood Josephus' Hebrew, or rather Chaldaic books of the Jewish War, before they were put into the Greek language.

thing to see the truth falsified in affairs of such great consequence, and to take no notice of it; but to suffer those Greeks and Romans that were not in the wars to be ignorant of these things, and to read either flatteries or fictions, while the Parthians, and the Babylonians, and the remotest Arabians, and those of our nation beyond Euphrates, with the Adiabeni, by my means, knew ·accurately both whence the war begun, what miseries it brought upon us, and after what manner it ended.

3. It is true, these writers have the confidence to call their accounts histories; wherein yet they seem to me to fail of their own purpose, as well as to relate nothing that is sound. For they have a mind to demonstrate the greatness of the Romans, while they still diminish and lessen the actions of the Jews; as not discerning how it cannot be that those must appear to be great who have only conquered those that were little. Nor are they ashamed to overlook the length of the war, the multitude of the Roman forces who so greatly suffered in it, or the might of the commanders; whose great labours about Jerusalem will be deemed inglorious, if what they achieved be reckoned but a small matter.

4. However, I will not go to the other extreme, out of opposition to those men who extol the Romans, nor will I determine to raise the actions of my countrymen too high; but I will prosecute the actions of both parties with accuracy. Yet shall I suit my language to the passions I am under, as to the affairs I describe, and must be allowed to indulge some lamentations upon the miseries undergone by my own country. For that it was a seditious temper of our own that destroyed it, and that they were the tyrants among the Jews who brought the Roman power upon us, who unwillingly attacked us, and

occasioned the burning of our holy temple; Titus
Cæsar, who destroyed it, is himself a witness, who,
during the entire war, pitied the people who were
kept under by the seditious, and did often voluntarily delay the taking of the city, and allowed time
to the siege, in order to let the authors have opportunity for repentance. But if any one makes an
unjust accusation against us, when we speak so
passionately about the tyrants, or the robbers, or
sorely bewail the misfortunes of our country, let him
indulge my affections herein, though it be contrary
to the rules for writing history; because it had so
come to pass, that our city, Jerusalem, had arrived
at a higher degree of felicity than any other city
under the Roman government, and yet at last fell
into the sorest of calamities again. Accordingly it
appears to me, that the misfortunes of all men, from
the beginning of the world, if they be compared to
these of the Jews, are not so considerable as they
were; while the authors of them were not foreigners
neither. This makes it impossible for me to contain
my lamentations. But, if any one be inflexible in
his censures of me, let him attribute the facts themselves to the historical part; and the lamentations to
the writer himself only.

5. However, I may justly blame the learned men
among the Greeks, who, when such great actions
have been done in their own times, which, upon the
comparison, quite eclipse the old wars, do yet sit
as judges of those affairs, and pass bitter censures
upon the labours of the best writers of antiquity;
which moderns, although they may be superior to
the old writers in eloquence, yet are they inferior
to them in the execution of what they intended to do.
While these also write new histories about the Assyrians and Medes; as if the ancient writers had

not described their affairs as they ought to have done; although these be as far inferior to them in abilities, as they are different in their notions from them. For of old, every one took upon them to write what happened in his own time; where their immediate concern in the actions made their promises of value; and where it must be reproachful to write lies, when they must be known by the readers to be such. But then, an undertaking to preserve the memory of what hath not been before recorded, and to represent the affairs of one's own time to those that come afterwards, is really worthy of praise and commendation. Now, he is to be esteemed to have taken good pains in earnest, not who does no more than change the disposition and order of other men's works, but he who not only relates what had not been related before, but composes an entire body of history of his own; accordingly, I have been at great charges, and have taken very great pains [about this history,] though I be a foreigner: and do dedicate this work, as a memorial of great actions, both to the Greeks and to the Barbarians. But, for some of our own principal men, their mouths are wide open, and their tongues loosed presently, for gain and law-suits, but quite muzzled up when they are to write history, where they must speak truth and gather facts together with a great deal of pains; and so they leave the writing such histories to weaker people, and to such as are not acquainted with the actions of princes. Yet shall the real truth of historical facts be preferred by us, how much soever it be neglected among the Greek historians.

6. To write concerning the Antiquities of the Jews, who they were [originally,] and how they revolted from the Egyptians, and what country they travelled over, and what countries they seized upon

afterward, and how they were removed out of them, I think this not to be a fit opportunity, and, on other accounts, also superfluous; and this because many Jews before me have composed the histories of our ancestors very exactly; as have some of the Greeks done it also, and have translated our histories into their own tongue, and have not much mistaken the truth in their histories. But then, where the writers of these affairs, and our prophets leave off, thence shall I take my rise, and begin my history. Now as to what concerns that war which happened in my own time, I will go over it very largely, and with all the diligence I am able; but, for what preceded mine own age, that I shall run over briefly.

7. [For example, I shall relate,] how Antiochus, who was named *Epiphanes,* took Jerusalem by force, and held it three years and three months, and was then ejected out of the country by the sons of Asamoneus; after that, how their posterity quarrelled about the government, and brought upon their settlement the Romans and Pompey; how Herod also, the son of Antipater, dissolved their government, and brought Sosius upon them; as also how our people made a sedition upon Herod's death, while Augustus was the Roman emperor, and Quintilius Varus was in that country; and how the war broke out in the twelfth year of Nero, with what happened to Cestius; and what places the Jews assaulted in a hostile manner in the first sallies of the war.

8. As also, [I shall relate] how they built walls about the neighbouring cities; and how Nero, upon Cestius' defeat, was in fear of the entire event of the war, and thereupon made Vespasian general in this war; and how this Vespasian, with the [1] elder of his sons, made an expedition into the country of

[1] Titus.

Judea; what was the number of the Roman army, that he made use of; and how many of his auxiliaries were cut off in all Galilee; and how he took some of its cities entirely, and by force, and others of them by treaty, and on terms. Now, when I come so far, I shall describe the good order of the Romans in war, and the discipline of their legions; the amplitude of both the Galilees, with its nature, and the limits of Judea. And, besides this, I shall particularly go over what is peculiar to the country, the lakes and fountains that are in them, and what miseries happened to every city as they were taken, and all this with accuracy as I saw the things done, or suffered in them. For I shall not conceal any of the calamities I myself endured, since I shall relate them to such as know the truth of them.

9. After this, [I shall relate] how, when the Jews' affairs were become very bad, Nero died, and Vespasian, when he was going to attack Jerusalem, was called back to take the government upon him; what signs happened to him relating to his gaining that government, and what mutations of government then happened at Rome, and how he was unwillingly made emperor by his soldiers, and how, upon his departure to Egypt, to take upon him the government of the empire, the affairs of the Jews became very tumultuous; as also how the tyrants rose up against them, and fell into dissensions amongst themselves.

10. Moreover, [I shall relate] how Titus marched out of Egypt into Judea the second time; as also how, and where, and how many forces he got together, and in what state the city was, by the means of the seditious, at his coming; what attacks he made, and how many ramparts he cast up: of the three walls that encompassed the city, and of their measures;

of the strength of the city, and the structure of the temple, and holy house; and besides the measures of those edifices, and of the altar, and all accurately determined. A description also of certain of their festivals, and [1] seven purifications of purity, and the sacred ministrations of the priests, with the garments of the priests, and of the high priests; and of the nature of the most holy place of the temple without concealing any thing, or adding any thing to the known truth of things.

11. After this, I shall relate the barbarity of the tyrants towards the people of their own nation, as well as the indulgence of the Romans in sparing foreigners; and how often Titus, out of his desire to preserve the city and the temple, invited the seditious to come to terms of accommodation. I shall also distinguish the sufferings of the people, and their calamities; how far they were afflicted by the sedition, and how far by the famine, and at length were taken. Nor shall omit to mention the misfortunes of the deserters, nor the punishments inflicted on the captives: as also how the temple was burnt, against the consent of Cæsar, and how many sacred things that had been laid up in the temple, were snatched out of the fire; and the destruction also of the entire city, with the signs and wonders that went before it; and the taking the tyrants captives, and the multitude of those that were made slaves, and into what different misfortunes they were every one distributed. Moreover, what the Romans did to the remains of the war; and how they demolished the strongholds that were in the country; and how Titus went over the whole country, and

---

[1] These seven, or rather five, degrees of purity or purification, are enumerated hereafter, B. V. ch. v. sect. 6. The rabbins make ten degrees of them, as Reland there informs us.

settled its affairs; together with his return into Italy, and his triumph.

12. I have comprehended all these things in seven books; and have left no occasion for complaint or accusation to such as have been acquainted with this war; and I have written it down for the sake of those that love truth, but not for those that please themselves [with fictitious relations.] And I will begin my account of these things, with what I call my First Chapter.

BOOK I.

CONTAINING THE INTERVAL OF ONE HUNDRED AND SIXTY-
SEVEN YEARS.

[FROM THE TAKING OF JERUSALEM BY ANTIOCHUS EPI-
PHANES, TO THE DEATH OF HEROD THE GREAT.]

CHAPTER I.

*How the city Jerusalem was taken, and the temple
pillaged [by Antiochus Epiphanes.] As also concerning the actions of the Maccabees, Matthias, and
Judas; and concerning the death of Judas.*

1. At the same time that Antiochus, who is called
Epiphanes, had a quarrel with the sixth Ptolemy
about his right to the whole country of Syria, a great
sedition fell among the men of power in Judea, and
they had a contention about obtaining the government; while each of those that were of dignity could
not endure to be subject to their equals. However,
Onias, one of the high priests, got the better, and
cast the sons of Tobias out of the city; who fled
to Antiochus, and besought him to make use of
them for his leaders, and to make an expedition into
Judea. The king being thereto disposed beforehand,
complied with them, and came upon the Jews with
a great army, and took their city bv force, and slew
a great multitude of those that favoured Ptolemy,

and sent out his soldiers to plunder them without mercy. He also spoiled the temple,· and put a stop to the constant practice of offering a daily sacrifice of expiation for three years and six months. But Onias, the high priest, fled to Ptolemy, and received a place from him in Nomus of Heliopolis, where he built a city resembling Jerusalem, and a temple that was like ¹ its temple; concerning which we shall speak more in its proper place hereafter.

2. Now Antiochus was not satisfied either with his unexpected taking the city, or with its pillage, or with the great slaughter he had made there; but being overcome with his violent passions, and remembering what he had suffered during the siege, he compelled the Jews to dissolve the laws of their country, and to keep their infants uncircumcised, and to sacrifice swine's flesh upon the altar; against which they all opposed themselves, and the most approved among them were put to death. Bacchides also, who was sent to keep the fortresses, having these wicked commands, joined to his own natural barbarity, indulged all sorts of the extremest wickedness, and tormented the worthiest of the inhabitants, man by man, and threatened the city every day with open destruction; till at length he provoked the poor sufferers, by the extremity of his wicked doings, to avenge themselves.

3. Accordingly, Matthias, the son of Asamoneus, one of the priests who lived in a village called Modin, armed himself, together with his own family, which had five sons of his in it, and slew Bacchides with

¹ I see little difference in the several accounts in Josephus about the Egyptian temple Onion, of which large complaints are made by his commentators. Onias, it seems, hoped to have it made very like that at Jerusalem, and of the same dimensions; and so he appears to have really done, as far as he was able and thought proper. Of this temple, see Antiq. B. XIII. ch. iii. sect. 1, 2, 3, and Of the War, Book VII. ch. 10, sect. 3.

daggers; and thereupon, out of the fear of the many garrisons [of the enemy,] he fled to the mountains, and so many of the people followed him, that he was encouraged to come down from the mountains, and to give battle to Antiochus' generals, when he beat them, and drove them out of Judea. So he came to the government by this his success, and became the prince of his own people by their own free consent, and then died, leaving the government to Judas, his eldest son.

4. Now Judas, supposing that Antiochus would not lie still, gathered an army out of his own countrymen, and was the first that made a league of friendship with the Romans, and drove Epiphanes out of the country when he had made a second expedition into it, and this by giving him a great defeat there; and when he was warmed by this great success, he made an assault upon the garrison that was in the city, for it had not been cut off hitherto; so he ejected them out of the Upper City, and drove the soldiers into the Lower, which part of the city was called the Citadel. He then got the temple under his power, and cleansed the whole place, and walled it round about, and made new vessels for sacred ministrations, and brought them into the temple, because the former vessels had been profaned. He also built another altar, and began to offer the sacrifices; and when the city had already received its sacred constitution again, Antiochus died; whose son Antiochus succeeded him in the kingdom, and in his hatred to the Jews also.

5. So this Antiochus got together fifty thousand footmen, and five thousand horsemen, and fourscore elephants, and marched through Judea into the mountainous parts. He then took Bethsura, which was a small city; but at a place called Bethzacharias.

where the passage was narrow, Judas met him with his army. However, before the forces joined battle, Judas' brother Eleazer, seeing the very highest of the elephants adorned with a large tower, and with military trappings of gold to guard him, and supposing that Antiochus himself was upon him, he ran a great way before his own army, and cutting his way through the enemies' troops he got up to the elephant; yet could not reach him who seemed to be the king, by reason of his being so high; but still he ran his weapon into the belly of the beast, and brought him down upon himself, and was crushed to death, having done no more than attempted great things, and showed that he preferred glory before life. Now he that governed the elephant was but a private man, and had he proved to be Antiochus, Eleazer had performed nothing more by this bold stroke than that it might appear he chose to die, when he had the bare hope of thereby doing a glorious action; nay, this disappointment proved an omen to his brother [Judas] how the entire battle would end. It is true that the Jews fought it out bravely for a long time, but the king's forces being superior in number, and having fortune on their side, obtained the victory. And when a great many of his men were slain, Judas took the rest with him, and fled to the toparchy of Gophra. So Antiochus went to Jerusalem, and stayed there but a few days, for he wanted provisions, and so he went his way. He left indeed a garrison behind him, such as he thought sufficient to keep the place, but drew the rest of his army off, to take their winter quarters in Syria.

6. Now, after the king was departed, Judas was not idle; for as many of his own nation came to him, so did he gather those that had escaped out of the battle together, and gave battle again to Antiochus'

generals at a village called Adasa; and being too hard for his enemies in the battle, and killing a great number of them, he was at last himself slain also. Nor was it many days afterward that his brother John had a plot laid against him by Antiochus' party, and was slain by them.

CHAPTER II.

Concerning the successors of Judas, who were Jonathan and Simeon, and John Hyrcanus.

1. When Jonathan, who was Judas' brother, succeeded him, he behaved himself with great circumspection in other respects, with relation to his own people; and he corroborated his authority by preserving his friendship with the Romans. He also made a league with Antiochus the son. Yet was not all this sufficient for his security; for the tyrant Trypho, who was guardian to Antiochus' son, laid a plot against him; and, besides that, endeavoured to take off his friends, and caught Jonathan by a wile, as he was going to Ptolemais to Antiochus, with a few persons in his company, and put them in bonds, and then made an expedition against the Jews; but when he was after ward driven away by Simeon, who was Jonathan's brother, and was enraged at his defeat, he put Jonathan to death.

2. However, Simeon managed the public affairs after a courageous manner, and took Gazara, and Joppa, and Jamina, which were cities in the neighbourhood. He also got the garrison under, and demolished the citadel. He was afterward an auxiliary to Antiochus, against Trypho, whom he besieged in Dora, before he went on his expedition against the

Medes; yet could not he make the king ashamed of his ambition, though he had assisted him in killing Trypho; for it was not long ere Antiochus sent Cendebeus his general with an army to lay waste Judea, and to subdue Simeon; yet he, though he were now in years, conducted the war, as if he were a much younger man. He also sent his sons with a band of strong men against Antiochus, while he took part of the army himself with him, and fell upon him from another quarter: he also laid a great many men in ambush in many places of the mountains, and was superior in all his attacks upon them, and when he had been conqueror after so glorious a manner, he was high priest, and also freed the Jews from the dominion of the Macedonians, after a hundred and seventy years of the empire of [Seleucus.]

3. This Simeon also had a plot laid against him, and was slain at a feast by his son-in-law Ptolemy, who put his wife and two sons into prison, and sent some persons to kill John, who was also [1] called *Hyrcanus.* But when the young man was informed of their coming beforehand, he made haste to get to the city, as having a very great confidence in the people there, both on account of the memory of the glorious actions of his father, and of the hatred they could not but bear to the injustice of Ptolemy. Ptolemy also made an attempt to get into the city by another gate; but was repelled by the people, who had just then admitted Hyrcanus; so he retired presently to one of the fortresses that were about Jericho, which was called *Dagon.* Now, when Hyrcanus had

---

[1] Why this John, the son of Simeon, the high priest and governor of the Jews, was called *Hyrcanus,* Josephus nowhere informs us; nor is he called other than *John* at the end of the first book of the Maccabees. However, Sixtus Senensis, when he gives us an epitome of the Greek version of the book here abridged by Josephus, or of the Chronicles of this John Hyrcanus, then extant, assures us that he was called Hyrcanus from his conquest of one of that name. See Authent. Rec. Part. I. p. 27.

received the high priesthood, which his father had
held before, and had offered sacrifice to God, he
made great haste to attack Ptolemy, that he might
afford relief to his mother and brethren.

4. So he laid siege to the fortress, and was superior to Ptolemy in other respects, but was overcome
by him as to the just affection [he had for his relations;] for when Ptolemy was distressed he brought
forth his mother, and his brethren, and set them
upon the wall, and beat them with rods in everybody's sight, and threatened, that unless he would
go away immediately he would throw them down
headlong; at which sight Hyrcanus' commiseration
and concern were too hard for his anger. But his
mother was not dismayed, neither at the stripes she
received, nor at the death with which she was threatened; but stretched out her hands, and prayed her
son not to be moved with the injuries that she had
suffered to spare the wretch; since it was to her
better to die by the means of Ptolemy than to live
ever so long, provided he might be punished for the
injuries he had done to their family. Now John's
case was this: when he considered the courage of his
mother, and heard her entreaty, he set about his
attacks; but when he saw her beaten, and torn to
pieces with the stripes, he grew feeble, and was
entirely overcome by his affections. And as the siege
was delayed by this means, the year of rest came on,
upon which the Jews rest every seventh year as they
do on every seventh day. On this year, therefore,
Ptolemy was freed from being besieged and slew
the brethren of John, with their mother, and fled to
Zeno, who was also called *Cotylas,* who was the
tyrant of Philadelphia.

5. And now Antiochus was so angry at what he
had suffered from Simeon, that he made an expedi-

tion into Judea, and sat down before Jerusalem, and besieged Hyrcanus; but Hyrcanus opened the sepulchre of David, who was the richest of all kings, and took thence about three thousand talents in money, and induced Antiochus, by the promise of three thousand talents, to raise the siege. Moreover, he was the first of the Jews that had money enough, and began to hire foreign auxiliaries also.

6. However at another time, when Antiochus was gone upon an expedition against the Medes, and so gave Hyrcanus an opportunity of being revenged upon him, he immediately made an attack upon the cities of Syria, as thinking, what proved to be the case with them, that they would find them empty of good troops. So he took Medeba and Samea, with the towns in their neighbourhood, as also Sechem and Gerizzim; and besides these [he subdued] the nation of the Chutheans, who dwelt round about that temple which was built in imitation of the temple at Jerusalem; he also took a great many other cities of Idumea, with Adoraon and Marissa.

7. He also proceeded as far as Samaria, where is now the city Sebaste, which was built by Herod the king, and encompassed it all round with a wall, and set his sons Aristobulus and Antigonus, over the siege; who pushed it on so hard, that a famine so far prevailed within the city, that they were forced to eat what never was esteemed food. They also invited Antiochus, who was called *Cyzicenus,* to come to their assistance; whereupon he got ready, and complied with their invitation, but was beaten by Aristobulus and Antigonus; and indeed he was pursued as far as Scythopolis by these brethren, and fled away from them. So they returned back to Samaria, and shut the multitude again within the wall; and when they had taken the city, they de-

molished it, and made slaves of its inhabitants. And, as they had still great success in their undertakings, they did not suffer their zeal to cool, but marched with an army as far as Scythopolis, and made an incursion upon it, and laid waste all the country that lay within Mount Carmel.

8. But then, these successes of John and of his sons made them be envied, and occasioned a sedition in the country, and many there were who got together, and would not be at rest till they broke out into open war, in which war they were beaten. So John lived the rest of his life very happily, and administered the government after a most extraordinary manner, and this for thirty-three entire years together. He died, leaving five sons behind him. He was certainly a very happy man, and afforded no occasion to have any complaint made of fortune on his account. He it was who alone had three of the most desirable things in the world, the government of his nation, and the high priesthood, and the gift of prophecy. For the Deity conversed with him, and he was not ignorant of any thing that was to come afterward; insomuch, that he foresaw and foretold that his two eldest sons would not continue masters of the government; and it will highly deserve our narration, to describe their catastrophe, and how far inferior these men were to their father in felicity.

CHAPTER III.

*How Aristobulus was the first that put a diadem
about his head, and after he had put his mother
and brother to death, died himself, when he had
reigned no more than a year.*

1. FOR after the death of their father, the elder
of them, Aristobulus, changed the government into
a kingdom, and was the first that put a diadem upon
his head, four hundred seventy and one years and
three months after our people came down into this
country; when they were set free from the Babylonian slavery. Now, of his brethren, he appeared to
have an affection for Antigonus, who was next to
him, and made him his equal; but for the rest, he
bound them, and put them in prison. He also put
his mother in bonds, for her contesting the government with him; for John had left her to be the gov-
erness of public affairs. He also proceeded to that
degree of barbarity as to cause her to be pined to
death in prison.

2. But vengeance circumvented him in the affair
of his brother Antigonus, whom he loved, and whom
he made his partner in the kingdom; for he slew
him by the means of the calumnies which ill men
about the palace contrived against him. At first,
indeed, Aristobulus would not believe their reports,
partly out of the affection he had for his brother,
and partly because he thought that a great part of
these tales were owing to the envy of their relaters;
however, as Antigonus came once in a splendid manner from the army to that festival, wherein our
ancient custom is to make tabernacles for God, it

happened, in those days, that Aristobulus was sick, and that, at the conclusion of the feast, Antigonus came up to it, with his armed men about him; and this, when he was adorned in the finest manner possible, and that, in a great measure, to pray to God on the behalf of his brother. Now, at this very time it was, that these ill men came to the king, and told him in what a pompous manner the armed men came, and with what insolence Antigonus marched, and that such his insolence was too great for a private person, and that accordingly he was come with a great band of men to kill him; for that he could not endure this bare enjoyment of royal honour, when it was in his power to take the kingdom himself.

3. Now Aristobulus, by degrees, and unwillingly, gave credit to these accusations; and accordingly he took care not to discover his suspicion openly, though he provided to be secure against any accidents: so he placed the guards of his body in a certain dark subterranean passage: for he lay sick in a place called formerly the Citadel, though afterwards its name was changed to Antonia; and he gave orders, that if Antigonus came unarmed, they should let him alone; but if he came to him in his armour, they should kill him. He also sent some to let him know beforehand, that he should come unarmed. But, upon this occasion, the queen very cunningly contrived the matter with those that plotted his ruin, for she persuaded those that were sent, to conceal the king's message; but to tell Antigonus how his brother had heard he had got a very fine suit of armour made with fine martial ornaments, in Galilee; and because his present sickness hindered him from coming and seeing all that finery, he very much desired to see him now in his armour; because, said he, in a little time thou art going away from me,

4. As soon as Antigonus heard this, the good temper of his brother not allowing him to suspect any harm from him, he came along with his armour on, to show it to his brother; but when he was going along that dark passage, which was called Strato's Tower, he was slain by the body guards, and became an eminent instance how calumny destroys all good-will and natural affection, and how none of our good affections are strong enough to resist envy perpetually.

5. And truly any one would be surprised at Judas upon this occasion. He was of the sect of the Essenes, and had never failed or deceived men in his predictions before. Now, this man saw Antigonus as he was passing along by the temple, and cried out to his acquaintance, (they were not a few who attended upon him as his scholars,) "O strange! it is good for me to die now, since truth is dead before me, and somewhat that I have foretold hath proved false; for this Antigonus is this day alive, who ought to have died this day; and the place where he ought to be slain, according to that fatal decree, was Strato's Tower, which is at the distance of six hundred furlongs from this place; and yet four hours of this day are over already, which point of time renders the prediction impossible to be fulfilled." And, when the old man had said this, he was dejected in his mind, and so continued. But, in a little time, news came, that Antigonus was slain in a subterraneous place, which was itself also called Strato's Tower, by the same name with that of Cæsarea which lay by the seaside, and this ambiguity it was which caused the prophet's disorder.

6. Hereupon Aristobulus repented of the great crime he had been guilty of, and this gave occasion to the increase of his distemper. He also grew worse and

worse, and his soul was constantly disturbed at the thoughts of what he had done, till his very bowels being torn to pieces by the intolerable grief he was under, he threw up a great quantity of blood. And, as one of those servants that attended him carried out that blood, he, by some supernatural providence, slipped and fell down in the very place where Antigonus had been slain; and so he spilt some of the murderer's blood upon the spots of the blood of him that had been murdered, which still appeared. Hereupon a lamentable cry arose among the spectators, as if the servant had spilled the blood on purpose in that place; and as the king heard the cry, he inquired what was the cause of it? and while nobody durst tell him, he pressed them so much the more to let him know what was the matter; so, at length, when he had threatened them, and forced them to speak out, they told; whereupon he burst into tears, and groaned, and said, "So I perceive I am not like to escape the all-seeing eye of God, as to the great crimes I have committed; but the vengeance of the blood of my kinsman pursues me hastily. O thou most impudent body! how long wilt thou retain a soul that ought to die on account of that punishment it ought to suffer for a mother and a brother slain! how long shall I myself spend my blood drop by drop? let them take it all at once; and let their ghosts no longer be disappointed by a few parcels of my bowels offered to them." As soon as he had said these words, he presently died, when he had reigned no longer than a year.

CHAPTER IV.

What actions were done by Alexander Janneus, who reigned twenty-seven years.

1. AND now the king's wife loosed the king's brethren, and made Alexander king, who appeared both elder in age, and more moderate in his temper than the rest; who, when he came to the government, slew one of his brethren, as affecting to govern himself; but had the other of them in great esteem, as loving a quiet life, without meddling with public affairs.

2. Now it happened, that there was a battle between him and Ptolemy, who was called Lathyrus, who had taken the city Asochis. He indeed slew a great many of his enemies, but the victory rather inclined to Ptolemy. But, when this Ptolemy was pursued by his mother Cleopatra, and retired into Egypt, Alexander besieged Gadara, and took it; as also he did Amathus, which was the strongest of all the fortresses that were about Jordan, and therein were the most precious of all the possessions of Theodorus, the son of Zeno. Whereupon Theodorus marched against him, and took what belonged to himself as well as the king's baggage, and slew ten thousand of the Jews. However, Alexander recovered this blow, and turned his force towards the maritime parts, and took Raphia and Gaza, with Anthedon also, which was afterwards called Agrippias by king Herod.

3. But when he had made slaves of the citizens of all these cities, the nation of the Jews made an insurrection against him at a festival; for at those

feasts seditions are generally begun, and it looked as if he should not be able to escape the plot they had laid for him, had not his foreign auxiliaries, the Pisidians and Cicilians assisted him: for, as to the Syrians, he never admitted them among his mercenary troops, on account of their innate enmity against the Jewish nation. And when he had slain more than six thousand of the rebels, he made an incursion into Arabia, and when he had taken that country, together with the Gileadites and Moabites, he enjoined them to pay him tribute, and returned to Amathus; and, as Theodorus was surprised at his great success, he took the fortress, and demolished it.

4. However, when he fought with Obodus, king of the Arabians, who laid an ambush for him near Golan, and a plot against him,. he lost his entire army, which was crowded together in a deep valley, and broken to pieces by the multitudes of camels. And, when he had made his escape to Jerusalem, he provoked the multitude, which hated him before, to make an insurrection against him, and this on account of the greatness of the calamity that he was under. However, he was then too hard for them, and in the several battles that were fought on both sides, he slew not fewer than fifty thousand of the Jews, in the interval of six years. Yet had he no reason to rejoice in these victories, since he did but consume his own kingdom; till at length he fell off fighting, and endeavoured to come to a composition with them, by talking with his subjects. But this mutability and irregularity of his conduct made them hate him still more. And, when he asked them why they so hated him; and what he should do in order to appease them? they said, by killing himself; for that it would be then all they could do to be reconciled to him, who had done such tragical things to them, even

when he was dead. At the same time they invited
Demetrius, who was called Eucerus, to assist them;
and, as he readily complied with their request in
hopes of great advantages, and came with his army,
the Jews joined with those their auxiliaries about
Shechem.

5. Yet did Alexander meet with these forces with
one thousand horsemen, and eight thousand mercenaries that were on foot. He had also with him
that part of the Jews which favoured him, to the
number of ten thousand; while the adverse party
had three thousand horsemen, and fourteen thousand
footmen. Now, before they joined battle, the kings
made proclamation, and endeavoured to draw off
each other's soldiers, and make them revolt: while
Demetrius hoped to induce Alexander's mercenaries
to leave him, and Alexander hoped to induce the
Jews that were with Demetrius to leave him. But,
since neither the Jews would leave off their rage, nor
the Greeks prove unfaithful, they came to an engagement, and to a close fight with their weapons. In
which battle Demetrius was the conqueror, although
Alexander's mercenaries showed the greatest exploits,
both in soul and body. Yet did the upshot of this
battle prove different from what was expected, as to
both of them; for neither did those that invited
Demetrius to come to them continue firm to him,
though he were conqueror; and six thousand Jews,
out of pity to the change of Alexander's condition,
when he was fled to the mountains, came over to him.
Yet could not Demetrius bear this turn of affairs,
but supposing that Alexander was already become
a match for him again, and that all the nation would
[at length] run to him, he left the country, and went
his way.

6. However, the rest of the [Jewish] multitude

did not lay aside their quarrels with him, when the [foreign] auxiliaries were gone; but they had a perpetual war with Alexander, until he had slain the greatest part of them, and driven the rest into the city Bemeselis; and when he had demolished that city, he carried the captives to Jerusalem. Nay, his rage was grown so extravagant, that his barbarity proceeded to the degree of impiety; for, when he had ordered eight hundred to be hung upon crosses in the midst of the city, he had the throats of their wives and children cut before their eyes; and these executions he saw as he was drinking and lying down with his concubines. Upon which so deep a surprise seized on the people, that eight thousand of his opposers fled away the very next night, out of all Judea, whose flight was only terminated by Alexander's death: so at last, though not till late, and with great difficulty, he, by such actions, procured quiet to his kingdom, and left off fighting any more.

7. Yet did that Antiochus, who was also called Dionysus, become an origin of troubles again. This man was the brother of Demetrius, and the [1] last of the race of the Seleucidæ. Alexander was afraid of him, when he was marching against the Arabians; so he cut a deep trench between Antipatris, which was near the mountains, and the shores of Joppa; he also erected a high wall before the trench, and built wooden towers, in order to hinder any sudden approaches. But still he was not able to exclude Antiochus, for he burnt the towers and filled up the trenches, and marched on with his army. And as he looked upon taking his revenge on Alexander, for

[1] Josephus here calls this Antiochus the last of the Seleucidæ, although there remained still a shadow of another king of that family, Antiochus Asiaticus; or Commagenus, who reigned, or rather lay hid, till Pompey quite turned him out, as Dean Aldrich here notes, from Apion and Justin.

endeavouring to stop him, as a thing of less consequence, he marched directly against the Arabians, whose king retired into such parts of the country as were fittest for engaging the enemy, and then on the sudden made his horse turn back, which were in number ten thousand, and fell upon Antiochus' army, while they were in disorder, and a terrible battle ensued. Antiochus' troops, so long as he was alive, fought it out, although a mighty slaughter was made among them by the Arabians; but when he fell, for he was in the fore-front, in the utmost danger in rallying his troops, they all gave ground, and the greatest part of his army were destroyed, either in the action or the flight; and for the rest, who fled to the village of Cana, it happened that they were all consumed by want of necessaries, a few only excepted.

8. About this time it was that the people of Damascus, out of their hatred to Ptolemy, the son of Menneus invited Aretas [to take the government,] and made him king of Celosyria. This man also made an expedition against Judea, and beat Alexander in battle; but afterwards retired by mutual agreement. But Alexander, when he had taken Pella, marched to Gerasa again, out of the covetous desire he had of Theodorus' possessions; and when he had built a triple wall about the garrison, he took the place by force. He also demolished Golan, and. Seleucia, and what was called *The Valley of Antiochus;* besides which, he took the strong fortress of Gamala, and stripped Demetrius, who was governor therein, of what he had, on account of the many crimes laid to his charge, and then returned into Judea, after he had been three whole years in this expedition. And now he was kindly received of the nation, because of the good success he had. So, when

he was at rest from war, he fell into a distemper; for he was afflicted with a quartan ague, and supposed that by exercising himself again in martial affairs, he should get rid of this distemper; but, by making such expeditions at unseasonable times, and forcing his body to undergo greater hardships than it was able to bear, he brought himself to his end. He died, therefore, in the midst of his troubles, after he had reigned seven and twenty years.

CHAPTER V.

Alexandra reigns nine years, during which time the Pharisees were the real rulers of the nation.

1. Now Alexander left the kingdom to Alexandra his wife, and depended upon it, that the Jews would now very readily submit to her, because she had been very averse to such cruelty as he had treated them with, and had opposed his violation of their laws, and had thereby got the good-will of the people. ˙Nor was he mistaken as to his expectations; for this woman kept the dominion, by the opinion that the people had of her piety; for she chiefly studied the ancient customs of her country, and cast those men out of the government that offended against their holy laws. And, as she had two sons by Alexander, she made Hyrcanus the elder high priest; on account of his age, as also, on account of his inactive temper, which no way disposed him to disturb the public. But she retained the younger Aristobulus with her, as a private person, by reason of the warmth of his temper.

2. And now the Pharisees joined themselves to her, to assist her in the government. These are a

certain sect of the Jews that appear more religious than others, and seem to interpret the laws more accurately. Now, Alexandra hearkened to them to an extraordinary degree, as being herself a woman of great piety towards God. But these Pharisees artfully insinuated themselves into her favour by little and little, and became themselves the real administrators of the public affairs: they banished and reduced whom they pleased; they bound and loosed [men] at their pleasure,[1] and, to say all at once, they had the enjoyment of the royal authority, whilst the expenses and the difficulties of it belonged to Alexandra. She was a sagacious woman in the management of great affairs, and intent always upon gathering soldiers together; so that she increased the army the one half, and procured a great body of foreign troops, till her own nation became not only very powerful at home, but terrible also to foreign potentates, while she governed other people, and the Pharisees governed her.

3. Accordingly they themselves slew Diogenes, a person of figure, and one that had been a friend to Alexander: and accused him as having assisted the king with his advice, for crucifying the eight hundred men [before mentioned.] They also prevailed with Alexandra to put to death the rest of those who had irritated him 'against them. Now, she was so superstitious as to comply with their desires, and accordingly they slew whom they pleased themselves; but the principal of those that were in danger fled to Aristobulus, who persuaded his mother to spare the men on account of their dignity, but to expel them out of the city, unless she took them to be innocent;

---

[1] Matt. xvi. 19, xviii. 18. Here we have the oldest and most authentic Jewish exposition of binding and loosing, for punishing or absolving men, not for declaring actions lawful or unlawful; as some modern Jews and Christians vainly pretend.

so they were suffered to go unpunished, and were dispersed all over the country. But, when Alexandra sent out her army to Damascus, under pretence that Ptolemy was always oppressing that city, she got possession of it; nor did it make any considerable resistance. She also prevailed with Tigranes, king of Armenia, who lay with his troops about Ptolemais, and besieged [1] Cleopatra, by agreements and presents, to go away. Accordingly Tigranes soon arose from the siege, by reason of those domestic tumults which happened upon Lucullus' expedition in Armenia.

4. In the meantime, Alexandra fell sick, and Aristobulus, her younger son, took hold of this opportunity with his domestics, of which he had a great many, who were all of them his friends, on account of the warmth of their youth, and got possession of all the fortresses. He also used the sums of money he found in them, to get together a number of mercenary soldiers, and made himself king; and besides this, upon Hyrcanus' complaint to his mother, she compassionated his case, and put Aristobulus' wife and sons under restraint in Antonia, which was a fortress that joined to the north part of the temple. It was, as I have already said, of old called the citadel; but afterwards got the name of Antonia, when Antony was lord [of the East,] just as the other cities, Sebaste and Agrippas, had their names changed, and these given them, from Sebastus and

[1] Strabo, B. XVI. p. 740, relates, that this Selene Cleopatra was besieged by Tigranes, not in Ptolemais, as here, but after she had left Syria in Seleucia, a citadel in Mesopotamia; and adds, that when he had kept her a while in prison, he put her to death. Dean Aldrich supposes here that Strabo contradicts Josephus, which does not appear to me; for although Josephus says both here and in the Antiquities, B. XIII. ch. xvi. sect. 4, that Tigranes besieged her now in Ptolemais, and that he took the city, the Antiquities inform us, yet does he nowhere intimate that he now took the queen herself; so that both the narrations of Strabo and Josephus may still be true notwithstanding.

Agrippa. But Alexandra died before she could punish Aristobulus, for his disinheriting his brother, after she had reigned nine years.

CHAPTER VI.

When Hyrcanus, who was Alexandra's heir, receded from his claim of the crown, Aristobulus is made king, and afterward the same Hyrcanus, by the means of Antipater, is brought back by Aretas. At last Pompey is made the arbitrator of the dispute between the brothers.

1. Now Hyrcanus was heir to the kingdom, and to him did his mother commit it before she died; but Aristobulus was superior to him in power and magnanimity; and when there was a battle between them, to decide the dispute about the kingdom, near Jericho, the greatest part deserted Hyrcanus, and went over to Aristobulus; but Hyrcanus, with those of his party who stayed with him, fled to Antonia, and got into his power the hostages that might be for his preservation (which were Aristobulus' wife, with her children;) but they came to an agreement, before things should come to extremities, that Aristobulus should be king, and Hyrcanus should resign that up, but retain all the rest of his dignities, as being the king's brother. Hereupon they were reconciled to each other in the temple, and embraced one another in a very kind manner, while the people stood round about them: they also changed their houses, while Aristobulus went to the royal palace, and Hyrcanus retired to the house of Aristobulus.

2. Now, those other people which were at variance

with Aristobulus were afraid upon his unexpected
obtaining the government; and especially this concerned [1] Antipater, whom Aristobulus hated of old.
He was by birth an Idumean, and one of the principal of that nation on account of his ancestors and
riches, and other authority to him belonging; he also
persuaded Hyrcanus to fly to Aretas, the king of
Arabia, and to lay claim to the kingdom; as also,
he persuaded Aretas to receive Hyrcanus, and to
bring him back to his kingdom: he also cast great
reproaches upon Aristobulus, as to his morals, and
gave great commendations to Hyrcanus, and exhorted Aretas to receive him, and told him how becoming a thing it would be for him, who ruled so
great a kingdom, to afford his assistance to such as
are injured; alleging that Hyrcanus was treated unjustly, by being deprived of that dominion which
belonged to him by the prerogative of his birth.   And
when he had predisposed them both to do what he
would have them, he took Hyrcanus by night, and
ran away from the city, and continuing his flight with
great swiftness, he escaped to the place called *Petra,*
which is the royal seat of the king of Arabia, where
he put Hyrcanus into Aretas' hand; and by discoursing much with him, and gaining upon him with
many presents, he prevailed with him to give him
an army that might restore him to his kingdom.   This
army consisted of fifty thousand footmen and horsemen, against which Aristobulus was not able to make
resistance, but was deserted in his first onset, and
was driven to Jerusalem: he also had been taken at
first by force, if Scaurus, the Roman general, had
not come and seasonably interposed himself, and
raised the siege.   This Scaurus was sent into Syria

---

[1] That this Antipater, the father of Herod the Great, was an Idumean,
as Josephus affirms here, see the note on Antiq. B. XIV. ch. xv. sect. 2.

from Armenia by Pompey the Great, when he fought against Tigranes: so Scaurus came to Damascus, which had been lately taken by Metellus and Lollius, and caused them to leave the place; and, upon his hearing how the affairs of Judea stood, he made haste thither as to a certain booty.

3. As soon, therefore, as he was come into the country, there came ambassadors from both the brothers, each of them desiring his assistance; but Aristobulus' three hundred talents had more weight with him than the justice of the cause; which sum, when Scaurus had received, he sent a herald to Hyrcanus and the Arabians, and threatened them with the resentment of the Romans, and of Pompey, unless they would raise the siege. So Aretas was terrified, and retired out of Judea to Philadelphia, as did Scaurus return to Damascus again: nor was Aristobulus satisfied with escaping [out of his brother's hands,] but gathered all his forces together, and pursued his enemies, and fought them at a place called Papyron, and slew about six thousand of them, and, together with them, Antipater's brother, Phalion.

4. When Hyrcanus and Antipater were thus deprived of their hopes from the Arabians, they transferred the same to their adversaries: and because Pompey had passed through Syria, and was come to Damascus, they fled to him for assistance; and, [1] without any bribes, they made the same equitable pleas that they had used to Aretas, and besought him to hate the violent behaviour of Aristobulus, and

---

[1] It is somewhat probable, as Havercamp supposes, and partly Spanheim also, that the Latin copy is here the truest; that Pompey did take the many persons offered him by Hyrcanus, as he would have done the others from Aristobulus, sect. 6, although his remarkable abstinence from the 2,000 talents that were in the Jewish temple, when he took it a little afterward, ch. vii. sect. 6, and Antiq. B. XIV. ch. iv. sect. 4, will hardly permit us to desert the Greek copies, all which agree that he did not take them.

to bestow the kingdom upon him to whom it justly belonged, both on account of his good character, and on account of his superiority in age. However, neither was Aristobulus wanting to himself in this case, as relying on the bribes that Scaurus had received: he was also there himself, and adorned himself after a manner the most agreeable to royalty that he was able. But he soon thought it beneath him to come in such a servile manner, and could not endure to serve his own ends in a way so much more abject than he was used to; so he departed from Diopolis.

5. At this his behaviour Pompey had great indignation; Hyrcanus also and his friends made great intercession to Pompey; so he took not only his Roman forces, but many of his Syrian auxiliaries, and marched against Aristobulus. But when he had passed by Pella and Scythopolis, and was come to Corea, where you enter into the country of Judea, when you go up to it through the Mediterranean parts, he heard that Aristobulus was fled to Alexandrium, which is a stronghold fortified with the utmost magnificence, and situated upon a high mountain, and he sent to him and commanded him to come down. Now his inclination was to try his fortune in a battle, since he was called in such an imperious manner, rather than to comply with that call. However he saw the multitude were in great fear, and his friends exhorted him to consider what the power of the Romans was, and how it was irresistible; so he complied with their advice, and came down to Pompey; and when he had made a long apology for himself, and for the justness of his cause in taking the government, he returned to the fortress. And when his brother invited him again [to plead his cause,] he came down and spoke about the justice of it, and then went away without any hinderance from

Pompey: so he was between hope and fear. And when he came down it was to prevail with Pompey to allow him the government entirely; and when he went up to the citadel, it was that he might not appear to debase himself too low. However, Pompey commanded him to give up his fortified places, and forced him to write to every one of their governors to yield them up; they having had this charge given them, to obey no letters but what were of his own handwriting. Accordingly he did what he was ordered to do; but had still an indignation in what was done, and retired to Jerusalem, and prepared to fight with Pompey.

6. But Pompey did not give him time to make any preparations [for a siege,] but followed him at his heels; he was also obliged to make haste in his attempt, by the death of Mithridates, of which he was informed about Jericho. Now here is the most fruitful country of Judea, which bears a vast number of palm-trees, besides the balsam-tree, whose sprouts they cut with sharp stones, and at the incisions they gather the juice, which drops down like tears. So Pompey pitched his camp in that place one night, and then hasted away the next morning to Jerusalem; but Aristobulus was so affrighted at his approach, that he came and met him by way of supplication. He also promised him money, and that he would deliver up both himself and the city into his disposal, and thereby mitigated the anger of Pompey. Yet did not he perform any of the conditions he had agreed to; for Aristobulus' party would not so much as admit Gabinius into the city, who was sent to receive the money that he had promised.

CHAPTER VII.

*How Pompey had the city Jerusalem delivered up
to him, but took the temple [by force.]   How he
went into the Holy of Holies; as also what were
his other exploits in Judea.*

1. AT this treatment Pompey was very angry,
and took Aristobulus into custody.   And when he was
come to the city he looked about where he might make
his attack; for he saw the walls were so firm that it
would be hard to overcome them, and that the valley
before the walls was terrible; and that the temple,
which was within that valley, was itself encompassed
with a very strong wall, insomuch that if the city
were taken, the temple would be a second place of
refuge for the enemy to retire to.

2. Now, as he was long in deliberating·about this
matter, a sedition arose among the people within the
city: Aristobulus' party being willing to fight, and to
set their king at liberty, while the party of Hyrcanus
were for opening the gates to Pompey; and the dread
people were in, occasioned these last to be a very
numerous party, when they looked upon the excellent
order the Roman soldiers were in.   So Aristobulus'
party was worsted, and retired into the temple, and
cut off the communication between the temple and
the city, by breaking down the bridge that joined
them together, and prepared to make an opposition
to the utmost; but as the others had received the
Romans into the city, and had delivered up the palace
to him, Pompey sent Piso, one of his great officers,
into that palace with an army, who distributed a
garrison about the city, because he could not per-

suade any one of those that had fled to the temple, to come to terms of accommodation; he then disposed all things that were round about them so as might favour their attacks, as having Hyrcanus' party very ready to afford them both counsel and assistance.

3. But Pompey himself filled up the ditch that was on the north side of the temple and the entire valley also, the army itself being obliged to carry the materials for that purpose. And indeed it was a hard thing to fill up that valley by reason of its immense depth, especially as the Jews used all the means possible to repel them from their superior station; nor had the Romans succeeded in their endeavours, had not Pompey taken notice of the seventh days, on which the Jews abstain from all sorts of work on a religious account, and raised his bank, but restrained his soldiers from fighting on those days; for the Jews only acted defensively on sabbath days. But as soon as Pompey had filled up the valley, he erected high towers upon the bank, and brought those engines which they had fetched from Tyre, near to the wall and tried to batter it down; and the slingers of stones beat off those that stood above them, and drove them away; but the towers on this side of the city made very great resistance, and were indeed extraordinary both for largeness and magnificence.

4. Now, here it was that upon the many hardships which the Romans underwent, Pompey could not but admire not only at the other instances of the Jews' fortitude, but especially that they did not at all intermit their religious services, even when they were encompassed with darts on all sides; for, as if the city were in full peace, their daily sacrifices and purifications, and every branch of their religious worship was still performed to God with the utmost exactness. Nor indeed, when the temple was actually

EXCAVATION; CITY WALL, NORTH.

It is the northern wall—the bend inclosing the high ground of Bezetha, and then running on from the Damascus gate toward the Latin Convent, that has, in every age, sustained the shock of besieging armies; for on this side the approach to the walls is much less acclivitous than on any other; and, at the same time, the level ground, affording room for military evolutions, is much more extensive in this direction than elsewhere. On this side also a broad swell of land, north of the valley of Jehoshaphat, rises—at Scopus, to a commanding height; and it is, therefore, a position which would always be chosen as the base of operations directed against the city.

The wall on this northern side—as appears in the plate— is itself of commanding altitude; and it runs, for the most part, upon a precipitous ridge, which in several places, as at this point, has been rendered more so artificially. A little further toward the east a wide fosse commences, and runs on to the corner, which it turns. What purpose precisely the excavation here represented was intended to subserve, or, indeed, to what age it should be attributed, or by whom effected, does not appear; but it is one of those spots to which it is well to direct the attention of travellers, inasmuch as it offers itself to exploration, which might probably reveal—if nothing more—the date of the foundations of the wall.

taken; and they were every day slain about the altar, did they leave off the instances of their divine worship that were appointed by their law; for it was in the third month of the siege before the Romans could even with great difficulty overthrow one of the towers and get into the temple. Now he that first of all ventured to get over the wall, was Faustus Cornelius, the son of Sylla; and next after him were two centurions, Furius and Fabius; and every one of these was followed by a cohort of his own, who encompassed the Jews on all sides, and slew them, some of them as they were running for shelter to the temple, and others as they, for a while, fought in their own defence.

5. And now did many of the priests, even when they saw their enemies assailing them with swords in their hands, without any disturbance, go on with their divine worship, and were slain while they were offering their drink-offerings, and burning their incense, as preferring the duties about their worship to God, before their own preservation. The greatest part of them were slain by their own countrymen, of the adverse faction, and an innumerable multitude threw themselves down precipices; nay, some there were who were so distracted among the insuperable difficulties they were under, that they set fire to the buildings that were near to the wall, and were burnt together with them. Now of the Jews were slain twelve thousand; but of the Romans very few were slain, but a great number were wounded.

6. But there was nothing that affected the nation so much, in the calamities they were then under, as that their holy place, which had been hitherto seen by none, should be laid open to strangers; for [1] Pom-

---

[1] Thus says Tacitus, Cn. Pompeius first of all subdued the Jews, and went into their temple, by right of conquest, Hist. B. V. ch. ix., nor did he touch any of its riches, as has been observed on the parallel place of the Antiquities, B. XIV. ch. iv. sect. 4, out of Cicero himself.

pey, and those that were about him, went into the temple itself, whither it was not lawful for any to enter but the high priest, and saw what was reposited therein, the candlestick with its lamps, and the table, and the pouring vessels, and the censers, all made entirely of gold, as also, a great quantity of spices heaped together, with two thousand talents of sacred money. Yet did not he touch that money, nor any thing else that was there reposited; but he commanded the ministers about the temple, the very next day after he had taken it, to cleanse it, and to perform their accustomed sacrifices. Moreover, he made Hyrcanus high priest, as one that not only in other respects had showed great alacrity, on his side, during the siege, but as he had been the means of hindering the multitude that was in the country from fighting for Aristobulus, which they were otherwise very ready to have done; by which means he acted the part of a good general, and reconciled the people to him more by benevolence than by terror. Now, among the captives, Aristobulus' father-in-law was taken, who was also his uncle: so those that were the most guilty he punished with decollation; but rewarded Faustus, and those with him that had fought so bravely, with glorious presents, and laid a tribute upon the country and upon Jerusalem itself.

7. He also took away from the nation all those cities they had formerly taken, and that belonged to Celosyria, and made them subject to him that was at that time appointed to be the Roman president there; and reduced Judea within its proper bounds. He also rebuilt [1] Gadara, that had been demolished by the Jews, in order to gratify one Demetrius, who

---

[1] The coin of this Gadara, still extant, with its date from this era, is a certain evidence of this its rebuilding by Pompey, as Spanheim here assures us.

was of Gadara, and was one of his own freed men. He also made other cities free from their dominion, that lay in the midst of the country, such, I mean, as they had not demolished before that time, Hippos, and Scythopolis, as also Pella, and Samaria, and Marissa; and besides these, Ashdod, and Jamnia, and Arethusa; and in like manner dealt he with the maritime cities, Gaza, and Joppa, and Dora, and that which was anciently called *Strato's Tower;* but was afterward rebuilt with the most magnificent edifices, and had its name changed to *Cæsarea* by king Herod. All which he restored to their own citizens, and put them under the province of Syria; which province, together with Judea, and the countries as far as Egypt and Euphrates, he committed to Scaurus as their governor, and gave him two legions to support him; while he made all the haste he could himself to go through Cilicia, in his way to Rome, having Aristobulus and his children along with him, as his captives. They were two daughters and two sons; the one of which sons, Alexander, ran away as he was going; but the younger, Antigonus, with his sisters, were carried to Rome.

CHAPTER VIII.

Alexander, the son of Aristobulus, who ran away from Pompey, makes an expedition against Hyrcanus; but being overcome by Gabinius, he delivers up the fortresses to him. After this Aristobulus escapes from Rome, and gathers an army together; but being beaten by the Romans, he is brought back to Rome; with other things relating to Gabinius, Crassus, and Cassius.

1. In the meantime, Scaurus made an expedition into Arabia, but was stopped by the difficulty of the places about Petra. However, he laid waste the country about Pella, though even there he was under great hardship; for his army was afflicted with famine. In order to supply which want, Hyrcanus afforded him some assistance, and sent him provisions by the means of Antipater; whom also Scaurus sent to Aretas, as one well acquainted with him, to induce him to pay him money to buy his peace. The king of Arabia complied with the proposal, and gave him three hundred talents; upon which Scaurus drew his army out of Arabia.

2. But as for Alexander, that son of Aristobulus who ran away from Pompey, in some time he got a considerable band of men together, and lay heavy upon Hyrcanus, and overran Judea, and was likely to overturn him quickly; and indeed he had come to Jerusalem, and had ventured to rebuild its wall that was thrown down by Pompey, had not Gabinius, who was sent as successor to Scaurus into Syria, showed his bravery, as in many other points, so in making

an expedition against Alexander; who, as he was afraid that he would attack him, so he got together a large army, composed of ten thousand armed footmen, and fifteen hundred horsemen. He also built walls about proper places, Alexandrium, and Hyr canium, and Macherus, that lay upon the mountains of Arabia.

3. However, Gabinius sent before him Marcus Antonius, and followed himself with his whole army; but for the select body of soldiers that were about Antipater, and another body of Jews under the command of Malithus and Pitholaus, these joined themselves to those captains that were about Marcus Antonius, and met Alexander; to which body came Gabinius, with his main army soon afterward; and as Alexander was not able to sustain the charge of the enemies' forces, now they were joined, he retired. But when he was come near to Jerusalem, he was forced to fight, and lost six thousand men in the battle; three thousand of whom fell down dead, and three thousand were taken alive; so he fled with the remainder to Alexandrium.

4. Now, when Gabinius was come to Alexandrium, because he found a great many there encamped, he tried, by promising them pardon for their former offences, to induce them to come over to him, before it came to a fight; but when they would hearken to no terms of accommodation, he slew a great number of them, and shut up a great number of them in the citadel. Now Marcus Antonius, their leader, signalized himself in this battle, who as he always showed great courage, so did he never show it so much as now; but Gabinius, leaving forces to take the citadel, went away himself, and settled the cities that had not been demolished, and rebuilt those that had been destroyed. Accordingly, upon his injunctions, the

following cities were restored: Scythopolis, and Samaria, and Anthedon, and Apolinia, and Jamnia, and
Raphia, and Marissa, and Adoreus, and Gamala, and
Ashdod, and many others; while a great number of
men readily ran to each of them, and became their
inhabitants.

5. When Gabinius had taken care of these cities,
he returned to Alexandrium, and pressed on the
siege. So when Alexander despaired of ever obtaining the government, he sent ambassadors to him, and
prayed him to forgive what he had offended him in,
and gave up to him the remaining fortresses, Hyrcanium and Macherus, as he put Alexandrium into
his hands afterwards: all which Gabinius demolished,
at the persuasion of Alexander's mother, that they
might not be receptacles of men in the second war.
She was now there in order to mollify Gabinius, out
of her concern for her relations that were captives
at Rome, which were her husband and her other
children. After this Gabinius brought Hyrcanus to
Jerusalem, and committed the care of the temple to
him; but ordained the other political government to
be by an aristocracy. He also parted the whole nation into five conventions, assigning one portion to
Jerusalem, another to Gadara, that another should
belong to Amathus, a fourth to Jericho, and to the
fifth division was allotted Sepphoris, a city of Galilee.
So the people were glad to be thus freed from
monarchical government, and were governed for the
future by an aristocracy.

6. Yet did Aristobulus afford another foundation
for new disturbances. He fled away from Rome,
and got together again many of the Jews that were
desirous of a change, such as had borne an affection
to him of old; and when he had taken Alexandrium
in the first place, he attempted to build a wall about

it; but as soon as Gabinius had sent an army against him under Sisenna, and Antonius, and. Servilius, he was aware of it, and retreated to Macherus. And as for the unprofitable multitude, he dismissed them, and only marched on with those that were armed, being to the number of eight thousand, among whom was Pitholaus, who had been the lieutenant at Jerusalem, but deserted to Aristobulus with a thousand of his men: so the Romans followed him, and when it came to a battle, Aristobulus' party for a long time fought courageously: but at length they were overborne by the Romans, and of them five thousand fell down dead, and about two thousand fled to a certain little hill, but the thousand that remained with Aristobulus broke through the Roman army, and marched together to Macherus; and, when the king had lodged the first night upon its ruins, he was in hopes of raising another army, if the war would but cease a while; accordingly, he fortified that stronghold, though it were done after a poor manner. But, the Romans falling upon him, he resisted, even beyond his abilities, for two days, and then was taken, and brought a prisoner to Gabinius, with Antigonus his son, who had fled away together with him from Rome, and from Gabinius he was carried to Rome again. Wherefore the senate put him under confinement, but returned his children back to Judea, because Gabinius informed them by letters, that he had promised Aristobulus' mother to do so, for her delivering the fortresses up to him.

7. But now as Gabinius was marching to the war against the Parthians, he was hindered by Ptolemy, whom, upon his return from Euphrates, he brought back into Egypt, making use of Hyrcanus and Antipater, to provide every thing that was necessary for this expedition; for Antipater furnished him with

money, and weapons, and corn, and auxiliaries; he also prevailed with the Jews that were there, and guarded the avenues at Pelusium, to let them pass. But now, upon Gabinius' absence, the other part of Syria was in motion, and Alexander, the son of Aristobulus, brought the Jews to revolt again. Accordingly, he got together a very great army, and set about killing all the Romans that were in the country; hereupon Gabinius was afraid, (for he was come back already out of Egypt, and obliged to come back quickly by these tumults,) and sent Antipater, who prevailed with some of the revolters to be quiet. However, thirty thousand still continued with Alexander, who was himself eager to fight also; accordingly, Gabinius went out to fight, when the Jews met him, and, as the battle was fought near Mount Tabor, ten thousand of them were slain, and the rest of the multitude dispersed themselves, and fled away. So Gabinius came to Jerusalem, and settled the government as Antipater would have it; thence he marched, and fought and beat the Nabateans; as for Mithridates and Orsanes, who fled out of Parthia, he sent them away privately, but gave it out among the soldiers that they had run away.

8. In the meantime, Crassus came as successor to Gabinius in Syria. He took away all the rest of the gold belonging to the temple of Jerusalem, in order to furnish himself for his expeditions against the Parthians. He also took away the two thousand talents which Pompey had not touched; but when he had passed over Euphrates, he perished himself, and his army with him; concerning which affairs this is not a proper time to speak [more largely.]

9. But now Cassius, after Crassus put a stop to the Parthians, who were marching in order to enter Syria, Cassius had fled into that province, and when

he had taken possession of the same, he made a hasty march into Judea; and, upon his taking Taricheæ, he carried thirty thousand Jews into slavery. He also slew Pitholaus, who had supported the seditious followers of Aristobulus, and it was Antipater who advised him so to do. Now this Antipater married a wife of an eminent family among the Arabians, whose name was Cypros, and had four sons born to him by her, Phasaelus and Herod, who was afterwards king, and, besides these, Joseph and Pheroras; and he had a daughter whose name was Salome. Now, as he made himself friends among the men of power every where, by the kind offices he did them, and the hospitable manner that he treated them; so did he contract the greatest friendship with the king of Arabia, by marrying his relation; insomuch, that when he made war with Aristobulus, he sent and intrusted his children with him. So, when Cassius had forced Alexander to come to terms and to be quiet, he returned to Euphrates, in order to prevent the Parthians from repassing it, concerning which matter [1] we shall speak elsewhere.

CHAPTER IX.

Aristobulus is taken off by Pompey's friends, as his son Alexander, by Scipio. Antipater cultivates a friendship with Cæsar, after Pompey's death; he also performs great actions in that war, wherein he assisted Mithridates.

1. Now, upon the flight of Pompey, and of the senate, beyond the Ionian Sea, Cæsar got Rome and

[1] This citation is now wanting.

the empire under his power, and released Aristobulus from his bonds. He also committed two legions to him, and sent him in haste into Syria, as hoping that by his means he should easily conquer that country, and the parts adjoining to Judea. But envy prevented any effect of Aristobulus' alacrity, and the hopes of Cæsar; for he was taken off by poison given him by those of Pompey's party, and, for a long while, he had not so much as a burial vouchsafed him in his own country; but his dead body lay [above ground,] preserved in honey, until it was sent to the Jews by Antony, in order to be buried in the royal sepulchres.

2. His son Alexander also was beheaded by Scipio at Antioch, and that by the command of Pompey, and upon an accusation laid against him before his tribunal, for the mischiefs he had done to the Romans. But Ptolemy, the son of Menneus, who was then ruler of Chalcis, under Libanus, took his brethren to him by sending his son Philippio for them to Ascalon, who took Antigonus, as well as his sisters, away from Aristobulus' wife, and brought them to his father; and falling in love with the younger daughter, he married her, and was afterwards slain by his father, on her account; for Ptolemy himself, after he had slain his son, married her, whose name was Alexandra; on account of which marriage, he took the greater care of her brother and sister.

3. Now, after Pompey was dead, Antipater changed sides, and cultivated a friendship with Cæsar. And, since Mithridates of Pergamus, with the forces he led against Egypt, was excluded from the avenues about Pelusium, and was forced to stay at Ascalon, he persuaded the Arabians, among whom he had lived, to assist him, and came himself to him, at the head of three thousand armed men. He also en-

couraged the men of power in Syria to come to his
assistance, as also of the inhabitants of Libanus,
Ptolemy, and Jamblicus, and another Ptolemy; by
which means the cities of that country came readily
into this war; insomuch, that Mithridates ventured
now, in dependence upon the additional strength that
he had gotten by Antipater, to march forward to
Pelusium; and, when they refused him a passage
through it, he besieged the city: in the attack of
which place, Antipater principally signalized himself,
for he brought down that part of the wall which was
over against him, and leaped first of all into the city,
with the men that were about him.

4. Thus was Pelusium taken. But still, as they
were marching on, those Egyptian Jews that inhabited the country, called the country of Onias,
stopped them. Then did Antipater not only persuade them not to stop them, but to afford provisions
for their army; on which account even the people
about Memphis would not fight against them, but, of
their own accord, joined Mithridates. Whereupon he
went round about Delta, and fought the rest of the
Egyptians at a place called the Jews' Camp: nay,
when he was in danger in the battle with all his right
wing, Antipater wheeled about, and came along the
bank of the river to him; for he had beaten those
that opposed him as he led the left wing. After which
success he fell upon those that pursued Mithridates,
and slew a great many of them, and pursued the remainder so far that he took their camp, while he lost
no more than fourscore of his own men; as Mithridates lost, during the pursuit that was made after
him, about eight hundred. He was also himself saved
unexpectedly, and became an unreproachable witness
to Cæsar of the great actions of Antipater.

6. Whereupon Cæsar encouraged Antipater to un-

dertake other hazardous enterprises for him, and that by giving him great commendations, and hopes of reward. In all which enterprises he readily exposed himself to many dangers, and became a most courageous warrior; and had many wounds, almost all over his body, as demonstrations of his valour. And, when Cæsar had settled the affairs of Egypt, and returning into Syria again, he gave him the privilege of a Roman citizen, and freedom from taxes, and rendered him an object of admiration by the honours and marks of friendship he bestowed upon him. On this account it was that he also confirmed Hyrcanus in the high priesthood.

CHAPTER X.

Cæsar makes Antipater procurator of Judea; as does Antipater appoint Phasaelus to be governor of Jerusalem, and Herod governor of Galilee; who, in some time, was called to answer for himself [before the Sanhedrim,] where he is acquitted. Sextus Cæsar is treacherously killed by Basus, and is succeeded by Marcus.

1. ABOUT this time it was that Antigonus, the son of Aristobulus, came to Cæsar, and became, in a surprising manner, the occasion of Antipater's farther advancement; for, whereas he ought to have lamented that his father appeared to have been poisoned on account of his quarrels with Pompey, and to have complained of Scipio's barbarity towards his brother, and not to mix any invidious passion when he was suing for mercy; besides those things, he came before Cæsar, and accused Hyrcanus and Antipater, how

they had driven him and his brethren entirely out of their native country, and had acted in a great many instances unjustly and extravagantly with relation to their nation, and that as to his assistance they had sent him into Egypt, it was not done out of good-will to him, but out of the fear they were in from former quarrels, and in order to gain pardon for their friendship to [his enemy Pompey.]

2. Hereupon Antipater threw away his garments, and showed the multitude of the wounds he had, and said, that "as to his good-will to Cæsar, he had no occasion to say a word, because his body cried aloud, though he said nothing himself: that he wondered at Antigonus' boldness, while he was himself no other than the son of an enemy to the Romans, and of a fugitive, and had it by inheritance from his father to be fond of innovations and seditions, that he should undertake to accuse other men before the Roman governor, and endeavour to gain some advantages to himself, when he ought to be contented that he was suffered to live; for that the reason of his desire of governing public affairs, was not so much because he was in want of it, but because, if he could once obtain the same he might stir up a sedition among the Jews, and use what they should gain from the Romans, to the disservice of those that gave it him."

3. When Cæsar heard this, he declared Hyrcanus to be the most worthy of the high priesthood, and gave leave to Antipater to choose what authority he pleased; but he left the determination of such dignity to him that bestowed the dignity upon him; so he was constituted procurator of all Judea, and obtained leave, moreover, to rebuild [1] those walls of his country

[1] What is here noted by Hudson and Spanheim, that this grant of leave to rebuild the walls of the cities of Judea was made by Julius Cæsar, not as here to Antipater, but to Hyrcanus, Antiq. B. XIV. ch. viii. sect. 5, has hardly an appearance of a contradiction; Antipater being

that had been thrown down. These honorary grants
Cæsar sent orders to have engraved in the capitol, that
they might stand there as indications of his own justice, and of the virtue of Antipater.

4. But as soon as Antipater had conducted Cæsar
out of Syria, he returned to Judea, and the first
thing he did, was to rebuild that wall of his own
country, [Jerusalem,] which Pompey had overthrown,
and then to go over the country, and to quiet the
tumults that were therein; where he partly threatened,
and partly advised every one, and told them, that,
"in case they would submit to Hyrcanus, they would
live happily and peaceably, and enjoy what they
possessed, and that with universal peace and quietness; but that, in case they hearkened to such as had
some frigid hopes; by raising new troubles to get
themselves some gain, they should then find him to
be their lord instead of their procurator; and find
Hyrcanus to be a tyrant instead of a king; and both
the Romans and Cæsar to be their enemies, instead
of rulers; for that they would not suffer him to be
removed from the government, whom they had made
their governor." And, at the same time that he said
this, he settled the affairs of the country by himself,
because he saw that Hyrcanus was inactive, and not
fit to manage the affairs of the kingdom. So he
constituted his eldest son, Phasaelus, governor of
Jerusalem, and of the parts about it; he also sent
his next son, Herod, who was ¹ very young, with
equal authority into Galilee.

5. Now Herod was an active man, and soon found

now perhaps considered only as Hyrcanus' deputy and minister; although
he afterwards made a cypher of Hyrcanus, and, under great decency of
behaviour to him, took the real authority to himself.
    ¹ Or 25 years of age. See the note on Antiq. B. I. ch. xii. sect. 3,
and on B. XIV. ch. ix. sect. 2, and Of the War, B. II. ch. xi. sect. 6,
and Polyb. B. XVII. p. 725.

proper materials for his active spirit to work upon. As therefore he found that Hezekias, the head of the robbers, ran over the neighbouring parts of Syria with a great band of men, he caught him and slew him and many more of the robbers with him; which exploit was chiefly grateful to the Syrians, insomuch that hymns were sung in Herod's commendation, both in the villages and in the cities, as having procured their quietness, and having preserved what they possessed to them; on which occasion he became acquainted with Sextus Cæsar, a kinsman of the great Cæsar, and president of Syria. A just emulation of his glorious actions excited Phasaelus also to imitate him. Accordingly, he procured the good-will of the inhabitants of Jerusalem, by his own management of the city affairs, and did not abuse his power in any disagreeable manner; whence it came to pass, that the nation paid Antipater the respects that were due only to a king, and the honours they all yielded him were equal to the honours due to an absolute lord; yet did he not abate any part of that good-will or fidelity which he owed to Hyrcanus.

6. However, he found it impossible to escape envy in such his prosperity; for the glory of these young men affected, even Hyrcanus himself already privately, though he said nothing of it to anybody: but what he principally was grieved at, was the great actions of Herod, and that so many messengers came one before another, and informed him of the great reputation he got in all his undertakings. There were also many people in the royal palace itself, who inflamed his envy at him: those, I mean, who were obstructed in their designs by the prudence either of the young men or of Antipater. These men said, that by committing the public affairs to the management of Antipater and of his sons, he sat down with

nothing but the bare name of a king, without any of its authority; and they asked him, how long he would so far mistake himself, as to breed up kings against his own interest? for that they did not now conceal their government of affairs any longer, but were plainly lords of the nation, and had thrust him out of his authority: that this was the case when Herod slew so many men without his giving him any command to do it, either by word of mouth, or by his letter, and this in contradiction to the law of the Jews; who, therefore, in case he be not a king, but a private man, still ought to come to his trial, and answer it to him, and to the laws of his country, which do not permit any one to be killed, till he hath been condemned in judgment.

7. Now Hyrcanus was, by degrees, inflamed with those discourses, and at length could bear no longer, but he summoned Herod to take his trial. Accordingly, by his father's advice, and as soon as the affairs of Galilee would give him leave, he came up to [Jerusalem,] when he had first placed garrisons in Galilee; however, he came with a sufficient body of soldiers, so many indeed that he might not appear to have with him an army able to overthrow Hyrcanus' government, nor yet so few as to expose him to the insults of those that envied him. However, Sextus Cæsar was in fear for the young man, lest he should be taken by his enemies, and brought to punishment; so he sent some to denounce expressly to Hyrcanus, that he should acquit Herod of the capital charge against him; who acquitted him accordingly, as being otherwise inclined also so to do, for he loved Herod.

8. But Herod, supposing that he had escaped punishment, with the consent of the king retired to Sextus, to Damascus, and got every thing ready in order not to obey him, if he should summon him again;

whereupon those that were evil disposed irritated Hyrcanus, and told him, that Herod was gone away in anger, and was prepared to make war upon him; and as the king believed what they said, he knew not what to do, since he saw his antagonist was stronger than he was himself. And now, since Herod was made general of Celosyria, and Samaria, by Sextus Cæsar, he was formidable, not only from the good-will which the nation bore him, but by the power he himself had; insomuch that Hyrcanus fell into the utmost degree of terror, and expected he would presently march against him with his army.

9. Nor was he mistaken in the conjecture he made, for Herod got his army together, out of the anger he bore him for his threatening him with the accusation in a public court, and led it to Jerusalem, in order to throw Hyrcanus down from his kingdom: and this he had soon done, unless his father and brother had gone out together and broken the force of his fury, and this by exhorting him to carry his revenge no farther than to threatening and affrighting, but to spare the king, under whom he had been advanced to such a degree of power; and that he ought not to be so much provoked at his being tried, as to forget to be thankful that he was acquitted; nor so long to think upon what was of a melancholy nature, as to be ungrateful for his deliverance; and if we ought to reckon that God is the arbitrator of success in war, an unjust cause is of more disadvantage than an army can be of advantage; and that therefore he ought not to be entirely confident of success in a case where he is to fight against his king, his supporter, and one that had often been his benefactor, and that had never been severe to him, any otherwise than as he had hearkened to evil counsellors, and this no farther than by bringing a shadow of

injustice upon him. So Herod was prevailed upon by these arguments, and supposed that what he had already done was sufficient for his future hopes, and that he had enough shown his power to the nation.

10. In the meantime, there was a disturbance among the Romans about Apamia, and a civil war occasioned by the treacherous [1] slaughter of Sextus Cæsar, by Cicilius Bassus, which he perpetrated out of his good-will to Pompey; he also took the authority over his forces: but, as the rest of Cæsar's commanders attacked Bassus with their whole army, in order to punish him for the murder of Cæsar, Antipater also sent them assistance by his sons, both on account of him that was murdered, and on account of that Cæsar who was still alive, both of which were their friends; and as this war grew to be of a considerable length, Marcus came from Italy as successor to Sextus.

CHAPTER XI.

Herod is made procurator of all Syria: Malichus is afraid of him, and takes Antipater off by poison; whereupon the tribunes of the soldiers are prevailed with to kill him.

1. THERE was at this time a mighty war raised among the Romans upon the sudden and treacherous slaughter of Cæsar by Cassius and Brutus, after he had held the government for [2] three years and seven

---

[1] Many writers of the Roman history give an account of this murder of Sextus Cæsar, and of the war at Apamia upon that occasion.

[2] In the Antiquities, B. XIV. ch. xi. sect. 1, the duration of the reign of Julius Cæsar, is three years six months; but here three years seven months, beginning rightly, says Dean Aldrich, from his second dictator-

months. Upon this murder there were very great
agitations, and the great men were mightily at difference one with another, and every one betook himself
to that party where they had the greatest hopes of
their own, of advancing themselves. Accordingly,
Cassius came into Syria, in order to receive the forces
that were at Apamia, where he procured a reconciliation between Bassus and Marcus, and the legions
which were at difference with him; so he raised the
siege of Apamia, and took upon him the command
of the army, and went about exacting tribute of the
cities, and demanding their money to such a degree
as they were not able to bear.

2. So he gave command that the Jews should
bring in seven hundred talents: whereupon Antipater,
out of his dread of Cassius' threats, parted the raising
of this sum among his sons, and among others of his
acquaintance, and to be done immediately, and among
them he required one Malichus, who was at enmity
with him, to do his part also, which necessity forced
him to do. Now Herod, in the first place, mitigated
the passion of Cassius, by bringing his share out of
Galilee, which was a hundred talents, on which account he was in the highest favour with him, and
when he reproached the rest for being tardy, he was
angry at the cities themselves; so he made slaves of
Gophna and Emmaus, and two others of less note,
nay, he proceeded as if he would kill Malichus, because he had not made greater haste in exacting his
tribute; but Antipater prevented the ruin of this
man, and of the other cities, and got into [1] Cassius'

ship. It is probable the real duration might be three years and between
six and seven months.

[1] It appears evidently by Josephus' accounts, both here and in his
Antiquities, B. XIV. ch. xi. sect. 2, that this Cassius, one of Cæsar's
murderers, was a bitter oppressor, and exactor of tribute in Judea; these
700 talents amount to about £300,000 sterling, and are about half the yearly
revenues of king Herod afterwards. See the note on Antiq B. XVII.

favour by bringing in a hundred talents immediately.

3. However, when Cassius was gone, Malichus forgot the kindness that Antipater had done him, and laid frequent plots against him that had saved him, as making haste to get him out of the way, who was an obstacle to his wicked practices; but Antipater was so much afraid of the power and cunning of the man, that he went beyond Jordan in order to get an army to guard himself against his treacherous designs; but when Malichus was caught in his plot, he put upon Antipater's sons by his impudence, for he thoroughly deluded Phasaelus, who was the guardian of Jerusalem, and Herod who was intrusted with the weapons of war, and this by a great many excuses and oaths, and persuaded them to procure his reconciliation to their father. Thus was he preserved again by Antipater, who dissuaded Marcus, the then president of Syria, from his resolution of killing Malichus, on account of his attempts for innovation.

4. Upon the war between Cassius and Brutus on one side, against the younger Cæsar [Augustus] and Antony on the other, Cassius and Marcus got together an army out of Syria; and because Herod was likely to have a great share in providing necessaries, they then made him procurator of all Syria, and gave him an army of foot and horse. Cassius promised him also, that after the war was over, he would make him king of Judea; but it so happened, that the power and hopes of his son became the cause of his perdition; for as Malichus was afraid of this, he corrupted one of the king's cupbearers with money, to give a poisoned potion to Antipater; so he became a sacrifice to Malichus' wickedness, and died at a feast. He was a man

ch. xi. sect. 4. It also appears that Galilee then paid no more than 100 talents, or the 7th part of the entire sum to be levied in all the country.

in other respects active in the management of affairs, and one that recovered the government to Hyrcanus, and preserved it in his hands.

5. However, Malichus, when he was suspected of poisoning Antipater, and when the multitude was angry with him for it, denied it, and made the people believe he was not guilty. He also prepared to make a great figure, and raised soldiers; for he did not suppose that Herod would be quiet, who indeed came upon him with an army presently, in order to revenge his father's death, but upon hearing the advice of his brother Phasaelus, not to punish him in an open manner, lest the multitude should fall into a sedition, he admitted of Malichus' apology, and professed that he cleared him of the suspicion; he also made a pompous funeral for his father.

6. So Herod went to Samaria, which was then in a tumult, and settled the city in peace; after which, at the [Pentecost] festival, he returned to Jerusalem, having his armed men with him; hereupon Hyrcanus, at the request of Malichus, who feared his reproach, forbade them to introduce foreigners to mix themselves with the people of the country, while they were purifying themselves; but Herod despised the pretence, and him that gave that command, and came in by night. Upon which Malichus came to him, and bewailed Antipater; Herod also made him believe [he admitted of his lamentations as real,] although he had much ado to restrain his passion at him; however, he did himself bewail the murder of his father, in his letters to Cassins, who, on other accounts, also hated Malichus; Cassius sent him word back that he should avenge his father's death upon him, and privately gave order to the tribunes that were under him, that they should assist Herod in a righteous action he was about.

7. And because, upon the taking of Laodicea by

Cassius, the men of power were gotten together from all quarters, with presents and crowns in their hands, Herod allotted this time for the punishment of Malichus. When Malichus suspected that, and was at Tyre, he resolved to withdraw his son privately from among the Tyrians, who was a hostage there, while he got ready to fly away into Judea; the despair he was in of escaping excited him to think of greater things; for he hoped that he should raise the nation to a revolt from the Romans, while Cassius was busy about the war against Antony, and that he should easily depose Hyrcanus, and get the crown for himself.

8. But fate laughed at the hopes he had; for Herod foresaw what he was so zealous about and invited both Hyrcanus and him to supper; but calling one of the principal servants that stood by him, to him, he sent him out, as though it were to get things ready for supper, but in reality to give notice beforehand, about the plot that was laid against him; accordingly they called to mind what orders Cassius had given them, and went out of the city with their swords in their hands upon the seashore, where they encompassed Malichus round about, and killed him with many wounds. Upon which Hyrcanus was immediately affrighted, till he swooned away, and fell down at the surprise he was in; and it was with difficulty that he was recovered, when he asked who it was that had killed Malichus? and when one of the tribunes replied that it was done by the command of Cassius, "Then, said he, Cassius hath saved both me and my country, by cutting off one that was laying plots against them both." Whether he spoke according to his own sentiments, or whether his fear was such, that he was obliged to commend the action by saying so, is uncertain; however, by this method Herod inflicted punishment upon Malichus.

CHAPTER XII.

*Phasaelus is too hard for Felix; Herod also over-
comes Antigonus in battle; and the Jews accuse
both Herod and Phasaelus, but Antonius acquits
them, and makes them tetrarchs.*

1. WHEN Cassius was gone out of Syria, another
sedition arose at Jerusalem, wherein Felix assaulted
Phasaelus with an army, that he might revenge the
death of Malichus upon Herod, by falling upon his
brother. Now Herod happened then to be with
Fabius, the governor of Damascus, and as he was
going to his brother's assistance, he was detained by
sickness; in the meantime, Phasaelus was by himself
too hard for Felix, and reproached Hyrcanus on account of his ingratitude, both for what assistance
he had afforded Malichus, and for overlooking Malichus' brother, when he possessed himself of the
fortresses; for he had gotten a great many of them
already, and among them the strongest of them all,
Masada.

2. However, nothing could be sufficient for him
against the force of Herod, who, as soon as he was
recovered, took the other fortresses again, and drove
him out of Masada in the posture of a supplicant; he
also drove away Marion, the tyrant of the Tyrians,
out of Galilee, when he had already possessed himself of three fortified places; but as to those Tyrians
whom he had caught, he preserved them all alive;
nay, some of them he gave presents to, and so sent
them away, and thereby procured good-will to him
self from the city, and hatred to the tyrant. Marion
had indeed obtained that tyrannical power of Cassius,

who [1] set tyrants over all Syria; and out of hatred to Herod it was that he assisted Antigonus, the son of Aristobulus, and principally on Fabius' account, whom Antigonus had made his assistant by money, and had him accordingly on his side when he made his descent; but it was Ptolemy, the kinsman of Antigonus, that supplied all that he wanted.

3. When Herod had fought against these in the avenues of Judea, he was conqueror in the battle, drove away Antigonus, and returned to Jerusalem beloved by everybody, for the glorious action he had done; for, those who did not before favour him, did join themselves to him now, because of his marriage into the family of Hyrcanus; for as he had formerly married a wife out of his own country of no ignoble blood, who was called Doris, of whom he begot Antipater; so did he marry Mariamne, the daughter of Alexander the son of Aristobulus, and the granddaughter of Hyrcanus, and was become thereby a relation of the king.

4. But when Cæsar and Antony had slain Cassius near Philippi, and Cæsar was gone to Italy, and Antony to Asia, amongst the rest of the cities which sent ambassadors to Antony, into Bithynia, the great men of the Jews came also, and accused Phasaelus and Herod, that they kept the government by force, and that Hyrcanus had no more than an honourable name. Herod appeared ready to answer this accusation, and, having made Antony his friend by the large sums of money which he gave him, he brought him to such a temper as not to hear the others speak against him, and thus did they part at this time.

5. However, after this there came a hundred of

---

[1] Here we see that Cassius set tyrants over all Syria: so that his assisting to destroy Cæsar does not seem to have proceeded from his true zeal for public liberty, but from a desire to be a tyrant himself.

the principal men among the Jews to Daphne by Antioch to Antony, who was already in love with Cleopatra to the degree of slavery; these Jews put those men that were the most potent, both in dignity and eloquence, foremost, and accused the [1] brethren. But Messala opposed them and defended the brethren, and that while Hyrcanus stood by him, on account of his relation to them. When Antony had heard both sides, he asked Hyrcanus what party was the fittest to govern? who replied, that Herod and his party were the fittest. Antony was glad of that answer, for he had been formerly treated in a hospitable and obliging manner by his father Antipater, when he marched into Judea with Gabinius; so he constituted the brethren tetrarchs, and committed to them the government of Judea.

6. But when the ambassadors had indignation at this procedure, Antony took fifteen of them and put them into custody, whom he was also going to kill presently, and the rest he drove away with disgrace, on which occasion a still greater tumult arose at Jerusalem, so they sent again a thousand ambassadors to Tyre, where Antony now abode, as he was marching to Jerusalem; upon these men, who made a clamour, he sent out the governor of Tyre, and ordered him to punish all that he could catch of them, and to settle those in the administration whom he had made tetrarchs.

7. But before this Herod and Hyrcanus went out upon the seashore, and earnestly desired of these ambassadors that they would neither bring ruin upon themselves, nor war upon their native country, by their rash contentions; and when they grew still more outrageous, Antony sent out armed men, and slew a great many, and wounded more of them; of whom those that were slain were buried by Hyrcanus, as

[1] Phasaelus and Herod.

were the wounded put under the care of physicians by him; yet would not those that had escaped be quiet still, but put the affairs of the city into such disorder, and so provoked Antony, that he slew those whom he had in bonds also.

CHAPTER XIII.

The Parthians bring Antigonus back into Judea, and cast Hyrcanus and Phasaelus into prison. The flight of Herod, and the taking of Jerusalem, and what Hyrcanus and Phasaelus suffered.

1. Now two years afterward, when Barzapharnes, a governor among the Parthians, and Pacorus, the king's son, had possessed themselves of Syria, and when Lysanius had already succeeded upon his father Ptolemy the son of Menneus' death, in the government [of Chalcis,] he prevailed with the governor, by a promise of a thousand talents, and five hundred women, to bring back Antigonus to his kingdom, and to turn Hyrcanus out of it. Pacorus was by these means induced so to do, and marched along the sea coast, while he ordered Barzapharnes to fall upon the Jews as he went along the Mediterranean part of the country; but of the maritime people the Tyrians would not receive Pacorus, although those of Ptolemais and Sidon had received him: so he committed a troop of his horse to a certain cupbearer belonging to the royal family, of his own name [Pacorus,] and gave him orders to march into Judea, in order to learn the state of affairs among their enemies, and to help Antigonus when he should want his assistance.

2. Now as these men were ravaging Carmel, many

of the Jews ran together to Antigonus, and showed
themselves ready to make an incursion into the country; so he sent them before into that place called
¹ *Drymus,* [the wood-land] to sieze upon the place;
whereupon a battle was fought between them, and
they drove the enemy away, and pursued them, and
ran after them as far as Jerusalem, and as their
numbers increased, they proceeded as far as the king's
palace; but as Hyrcanus and Phasaelus received them
with a strong body of men, there happened a battle
in the market-place, in which Herod's party beat the
enemy, and shut them up in the temple, and set
sixty men in the houses adjoining as a guard on them.
But the people that were tumultuous against the
brethren came in, and burnt those men; while Herod,
in his rage for killing them, attacked and slew many
of the people, till one party made incursions on the
other by turns, day by day, in the way of ambushes,
and slaughters were made continually among them.

3. Now, when that festival which we call *Pentecost*
was at hand, all the places about the temple, and the
whole city, was full of a multitude of people that
were come out of the country, and which were the
greatest part of them armed also, at which time
Phasaelus guarded the wall, and Herod, with a few,
guarded the royal palace; and when he made an
assault upon his enemies, as they were out of their
ranks, on the north quarter of the city he slew a very
great number of them, and put them all to flight, and
some of them he shut up within the city, and others
within the outward rampart. In the meantime Antigonus desired that Pacorus might be admitted to
be a reconciler between them; and Phasaelus was

---

¹ This large and noted wood, or wood-land, belonging to Carmel, called
δρυμος by the Septuagint, is mentioned in the Old Testament, 2 Kings
xix. 23, and Isa. xxxviii. 24, and by Strabo, B. XIV. p. 758, as both
Aldrich and Spanheim here remark very pertinently.

prevailed upon to admit the Parthian into the city
with five hundred horse, and to treat him in a hospitable manner, who pretended that he came to quell
the tumult, but in reality he came to assist Antigonus; however, he laid a plot for Phasaelus, and
persuaded him to go as an ambassador to Barzapharnes, in order to put an end to the war, although
Herod was very earnest with him to the contrary,
and exhorted him to kill the plotter, but not expose
himself to the snares he had laid for him, because the
barbarians are naturally perfidious. However Pacorus went out and took Hyrcanus with him, that he
might be the less suspected; he also left some of the
horsemen, [1] called the *Freemen,* with Herod, and conducted Phasaelus with the rest.

4. But now, when they were come to Galilee, they
found that the people of that country had revolted,
and were in arms, who came very cunningly to their
leader, and besought him to conceal his treacherous
intentions by an obliging behaviour to them; accordingly, he at first made them presents; and afterward,
as they went away, laid ambushes for them; and, when
they were come to one of the maritime cities called
Ecdippon, they perceived that a plot was laid for
them; for they were there informed of the promise
of a thousand talents, and how Antigonus had devoted the greatest number of the women that were
there with them, among the five hundred, to the Parthians; they also perceived that an ambush was always
laid for them by the barbarians in the night time;
they had also been seized on before this, unless they
had waited for the seizure of Herod first at Jerusalem, because if he were once informed of this

[1] These accounts, both here and Antiq. B. XIV. ch. xiii. sect. 5, that
the Parthians fought chiefly on horseback, and that only some few of
their soldiers were freemen, perfectly agree with Trogus Pompeius, in
Justin, B. XLI. 2.

treachery of theirs, he would take care of himself; nor was this a mere report, but they saw the guards already not far off them.

5. Nor would Phasaelus think of forsaking Hyrcanus and flying away, although Ophellius earnestly persuaded him to it: for this man had learned the whole scheme of the plot from Saramalla, the richest of all the Syrians. But Phasaelus went up to the Parthian governor, and reproached him to his face, for laying this treacherous plot against them, and chiefly because he had done it for money; and he promised him, that he would give him more money for their preservation than Antigonus had promised to give for the kingdom. But the sly Parthian endeavoured to remove all this suspicion by apologies and by oaths, and then went to [the other] Pacorus; immediately after which those Parthians who were left, and had it in charge, seized upon Phasaelus and Hyrcanus, who could do no more than curse their perfidiousness and their perjury.

6. In the meantime the cupbearer was sent [back,] and laid a plot how to seize upon Herod, by deluding him, and getting him out of the city, as he was commanded to do. But Herod suspected the barbarians from the beginning, and having then received intelligence that a messenger, who was to bring him the letters that informed him of the treachery intended, had fallen among the enemy, he would not go out of the city; though Pacorus said very positively, that he ought to go out, and meet the messengers that brought the letters, for that the enemy had not taken them, and that the contents of them were not accounts of any plots upon them, but of what Phasaelus had done; yet had he heard from others that his brother was seized; and Alexandra,[1]

---

[1] Mariamne here, in the copies.

the shrewdest woman in the world, Hyrcanus' daughter, begged of him that he would not go out, nor trust himself to those barbarians who were now come to make an attempt upon him openly.

7. Now as Pacorus and his friends were considering how they might bring their plot to bear privately, because it was not possible to circumvent a man of so great prudence, by openly attacking him, Herod prevented them, and went off with the persons that were the most nearly related to him by night, and this without their enemies being apprised of it. But, as soon as the Parthians perceived it, they pursued after them, and, as he gave orders for his mother, and sister, and the young woman who was betrothed to him, with her mother, and his youngest brother, to make the best of their way, he himself, with his servants, took all the care they could to keep off the barbarians; and when at every assault, he had slain a great many of them, he came to the stronghold of Masada.

8. Nay, he found by experience that the Jews fell more heavily upon him than did the Parthians, and created him troubles perpetually, and this ever since he was gotten sixty furlongs from the city; these sometimes brought it to a sort of regular battle. Now, in the place where Herod beat them, and killed a great number of them, there he afterward built a citadel, in memory of the great actions he did there, and adorned it with the most costly palaces, and erected very strong fortifications, and called it from his own name *Herodium*. Now, as they were in their flight, many joined themselves to him every day; and at a place called *Thresa* of *Idumea*, his brother Joseph met him, and advised him to ease himself of a great number of his followers; because Masada would not contain so great a multitude, which were

SUPPOSED REMAINS OF HERODIUM.

What Josephus affirms concerning that Herodium which, of the two he mentions, was nearest to Jerusalem, entirely consists, as well with the position, as with the present appearance of the remains before us. He says that two fortress-palaces were constructed by Herod, each with the intention, as it seems, of affording him—like Masada—a place of refuge in the event of popular commotions, and of perpetuating his name; and one of them was to serve as his place of sepulture. And it was the one now in question, probably, (not that towards Arabia,) which was to receive, and which in fact did receive, his remains. This Herodium is said to have been an artificial mound—κολωνὸν ὄντα χειροποίητον, and so may have been the actual apex, or truncated cone, of what is called the Frank Mountain. This apex is stated to rise about 300 feet above the level of the broader hill, of which it forms the central point, and which itself has an elevation of 300 or 400 feet above the level of the adjoining Wady. On what account it might merit the epithet bestowed upon it—μαστοειδῆ, better than does almost any even-surfaced rotund hill, does not appear; and it is probable that ample justice would be done to the phrase, here employed by Josephus, and its whole import conveyed, if it were rendered with a less rigid regard to its etymology. In translating this word somewhat more laxly, we should be sustained by a passage in Polybius (V. 70), who, in speaking of Itabyrium, says it is situated upon a round hill (Tabor), ἐπὶ λόφου μαστοειδοῦς—*in rotundo colle.* The Frank Mountain, now assumed to be the Herodium of Josephus, although not to be compared with Tabor, and not rising to half its height, is yet such as that to it, and with nearly equal propriety, may be applied the term which Josephus employs in describing it, as Polybius does in speaking of the other. The Frank Mountain, in fact, is seen far and wide, and it attracts the eye from almost every eminence of this district, south of Jerusalem.

above nine thousand. Herod complied with this advice, and sent away the most cumbersome part of his
retinue, that they might go into Idumea, and gave
them provisions for their journey; but he got safe to
the fortress with his nearest relations, and retained
with him only the stoutest of his followers; and there
it was that he left eight hundred of his men as a
guard for the women, and provisions sufficient for
a siege, but he made haste himself to Petra of Arabia.

9. As for the Parthians in Jerusalem, they betook
themselves to plundering, and fell upon the houses
of those that were· fled, and upon the king's palace;
and spared nothing but Hyrcanus' money, which was
not above three hundred talents. They lighted on
other men's money also, but not so much as they
hoped for, for Herod, having a long while had a
suspicion of the perfidiousness of the barbarians, had
taken care to have what was most splendid among
his treasures conveyed into Idumea, as every one
belonging to him had in like manner done also. But
the Parthians proceeded to that degree of injustice,
as to fill all the country with war without denouncing
it, and to demolish the city Marissa, and not only
set up Antigonus for king, but to deliver Phasaelus
and Hyrcanus bound into his hands, in order to their
being tormented by him. Antigonus himself also bit
off Hyrcanus' ears with his own teeth, as he fell down
upon his knees to him, that so he might never be able,
upon any mutation of affairs, to take the high priesthood again, for the high priests that officiated were
to be complete and without blemish.

10. However, he failed in his purpose of abusing
Phasaelus by reason of his courage, for though he
neither had the command of his sword nor of his
hands, be prevented all abuses by dashing his head
against a stone; so he demonstrated himself to be

Herod's own brother, and Hyrcanus a most degenerate relation, and died with great bravery, and made the end of his life agreeable to the actions of it. There is also another report about his end, viz. that he recovered of that stroke, and that a surgeon, who was sent by Antigonus to heal him, filled the wound with poisonous ingredients, and so killed him; whichsoever of these deaths he came to, the beginning of it was glorious. It is also reported, that before he expired he was informed by a certain poor woman how Herod had escaped out of his hands, and that he said thereupon, "I now die with comfort, since I leave behind me one alive, that will avenge me of mine enemies."

11. This was the death of Phasaelus; but the Parthians, although they had failed of the women they chiefly desired, yet did they put the government of Jerusalem into the hands of Antigonus, and took away Hyrcanus, and bound him, and carried him to Parthia.

CHAPTER XIV.

When Herod is rejected in Arabia, he makes haste to Rome, where Antony and Cæsar join their interest to make him king of the Jews.

1. Now Herod did the more zealously pursue his journey into Arabia, as making haste to get money of the king, while his brother was yet alive, by which money alone it was that he hoped to prevail upon the covetous temper of the barbarians to spare Phasaelus; for he reasoned thus with himself, that if the Arabian king was too forgetful of his father's friendship with him, and was too covetous to make

him a free gift, he would however borrow of him
as much as might redeem his brother, and put into
his hands, as a pledge, the son of him that was to
be redeemed; accordingly he led his brother's son
along with him, who was of the age of seven years.
Now he was ready to give three hundred talents for
his brother, and intended to desire the intercession
of the Tyrians, to get them accepted; however fate
had been too quick for his diligence; and since
Phasaelus was dead, Herod's brotherly love was now
in vain. Moreover, he was not able to find any lasting friendship among the Arabians; for their king,
Malichus, sent to him immediately and commanded
him to return back out of his country, and used the
name of the Parthians as a pretence for so doing,
as though these had denounced to him by their ambassadors to cast Herod out of Arabia; while in
reality they had a mind to keep back what they owed
to Antipater, and not be obliged to make requitals
to his sons for the free gifts the father had made
them. He also took the imprudent advice of those
who, equally with himself, were willing to deprive
Herod of what Antipater had deposited among them;
and these men were the most potent of all whom
he had in his kingdom.

2. So when Herod had found that the Arabians
were his enemies, and this for those very reasons
whence he hoped they would have been the most
friendly, and had given them such an answer as his
passion suggested, he returned back and went for
Egypt. Now he lodged the first evening at one of
the temples of that country, in order to meet with
those whom he left behind; but on the next day
word was brought him as he was going to Rhinocu-
lura, that his brother was dead, and how he came
by his death; and when he had lamented him as much

as his present circumstances could bear, he soon laid
aside such cares, and proceeded on his journey. But
now, after some time, the king of Arabia repented
of what he had done, and sent presently away messengers to call him back: Herod had prevented them,
and was come to Pelusium, where he could not obtain
a passage from those that lay with the fleet, so he
besought their captains to let him go by them; accordingly, out of the reverence they bore to the fame
and dignity of the man, they conducted him to Alexandria; and when he came into the city he was received by Cleopatra with great splendour, who hoped
he might be persuaded to be commander of her forces
in the expedition she was now about; but he rejected
the queen's solicitations, and being neither affrighted
at the height of that storm which then happened,
nor at the tumults that were now in Italy, he sailed
for Rome.

3. But as he was in peril about Pamphilia, and
obliged to cast out the greatest part of the ship's
lading, he, with difficulty, got safe to Rhodes, a place
which had been grievously harassed in the war with
Cassius. He was there received by his friends, Ptolemy and Sappinius; and, although he was then in
want of money, he fitted up a three decked ship of
very great magnitude, wherein he and his friends
sailed to Brundusium, and went thence to Rome with
all speed; where he first of all went to Antony, on
account of the friendship his father had with him,
and laid before him the calamities of himself and his
family, and that he had left his nearest relations besieged in a fortress, and had sailed to him through
a storm, to make supplication to him for assistance.

4. Hereupon Antony was moved to compassion
at the change that had been made in Herod's affairs,
and this both upon his calling to mind how hospitably

he had been treated by Antipater, but more especially on account of Herod's own virtue; so he then resolved to get him made king of the Jews, whom he had himself formerly made tetrarch. The contest also that he had with Antigonus was another inducement, and that of no less weight than the great regard he had for Herod; for he looked upon Antigonus as a seditious person, and an enemy of the Romans; and as for Cæsar, Herod found him better prepared than Antony, as remembering very fresh the wars he had gone through together with his father, the hospitable treatment he had met with from him, and the entire good-will he had showed to him; besides the activity which he saw in Herod himself. So he called the senate together, wherein Messales, and after him Atratinus, produced Herod before them, and gave a full account of the merits of his father, and his own good-will to the Romans. At this same time they demonstrated that Antigonus was their enemy, not only because he soon quarrelled with them, but because he now overlooked the Romans, and took the government by the means of the Parthians. These reasons greatly moved the senate; at which juncture Antony came in and told them that it was for their advantage in the Parthian war that Herod should be king; so they all gave their votes for it. And when the senate was separated, Antony and Cæsar went out, with Herod between them; while the consul and the rest of the magistrates went before them in order to offer sacrifices, and to lay the decree in the capitol: Antony also made a feast for Herod on the first day of his reign.

CHAPTER XV.

Antigonus besieges those that are in Masada, whom Herod frees from confinement when he comes back from Rome, and presently marches to Jerusalem, where he finds Silo corrupted by bribes.

1. Now during this time Antigonus besieged those that were in Masada, who had all other necessaries in sufficient quantity, but were in want of water; on which account Joseph, Herod's brother, was disposed to run away to the Arabians, with two hundred of his own friends, because he had heard that Malichus repented of his offences with regard to Herod; and he had been so quick as to have been gone out of the fortress already, unless on that very night when he was going away, there had fallen a great deal of rain, insomuch that his reservoirs were full of water, and so he was under no necessity of running away. After which, therefore, they made an irruption upon Antigonus' party, and slew a great many of them, some in open battles, and some in private ambush; nor had they always success in their attempts, for sometimes they were beaten and ran away.

2. In the meantime Ventidius, the Roman general, was sent out of Syria, to restrain the incursions of the Parthians, and after he had done that, he came into Judea, in pretence indeed to assist Joseph and his party, but in reality to get money of Antigonus and when he had pitched his camp very near to Jerusalem, as soon as he had got money enough, he went away with the greatest part of his force; yet still did he leave Silo with some part of them, lest if he had taken them all away, his taking of bribes might have been too

openly discovered. Now Antigonus hoped that the Parthians would come again to his assistance, and therefore
cultivated a good understanding with Silo in the meantime, lest any interruption should be given to his hopes.
3. Now by this time Herod had sailed out of
Italy, and was come to Ptolemais: and as soon as
he had gotten together no small army of foreigners,
and of his own countrymen, he marched through
Galilee against Antigonus, wherein he was assisted
by Ventidius and Silo, both whom [1] Dellius, a person
sent by Antony, persuaded to bring Herod [into
his kingdom.] Now Ventidius was at this time
among the cities, and composing the disturbances
which had happened by means of the Parthians, as
was Silo in Judea corrupted by the bribes that Antigonus had given him; yet was not Herod himself
destitute of power, but the number of his forces increased every day as he went along, and all Galilee
with few exceptions joined themselves to him. So
he proposed to himself to set about his most necessary
enterprise, and that was Masada, in order to deliver
his relations from the siege they endured. But still
Joppa stood in his way, and hindered his going thither;
for it was necessary to take that city first, which
was in the enemies' hands, that when he should go
to Jerusalem, no fortress might be left in the enemies'
power behind him. Silo also willingly joined him,
as having now a plausible occasion of drawing off
his forces [from Jerusalem;] and when the Jews
pursued him and pressed upon him [in his retreat,]
Herod made an excursion upon them with a small
body of his men, and soon put them to flight, and
saved Silo when he was in distress.

---

[1] This Dellius is famous, or rather infamous, in the History of Mark
Antony, as Spanheim and Aldrich here note, from the coins, from Plutarch and Dio.

4. After this Herod took Joppa, and then made haste to Masada to free his relations. Now as he was marching, many came in to him, induced some by their friendship to his father, some by the reputation he had already gained himself, and some in order to repay the benefits they had received from them both; but still what engaged the greatest number on his side, was the hopes from him, when he should be established in his kingdom; so that he had gotten together already an army hard to be conquered. But Antigonus laid an ambush for him as he marched out, in which he did little or no harm to his enemies. However, he easily recovered his relations again that were in Masada, as well as the fortress Ressa, and then marched to Jerusalem, where the soldiers that were with Silo joined themselves to his own, as did many out of the city, from a dread of his power.

5. Now when he had pitched his camp on the west side of the city, the guards that were there shot their arrows, and threw their darts at them, while others ran out in companies, and attacked those in the forefront; but Herod commanded proclamation to be made at the wall, that "he was come for the good of the people and the preservation of the city without any design to be revenged on his open enemies, but to grant oblivion to them, though they had been the most obstinate against him." Now the soldiers that were for Antigonus made a contrary clamour, and did neither permit anybody to hear that proclamation, nor to change their party; so Antigonus gave order to his forces to beat the enemy from the walls; accordingly, they soon threw their darts at them from the towers, and put them to flight.

6. And here it was that Silo discovered he had taken bribes; for he set many of the soldiers to

clamour about their want of necessaries, and to require their pay, in order to buy themselves food, and
to demand that he would lead them into places convenient for their winter quarters; because all the
parts about the city were laid waste by the means of
Antigonus' army, which had taken all things away.
By this he moved the army, and attempted to get
them off the siege; but Herod went to the captains
that were under Silo, and to a great many of the
soldiers, and begged of them not to leave him who
was sent thither by Cæsar, and Antony, and the
senate; for that he would take care to have their
wants supplied that very day. After the making of
which entreaty, he went hastily into the country, and
brought thither so great an abundance of necessaries,
that he cut off all Silo's pretences; and in order to
provide that for the following days they should not
want supplies, he sent to the people that were about
Samaria (which city had joined itself to him), to
bring corn, and wine, and oil, and cattle to Jericho.
When Antigonus heard of this, he sent some of his
party with orders to hinder, and lay ambushes for
these collectors of corn. This command was obeyed,
and a great multitude of armed men were gathered
together about Jericho, and lay upon the mountains,
to watch those that brought the provisions. Yet was
Herod not idle, he took with him ten cohorts, five of
them were Romans, and five were Jewish cohorts,
together with some mercenary troops intermixed
among them, and besides those a few horsemen, and
came to Jericho; and when he came he found the
city deserted, but that there were five hundred men,
with their wives and children, who had taken possession of the tops of the mountains, these he took
and dismissed them, while the Romans fell upon the
rest of the city, and plundered it, having found the

houses full of all sorts of good things. So the king left a garrison at Jericho, and came back and sent the Roman army into those cities which were come over to him, to take their winter quarters there, viz. into Judea, [or Idumea,] and Galilee, and Samaria. Antigonus also by bribes obtained of Silo to let a part of · his army be received at Lydda, as a compliment to Antonius.

CHAPTER XVI.

Herod takes Sepphoris, and subdues the robbers that were in the caves: he after that avenges himself upon Macheras, as upon an enemy of his, and goes to Antony, as he was besieging Samosata.

1. So the Romans lived in plenty of all things, and rested from war. However, Herod did not lie at rest, but seized upon Idumea, and kept it, with two thousand footmen, and four hundred horsemen: and this he did by sending his brother Joseph thither, that no innovation might be made by Antigonus. He also removed his mother, and all his relations, who had been in Masada, to Samaria, and when he had settled them securely, he marched to take the remaining parts of Galilee, and to drive away the garrisons placed there by Antigonus.

2. But when Herod had reached Sepphoris, in a very great snow, he took the city without any difficulty; the guards that should have kept it, flying away before it was assaulted; where he gave an opportunity to his followers that had been in distress to refresh themselves, there being in that city a great abundance of necessaries. After which he hasted

away to the robbers that were in the caves, who over-ran a great part of the country, and did as great mischief to its inhabitants as a war itself could have done. Accordingly, he sent beforehand three cohorts of footmen, and one troop of horsemen to the village Arbela, and came himself [1] forty days afterwards with the rest of his forces. Yet were not the enemy affrighted at his assault, but met him in arms; for their skill was not that of warriors, but their boldness was the boldness of robbers: when, therefore, it came to a pitched battle, they put to flight Herod's left wing with their right one; but Herod, wheeling about on the sudden from his own right wing, came to their assistance, and both made his own left wing return back from its flight, and fell upon the pursuers, and cooled their courage, till they could not bear the at-tempts that were made directly upon them, and so turned back and ran away.

3. But Herod followed them, and slew them as he followed them, and destroyed a great part of them, till those that remained were scattered beyond the river [Jordan,] and Galilee was freed from the terrors they had been under, excepting from those that remained, and lay concealed in caves, which required longer time ere they could be conquered. In order to which, Herod, in the first place, distributed the fruits of their former labours to the soldiers, and gave every one of them a hundred and fifty drachmæ of silver, and a great deal more to their commanders, and set them into their winter quarters. He also sent to his youngest brother Pheroras, to take care of a good

---

[1] This way of speaking after 40 days, is interpreted by Josephus him-self, on the 40th day; Antiq. B. XIV. ch. xv. sect. 4, Vol. II. In like manner, when Josephus says, ch. xxxiii. sect. 8, that Herod lived after he had ordered Antipater to be slain 5 days; this is by himself in-terpreted, Antiq. B. XVII. ch. viii. sect. 1, Vol. III. that he died on the 5th day afterward. See also what is in this book, ch. xiii. sect. 1, after two years, is Antiq. B. XIV. ch. xiii. sect. 3, Vol. II. on the second year.

market for them, where they might buy themselves
provisions, and to build a wall about Alexandrium,
who took care of both those injunctions accordingly.

4. In the meantime Antony abode at Athens,
while Ventidius called for Silo and Herod to come
to the war against the Parthians, but ordered them
first to settle the affairs of Judea; so Herod willingly
dismissed Silo to go to Ventidius, but he made an
expedition himself against those that lay in the caves.
Now these caves were in the precipices of craggy
mountains, and could not be come at from any side,
since they had only some winding pathways, very
narrow, by which they got up to them; but the rock
that lay on their front had beneath it valleys of a
vast depth, and of an almost perpendicular declivity;
insomuch that the king was doubtful for a long time
what to do, by reason of a kind of impossibility there
was of attacking the place. Yet did he at length
make use of a contrivance that was subject to the
utmost hazard; for he let down the most hardy of
his men in chests, and set them at the mouths of the
dens. Now these men slew the robbers and their
families, and when they made resistance, they sent
in fire upon them, [and burnt them;] and as Herod
was desirous of saving some of them, he had proclamation made, that they should come and deliver themselves up to him; but not one of them came willingly
to him, and of those that were compelled to come,
many preferred death to captivity. And here a certain old man, the father of seven children, whose
children, together with their mother, desired him to
give them leave to go out, upon the assurance and
right hand that was offered them, slew them after
the following manner: he ordered every one of them
to go out, while he stood himself at the cave's mouth,
and slew that son of his perpetually who went out.

Herod was near enough to see this sight, and his bowels of compassion were moved at it, and he stretched out his right hand to the old man, and besought him to spare his children; yet did he not relent at all upon what he said, but over and above reproached Herod on the lowness of his descent, and slew his wife as well as his children; and when he had thrown their dead bodies down the precipice, he at last threw himself down after them.

5. By this means Herod subdued these caves, and the robbers that were in them. He then left there a part of his army, as many as he thought sufficient to prevent any sedition, and made Ptolemy their general, and returned to Samaria: he led also with him three thousand armed footmen, and six hundred horsemen against Antigonus. Now here those that used to raise tumults in Galilee, having liberty so to do upon his departure, fell unexpectedly upon Ptolemy, the general of his forces, and slew him: they also laid the country waste, and then retired to the bogs, and to places not easily to be found. But when Herod was informed of this insurrection, he came to the assistance of the country immediately, and destroyed a great number of the seditious, and raised the sieges of all those fortresses they had besieged; he also exacted the tribute of a hundred talents of his enemies, as a penalty for the mutations they had made in the country.

6. By this time the Parthians being already driven out of the country and Pacorus slain, Ventidius, by Antony's command, sent a thousand horsemen and two legions, as auxiliaries to Herod, against Antigonus. Now Antigonus besought Macheras, who was their general, by letter, to come to his assistance, and made a great many mournful complaints about Herod's violence, and about the injuries he did to

the kingdom; and promised to give him money for
such his assistance: but he complied not with his invitation to betray his trust, for he did not contemn
him that sent him, especially while Herod gave him
more money [than the other offered.] So he pretended friendship to Antigonus, but came as a spy
to discover his affairs: although he did not herein
comply with Herod, who dissuaded him from so doing.
But Antigonus perceived what his intentions were
beforehand, and excluded him out of the city, and
defended himself against him, as against an enemy
from the walls; till Macheras was ashamed of what
he had done, and retired to Emmaus to Herod; and,
as he was in a rage at his disappointment, he slew
all the Jews whom he met with, without sparing those
that were for Herod, but using them all as if they
were for Antigonus.

7.   Hereupon Herod was very angry at him, and
was going to fight against Macheras as his enemy;
but he restrained his indignation, and marched to
Antony to accuse Macheras of maladministration.
But Macheras was made sensible of his offences, and
followed after the king immediately, and earnestly
begged and obtained that he would be reconciled to
him.   However, Herod did not desist from his resolution of going to Antony; but when he heard that
he was besieging Samosata with a great army, which
is a strong city near to Euphrates, he made the
greater haste, as observing that this was a proper
opportunity for showing at once his courage, and
for doing what would greatly oblige Antony.   Indeed
when he came, he soon made an end of that siege,
and slew a great number of the barbarians, and took
from them a large prey; insomuch that Antony, who
admired his courage formerly, did now admire it still
more.   Accordingly he heaped many more honours

upon him, and gave him more assured hopes that he should gain his kingdom: and now king Antiochus was forced to deliver up ᐧSamosata.

CHAPTER XVII.

The death of Joseph, [Herod's brother,] which had been signified to Herod in dreams. How Herod was preserved twice, after a wonderful manner. He cuts off the head of Pappus, who was the murderer of his brother, and sends that head to [his other brother] Pheroras. And in no long time he besieges Jerusalem, and marries Mariamne.

1. In the meantime, Herod's affairs in Judea were in an ill state. He had left his brother Joseph with full power, but had charged him to make no attempts against Antigonus, till his return; for that Macheras would not be such an assistant as he could depend on, as it appeared by what he had done already; but as soon as Joseph heard that his brother was at a very great distance, he neglected the charge he had received, and marched towards Jericho with five cohorts, which Macheras sent with him. This movement was intended for seizing on the corn, as it was now in the midst of summer; but when his enemies attacked him in the mountains, and in places which were difficult to pass, he was both killed himself, as he was very bravely fighting in the battle, and the entire Roman cohorts were destroyed; for these cohorts were new raised men, gathered out of Syria, and there was no mixture of those called veteran soldiers among them, that might have supported those that were unskilful in war.

2. This victory was not sufficient for Antigonus, but he proceeded to that degree of rage, as to treat the dead body of Joseph barbarously; for when he had gotten possession of the bodies of those that were slain, he cut off his head, although his brother Pheroras would have given fifty talents as a price of redemption for it. And now the affairs of Galilee were put in such disorder after this victory of Antigonus', that those of Antigonus' party brought the principal men that were on Herod's side to the lake, and there drowned them. There was a great change made also in Idumea where Macheras was building a wall about one of the fortresses, which was called *Gittha*. But Herod had not yet been informed of these things; for after the taking of Samosata, and when Antony had set Sosius over the affairs of Syria, and given him orders to assist Herod against Antigonus, he departed into Egypt; but Sosius sent two legions before him into Judea to assist Herod, and followed himself soon after with the rest of his army.

3. Now when Herod was at Daphne, by Antioch, he had some dreams which clearly foreboded his brother's death, and as he leaped out of his bed in a disturbed manner, there came messengers that acquainted him with that calamity. So when he had lamented this misfortune for a while, he put off the main part of his mourning, and made haste to march against his enemies; and when he had performed a march that was above his strength, and was gone as far as Libanus, he got him eight hundred men of those that lived near to that mountain, as his assistants, and joined with them one Roman legion, with which, before it was day, he made an irruption into Galilee, and met his enemies, and drove them back to the place which they had left. He also made an immediate and continual attack upon the fortress. Yet

was he forced by a most terrible storm to pitch his camp in the neighbouring villages, before he could take it: but when, after a few days' time, the second legion, that came from Antony, joined themselves to him, the enemy were affrighted at his power, and left their fortifications in the night time.

4. After this he marched through Jericho as making what haste he could to be avenged on his brother's murderers; where happened to him a providential sign, out of which, when he had unexpectedly escaped, he had the reputation of being very dear to God; for that evening there feasted with him many of the principal men, and after that feast was over, and all the guests were gone out, the house fell down immediately. And as he judged this to be a common signal of what dangers he should undergo, and how he should escape them in the war that he was going about, he, in the morning, set forward with his army, when about six thousand of his enemies came running down from the mountains, and began to fight with those in his forefront; yet durst they not be so very bold as to engage the Romans hand to hand, but threw stones and darts at them at a distance; by which means they wounded a considerable number; in which action Herod's own side was wounded with a dart.

5. Now as Antigonus had a mind to appear to exceed Herod, not only in the courage, but in the number of his men, he sent Pappus, one of his companions, with an army against Samaria, whose fortune it was to oppose Macheras; but Herod overran the enemies' country, and demolished five little cities, and destroyed two thousand men that were in them, and burned their houses, and then returned to his camp; but his head quarters were at a village called *Cana.*

6. Now a great multitude of Jews resorted to him every day, both out of Jericho, and the other parts of the country. Some were moved so to do out of their hatred to Antigonus, and some out of regard to the glorious actions Herod had done; but others were led on by an unreasonable desire of change; so he fell upon them immediately. As for Pappus and his party, they were not terrified either at their number, or at their zeal, but marched out with great alacrity to fight them, and it came to a close fight. Now other parts of their army made resistance for a while; but Herod running the utmost hazard out of the rage he was in at the murder of his brother, that he might be avenged on those that had been the authors of it, soon beat those that opposed him, and, after he had beaten them, he always turned his forces against those that stood to it still, and pursued them all; so that a great slaughter was made, while some were forced back into that village whence they came out; he also pressed hard upon the hindermost, and slew a vast number of them; he also fell into the village with the enemy, where every house was filled with armed men, and the upper rooms were crowded above with soldiers for their defence; and when he had beaten those that were on the outside, he pulled the houses to pieces, and plucked out those that were within; upon many he had the roofs shaken down, whereby they perished by heaps, and as for those that fled out of the ruins, the soldiers received them with their swords in their hands, and the multitude of those slain, and lying on heaps, was so great that the conquerors could not pass along the roads. Now the enemy could not bear this blow, so that when the multitude of them which were gathered together, saw that those in the village were slain, they dispersed themselves and fled away, upon the con-

fidence of which victory, Herod had marched immediately to Jerusalem, unless he had been hindered by the depth of winter's [coming on.] This was the impediment that lay in the way of this his entire glorious progress, and was what hindered Antigonus from being now conquered, who was already disposed to forsake the city.

7. Now when at the evening Herod had already dismissed his friends to refresh themselves after their fatigue, and when he was gone himself, while he was still hot in his armour, like a common soldier, to bathe himself, and had but one servant that attended him, and before he was gotten into the bath, one of the enemies met him in the face with a sword in his hand, and then a second, and then a third, and after that more of them; these were men who had run away out of the battle into the bath in their armour, and they had lain there for some time in great terror, and in privacy, and when they saw the king, they trembled for fear, and ran by him in a fright, although he were naked, and endeavoured to get off into the public road: now there was by chance nobody else at hand that might seize upon these men, and for Herod, he was contented to have come to no harm himself, so that they all got away in safety.

8. But on the next day Herod had Pappus' head cut off, who was the general for Antigonus, and was slain in the battle, and sent it to his brother Pheroras by way of punishment for their slain brother, for he was the man that slew Joseph. Now as winter was going off, Herod marched to Jerusalem, and brought his army to the wall of it; this was the third year since he had been made king at Rome; so he pitched his camp before the temple, for on that side it might be besieged, and there it was that Pompey took the city. So he parted the work among the army, and

demolished the suburbs, and raised three banks, and gave orders to have towers built upon those banks, and left the most laborious of his acquaintance at the works. But he went himself to Samaria, to take the daughter of Alexander, the son of Aristobulus, to wife, who had been betrothed to him before, as we have already said; and thus he accomplished this by the by, during the siege of the city, for he had his enemy in great contempt already.

9. When he had thus married Mariamne, he came back to Jerusalem with a greater army; Sosius also joined him with a large army, both of horsemen and footmen, which he sent before him through the midland parts, while he marched himself along Phenicia; and when the whole army was gotten together, which were eleven regiments of footmen, and six thousand horsemen, besides the Syrian auxiliaries, which was no small part of the army, they pitched their camp near to the north wall. Herod's dependance was upon the decree of the senate, by which he was made king, and Sosius relied upon Antony, who sent the army that was under him to Herod's assistance.

CHAPTER XVIII.

How Herod and Sosius took Jerusalem by force; and what death Antigonus came to. Also concerning Cleopatra's avaricious temper.

1. Now the multitude of the Jews that were in the city were divided into several factions; for the people that crowded about the temple, being the weaker part of them, gave it out, that, as times were, he was the happiest and most religious man who

should die first. But as to the more bold and hardy
men, they got together in bodies, and fell a-robbing
others after various manners, and these particularly
plundered the places that were about the city, and
this because there was no food left either for the
horses or the men; yet some of the warlike men who
were used to fight regularly, were appointed to defend the city during the siege, and these drove those
that raised the banks away from the wall, and these
were always inventing one engine or another to be
a hinderance to the engines of the enemy, nor had
they so much success any way as in the mines under
ground.

2. Now, as for the robberies which were committed
the king contrived that ambushes should be so laid,
that they might restrain their excursions; and as
for the want of provisions, he provided that they
should be brought to them from great distances. He
was also too hard for the Jews, by the Romans' skill
in the art of war; although they were bold to the
utmost degree, now they durst not come to a plain
battle with the Romans, which was certain death, but
through their mines under ground they would appear
in the midst of them on the sudden, and before they
could batter down one wall, they built them another
in its stead; and to sum up all at once, they did not
show any want either of pains taking, or of contrivances, as having resolved to hold out to the very
last. Indeed though they had so great an army lying
round about them, they bore a siege of five months,
till some of Herod's chosen men ventured to get upon
the wall, and fell into the city, as did Sosius' centurions after them; and now they first of all seized
upon what was about the temple, and upon the pouring in of the army, there was slaughter of vast multitudes every where, by reason of the rage the Ro-

mans were in at the length of this siege, and by reason that the Jews who were about Herod earnestly endeavoured that none of their adversaries might remain; so they were cut to pieces by great multitudes, as they were crowded together in narrow streets, and in houses, or were running away to the temple; nor was there any mercy showed either to infants, or to the aged, or to the weaker sex; insomuch, that although the king sent about and desired them to spare the people, nobody could be persuaded to withhold their right hand from slaughter, but they slew people of all ages like madmen. Then it was that Antigonus, without any regard to his former or to his present fortune, came down from the citadel and fell down at Sosius' feet, who, without pitying him at all upon the change of his condition, laughed at him beyond measure, and called him *Antigona*.[1] Yet did he not treat him like a woman, or let him go free, but put him into bonds, and kept him in custody.

3. But Herod's concern at present, now he had gotten his enemies under his power, was to restrain the zeal of his foreign auxiliaries; for the multitude of the strange people were very eager to see the temple, and what was sacred in the holy house itself; but the king endeavoured to restrain them, partly by his exhortations, partly by his threatening, nay, partly by force, as thinking the victory worse than a defeat to him, if any thing that ought not to be seen were seen by them. He also forbade, at the same time, the spoiling of the city, asking Sosius in the most earnest manner, whether the Romans, by thus emptying the city of money and men, had a mind to leave him king of a desert? and told him, "That he judged the dominion of the habitable earth too small a compensation for the slaughter of so many citizens." And

[1] That is, a woman, not a man.

when Sosius said, "That it was but just to allow the soldiers this plunder as a reward for what they suffered during the siege," Herod made answer, that "he would give every one of the soldiers a reward out of his own money." So he purchased the deliverance of his country, and performed his promises to them, and made presents after a magnificent manner to each soldier, and proportionably to their commanders, and with a most royal bounty to Sosius himself, whereby nobody went away but in a wealthy condition. Hereupon Sosius dedicated a crown of gold to God, and then went away from Jerusalem, leading Antigonus away in bonds to Antony; then did the [1] axe bring him to his end, who still had a fond desire of life, and some frigid hopes of it to the last, but by his cowardly behaviour well deserved to die by it.

4. Hereupon king Herod distinguished the multitude that was in the city, and for those that were of his side, he made them still more his friends by the honours he conferred on them; but for those of Antigonus' party he slew them, and as his money ran low, he turned all the ornaments he had into money, and sent it to Antony, and to those about him. Yet could he not hereby purchase an exemption from all sufferings; for Antony was now bewitched by his love to Cleopatra, and was entirely conquered by her charms. Now, Cleopatra had put to death all her kindred, till no one near her in blood remained alive, and after that she fell a-slaying those no way related to her. So she calumniated the principal men among the Syrians to Antony, and persuaded him to have them slain, that so she might

---

[1] This death of Antigonus is confirmed by Plutarch and Strabo; the latter of whom is cited for it by Josephus himself, Antiq. B. XV. ch. i. sect. 2, Vol. II.

easily gain to be mistress of what they had; nay, she extended her avaricious humour to the Jews and Arabians, and secretly laboured to have Herod and Malichus, the kings of both those nations, slain by his order.

5. Now as to these her injunctions to Antony, he complied in part: for though he esteemed it too abominable a thing to kill such good and great kings, yet was he thereby alienated from the friendship he had for them. He also took away a great deal of their country: nay, even the plantation of palm-trees at Jericho, where also grows the balsam-tree, and bestowed them upon her: as also all the cities on this side the river Eleutherus, Tyre and Sidon [1] excepted. And when she was become mistress of these, and had conducted Antony in his expedition against the Parthians, as far as Euphrates, she came by Apamia and Damascus into Judea: and there did Herod pacify her indignation at him by large presents. He also hired of her those places that had been torn away from his kingdom, at the yearly rent of two hundred talents. He conducted her also as far as Pelusium, and paid her all the respects possible. Now it was not long after this that Antony was come back from Parthia, and led with him Artabazes, Tigranes' son, captive, as a present for Cleopatra; for this Parthian was presently given her, with his money, and all the prey that was taken with him.

---

[1] This ancient liberty of Tyre and Sidon under the Romans, taken notice of by Josephus, both here and Antiq. B. XV. ch. iv. sect. 1, Vol. II. is confirmed by the testimony of Strabo, B. XVI. p. 757, although this liberty lasted but a little while longer, when Augustus took it away from them.

CHAPTER XIX.

How Antony, at the persuasion of Cleopatra, sent Herod to fight against the Arabians; and how, after several battles, he at length got the victory. As also concerning a great earthquake.

1. Now when the war about Actium was begun, Herod prepared to come to the assistance of Antony, as being already freed from his troubles in Judea, and having gained Hyrcania, which was a place that was held by Antigonus' sister. However, he was cunningly hindered from partaking of the hazards that Antony went through by Cleopatra; for since, as we have already noted, she laid a plot against the kings [of Judea and Arabia,] she prevailed with Antony to commit the war against the Arabians to Herod; that so, if he got the better, she might become mistress of Arabia, or, if he were worsted, of Judea; and that she might destroy one of those kings by the other.

2. However, this contrivance tended to the advantage of Herod; for at the very first he took hostages from the enemy, and got together a great body of horse, and ordered them to march against them about Diospolos, and he conquered that army although it fought resolutely against him. After which defeat, the Arabians were in great motion, and assembled themselves together at Kanatha, a city of Celosyria, in vast multitudes, and waited for the Jews. And when Herod was come thither, he tried to manage this war with particular prudence, and gave orders that they should build a wall about their camp; yet did not the multitude comply with those orders, but were

so emboldened by their foregoing victory, that they presently attacked the Arabians, and beat them at the first onset, and then pursued them; yet there were snares laid for Herod in that pursuit; while Athenio, who was one of Cleopatra's generals, and always an antagonist to Herod, sent out of Kanatha the men of that country against him, for, upon this fresh onset, the Arabians took courage, and returned back, and both joined their numerous forces about stony places, that were hard to be gone over, and there put Herod's men to the rout, and made a great slaughter of them; but those that escaped out of the battle fled to Ormiza, where the Arabians surrounded their camp, and took it, with all the men in it.

3. In a little time after this calamity, Herod came to bring them succours; but he came too late. Now the occasion of that blow was this, that the officers would not obey orders; for had not the fight began so suddenly, Athenio had not found a proper season for the snares he laid for Herod; however, he was even with the Arabians afterward, and overrun their country, and did them more harm than their single victory could compensate. But as he was avenging himself on his enemies, there fell upon him another providential calamity; for in the [1] seventh year of his reign, when the war about Actium was at the height, at the beginning of the spring, the earth was

---

[1] This seventh year of the reign of Herod [from the conquest, or death of Antigonus,] with the great earthquake in the beginning of the same spring, which are here fully implied to be not much before the fight at Actium, between Octavius and Antony, and which is known from the Roman historians to have been in the beginning of September, in the 31st year before the Christian era, determines the chronology of Josephus as to the reign of Herod, viz that he began in the year 37, beyond rational contradiction. Nor is it quite unworthy of our notice, that this seventh year of the reign of Herod, or the 31st before the Christian era, contained the latter part of a Sabbatic year, on which Sabbatic year, therefore, it is plain this great earthquake happened in Judea.

shaken, and destroyed an immense number of cattle, with thirty thousand men; but the army received no harm, because it lay in the open air. In the meantime, the fame of this earthquake elevated the Arabians to greater courage, and this by augmenting it to fabulous height, as is constantly the case in melancholy accidents, and pretending that all Judea was overthrown; upon this supposal, therefore, that they should easily get a land that was destitute of inhabitants into their power, they first sacrificed those ambassadors who were come to them from the Jews, and then marched into Judea immediately. Now the Jewish nation were affrighted at this invasion, and quite dispirited at the greatness of their calamities one after another; whom yet Herod got together, and endeavoured to persuade them to defend themselves by the following speech which he made to them.

4. "The present dread you are under, seems to me to have seized upon you very unreasonably. It is true, you might justly be dismayed at that providential chastisement which hath befallen you; but to suffer yourselves to be equally terrified at the invasion of men, is unmanly. As for myself, I am so far from being affrighted at our enemies after this earthquake, that I imagine that God hath thereby laid a bait for the Arabians, that we may be avenged on them, for their present invasion proceeds more from our accidental misfortunes, than that they have any great dependance on their weapons, or their own fitness for action. Now that hope which depends not on men's own power, but on others' ill success, is a very ticklish thing: for there is no certainty among men, either in their bad or good fortunes; but we may easily observe that fortune is mutable, and goes from one side to another; and this you may readily learn from examples -among ourselves; for when you were once victors in

the former fights, your enemies overcame you at last;
and very likely it will now happen so, that these who
think themselves sure of beating you, will themselves
be beaten. For, when men are very confident, they
are not upon their guard, while fear teaches men to
act with caution; insomuch, that I venture to prove
from your very timorousness, that you ought to take
courage: for when you were more bold than you
ought to have been, and than I would have had you,
and marched on, Athenio's treachery took place; but
your present slowness and seeming dejection of mind,
is to me a pledge and assurance of victory. And
indeed it is proper beforehand to be thus provident;
but when we come to action, we ought to erect our
minds, and to make our enemies, be they ever so
wicked, believe, that neither any human, no, nor any
providential misfortune, can ever depress the courage
of the Jews while they are alive; nor will any of
them ever overlook an Arabian, or suffer such a one
to become lord of his good things, whom he has in
a manner taken captive, and that at many times also.
And do not you disturb yourselves at the quaking
of inanimate creatures, nor do you imagine that this
earthquake is another sign of another calamity; for
such affections of the elements are according to the
course of nature, nor does it import any thing farther
to men, than what mischief it does immediately of
itself. Perhaps there may come some short sign
beforehand in the case of pestilences, and famines,
and earthquakes; but these calamities themselves have
their force limited by themselves, [without foreboding
any other calamity.] And indeed what greater mischief can the war, though it should be a violent one,
do to us, than the earthquake has done? Nay, there
is a signal of our enemies' destruction visible, and
that a very great one also; and this is not a natural

one, nor derived from the hand of foreigners neither, but it is this, that they have barbarously murdered our ambassadors, contrary to the common law of mankind; and they have destroyed so many, as if they esteemed them sacrifices for God, in relation to this war. But they will not avoid his great eye, nor his invincible right hand; and we shall be revenged of them presently, in case we still retain any of the courage of our forefathers, and rise up boldly to punish these covenant breakers. Let every one therefore go on and fight, not so much for his wife or his children, or for the danger his country is in, as for these ambassadors of ours; those dead ambassadors will conduct this war of ours better than we ourselves who are alive. And if you will be ruled by me, I will myself go before you into danger; for you know this well enough, that your courage is irresistible, unless you hurt yourselves by acting rashly." [1]

5. When Herod had encouraged them by this speech, and he saw with what alacrity they went, he offered sacrifice to God, and after that sacrifice, he passed over the river Jordan with his army, and pitched his camp about Philadelphia; near the enemy; and about a fortification that lay between them. He then shot at them at a distance, and was desirous to come to an engagement presently; for some of them had been sent beforehand to seize upon that fortification: but the king sent some who immediately beat them out of the fortification, while he himself went in the forefront of the army, which he put in battle array every day, and invited the Arabians to fight. But as none of them came out of their camp, for they were in a terrible fright, and their general, Elthimus,

---

[1] This speech of Herod's is set down twice by Josephus, here and Antiq. B. XV. ch. v. sect. 3, Vol. II., to the very same purpose, but by no means in the same words; whence it appears, that the sense was Herod's, but the composition Josephus'.

was not able to say a word for fear; so Herod came upon them, and pulled their fortification to pieces, by which means they were compelled to come out to fight, which they did in disorder, and so that the horsemen and footmen were mixed together. They were indeed superior to the Jews in number, but inferior as to their alacrity, although they were obliged to expose themselves to danger by their very despair of victory.

6. Now while they made opposition, they had not a great number slain; but as soon as they turned their backs, a great many were trodden to pieces by the Jews, and a great many by themselves, and so perished, till five thousand were fallen down dead in their flight, while the rest of the multitude prevented their immediate death, by crowding into the fortification. Herod encompassed these round, and besieged them; and while they were ready to be taken by their enemies in arms; they had another additional distress upon them, which was thirst and want of water: for the king was above hearkening to their ambassadors, and when they offered five hundred talents, as the price of their redemption, he pressed still harder upon them. And as they were burnt up by their thirst, they came out and voluntarily delivered themselves up by multitudes to the Jews, till in five days' time four thousand of them were put into bonds; and on the sixth day the multitude that were left despaired of saving themselves, and came out to fight; with these Herod fought, and slew again about seven thousand, insomuch, that he punished Arabia so severely, and so far extinguished the spirits of the men, that he was chosen by the nation for their ruler.

CHAPTER XX.

*Herod is confirmed in his kingdom by Cæsar, and cul-
tivates a friendship with the emperor by magnificent
presents; while Cæsar returns his kindness by bestowing on him that part of his kingdom which had
been taken away from it by Cleopatra, with the
addition of Zenodorus' country also.*

1. BUT now Herod was under immediate concern
about a most important affair, on account of his
friendship with Antony, who was already overcome at
Actium by Cæsar; yet he was more afraid than hurt;
for Cæsar did not think he had quite undone Antony
while Herod continued his assistance to him. However, the king resolved to expose himself to dangers:
accordingly he sailed to Rhodes, where Cæsar then
abode, and came to him without his diadem, and in the
habit and appearance of a private person, but in his
behaviour as a king. So he concealed nothing of the
truth, but spoke thus before his face, "O Cæsar, as I
was made king of the Jews by Antony, so do I profess that I have used my royal authority in the best
manner, and entirely for his advantage; nor will I
conceal this farther, that thou hadst certainly found
me in arms, and an inseparable companion of his, had
not the Arabians hindered me. However, I sent him
as many auxiliaries as I was able, and many ten
thousand [cori] of corn. Nay, indeed, I did not
desert my benefactor after the blow that was given
him at Actium; but I gave him the best advice I was
able, when I was no longer able to assist him in the
war; and I told him that there was but one way of
recovering his affairs, and that was to kill Cleopatra;

and I promised him, that if she were once dead, I would afford him money and walls for his security, with an army and myself to assist him in his war against thee: but his affections for Cleopatra stopped his ears, as did God himself also, who hath bestowed the government on thee. I own myself also to be overcome together with him, and with his last fortune I have laid aside my diadem, and am come hither to thee, having my hopes of safety in thy virtue; and I desire that thou wilt first consider how faithful a friend, and not whose friend, I have been."

2. Cæsar replied to him thus: "Nay, thou shalt not only be in safety, but shalt be a king; and that more firmly than thou wert before; for thou art worthy to reign over a great many subjects, by reason of the fastness of thy friendship: and do thou endeavour to be equally constant in thy friendship to me, upon my good success, which is what I depend upon from the generosity of thy disposition. However, Antony hath done well in preferring Cleopatra to thee; for by this means we have gained thee by her madness, and thus thou hast begun to be my friend before I began to be thine; on which account Quintus Dedius hath written to me that thou sentest him assistance against the gladiators. I do therefore assure thee, that I will confirm the kingdom to thee by decree: I shall also endeavour to do thee some farther kindness hereafter, that thou mayest find no loss in the want of Antony."

3. When Cæsar had spoken such obliging things to the king, and had put the diadem again about his head, he proclaimed what he had bestowed on him by a decree, in which he enlarged in the commendation of the man after a magnificent manner. Whereupon Herod obliged him to be kind to him by the presents he gave him, and he desired him to forgive Alexander, one of Antony's friends, who was become a supplicant

to him. But Cæsar's anger against him prevailed, and
he complained of the many and very great offences the
man whom he petitioned for had been guilty of; and
by what means he rejected his petition. After this,
Cæsar went from Egypt through Syria, when Herod
received him with royal and rich entertainments; and
then did he first of all ride along with Cæsar, as he
was reviewing his army about Ptolemais; and feasted
him with all his friends, and then distributed among
the rest of the army what was necessary to feast them
withal. He also made a plentiful provision of water
for them, when they were to march as far as Pelusium, through a dry country, which he did also in
like manner at their return thence; nor were there
any necessaries wanting to that army. It was therefore the opinion, both of Cæsar and of his soldiers,
that Herod's kingdom was too small for those generous presents he made them; for which reason, when
Cæsar was come into Egypt, and Cleopatra and Antony were dead, he did not only bestow other marks
of honour upon him, but made an addition to his
kingdom, by giving him, not only the country which
had been taken from him by Cleopatra, but besides
that, Gadara, and Hippos, and Samaria; and moreover, of the maritime cities, [1] Gaza, and Anthedon, and
Joppa, and Strato's Tower. He also made him a present of four hundred Galls [Galatians] as a guard for his
body, which they had been to Cleopatra before. Nor
did any thing so strongly induce Cæsar to make these
presents as the generosity of him that received them.

[1] Since Josephus, both here, and in his Antiq. B. XV. ch. vii. sect. 3,
Vol. II. reckons Gaza, which had been a free city, among the cities
given Herod by Augustus, and yet implies that Herod had made Costobarus a governor of it before, Antiq. B. XV. ch. vii. sect. 9, Hardum
has some pretence for saying that Josephus here contradicted himself.
But perhaps Herod thought he had sufficient authority to put a governor
into Gaza, after he was made tetrarch or king, in times of war, ere the
city was entirely delivered into his hands by Augustus.

4. Moreover, after the first games at Actium, he added to his kingdom both the region called *Trachonitis,* and what lay in its neighbourhood, Batanea, and the country of Auranitis: and that on the following occasion: Zenodorus, who had hired the house of Lysanias, had all along sent robbers out of Trachonitis among the Damascenes; who thereupon had recourse to Varro, the president of Syria, and desired of him that he would represent the calamity they were in to Cæsar; when Cæsar was acquainted with it, he sent back orders that this nest of robbers should be destroyed. Varro therefore made an expedition against them, and cleared the land of those men, and took it away from Zenodorus. Cæsar did also afterward bestow it on Herod, that it might not again become a receptacle for those robbers that had come against Damascus. He also made him procurator of all Syria, and this on the tenth year afterward when he came again into that province; and this was so established, that the other procurators could not do any thing in the administration without his advice; but when Zenodorus was dead, Cæsar bestowed on him all that land which lay between Trachonitis and Galilee. Yet what was still of more consequence to Herod, he was beloved by Cæsar next after Agrippa, and by Agrippa next after Cæsar; whence he arrived at a very great degree of felicity. Yet did the greatness of his soul exceed it, and the main part of his magnanimity was extended to the promotion of piety.

CHAPTER XXI.

*Of the [temple and] cities that were built by Herod,
and erected from the very foundations; as also, of
those other edifices that were erected by him: and
what magnificence he showed to foreigners; and
how fortune was in all things favourable to him.*

1. ACCORDINGLY, in the sixteenth year of his reign,
Herod rebuilt the temple, and encompassed a piece
of land about it with a wall, which land was twice
as large as that before enclosed. The expenses he
laid out upon it were vastly large; and the riches
about it were also unspeakable. A sign of which you
have in the great cloisters that were erected about
the temple and ¹ the citadel which was on its north
side. The cloisters he built from the foundation, but
the citadel he repaired at a vast expense, nor was it
other than a royal palace, which he called *Antonia,*
in honour of Antony. He also built himself a palace
in the upper city, containing two very large and most
beautiful apartments; to which the holy house itself
could not be compared [in largeness.] The one
apartment he named *Cæsareum,* and the other he
named *Agrippium,* from his [two great] friends.

2. Yet did he not preserve their memory by particular buildings only, with their names given them,
but his generosity went as far as entire cities; for

¹ This fort was first built, as it is supposed, by John Hyrcanus, see
Prid. at the year 207, and called *Baris,* the tower or citadel. It was
afterwards rebuilt, with great improvements, by Herod, under the government of Antonius, and was named from him *the Tower of Antonia;*
and about the time when Herod rebuilt the temple, he seems to have
put his last hand to it. See Antiq. B. XVIII. ch. v. sect. 4, Vol. III.
Of the War, B. I. ch. iii. sect. 4. It lay on the north-west side of the
temple, and was a quarter as large.

when he had built a most beautiful wall round a country in Samaria, twenty furlongs long, and had brought six thousand inhabitants into it, and had allotted to it a most fruitful piece of land, and in the midst of this city, thus built, had erected a very large temple to Cæsar, and had laid round about it a portion of sacred land of three furlongs and a half, he called the city *Sebaste,* from Sebastus or Augustus, and settled the affairs of the city after a most regular manner.

3. And when Cæsar had further bestowed upon him another additional country, he built there also a temple of while marble, hard by the fountains of Jordan: the place is called Panium, where is a top of a mountain that is raised to an immense height, and at its side, beneath, or at its bottom, a dark cave opens itself; within which there is a horrible precipice, that descends abruptly to a vast depth; it contains a mighty quantity of water, which is immovable; and when anybody lets down any thing to measure the depth of the earth beneath the water, no length of cord is sufficient to reach it. Now the fountains of Jordan rise at the roots of this cavity outwardly; and, as some think, this is the utmost origin of Jordan: but we shall speak of that matter more accurately in our following history.

4. But the king erected other places at Jericho, also, between the citadel Cypros and the former place, such as were better and more useful than the former for travellers, and named them from the same friends of his. To say all at once, there was not any place of his kingdom fit for the purpose, that was permitted to be without somewhat that was for Cæsar's honour, and when he had filled his own country with temples, he poured out the like plentiful marks of his esteem into his provinces, and built many cities which he called *Cæsareas.*

5. And when he observed that there was a city by the seaside, that was much decayed (its name was Strato's Tower,) but that the place, by the happiness of its situation, was capable of great improvements from his liberality, he rebuilt it all with white stone, and adorned it with several most splendid palaces, wherein he especially demonstrated his magnanimity: for the case was this, that all the seashore between Dora and Joppa, in the middle, between which this city is situated, had no good haven, insomuch that every one that sailed from Phenicia for Egypt was obliged to lie in the stormy sea, by reason of the south wind that threatened them; which wind, if it blow but a little fresh, such vast waves are raised, and dash upon the rocks, that upon their retreat, the sea is in a great ferment for a long way. But the king, by the expenses he was at, and the liberal disposal of them, overcame nature, and built a haven larger than was the Pyreeum [1] [at Athens;] and in the other retirements of the water he built other deep stations [for the ships also.]

6. Now although the place where he built was greatly opposite to his purposes, yet did he so fully struggle with that difficulty, that the firmness of his building could not easily be conquered by the sea; and the beauty and ornament of the works was such, as though he had not had any difficulty in the operation; for when he had measured out as large a space as we have before mentioned, he let down stones into twenty fathom water, the greatest part of which were fifty feet in length, and nine in depth, and ten in

[1] That Josephus speaks truth, when he assures us that "the haven of this Cæsarea was made by Herod not less, nay rather larger, than that famous haven at Athens called *the Pyreeum*," will appear, says Dean Aldrich, to him who compares the descriptions of that at Athens in Thucydides and Pausanias, with this of Cæsarea in Josephus here, and in the Antiq. B. XV. ch. ix. sect. 6, Vol. II. and B. XVII. ch. ix. sect. 1, Vol. III.

breadth, and some still larger. But when the haven
was filled up to that depth, he enlarged that wall
which was thus already extant above the sea, till it
was two hundred feet wide; one hundred of which
had buildings before it, in order to break the force
of the waves, whence it was called *Procumatia*, or the
first breaker of the waves; but the rest of the space
was under a stone wall that ran round it. On this
wall were very large towers, the principal and most
beautiful of which was called *Drusium*, from Drusus,
who was son-in-law to Cæsar.

7. There were also a great number of arches,
where the mariners dwelt; and all the places before
them round about was a large valley, or walk, for a
quay [or landing place] to those that came on shore;
but the entrance was on the north, because the north
wind was there the most gentle of all the winds. At
the mouth of the haven were on each side three great
Colossi, supported by pillars, where those Colossi that
are on your left hand as you sail into the port, are
supported by a solid tower, but those on the right
hand are supported by two upright stones joined together, which stones were larger than that tower which
was on the other side of the entrance. Now there
were continual edifices joined to the haven, which were
also themselves of white stone; and to this haven did
the narrow streets of the city lead, and were built at
equal distances one from another. And over against
the mouth of the haven, upon an elevation, there was
a temple for Cæsar, which was excellent both in
beauty and largeness; and therein was a Colossus of
Cæsar, not less than that of Jupiter Olympius, which
it was made to resemble. The other Colossus of
Rome was equal to that of Juno at Argos. So he
dedicated the city to the province, and the haven to
the sailors there, but the honour of the building he

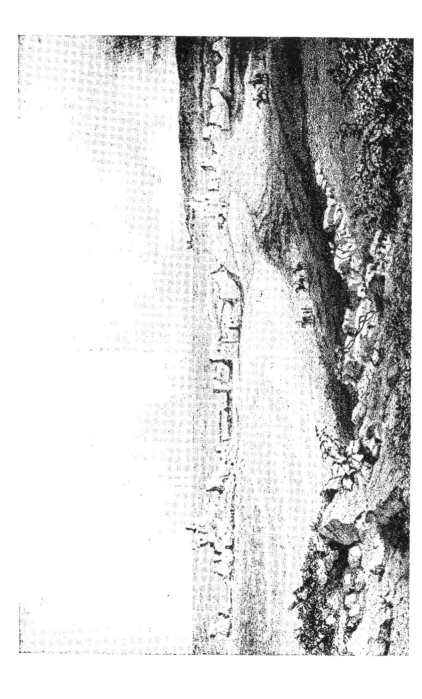

CÆSAREA.

This view shows the existing remains of the ancient Cæsarea and of its mole, as they occupy a large area upon the mainland and stretch out some distance to seaward. A large portion of the masonry or foundations of the mole are now buried far below the sea level. The promontory on the horizon at a distance of about twelve miles is the Castellum Perigrinorum, where there are extensive ruins, and beyond this, eight miles further north, is the headland of Carmel.

Josephus' descriptions of Cæsarea, as built and adorned in ten years by Herod—War, I. xxi. 5, 6, 7, and Antiquities, XV. ix. 6, nearly identical as they are, while they perfectly consist with contemporaneous testimonies, are the more to be regarded as furnishing an instance of his trustworthiness, inasmuch as no other account of this port and city, comprising details, has come down to us from that age. The greatness of the place, in the time of Josephus, we might indeed *infer* from the brief allusions of other writers; but we must turn to Josephus as our sole authority, if we wish for more information.

ascribed to ¹ Cæsar, and named it Cæsarea accordingly.

8.   He also built the other edifices, the amphitheatre, and theatre, and market-place, in a manner
agreeable to that denomination; and appointed games
every fifth year, and called them in like manner,
Cæsar's Games; and he first himself proposed the
largess prizes upon the hundred ninety-second Olym-
piad; in which not only the victors themselves, but
those that came next to them, and even those that
came in the third place, were partakers of his royal
bounty.   He also rebuilt Anthedon, a city that lay
on the coast, and had been demolished in the wars,
and named it *Agrippium.*   Moreover, he had so very
great a kindness for his friend Agrippa, that he had
his name engraven upon that gate which he had himself erected in the temple.

9.   Herod was also a lover of his father, if any
other person ever was so; for he made a monument
for his father, even that city which he built in the
finest plain that was in his kingdom, and which had
rivers and trees in abundance, and named it *Antipatris.*   He also built a wall about a citadel that
lay above Jericho, and was a very strong and very
fine building, and dedicated it to his mother, and
called it *Cypros.*   Moreover, he dedicated a tower
that was at Jerusalem, and called it by the name of
his brother Phasaelus, whose structure, largeness, and
magnificence, we shall describe hereafter.   He also
built another city in the valley that leads northward
from Jericho, and named it *Phasaelis.*

10.   And as he transmitted to eternity his family
and friends, so did he not neglect a memorial for
himself, but built a fortress upon a mountain towards

¹ These buildings of cities by the name of Cæsar, and institution of
solemn games in honour of Augustus Cæsar, as here, and in the Antiquities, related of Herod by Josephus, the Roman historians attest
to, as things then frequent in the provinces of that empire.

Arabia, and named it from himself [1] *Herodium;* and he called that hill that was the shape of a woman's breast, and was sixty furlongs distant from Jerusalem, by the same name. He also bestowed much curious art upon it, with great ambition, and built round towers all about the top of it, and filled up the remaining space with the most costly palaces round about, insomuch, that not only the sight of the inner apartments was splendid but great wealth was laid out on the outward walls, and partitions, and roofs also. Besides this, he brought a mighty quantity of water from a great distance, and at vast charges, and raised an ascent to it of two hundred steps of the whitest marble, for the hill was itself moderately high, and entirely factitious. He also built other palaces about the roots of the hill, sufficient to receive the furniture that was put into them, with his friends also; insomuch, that on account of its containing all necessaries, the fortress might seem to be a city, but, by the bounds it had, a palace only.

11. And when he had built so much, he showed the greatness of his soul to no small number of foreign cities. He built places for exercise at Tripoli, and Damascus, and Ptolemais; he built a wall about Byblus, as also large rooms, and cloisters, and temples, and market-places at Berytus and Tyre, with theatres at Sidon and Damascus. He also built aqueducts for those Laodiceans who have lived by the seaside; and for those of Ascalon he built baths and costly fountains, as also cloisters round a court that were admirable, both for their workmanship and largeness.

---

[1] There were two cities, or citadels, called Herodium, in Judea, and both mentioned by Josephus, not only here, but Antiq. B. XIV. ch. xiii. sect. 9, B. XV. ch. ix. sect. 6, Vol. II. Of the War, B. I. ch. xiii. sect. 8, B. III. ch. iii. sect. 5. One of them was 200, and the other 60 furlongs distant from Jerusalem. One of them is mentioned by Pliny. Hist. Nat. B. V. ch. xiv.

Moreover, he dedicated groves and meadows to some
people; nay, not a few cities there were who had lands
of his donation, as if they were parts of his own
kingdom. He also bestowed annual revenues, and
those for ever also, on the settlements for exercises,
and appointed for them, as well as for the people of
Cos, that such rewards should never be wanting. He
also gave corn to all such as wanted it, and conferred
upon Rhodes large sums of money for building ships,
and this he did in many places, and frequently also.
And when Apollo's temple had been burnt down, he
rebuilt it at his own charges, after a better manner
than it was before. What need I speak of the presents he made to the Lyceans and Samnians? or of his
great liberality through all Ionia? and that according
to everybody's wants of them. And are not the
Athenians, and Lacedemonians, and Nicopolitans,
and that Pergamus which is in Mysia, full of donations that Herod presented them withal? And as
for that large open place belonging to Antioch in
Syria, did not he pave it with polished marble, though
it were twenty furlongs long? and this when it was
shunned by all men before, because it was full of
dirt and filthiness, when he besides adorned the same
place with a cloister of the same length.

12. It is true, a man may say, these were favours
peculiar to those particular places, on which he be
stowed his benefits; but then what favours he be
stowed on the Eleans was a donation not only in
common to all Greece, but to all the habitable earth,
as far as the glory of the Olympic games reached.
For when he perceived that they were come to nothing,
for want of money, and that the only remains of
ancient Greece were in a manner gone, he not only
became one of the combatants in that return of the
fifth-year games, which in his sailing to Rome he

happened to be present at, but he settled upon them revenues of money for perpetuity, insomuch, that his memorial as a combatant there can never fail. It would be an infinite task if I should go over his payments of people's debts, or tributes, for them, as he eased the people of Phasaelus, of Batanea, and of the small cities about Cilicia, of those annual pensions they before paid. However, the fear he was in much disturbed the greatness of his soul, lest he should be exposed to envy, or seem to hunt after greater things than he ought, while he bestowed more liberal gifts upon the cities, than did their owners themselves.

13. Now Herod had a body suited to his soul, and was ever a most excellent hunter, where he generally had good success, by the means of his great skill in riding horses; for in one day he caught forty wild [1] beasts; that country breeds also bears, and the greatest part of it is replenished with stags, and wild asses. He was also such a warrior as could not be withstood: many men therefore there are who have stood amazed at his readiness in his exercises, when they saw him throw the javelin directly forward, and to shoot the arrow upon the mark. And then besides these performances of his, depending on his own strength of mind and body, fortune was also very favourable to him; for he seldom failed of success in his wars; and when he failed, he was not himself the occasion of such failings, but he either was betrayed by some, or the rashness of his own soldiers procured his defeat.

---

[1] Here seems to be a small defect in the copies, which describe the wild beasts which were hunted in a certain country by Herod, without naming any such country at all.

CHAPTER XXII.

The murder of Aristobulus and Hyrcanus, the high priests, as also of Mariamne the queen.

1. HOWEVER, fortune was avenged on Herod in his eternal great successes, by raising him up domestic troubles, and he began to have wild disorders in his family on account of his wife, of whom he was so very fond. For when he came to the government, he sent away her whom he had before married, when he was a private person, and who was born at Jerusalem, whose name was *Doris,* and married Mariamne, the daughter of Alexander the son of Aristobulus; on whose account disturbances arose in his family, and that in part very soon, but chiefly after his return from Rome. For first of all, he expelled Antipater the son of Doris, for the sake of his sons by Mariamne, out of the city, and permitted him to come thither at no other times than at the festivals. After this he slew his wife's grandfather, Hyrcanus, when he was returned out of Parthia to him, under this pretence, that he suspected him of plotting against him. Now this Hyrcanus had been carried captive to Barzapharnes, when he overran Syria; but those of his own country beyond Euphrates were desirous he would stay with them, and this out of the commiseration they had for his condition; and had he complied with their desires, when they exhorted him not to go over the river to Herod, he had not perished, but the marriage of his granddaughter [to Herod] was his temptation; for as he relied upon him, and was overfond of his own country, he came back to it. Herod's provocation was this, not that Hyrcanus made any

attempt to gain the kingdom, but that it was fitter for
him to be their king than for Herod.

2. Now of the five children which Herod had by
Mariamne, two of them were daughters, and three
were sons; and the youngest of these sons was educated at Rome, and there died; but the two eldest he
treated as those of royal blood, on account of the
nobility of their mother, and because they were not
born till he was king. But then what was stronger
than all this, was the love that he bore to Mariamne,
and which inflamed him every day to a great degree,
and so far conspired with the other motives, that he
felt no other troubles on account of her he loved so
entirely. But Mariamne's hatred to him was not
inferior to his love for her. She had indeed but too
just a cause of indignation, from what he had done,
while her boldness proceeded from his affection to
her; so she openly reproached him with what he had
done to her grandfather Hyrcanus, and to her brother
Aristobulus; for he had not spared this Aristobulus,
though he were but a child, for when he had given
him the high priesthood at the age of seventeen, he
slew him quickly after he had conferred that dignity
upon him; but when Aristobulus had put on the holy
vestments, and had approached to the altar, at a
festival, the multitude, in great crowds, fell into
tears; whereupon the child was sent by night to Jericho, and was there dipped by the Galls, at Herod's
command, in a pool till he was drowned.

3. For these reasons Mariamne reproached Herod,
and his sister and mother, after a most contumelious
manner, while he was dumb on account of his affection for her; yet had the women great indignation at
her, and raised a calumny against her, that she was
false to his bed: which thing they thought most likely
to move Herod to anger. They also contrived to

have many other circumstances believed, in order to
make the thing more credible, and accused her of
having sent her picture into Egypt to Antony, and
that her lust was so extravagant, as to have thus
showed herself, though she was absent, to a man that
ran mad after women, and to a man that had it in
his power to use violence to her. This charge fell
like a thunderbolt upon Herod, and put him into
disorder; and that especially, because his love to her
occasioned him to be jealous, and because he considered with himself that Cleopatra was a shrewd
woman, and that on her account Lysanias the king
was taken off, as well as Malichus the Arabian: for
his fear did not only extend to the dissolving of his
marriage, but to the danger of his life.

4. When therefore he was about to take a journey
abroad, he committed his wife to Joseph, his sister
Salome's husband, as to one who would be faithful
to him, and bore him good-will on account of their
kindred; he also gave him a secret injunction, that
if Antony slew him, he would slay her. But Joseph,
without any ill design, and only in order to demonstrate the king's love to his wife, how he could not
bear to think of being separated from her, even by
death itself, discovered this grand secret to her; upon
which, when Herod was come back, and as they talked
together, confirmed his love to her by many oaths,
and assured her that he had never such an affection
for any other woman as he had for her. [1] "Yes,
says she, thou didst, to be sure, demonstrate thy love

---

[1] Here is either a defect, or a great mistake in Josephus' present
copies, or memory, for Mariamne did not now reproach Herod with this
his first injunction to Joseph to kill her, if he himself were slain by
Antony, but that he had given the like command a second time to
Sohemus also, when he was afraid of being slain by Augustus. Antiq.
B. XV. ch. iii. sect. 5, Vol. II., etc.

to me by the injunctions thou gavest Joseph, when thou commandedst him to kill me."

5. When he heard that this grand secret was discovered, he was like a distracted man, and said, that Joseph would never have disclosed that injunction of his, unless he had debauched her. His passion also made him stark mad, and leaping out of his bed, he ran about the palace after a wild manner; at which time his sister Salome took the opportunity also to blast her reputation, and confirmed his suspicion about Joseph; whereupon out of his ungovernable jealousy and rage, he commanded both of them to be slain immediately; but as soon as ever his passion was over, he repented of what he had done, and as soon as his anger was worn off, his affections were kindled again. And, indeed, the flame of his desires for her was so ardent, that he could not think she was dead, but would appear under his disorders to speak to her as if she were still alive, till he were better instructed by time, when his grief and trouble, now she was dead, appeared as great as his affection had been for her while she was living.

CHAPTER XXIII.

Calumnies against the sons of Mariamne. Antipater is preferred before them. They are accused before Cæsar, and Herod is reconciled to them.

1. Now Mariamne's sons were heirs to that hatred which had been borne their mother, and when they considered the greatness of Herod's crime towards her, they were suspicious of him as of an enemy of theirs; and this first while they were educated at

Rome, but still more when they were returned to Judea. This temper of theirs increased upon them, as they grew up to be men, and when they were come to an age fit for marriage, the one of them married their aunt Salome's daughter, which Salome had been the accuser of their mother; the other married the daughter of Archelaus, king of Cappadocia. And now they used boldness in speaking, as well as bore hatred in their minds. Now those that calumniated them took a handle from such their boldness, and certain of them spoke now more plainly to the king that there were treacherous designs laid against him by both his sons, and that he who was son-in-law to Archelaus, relying upon his father-in-law, was preparing to fly away, in order to accuse Herod before Cæsar; and when Herod's head had been long enough filled with these calumnies, he brought Antipater, whom he had by Doris, into favour again, as a defence to him against his other sons, and began all the ways he possibly could to prefer him before them.

2. But these sons were not able to bear this change in their affairs, but when they saw him that was born of a mother of no family, the nobility of their birth made them unable to contain their indignation; but whensoever they were uneasy, they showed the anger they had at it. And as these sons did day after day improve in that their anger, Antipater already exercised all his own abilities, which were very great, in flattering his father, and in contriving many sorts of calumnies against his brethren, while he told some stories of them himself, and put it upon other proper persons to raise other stories against them, till at length he entirely cut his brethren off from all hopes of succeeding to the kingdom; for he was already publicly put into his father's will as his successor. Accordingly, he was sent with royal ornaments, and

other marks of royalty, to Cæsar, excepting the diadem. He was also able in time to introduce his mother again into Mariamne's bed. The two sorts of weapons he made use of against his brethren, were flattery and calumny, whereby he brought matters privately to such a pass, that the king had thoughts of putting his sons to death.

3. So the father drew Alexander as far as Rome, and charged him with an attempt of poisoning him before Cæsar. Alexander could hardly speak for lamentation, but having a judge that was more skilful than Antipater, and more wise than Herod, he modestly avoided laying any imputation upon his father, but with great strength of reason confuted the calumnies laid against him; and when he had demonstrated the innocency of his brother, who was in the like danger with himself, he at last bewailed the craftiness of Antipater, and the disgrace they were under. He was enabled also to justify himself, not only by a clear conscience, which he carried with him, but by his eloquence; for he was a shrewd man in making speeches. And upon his saying at last, that if his father objected this crime to them, it was in his power to put them to death, he made all the audience weep; and he brought Cæsar to that pass, as to reject the accusations, and to reconcile their father to them immediately. But the conditions of their reconciliation were these, that they should in all things be obedient to their father, and that he should have power to leave the kingdom to which of them he pleased.

4. After this the king came back from Rome, and seemed to have forgiven his sons upon these accusations; but still so, that he was not without his suspicions of them. They were followed by Antipater, who was the fountain-head of these accusations; yet did not he openly discover his hatred to them, as

revering him that had reconciled them. But as Herod sailed by Cilicia, he touched at [1] Eleusa, where Archelaus treated them in the most obliging manner, and gave him thanks for the deliverance of. his son-in-law, and was much pleased at their reconciliation; and this the more, because he had formerly written to his friends at Rome, that they should be assisting to Alexander at his trial. So he conducted Herod as far as Zephyrium, and made him presents to the value of thirty talents.

5. Now when Herod was .come to Jerusalem, he gathered the people together and presented to them his three sons, and gave them an apologetic account of his absence, and "thanked God greatly, and thanked Cæsar greatly also, for settling his house when it was under disturbances, and had procured concord among his sons, which was of greater consequence than the kingdom itself, and which I will render still more firm; for Cæsar hath put into my power to dispose of the government, and to appoint my successor. Accordingly, in way of requital for his kindness, and in order to provide for mine own advantage, I do declare, that these three sons of mine shall be kings. And, in the first place, I pray for the approbation of God to what I am about; and, in the next place, I·desire your approbation also. The age of one of them, and the nobility of the other two, should procure them the succession. Nay, indeed, my kingdom is so large, that it may be sufficient for more kings. Now do you keep those in their places whom Cæsar hath joined, and their father hath appointed; and do not you pay undue or unequal re-

---

[1] That this island Eleusa, afterwards called Sebaste, near Cilicia, had in it the royal palace of this Archelaus, king of Cappadocia, Strabo testifies, B. XV. p. 671. Stephanus of Byzantium also calls it "an island of Cilicia, which is now Sebaste." See the same history, Antiq. B. XVI. ch. x. sect. 7, Vol. II.

spects to them, but to every one according to the prerogative of their births; for he that pays such respects unduly, will thereby not make him that is honoured beyond what his age requires so joyful, as he will make him that is dishonoured sorrowful. As for the kindred and friends that are to converse with them, I will appoint them to each of them, and will so constitute them, that they may be securities for their concord: as well knowing, that the ill tempers of those with whom they converse, will produce quarrels and contentions among them; but that, if those with whom they converse be of good tempers, they will preserve their natural affections for one another. But still I desire, that not these only, but all the captains of my army, have, for the present, their hopes placed on me alone; for I do not give away my kingdom to these my sons, but give them royal honours only; whereby it will come to pass, that they will enjoy the sweet parts of government as rulers themselves, but that the burden of administration will rest upon myself, whether I will or not. And let every one consider what age I am of, how I have conducted my life, and what piety I have exercised: for my age is not so great, that men may soon expect the end of my life; nor have I indulged such a luxurious way of living as cuts men off when they are young; and we have been so religious towards God, that we [have reason to hope we] may arrive at a very great age. But for such as cultivate a friendship with my sons, so as to aim at my destruction, they shall be punished by me on their account. I am not one who envy my own children, and therefore forbid men to pay them great respect; but I know that such [extravagant] respects are the way to make them insolent. And if every one that comes near them does but revolve this in his mind, that if he proves a good man, he shall receive a reward from me, that if he proves seditious, his ill intended complaisance shall get him nothing from him to whom it is shown. I suppose they will all be of my side, that is of my sons' side; for it will be for their advantage that I reign, and that I be at concord with them. But do you, O my good children, reflect upon the holiness of nature itself, by whose means natural affection is preserved, even among wild beasts; in the next place reflect upon Cæsar, who hath made this reconciliation among us; and, in the third place, reflect upon me who entreat you to do what I have power to command you; continue brethren. I give you royal garments, and royal honours; and I pray to God to preserve what I have determined, in case you be at concord one with another." When the king had thus spoken, and had saluted every one of his sons after an obliging manner, he dismissed the multitude; some of which gave their assent to what he had said, and wished it might take effect accordingly; but for those who wished for a change of affairs, they pretended they did not so much as hear what he said.

CHAPTER XXIV.

The malice of Antipater and Doris. Alexander is very uneasy on Glaphyra's account. Herod pardons Pheroras whom he suspected, and Salome, whom he knew to make mischief among them. Herod's eunuchs are tortured, and Alexander is bound.

1. BUT now the quarrel that was between them, still accompanied these brethren when they parted,

and the suspicions they had one of the other grew worse. Alexander and Aristobulus were much grieved that the privilege of the first-born was confirmed to Antipater, as was Antipater very angry at his brethren, that they were to succeed him. But then this last being of a disposition that was mutable and politic, he knew how to hold his tongue, and used a great deal of cunning, and thereby concealed the hatred he bore to them; while the former, depending on the nobility of their births, had every thing upon their tongues which was in their minds. Many also there were who provoked them farther, and many of their [seeming] friends insinuated themselves into their acquaintance, to spy out what they did. Now every thing that was said by Alexander was presently brought to Antipater, and from Antipater it was brought to Herod with additions. Nor could the young man say any thing in the simplicity of his heart, without giving offence, but what he said was still turned to calumny against him. And if he had been at any time a little free in his conversation, great imputations were forged from the smallest occasions. Antipater also was perpetually setting some to provoke him to speak, that the lies he raised of him might seem to have some foundation of truth; and if, among the many stories that were given out, but one of them could be proved true, that was supposed to imply the rest to be true also. And as to Antipater's friends, they were all either naturally so cautious in speaking, or had been so far bribed to conceal their thoughts, that nothing of these grand secrets got abroad by their means. Nor should one be mistaken if he called the life of Antipater a mystery of wickedness; for he either corrupted Alexander's acquaintance with money, or got into their favour by flatteries; by which two means he gained all his designs, and brought them to betray their master, and to steal away, and reveal what he either did or said. Thus did he act a part very cunningly in all points, and wrought himself a passage by his calumnies, with the greatest shrewdness; while he put on a face as if he were a kind brother to Alexander and Aristobulus, but suborned other men to inform of what they did to Herod. And when any thing was told against Alexander, he would come in and pretend [to be of his side,] and would begin to contradict what was said; but would afterward contrive matters so privately, that the king should have an indignation at him. His general aim was this, to lay a plot, and to make it believed that Alexander lay in wait to kill his father; for nothing afforded so great a confirmation to these calumnies as did Antipater's apologies for him.

2. By these methods Herod was inflamed, and, as much as his natural affection to the young men did every day diminish, so much did it increase toward Antipater. The courtiers also inclined to the same conduct, some of their own accord, and others by the king's injunction, as particularly did Ptolemy, the king's dearest friend, as also the king's brethren, and all his children; for Antipater was all in all: and what was the bitterest part of all to Alexander, Antipater's mother was also all in all; she was one that gave counsel against them, and was more harsh than a stepmother, and one that hated the queen's sons more than is usual to hate sons-in-law. All men did therefore already pay their respects to Antipater, in hopes of advantage; and it was the king's command which alienated everybody [from the brethren,] he having given this charge to his most intimate friends, that they should not come near, nor pay any regard to Alexander, or to his friends. Herod was also be-

come terrible, not only to his domestics about the court, but to his friends abroad; for Cæsar had given such a privilege to no other king as he had given to him, which was this, that he might fetch back any one that fled from him, even out of a city that was not under his own jurisdiction. Now the young men were not acquainted with the calumnies raised against them; for which reason they could not guard themselves against them, but fell under them; for their father did not make any public complaints against either of them; though in a little time they perceived how things were by his coldness to them, and by the great uneasiness he showed upon any thing that troubled him. Antipater had also made their uncle Pheroras to be their enemy, as well as their aunt Salome, while he was always talking with her, as with a wife, and irritating her against them. Moreover, Alexander's wife, Glaphyra, augmented this hatred against them, by deriving her nobility and genealogy [from great persons,] and pretending that she was a lady superior to all others in that kingdom, as being derived by her father's side from Temenus, and by her mother's side from Darius, the son of Hystaspes. She also frequently reproached Herod's sister and wives, with the ignobility of their descent; and that they were every one chosen by him for their beauty, but not for their family. Now those wives of his were not a few; it being of old permitted to the Jews to ¹ marry many wives; and this king delighted in many, all of whom hated Alexander, on account of Glaphyra's boasting and reproaches.

¹ That it was an immemorial custom among the Jews, and their forefathers, the patriarchs, to have sometimes more wives, or wives and concubines, than one at the same time, and that this polygamy was not directly *forbidden* in the law of Moses, is evident; but that *polygamy* was ever properly and distinctly *permitted* in that law of Moses, in the places here cited by Dean Aldrich, Deut. xvii. 16, 17, or xxi. 15, or indeed any where else, does not appear to me.

3. Nay, Aristobulus had raised a quarrel between himself and Salome, who was his mother-in-law, besides the anger he had conceived at Glaphyra's reproaches; for he perpetually upbraided his wife with the meanness of her family, and complained, that as he had married a woman of a low family, so had his brother Alexander married one of royal blood. At this Salome's daughter wept, and told it her with this addition, that Alexander threatened the mothers of his other brethren, that when he should come to the crown, he would make them weave with their maidens, and would make those brothers of his country schoolmasters; and broke this jest upon them, that they had been very carefully instructed to fit them for such an employment. Hereupon Salome could not contain her anger, but told all to Herod: nor could her testimony be suspected, since it was against her own son-in-law. There was also another calumny that ran abroad, and inflamed the king's mind; for he heard that these sons of his were perpetually speaking of their mother, and, among their lamentations for her, did not abstain from cursing him; and that when he made presents of any of Mariamne's garments to his later wives, these threatened, that in a little time, instead of royal garments, they would clothe them in no better than haircloth.

4. Now upon these accounts, though Herod was somewhat afraid of the young men's high spirit, yet did he not despair of reducing them to a better mind; but before he went to Rome, whither he was now going by sea, he called them to him, and partly threatened them a little, as a king; but for the main, he admonished them as a father, and exhorted them to love their brethren, and told them that he would pardon their former offences, if they would amend for the time to come. But they refuted the calumnies

that had been raised of them, and said they were false, and alleged that their actions were sufficient for their vindication, and said withal, that he himself ought to shut his ears against such tales, and not to be too easy in believing them, for that there would never be wanting those that would tell lies to their disadvantage, as long as any would give ear to them.

5. When they had thus soon pacified him, as being their father, they got clear of the present fear they were in. Yet did they see occasion for sorrow in some time afterward; for they knew that Salome, as well as their uncle Pheroras, were their enemies; who were both of them heavy and severe persons, and especially Pheroras, who was a partner with Herod in all the affairs of the kingdom, excepting his diadem. He had also a hundred talents of his own revenue, and enjoyed the advantage of all the land beyond Jordan, which he had received as a gift from his brother, who had asked of Cæsar to make him a tetrarch, as he was made accordingly. Herod had also given him a wife out of the royal family, who was no other than his own wife's sister, and after her death had solemnly espoused to him his own eldest daughter, with a dowry of three hundred talents: but Pheroras refused to consummate this royal marriage out of his affection to a maid-servant of his. Upon which account Herod was very angry, and gave that daughter in marriage to a brother's son of his [Joseph,] who was slain afterward by the Parthians; but in some time he laid aside his anger against Pheroras, and pardoned him, as one not able to overcome his foolish passion for the maid-servant.

6. Nay, Pheroras had been accused long before, while the queen Mariamne was alive, as if he were in a plot to poison Herod; and there came then so great a number of informers, that Herod himself, though

he was an exceeding lover of his brethren, was brought
to believe what was said, and to be afraid of it also;
and when he had brought many of those that were
under suspicion to the torture, he came at last to
Pheroras' own friends; none of which did openly
confess the crime, but they owned that he had made
preparation to take her whom he loved, and run away
to the Parthians. Costobarus also, the husband of
Salome, to whom the king had given her in marriage,
after her former husband had been put to death for
adultery, was instrumental in bringing about this
contrivance and flight of his. Nor did Salome escape
all calumny upon herself; for her brother Pheroras
accused her, that she had made an agreement to marry
Silleus, the procurator of Obodas, king of Arabia,
who was at bitter enmity with Herod; but when she
was convicted of this, and of all that Pheroras had
accused her of, she obtained her pardon. The king
also pardoned Pheroras himself the crimes he had
been accused of.

7. But the storm of the whole family was removed
to Alexander, and all of it rested upon his head.
There were three eunuchs who were in the highest
esteem with the king, as was plain by the offices they
were in about him; for one of them was appointed
to be his butler, another of them got his supper ready
for him, and the third put him into bed, and lay down
by him. Now Alexander had prevailed with these
men, by large gifts, to let him use them after an
obscene manner: which, when it was told to the king,
they were tortured, and found guilty, and presently
confessed the criminal conversation he had with them.
They also discovered the promises by which they were
induced so to do, and how they were deluded by
Alexander, who had told them, That "they ought not
to fix their hopes upon Herod, an old man, and one

so shameless as to colour his hair, unless they thought
that would make him young again; but that they
ought to fix their attention on him, who was to be
his successor in the kingdom whether he would or not;
and who in no long time would avenge himself on his
enemies, and make his friends happy and blessed, and
themselves in the first place: that the men of power
did already pay respects to Alexander privately; and
that the captains of the soldiery, and the officers, did
secretly come to him."

8. These confessions did so terrify Herod that he
durst not immediately publish them; but he sent spies
abroad privately by night and by day, who should
make a close inquiry after all that was done and said;
and when any were but suspected [of treason] he put
them to death, insomuch that the palace was full of
horribly unjust proceedings, for everybody forged
calumnies, as they were themselves in a state of enmity
or hatred against others; and many there were who
abused the king's bloody passion to the disadvantage
of those with whom they had quarrels, and lies were
easily believed, and punishments were inflicted sooner
than the calumnies were forged: he who had just then
been accusing another, was accused himself, and was
led away to execution together with him whom he
had convicted; for the danger the king was in of his
life made examinations be very short. He also proceeded to such a degree of bitterness, that he could
not look on any of those that were not accused with
a pleasant countenance, but was in the most barbarous
disposition towards his own friends. Accordingly, he
forbade a great many of them to come to court, and
to those whom he had not power to punish actually,
he spoke harshly; but for Antipater, he insulted
Alexander, now he was under his misfortunes, and
got a stout company of his kindred together, and

raised all sorts of calumny against him: and for the king, he was brought to such a degree of terror by those prodigious slanders and contrivances, that he fancied he saw Alexander coming to him with a drawn sword in his hand; so he caused him to be seized upon immediately and bound, and fell to examining his friends by torture, many of whom died [under the torture] but would discover nothing, nor say any thing against their consciences; but some of them, being forced to speak falsely by the pains they endured, said that Alexander, and his brother Aristobulus, plotted against him, and waited for an opportunity to kill him as he was hunting, and then fly away to Rome. These accusations, though they were of an incredible nature, and only framed upon the great distress they were in, were readily believed by the king, who thought it some comfort to him, after he had bound his son, that it might appear he had not done it unjustly.

CHAPTER XXV.

Archelaus procures a reconciliation between Alexander, Pheroras, and Herod.

1. Now as to Alexander, since he perceived it impossible to persuade his father [that he was innocent,] he resolved to meet his calamities, how severe soever they were; so he composed four books against his enemies, and confessed that he had been in a plot; but declared withal that the greatest part [of the courtiers] were in a plot with him, and chiefly Pheroras, and Salome; nay, that Salome once came and forced him to lie with her in the night time, whether

he would or no. These books were put into Herod's hands, and made a great clamour against the men in power. And now it was that Archelaus came hastily into Judea, as being affrighted for his son-in-law, and his daughter; and he came as a proper assistant, and in a very prudent manner, and by a stratagem he obliged the king not to execute what he had threatened; for when he was come to him, he cried out, "Where in the world is this wretched son-in-law of mine? Where shall I see the head of him who contrived to murder his father, which I will tear to pieces with my own hands? I will do the same also to my daughter, who hath such a fine husband: for although she be not a partner in the plot, yet, by being the wife of such a creature, she is polluted. And I cannot but admire at thy patience, against whom this plot is laid, if Alexander be still alive; for as I came with what haste I could from Cappadocia, I expected to find him put to death for his crimes long ago; but still in order to make an examination with thee about my daughter, whom out of regard to thee, and thy dignity, I had espoused to him in marriage; but now we must take counsel about them both; and if thy paternal affection be so great, that thou canst not punish thy son, who hath plotted against thee, let us change our right hands, and let us succeed one to the other in expressing our rage upon this occasion."

2. When he had made this pompous declaration, he got Herod to remit of his anger, though he were in disorder, who thereupon gave him the books which Alexander had composed to be read by him, and as he came to every head, he considered of it, together with Herod. So Archelaus took hence the occasion for that stratagem which he made use of, and by degrees he laid the blame on those men whose names

were in these books, and especially upon Pheroras;
and when he saw that the king believed him [to be
in earnest,] he said, "We must consider whether the
young man be not himself plotted against by such
a number of wicked wretches, and not thou plotted
against by the young man; for I cannot see any
occasion for his falling into so horrid a crime, since
he enjoys the advantages of royalty already, and has
the expectation of being one of thy successors; I mean
this, unless there were some persons that persuade
him to it, and such persons as make an ill use of the
facility they know there is to persuade young men;
for by such persons, not only young men are sometimes imposed upon, but old men also, and by them
sometimes are the most illustrious families and kingdoms overturned."

3. Herod assented to what he had said, and, by
degrees, abated of his anger against Alexander; but
was more angry at Pheroras: for the principal subject of the four books was Pheroras, who perceiving
that the king's inclinations changed on a sudden, and
that Archelaus' friendship could do every thing with
him, and that he had no honourable method of preserving himself, he procured his safety by his impudence. So he left Alexander, and had recourse to
Archelaus, who told him, That "he did not see how
he could get him excused, now he was directly caught
in so many crimes, whereby it was evidently demonstrated that he had plotted against the king, and had
been the cause of those misfortunes which the young
man was now under, unless he would moreover leave
off his cunning knavery, and his denials of what he
was charged withal, and confess the charge, and im-
plore pardon of his brother, who still had a kindness
for him; but that if he would do so, he would afford
him all the assistance he was able."

4. With this advice Pheroras complied, and, putting himself into such a habit as might most move compassion, he came with black cloth upon his body and tears in his eyes, and threw himself down at Herod's feet, and begged his pardon for what he had done, and confessed that he had acted very wickedly, and was guilty of every thing that he had been accused of, and lamented that disorder of his mind, and distraction which his love to a woman, he said, had brought him to. So when Archelaus had brought Pheroras to accuse and bear witness against himself, he then made an excuse for him, and mitigated Herod's anger towards him, and this by using certain domestical examples, "For that when he had suffered much greater mischiefs from a brother of his own, he preferred the obligations of nature, before the passion of revenge; because it is in kingdoms, as it is in gross bodies, where some member or other is ever swelled by the body's weight, in which case it is not proper to cut off such member, but to heal it by a gentle method of cure."

5. Upon Archelaus' saying this, and much more to the same purpose, Herod's displeasure against Pheroras was mollified; yet did he persevere in his own indignation against Alexander, and said, he would have his daughter divorced, and taken away from him, and this till he had brought Herod to that pass, that, contrary to his former behaviour to him, he petitioned Archelaus for the young man, and that he would let his daughter continue espoused to him; but Archelaus made him strongly believe that he would permit her to be married to any one else, but not to Alexander, because he looked upon it as a very valuable advantage, that the relation they had contracted by that affinity, and the privileges that went along with it might be preserved. And when the king said,

that his son would take it for a great favour to him, if he would not dissolve that marriage, especially since they had already children between the young man and her, and since that wife of his was so well beloved by him, and that as while she remains his wife she would be a great preservative to him, and keep him from offending, as he had formerly done; so if she should be once torn away from him, she would be the cause of his falling into despair; because such young men's attempts are best mollified, when they are diverted from them by settling their affections at home. So Archelaus complied with what Herod desired, but not without difficulty, and was both himself reconciled to the young man, and reconciled his father to him also. However, he said he must, by all means, be sent to Rome to discourse with Cæsar, because he had already written a full account to him of this whole matter.

6. Thus a period was put to Archelaus' stratagem, whereby he delivered his son-in-law out of the dangers he was in: but when these reconciliations were over, they spent their time in feastings and agreeable entertainments. And when Archelaus was going away, Herod made him a present of seventy talents, with a golden throne set with precious stones, and some eunuchs, and a concubine who was called *Pannychis*. He also paid due honours to every one of his friends according to their dignity. In like manner did all the king's kindred, by his command, make glorious presents to Archelaus; and so he was conducted on his way by Herod and his nobility as far as Antioch.

CHAPTER XXVI.

How [1] Eurycles calumniated the sons of Mariamne: and how Euaratus of Cos' apology for them had no effect.

1. Now a little afterward there came into Judea a man that was much superior to Archelaus' stratagems, who did not only overturn that reconciliation that had been so wisely made with Alexander, but proved the occasion of his ruin. He was a Lacedemonian, and his name was *Eurycles*. He was so corrupt a man, that out of the desire of getting money, he chose to live under a king, for Greece could not suffice his luxury. He presented Herod with splendid gifts, as a bait which he laid in order to compass his ends, and quickly receiving them back again manifold; yet did he esteem bare gifts as nothing, unless he imbrued the kingdom in blood by his purchases. Accordingly, he imposed upon the king by flattering him, and by talking subtilely to him, as also by the lying encomiums which he made upon him; for as he soon perceived Herod's blind side, so he said and did every thing that might please him, and thereby became one of his most intimate friends; for both the king and all that were about him, had a great regard [2] for this Spartan, on account of his country.

---

[1] This vile fellow, Eurycles the Lacedemonian, seems to have been the same who is mentioned by Plutarch, as 25 years before a companion to Mark Antony, and as living with Herod; whence he might easily insinuate himself into the acquaintance of Herod's sons, Antipater and Alexander. The reason why his being a Spartan rendered him acceptable to the Jews, as we here see he was, is visible from the public records of the Jews and Spartans, owning those Spartans to be of kin to the Jews, and derived from their common ancestor Abraham, the first patriarch of the Jewish nation. Antiq. B. XII. ch. iv. sect. 10, B. XIII. ch. v. sect. 8, Vol II. and 1 Mac. xii. 7.

[2] See the preceding note.

2. Now as soon as this fellow perceived the rotten parts of the family, and what quarrels the brothers had one with another, and in what disposition the father was towards each of them, he chose to take his lodging at the first in the. house of Antipater, but deluded Alexander with a pretence of friendship to him, and falsely claimed to be an old acquaintance of Archelaus'; for which reason he was presently admitted into Alexander's familiarity as a faithful friend. He also soon recommended himself to his brother Aristobulus. And when he had thus made trial of these several persons, he imposed upon one of them by one method, and upon another by another. But he was principally hired by Antipater, and so betrayed Alexander, and this by reproaching Antipater, because while he was the eldest son, he overlooked the intrigues of those who stood in the way of his expectations; and by reproaching Alexander, because he who was born of a queen, and was married to a king's daughter, permitted one that was born of a mean woman to lay claim to the succession, and this when he had Archelaus to support him in the most complete manner. Nor was his advice thought to be other than faithful by the young man, because of his pretended friendship with Archelaus: on which account it was that Alexander lamented to him Antipater's behaviour with regard to himself, and this without concealing any thing from him; and how it was no wonder if Herod, after he had killed their mother, should deprive them of her kingdom. Upon this Eurycles pretended to commiserate his condition and to grieve with him. He also, by a bait that he laid for him, procured Aristobulus to say the same things. Thus did he inveigle both the brothers to make complaints of their father, and then went to Antipater, and carried these grand secrets to him.

He also added a fiction of his own, as if his brothers had laid a plot against him, and were almost ready to come upon him with their drawn swords. For this intelligence he received a great sum of money, and on that account he commended Antipater before his father, and at length undertook the work of bringing Alexander and Aristobulus to their graves, and accused them before their father. So he came to Herod and told him, That "he would save his life, as a requital for the favours he had received from him, and would preserve his light [of life] by way of retribution for his kind entertainment: for that a sword had been long whetted, and Alexander's right hand had been long stretched out against him; but that he had laid impediments in his way, prevented his speed, and that by pretending to assist him in his design: how Alexander said that Herod was not contented to reign in a kingdom that belonged to others, and to make dilapidations in their mother's government, after he had killed her; but besides all this, that he introduced a spurious successor, and proposed to give the kingdom of their ancestors to that pestilent fellow Antipater; that he would now appease the ghosts of Hyrcanus and Mariamne, by taking vengeance on him; for that it was not fit for him to take the succession to the government from such a father without bloodshed: that many things happen every day to provoke him so to do, insomuch that he can say nothing at all but it affords occasion for calumny against him; for that if any mention be made of nobility of birth, even in other cases he is abused unjustly, while his father would say, that nobody, to be sure, is of noble birth but Alexander, and that his father was inglorious for want of such nobility. If they be at any time hunting, and he says nothing, he gives offence; and if he commends anybody, they take it in way of jest; that they always find their father unmercifully severe, and have no natural affection for any of them but for Antipater; on which accounts, if his plot does not take, he is very willing to die; but that in case he kill his father, he hath sufficient opportunities for saving himself. In the first place, he hath Archelaus his father-in-law to whom he can easily fly; and in the next place he hath Cæsar, who hath never known Herod's character to this day; for that he shall not appear then before him with that dread he used to do, when his father was there to terrify him; and that he will not then produce the accusations that concerned himself alone, but would, in the first place, openly insist on the calamities of their nation, and how they are taxed to death, and in what ways of luxury and wicked practices that wealth is spent which was gotten by bloodshed; what sort of persons they are that get our riches, and to whom those cities belong, upon whom he bestows his favours; that he would have inquiry made what became of his grandfather [Hyrcanus,] and his mother [Mariamne,] and would openly proclaim the gross wickedness that was in the kingdom; on which accounts he should not be deemed a parricide."

3. When Eurycles had made this portentous speech, he greatly commended Antipater, as the only child that had an affection for his father, and on that account was an impediment to the others' plot against him. Hereupon the king, who had hardly repressed his anger upon the former accusations, was exasperated to an incurable degree. At which time Antipater took another occasion to send in other persons to his father, to accuse his brethren, and to tell him, that they had privately discoursed with Jucundus and Tyrannus, who had once been masters of the

horse to the king, but for some offences had been
put out of that honourable employment. Herod was
in a very great rage at these informations, and presently ordered these men to be tortured: yet did not
they confess any thing of what the king had been
informed, but a certain letter was produced, as written
by Alexander to the governor of a castle, to desire
him to receive him and Aristobulus into the castle
when he had killed his father, and to give them
weapons, and what other assistance he could upon
that occasion. Alexander said, that this letter was
a forgery of Diophantus. This Diophantus was the
king's secretary, a bold man, and cunning in counter-
feiting any one's hand, and after he had counterfeited a great number, he was at last put to death for
it. Herod did also order the governor of the castle
to be tortured, but got nothing out of him of what
the accusation suggested.

4. However, although Herod found the proofs
too weak, he gave order to have his sons kept in
custody: for till now they had been at liberty. He
also called that pest of his family, and forger of all
this vile accusation, Eurycles, his saviour and benefactor, and gave him a reward of fifty talents. Upon
which he prevented any accurate accounts that could
come of what he had done, by going immediately into
Cappadocia, and there he got money of Archelaus,
having the impudence to pretend that he had reconciled Herod to Alexander. He thence passed over
into Greece, and used what he had thus wickedly
gotten to the like wicked purposes. Accordingly, he
was twice accused before Cæsar, that he had filled
Achaia with sedition, and had plundered its cities;
and so he was sent into banishment. And thus was
he punished for what wicked actions he had been
guilty of about Aristobulus and Alexander,

5. But it will now be worth while to put Euaratus of Cos in opposition to this Spartan; for as he was one of Alexander's most intimate friends, and came to him in his travels at the same time that Eurycles came, so the king put the question to him, whether those things of which Alexander was accused were true? He assured him upon oath, that he had never heard any such things from the young men; yet did this testimony avail nothing for the clearing those miserable creatures; for Herod was only disposed and most ready to hearken to what made against them, and every one was most agreeable to him, that would believe they were guilty, and showed their indignation at them.

CHAPTER XXVII.

*Herod, by Cæsar's direction, accuses his sons at Bery-
tus. They are not produced before the court, but
yet are condemned; and in a little time they are sent
to Sebaste, and strangled there.*

1. Moreover Salome exasperated Herod's cruelty against his sons; for Aristobulus was desirous to bring her, who was his mother-in-law and his aunt, into the like dangers with themselves: so he sent to her to take care of her own safety, and told her, that the king was preparing to put her to death, on account of the accusation that was laid against her, as if when she formerly endeavoured to marry herself to Sylleus the Arabian, she had discovered the king's grand secrets to him, who was the king's enemy; and this it was that came as the last storm, and entirely sunk the young men when they were in great danger before.

For Salome came running to the king, and informed him of what admonition had been given her, whereupon he could bear no longer, but commanded both the young men to be bound, and kept the one asunder from the other. He also sent Volumnius, the general of his army, to Cæsar immediately, as also his friend Olympus with him, who carried the informations in writing along with them. Now as soon as they had sailed to Rome, and delivered the king's letters to Cæsar, Cæsar was mightily troubled at the case of the young men; yet did not he think he ought to take the power from the father of condemning his sons: so he wrote back to him, and appointed him to have the power over his sons; but said withal, that "he would do well to make an examination into this matter of the plot against him, in a public court, and to take for his assessors his own kindred, and the governors of the province. And if ' those sons be found guilty, to put them to death, but if they appear to have thought of no more than flying away from him, that he should moderate their punishment."

2. With these directions Herod complied, and came to Berytus, where Cæsar had ordered the court to be assembled, and got the judicature together. The presidents sat first, as Cæsar's letters had appointed, who were Saturninus, and Pedanius, and their lieutenants that were with them, with whom was the procurator Volumnius also; next to them sat the king's kinsmen and friends, with Salome also, and Pheroras; after whom sat the principal men of all Syria, excepting Archelaus; for Herod had a suspicion of him, because he was Alexander's father-in-law. Yet did not he produce his sons in open court; and this was done very cunningly, for he knew well enough that had they but appeared only, they would certainly have been pitied; and if withal they had been suffered to

speak, Alexander would easily have answered what they were accused of; but they were in custody at Platane, a village of the Sidonians.

3. So the king got up, and inveighed against his sons, as if they were present; and as for that part of the accusation that they had plotted against him, he urged it but faintly, because he was destitute of proofs; but he insisted before the assessors on the reproaches, and jests, and injurious carriage, and ten thousand the like offences against him, which were heavier than death itself, and when nobody contradicted him, he moved them to pity his case, as though he had been condemned himself, now he had gained a bitter victory against his sons. So he asked every one's sentence, which sentence was first of all given by Saturninus, and was this, That he condemned the young men, but not to death; for that it was not fit for him, who had three sons of his own now present, to give his vote for the destruction of the sons of another. The two lieutenants also gave the like vote; some others there were also who followed their example; but Volumnius began to vote on the more melancholy side, and all those that came after him condemned the young men to die, some out of flattery, and some out of hatred to Herod; but none out of indignation at their crimes. And now all Syria and Judea was in great expectation, and waited for the last act of this tragedy; yet did nobody suppose that Herod would be so barbarous as to murder his children; however, he carried them away to Tyre, and thence sailed to Cæsarea; and deliberated with himself what sort of death the young men should suffer.

4. Now there was a certain old soldier of the king's, whose name was Tero, who had a son that was very familiar with, and a friend to Alexander, and who himself particularly loved the young men. This

soldier was in a manner distracted out of the excess
of the indignation he had at what was doing; and at
first he cried out aloud, as he went about, "That jus
tice was trampled under foot; that truth was perished,
and nature confounded; and that the life of man was
full of iniquity," and every thing else that passion
could suggest to a man who spared not his own life,
and at last he ventured to go to the king, and said,
"Truly, I think, thou art a most miserable man, when
thou hearkenest to most wicked wretches, against
those that ought to be dearest to thee; since thou hast
frequently resolved that Pheroras and Salome should
be put to death, and yet believest them against thy
sons; while these, by cutting off the succession of thine
own sons, leave all wholly to Antipater, and thereby
choose to have thee such a king as may be thoroughly
in their own power. However, consider whether this
death of Antipater's brethren, will not make him
hated by the soldiers; for there is nobody but com-
miserates the young men, and of the captains a great
many show their indignation at it openly." Upon
his saying this, he named those that had such indignation; but the king ordered those men, with Tero himself, and his son, to be seized upon immediately.

5. At which time there was a certain barber, whose
name was *Trypho*. This man leaped out from among
the people in a kind of madness, and accused himself,
and said, "This Tero endeavoured to persuade me also
to cut thy throat with my razor, when I trimmed thee,
and promised that Alexander should give me large
presents for so doing." When Herod heard this, he
examined Tero, with his son and the barber, by the
torture; but as the others denied the accusation, and
he said nothing farther, Herod gave order that Tero
should be racked more severely; but his son, out of
pity to his father, promised to discover the whole to

the king, if he would grant [that his father should
be no longer tortured;] when he had agreed to this,
he said, That "his father, at the persuasion of Alexander, had an intention to kill him." Now some said
this was forged, in order to free his father from his
torments, and some said it was true.

6. And now Herod accused the captains, and Tero,
in an assembly of the people, and brought the people
together in a body against them; and accordingly
there were they put to death, together with [Trypho]
the barber; they were killed by the pieces of wood
and the stones that were thrown at them. He also sent
his sons to Sebaste, a city not far from Cæsarea, and
ordered them to be there strangled: and as what he
had ordered was executed immediately, so he commanded that their dead bodies should be brought to the
fortress Alexandrium, to be buried with Alexander,
their grandfather by the mother's side. And this was
the end of Alexander and Aristobulus.

CHAPTER XXVIII.

How Antipater is hated of all men; and how the king
espouses the sons of those that had been slain to
his kindred: but that Antipater made him change
them for other women. Of Herod's marriages and
children.

1. But an intolerable hatred fell upon Antipater
from the nation, though he had now an indisputable
title to the succession; because they all knew that he
was the person who contrived all the calumnies against
his brethren. However, he began to be in a terrible
fear, as he saw the posterity of those that had been

slain growing up; for Alexander had two sons by Glaphyra, Tigranes and Alexander; and Aristobulus had Herod, and Agrippa, and Aristobulus, his sons, with Herodias and Mariamne, his daughters, and all by Bernice, Salome's daughter; as for Glaphyra, Herod, as soon as he had killed Alexander, sent her back, together with her portion, to Cappadocia. He married Bernice, Salome's daughter, to Antipater's uncle by his mother, and it was Antipater, who, in order to reconcile her to him, when she had been at variance with him, contrived this match; he also got into Pheroras' favour, and into the favour of Cæsar's friends by presents, and other ways of obsequiousness, and sent no small sums of money to Rome: Saturninus also, and his friends in Syria, were all well replenished with the presents he made them; yet the more he gave, the more he was hated, as not making these presents out of generosity, but spending his money out of fear. Accordingly, it so fell out, that the receivers bore him no more good-will than before, but that those to whom he gave nothing were his more bitter enemies. However, he bestowed his money every day more and more profusely, on observing that, contrary to his expectations, the king was taking care about the orphans, and discovering at the same time his repentance for killing their fathers, by his commiseration of those that sprang from them.

2. Accordingly, Herod got together his kindred and friends, and set before them the children, and with his eyes full of tears, said thus to them: "It was an unlucky fate that took away from me these children's fathers, which children are recommended to me by that natural commiseration which their orphan condition requires; however, I will endeavour, though I have been a most unfortunate father, to appear a better grandfather, and to leave these children such

curators after myself as are dearest to me. I therefore betroth thy daughter, Pheroras, to the elder of
these brethren, the children of Alexander, that thou
mayest be obliged to take care of them. I also
betroth to thy son, Antipater, the daughter of Aristobulus; be thou therefore a father to that orphan,
and my son Herod [Philip] shall have her sister,
whose grandfather, by the mother's side, was high
priest. And let every one that loves me be of my
sentiments in these dispositions, which none that hath
an affection for me will abrogate. And I pray God,
that he will join these children together in marriage,
to the advantage of my kingdom, and of my posterity,
and may he look down with eyes more serene upon
them than he looked upon their fathers."

3. While he spoke these words, he wept, and joined
the children's right hands together; after ·which he embraced them every one after an affectionate manner,
and dismissed the assembly. Upon this, Antipater
was in great disorder immediately, and lamented
publicly at what was done; for he supposed that
this dignity which was conferred on these orphans
was for his own destruction, even in his father's lifetime, and that he should run another risk of losing
the government, if Alexander's sons should have both
Archelaus [a king] and Pheroras a tetrarch, to support them. He also considered how he was himself
hated by the nation, and how they pitied these orphans;
how great affection the Jews bore to those brethren of
his when they were alive, and how gladly they remembered them now they had perished by his means. So
he resolved by all the ways possible to get these
espousals dissolved.

4. Now he was afraid of going subtilely about this
matter with his father, who was hard to be pleased,
and was presently moved upon the least suspicion: so

he ventured to go to him directly, and to beg of him before his face, not to deprive him of that dignity which he had been pleased to bestow upon him, and that he might not have the bare name of a king, while the power was in other persons: for that he should never be able to keep the government, if Alexander's son was to have both his grandfather Archelaus, and Pheroras for his curators; and he besought him earnestly, since there were so many of the royal family alive, that he would change those [intended] marriages. Now the king had [1] nine wives, and children by seven of them; Antipater was himself born of Doris, and Herod [Philip] of Mariamne, the high priest's daughter, Antipas also and Archelaus were by Malthace, the Samaritan, as was his daughter Olympias, which his brother Joseph's [2] son had married; by Cleopatra of Jerusalem he had Herod and Philip, and by Pallas, Phasaelus; he had also two daughters, Roxana and Salome, the one by Phedra, and the other by Elpis: he had also two wives that had no children, the one his first cousin, and the other his niece; and besides these he had two daughters, the sisters of Alexander and Aristobulus, by Mariamne. Since, therefore, the royal family was so numerous, Antipater prayed him to change these [intended] marriages.

5. When the king perceived what disposition he was in towards these orphans, he was angry at it,

---

[1] These nine wives of Herod were alive at the same time, and if the celebrated Mariamne, who was now dead, be reckoned, those wives were in all ten. Yet it is remarkable that he had no more than fifteen children by them all.

[2] To prevent confusion, it may not be amiss, to distinguish between four Josephs in the history of Herod. 1. Joseph, Herod's uncle, and the [second] husband of his sister Salome, slain by Herod, on account of Mariamne. 2. Joseph, Herod's quæstor, or treasurer, slain on the same account. 3. Joseph, Herod's brother, slain in battle against Antigonus. 4. Joseph, Herod's nephew, the husband of Olympias, mentioned in this place.

and a suspicion came into his mind, as to those sons whom he had put to death, whether that had not been brought about by the false tales of Antipater; so at that time he made Antipater a long and a peevish answer, and bid him begone. Yet was he afterwards prevailed upon cunningly by his flatteries, and changed the marriages; he married Aristobulus' daughter to him, and his son to Pheroras' daughter.

6. Now one may learn, in this instance, how very much this flattering Antipater could do, even what Salome in the like circumstances could not do; for when she, who was his sister, and who, by the means of Julia, Cæsar's wife, earnestly desired leave to be married to Sylleus the Arabian, Herod swore he would esteem her his bitter enemy, unless she would leave off that project: he also caused her, against her own consent, to be married to Alexas, a friend of his, and that one of her daughters should be married to Alexas' son, and the other to Antipater's uncle by the mother's side. And for the daughters the king had by Mariamne, the one was married to Antipater, his sister's son, and the other to his brother's son, Phasaelus.

CHAPTER XXIX.

Antipater becomes intolerable. He is sent to Rome, and carries Herod's testament with him. Pheroras leaves his brother, that he may keep his wife. He dies at home.

1. Now when Antipater had cut off the hopes of the orphans, and had contracted such affinities as would be most for his own advantage, he proceeded briskly, as having a certain expectation of the king-

dom, and as he had now assurance added to his wickedness, he became intolerable, for not being able to avoid the hatred of all people, he built his security upon the terror he struck into them. Pheroras also assisted him in his designs, looking upon him as already fixed in the kingdom. There was also a company of women in the court, which excited new disturbances; for Pheroras' wife, together with her mother and sister, as also Antipater's mother, grew very impudent in the palace. She also was so insolent as to affront the king's [1] two daughters, on which account the king hated her to a great degree; yet although these women were hated by him, they domineered over others: there was only Salome who opposed their good agreement, and informed the king of their meetings, as not being for the advantage of his affairs. And when those women knew what calumnies she had raised against them, and how much Herod was displeased, they left off their public meetings, and friendly entertainments of one another; nay, on the contrary, they pretended to quarrel one with another when the king was within hearing. The like dissimulation did Antipater make use of, and when matters were public, he opposed Pheroras; but still they had private cabals, and merry meetings in the night time; nor did the observation of others do any more than confirm their mutual agreement. However, Salome knew every thing they did, and told every thing to Herod.

2. But he was inflamed with anger at them, and chiefly at Pheroras' wife; for Salome had principally accused her. So he got an assembly of his friends and kindred together, and there accused this woman of many things, and particularly of the affronts she

[1] These daughters of Herod, whom Pheroras' wife affronted, were Salome and Roxana, two virgins, who were born to him of his two wives, Elpis and Phedra. See Herod's genealogy, Antiq. B. XVII. ch. i. sect. 3. Vol. III.

had offered his daughters; and that she had supplied the Pharisees with money, by way of rewards for what they had done against him, and had procured his brother to become his enemy, by giving him. love potions. At length he turned his speech to Pheroras, and told him, That "he would give him his choice of these two things, whether he would keep in with his brother, or with his wife?" And when Pheroras said, that he would ¹ die rather than forsake his wife, Herod, not knowing what to do farther in that matter, turned his speech to Antipater, and charged him to have no intercourse either with Pheroras' wife, or with Pheroras himself, or with any one belonging to her. Now, though Antipater did not transgress that his injunction publicly, yet did he in secret come to their night meetings; and because he was afraid that Salome observed what he did, he procured, by the means of his Italian friends, that he might go and live at Rome: for when they wrote that it was proper for Antipater to be sent to Cæsar for some time, Herod made no delay, but sent him, and that with a splendid attendance, and a great deal of money, and gave him his testament to carry with him, wherein Antipater had the kingdom bequeathed to him, and wherein Herod was named for Antipater's successor, that Herod, I mean, who was the son of Mariamne, the high priest's daughter.

¹ This strange obstinacy of Pheroras in retaining his wife, who was one of a low family, and refusing to marry one nearly related to Herod, though he so earnestly desired it, as also that wife's admission to the counsels of the other great court ladies, together with Herod's own importunity as to Pheroras' divorce and other marriage, all so remarkable here, or in the Antiquities, B. XVII. ch. ii. sect. 4, Vol. III. and ch. iii. sect. 3, cannot be well accounted for, but on the supposal that Pheroras believed, and Herod suspected, that the Pharisees' prediction, as if the crown of Judea should be translated from Herod to Pheroras' posterity, and that most probably to Pheroras' posterity by this his wife, also would prove true. See Antiq. B. XVII. ch. ii. sect. 4, and ch. iii. sect. 1, Vol. III.

3. Sylleus also, the Arabian, sailed to Rome, without any regard to Cæsar's injunctions, and this in order to oppose Antipater with all his might, as to that law-suit which Nicolaus had with him before. This Sylleus had also a great contest with Aretas his own king; for he had slain many others of Aretas' friends, and particularly Sohemus, the most potent man in the city Petra. Moreover, he had prevailed with Phabatus, who was Herod's steward, by giving him a great sum of money to assist him against Herod; but when Herod gave him more, he induced him to leave Sylleus, and by his means he demanded of him all that Cæsar had required of him to pay. But when Sylleus paid nothing of what he was to pay, and did also accuse Phabatus to Cæsar, and said that he was not a steward for Cæsar's advantage, but for Herod's, Phabatus was angry at him on that account, but was still in very great esteem with Herod, and discovered Sylleus' grand secrets, and told the king that Sylleus had corrupted Corinthus, one of the guards of his body, by bribing him, and of whom he must therefore have a care. Accordingly the king complied, for this Corinthus, though he were brought up in Herod's kingdom, yet was he by birth an Arabian, so the king ordered him to be taken up immediately, and not only him, but two other Arabians, who were caught with him; the one of them was Sylleus' friend, the other the head of a tribe. The last being put to the torture, confessed that they had prevailed with Corinthus, for a large sum of money to kill Herod; and when they had been farther examined before Saturninus the president of Syria, they were sent to Rome.

4. However, Herod did not leave off importuning Pheroras, but proceeded to force him to put away his wife; yet could he not devise any way by which

he could bring the woman herself to punishment,
although he had many causes of hatred to her; till
at length he was in such great uneasiness at her,
that he cast both her and his brother out of his kingdom. Pheroras took this injury very patiently, and
went away into his own tetrarchy [Perea beyond
Jordan,] and swore that there should be but one end
put to his flight, and that should be Herod's death;
and that he would never return while he was alive.
Nor indeed would he return when his brother was
sick, although he earnestly sent for him to come to
him, because he had a mind to leave some injunctions
with him before he died; but Herod unexpectedly
recovered. A little afterward Pheroras himself fell
sick, when Herod showed great moderation: for he
came to him and pitied his case, and took care of
him; but his affection for him did him no good, for
Pheroras died a little afterward. Now, though Herod
had so great an affection for him to the last day of
his life, yet was a report spread abroad that he had
killed him by poison. However, he took care to have
his dead body carried to Jerusalem, and appointed a
very great mourning to the whole nation for him, and
bestowed a most pompous funeral upon him. And
this was the end that one of Alexander's and Aristobulus' murderers came to.

CHAPTER XXX.

When Herod made inquiry about Pheroras' death, a discovery was made that Antipater had prepared a poisonous draught for him. Herod casts Doris and her accomplices, as also Mariamne, out of the palace, and blots her son Herod out of his testament.

1. BUT now the punishment was transferred unto the original author, Antipater, and took its rise from the death of Pheroras: for certain of his freed men came with a sad countenance to the king, and told him, That "his brother had been destroyed by poison, and that his wife had brought him somewhat that was prepared after an unusual manner, and that, upon his eating it, he presently fell into his distemper; that Antipater's mother and sister, two days before, brought a woman out of Arabia that was skilful in mixing such drugs, that she might prepare a love potion for Pheroras; and that, instead of a love potion, she had given him deadly poison; and that this was done by the management of Sylleus, who was acquainted with that woman."

2. The king was deeply affected with so many suspicions, and had the maid-servants and some of the free women also tortured, one of whom cried out in her agonies, "May that God that governs the earth and the heaven, punish this author of all these our miseries: Antipater's mother!" The king took a handle from this confession, and proceeded to inquire farther into the truth of the matter. So this woman discovered the friendship of Antipater's mother to Pheroras and Antipater's women, as also their secret meetings, and that Pheroras and Antipater had drunk

with them for a whole night together as they returned
from the king, and would not suffer anybody, either
man-servant or maid-servant, to be there; while one
of the free women discovered the matter.

3. Upon this Herod tortured the maid-servants
every one by themselves separately, who all unani-
mously agreed in the foregoing discoveries, and that
accordingly by agreement they went away, Antipater
to Rome, and Pheroras to Perea: for that they oftentimes talked to one another thus, "That after Herod
had slain Alexander and Aristobulus, he would fall
upon them, and upon their wives, because, after he
had not spared Mariamne and her children, he would
spare nobody; and that for this reason it was best to
get as far off the wild beast as they were able." And
that Antipater oftentimes lamented his own case before his mother, and said to her, That "he had already grey hairs upon his head, and that his father
grew younger again every day, and that perhaps
death would overtake him before he should begin to
be a king in earnest; and that in case Herod should
die, which yet nobody knew when it would be, the
enjoyment of the succession could certainly be but
for a little time; for that these heads of Hydra, the
sons of Alexander and Aristobulus, were growing
up: that he was deprived by his father of the hopes
of being succeeded by his children, for that his successor after his death was not to be any one of his
own sons, but Herod the son of Mariamne; that in
this point Herod was plainly distracted, to think that
his testament should therein take place; for he would
take care that not one of his posterity should remain,
because he was of all fathers the greatest hater of his
children. Yet does he hate his brother still worse,
whence it was that he a while ago gave himself a
hundred talents, that he should not have any inter-

course with Pheroras. And when Pheroras said,
Wherein have we done him any harm? Antipater
replied, I wish he would but deprive us of all we
have, and leave us naked and alive only; but it is
indeed impossible to escape this wild beast, who is
thus given to murder, who will not permit us to love
any person openly, although we be together privately,
yet may we be so openly too, if we have but the
courage and the hands of men."

4. These things were said by the women upon
the torture, as also that Pheroras resolved to fly with
them to Perea. Now Herod gave credit to all they
said on account of the affair of the hundred talents;
for he had no discourse with anybody about them,
but only with Antipater. So he vented his anger first
of all against Antipater's mother, and took away from
her all the ornaments which he had given her, which
cost a great many talents, and cast her out of the
palace a second time. He also took care of Pheroras
women after their tortures, as being now reconciled to
them; but he was in great consternation himself, and
inflamed upon every suspicion, and had many innocent persons led to the torture out of his fear, lest
he should leave any guilty person untortured.

5. And now it was that he betook himself to examine Antipater of Samaria, who was the steward
of [his son] Antipater; and upon torturing him, he
learned, that Antipater had sent for a potion of
deadly poison for him out of Egypt, by Antiphilus,
a companion of his; that Theudio, the uncle of Antipater, had it from him, and delivered it to Pheroras;
for that Antipater had charged him to take his father
off while he was at Rome, and so free him from the
suspicion of doing it himself: that Pheroras also committed this potion to his wife. Then did the king
send for her, and bid her bring to him what she had

received immediately. So she came out of her house as if she would bring it with her, but threw herself down from the top of the house, in order to prevent any examination and torture from the king. However, it came to pass, as it seems by the providence of God, when he intended to bring Antipater to punishment, that she fell not upon her head, but upon other parts of her body, and escaped. The king, when she was brought to him, took care of her, (for she was at first quite senseless upon her fall,) and asked her why she had thrown herself down? and gave her his oath, that if she would speak the real truth, he would excuse her from punishment; but that if she concealed any thing, he would have her body torn to pieces by torments, and leave no part of it to be buried.

6. Upon this the woman paused a little, and then said, "Why do I spare to speak of these grand secrets, now Pheroras is dead, that would only tend to save Antipater, who is all our destruction. Hear then, O king, and be thou, and God himself, who cannot be deceived, witnesses to the truth of what I am going to say. When thou didst sit weeping by Pheroras as he was dying, then it was that he called me to him, and said, My dear wife, I have been greatly mistaken as to the disposition of my brother towards me, and have hated him that is so affectionate to me, and have contrived to kill him who is in such disorder for me before I am dead. As for myself, I receive the recompense of my impiety; but do thou bring what poison was left with us by Antipater, and which thou keepest in order to destroy him, and consume it immediately in the fire in my sight, that I may not be liable to the avenger in the invisible world. This I brought as he bid me, and emptied the greatest part of it into the fire, but reserved a little of it for

my own use against uncertain futurity, and out of my fear of thee."

7. When she had said this, she brought the box, which had a small quantity of this potion in it: but the king let her alone, and transferred the tortures to Antiphilus' mother and brother, who both confessed that Antiphilus brought the box out of Egypt, and that they had received the potion from a brother of his who was a physician at Alexandria. Then did the ghosts of Alexander and Aristobulus go round all the palace, and became the inquisitors and discoverers of what could not otherwise have been found out, and brought such as were the freest from suspicion to be examined; whereby it was discovered that Mariamne, the high priest's daughter, was conscious of this plot, and her very brothers, when they were tortured, declared it so to be. Whereupon the king avenged this insolent attempt of the mother upon her son, and blotted Herod, whom he had by her, out of his testament who had been before named therein as successor to Antipater.

CHAPTER XXXI.

Antipater is convicted by Bathyllus: but he still returns from Rome without knowing it. Herod brings him to his trial.

1. AFTER. these things were over, Bathyllus came under examination, in order to convict Antipater, who proved the concluding attestation to Antipater's designs; for indeed he was no other than his freed man. This man came, and brought another deadly potion, the poison of asps, and the juices of other

serpents, that if the first potion did not do the business, Pheroras and his wife might be armed with this also to destroy the king. He brought also an addition to Antipater's insolent attempt against his father, which was the letters which he wrote against his brethren, Archelaus and Philip, who were the king's sons and educated at Rome, being yet youths, but of generous dispositions. Antipater set himself to get rid of these as soon as he could, that they might not be prejudicial to his hopes, and to that end he forged letters against them in the name of his friends at Rome. Some of these he corrupted by bribes to write how they grossly reproached their father, and did openly bewail Alexander and Aristobulus, and were uneasy at their being recalled, for their father had already sent for them, which was the very thing that troubled Antipater.

2. Nay, indeed while Antipater was in Judea, and before he was upon his journey to Rome, he gave money to have the like letters against them sent from Rome, and then came to his father, who as yet had no suspicion of him, and apologized for his brethren, and alleged on their behalf, that some of the things contained in those letters were false, and others of them were only youthful errors. Yet at the same time that he expended a great deal of his money, by making presents to such as wrote against his brethren, did he aim to bring his accounts into confusion, by buying costly garments, and carpets of various contextures, with silver and gold cups and a great many more curious things, that so, among the very great expenses laid out upon such furniture, he might conceal the money he had used in hiring men [to write the letters;] for he brought in an account of his expenses, amounting to two hundred talents, his main pretence for which was the lawsuit he had been in

with Sylleus. So while all his rogueries, even those of a lesser sort also, were covered by his greater villainy, while all the examinations by torture proclaimed his attempt to murder his father, and the letters proclaimed his second attempt to murder his brethren; yet did no one of those that came to Rome inform him of his misfortunes in Judea, although seven months had intervened between his conviction and his return, so great was the hatred which they all bore to him. And perhaps they were the ghosts of those brethren of his that had been murdered, that stopt the mouths of those that intended to have told him. He then wrote from Rome, and informed [his friends] that he would soon come to them, and how he was dismissed with honour by Cæsar.

3. Now the king being desirous to get this plotter against him into his hands, and being also afraid lest he should some way come to the knowledge how his affairs stood, and be upon his guard, he dissembled his anger in his epistle to him, as in other points, he wrote kindly to him, and desired him to make haste, because if he came quickly, he would then lay aside the complaints he had against his mother; for Antipater was not ignorant that his mother had been expelled out of the palace. However, he had before received a letter, which contained an account of the death of Pheroras, at Tarentum, and made great lamentations at it; for which some commended him, as being for his own uncle; though probably this confusion arose on account of his having thereby failed in his plot [on his father's life,] and his tears were more for the loss of him that was to have been subservient therein, than for [an uncle] Pheroras: moreover, a sort of fear came upon him as to his designs, lest the poison should have been discovered. However, when he was in Cilicia, he received the fore-

mentioned epistle from his father, and made great
haste accordingly. But when he had sailed to Celenderis, a suspicion came into his mind relating to his
mother's misfortune; as if his soul foreboded some
mischief to itself. Those therefore of his friends who
were the most considerate, advised him not rashly to
go to his father till he had learned what were the
occasions why his mother had been ejected, because
they were afraid that he might be involved in the
calumnies that had been cast upon his mother: but
those that were less considerate, and had more regard
to their own desires of seeing their native country,
than to Antipater's safety, persuaded him to make
haste home, and not by delaying his journey, afford
his father ground for an ill suspicion, and give a
handle to those that raised stories against him; for
that in case any thing had been moved to his disadvantage, it was owing to his absence, which durst
not have been done had he been present. And they
said, it was absurd to deprive himself of certain happiness, for the sake of an uncertain suspicion, and
not rather to return to his father, and take the royal
authority upon him, which was in a state of fluctua-
tion on his account only. Antipater complied with
this last advice; for Providence hurried him on [to
his destruction.] So he passed over the sea, and
landed at Sebastus, the haven of Cæsarea.

4. And here he found a perfect and unexpected
solitude, while everybody avoided him, and nobody
durst come at him; for he was equally hated by all
men; and now that hatred had liberty to show itself,
and the dread men were in at the king's anger made
men keep from him; for the whole city [of Jeru-
salem] was filled with the rumours about Antipater,
and Antipater himself was the only person who was
ignorant of them; for as no man was dismissed more

magnificently when he began his voyage to Rome, so was no man now received back with greater ignominy. And indeed he began already to suspect what misfortunes there were in Herod's family; yet did he cunningly conceal his suspicion; and while he was inwardly ready to die for fear, he put on a forced boldness of countenance. Nor could he now fly any whither, nor had he any way of emerging out of the difficulties which encompassed him, nor indeed had he even there any certain intelligence of the affairs of the royal family, by reason of the threats the king had given out: yet had he some small hopes of better tidings; for perhaps nothing had been discovered; or, if any discovery had been made, perhaps he should be able to clear himself by impudence, and artful tricks, which were the only things he relied upon for his deliverance.

5. And with these hopes did he screen himself, till he came to the palace, without any friends with him; for these were affronted and shut out at the first gate. Now Varus, the president of Syria, happened to be in the palace [at this juncture:] so Antipater went in to his father, and, putting on a bold face, he came near to salute him: but Herod stretched out his hands, and turned his head away from him, and cried out, "Even this is an indication of a parricide, to be desirous to get me into his arms, when he is under such heinous accusations. God confound thee, thou vile wretch, do not thou touch me, till thou hast cleared thyself of these crimes that are charged upon thee. I appoint thee a court where thou art to be judged, and this Varus, who is very seasonably here, to be thy judge; and get thou thy defence ready against to-morrow; for I give thee so much time to prepare suitable excuses for thyself." And as Antipater was so confounded, that he was able to make no answer

to this charge, he went away; but his mother and wife came to him, and told him of all the evidence they had gotten against him. Hereupon he recollected himself and considered what defence he should make against the accusations.

CHAPTER XXXII.

Antipater is accused before Varus, and is convicted of laying a plot [against his father] by the strongest evidence. Herod puts off his punishment till he should be recovered, and, in the meantime, alters his testament.

1. Now the day following the king assembled a court of his kinsmen and friends, and called in Antipater's friends also: Herod himself, with Varus, were the presidents; and Herod called for all the witnesses, and ordered them to be brought in; among whom some of the domestic servants of Antipater's mother were brought in also, who had but a little while before been caught, as they were carrying the following letter from her to her son: "Since all those things have been already discovered to thy father, do not thou come to him, unless thou canst procure some assistance from Cæsar." When this and the other witnesses were introduced, Antipater came in, and falling on his face before his father's feet, he said, "Father, I beseech thee do not condemn me beforehand, but let thy ears be unbiassed, and attend to my defence; for if thou wilt give me leave, I will demonstrate that I am innocent."

2. Hereupon Herod cried out to him to hold his peace, and spoke thus to Varus: "I cannot but think

that thou, Varus, and every other upright judge, will
determine that Antipater is a vile wretch. I am also
afraid that thou wilt abhor my ill fortune, and judge
me also myself worthy of all sorts of calamity, for
begetting such children; while yet I ought rather to
be pitied, who have been so affectionate ·a father to
such wretched sons; for when I had settled the kingdom on my former sons, even when they were young,
and when, besides the charges of their education at
Rome, I had made them the friends of Cæsar, and
made them envied by other kings, I found them
plotting against me; those have been put to death,
and that, in a great measure, for the sake of Antipater; for as he was then young, and appointed to be
my successor, I took care chiefly to secure him from
danger: but this profligate wild beast, when he had
been over and above satiated with that patience which
I showed him, he made use of that abundance I had
given him against myself; for I seemed to him to
live too long, and he was very uneasy at the old age
I was arrived at; nor could he stay any longer, but
would be a king by parricide. And justly I am
served by him for bringing him back out of the country to court, when he was of no esteem before, and
for thrusting out those sons of mine that were born
of the queen, and for making him a successor to my
dominions. I confess to thee, O Varus, the great
folly I was guilty of: for I provoked those sons of
mine to act against me, and cut off their just expectations for the sake of Antipater; and indeed what
kindness did I do to them, that could equal what I
have done to Antipater? to whom I have, in a manner,
yielded up my royal authority while I am alive, and
whom I have openly named for the successor to my
dominions in my testament, and given him a yearly
revenue of his own, fifty talents, and supplied him

with money to an extravagant degree out of my own
revenue; and when he was about to sail to Rome, I
gave him three hundred talents, and recommended
him, and him alone of all my children, to Cæsar, as
his father's deliverer. Now what crimes were those
other sons of mine guilty of like these of Antipater?
and what evidence was there brought against them so
strong as there is to demonstrate this son to have
plotted against me? Yet does this parricide presume
to speak for himself, and hopes to obscure the truth
by his cunning tricks. Thou, O Varus, must guard
thyself against him; for I know the wild beast, and
I foresee how plausibly he will talk, and his counterfeit lamentation. This was he who exhorted me to
have a care of Alexander when he was alive, and not
to intrust my body with all men! This was he who
came to my very bed, and looked about lest any one
should lay snares for me! This was he who took care
of my sleep, and secured me from any fear of danger,
who comforted me under the trouble I was in upon
the slaughter of my sons, and looked to see what
affection my surviving brethren bore me! This was
my protector, and the guardian of my body! And
when I call to mind, O Varus, his craftiness upon
every occasion, and his art of dissembling, I can
hardly believe that I am still alive, and I wonder how
I have escaped such a deep plotter of mischief. However, since some fate or other makes my house desolate, and perpetually raises up those that are dearest
to me against me, I will with tears lament my hard
fortune, and privately groan under my lonesome condition; yet I am resolved that no one who thirsts after
my blood shall escape punishment, although the evidence should extend itself to all my sons.

3.· Upon Herod's saying this, he was interrupted
by the confusion he was in; but ordered Nicolaus, one

of his friends, to produce the evidence against Antipater. But in the meantime Antipater lifted up his head, (for he lay on the ground before his father's feet,) and cried out aloud, "Thou, O father, hast made my apology for me; for how can I be a parricide, whom thou thyself confessest to have always had for thy guardian? Thou callest my filial affection prodigious lies, and hypocrisy; how then could it be that I, who was so subtle in other matters, should here be so mad as not to understand that it was not easy that he who committed so horrid a crime should be concealed from men, but impossible that he should be concealed from the Judge of heaven, who sees all things, and is present everywhere? or did not I know what end my brethren came to, on whom God inflicted so great a punishment for their evil designs against thee? and indeed what was there that could possibly provoke me against thee? Could the hope of being a king do it? I was a king already. Could I suspect hatred from thee? No: was not I beloved by thee? And what other fear could I have? Nay, by preserving thee safe, I was a terror to others. Did I want money? No; for who was able to expend so much as myself? Indeed, father, had I been the most execrable of all mankind, and had I had the soul of the most cruel wild beast, must I not have been overcome with the benefits thou hadst bestowed upon me? whom, as thou thyself sayest, thou broughtest [into the palace;] whom thou didst prefer before so many of thy sons; whom thou madest a king in thine own lifetime, and by the vast magnitude of the other advantages thou bestowedst on me, thou madest me an object of envy. O miserable man! that thou shouldst undergo this bitter absence, and thereby afford a great opportunity for envy to rise against thee! and a long space for such as were laying designs against

thee! Yet was I absent, father, on thy affairs, that
Sylleus might not treat thee with contempt in thine
old age. Rome is a witness to my filial affection, and
so is Cæsar, the ruler of the habitable earth, who
oftentimes called me ¹ *Philopater*. Take here the
letters he hath sent thee, they are more to be believed
than the calumnies raised here; these letters are my
only apology; these I use as the demonstration of
that natural affection I have to thee. Remember that
it was against my own choice that I sailed [to Rome,]
as knowing the latent hatred that was in the kingdom
against me. It was thou, O father, however unwillingly, who hast been my ruin, by forcing me to
allow time for calumnies against me, and envy at me.
However, I am come hither, and am ready to hear
the evidence there is against me. If I be a parricide,
I have passed by land and by sea, without suffering
any misfortune on either of them: but this method of
trial is no advantage to me; for it seems, O father,
that I am already condemned, both before God and
before thee; and as I am already condemned I beg
that thou wilt not believe the others that have been
tortured, but let fire be brought to torment me; let
the racks march through my bowels; have no regard
to any lamentations that this polluted body can make;
for if I be a parricide, I ought not to die without
torture " Thus did Antipater cry out with lamentation and weeping, and moved all the rest, and
Varus in particular, to commiserate his case. Herod
was the only person whose passion was too strong to
permit him to weep, as knowing that the testimonies
against him were true.

4. And now it was, that at the king's command,
Nicolaus, when he had premised a great deal about
the craftiness of Antipater, and had prevented the

¹ A lover of his father.

effect of their commiseration to him, afterwards brought in a bitter and large accusation against him, ascribing all the wickedness that had been in the kingdom to him, and especially the murder of his brethren, and demonstrated that they had perished by the calumnies he had raised against them. He also said that he had laid designs against them that were still alive, as if they were laying plots for the succession; and, said he, how can it be supposed that he who prepared poison for his father, should abstain from mischief as to his brethren? He then proceeded to convict him of the attempt to poison Herod, and gave an account in order of the several discoveries that had been made, and had great indignation as to the affair of Pheroras, because Antipater had been for making him murder his brother, and had corrupted those that were dearest to the king, and filled the whole palace with wickedness; and when he had insisted on many other accusations, and the proofs for them, he left off.

5. Then Varus bid Antipater make his defence; but he lay along in silence, and said no more but this, "God is my witness that I am entirely innocent." So Varus asked for the potion, and gave it to be drunk by a condemned malefactor, who was then in prison, who died upon the spot. So Varus, when he had had a very private discourse with Herod, and had written an account of this assembly to Cæsar, went away after a day's stay. The king also bound Antipater, and sent away to inform Cæsar of his misfortunes.

6. Now after this, it was discovered that Antipater had laid a plot against Salome also; for one of Antiphilus' domestic servants came, and brought letters from Rome, from a maid-servant of Julia, Cæsar's wife, whose name was *Acme.* By her a message was

sent to the king, that she had found a letter written
by Salome, among Julia's papers, and had sent it to
him privately, out of her good-will to him. This
letter of Salome's contained the most bitter reproaches
of the king, and the highest accusations against him.
Antipater had forged this letter, and had corrupted
Acme, and persuaded her to send it to Herod. This
was proved by her letter to Antipater, for thus did
this woman write to him: "As thou desirest, I have
written a letter to thy father, and have sent that letter,
and am persuaded that the king will not spare his sister
when he reads it. Thou wilt do well to remember
what thou hast promised when all is accomplished."

7. When this epistle was discovered, and what the
epistle forged against Salome contained, a suspicion
came into the king's mind, that perhaps the letters
against Alexander were also forged: he was moreover greatly disturbed, and in a passion, because he
had almost slain his sister on Antipater's account.
He did no longer delay therefore to bring him to
punishment for all his crimes; yet when he was eagerly
pursuing . Antipater, he was restrained by a severe
distemper he fell into. However, he sent an account
to Cæsar about Acme, and the contrivances against
Salome; he sent also for his testament, and altered it,
and therein made Antipas king, as taking no care
of Archelaus and Philip, because Antipater had
blasted their reputations with him; but he bequeathed
to Cæsar, besides other presents that he gave him, a
thousand talents; as also to his wife and children, and
friends, and freed-men, about five hundred: he also
bequeathed to all others a great quantity of land, and
of other money, and showed his respects to Salome
his sister, by giving her most splendid gifts. And
this was what was contained in his testament, as it was
now altered.

CHAPTER XXXIII.

*The golden eagle is cut to pieces. Herod's barbarity
when he was ready to die. He attempts to kill
himself. He commands Antipater to be slain. He
survives him five days, and then dies.*

1. Now Herod's distemper became more and more
severe to him, and this because these his disorders fell
upon him in his old age, and when he was in a melancholy condition; for he was already almost seventy
years of age, and had been brought low by the
calamities that happened to him about his children,
whereby he had no pleasure in life, even when he
was in health; the grief also that Antipater was still
alive aggravated his disease, whom he resolved to put
to death now not at random, but as soon as he should
be well again, and resolved to have him slain [in a
public manner.]

2. There also now happened to him, among his
other calamities, a certain popular sedition. There
were two men of learning in the city [Jerusalem,]
who were thought the most skilful in the laws of their
country, and were on that account had in very great
esteem all over the nation; they were, the one Judas,
the son of Sephoris, and the other Matthias, the son
of Margalus. There went a great concourse of the
young men to these men, when they expounded the
laws, and there got together every day a kind of an
army of such as were growing up to be men. Now
when these men were informed that the king was
wearing away with melancholy, and with a distemper,
they dropped words to their acquaintance, how it
was now a very proper time to defend the cause of

God, and to pull down what had been erected contrary to the laws of their country; for it was unlawful
there should be any such thing in the temple as
images, or faces, or the like representation of any
animal whatsoever. Now the king had put up a
golden eagle over the great gate of the temple, which
these learned men exhorted them to cut down, and
told them, that if there should any danger arise, it
was a glorious thing to die for the laws of their
country; because that the soul was immortal, and that
an eternal enjoyment of happiness did await such
as died on that account: while the mean spirited, and
those that were not wise enough to show a right love
of their souls, preferred a death by a disease, before
that which is the result of a virtuous behaviour.

3. At the same time that these men made this
speech to their disciples, a rumour was spread abroad,
that the king was dying, which made the young men
set about the work with greater boldness; they therefore let themselves down from the top of the temple
with thick cords, and this at midday, and while a
great number of people were in the temple, and cut
down that golden eagle with axes. This was presently told to the king's captain of the temple, who
came running with a great body of soldiers, and
caught about forty of the young men, and brought
them to the king. And when he asked them, first of
all, whether they had been so hardy as to cut down
the golden eagle? they confessed they had done so;
and when he asked them by whose command they
had done it, they replied, at the command of the law
of their country; and when he farther asked them,
how they could be so joyful when they were to be
put to death, they replied, Because they should enjoy
greater happiness after they were dead.

4. At this the king was in such an extravagant

passion, that he overcame his disease [for the time,]
and went out, and spoke to the people; wherein he
made a terrible accusation against those men, as being
guilty of sacrilege, and as making greater attempts
under pretence of their law, and he thought they
deserved to be punished as impious persons. Whereupon the people were afraid lest a great number
should be found guilty, and desired that when he
had first punished those that put them upon this
work, and then those that were caught in it, he would
leave off his anger as to the rest. With this the king
complied, though not without difficulty, and ordered
those that had let themselves down, together with the
Rabbins, to be burnt alive, but delivered the rest that
were caught to the proper officers to be put to death
by them.

5. After this, the distemper seized upon his whole
body, and greatly disordered all his parts with various
symptoms; for there was a great fever upon him, and
an intolerable itching over all the surface of his body,
and continual pains in his colon, and dropsical tumours
about his feet, and an inflammation of the abdomen,
and a putrefaction of his privy member, that produced worms. Besides which, he had a difficulty of
breathing upon him, and could not breathe but when
he sat upright, and had a convulsion of all his members, insomuch that the diviners said, those diseases
were a punishment upon him for what he had done
to the Rabbins. Yet did he struggle with his numerous disorders, and still had a desire to live, and hoped
for recovery, and considered of several methods of
cure. Accordingly he went over Jordan, and made
use of those hot baths at Callirhoe, which run into
the lake Asphaltitis, but are themselves sweet enough
to be drunk. And here the physicians thought proper
to bathe his whole body in warm oil, by letting it

down into a large vessel full of oil; whereupon his eyes failed him, and he came and went as if he were dying; and as a tumult was then made by his servants, at their voice he revived again. Yet did he after this despair of recovery, and gave orders that each soldier should have fifty drachmæ a-piece, and that his commanders and friends should have great sums of money given them.

6. He then returned back and came to Jericho, in such a melancholy state of body as almost threatened him with present death, when he proceeded to attempt a horrid wickedness; for he got together the most illustrious men of the whole Jewish nation, out of every village, into a place called the Hippodrome, and there shut them in. He then called for his sister Salome, and her husband Alexas, and made this speech to them: "I know well enough that the Jews will keep a festival upon my death; however it is in my power to be mourned for on other accounts, and to have a splendid funeral, if you will be but subservient to my commands. Do you but take care to send soldiers to encompass these men that are now in custody and slay them immediately upon my death, and then all Judea, and every family of them will weep at it, whether they will or no."

7. These were the commands he gave them; when there came letters from his ambassadors at Rome, whereby information was given that Acme was put to death at Cæsar's command, and that Antipater was condemned to die: however, they wrote withal, that if Herod had a mind rather to banish him, Cæsar permitted him so to do. So he for a little while revived, and had a desire to live; but presently after he was overborne by his pains, and was disordered by want of food, and by a convulsive cough, and endeavoured to prevent a natural death; so he took an

apple and asked for a knife, for he used to pare apples and eat them; he then looked round about to see that there was nobody to hinder him, and lifted up his right hand as if he would stab himself; but Achiabus, his first cousin, came running to him, and held his hand, and hindered him from so doing; on which occasion a very great lamentation was made in the palace, as if the king was expiring. As soon as ever Antipater heard that, he took courage, and with joy in his looks, besought his keepers, for a sum of money, to loose him and let him go; but the principal keeper of the prison did not only obstruct him in that his intention, but ran and told the king what his design was; hereupon the king cried out louder than his distemper would well bear, and immediately sent some of his guards and slew Antipater; he also gave order to have him buried at Hyrcanium, and altered his testament again, and therein made Archelaus, his eldest son, and the brother of Antipas, his successor, and made Antipas tetrarch.

8. So Herod having survived the slaughter of his son five days, died, having reigned thirty-four years, since he had caused Antigonus to be slain, and obtained his kingdom: but thirty-seven years since he had been made king by the Romans. Now as for his fortune it was prosperous in all other respects, if ever any other man could be so, since, from a private man he' obtained the kingdom, and kept it so long, and left it to his own sons; but still in his domestic affairs, he was a most unfortunate man. Now before the soldiers knew of his death, Salome and her husband came out and dismissed those that were in bonds, whom the king had commanded to be slain, and told them that he had altered his mind and would have every one of them sent to their own homes. When these men were gone, Salome told the soldiers

[the king was dead,] and got them and the rest of the multitude together to an assembly, in the amphitheatre in Jericho, where Ptolemy, who was intrusted by the king with his signet-ring, came before them, and spoke of the happiness the king had attained, and comforted the multitude, and read the epistle which had been left for the soldiers, wherein he earnestly exhorted them to bear good-will to his successor; and after he had read the epistle, he opened and read his testament, wherein Philip was to inherit Trachonitis, and the neighbouring countries, and Antipas was to be tetrarch, as we said before, and Archelaus was made king. He had also been commanded to carry Herod's ring to Cæsar, and the settlements he had made sealed up, because Cæsar was to be lord of all the settlements he had made, and was to confirm his testament; and he ordered that the dispositions he had made were to be kept as they were in his former testament.

9. So there was an acclamation made to Archelaus, to congratulate him upon his advancement, and the soldiers, with the multitude, went round about in troops, and promised him their good-will, and besides, prayed God to bless his government. After this they betook themselves to prepare for the king's funeral; and Archelaus omitted nothing of magnificence therein, but brought out all the royal ornaments to augment the pomp of the deceased. There was a bier all of gold, embroidered with precious stones, and a purple bed of various contexture, with the dead body upon it, covered with purple; and a diadem was put upon his head, and a crown of gold above it, and a sceptre in his right hand; and near to the bier were Herod's sons, and a multitude of his kindred; next to which came his guards and the regiments of Thracians, the Germans also and Gauls, all accoutered

as if they were going to war; but the rest of the army went foremost, armed, and following their captains and officers in a regular manner; after whom five hundred of his domestic servants and freed men followed with sweet spices in their hands: and the body was carried two hundred furlongs to Herodium, where he had given orders to be buried. And this shall suffice for the conclusion of the life of Herod.

BOOK II.

CONTAINING THE INTERVAL OF SIXTY-NINE YEARS.

[FROM THE DEATH OF HEROD TILL VESPASIAN WAS SENT
TO SUBDUE THE JEWS BY NERO.]

CHAPTER I.

Archelaus makes a funeral feast for the people, on the account of Herod. After which a great tumult is raised by the multitude, and he sends the soldiers out upon them, who destroy about three thousand of them.

1. Now the necessity which Archelaus was under of taking a journey to Rome was the occasion of new disturbances; for when he had mourned for his father seven [1] days, and had given a very expensive funeral feast to the multitude, (which custom is the occasion of poverty to many of the Jews, because they are

---

[1] The law or custom of the Jews requires seven days' mourning for the dead, Antiq. B. XVII. ch. viii. sect. iv. Vol. III. Whence the author of the book of Ecclesiasticus, ch. xxii. 12, assigns seven days as the proper time of mourning for the dead, and ch. xxxviii. 17, enjoins men to mourn for the dead, that they may not be evil spoken of; for as Josephus says presently, if any one omits this mourning [funeral feast] he is not esteemed a holy person. Now it is certain that such a seven days' mourning has been customary from times of the greatest antiquity, Gen. i. 10. Funeral feasts are also mentioned as of considerable antiquity, Ezek. xxiv. 17, Jer. xvi. 9, Prov. xxxi. 6, Deut. xxvi. 14, Josephus, Of the War, B. III. ch. ix. sect. 5, Vol. IV.

forced to feast the multitude; for if any one omits it, he is not esteemed a holy person,) he put on a white garment and went up to the temple, where the people accosted him with various acclamations. He also spoke kindly to the multitude from an elevated seat, and a throne of gold, and returned them thanks for the zeal they had shown about his father's funeral, and the submission they had made to him, as if he were already settled in the kingdom; but he told them withal, that "he would not at present take upon him either the authority of a king, or the names thereto belonging, until Cæsar, who is made lord of this whole affair by the testament, confirm the succession; for that when the soldiers would have set the diadem on his head at Jericho, he would not accept of it; but that he would make abundant requitals, not to the soldiers only, but to the people for their alacrity and good-will to him, when the superior lords [the Romans] should have given him a complete title to the kingdom; for that it should be his study to appear in all things better than his father."

2. Upon this the multitude were pleased, and presently made a trial of what he intended, by asking great things of him; for some made a clamour that he would ease them in their taxes, others, that he would take off the duties upon commodities, and some, that he would loose those that were in prison; in all which cases he answered readily to their satisfaction, in order to get the good-will of the multitude; after which he offered [the proper] sacrifices, and feasted with his friends. And here it was that a great many of those that desired innovations, came in crowds towards the evening, and began then to mourn on their own account, when the public mourning for the king was over. These lamented those that were put to death by Herod, because they had cut down the

golden eagle that had been over the gate of the temple.
Nor was this mourning of a private nature, but the
lamentations were very great, the mourning solemn,
and the weeping such as was loudly heard all over
the city, as being for those men who had perished for
the laws of their country, and for the temple. They
cried out, that a punishment ought to be inflicted for
these men upon those that were honoured by Herod,
and that, in the first place, the man whom he had made
high priest should be deprived, and that it was fit
to choose a person of greater piety and purity than
he was.

3. At these clamours Archelaus was provoked, but
restrained himself from taking vengeance on the
authors, on account of the haste he was in of going
to Rome, as fearing lest, upon his making war on
the multitude, such an action might detain him at
home. Accordingly, he made trial to quiet the innovators by persuasion, rather than by force, and sent
his general in a private way to them, and by him exhorted them to be quiet. But the seditious threw
stones at him, and drove him away, as he came into
the temple, and before he could say any thing to
them. The like treatment they showed to others, who
came to them after him, many of whom were sent by
Archelaus, in order to reduce them to sobriety, and
these answered still on all occasions after a passionate
manner; and it openly appeared that they would not
be quiet, if their numbers were but considerable. And
indeed, at the feast of unleavened bread, which was
now at hand, and is by the Jews called the Passover,
and used to be celebrated with a great number of
sacrifices, an innumerable multitude of the people
came out of the country to worship: some of these
stood in the temple bewailing the Rabbins [that had
been put to death,] and procured their sustenance by

begging, in order to support their sedition. At this Archelaus was affrighted, and privately sent a tribune, with his cohort of soldiers, upon them, before the disease should spread over the whole multitude, and gave orders that they should constrain those that began the tumult, by force, to be quiet. At these the whole multitude were irritated, and threw stones at many of the soldiers, and killed them: but the tribune fled away wounded, and had much ado to escape so. After which they betook themselves to their sacrifices, as if they had done no mischief; nor did it appear to Archelaus that the multitude could be restrained without bloodshed; so he sent his whole army upon them, the footmen in great multitudes, by the way of the city, and the horsemen by the way of the plain, who, falling upon them on the sudden, as they were offering their sacrifices, destroyed about three thousand of them; but the rest of the multitude were dispersed upon the adjoining mountains; these were followed by Archelaus' heralds, who commanded every one to retire to their own homes, whither they all went, and left the festival.

CHAPTER II.

Archelaus goes to Rome with a great number of his kindred. He is there accused before Cæsar by Antipater; but is superior to his accusers in judgment, by the means of that defence which Nicolaus made for him.

1. ARCHELAUS went down now to the seaside, with his mother and his friends, Poplas, and Ptolemy, and Nicolaus, and left behind him Philip, to be his steward.

in the palace, and to take care of his domestic affairs. Salome went also along with him with her sons, as did also the king's brethren and sons-in-law. These, in appearance, went to give him all the assistance they were able, in order to secure his succession, but in reality to accuse him for his breach of the laws, by what he had done at the temple.

2. But as they were come to Cæsarea, Sabinus, the procurator of Syria, met them: he was going up to Judea, to secure Herod's effects: but Varus, [president of Syria,] who was come thither, restrained him from going any farther. This Varus Archelaus had sent for, by the earnest entreaty of Ptolemy. At this time indeed, Sabinus, to gratify Varus, neither went to the citadels, nor did he shut up the treasuries where his father's money was laid up, but promised that he would lie still, until Cæsar should have taken cognizance of the affair. So he abode at Cæsarea; but as soon as those that were his hinderance were gone, when Varus was gone to Antioch, and Archelaus was sailed to Rome, he immediately went on to Jerusalem, and seized upon the palace. And when he had called for the governors of the citadels, and the stewards [of the king's private affairs,] he tried to sift out the accounts of the money, and so take possession of the citadels. But the governors of those citadels were not unmindful of the commands laid upon them by Archelaus, and continued to guard them, and said, the custody of them rather belonged to Cæsar than to Archelaus.

3. In the meantime Antipas went also to Rome, to strive for the kingdom, and to insist that the former testament, wherein he was named to be king, was valid before the latter testament. Salome had also promised to assist him, as had many of Archelaus' kindred, who sailed along with Archelaus himself also.

He also carried along with him his mother, and Ptolemy the brother of Nicolaus, who seemed one of great weight, on account of the great trust Herod put in him, he having been one of his most honoured friends. However, Antipas depended chiefly upon Ireneus, the orator, upon whose authority he had rejected such as advised him to yield to Archelaus, because he was his eldest brother, and because the second testament gave the kingdom to him. The inclinations also of all Archelaus' kindred, who hated him, were removed to Antipas, when they came to Rome, although in the first place every one rather desired to live under their own laws, [without a king,] and to be under a Roman governor; but if they should fail in that point, these desired that Antipas might be their king.

4. Sabinus did also afford these his assistance to the same purpose, by the letters he sent, wherein he accused Archelaus before Cæsar, and highly commended Antipas. Salome also, and those with her, put the crimes which they accused Archelaus of in order, and put them into Cæsar's hands: and after they had done that, Archelaus wrote down the reasons of his claim, and, by Ptolemy, sent in his father's ring, and his father's accounts. And when Cæsar had maturely weighed by himself what both had to allege for themselves, as also had considered of the great burden of the kingdom, and largeness of the revenues, and withal the number of the children Herod had left behind him, and had moreover read the letters he had received from Varus and Sabinus on this occasion, he assembled the principal persons among the Romans together, (in which assembly Caius, the son of Agrippa, and his daughter Julia's, but by himself adopted for his own son, sat in the first seat;) and gave the pleaders leave to speak.

5. Then stood up Salome's son, Antipater, (who of all Archelaus' antagonists was the shrewdest pleader,) and accused him in the following speech: "That Archelaus did in words contend for the kingdom, but that in deeds he had long exercised royal authority, and so did but insult Cæsar in desiring to be now heard on that account; since he had not stayed for his determination about the succession, and since he had suborned certain persons, after Herod's death, to move for putting the diadem upon his head; since he had set himself down in the throne, and given answers as a king, and altered the disposition of the army, and granted to some higher dignities: that he had also complied in all things with the people in the requests they had made to him as to their king, and had also dismissed those that had been put into bonds by his father, for most important reasons. Now after all this, he desires the shadow of that royal authority, whose substance he had already seized to himself, and so hath made Cæsar lord, not of things, but of words. He also reproached him farther, that his mourning for his father was only pretended, while he put on a sad countenance in the daytime, but drank to great excess in the night, from which behaviour, he said, the late disturbance among the multitude came, while they had an indignation thereat. And indeed the purport of his whole discourse was to aggravate Archelaus' crime in slaying such a multitude about the temple, which multitude came to the festival, but were barbarously slain in the midst of their own sacrifices; and he said, there was such a vast number of dead bodies heaped together in the temple, as even a foreign war, that should come upon them [suddenly,] before it was denounced, could not have heaped together. And he added, that it was the foresight his father had of that his bar-

barity, which made him never give him any hopes
of the kingdom, but when his mind was more infirm
than his body, and he was not able to reason soundly,
and did not well know what was the character of that
son, whom in his second testament he made his successor; and this was done by him at a time when he
had no complaints to make of him whom he had
named before when he was sound in body, and when
his mind was free from all passion. That, however,
if any one should suppose Herod's judgment, when
he was sick, was superior to that at another time, yet
had Archelaus forfeited his kingdom by his own
behaviour, and those his actions, which were contrary
to the law, and to its disadvantage. Or what sort
of a king will this man be, when he hath obtained the
government from Cæsar, who hath slain so many before he hath obtained it?"

6. When Antipater had spoken largely to this
purpose, and had produced a great number of Archelaus' kindred as witnesses, to prove every part of
the accusation, he ended his discourse. Then stood
up Nicolaus to plead for Archelaus. He alleged
that "the slaughter in the temple could not be
avoided; that those that were slain were become enemies not to Archelaus' kingdom only, but to Cæsar,
who was to determine about him. He also demonstrated, that Archelaus' accusers had advised him to
perpetrate other things of which he might have been
accused. But he insisted that the latter testament
should, for this reason, above all others, be esteemed
valid, because Herod had therein appointed Cæsar to
be the person who should confirm the succession; for
he who showed such prudence as to recede from his
own power and yield it up to the lord of the world,
cannot be supposed mistaken in his judgment about
him that was to be his heir; and he that so well knew

whom to choose for arbitrator of the succession, could not be unacquainted with him whom he chose for his successor."

7. When Nicolaus had gone through all he had to say, Archelaus came, and fell down before Cæsar's knees, without any noise. Upon which he raised him up, after a very obliging manner, and declared that truly he was worthy to succeed his father. However, he still made no firm determination in his case; but when he had dismissed those assessors that had been with him that day, he deliberated by himself about the allegations which he had heard, whether it were fit to constitute any of those named in the testaments for Herod's successor, or whether the government should be parted among all his posterity, and this because of the number of those that seemed to stand in need of support therefrom.

CHAPTER III.

The Jews fight a great battle with Sabinus' soldiers, and a great destruction is made at Jerusalem.

1. Now before Cæsar had determined any thing about these affairs, Malthace, Archelaus' mother, fell sick and died. Letters also were brought out of Syria from Varus, about a revolt of the Jews. This was foreseen by Varus, who accordingly, after Archelaus was sailed, went up to Jerusalem to restrain the promoters of the sedition, since it was manifest that the nation would not be at rest; so he left one of those legions which he brought with him out of Syria into the city, and went himself to Antioch. But Sabinus came, after he was gone, and gave them an occasion of making innovations; for he compelled

the keepers of the citadels to deliver them up to him, and made a bitter search after the king's money, as depending not only on the soldiers who were left by Varus, but on the multitude of his own servants, all of whom he armed and used as the instruments of his covetousness. Now when that feast, which was observed after seven weeks, and which the Jews call Pentecost, (i. e. the 50th day) was at hand, its name being taken from the number of days [after the passover,] the people got together, but not on account of the accustomed divine worship, but of the indignation they had [at the present state of affairs.] Wherefore an immense multitude ran together, out of Galilee, and Idumea, and Jericho, and Perea, that was beyond Jordan; but the people that naturally belonged to Judea itself were above the rest, both in number, and in the alacrity of the men. So they distributed themselves into three parts, and pitched their camps in three places; one at the north side of the temple, another at the south side, by the Hippodrome, and the third part were at the palace on the west. So they lay round about the Romans on every side, and besieged them.

2. Now Sabinus was affrighted, both at the multitude, and at their courage, and sent messengers to Varus continually, and besought him to come to his succour quickly, for that, if he delayed, his legion would be cut to pieces. As for Sabinus himself, he got up to the highest tower of the fortress, which was called Phasaelus: it is of the same name with Herod's brother, who was destroyed by the Parthians: and then he made signs to the soldiers of that legion to attack the enemy; for his astonishment was so great, that he durst not go down to his own men. Hereupon the soldiers were prevailed upon, and leaped out into the temple, and fought a terrible

battle with the Jews; in which, while there were none over their heads to distress them, they were too hard for them, by their skill, and the others' want of skill, in war; but when once many of the Jews had gotten up to the top of the cloisters, and threw their darts downwards, upon the heads of the Romans, there were a great many of them destroyed. Nor was it easy to avenge themselves upon those that threw their weapons from on high, nor was it more easy for them to sustain those who came to fight them hand to hand.

3. Since therefore the Romans were sorely afflicted by both these circumstances, they set fire to the cloisters, which were works to be admired, both on account of their magnitude and costliness. Whereupon those that were above them were presently encompassed with the flame, and many of them perished therein; as many of them also were destroyed by the enemy, who came suddenly upon them; some of them also threw themselves down from the walls backward, and some there were who, from the desperate condition they were in, prevented the fire, by killing themselves with their own swords; but so many of them as crept out from the walls, and came upon the Romans, were easily mastered by them, by reason of the astonishment they were under; until at last, some of the Jews being destroyed and others dispersed by the terror they were in, the soldiers fell upon the treasure of God, which was now deserted, and plundered about four hundred talents, of which sum Sabinus got together all that was not carried away by the soldiers. •

4. However this destruction of the works [about the temple,] and of the men, occasioned a much greater number, and those of a more warlike sort, to get together, to oppose the Romans. These encom-

passed the palace round, and threatened to destroy all that were in it, unless they went their ways quickly; for they promised that Sabinus should come to no harm, if he would go out with his legion. There were also a great many of the king's party who deserted the Romans, and assisted the Jews; yet did the most warlike body of them all, who were three thousand of the men of Sebaste, go over to the Romans. Rufus also, and Gratus, their captains, did the same, (Gratus having the foot of the king's party under him, and Rufus the horse,) each of whom even without the forces under them, were of great weight, on account of their strength and wisdom, which turn the scales in war. Now the Jews persevered in the siege, and tried to break down the walls of the fortress, and cried out to Sabinus and his party, that they should go their ways, and not prove a hinderance to them, now they hoped, after a long time, to recover that ancient liberty which their forefathers had enjoyed. Sabinus indeed was well contented to get out of the danger he was in, but he distrusted the assurances the Jews gave him, and suspected such gentle treatment was but a bait laid as a snare for them: this consideration, together with the hopes he had of succour from Varus, made him bear the siege still longer.

CHAPTER IV.

Herod's veteran soldiers become tumultuous. The robberies of Judas. Simon and Athrongeus take the name of king upon them.

1. AT this time there were great disturbances in the country, and that in many places; and the opportunity that now offered itself induced a great many

to set up for kings. And indeed in Idumea two thousand of Herod's veteran soldiers got together, and armed themselves, and fought against those of the king's party; against whom Achiabus, the king's first cousin, fought, and that out of some of the places that were the most strongly fortified; but so as to avoid a direct conflict with them in the plains. In Sepphoris also, a city of Galilee, there was one Judas, the son of that arch-robber Hezekias, who formerly overran the country, and had been subdued by king Herod; this man got no small multitude together, and broke open the place where the royal armour was laid up, and armed those about him, and attacked those that were so earnest to gain the dominion.

2. In Perea also, Simon, one of the servants to the king, relying upon the handsome appearance, and tallness of his body, put a diadem upon his own head also; he also went about with a company of robbers that he had gotten together, and burnt down the royal palace that was at Jericho, and many other costly edifices besides, and procured himself very easily spoils by rapine, as snatching them out of the fire. And he had soon burnt down all the fine edifices, if Gratus, the captain of the foot of the king's party, had not taken the Trachonite archers, and the most warlike of Sebaste, and met the man. His footmen were slain in the battle in abundance, Gratus also cut to pieces Simon himself, as he was flying along a strait valley, when he gave him an oblique stroke upon his neck, as he ran away, and broke it. The royal palaces that were near Jordan at Betheramptha were also burnt down by some other of the seditious that came out of Perea.

3. At this time it was that a certain shepherd ventured to set himself up for a king; he was called

Athrongeus. It was his strength of body that made him expect such a dignity, as well as his soul, which despised death; and besides these qualifications, he had four brethren like himself. He put a troop of armed men under each of these his brethren, and made use of them as his generals and commanders, when he made his incursions, while he did himself act like a king, and meddled only with the more important affairs: and at this time he put a diadem about his head, and continued after that to overrun the country for no little time with his brethren, and became their leader in killing both the Romans and those of the king's party; nor did any Jew escape him, if any gain could accrue to him thereby. He once ventured to encompass a whole troop of Romans at Emmaus, who were carrying corn and weapons to their legion; his men therefore shot their arrows and darts, and thereby slew their centurion Arius, and forty of the stoutest of his men, while the rest of them who were in danger of the same fate, upon the coming of Gratus, with those of Sebaste, to their assistance, escaped. And when these men had thus served both their own countrymen and foreigners, and that through this whole war, three of them were after some time subdued, the eldest by Archelaus, the two next by falling into the hand of Gratus and Ptolemeus; but the fourth delivered himself up to Archelaus, upon his giving him his right hand for his security. However, this their end was not till afterward, while at present they filled all Judea with a piratic war.

CHAPTER V.

Varus composes the tumults in Judea, and crucifies about two thousand of the seditious.

1. Upon Varus' reception of the letters that were written by Sabinus, and the captains, he could not avoid being afraid for the whole legion [he had left there.] So he made haste to their relief, and took with him the other two legions, with the four troops of horsemen to them belonging, and marched to Ptolemais; having given orders for the auxiliaries that were sent by the kings and governors of cities to meet him there. Moreover, he received from the people of Berytus, as he passed through their city, fifteen hundred armed men. Now as soon as the other body of auxiliaries were come to Ptolemais, as well as Aretas the Arabian, (who, out of the hatred he bore to Herod, brought a great army of horse and foot,) Varus sent a part of his army presently to Galilee, which lay near to Ptolemais, and Caius one of his friends, for their captain. This Caius put those that met him to flight, and took the city Sepphoris, and burnt it, and made slaves of its inhabitants; but as for Varus himself, he marched to Samaria with his whole army, where he did not meddle with the city itself, because he found that it had made no commotion during these troubles, but pitched his camp about a certain village which was called *Arus;* it belonged to Ptolemy, and on that account was plundered by the Arabians, who were very angry even at Herod's friends also. He thence marched on to the village Sampho, another fortified place, which they plundered, as they had done the other. As they

carried off all the money they lighted upon belonging to the public revenues, all was now full of fire and bloodshed, and nothing could resist the plunders of the Arabians. Emmaus was so burnt, upon the flight of its inhabitants, and this at the command of Varus, out of his rage at the slaughter of those that were about Arius.

2. Thence he marched on to Jerusalem, and as soon as he was but seen by the Jews, he made their camps disperse themselves: they also went away, and fled up and down the country; but the citizens received him and cleared themselves of having any hand in this revolt; and said, that they had raised no commotions, but had only been forced to admit the multitude because of the festival, and that they were rather besieged together with the Romans, than assisted those that had revolted. There had before this met him Joseph the first cousin of Archelaus, and Gratus, together with Rufus, who led those of Sebaste, as well as the king's army: there also met him those of the Roman legion, armed after their accustomed manner: for as to Sabinus he durst not come into Varus' sight, but was gone out of the city before this, to the seaside; but Varus sent a part of his army into the country, against those that had been the authors of this commotion, and as they caught great numbers of them, those that appeared to have been the least concerned in these tumults he put into custody, but such as were the most guilty he crucified; these were in number about two thousand.

3. He was also informed, that there continued in Idumea ten thousand men still in arms; but when he found that the Arabians did not act like auxiliaries, but managed the war according to their own passions, and did mischief to the country otherwise than he intended, and this out of their hatred to Herod, he

sent them away, but made haste, with his own legions,
to march against those that had revolted; but these,
by the advice of Achiabus, delivered themselves up to
him before it came to a battle. Then did Varus forgive the multitude their offences, but sent their captains to Cæsar to be examined by him. Now Cæsar
forgave the rest, but gave orders that certain of the
king's relations (for some of those that were among
them were Herod's kinsmen) should be put to death,
because they had engaged in a war against a king
of their own family. When therefore Varus had
settled matters at Jerusalem after this manner, and
had left the former legion there as a garrison, he
returned to Antioch.

CHAPTER VI.

*The Jews greatly complain of Archelaus, and desire
that they may be made subject to Roman governors.
But when Cæsar had heard what they had to say,
he distributed Herod's dominions among his sons,
according to his own pleasure.*

1. BUT now came another accusation from the
Jews against Archelaus at Rome, which he was to
answer to. It was made by those ambassadors, who
before the revolt, had come, by Varus' permission, to
plead for the liberty of their country; those that came
were fifty in number, but there were more than eight
thousand of the Jews at Rome who supported them.
And when Cæsar had assembled a council of the
principal Romans in [1] Apollo's temple, that was in

---

[1] This holding a council in the temple of Apollo, in the emperor's
palace at Rome, by Augustus, and even the building of this temple

the palace, (this was what he had himself built and adorned, at a vast expense,) the multitude of the Jews stood with the ambassadors, and on the other side stood Archelaus, with his friends; but as for the kindred of Archelaus, they stood on neither side; for to stand on Archelaus' side, their hatred to him, and envy at him, would not give them leave, while yet they were afraid to be seen by Cæsar with his accusers. Besides these, there were present Archelaus' brother Philip, being sent thither beforehand out of kindness by Varus, for two reasons; the one was this, that he might be assisting to Archelaus, and the other was this, that in case Cæsar should make a distribution of what Herod possessed among his posterity, he might obtain some share of it.

2. And now, upon the permission that was given the accusers to speak, they in the first place, went over Herod's breaches of their law, and said, "that he was not a king, but the most barbarous of all tyrants, and that they had found him to be such by the sufferings they underwent from him; that when a very great number had been slain by him, those that were left had endured such miseries, that they called those that were dead happy men; that he had not only tortured the bodies of his subjects, but entire cities, and had done much harm to the cities of his own country, while he adorned those that belonged to foreigners, and he shed the blood of Jews, in order to do kindness to those people that were out of their bounds; that he had filled the nation full of poverty, and of the greatest iniquity, instead of that happiness, and those laws which they had anciently enjoyed; that, in short, the Jews had borne more calamities

magnificently by himself in that palace, are exactly agreeable to Augustus, in his elder years, as Aldrich and Spanheim observe and prove, from Suetonius and Propertius.

from Herod, in a few years, than had their forefathers during all that interval of time that had
passed since they had come out of Babylon, and returned home, in the reign of [1] Xerxes: that, however,
the nation was come to so low a condition, by being
inured to hardships, that they submitted to his successor of their own accord, though he brought them
into bitter slavery: that accordingly they readily called
Archelaus, though he was the son of so great a
tyrant, *king,* after the decease of his father, and
joined with him in mourning for the death of Herod,
and in wishing him good success in that his succession;
while yet this Archelaus, lest he should be in danger
of not being thought the genuine son of Herod, began
his reign with the murder of three thousand citizens;
as if he had a mind to offer so many bloody sacrifices
to God for his government, and to fill the temple
with the like number of dead bodies at the festival:
that, however, those that were left after so many
miseries, had just reason to consider now at last the
calamities they had undergone, and to oppose themselves, like soldiers in war, to receive those stripes
upon their faces, [but not upon their backs, as
hitherto.] Whereupon they prayed that the Romans
would have compassion upon the [poor] remains of
Judea, and not expose what was left of them to such
as barbarously tore them to pieces, and that they
would join their country to Syria, and administer the
government by their own commanders, whereby it
would [soon] be demonstrated that those who are
under the calumny of seditious persons, and lovers
of war, know how to bear governors that are set
over them, if they be but tolerable ones." So the

[1] Here we have a strong confirmation that it was Xerxes and not
Artaxerxes, under whom the main part of the Jews returned out of
the Babylonian captivity, i.e. in the days of Ezra and Nehemiah The
same thing is in the Antiquities, B. XI. ch. v. sect. 1, Vol. II.

Jews concluded their accusation with this request. Then rose up Nicolaus, and confuted the accusations which were brought against the kings, and himself accused the Jewish nation, as hard to be ruled, and as naturally disobedient to kings. He also reproached all those kinsmen of Archelaus' who had left him, and were gone over to his accusers.

3. So Cæsar, after he had heard both sides, dissolved the assembly for that time, but a few days afterward, he gave the one half of Herod's kingdom to Archelaus, by the name of *Ethnarch,* and promised to make him king also afterward, if he rendered himself worthy of that dignity. But as to the other half, he divided it into two tetrarchies, and gave them to two other sons of Herod, the one of them to Philip, and the other to that Antipas who contested the kingdom with Archelaus. Under this last was Perea, and Galilee, with a revenue of two hundred talents: but Batanea, and Trachonitis, and Auranitis, and certain parts of Zeno's house about Jamnia, with a revenue of a hundred talents, were made subject to Philip; while Idumea, and all Judea, and Samaria, were parts of the ethnarchy of Archelaus, although Samaria was eased of one quarter of its taxes, out of regard to their not having revolted with the rest of the nation. He also made subject to him the following cities, viz. Strato's Tower, and Sebaste, and Joppa, and Jerusalem; but as to the Grecian cities, Gaza, and Gadara, and Hippos, he cut them off from the kingdom, and added them to Syria. Now the revenue of the country that was given to Archelans, was four hundred talents. Salome also, besides what the king had left her in his testaments, was now made mistress of Jamnia, and Ashdod, and Phasaelis. Cæsar did moreover bestow upon her the royal palace of Ascalon; by all which she got to-

OM KEIS.

(GADARA.)

The architectural remains embraced in this view demand some attention. Thev mark, as it is believed, the site of Gadara, a place very frequently mentioned by Josephus. They occur at a spot bearing S.E. by E. from the southern extremity of the Sea of Galilee, at the distance of about six miles from its borders, and very near to a bend of the Yarmak—the principal tributary of the Jordan—being a confluence, collecting the streams that drain the East Country, or Bashan, far and wide.

In the plate before us the direction of sight is nearly east. The reader is referred to a passage from the Journal of Irby and Ⅿangles distinctly describing the objects which are presented in this plate. The "street" there mentioned is here seen in front, and on the face of its dislocated pavement it exhibits the tracks of wheels which, nineteen centuries ago, rumbled through the crowded ways of a populous city. On either side of this pavement the fallen columns show where stood its temples, halls, and palaces. Similar remains of the architectural magnificence of the place are scattered over the uneven surface around, far and wide.

Josephus tells us, Book III, c. 7, that Vespasian not only abandoned the inhabitants to an indiscriminate slaughter; but overthrew the city itself. That it was however afterwards restored appears from the fact of its having long held an important rank among the metropolitan cities of Syria, after the establishment of Christianity. Some confusion, however, attaches to the historical notices of this place, from the circumstance that there were one or two other cities of Palestine of the same name.

gether a revenue of sixty talents; but he put her house under the ethnarchy of Archelaus. And for the rest of Herod's offspring, they received what was bequeathed to them in his testaments; but besides that, Cæsar granted to Herod's two virgin daughters five hundred thousand [drachmæ] of silver, and gave them in marriage to the sons of Pheroras: but after this family distribution, he gave between them what had been bequeathed to him by Herod, which was a thousand talents, reserving to himself only some inconsiderable presents in honour of the deceased.

CHAPTER VII.

The history of the spurious Alexander. Archelaus is banished, and Glaphyra dies, after what was to happen to both of them had been showed them in dreams.

1. IN the meantime there was a man, who was by birth a Jew, but brought up at Sidon with one of the Roman freed men, who falsely pretended, on account of the resemblance of their countenances, that he was that Alexander who was slain by Herod. This man came to Rome, in hopes of not being detected. He had one who was his assistant, of his own nation, and who knew all the affairs of the kingdom, and instructed him to say, how those that were sent to kill him and Aristobulus had pity upon them and stole them away, by putting bodies that were like theirs in their places. This man deceived the Jews that were at Crete, and got a great deal of money of them for travelling in splendour: and thence sailed to Melos, where he was thought so certainly

genuine, that he got a great deal more money, and prevailed with those that had treated him to sail along with him to Rome. So he landed at Dicearchia, [Puteoli,] and got very large presents from the Jews who dwelt there, and was conducted by his father's friends as if he were a king; nay, the resemblance in his countenance procured him so much credit, that those who had seen Alexander, and had known him very well, would take their oaths that he was the very same person. Accordingly, the whole body of the Jews that were at Rome, ran out in crowds to see him, and an innumerable multitude there was who stood in the narrow places, through which he was carried; for those of Melos were so far distracted, that they carried him in a sedan, and maintained a royal attendance for him at their own proper charges.

2. But Cæsar, who knew perfectly well the lineaments of Alexander's face, because he had been accused by Herod before him, doubted the truth of the story, even before he saw the man. However, he suffered the agreeable fame that went of him to have some weight with him, and sent Celedus, one who well knew Alexander, and ordered him to bring the young man to him. But when Cæsar saw him, he immediately discerned a difference in his countenance, and when he had discovered that his whole body was of a more robust texture, and like that of a slave, he understood the whole was a contrivance. But the impudence of what he said greatly provoked him to be angry at him; for when he was asked about Aristobulus, he said, That "he was also preserved alive, and was left on purpose in Cyprus for fear of treachery, because it would be harder for plotters to get them both into their power while they were separate." Then did Cæsar take him by himself privately, and said to him, "I will give thee thy life, if

thou wilt discover who it was that persuaded thee to forge such stories." So he said, that he would discover him, and followed Cæsar, and pointed to that Jew who abused the resemblance of his face to get money; for that he had received more presents in every city than ever Alexander did when he was alive. Cæsar laughed at the contrivance, and put this spurious Alexander among his rowers, on account of the strength of his body, but ordered him that persuaded him to be put to death. But for the people of Melos, they had been sufficiently punished for their folly, by the expenses they had been at on his account.

3. And now Archelaus took possession of his ethnarchy, and used not the Jews only, but the Samaritans also, barbarously; and this out of his resentment of their old quarrels with him. Whereupon they both of them sent ambassadors against him to Cæsar, and in the ninth year of his government he was banished to Vienna, a city of Gaul, and his effects were put into Cæsar's treasury. But the report goes, that before he was sent for by Cæsar, he seemed to see nine ears of corn, full and large, but devoured by oxen. When, therefore, he had sent for the diviners, and some of the Chaldeans, and inquired of them what they thought it portended, and when one of them had one interpretation, and another had another, Simon, one of the sect of the Essens, said, That "he thought the ears of corn denoted years, and the oxen denoted a mutation of things, because by their ploughing they made an alteration of the country. That therefore he should reign as many years as there were ears of corn, and after he had passed through various alterations of fortune, should die." Now five days after Archelaus had heard this interpretation, he was called to his trial.

4. I cannot also but think it worthy to be recorded, what dream Glaphyra, the daughter of Archelaus, king of Cappadocia, had, who had at first been wife to Alexander, who was the brother of Archelaus, concerning whom we have been discoursing. This Alexander was the son of Herod the king, by whom he was put to death, as we have already related. This Glaphyra was married, after his death, to Juba, king of Lybia, and after his death, was returned home, and lived a widow with her father. Then it was that Archelaus, the ethnarch, saw her, and fell so deeply in love with her, that he divorced Mariamne, who was then his wife, and married her. When, therefore, she was come into Judea, and had been there for a little while, she thought she saw Alexander stand by her, and that he said to her, "Thy marriage with the king of Lybia might have been sufficient for thee; but thou wast not contented with him, but art returned again to my family, to a third husband, and him, thou impudent woman, hast thou chosen for thine husband, who is my brother. However, I shall not overlook the injury thou hast offered me; I shall [soon] have thee again, whether thou wilt or no." Now Glaphyra hardly survived the narration of this dream of hers two days.

CHAPTER VIII.

Archelaus' ethnarchy is reduced into a [Roman] province. The sedition of Judas of Galilee. The three sects of the Jews.

1. AND now Archelaus' part of Judea was reduced into a province; and Coponius, one of the equestrian order among the Romans, was sent as a procurator,

having the power of [life and death] put into his hands by Cæsar. Under his administration it was, that a certain Galilean, whose name was Judas, prevailed with his countrymen to revolt, and said they were cowards if they would endure to pay a tax to the Romans, and would, after God, submit to mortal men as their lords. This man was a teacher of a peculiar sect of his own, and was not at all like the rest of those their leaders.

2. For there are three philosophical sects among the Jews. The followers of the first of which are the Pharisees, of the second the Sadducees, and the third sect, which pretends to a severe discipline, are called Essens. These last are Jews by birth, and seem to have a greater affection for one another than the other sects have. These Essens reject pleasures as an evil, but esteem continence, and the conquest over our passions to be virtue. They neglect wedlock, but choose out other persons' children while they are pliable and fit for learning, and esteem them to be of their kindred, and form them according to their own manners. They do not absolutely deny the fitness of marriage, and the succession of mankind thereby continued; but they guard against the lascivious behaviour of women, and are persuaded that none of them preserve their fidelity to one man.

3. These men are despisers of riches, and so very communicative as raises our admiration. Nor is there any one to be found among them who hath more than another; for it is a law among them, that those who come to them must let what they have be common to the whole order, insomuch that among them all there is no appearance of poverty, or excess of riches, but every one's possessions are intermingled with every other's possessions, and so there is, as it were, one patrimony among all the brethren. They think that oil is a

defilement; and if any one of them be anointed, without his own approbation, it is wiped off his body; for they think to be sweaty is a good thing, as they do also to be clothed in white garments. They also have stewards appointed to take care of their common affairs, who, every one of them, have no separate business for any, but what is for the uses of them all.

4. They have no one certain city, but many of them dwell in every city; and if any of their sect come from other places, what they have lies open for them, just as if it were their own, and they go into such as they never knew before, as if they had been ever so long acquainted with them. For which reason they carry nothing at all with them when they travel into remote parts, though still they take their weapons with them, for fear of thieves. Accordingly, there is, in every city where they live, one appointed particularly to take care of strangers, and to provide garments and other necessaries for them. But the habit and management of their bodies is such as children use who are in fear of their masters. Nor do they allow of the change of garments or of shoes, till they first be entirely torn to pieces, or worn out by time. Nor do they either buy or sell any thing to one another, but every one of them gives what he hath to him that wanteth it, and receives from him again in lieu of it what may be convenient for himself; and although there be no requital made, they are fully allowed to take what they want of whomsoever they please.

5. And as for their piety towards God, it is very extraordinary; for, before sun-rising, they speak not a word about profane matters, but put up certain prayers, which they have received from their forefathers, as if they made a supplication for its rising. After this every one of them is sent away by their

curators to exercise some of those arts wherein they
are skilled, in which they labour with great diligence
till the fifth hour. After which they assemble themselves together again into one place, and when they
have clothed themselves in white veils, they then
bathe their bodies in cold water. And after this
purification is over, they every one meet together in
an apartment of their own, into which it is not permitted to any of another sect to enter; while they
go, after a pure manner, into the dining-room, as
into a certain holy temple, and quietly set themselves
down: upon which the baker lays them loaves in order;
the cook also brings a single plate of one sort of good,
and sets it before every one of them; but a priest
says grace before meat, and it is unlawful for any
one to taste of the food before grace be said. The
same priest, when he hath dined, says grace again
after meat, and when they begin, and when they end,
they praise God, as he that bestows their food upon
them; after which they lay aside their [white] garments, and betake themselves to their labours again
till the evening, then they return home to supper,
after the same manner, and if there be any strangers
there, they sit down with them. Nor is there ever
any clamour or disturbance to pollute their house,
but they give every one leave to speak in their turn;
which silence thus kept in their house, appears to
foreigners like some tremendous mystery; the cause
of which is that perpetual sobriety they exercise, and
the same settled measure of meat and drink that is
allotted them, and that such as is abundantly sufficient
for them.

6. And truly, as for other things they do nothing
but according to the injunctions of their curators;
only these two things are done among them at every
one's own free-will, which are to assist those that want

it, and to show mercy; for they are permitted of their own accord to afford succour to such as deserve it, when they stand in need of it, and to bestow food on those that are in distress; but they cannot give any thing to their kindred without the curators. They dispense their anger after a just manner, and restrain their passion. They are eminent for fidelity, and are the ministers of peace; whatsoever they say also is firmer than an oath; but swearing is avoided by them, and they esteem it worse than perjury; for they say, that he who cannot be believed, without [swearing by] God, is already condemned. They also take great pains in studying the writings of the ancients, and choose out of them what is most for the advantage of their soul and body, and they inquire after such roots and medicinal stones as may cure their distempers.

7. But now, if any one hath a mind to come over to their sect, he is not immediately admitted, but he is prescribed the same method of living which they use, for a year, while he continues excluded, and they give also a small hatchet, and the forementioned girdle, and the white garment. And when he hath given evidence, during that time, that he can observe their continence, he approaches nearer to their way of living, and is made a partaker of the waters of purification; yet he is not even now admitted to live with them; for after this demonstration of his fortitude, his temper is tried two more years, and if he appear to be worthy, they then admit him into their society. And before he is allowed to touch their common food, he is obliged to take tremendous oaths, that in the first place he will exercise piety towards God, and then that he will observe justice towards men, and that he will do no harm to any one, either of his own accord, or by the command of others; that he will always hate the

wicked, and be an assistant to the righteous, that he will ever show fidelity to all men, and especially to those in authority; because no one obtains the government, without God's assistance; and that if he be in authority, he will in no time whatever abuse his authority, nor endeavour to outshine his subjects, either in his garments or any other finery; that he will be perpetually a lover of truth, and propose to himself to reprove those that tell lies; that he will keep his hands clear from theft, and his soul from unlawful gains; and that he will neither conceal any thing from those of his own sect, nor discover any of their doctrines to others; no, not though any one should compel him so to do at the hazard of his life. Moreover he swears to communicate their doctrines to no one any otherwise than as he received them himself; that he will abstain from robbery, and will equally preserve the books belonging to their sect, and the names of the [1] angels [or messengers.] These are the oaths by which they secure their proselytes to themselves.

8. But for those that are caught in any heinous sins, they cast them out of their society, and he who is thus separated from them, does often die after a miserable manner; for as he is bound by the oath he had taken, and by the customs he hath been engaged in, he is not at liberty to partake of that food that he meets

---

[1] This mention of the *names of angels,* so particularly preserved by the Essens (if it meant more than those *messengers* which were employed to bring them the peculiar books of their sect,) looks like a prelude to that *worshipping of angels,* blamed by St. Paul, as superstitious and unlawful, in some such sort of people as these Essens were, Col. ii. 8, as is the prayer to, or towards the sun for his rising every morning, mentioned before, sect. 5, very like those not much later observances made mention of in the preaching of Peter, Authent. Rec. Part II. p. 669, and regarding a kind of worship of angels, of the month, and of the moon, and not celebrating the new moons, or other festivals, unless the moon appeared. Which indeed seems to me the earliest mention of any regard to the moon's phasis in fixing the Jewish calendar, of which the Talmud and later Rabbins talk so much, and upon so very little ancient foundation.

with elsewhere, but is forced to eat grass, and to famish his body with hunger, till he perish; for which reason they receive many of them again, when they are at their last gasp, out of compassion to them, as thinking the miseries they have endured till they came to the very brink of death, to be a sufficient punishment for the sins they had been guilty of.

9. But in the judgments they exercise they are most accurate and just, nor do they pass sentence by the votes of a court that is fewer than a hundred. And as to what is once determined by that number it is unalterable. What they most of all honour, after God himself, is the name of their legislator [Moses,] whom if any one blaspheme, he is punished capitally. They also think it a good thing to obey their elders and the major part. Accordingly, if ten of them be sitting together, no one of them will speak while the other nine are against it. They also avoid spitting in the midst of them, or on the right side. Moreover, they are stricter than any other of the Jews in resting from their labours on the seventh day; for they not only get their food ready the day before, that they may not be obliged to kindle a fire on that day, but they will not remove any vessel out of its place, nor go to stool thereon. Nay, on other days they dig a small pit, a foot deep, with a paddle, (which kind of hatchet is given them, when they are first admitted among them,) and covering themselves round with their garment, that they may not affront the divine rays of light, they ease themselves into that pit, after which they put the earth that was dug out again into the pit, and even this they do only in the more lonely places, which they choose out for this purpose; and although this easement of the body be natural, yet it is a rule with them to wash themselves after it, as if it were a defilement to them.

10. Now after the time of their preparatory trial is over, they are parted into four classes; and so far are the juniors inferior to the seniors, that if the seniors should be touched by the juniors, they must wash themselves, as if they had intermixed themselves with the company of a foreigner. They are long-lived also, insomuch that many of them live above a hundred years, by means of the simplicity of their diet, nay, as I think, by means of the regular course of life they observe also. They contemn the miseries of life, and are above pain, by the generosity of their mind. And as for death, if it will be for their glory, they esteem it better than living always; and indeed our war with the Romans gave abundant evidence what great souls they had in their trials, wherein, although they were tortured and distorted, burnt and torn to pieces, and went through all kinds of instruments of torment, that they might be forced either to blaspheme their legislator, or to eat what was forbidden them, yet could they not be made to do either of them, no, nor once to flatter their tormentors, or to shed a tear; but they smiled in their very pains, and laughed those to scorn who inflicted the torments upon them, and resigned up their souls with great alacrity, as expecting to receive them again.

11. For their doctrine is this, That bodies are corruptible, and that the matter they are made of is not permanent; but that the souls are immortal, and continue for ever, and that they come out of the most subtile air, and are united to their bodies as to prisons, into which they are drawn by a certain natural enticement; but that when they are set free from the bands of the flesh, they then, as released from a long bondage, rejoice and mount upward. And this is like the opinions of the Greeks, that good souls have their habitations beyond the ocean, in a

region that is neither oppressed with storms of rain or snow, or with intense heat, but that this place is such as is refreshed by the gentle breathing of a west wind, that is perpetually blowing from the ocean; while they allot to bad souls a dark and tempestuous den, full of never ceasing punishments. And indeed the Greeks seem to me to have followed the same notion, when they allot the islands of the blessed to their brave men, whom they call heroes, and demigods; and to the souls of the wicked, the region of the ungodly, in Hades, where their fables relate that certain persons, such as Sisyphus, and Tantalus, and Ixon, and Tityus, are punished; which is built on this first supposition, that souls are immortal; and thence are those exhortations to virtue, and dehortations from wickedness collected, whereby good men are bettered in the conduct of their life by the hopes they have of reward after their death, and whereby the vehement inclinations of bad men to vice are restrained, by the fear and expectation they are in, that although they should lie concealed in this life, they should suffer immortal punishment after their death. These are the divine doctrines of the Essens [1] about the soul, which lay an unavoidable bait for such as have once had a taste of their philosophy.

12. There are also those among them who undertake to [2] foretell things to come, by reading the holy books, and using several sorts of purifications, and

---

[1] Of these Jewish or Essene, and indeed Christian, doctrines, concerning souls, both good and bad in Hades, see that excellent discourse or homily of our Josephus' concerning Hades, at the end of Vol. IV.

[2] Dean Aldrich reckons up three examples of this gift of prophecy in several of these Essens out of Josephus himself, viz. in the History of the War, B. I. ch. iii. sect. 5, Vol. III., Judas foretold the death of Antigonus at Strato's Tower; B. II. ch. vii. sect. 3, Simon foretold that Archelaus should reign but nine or ten years; and Antiq. B. XV. ch. x. sect. 4, 5, Vol. II., Manahem foretold that Herod should be king, and should reign tyrannically, and that for more than twenty or even thirty years. All which came to pass accordingly.

being perpetually conversant in the discourses of the prophets: and it is but seldom that they miss in their predictions.

13. Moreover, there in another order of Essens, who agree with the rest as to their way of living, and customs, and laws, but differ from them in the point of marriage, as thinking that by not marrying they cut off the principal part of human life, which is the prospect of succession; nay rather, that if all men should be of the same opinion, the whole race of mankind would fail. However, they try their spouses for three years, and if they find that they have their natural purgations thrice, as trials that they are likely to be fruitful, they then actually marry them. But they do not use to accompany with their wives when they are with child, as a demonstration that they do not marry out of regard to pleasure, but for the sake of posterity. Now the women go into the baths with some of their garments on, as the men do with somewhat girded about them. And these are the customs of this order of Essens.

14. But then as to the two other orders at first mentioned, the Pharisees are those who are esteemed most skilful in the exact explication of their laws, and introduce the first sect. These ascribe all to fate, [or providence,] and to God, and yet allow, that to act what is right, or the contrary, is principally in the power of men: although fate does co-operate in every action. They say, that all souls are incorruptible, but that the [1] souls of good men only are

---

[1] There is so much more here about the Essens, than is cited from Josephus in Porphyry and Eusebius, and yet so much less about the Pharisees and Sadducees, the two other Jewish sects, than would naturally be expected in proportion to the Essens or third sect, nay, than seems to be referred to by himself elsewhere, that one is tempted to suppose Josephus had at first written less of the one, and more of the two others than his present copies afford us; as also that, by some unknown accident, our present copies are here made up of the larger edition in the first

removed into other bodies, but that the souls of bad men are subject to eternal punishment. But the Sadducees are those that compose the second order, and take away fate entirely, and suppose that God is not concerned in our doing or not doing what is evil; and they say, that to act what is good or what is evil, is at men's own choice, and that the one or the other belongs so to every one, that they may act as they please. They also take away the belief of the immortal duration of the soul, and the punishments and rewards in Hades. Moreover, the Pharisees are friendly to one another, and are for the exercise of concord, and regard for the public; but the behaviour of the Sadducees one towards another is in some degree wild, and their conversation with those that are of their own party is as barbarous as if they were strangers to them. And this is what I had to say concerning the philosophic sects among the Jews.

case, and of the smaller in the second. However, what Josephus says in the name of the Pharisees, that only the souls of good men go out of one body into another, although all souls be immortal, and still the souls of the bad are liable to eternal punishment; as also what he says afterwards, Antiq. B. XVIII. ch. 1, sect 3, Vol. III., that the soul's vigour is immortal, and that under the earth they receive rewards or punishments according as their lives have been virtuous or vicious in the present world; that to the bad is allotted an eternal prison, but that the good are permitted to live again in this world, are nearly agreeable to the doctrines of Christianity. Only Josephus' rejection of the return of the wicked into other bodies, or into this world, which he grants to the good, looks somewhat like a contradiction to St. Paul's account of the doctrine of the Jews, that "they themselves allowed that there should be a resurrection of the dead, both 'of the just and unjust,'" Acts xxiv. 15. Yet because Josephus' account is that of the Pharisees, and St. Paul's that of the Jews in general, and of himself, the contradiction is not very certain.

CHAPTER IX.

The death of Salome. The cities which Herod and
Philip built. Pilate occasions disturbances. Ti-
berius puts Agrippa into bonds, but Caius frees
him from them, and makes him king. Herod An-
tipas is banished.

1. AND now as the ethnarchy of Archelaus was
fallen into a Roman province, the other sons of Herod,
Philip, and that Herod who was called Antipas,
each of them took upon them the administration of
their own tetrarchies; for when Salome died, she bequeathed to Julia, the wife of Augustus, both her
toparchy, and Jamnia, as also her plantation of palm-
trees that were in Phasaelis. ˙But when the Roman
empire was translated to Tiberius, the son of Julia,
upon the death of Augustus, who had reigned fifty-
seven years, six months, and two days, both Herod
and Philip continued in their tetrarchies, and the
latter of them built the city Cæsarea, at the fountains of Jordan, and in the region of Paneas; as also
the city Julias, in the lower Gaulanitis. Herod also
built the city Tiberias in Galilee, and in Perea [be-
yond Jordan] another that was also called Julias.

2. Now Pilate, who was sent as a procurator into
Judea by Tiberius, sent by night those images of
Cæsar that are called *ensigns,* into Jerusalem. This
excited a very great tumult among the Jews when
it was day; for those that were near them were astonished at the sight of them, as indications that their
laws were trodden under foot; for those laws do not
permit any sort of image to be brought into the city.
Nay, besides the indignation which the citizens had

themselves at this procedure, a vast number of people came running out of the country. These came zealously to Pilate to Cæsarea, and besought him to carry those ensigns out of Jerusalem, and to preserve them their ancient laws inviolable; but upon Pilate's denial of their request, they fell down prostrate upon the ground, and continued immovable in that posture for five days and as many nights.

3. On the next day Pilate sat upon his tribunal, in the open market-place, and called to him the multitude, as desirous to give them an answer; and then gave a signal to the soldiers, that they should all by agreement at once encompass the Jews with their weapons; so the band of soldiers stood round about the Jews in three ranks. The Jews were under the utmost consternation at that unexpected sight. Pilate also said to them, that they should be cut in pieces, unless they would admit of Cæsar's images, and gave intimation to the soldiers to draw their naked swords. Hereupon the Jews, as it were at one signal, fell down in vast numbers together, and exposed their necks bare, and cried out that they were sooner ready to be slain, than that their law should be transgressed. Hereupon Pilate was greatly surprised at their prodigious superstition, and gave order that the ensigns should be presently carried out of Jerusalem.

4. After this he raised another disturbance, by expending that sacred treasure which is called Corban upon aqueducts, whereby he brought water from the distance of four hundred furlongs. At this the multitude had indignation; and when Pilate was come to Jerusalem, they came about his tribunal, and made a clamour at it. Now when he was apprised aforehand of this disturbance, he mixed his own soldiers in their armour with the multitude, and ordered them to conceal themselves under the habits of private

men, and not indeed to use their swords, but with their staves to beat those that made the clamour. He then gave the signal from his tribunal [to do as he had bidden them.] Now the Jews were so sadly beaten, that many of them perished by the stripes they received, and many of them perished as trodden to death by themselves; by which means the multitude was astonished at the calamity of those that were slain, and held their peace.

5. In the meantime Agrippa, the son of that Aristobulus, who had been slain by his father Herod, came to Tiberius, to accuse Herod the tetrarch; who not admittting of his accusation, he stayed at Rome, and cultivated a friendship with others of the men of note, but principally with Caius the son of Germanicus, who was then but a private person. Now this Agrippa, at a certain time, feasted Caius, and as he was very complaisant to him on several other accounts, he at length stretched out his hands, and openly wished that Tiberius might die, and that he might quickly see him emperor of the world. This was told to Tiberius by one of Agrippa's domestics, who thereupon was very angry, and ordered Agrippa to be bound, and had him very ill treated in the prison for six months, until Tiberius died, after he had reigned twenty-two years, six months, and three days.

6. But when Caius was made Cæsar, he released Agrippa from his bonds, and made him king of Philip's tetrarchy, who was now dead; but when Agrippa had arrived at that degree of dignity, he inflamed the ambitious desires of Herod the tetrarch, who was chiefly induced to hope for the royal authority by his wife Herodias, who reproached him for his sloth, and told him that it was only because he would not sail to Cæsar, that he was destitute of that great dignity; for since Cæsar had made Agrippa a

king, from a private person, much more would he
advance him from a tetrarch to that dignity. These
arguments prevailed with Herod, so that he came
to Caius, by whom he was punished for his ambition,
by being banished into Spain; for Agrippa followed
him, in order to accuse him: to whom also Caius gave
his tetrarchy, by way of addition. So Herod died
in Spain, whither his wife had followed him.

CHAPTER X.

*Caius commands that his statue should be set up in
the temple itself; and what Petronius did thereupon.*

1. Now Caius Cæsar did so grossly abuse the
fortune he had arrived at, as to take himself to be
a god, and to desire to be so called also, and to cut
off those of the greatest nobility out of his country.
He also extended his impiety as far as the Jews.
Accordingly, he sent Petronius with an army to
Jerusalem, to place his [1] statues in the temple, and
commanded him that in case the Jews would not
admit of them, he should slay those that opposed it,
and carry all the rest of the nation into captivity;
but God concerned himself with these his commands.
However, Petronius marched out of Antioch into
Judea, with three legions, and many Syrian auxiliaries.
Now as to the Jews, some of them could not believe
the stories that spoke of a war, but those that did
believe them were in the utmost distress how to defend themselves, and the terror diffused itself pres-

---

[1] Tacitus owns that Caius commanded the Jews to place his effigies
in their temple, though he be mistaken when he adds, that the Jews
thereupon took arms.

ently through them all; for the army was already come
to Ptolemais.

2. This Ptolemais is a maritime city of Galilee,
built in the great plain. It is encompassed with
mountains; that on the east side, sixty furlongs off,
belongs to Galilee; but that on the south belongs to
Carmel, which is distant from it a hundred and twenty
furlongs; and that on the north is the highest of them
all, and is called by the people of the country, *the
Ladder of the Tyrians,* which is at the distance of a
hundred furlongs. The very small river [1] Belus runs
by it, at the distance of two furlongs; near which
there is [2] Memnon's monument, and hath near it a
place no larger than a hundred cubits, which deserves
admiration; for the place is round and hollow, and
affords such sand as glass is made of, which place,
when it hath been emptied by the many ships there
loaded, it is filled again by the winds, which bring
into it, as it were on purpose, that sand which lay
remote, and was no more than bare common sand,
while this mine presently turns it into glassy sand.
And what is to me still more wonderful, that glassy
sand which is superfluous, and is once removed out
of the place, becomes bare common sand again. And
this is the nature of the place we are speaking of.

3. But now the Jews got together in great num--
bers with their wives and children into that plain
that was by Ptolemais, and made supplication to
Petronius, first for their laws, and, in the next place,
for themselves. So he was prevailed upon by the
multitude of the suppliants, and by their supplica-

---

[1] This account of a place near the mouth of the river Belus in
Phœnicia, whence came that sand out of which the ancients made their
glass, is a thing known in history, particularly in Tacitus and Strabo,
and more largely in Pliny.

[2] This Memnon had several monuments, and one of them appears,
both by Strabo and Diodorus, to have been in Syria and not improbably
in this very place.

tions, and left his army and the statues at Ptolemais, and then went forward into Galilee, and called together the multitude, and all the men of note to Tiberias, and showed them the power of the Romans, and the threatenings of Cæsar; and, besides this, proved that their petition was unreasonable; because while all the nations in subjection to them had placed the images of Cæsar in their several cities, among the rest of their gods, for them alone to oppose it, was almost like the behaviour of revolters, and was injurious to Cæsar.

4. And when they insisted on their law, and the custom of their country, and how it was not only not permitted them to make either an image of God, or indeed of a man, and to put it in any despicable part of their country, much less in the temple itself; Petronius replied, "And am not I also," said he, "bound to keep the law of my own lord? For if I transgress it, and spare you, it is but just that I perish; while he that sent me, and not I, will commence a war against you; for I am under command as well as you." Hereupon the whole multitude cried out, That "they are ready to suffer for their law." Petronius then quieted them, and said to them, "Will you then make war against Cæsar?" The Jews said, "We offer sacrifices twice every day for Cæsar, and for the Roman people; but that if he would place the images among them, he must first sacrifice the whole Jewish nation; and that they were ready to expose themselves, together with their children and wives, to be slain." At this Petronius was astonished, and pitied them on account of the inexpressible sense of religion the men were under, and that courage of theirs which made them ready to die for it; so they were dismissed without success.

5. But on the following days he got together the

men of power privately, and the multitude publicly, and sometimes he used persuasions to them, and sometimes he gave them his advice; but he chiefly made use of threatening to them, and insisted upon the power of the Romans, and the anger of Caius; and besides, upon the necessity he was himself under [to do as he was enjoined.] But as they could be no way prevailed upon, and he saw that the country was in danger of lying without tillage; for it was about seed-time that the multitude continued for fifty days together idle; so he at last got them together, and told them, That "it was best for him to run some hazard himself; for either, by the divine assistance, I shall prevail with Cæsar, and shall myself escape the danger as well as you, which will be matter of joy to us both; or, in case Cæsar continue in his rage, I will be ready to expose my own life for such a great number as you are." Whereupon he dismissed the multitude, who prayed greatly for his prosperity; and he took the army out of Ptolemais, and returned to Antioch; from whence he presently sent an epistle to Cæsar, and informed him of the irruption he had made into Judea, and of the supplications of the nation; and that unless he had a mind to lose both the country, and the men in it, he must permit them to keep their law, and must countermand his former injunction. Caius answered that epistle in a violent way, and threatened to have Petronius put to death for his being so tardy in the execution of what he had commanded. But it happened that those who brought Caius' epistle were tossed by a storm, and were detained on the sea for three months, while others that brought the news of Caius' death had a good voyage. Accordingly, Petronius received the epistle concerning Caius seven and twenty days before he received that which was against himself.

CHAPTER XI.

Concerning the government of Claudius, and the reign of Agrippa. Concerning the deaths of Agrippa, and of Herod, and what children they both left behind them.

1. Now when Caius had reigned three years and eight months, and had been slain by treachery, Claudius was hurried away by the armies that were at Rome to take the government upon him: but the senate, upon the reference of the consuls, Sentius Saturninus, and Pomponius Secundus, gave orders to the three regiments of soldiers that stayed with them to keep the city quiet, and went up into the capitol in great numbers, and resolved to oppose Claudius by force, on account of the barbarous treatment they had met with from Caius; and they determined either to settle the nation under an aristocracy, as they had of old been governed, or at least to choose by vote such a one for emperor as might be worthy of it.

2. Now it happened that at this time Agrippa sojourned at Rome, and that both the senate called him to consult with them, and at the same time Claudius sent for him out of the camp, that he might be serviceable to him, as he should have occasion for his service. So he, perceiving that Claudius was in effect made Cæsar already, went to him, who sent him as an ambassador to the senate, to let them know what his intentions were: That "in the first place, it was without his seeking, that he was hurried away by the soldiers; moreover, that he thought it was not just to desert those soldiers in such their zeal

for him, and that if he should do so, his own fortune would be in uncertainty: for that it was a dangerous case to have been once called to the empire. He added farther, that he would administer the government as a good prince, and not like a tyrant; for that he would be satisfied with the honour of being called emperor, but would, in every one of his actions, permit them all to give him their advice: for that although he had not been by nature for moderation, yet would the death of Caius afford him a sufficient demonstration how soberly he ought to act in that station."

3. This message was delivered by Agrippa; to which the senate replied, That "since they had an army, and the wisest consuls on their side, they would not endure a voluntary slavery." And when Claudius heard what answer the senate had made, he sent Agrippa to them again, with the following message, That "he could not bear the thoughts of betraying them that had given their oaths to be true to him; and that he saw he must fight, though unwillingly, against such as he had no mind to fight; that however, [if it must come to that,] it was proper to choose a place without the city for the war; because it was not agreeable to piety to pollute the temples of their own city with the blood of their own countrymen, and this only on occasion of their imprudent conduct." And when Agrippa had heard this message, he delivered it to the senators.

4. In the meantime, one of the soldiers belonging to the senate drew his sword, and cried out, "O my fellow-soldiers, what is the meaning of this choice of ours, to kill our brethren, and to use violence to our kindred that are with Claudius? while we may have him for our emperor whom no one can blame, and who hath so many just reasons [to lay claim to the

government;] and this with regard to those against
whom we are going to fight." When he had said
this, he marched through the whole senate, and carried
all the soldiers along with him. Upon which all the
patricians were immediately at a great fright at their
being thus deserted. But still, because there appeared no other way whither they could turn themselves for deliverance, they made haste the same way
with the soldiers, and went to Claudius. But those
that had the greatest luck in flattering the good fortune of Claudius betimes, met them before the walls
with their naked swords, and there was reason to
fear that those that came first might have been in
danger, before Claudius could know what violence
the soldiers were going to offer them, had not Agrippa
ran before, and told him what a dangerous thing
they were going about, and that unless he restrained
the violence of these men, who were in a fit of madness against the patricians, he would lose those on
whose account it was most desirable to rule, and
would be emperor over a desert.

5. When Claudius heard this, he restrained the
violence of the soldiery, and received the senate into
the camp, and treated them after an obliging manner,
and went out with them presently to offer their
thank-offerings to God, which were proper upon his
first coming to the empire. Moreover, he bestowed
on Agrippa his whole paternal kingdom immediately,
and added to it, besides those countries that had been
given by Augustus to Herod, Trachonitis and Auranitis, and still besides these, that kingdom which was
called *the kingdom of Lysanias.* This gift he declared to the people by a decree, but ordered the
magistrates to have the donation engraved on tables
of brass, and to be set up in the capitol. He bestowed on his brother Herod, who was also his son-

in-law, by marrying [his daughter] Bernice, the kingdom of Chalcis.

6. So now riches flowed in to Agrippa by his enjoyment of so large a dominion, nor did he abuse the money he had on small matters, but he began to encompass Jerusalem with such a wall, which, had it been brought to perfection, had made it impracticable for the Romans to take it by siege; but his death, which happened at Cæsarea, before he had raised the walls to their due height, prevented him. He had then reigned three years, as he had governed his tetrarchies three other years. He left behind him three daughters, born to him by Cypros, viz. Bernice, Mariamne, and Drusilla, and a son born of the same mother, whose name was Agrippa: he was left a very young child, so that Claudius made the country a Roman province, and sent Cuspius Fadus to be its procurator, and after him Tiberius Alexander, who, making no alterations of the ancient laws, kept the nation in tranquillity. Now after this, Herod the king of Chalcis died, and left behind him two sons, born to him of his brother's daughter Bernice; their names were *Bernicianus* and *Hyrcanus.* [He also left behind him] Aristobulus, whom he had by his former wife, Mariamne. There was besides another brother of his that died a private person; his name was also *Aristobulus,* who left behind him a daughter, whose name was *Jotape:* and these, as I have formerly said, were the children of Aristobulus the son of Herod, which Aristobulus and Alexander were born to Herod by Mariamne, and were slain by him. But as for Alexander's posterity, they reigned in Armenia.

CHAPTER XII.

Many tumults under Cumanus, which were composed by Quadratus. Felix is procurator of Judea. Agrippa is advanced from Chalcis to a greater kingdom.

1. Now after the death of Herod, king of Chalcis, Claudius set Agrippa, the son of Agrippa, over his uncle's kingdom, while Cumanus took upon him the office of procurator of the rest, which was a Roman province, and therein he succeeded Alexander, under which Cumanus began the troubles, and the Jews' ruin came on; for when the multitude were come together to Jerusalem, to the feast of unleavened bread, and a Roman cohort stood over the cloisters of the temple, (for they always were armed and kept guard at the festivals, to prevent any innovation, which the multitude thus gathered together might make,) one of the soldiers pulled back his garment, and, couring down after an indecent manner, turned his breech to the Jews, and spoke such words as you may expect upon such a posture. At this the whole multitude had indignation, and made a clamour to Cumanus, that he would punish the soldier; while the rasher part of the youth, and such as were naturally the most tumultuous, fell to fighting, and caught up stones, and threw them at the soldiers. Upon which Cumanus was afraid lest all the people should make an assault upon him, and sent to call for more armed men, who, when they came in great numbers into the cloisters, the Jews were in a very great consternation, and being beaten out of the temple, they ran into the city, and the violence with which they

crowded to get out was so great, that they trode upon each other, and squeezed one another, till ten thousand of them were killed, insomuch that this feast became the cause of mourning to the whole nation, and every family lamented [their own relations.]

2. Now there followed after this another calamity, which arose from a tumult made by robbers; for at the public road of Beth-horon, one Stephen, a servant of Cæsar, carried some furniture, which the robbers fell upon, and seized; upon this Cumanus sent men to go round about to the neighbouring villages, and to bring their inhabitants to him bound, as laying it to their charge that they had not pursued after the thieves, and caught them. Now here it was that a certain soldier, finding the sacred book of the law, tore it to pieces, and [1] threw it into the fire. Hereupon the Jews were in great disorder, as if their whole country were in a flame, and assembled themselves so many of them by their zeal for their religion, as by an engine, and ran together with united clamour to Cæsarea, to Cumanus, and made supplication to him, that he would not overlook this man, who had offered such an affront to God, and to his law, but punish him for what he had done. Accordingly, he, perceiving that the multitude would not be quiet unless they had a comfortable answer from him, gave order that the soldier should be brought, and drawn through those that required to have him punished to execution, which being done, the Jews went their ways.

3. After this there happened a fight between the Galileans and the Samaritans; it happened at a village called *Geman,* which is situate in the great plain of Samaria, where, as a great number of Jews

---

[1] Reland notes here, that the Talmud, in recounting ten sad accidents for which the Jews ought to rend their garments, reckons this for one, "When they hear that the law of God is burnt."

were going up to Jerusalem to the feast [of tabernacles,] a certain Galilean was slain; and besides
a vast number of people ran together out of Galilee,
in order to fight with the Samaritans; but the principal men among them came to Cumanus, and besought him, that before the evil became incurable,
he would come into Galilee, and bring the authors
of this murder to punishment, for that there was no
other way to make the multitude separate without
coming to blows. However, Cumanus postponed
their supplications to the other affairs he was then
about, and sent the petitioners away without success.

4. But when the affair of this murder came to be
told at Jerusalem, it put the multitude into disorder,
and they left the feast, and without any generals to
conduct them, they marched with great violence to
Samaria; nor would they be ruled by any of the
magistrates that were set over them, but they were
managed by one Eleazar, the son of Dineus, and by
Alexander, in these their thievish and seditious attempts. These men fell upon those that were in
the neighbourhood of the Acrabatene toparchy, and
slew them, without sparing any age, and set the villages on fire.

5. But Cumanus took one troop of horsemen,
called *the troop of Sebaste,* out of Cæsarea, and came
to the assistance of those that were spoiled; he also
seized upon a great number of those that followed
Eleazar, and slew more of them. And as for the
rest of the multitude of those that went so zealously
to fight with the Samaritans, the rulers of Jerusalem
ran out clothed with sackcloth, and having ashes on
their heads, and begged of them to go their ways, lest
by their attempt to revenge themselves upon the Samaritans, they should provoke the Romans to come
against Jerusalem; to have compassion upon their

country and temple, their children and their wives,
and not bring the utmost dangers of destruction upon
them, in order to avenge themselves upon one Galilean only. The Jews complied with these persuasions of theirs, and dispersed themselves; but still
there were a great number who betook themselves to
robbing, in hopes of impunity, and rapines and insurrections of the bolder sort happened over the whole
country; and the men of power among the Samaritans
came to Tyre, to [1] Ummidius Quadratus, the president of Syria, and desired that they that had laid
waste the country might be punished: the great men
also of the Jews, and Jonathan the son of Ananus,
the high priest, came thither, and said, that the Samaritans were the beginners of the disturbance, on
account of that murder they had committed, and that
Cumanus had given occasion to what had happened,
by his unwillingness to punish the original authors
of that murder.

6. But Quadratus put both parties off for that
time, and told them, that when he should come to
those places he would make a diligent inquiry after
every circumstance. After which he went to Cæsarea,
and crucified all those whom Cumanus had taken
alive; and when from thence he was come to the city
Lydda, he heard the affair of the Samaritans, and
sent for eighteen of the Jews whom he had learned
to have been concerned in that fight, and beheaded
them; but he sent two others of those that were of
the greatest power among them, and both Jonathan
and Ananias, the high priests, as also Ananus the
son of this Ananias, and certain others that were
eminent among the Jews, to Cæsar; as he did in like

---

[1] This Ummidius, or Numidius, or, as Tacitus calls him, *Vinidius
Quadratus*, is mentioned in an ancient inscription still preserved, as
Spanheim here informs us, which calls him Ummidius Quadratus.

manner by the most illustrious of the Samaritans.
He also ordered that Cumanus [the procurator] and
Celer the tribune should sail to Rome, in order to
give an account of what had been done to Cæsar.
When he had finished these matters, he went up from
Lydda to Jerusalem, and finding the multitude cele-
brating their feast of unleavened bread without any
tumult, he returned to Antioch.

7. Now when Cæsar at Rome had heard what
Cumanus and the Samaritans had to say, (where it
was done in the hearing of Agrippa, who zealously
espoused the cause of the Jews, as, in like manner,
many of the great men stood by Cumanus,) he condemned the Samaritans, and commanded that three of
the most powerful men among them should be put to
death: he banished Cumanus, and sent Celer bound
to Jerusalem, to be delivered over to the Jews to be
tormented, that he should be drawn round the city,
and then beheaded.

8. After this Cæsar sent Felix,[1] the brother of

---

[1] Take the character of this Felix, (who is well known from the
Acts of the Apostles, particularly from his *trembling* when St. Paul
discoursed of "righteousness, charity, and judgment to come," Acts xxiv.
25, and no wonder, when we have elsewhere seen, that he lived in adultery
with Drusilla, another man's wife, Antiq. B. XX. ch. vii. sect. 1, Vol. III.)
in the words of Tacitus: "Felix exercised," says Tacitus, "the authority
of a king, with the disposition of a slave, and relying upon the great
power of his brother Pallas at court, thought he might safely be guilty
of all kinds of wicked practices." Observe also the time when he was
made procurator, A.D. 52, that when St. Paul pleaded his cause before
him, A.D. 58, he might have been "many years a judge unto that nation;"
as St. Paul says he had been, Acts xxiv. 10. But as to what Tacitus
here says, that before the death of Cumanus, Felix was procurator over
Samaria only, does not well agree with St. Paul's words, who would
hardly have called Samaria a *Jewish nation*. In short, since what Tacitus
here says, is about countries very remote from Rome, where he lived;
since what he says of two Roman procurators, the one over Galilee, the
other over Samaria at the same time, is without all example elsewhere,
and since Josephus, who lived at that very time in Judea, appears to
have known nothing of this procuratorship of Felix, before the death
of Cumanus, I must suspect the story itself as nothing better than a
mistake of Tacitus, especially when it seems not only omitted, but
contradicted by Josephus, as any one may find who compares their his-

Pallas, to be procurator of Galilee, and Samaria, and Perea, and removed Agrippa from Chalcis unto a greater kingdom; for he gave him the tetrarchy which had belonged to Philip, which contained Batanea, Trachonitis, and Gaulanitis: he added to it the kingdom of Lysanias, and that province [Abilene] which Varus had governed. But Claudius himself, when he had administered the government thirteen years, eight months, and twenty days, died, and left Nero to be his successor in the empire, whom he had adopted by his wife Agrippina's delusions in order to be his successor, although he had a son of his own, whose name was *Britannicus,* by Messalina his former wife, and a daughter whose name was *Octavio,* whom he had married to Nero; he had also another daughter by Petina, whose name was *Antonia.*

CHAPTER XIII.

Nero adds four cities to Agrippa's kingdom; but the other parts of Judea were under Felix. The disturbances which were raised by the Sicarii, the magicians, and an Egyptian false prophet. The Jews and Syrians have a contest at Cæsarea.

1. Now as to the many things in which Nero acted like a madman, out of the extravagant degree of the felicity and riches which he enjoyed, and by that means used his good fortune to the injury of others; and after what manner he slew his brother, and wife, and mother, from whom his barbarity spread

tories together. Possibly Felix might have been a subordinate judge among the Jews some time before under Cumanus, but that he was in earnest a procurator of Samaria before, I do not believe.

itself to others that were most nearly related to him; and how, at last, he was so distracted that he became an actor in the scenes, and upon the theatre, I omit to say any more about them, because there are writers enough upon those subjects everywhere; but I shall turn myself to those actions of his time in which the Jews were concerned.

2. Nero, therefore, bestowed the kingdom of the lesser Armenia upon Aristobulus,[1] Herod's son, and he added to Agrippa's kingdom four cities, with the toparchies to them belonging: I mean Abila, and that Julius which is in Perea, Tarichea also, and Tiberias of Galilee; but over the rest of Judea he made Felix procurator. This Felix took Eleazar the arch robber, and many that were with him, alive, when they had ravaged the country for twenty years together, and sent them to Rome; but as to the number of the robbers he caused to be crucified, and of those who were caught among them, and whom he brought to punishment, they were a multitude not to be enumerated.

3. When the country was purged of these, there sprang up another sort of robbers in Jerusalem, who were called Sicarii, who slew men in the daytime, and in the midst of the city; this they did chiefly at the festivals, when they mingled themselves among the multitude, and concealed daggers under their garments, with which they stabbed those that were their enemies; and when any fell down dead, the murderers became a part of those that had indignation against them, by which means they appeared persons of such reputation that they could by no means be discovered. The first man who was slain by them was Jonathan the high priest, after whose death many were slain every day, while the fear

_____
[1] I. e. Herod king of Chalcis.

men were in of being so served was more afflicting than the calamity itself, and while everybody expected death every hour, as men do in war, so men were obliged to look before them, and to take notice of their enemies at a great distance; nor, if their friends were coming to them, durst they trust them any longer; but, in the midst of their suspicions and guarding of themselves, they were slain. Such was the celerity of the plotters against them, and so cunning was their contrivance.

4. There was also another body of wicked men gotten together, not so impure in their actions, but more wicked in their intentions, who laid waste the happy state of the city no less than did these murderers. These were such men as deceived and deluded the people under pretence of divine inspiration, but were for procuring innovations and changes of the government; and these prevailed with the multitude to act like madmen, and went before them into the wilderness, as pretending that God would there show them the signals of liberty. But Felix thought this procedure was to be the beginning of a revolt; so he sent some horsemen and footmen both armed, who destroyed a great number of them.·

5. But there was an Egyptian false prophet that did the Jews more mischief than the former; for he was a cheat, and pretended to be a prophet also, and got together thirty thousand men that were deluded by him; these he led round. about from the wilderness to the mount which was called the Mount of Olives, and was ready to break into Jerusalem by force from that place; and if he could but once conquer the Roman garrison and the people, he intended to domineer over them by the assistance of those guards of his that were to break into the city with him. But Felix prevented his attempt, and met him

with his Roman soldiers, while all the people assisted him in his attack upon them, insomuch that, when it came to a battle, the Egyptian ran away, with a few others, while the greatest part of those that were with him were either destroyed or taken alive; but the rest of the multitude were dispersed every one to their own homes, and there concealed themselves.

6. Now, when these were quieted, it happened, as it does in a diseased body, that another part was subject to an inflammation, for a company of deceivers and robbers got together, and persuaded the Jews to revolt, and exhorted them to assert their liberty, inflicting death on those that continued in obedience to the Roman government, and saying, that such as willingly chose slavery, ought to be forced from such their desired inclinations; for they parted themselves into different bodies, and lay in wait up and down the country, and plundered the houses of the great men, and slew the men themselves, and set the villages on fire; and this till all Judea was filled with the effects of their madness. And thus the flame was every day more and more blown up, till it came to a direct war.

7. There was also another disturbance at Cæsarea, those Jews who were mixed with the Syrians that lived there, raising a tumult against them. The Jews pretended that the city was theirs, and said, that he who built it was a Jew, meaning king Herod. The Syrians confessed also that its builder was a Jew, but they still said, however, that the city was a Grecian city; for that he who set up statues and temples in it could not design it for Jews. On which account both parties had a contest with one another; and this contest increased so much, that it came at last to arms, and the bolder sort of them marched out to fight; for the elders of the Jews were not

able to put a stop to their own people that were disposed to be tumultuous, and the Greeks thought it a shame for them to be overcome by the Jews. Now these Jews exceeded the others in riches, and strength of body; but the Grecian part had the advantage of assistance from the soldiery; for the greatest part of the Roman garrison was raised out of Syria, and being thus related to the Syrian part, they were ready to assist it. However, the governors of the city were concerned to keep all quiet, and whenever they caught those that were most for fighting on either side, they punished them with stripes and bands. Yet did not the sufferings of those that were caught affright the remainder, or make them desist; but they were still more and more exasperated, and deep engaged in the sedition. And as Felix came once into the market-place, and commanded the Jews, when they had beaten the Syrians, to go their ways, and threatened them if they would not, and they would not obey him, he sent his soldiers out upon them, and slew a great many of them, upon which it fell out that what they had was plundered. And as the sedition still continued, he chose out the most eminent men on both sides as ambassadors to Nero, to argue about their several privileges.

CHAPTER XIV.

Festus succeeds Felix, who is succeeded by Albinus, as he is by Florus; who, by the barbarity of his government, forces the Jews into the war.

1. Now it was that Festus succeeded Felix, as procurator, and made it his business to correct those

that made disturbances in the country. So he caught the greatest part of the robbers, and destroyed a great many of them. But then Albinus, who succeeded Festus, did not execute his office as the other had done; nor was there any sort of wickedness that could be named but he had a hand in it. Accordingly, he did not only, in his political capacity, steal and plunder every one's substance, nor did he only burden the whole nation with taxes, but he permitted the relations of such as were in prison for robbery, and had been laid there, either by the senate of every city, or by the former procurators, to redeem them for money; and nobody remained in the prisons, as a malefactor, but he who gave him nothing. At this time it was, that the enterprises of the seditious at Jerusalem, were very formidable: the principal men among them purchasing leave of Albinus to go on with their seditious practices; while that part of the people who delighted in disturbances joined themselves to such as had fellowship with Albinus: and every one of those wicked wretches was encompassed with his own band of robbers, while himself, like an arch robber, or a tyrant, made a figure among his company and abused his authority over those about him, in order to plunder those that lived quietly. The effect of which was this, that those who lost their goods were forced to hold their peace, when they had reason to show great indignation at what they had suffered, but those who had escaped, were forced to flatter him that deserved to be punished, out of the fear they were in of suffering equally with the others. Upon the whole, nobody durst speak their minds, but tyranny was generally tolerated; and at this time were those seeds sown which brought the city to destruction.

2   And though such was the character of Albinus,

yet did [1] Gessius Florus, who succeeded him, demonstrate him to have been a most excellent person, upon the comparison; for the former did the greatest part of his rogueries in private, and with a sort of dissimulation; but Gessius did his unjust actions to the harm of the nation after a pompous manner: and as though he had been sent as an executioner to punish condemned malefactors, he omitted no sort of rapine or of vexation; where the case was really pitiable, he was most barbarous, and in things of the greatest turpitude he was most impudent. Nor could any one outdo him in disguising the truth, nor could any one contrive more subtle ways of deceit than he did. He indeed thought it but a petty offence to get money out of single persons, so he spoiled whole cities, and ruined entire bodies of men at once, and did almost publicly proclaim it all the country over; that they had liberty given them to turn robbers, upon this condition, that he might go shares with them in the spoils they got. Accordingly, this his greediness of gain was the occasion that entire toparchies were brought to desolation, and a great many of the people left their own country, and fled into foreign provinces.

3. And truly, while Cestius Gallus was president of the province of Syria, nobody durst do so much as send an embassage to him against Florus; but when he was come to Jerusalem, upon the approach of the feast of unleavened bread, the people came about

[1] Not long after this beginning of Florus, the wickedest of all the Roman procurators of Judea, and the immediate occasion of the Jewish war, at the 12th year of Nero, and the 17th of Agrippa, or a. d. 66, the history in the twenty books of Josephus' Antiquities ends; although Josephus did not finish these books till the 13th of Domitian, or a. d. 93, twenty-seven years afterward; as he did not finish their Appendix, containing an account of his own life, till Agrippa was dead, which happened in the third year of Trajan, or a. d. 100, as I have several times observed before.

him not fewer in number than [1] three millions: these besought him to commiserate the calamities of their nation, and cried out upon Florus as the bane of their country. But as he was present, and stood by Cestius, he laughed at their words. However Cestius, when he had quieted the multitude, and had assured them, that he would take care that Florus should hereafter treat them in a more gentle manner, returned to Antioch: Florus also conducted him as far as Cæsarea, and deluded him, though he had at that very time the purpose of showing his anger at the nation, and procuring a war upon them, by which means alone it was that he supposed he might conceal his enormities; for he expected that, if the peace continued, he should have the Jews for his accusers before Cæsar; but that if he could procure them to make a revolt,. he should divert their laying lesser crimes to his charge, by a misery which was so much greater; he therefore did every day augment their calamities, in order to induce them to a rebellion.

4. Now at this time it happened, that the Grecians at Cæsarea had been too hard for the Jews, and had obtained of Nero the government of the city, and had brought the judicial determination; at the same time began the war, in the twelfth year of the reign of Nero and the seventeenth of the reign of Agrippa, in the month of Artemisius [Jyar.] Now the occasion of this war was by no means proportionable to those heavy calamities which it brought upon us. For the Jews that dwelt at Cæsarea had a synagogue near the place, whose owner was a certain Cæsarean Greek; the Jews had endeavoured frequently to have pur-

---

[1] Here we may note, that 3,000,000 of the Jews were present at the passover, A. D. 65, which confirms what Josephus elsewhere informs us of, that at a passover a little later, they counted 256,500 paschal lambs, which, at twelve to each lamb, which is no immoderate calculation, come to 3,078,000. See B. VI. ch. 9, sect. 8.

chased the possession of the place, and had offered
many times its value for its price; but as the owner
overlooked their offers, so did he raise other buildings
upon the place, in way of affront to them, and made
working shops of them, and left them but a narrow
passage, and such as was very troublesome for them
to go along to their synagogue. Whereupon the
warmer part of the Jewish youth went hastily to the
workmen, and forbade them to build there: but as
Florus would not permit them to use force, the great
men of the Jews, with John the publican, being in
the utmost distress what to do, persuaded Florus,
with the offer of eight talents, to hinder the work.
He then, being intent upon nothing but getting
money, promised he would do for them all they desired
of him, and then went away from Cæsarea to Sebaste,
and left the sedition to take its full course, as if he
had sold a license to the Jews to fight it out.

5. Now on the next day, which was the seventh
day of the week, when the Jews were crowding apace
to their synagogue, a certain man of Cæsarea of a
seditious temper, got an earthen vessel, and set it
with the bottom upward at the entrance of that synagogue, and sacrificed birds. This thing provoked the
Jews to an incurable degree, because their laws were
affronted, and the place was polluted. Whereupon
the sober and moderate part of the Jews thought it
proper to have recourse to their governors .again'
while the seditious part, and such as were in the
fervour of their youth, were vehemently inflamed to
fight. The seditious also among the [Gentiles of]
Cæsarea stood ready for the same purpose; (for they
had by agreement, sent the man to sacrifice beforehand, as ready to support him;) so that it soon came
to blows. Hereupon Jucundus, the master of the
horse, who was ordered to prevent the fight, came

thither, and took away the earthen vessel, and endeavoured to put a stop to the sedition; but when
he was overcome by the violence of the people of
Cæsarea, the Jews caught up their books of the law,
and retired to Narbata, which was a place to them
belonging, distant from Cæsarea sixty furlongs. But
John, and twelve of the principal men with him, went
to Florus, to Sebaste, and made a lamentable complaint of their case, and besought him to help them;
and with all possible decency put him in mind of
the eight talents they had given him; but he had the
men seized upon, and put in prison, and accused them
for carrying the books of the law out of Cæsarea.

6. Moreover, as to the citizens of Jerusalem, although they took this matter very ill, yet did they
restrain their passion; but Florus acted herein as if
he had been hired, and blew up the war into a flame,
and sent some to take seventeen talents out of the
sacred treasure, and pretended that Cæsar wanted
them. At this the people were in confusion immediately, and ran together to the temple, with prodigious
clamours, and called upon Cæsar by name, and besought him to free them from the tyranny of Florus.
Some also of the seditious cried out upon Florus,
and cast the greatest reproaches upon him, and
carried a basket about and begged some spills of
money for him, as for one that was destitute of possessions, and in a miserable condition. Yet was not
he made ashamed hereby of his love of money, but
was more enraged, and provoked to get still more;
and instead of coming to Cæsarea, as he ought to have
done, and quenching the flame of war which was
beginning thence, and so taking away the occasion
of any disturbances, on which account it was that
he had received a reward [of eight talents,] he
marched hastily with an army of horsemen and foot-

men against Jerusalem, that he might gain his will
by the arms of the Romans, and might by his terror,
and by his threatenings, bring the city into subjection.
7. But the people were desirous of making Florus
ashamed of his attempt, and met his soldiers with
acclamations, and put themselves in order to receive
him very submissively. But he sent Capito, a centurion, beforehand, with fifty soldiers, to bid them
go back, and not now make a show of receiving him
in an obliging manner, whom they had so fondly
reproached before; and said, that it was incumbent
on them, in case they had generous souls, and were
free speakers, to jest upon him to his face, and appear
to be lovers of liberty, not only in words, but with
their weapons also. With this message was the multitude amazed, and upon the coming of Capito's
horsemen into the midst of them, they were dispersed
before they could salute Florus, or manifest their
submissive behaviour to him. Accordingly, they retired to their own houses, and spent that night in
fear and confusion of face.

8. Now at this time Florus took up his quarters
at the palace; and on the next day he had his tribunal
set before it, and sat upon it, when the high priests,
and the men of power, and those of the greatest
eminence in the city, came all before that tribunal;
upon which Florus commanded them to deliver up
to him those that had reproached him, and told them
that they should themselves partake of the vengeance
to them belonging, if they did not produce the criminals; but these demonstrated that the people were
peaceably disposed, and they begged forgiveness for
those that had spoken amiss; for that it was no
wonder at all that in so great a multitude there should
be some more daring than they ought to be, and
by reason of their younger age foolish also; and that

it was impossible to distinguish those that offended from the rest, while every one was sorry for what he had done, and denied it out of fear of what would follow; that he ought, however, to provide for the peace of the nation, and to take such counsels as might preserve the city for the Romans, and rather for the sake of a great number of innocent people, to forgive a few that were guilty, than for the sake of a few of the wicked, to put so large and good a body of men into disorder.

9. Florus was more provoked at this, and called out aloud to the soldiers to plunder that which was called *The Upper Market Place,* and to slay such as they met with. So the soldiers, taking this exhortation of their commander in a sense agreeable to their desire of gain, did not only plunder the place they were sent to, but forcing themselves into every house, they slew its inhabitants; so the citizens fled along the narrow lanes, and the soldiers slew those that they caught, and no method of plunder was omitted; they also caught many of the quiet people, and brought them before Florus, whom he first chastised with stripes, and then crucified. Accordingly, the whole number of those that were destroyed that day, with their wives and children, (for they did not spare even the infants themselves,) was about three thousand and six hundred. And what made this calamity the heavier, was this new method of Roman barbarity: for Florus ventured then to do what no one had done before, that is, to have men of the [1] equestrian order whipped and nailed to the cross before his tribunal; who although they were by birth Jews, yet were they of Roman dignity notwithstanding.

[1] Here we have examples of native Jews who were of the equestrian order among the Romans, and so ought never to have been whipped or crucified, according to the Roman laws. See almost the like case in St. Paul himself, Acts xxii. 25-29.

CHAPTER XV.

Concerning Bernice's petition to Florus, to spare the Jews, but in vain, as also how, after the seditious flame was quenched, it was kindled again by Florus.

1. ABOUT this very time king Agrippa was going to Alexandria, to congratulate Alexander upon his having obtained the government of Egypt from Nero; but as his sister Bernice was come to Jerusalem, and saw the wicked practices of the soldiers, she was sorely affected at it, and frequently sent the masters of her horse, and her guards, to Florus, and begged of him to leave off these slaughters; but he would not comply with her request, nor have any regard either to the multitude of those already slain, or to the nobility of her that interceded, but only to the advantage he should make by this plundering; nay, this violence of the soldiers broke out to such a degree of madness, that it spent itself on the queen herself, for they did not only torment and destroy those whom they had caught under her very eyes, but indeed had killed herself also, unless she had prevented them by flying to the palace, and had stayed there all night with her guards, which she had about her for fear of an insult from the soldiers. Now she dwelt then at Jerusalem, in order to perform a [1] vow which she

---

[1] This vow which Bernice (here and elsewhere called queen, not only as daughter and sister to two kings, Agrippa the Great, and Agrippa junior, but the widow of Herod king of Chalcis) came now to accomplish at Jerusalem, was not that of a Nazarite, but such a one as religious Jews used to make in hopes of any deliverance from a disease, or other danger, as Josephus here intimates. However, these thirty days' abode at Jerusalem, for fasting and preparation against the oblation of a proper sacrifice, seems to be too long, unless it were wholly voluntary in this great lady. It is not required in the law of Moses relating

had made to God; for it is usual with those that had
been either afflicted with a distemper, or with any
other distresses, to make vows; and for thirty days
before they are to offer their sacrifices, to abstain
from wine, and to shave the hair of their head. Which
things Bernice was now performing, and stood barefoot before Florus' tribunal, and besought him [to
spare the Jews.] Yet could she neither have any
reverence paid to her, nor could she escape without
some danger of being slain herself.

2. This happened upon the sixteenth day of the
month Artemisius, [Jyar.] Now on the next day,
the multitude who were in a great agony, ran together
to the upper market-place, and made the loudest
lamentations for those that had perished; and the
greatest part of the cries were such as reflected on
Florus; at which the men of power were affrighted,
together with the high priests, and rent their garments,
and fell down before each of them, and besought
them to leave off, and not to provoke Florus to some
incurable procedure, besides what they had already
suffered. Accordingly, the multitude complied immediately, out of reverence to those that had desired
it of them, and out of the hope they had that Florus
would do them no more injuries.

3. So Florus was troubled that the disturbances
were over, and endeavoured to kindle that flame

to Nazarites, Numb. vi. and is very different from St. Paul's time for
such preparation, which was but one day, Acts xxi. 26. So we want
already the continuation of the Antiquities to afford us light here, as
they have hitherto done, on so many occasions elsewhere. Perhaps in
this age the traditions of the Pharisees had obliged the Jews to this
degree of rigour, not only as to these thirty days' preparation, but as
to the going barefoot all that time, which here Bernice submitted to also.
Noldius well observes, De Herod, No. 404, 414, that Juvenal, in his
sixth satire, alludes to this remarkable penance of submission of this
Bernice to Jewish discipline, and jests upon her for it, as do Tacitus,
Dio, Suetonius, and Sextus Aurelius mention her as well known at
Rome. ibid.

again, and sent for the high priests, with the other
eminent persons, and said, The only demonstration
that the people would not make any other innovations
should be this, that they must go out and meet the
soldiers that were ascending from Cæsarea, whence
two cohorts were coming; and while these men were
exhorting the multitude so to do, he sent beforehand,
and gave directions to the centurions of the cohorts,
that they should give notice to those that were under
them, not to return the Jews' salutations, and that
if they made any reply to his disadvantage, they
should make use of their weapons. Now the high
priests assembled the multitude in the temple, and
desired them to go and meet the Romans and to
salute the cohorts very civilly, before their miserable
case should become incurable. Now the seditious part
would not comply with these persuasions, but the
consideration of those that had been destroyed made
them incline to those that were the boldest for action.

4. At this time it was that every priest, and every
servant of God, brought out the holy vessels, and the
ornamental garments wherein they used to minister
in sacred things. The harpers also, and the singers
of hymns, came out with their instruments of music,
and fell down before the multitude, and begged of
them that they would preserve those holy ornaments
to them, and not provoke the Romans to carry off
those sacred treasures. You might also see then the
high priests themselves, with dust sprinkled in great
plenty upon their heads, with bosoms deprived of
any covering, but what was rent; these besought
every one of the eminent men by name, and the multitude in common, that they would not for a small
offence betray their country to those that were desirous to have it laid waste; saying, "What benefit
will it bring to the soldiers to have a salutation from

the Jews? or what amendment of your affairs will
it bring you, if you do not now go out to meet them?
and that if they saluted them civilly, all handle would
be cut off from Florus to begin a war; that they
should thereby gain their country, and freedom from
all farther sufferings; and that, besides, it would be
a sign of great want of command of themselves, if
they should yield to a few seditious persons, while
it was fitter for them, who were so great a people,
to force the others to act soberly."

5. By these persuasions, which they used to the
multitude, and to the seditious, they restrained some
by threatenings, and others by the reverence that was
paid them. After this they led them out, and they
met the soldiers quietly, and after a composed manner,
and when they were come up with them, they saluted
them, but when they made no answer, the seditious
exclaimed against Florus, which was the signal given
for falling upon them. The soldiers therefore encompassed them presently, and struck them with
their clubs, and as they fled away, the horsemen
trampled them down, so that a great many fell down
dead by the strokes of the Romans, and more by their
own violence in crushing one another. Now there
was a terrible crowding about the gates, and while
everybody was making haste to get before another,
the flight of them all was retarded, and a terrible
destruction there was among those that fell down,
for they were suffocated, and broken to pieces by
the multitude of those that were uppermost; nor
could any of them be distinguished by his relations in
order to the care of his funeral; the soldiers also who
beat them, fell upon those whom they overtook, without showing them any mercy, and thrust the multitude through the place called Bezetha, as they forced
their way in order to get it and seize upon the temple,

and the tower Antonia. Florus also being desirous
to get those·places into his possession, brought such
as were with him out of the king's palace, and would
have compelled them to get as far as the citadel
[Antonia;] but his attempt failed, for the people
immediately turned back upon him, and stopped the
violence of his attempt, and as they stood upon the
tops of their houses, they threw their darts at the
Romans, who, as they were sorely galled thereby,
because those weapons came from above, and they
were not able to make a passage through the multitude, which stopped up the narrow passages, they
retired to the camp which was at the palace.

6. But for the seditious, they were afraid lest
Florus should come again, and get possession of the
temple, through Antonia; so they got immediately
upon those cloisters of the temple that joined to
Antonia, and cut them down. This cooled the avarice
of Florus, for whereas he was eager to obtain the
treasures of God [in the temple,] and on that account was desirous of getting into Antonia, as soon
as the cloisters were broken down, he left off his
attempt; he then sent for the high priests and the
sanhedrim, and told them that he was indeed himself going out of the city, but that he would leave
them as large a garrison as they should desire: hereupon they promised that they would make no innovations, in case he would leave them one band; but
not that which had fought with the Jews, because
the multitude bore ill will against that band on account
of what they had suffered from it; so he changed
the band as they desired, and, with the rest of his
forces, returned to Cæsarea.

CHAPTER XVI.

*Cestius sends Neopolitanus the tribune to see in what
condition the affairs of the Jews were. Agrippa
makes a speech to the people of the Jews, that he
may divert them from their intentions of making
war with the Romans.*

1. However, Florus contrived another way to
oblige the Jews to begin the war, and sent to Cestius,
and accused the Jews falsely of revolting [from the
Roman government,] and imputed the beginning of
the former fight to them, and pretended they had
been the authors of that disturbance, wherein they
were only the sufferers. Yet were not the governors
of Jerusalem silent upon this occasion, but did themselves write to Cestius, as did Bernice also, about the
illegal practices of which Florus had been guilty
against the city; who, upon reading both accounts,
consulted with his captains [what he should do.] Now
some of them thought it best for Cestius to go up
with his army, either to punish the revolt, if it was
real, or to settle the Roman affairs on a surer foundation, if the Jews continued quiet under them: but he
thought it best himself to send one of his intimate
friends beforehand, to see the state of affairs, and to
give him a faithful account of the intention of the
Jews. Accordingly he sent one of his tribunes, whose
name was Neopolitanus, who met with king Agrippa,
as he was returning from Alexandria at Jamnia, and
told him who it was that sent him, and on what errand
he was sent.

2. And here it was that the high priests, and men
of power among the Jews, as well as the sanhedrim,

came to congratulate the king [upon his safe return,]
and after they had paid him their respects, they
lamented their own calamities, and related to him
what barbarous treatment they had met with from
Florus. At which barbarity Agrippa had great indignation, but transferred, after a subtle manner, his
anger towards those Jews whom he really pitied,
that he might beat down their high thoughts of themselves, and would have them believe that they had not
been so unjustly treated, in order to dissuade them
from avenging themselves. So these great men, as
of better understanding than the rest, and desirous
of peace, because of the possessions they had, understood that this rebuke which the king gave them was
intended for their good; but, as to the people, they
came sixty furlongs out of Jerusalem, and congratulated both Agrippa and Neopolitanus; but the wives
of those that had been slain, came running first of
all and lamenting. The people also, when they heard
their mourning, fell into lamentations also, and besought Agrippa to assist them: they also cried out
to Neopolitanus, and complained of the many miseries
they had endured under Florus, and they showed
them, when they were come into the city, how the
market-place was made desolate, and the houses plundered. They then persuaded Neopolitanus, by the
means of Agrippa, that he would walk round the
city, with one only servant, as far as Siloam, that
he might inform himself that the Jews submitted to
all the rest of the Romans, and were only displeased
at Florus, by reason of his exceeding barbarity to
them. So he walked round, and had sufficient experience of the good temper the people were in, and
then went up to the temple, where he called the
multitude together, and highly commended them for
their fidelity to the Romans, and earnestly exhorted

them to keep the peace, and having performed such parts of divine worship at the temple as he was allowed to do, he returned to Cestius.

3. But as for the multitude of the Jews, they addressed themselves to the king, and to the high priests, and desired they might have leave to send ambassadors to Nero against Florus, and not by their silence afford a suspicion that they had been the occasions of such great slaughter, as had been made, and were disposed to revolt, alleging, that they should seem to have been the first beginners of the war, if they did not prevent the report by showing who it was that began it; and it appeared openly that they would not be quiet, if anybody should hinder them from sending such an embassage. But Agrippa, although he thought it too dangerous a thing for them to appoint men to go as the accusers of Florus, yet did he not think it fit for him to overlook them as they were in a disposition for war. He therefore called the multitude together into a large gallery, and placed his sister Bernice in the house of the Asamoneans, that she might be seen by them, (which house was over the gallery, at the passage to the upper city, where the bridge joined the temple to the gallery,) and spoke to them as follows.

4. [1] "Had I perceived that you were all zealously

---

[1] In this speech of king Agrippa we have an authentic account of the extent and strength of the Roman empire when the Jewish war began. And this speech, with other circumstances in Josephus, demonstrate how wise, and how great a person Agrippa was, and why Josephus elsewhere calls him a "most wonderful" or "admirable man," Contr. Ap. I. 9. He is the same Agrippa who said to Paul, "Almost thou persuadest me to be a Christian," Acts xxvi. 28, and of whom St. Paul said, "He was expert in all the customs and questions of the Jews," ver. 3. See another intimation of the limits of the same Roman empire, Of the War, B. III. ch. v. sect. 7, Vol. III. But what seems to me very remarkable here is this, that when Josephus, in imitation of the Greeks and Romans, for whose use he wrote his Antiquities, did himself frequently compose the speeches which he put into their mouth; they appear, by the politeness of their composition, and their flights of oratory, to be not the real

disposed to go to war with the Romans, and that
the purer and more sincere part of the people did not
purpose to live in peace, I had not come out to you,
nor been so bold as to give you counsel; for all discourses that tend to persuade men to do what they
ought to do is superfluous, when the hearers are agreed
to do the contrary. But because some are earnest to
go to war, because they are young, and without
experience of the miseries it brings, and because some
are for it, out of an unreasonable expectation of
regaining their liberty, and because others hope to
get by it, and are therefore earnestly bent upon it,
that in the confusion of your affairs they may gain
what belongs to those that are too weak to resist
them, I have thought proper to get you all together,
and to say to you what I think to be for your advantage; that so the former may grow wiser, and
change their minds, and that the best men may come
to no harm by the ill conduct of some others. And
let not any one be tumultuous against me, in case
what they hear me say do not please them; for as to
those that admit of no cure, but are resolved upon a
revolt, it will still be in their power to retain the
same sentiments after my exhortation is over; but
still my discourse will fall to the ground, even with
relation to those that have a mind to hear me, unless
you will all keep silence. I am well aware that they
make a tragical exclamation concerning the injuries
that have been offered you by your procurators, and

speeches of the persons concerned, who usually were no orators, but of
his own elegant composure: the speech before us is of another nature
full of undeniable facts, and composed in a plain and unartful, but
moving way; so it appears to be king Agrippa's own speech, and to
have been given Josephus by Agrippa himself, with whom Josephus had
the greatest friendship. Nor may we omit Agrippa's constant doctrine
here, that this vast Roman empire was raised and supported by divine
providence, and that therefore it was in vain for the Jews, or any others,
to think of destroying it.

concerning the glorious advantages of liberty; but before I begin the inquiry, who are you that must go to war? and who they are against whom you must fight? I shall first separate those pretences that are by some connected together; for if you aim at avenging yourselves on those that have done you injury, why do you pretend this to be a war for recoving your liberty? but if you think all servitude intolerable, to what purpose serve your complaints against your particular governors? for if they treated you with moderation, it would still be equally an unworthy thing to be in servitude. Consider now the several cases that may be supposed, how little occasion there is for your going to war. Your first occasion is the accusations you have to make against your procurators: now here you ought to be submissive to those in authority, and not give them any provocation; but when you reproach men greatly for small offences, you excite those whom you reproach to be your adversaries; for this will only make them leave off hurting you privately, and with some degree of modesty, and to lay what you have waste openly. Now nothing so much damps the force of strokes as bearing them with patience; and the quietness of those who are injured diverts the injurious persons from afflicting. But let us take it for granted, that the Roman ministers are injurious to you, and are incurably severe; yet are they not at all the Romans who thus injure you; nor hath Cæsar, against whom you are going to make war, injured you; it is not by their command that any wicked governor is sent to you; for they who are in the west cannot see those that are in the east; nor indeed is it easy for them there, even to hear what is done in those parts. Now it is absurd to make war with a great many for the sake of one; to do so with such mighty people, for

a small cause: and this when these people are not
able to know of what you complain; nay, such crimes
as we complain of may soon be corrected, for the
same procurator will not continue for ever; and
probable it is, that the successors will come with more
moderate inclinations. But as for war, if it be once
begun, it is not easily laid down again, nor borne
without calamities coming therewith. However, as to
the desire of recovering your liberty, it is unseasonable to indulge it so late; whereas you ought to have
laboured earnestly in old time that you might never
have lost it; for the first experience of slavery was
hard to be endured, and the struggle that you might
never have been subject to it would have been just;
but that slave who hath been once brought into sub
jection, and then runs away, is rather a refractory
slave than a lover of liberty, for it was then the
proper time for doing all that was possible, that you
might never have admitted the Romans [into your
city,] when Pompey came first into the country.
But so it was, that so our ancestors and their kings,
who were in much better circumstances than we are,
both as to money and [strong] bodies, and [valiant]
souls, did not bear the onset of a small body of the
Roman army. And yet you who have not accustomed yourselves to obedience from one generation
to another, and who are so much inferior to those
who first submitted, in your circumstances, will venture to oppose the entire empire of the Romans;
while those Athenians, who, in order to preserve the
liberty of Greece, did once set fire to their own city,
who pursued Xerxes, that proud prince, when he
sailed upon the land, and walked upon the sea, and
could not be contained by the seas, but conducted
such an army as was too broad for Europe, and
made him run away like a fugitive in a single ship,

and broke so great a part of Asia, at the lesser
Salamis, are yet at this time servants to the Romans;
and those injunctions which are sent from Italy, become laws to the principal governing city of Greece.
Those Lacedemonians also, who got the great victories at Thermopylæ and Platea, and had Agesilaus
[for their king,] and searched every corner of Asia, are
contented to admit the same lords. These Macedonians
also, who still fancy what great men their Philip and
Alexander were, and see that the latter had promised
them the empire over the world, these bear so great
a change, and pay their obedience to those whom
fortune hath advanced in their stead. Moreover, ten
thousand other nations there are, who had greater
reason than we to claim their entire liberty, and yet
do submit. You are the only people who think it a
disgrace to be servants to those to whom all the world
hath submitted. What sort of an army do you rely
on? What are the arms you depend on? Where
is your fleet, that may seize upon the Roman seas,
and where are those treasures which may be sufficient
for your undertakings? Do you suppose, I pray
you, that you are to make war with the Egyptians,
and with the Arabians? Will you not carefully reflect upon the Roman empire? Will you not estimate
your own weakness? Hath not your army been often
beaten even by your neighbouring nations? while the
power of the Romans is invincible in all parts of the
habitable earth; nay, rather, they seek for somewhat
still beyond that, for all Euphrates is not a sufficient
boundary for them on the east side, nor the Danube
on the north, and for their southern limit, Libya hath
been searched over by them, as far as countries uninhabited, as is Cadiz their limit on the west; nay,
indeed, they have sought for another habitable earth,
beyond the ocean, and have carried their arms as far

as such British islands as were never known before.
What therefore do you pretend to? Are you richer
than the Gauls, stronger than the Germans, wiser
than the Greeks, more numerous than all men upon
the habitable earth? What confidence is it that
elevates you to oppose the Romans? Perhaps it will
be said, it is hard to endure slavery. Yes, but how
much harder is this to the Greeks, who were esteemed
the noblest of all people under the sun. These,
though they inhabit in a large country, are in subjection to six bundles of Roman rods? It is the
same case with the Macedonians, who have juster
reason to claim their liberty than you have. What is
the case of five hundred cities of Asia? do they not
submit to a single governor, and to the consular
bundle of rods? What need I speak of the Heniochi,
and Cholchi, and the nation of Tauri, those that
inhabit the Bosphorus, and the nations about Pontus,
and Meotis, who formerly knew not so much as a
lord of their own, but are now subject to three
thousand armed men, and where forty long ships
kept the sea in peace, which before was not navigable,
and very tempestuous? How strong a plea may
Bithynia, and Cappadocia, and the people of Pam-
phylia, the Lycians, and Cilicians, put in for liberty?
But they are made tributary without an army. What
are the circumstances of the Thracians? whose country
extends in breadth five days' journey, and in length
seven, and is of a much more harsh constitution, and
much more defensible than yours, and by the rigour
of its cold sufficient to keep off armies from attacking
them; do not they submit to two thousand men of the
Roman garrisons? Are not the Illyrians, who inhabit the country adjoining, as far as Dalmatia and
the Danube, governed by barely two legions! by
which also they put a stop to the incursions of the

Dacians. And for the Dalmatians, who have made such frequent insurrections in order to regain their liberty, and who could never before be so thoroughly subdued, but that they always gathered their forces together again, and revolted, yet are they now very quiet under one Roman legion. Moreover, if great advantages might provoke any people to revolt, the Gauls might do it best of all, as being so thoroughly walled round by nature. On the east side by the Alps, on the north by the river Rhine, on the south by the Pyrenean mountains, and on the west by the ocean. Now although these Gauls have such obstacles before them to prevent any attack upon them, and have no fewer than three hundred and five nations among them, nay have, as one may say, the fountains of domestic happiness within themselves, and send out plentiful streams of happiness over almost the whole world, these bear to be tributary to the Romans, and derive their prosperous condition from them; and they undergo this, not because they are of effeminate minds, or because they are of an ignoble stock, as having borne a war of eighty years, in order to preserve their liberty: but by reason of the great regard they have to the power of the Romans, and their good fortune, which is of greater efficacy than their arms. These Gauls, therefore, are kept in servitude by twelve hundred soldiers, which are hardly so many as are their cities; nor hath the gold dug out of the mines of Spain been sufficient for the support of a war to preserve their liberty, nor could their vast distance from the Romans by land and by sea do it; nor could the martial tribes of the Lusitanians and Spaniards escape; no more could the ocean, with its tide, which yet was terrible to the ancient inhabitants. Nay, the Romans have extended their arms beyond the pillars of Hercules, and have

walked among the clouds, upon the Pyrenean mountains, and have subdued these nations. And one
legion is a sufficient guard for these people, although
they were so hard to be conquered, and at a distance
so remote from Rome. Who is there among you
who hath not heard of the great number of the
Germans? You have, to be sure, yourselves seen
them to be strong and tall, and that frequently, since
the Romans have them among their captives, everywhere; yet these Germans who dwell in an immense
country, who have minds greater than their bodies,
and a soul that despiseth death, and who are in rage
more fierce than wild beasts, have the Rhine for the
boundary of their enterprises, and are tamed by
eight Roman legions. Such of them as were taken
captive became their servants; and the rest of the
entire nation were obliged to save themselves by flight.
Do you also, who depend on the walls of Jerusalem,
consider what a wall the Britons had; for the Romans
sailed away to them, and subdued them while they
were encompassed by the ocean, and inhabited an
island that is not less than the [continent of this]
habitable earth; and four legions are a sufficient guard
to so large an island. And why should I speak
much more about this matter? while the Parthians,
that most warlike body of men, and lords of so many
nations, and encompassed with such mighty forces,
send hostages to the Romans; whereby you may see
if you please, even in Italy, the noblest nation of the
east, under the notion of peace submitting to serve
them. Now when almost all people under the sun
submit to the Roman arms, will you be the only
people that make war against them? and this without
regarding the fate of the Carthaginians, who, in the
midst of the brags of the great Hannibal, and the
nobility of their Phenician original, fell by the hand

of Scipio. Nor indeed have the Cyrenians, derived
from the Lacedemonians, nor the Marmaridæ: a
nation extended as far as the regions uninhabitable
for want of water, nor have the Syrtes, a place terrible to such as barely hear it described, the Nasamons
and Moors, and the immense multitude of the Nu-
midians, being able to put a stop to the Roman valour.
And as for the third part of the habitable earth,
[Africa,] whose nations are so many that it is not
easy to number them, and which is bounded by the
Atlantic sea and the pillars of Hercules, and feeds
an innumerable multitude of Ethiopians, as far as
the Red Sea, these have the Romans subdued entirely.
And besides the annual fruits of the earth, which
maintain the multitude of the Romans for eight
months in the year, this, over and above, pays all
sorts of tribute, and affords revenues suitable to the
necessities of the government. Nor do they, like
you, esteem such injunctions a disgrace to them,
although they have but one Roman legion that abides
among them. And indeed what occasion is there
for showing you the power of the Romans over remote countries, when it is so easy to learn it from
Egypt, in your neighbourhood? This country is extended as far as the Ethiopians, and Arabia the
Happy, and borders upon India; it hath seven millions
five hundred thousand men, besides the inhabitants
of Alexandria, as may be learned from the revenue
of the pole tax; yet it is not ashamed to submit to
the Roman government, although it hath Alexandria
as a grand temptation to a revolt, by reason it is
so full of people and of riches, and is besides exceeding large, its length being thirty furlongs, and
its breadth no less than ten; and it pays more tribute
to the Romans in one month than you do in a year;
nay, besides what it pays in money, it sends corn to

Rome that supports it for four months [in the year:]
it is also walled round on all sides, either by almost
impassable deserts, or seas that have no havens, or by
rivers, or by lakes; yet have none of these things
been found too strong for the Roman good fortune;
however, two legions that lie in that city are a bridle
both for the remoter parts of Egypt, and for the
parts inhabited by the more noble Macedonians.
Where then are those people whom you are to have
for your auxiliaries? Must they come from the parts
of the world that are uninhabited? for all that are
in the habitable earth are [under the] Romans. Unless any of you extend his hopes as far as beyond
the Euphrates, and suppose that those of your own
nation that dwell in Adiabene will come to your
assistance; but certainly these will not embarrass themselves with an unjustifiable war, nor, if they should
follow such ill advice, will the Parthians permit them
so to do; for it is their concern to maintain the truce
that is between them and the Romans, and they will
be supposed to break the covenants between them,
if any under their government march against the
Romans. What remains, therefore, is this, that you
have recourse to divine assistance; but this is already
on the side of the Romans: for it is impossible that
so vast an empire should be settled without God's
providence. Reflect upon it, how impossible it is
for your zealous observation of your religious customs to be here preserved, which are hard to be observed even when you fight with those whom you
are able to conquer; and how can you then most of
all hope for God's assistance, when, by being forced
to transgress his law, you will make him turn his face
from you? and if you do observe the custom of the
sabbath days, and will not be prevailed on to do any
thing thereon, you will easily be taken, as were your

forefathers by Pompey, who was the busiest in his
siege on those days on which the besieged rested.
But if in time of war you transgress the law of your
country, I cannot tell on whose account you will
afterward go to war; for your concern is but one,
that you do nothing against any of your forefathers;
and how will you call upon God to assist you, when
you are voluntarily transgressing against his religion?
Now all men that go to war do it either as depending
on divine, or on human assistance; but since your
going to war will cut off both those assistances, those
that are for going to war choose evident destruction.
What hinders you from slaying your children and
wives with your own hands, and burning this most
excellent native city of yours? for by this mad prank
you will, however, escape the reproach of being beaten.
But it were best, O my friends, it were best, while
the vessel is still in the haven, to foresee the impend-
ing storm, and not to set sail out of the port into the
middle of the hurricanes, for we justly pity those
who fall into great misfortunes without foreseeing
them; but for him who rushes into manifest ruin, he
gains reproaches [instead of commiseration.] But
certainly no one can imagine that you can enter into
a war as by agreement, or that when the Romans have
got you under their power, they will use you with
moderation, or will not rather, for an example to
other nations, burn your holy city, and utterly destroy your whole nation; for those of you who shall
survive the war, will not be able to find a place
whither to flee, since all men have the Romans for
their lords already, or are afraid they shall have
hereafter. Nay, indeed the danger concerns not those
Jews that dwell here only, but those of them who
dwell in other cities also; for there is no people upon
the habitable earth which have not some portion of

you among them, whom your enemies will slay, in
case you go to war, and on that account also; and
so every city which hath Jews in it will be filled with
slaughter for the sake of a few men, and they who
slay them will be pardoned: but if that slaughter be
not made by them, consider how wicked a thing it
is to take arms against those that are so kind to you.
Have pity, therefore, if not on your children and
wives, yet upon this your metropolis, and its sacred
walls; spare the temple, and preserve the holy house,
with its holy furniture, for yourselves: for if the
Romans get you under their power, they will no
longer abstain from them when their former abstinence
shall have been so ungratefully requited. I call to
witness your sanctuary, and the holy angels of God,
and this country common to us all, that I have not
kept back any thing that is for your preservation;
and if you will follow that advice which you ought
to do, you will have that peace which will be common
to you and to me; but if you indulge your passions,
you will run those hazards which I shall be free from."

5. When Agrippa had spoken thus, both he and
his sister wept, and by their tears repressed a great
deal of the violence of the people, but still they cried
out, That "they would not fight against the Romans,
but against Florus, on account of what they had
suffered by his means." To which Agrippa replied,
"that what they had already done was like such as
make war against the Romans; for you have not
paid the [1] tribute which is due to Cæsar; and you
have cut off the cloisters [of the temple] from joining
to the tower Antonia. You will therefore prevent
any occasion of revolt if you will but join these to-

---

[1] Julius Cæsar had decreed, that the Jews of Jerusalem should pay
an annual tribute to the Romans, excepting the city Joppa, and for the
Sabbatical year, Antiq. B, XIV, ch. x. sect, 6, Vol. II,

gether again, and if you will but pay your tribute; for the citadel does not now belong to Florus, nor are you to pay the tribute money to Florus."

CHAPTER XVII.

How the war of the Jews with the Romans began. And concerning Manahem.

1. THIS advice the people hearkened to, and went up into the temple with the king and Bernice, and began to rebuild the cloisters: the rulers also and senators divided themselves into the villages, and collected the tributes, and soon got together forty talents, which was the sum that was deficient. And thus did Agrippa then put a stop to that war which was threatened. Moreover, he attempted to persuade the multitude to obey Florus, until Cæsar should send one to succeed him; but they were hereby more provoked, and cast reproaches upon the king, and got him excluded out of the city; nay, some of the seditious had the impudence to throw stones at him. So when the king saw that the violence of those that were for innovations was not to be restrained, and being very angry at the contumelies he had received, he sent their rulers, together with their men of power, to Florus, to Cæsarea, that he might appoint whom he thought fit to collect the tribute in the country, while he retired into his own kingdom.

2. And at this time it was that some of those that principally excited the people to go to war, made an assault upon a certain fortress called Massada. They took it by treachery, and slew the Romans that were there, and put others of their own party to keep it.

At the same time Eleazar, the son of Ananias the
high priest, a very bold youth, who was at that time
governor of the temple, persuaded those that officiated
in the divine service to receive no gift or sacrifice for
any foreigner. And this was the true beginning of
our war with the Romans; for they rejected the sacrifice of Cæsar on this account; and when many of
the high priests and principal men besought them
not to omit the sacrifice, which it was customary for
them to offer for their princes, they would not be
prevailed upon. These relied much upon their multitude, for the most flourishing part of the innovators
assisted them; but they had the chief regard to
Eleazar, the governor of the temple.

3. Hereupon the men of power got together, and
conferred with the high priests, as did also the principal men of the Pharisees; and thinking all was at
stake, and that their calamities were becoming incurable, took counsel what was to be done. Accord
ingly they determined to try what they could do with
the seditious by words, and assembled the people before the brazen gate, which was that gate of the
inner temple [court of the priests] which looked
toward the sun rising. And, in the first place, they
showed the great indignation they had at this attempt
for a revolt, and for their bringing so great a war
upon their country: after which they confuted their
pretence as unjustifiable, and told them, That "their
forefathers had adorned their temple in great part
with donations bestowed on them by foreigners, and
had always received what had been presented to them
from foreign nations; and that they had been so far
from rejecting any person's sacrifice, (which would
be the highest instance of impiety,) that they had
themselves placed those donations about the temple
which were still visible, and had remained there so

long a time: that they did now irritate the Romans to take arms against them, and invited them to make war upon them, and brought up novel rules of a strange divine worship, and determined to run the hazard of having their city condemned for impiety, while they would not allow any foreigner, but Jews only, either to sacrifice or to worship therein. And if such a law should be introduced in the case of a single private person only, he would have indignation at it, as an instance of inhumanity determined against him; while they have no regard to the Romans or to Cæsar, and forbid even their oblations to be received also: that however they cannot but fear, lest by their rejecting his sacrifices, they shall not be allowed to offer their own; and that this city will lose its principality, unless they grow wiser quickly, and restore the sacrifices as formerly, and indeed amend the injury they have offered foreigners before the report of it comes to the ears of those that have been injured."

4. And as they said these things, they produced those priests that were skilful in the customs of their country, who made the report, That "all their forefathers had received the sacrifices from foreign nations." But still not one of the innovators would hearken to what was said; nay, those that ministered about the temple would not attend their divine service, but were preparing matters for beginning the war. So the men of power perceiving that the sedition was too hard for them to subdue, and that the danger which would arise from the Romans, would come upon them first of all, endeavoured to save themselves, and sent ambassadors, some to Florus, the chief of which was Simon the son of Ananias; and others to Agrippa, among whom the most eminent were Saul, and Antipas, and Costobarus, who were

of the king's kindred: and they desired of them both
that they would come with an army to the city, and
cut off the sedition before it should be too hard to
be subdued. Now this terrible message was good
news to Florus; and because his design was to have
a war kindled, he gave the ambassadors no answer
at all. But Agrippa was equally solicitous for those
that were revolting, and for those against whom the
war was to be made, and was desirous to preserve
the Jews for the Romans, and the temple and metropolis for the Jews; he was also sensible that it was
not for his own advantage that the disturbances
should proceed; so he sent three thousand horsemen
to the assistance of the people out of Auranitis, and
Batanea, and Trachonitis, and these under Darius
the master of his horse, and Philip the son of Jacimus,
the general of his army.

5. Upon this the men of power, with the high
priests, as also all the part of the multitude that were
desirous of peace, took courage, and seized upon the
upper city [Mount Sion;] for the seditious part had
the lower city and the temple in their power: so they
made use of stones and slings perpetually against one
another, and threw darts continually on both sides;
and sometimes it happened that they made incursions
by troops, and fought it out hand to hand, while the
seditious were superior in boldness, but the king's
soldiers in skill. These last strove chiefly to gain
the temple, and to drive those out of it who profaned
it; as did the seditious, with Eleazar, besides what
they had already, labour to gain the upper city. Thus
were there perpetual slaughters on both sides for
seven days' time; but neither side would yield up
the parts they had seized on.

6. Now the next day was the festival of Xylo-
phory, upon which the custom was for every one to

bring wood for the altar, (that there might never be a want of fuel for that fire which was unquenchable and always burning;) upon that day they excluded the opposite party from the observation of this part of religion. And when they had joined to themselves many of the Sicarii, who crowded in among the weaker people (that was the name for such robbers as had under their bosoms swords called *Sicæ*) they grew bolder, and carried their undertaking farther; insomuch, that the king's soldiers were overpowered by their multitude and boldness, and so they gave way, and were driven out of the upper city by force. The others then set fire to the house of Ananias the high priest, and to the palaces of Agrippa and Bernice: after which they carried the fire to the place where the archives were reposited, and made haste to burn the contracts belonging to their creditors, and thereby to dissolve their obligations for paying their debts, and this was done in order to gain the multitude of those who had been debtors, and that they might persuade the poorest sort to join in their insurrection with safety, against the more wealthy; so the keepers of the records fled away, and the rest set fire to them. And when they had thus burnt down the nerves of the city, they fell upon their enemies; at which time some of the men of power, and of the high priests, went into the vaults under ground, and concealed themselves, while others fled with the king's soldiers to the upper palace, and shut the gates immediately; among whom were Ananias the high priest, and the ambassadors that had been sent to Agrippa. And now the seditious were contented with the victory they had gotten, and the buildings they had burnt down, and proceeded no farther.

7. But on the next day, which was the fifteenth

of the month Lous, [Ab,] they made an assault upon
Antonia, and besieged the garrison which was in it
two days, and then took the garrison, and slew them,
and set the citadel on fire; after which they marched
to the palace, whither the king's soldiers were fled,
and parted themselves into four bodies, and made
an attack upon the walls. As for those that were
within it, no one had the courage to sally out, because those that assaulted them were so numerous,
but they distributed themselves into the breast-works
and turrets, and shot at the besiegers, whereby many
of the robbers fell under the walls; nor did they cease
to fight one with another either by night or by day,
while the seditious supposed that those within would
grow weary for want of food, and those within supposed the others would do the like by the tediousness
of the siege.

8. In the meantime one Manahem, the son of
Judas, that was called the *Galilean,* (who was a very
cunning sophister, and had formerly reproached the
Jews under Cyrenius, that after God they were subject to the Romans,) took some of the men of note
with him, and retired to Massada, where he broke
open king Herod's armoury, and gave arms not only
to his own people, but to other robbers also. These
he made use of for a guard, and returned in the
state of a king to Jerusalem; he became the leader
of the sedition, and gave orders for continuing the
siege, but they wanted proper instruments, and it
was not practicable to undermine the wall, because
the darts came down upon them from above. But
still they dug a mine from a great distance under
one of the towers and made it totter, and having
done that, they set fire on what was combustible, and
left it, and when the foundations were burnt below,
the tower fell down suddenly. Yet did they then

meet with another wall that had been built within;
for the besieged were sensible beforehand of what
they were doing, and probably the tower shook as it
was undermining, so they provided themselves of
another fortification; which, when the besiegers unexpectedly saw, while they thought they had already
gained the place, they were under some consternation. However, those that were within sent to Manahem, and to the other leaders of the sedition, and
desired they might go out upon a capitulation: this
was granted to the king's soldiers, and their own
countrymen only, who went out accordingly; but the
Romans that were left alone were greatly dejected,
for they were not able to force their way through
such a multitude; and to desire them to give them
their right hand for their security, they thought it
would be a reproach to them, and besides, if they
should give it them, they durst not depend upon it;
so they deserted their camp, as easily taken, and ran
away to the royal towers, that called *Hippicus,* that
called *Phasaelus,* and that called *Mariamne.* But
Manahem and his party fell upon the place whence
the soldiers were fled, and slew as many of them as
they could catch, before they got up to the towers,
and plundered what they left behind them, and set
fire to their camp. This was executed on the sixth
day of the month Gorpieus, [Elul.]

9. But on the next day the high priest was caught,
where he had concealed himself in an aqueduct; he
was slain, together with Hezekiah his brother, by
the robbers: hereupon the seditious besieged the
towers, and kept them guarded, lest any one of the
soldiers should escape. Now the overthrow of the
places of strength, and the death of the high priest
Ananias, so puffed up Manahem, that he became
barbarously cruel, and, as he thought he had no an-

tagonists to dispute the management of affairs with him, he was no better than an insupportable tyrant; but Eleazar and his party, when words had passed between them, how "It was not proper when they revolted from the Romans, out of the desire of liberty, to betray that liberty to any of their own people, and to bear a lord, who, though he should be guilty of no violence, was yet meaner than themselves; as also, that in case they were obliged to set some one over their public affairs, it was fitter they should give that privilege to any one rather than to him," they made an assault upon him in the temple; for he went up thither to worship in a pompous manner, and adorned with royal garments, and had his followers with him in their armour. But Eleazar and his party fell violently upon him, as did also the rest of the people, and taking up stones to attack him withal, they threw them at the sophister, and thought, that if he were once ruined, the entire sedition would fall to the ground. Now Manahem and his party made resistance for a while, but when they perceived that the whole multitude were falling upon them, they fled which way every one was able, those that were caught were slain, and those that hid themselves were searched for. A few there were of them who privately escaped to Masada, among whom was Eleazar, the son of Jairus, who was of kin to Manahem, and acted the part of a tyrant at Masada afterward: as for Manahem himself, he ran away to the place called *Ophla,* and there lay skulking in private; but they took him alive, and drew him out before them all; they then tortured him with many sorts of torments, and after all slew him, as they did by those that were captains under him also, and particularly bv the principal instrument of his tyranny, whose name was *Apsalom.*

10. And, as I said, so far truly the people assisted them, while they hoped this might afford some amendment to the seditious practices; but the others were not in haste to put an end to the war, but hoped to prosecute it with less danger, now they had slain Manahem. It is true, that when the people earnestly desired that they would leave off besieging the soldiers, they were the more earnest in pressing it forward, and this till Metilius, who was the Roman general, sent to Eleazar, and desired that they would give them security to spare their lives only, but agreed to deliver up their arms, and what else they had with them. The others readily complied with their petition, sent to them Gorion, the son of Nicodemus, and Ananias, the son of Sadduk, and Judas, the son of Jonathan, that they might give them the security of their right hands, and of their oaths; after which Metilius brought down his soldiers, which soldiers while they were in arms, were not meddled with by any of the seditious, nor was there any appearance of treachery; but as soon as, according to the articles of capitulation, they had all laid down their shields, and their swords, and were under no farther suspicion of any harm, but were going away, Eleazar's men attacked them after a violent manner, and encompassed them round, and slew them, while they neither defended themselves, nor entreated for mercy, but only cried out upon the breach of their articles of capitulation, and their oaths. And thus were all these men barbarously murdered, excepting Metilius; for when he entreated for mercy, and promised that he would turn Jew, and be circumcised, they saved him alive, but none else. This loss to the Romans was but light, there being no more than a few slain out of an immense army; but still it appeared to be a prelude to the Jews' own destruction, while men

made public lamentation when they saw that such
occasions were afforded for a war as were incurable;
that the city was all over polluted with such abomina-
tions, from which it was but reasonable to expect
some vengeance, even though they should escape
vengeance from the Romans; so that the city was
filled with sadness, and every one of the moderate men
in it were under great disturbance, as likely themselves to undergo punishment for the wickedness of
the seditious; for indeed it so happened, that this
murder was perpetrated on the Sabbath day, on which
day the Jews have a respite from their works on
account of divine worship.

CHAPTER XVIII.

The calamities and slaughters that came upon the Jews.

1. Now the people of Cæsarea had slain the
Jews that were among them on the very same day
and hour [when the soldiers were slain,] which one
would think must have come to pass by the direction
of providence; insomuch, that in one hour's time
above twenty thousand Jews were killed, and all
Cæsarea was emptied of its Jewish inhabitants; for
Florus caught such as ran away, and sent them in
bonds to the gallies. Upon which stroke that the
Jews received at Cæsarea, the whole nation was greatly
enraged; so they divided themselves into several
parties, and laid waste the villages of the Syrians,
and their neighbouring cities, Philadelphia, and Se-
bonitis, and Gerasa, and Pella, and Scythopolis, and
after them Gadara, and Hippos; and falling upon
Gaulanitis, some cities they destroyed there, and some
they set on fire, and then went to Kedasa, belonging

to the Tyrians, and to Ptolemais; and to Gaba, and to Cæsarea; nor was either Sebaste [Samaria,] or Askelon able to oppose the violence with which they were attacked; and when they had burnt these to the ground, they entirely demolished Anthedon and Gaza; many also of the villages that were about every one of those cities were plundered, and an immense slaughter was made of the men who were caught in them.

2. However the Syrians were even with the Jews in the multitude of the men whom they slew: for they killed those whom they caught in their cities, and that not only out of the hatred they bore them, as formerly, but to prevent the danger under which they were from them; so that the soldiers in all Syria were terrible, and every city was divided into two armies encamped one against another, and the preservation of the one party was in the destruction of the other; so the day time was spent in shedding of blood, and the night in fear, which was of the two the more terrible; for when the Syrians thought they had ruined the Jews, they had the Judaizer's in suspicion also, and as each side did not care to slay those whom they only suspected on the other, so did they greatly fear them when they were mingled with the other, as if they were certainly foreigners. Moreover, greediness of gain was a provocation to kill the opposite party, even to such of old as had appeared very mild and gentle towards them; for they without fear plundered the effects of the slain, and carried off the spoils of those whom they slew to their own houses, as if they had been gained in a set battle; and he was esteemed a man of honour who got the greatest share, as having prevailed over the greatest number of his enemies. It was then common to see cities filled with dead bodies, still lying unburied, and those

of old men, mixed with infants, all dead, and scattered about together; women also lay amongst them, without any covering for their nakedness; you might then see the whole province full of inexpressible calamities, while the dread of still more barbarous practices which were threatened, were everywhere greater than what had been already perpetrated.

3. And thus far the conflict had been between Jews and foreigners, but when they made excursions to Scythopolis, they found Jews that acted as enemies; for as they stood in battle array with those of Scythopolis, and preferred their own safety before their relation to us, they fought against their own countrymen; nay, their alacrity was so very great, that those of Scythopolis suspected them. These were afraid, therefore, lest they should make an assault upon the city in the night time, and, to their great misfortune, should thereby make an apology for themselves to their people for their revolt from them. So they commanded them, that in case they would confirm their agreement and demonstrate their fidelity to them, who were of a different nation, they should go out of the city, with their families to a neighbouring grove; and when they had done as they were commanded, without suspecting any thing, the people of Scythopolis lay still for the interval of two days, to tempt them to be secure; but on the third night they watched their opportunity, and cut all their throats, some as they lay unguarded, and some as they lay asleep. The number that was slain was above thirteen thousand, and then they plundered them of all that they had.

4. It will deserve our relation what befell Simon: he was the son of one Saul, a man of reputation among the Jews. This man was distinguished from the rest by the strength of his body and the boldness

of his conduct, although he abused them both to the mischieving of his countrymen; for he came every day and slew a great many of the Jews of Scythopolis, and he frequently put them to flight, and became himself alone the cause of his army's conquering. But a just punishment overtook him for the murders he had committed upon those of the same nation with him; for when the people of Scythopolis threw their darts at them in the grove, he drew his sword, but did not attack any of the enemy; for he saw that he could do nothing against such a multitude; but he cried out after a very moving manner, and said, "O, ye people of Scythopolis, I deservedly suffer for what I have done with relation to you, when I gave you such security of my fidelity to you, by slaying so many of those that were related to me. Wherefore we very justly experience the perfidiousness of foreigners, while we acted after a most wicked manner against our own nation. I will therefore die, polluted wretch as I am, by mine own hands; for it is not fit I should die by the hand of our enemies; and let the same action be to me both a punishment for my great crimes, and a testimony of my courage to my commendation, that so no one of our enemies may have it to brag of, that he it was that slew me, and no one may insult upon me as I fall" Now when he had said this, he looked round about him upon his family, with eyes of commiseration, and of rage, (that family consisted of a wife, and children, and his aged parents;) so, in the first place, he caught his father by the grey hairs, and ran his sword through him, and after him he did the same to his mother, who willingly received it; and after them he did the like to his wife and children, every one almost offering themselves to his sword, as desirous to prevent being slain by their enemies; so when he had gone over all his family, he stood upon their bodies to be seen by all, and stretching out his right hand, that his action might be observed by all, he sheathed his entire sword into his own bowels. This young man was to be pitied on account of the strength of his body and the courage of his soul; but since he had assured foreigners of his fidelity [against his own countrymen,] he suffered deservedly.

5. Besides this murder at Scythopolis, the other cities rose up against the Jews that were among them; those of Askelon slew two thousand, five hundred, and those of Ptolemais two thousand, and put not a few into bonds; those of Tyre also put a great number to death, but kept a greater number in prison; moreover, those of Hippos, and those of Gadara did the like, while they put to death the boldest of the Jews, but kept those of whom they were afraid in custody; as did the rest of the cities of Syria, according as they every one either hated them, or were afraid of them; only the Antiochians, the Sidonians, and Apamians spared those that dwelt with them, and would not endure either to kill any of the Jews, or to put them in bonds. And perhaps they spared them, because their own number was so great that they despised their attempts; but I think the greatest part of this favour was owing to their commiseration of those whom they saw to make no innovations. As for the Gerasans, they did no harm to those that abode with them, and for those who had a mind to go away, they conducted them as far as their borders reached.

6. There was also a plot laid against the Jews in Agrippa's kingdom; for he was himself gone to Cestius Gallus, to Antioch, but had left one of his companions, whose name was *Noarus,* to take care of the public affairs; which Noarus was of kin to king

Soheinus.[1] Now there came certain men, seventy in
number, out of Batanea, who were the most considerable for their families and prudence of the rest of
the people; these desired to have an army put into
their hands, that if any tumult should happen, they
might have about them a guard sufficient to restrain
such as might rise up against them. This Noarus
sent out some of the king's armed men by night, and
slew all those [seventy] men; which bold action he
ventured upon without the consent of Agrippa, and
was such a lover of money, that he chose to be so
wicked to his own countrymen, though he brought
ruin on the kingdom thereby: and thus cruelly did
he treat that nation, and this contrary to the laws
also, until Agrippa was informed of it, who did not
indeed dare to put him to death, out of regard to
Soheinus, but still he put an end to his procuratorship immediately. But as to the seditious, they took
the citadel which was called *Cypros,* and was above
Jericho, and cut the throats of the garrison, and
utterly demolished the fortifications; this was about
the same time that the multitude of the Jews that
were at Macherus persuaded the Romans who were
in garrison to leave the place, and deliver it up to
them. These Romans being in great fear, lest the
place should be taken by force, made an agreement
with them to depart upon certain conditions; and
when they had obtained the security they desired,
they delivered up the citadel, into which the people
of Macherus put a garrison for their own security,
and held it in their own power.

7. But for Alexandria, the sedition of the people
of the place against the Jews was perpetual, and

---

[1] Of this Soheinus we have mention made by Tacitus. We also learn
from Dio, that his father was king of the Arabians of Iturea, [which
Iturea is mentioned by St. Luke iii. 1.] See Noldius, No. 371.

this from that very time when Alexander [the Great,]
upon finding the readiness of the Jews in assisting
him against the Egyptians, and as a reward for such
their assistance, gave them equal privileges in this
city with the Grecians themselves. Which honorary
reward continued among them under his successors,
who also set apart for them a particular place, that
they might live without being polluted [by the Gentiles,] and were thereby not so much intermixed with
foreigners as before: they also gave them this farther
privilege, that they should be called *Macedonians*.
Nay, when the Romans got possession of Egypt,
neither the first Cæsar, nor any one that came after
him, thought of diminishing the honours which Alexander had bestowed on the Jews. But still conflicts
perpetually arose with the Grecians; and although
the governors did every day punish many of them,
yet did the sedition grow worse; but at this time
especially, when there were tumults in other places
also, the disorders among them were put into a
greater flame: for when the Alexandrians had once
a public assembly, to deliberate about an embassage
they were sending to Nero, a great number of Jews
came flocking to the theatre; but when their adversaries saw them, they immediately cried out, and
called them their enemies, and said they came as
spies upon them; upon which they rushed out, and
laid violent hands upon them; and as for the rest
they were slain as they ran away; but there were
three men whom they caught, and hauled them along,
in order to have them burnt alive; but all the Jews
came in a body to defend them, who at first threw
stones at the Grecians, but after that they took lamps,
and rushed with violence into the theatre, and threatened that they would burn the people to a man; and
this they had soon done, unless Tiberius Alexander,

the governor of the city, had restrained their passions. However, this man did not begin to teach them wisdom by arms, but sent among them privately some of the principal men, and thereby entreated them to be quiet and not provoke the Roman army against them; but the seditious made a jest of the entreaties of Tiberius, and reproached him for so doing.

8. Now when he perceived that those who were for innovations would not be pacified till some great calamity should overtake them, he sent out upon them those two Roman legions that were in the city, and together with them five thousand other soldiers, who by chance were come together out of Libya, to the ruin of the Jews. They were also permitted not only to kill them, but to plunder them of what they had, and to set fire to their houses. These soldiers rushed violently into that part of the city that was called *Delta* where the Jewish people lived together, and did as they were bidden, though not without bloodshed on their own side also; for the Jews got together, and set those that were the best armed among them in the forefront, and made resistance for a great while, but when once they gave back, they were destroyed unmercifully, and thus their destruction was complete, some being caught in the open field, and others forced into their houses, which houses were first plundered of what was in them, and then set on fire by the Romans; wherein no mercy was shown to the infants, and no regard had to the aged; but they went on in the slaughter of persons of every age, till all the place was overflowed with blood, and fifty thousand of them lay dead upon heaps; nor had the remainder been preserved had they not betaken themselves to supplication. So Alexander commiserated their condition, and gave orders to the Romans to retire: accordingly, these

being accustomed to obey orders, left off killing at
the first intimation; but the populace of Alexandria
bore so very great hatred to the Jews, that it was
difficult to recall them, and it was a hard thing to
make them leave their dead bodies.

9. And this was the miserable calamity which at
this time befell the Jews at Alexandria. Hereupon
Cestius thought fit no longer to lie still, while the
Jews were everywhere up in arms, so he took out
of Antioch the twelfth legion entire, and out of each
of the rest he selected two thousand, with six cohorts
of footmen, and four troops of horsemen, besides
those auxiliaries which were sent by the kings; of
which [1] Antiochus sent two thousand horsemen, and
three thousand footmen, with as many archers; and
Agrippa sent the same number of footmen, and one
thousand horsemen; Sohemus also followed with four
thousand, a third part whereof were horsemen, but
most part were archers, and thus did he march to
Ptolemais. There were also great numbers of auxiliaries gathered together from the [free] cities, who
indeed had not the same skill in martial affairs but
made up in their alacrity, and in their hatred to the
Jews what they wanted in skill. There came also
along with Cestius, Agrippa himself, both as a guide
in his march of the country, and a director what was
fit to be done; so Cestius took part of his forces, and
marched hastily to Zabulon, a strong city of Galilee,
which was called *the city of men,* and divides the
country of Ptolemais from our nation: this he found
deserted by its men, the multitude having fled to the
mountains, but full of all sorts of good things; those
he gave leave to the soldiers to plunder, and set fire

---

[1] Spanheim notes on the place, that this latter Antiochus, who was
called *Epiphanes,* is mentioned by Dio, LIX. p. 645, and that he is mentioned by Josephus elsewhere twice also, B. V. ch. xi. sect. 3, Vol III.
and Antiq. B. XIX. ch. viii. sect. 1, Vol. III.

to the city, although it was of admirable beauty, and had its houses built like those in Tyre, and Sidon, and Berytus. After this he overran all the country, and seized upon whatsoever came in his way, and set fire to the villages that were round about them, and then returned to Ptolemais. But when the Syrians, and especially those of Berytus, were busy in plundering, the Jews pulled up their courage again, for they knew that Cestius was retired, and fell upon those that were left behind unexpectedly, and destroyed about two thousand of them.

10. And now Cestius himself marched from Ptolemais and came to Cæsarea; but he sent part of his army before him to Joppa, and gave order, that if they could take that city [by surprise] they should keep it; but that in case the citizens should perceive they were coming to attack them, that they then should stay for him, and for the rest of the army. So some of them made a brisk march by the seaside, and some by land, and so coming upon them on both sides, they took the city with ease: and as the inhabitants had made no provision aforehand for a flight, nor had gotten anything ready for fighting, the soldiers fell upon them, and slew them all, with their families, and then plundered and burnt the city. The number of the slain was eight thousand, four hundred. In like manner Cestius sent also a considerable body of horsemen to the toparchy of Narbatene, that adjoined to Cæsarea, who destroyed the country, and slew a great multitude of its people; they also plundered what they had, and burnt their villages.

11. But Cestius sent Gallus, the commander of the twelfth legion, into Galilee, and delivered to him as many of his forces as he supposed sufficient to subdue that nation. He was received by the strongest

city of Galilee, which was Sepphoris, with acclamations of joy; which wise conduct of that city occasioned the rest of the cities to be quiet; while the seditious part, and the robbers ran away to that moun tain which lies in the very middle of Galilee, and is situated over against Sepphoris; it is called *Asamon*. So Gallus brought his forces against them, but while those men were in the superior parts above the Romans, they easily threw their darts upon the Romans, as they made their approaches, and slew about two hundred of them: but when the Romans had gone round the mountains, and were gotten into the parts above their enemies, the others were soon beaten, nor could they who had only light armour on, sustain the force of them that fought them armed all over; nor when they were beaten could they escape the enemy's horsemen; insomuch, that only some few concealed themselves in certain places hard to be come at, among the mountains, while the rest, above two thousand in number, were slain.

CHAPTER XIX.

What Cestius did against the Jews; and how, upon his besieging Jerusalem, he retreated from the city, without any just occasion in the world. As also what severe calamities he underwent from the Jews in his retreat.

1. AND now Gallus, seeing nothing more that looked towards an innovation in Galilee, returned with his-army to Cæsarea; but Cestius removed with his whole army, and marched to Antipatris. And when he was informed that there was a great body

of Jewish forces gotten together in a certain tower called *Aphek,* he sent a party before to fight them; but this party dispersed the Jews by affrighting them before it came to a battle: so they came, and finding their camp deserted they burnt it, as well as the villages that lay about it. But when Cestius had marched from Antipatris to Lydda, he found the city empty of its men, for the [1] whole multitude were gone up to Jerusalem to the feast of tabernacles; yet did he destroy fifty of those that showed themselves, and burnt the city, and so marched forwards; and ascending by Beth-horon, he pitched his camp at a certain place called *Gabao,* fifty furlongs distant from Jerusalem.

2. But as for the Jews, when they saw the war approaching to their metropolis, they left the feast, and betook themselves to their arms: and taking courage greatly from their multitude, went in a sudden and disorderly manner to the fight, with a great noise, and without any consideration had of the rest of the seventh day, although the Sabbath was the day to which they had the greatest regard; but

[1] Here we have an eminent example of that Jewish language, which Dr. Wall truly observes we several times find used in the sacred writings; I mean where the words *all* or *whole multitude,* etc. are used for much the greatest part only; but not so as to include every person, without exception; for when Josephus had said, that the *whole multitude* [all the males] of Lydda were gone to the feast of tabernacles, he immediately adds, that however no fewer than fifty of them appeared, and were slain by the Romans. Other examples somewhat like this I have observed elsewhere in Josephus, but, as I think, none so remarkable as this. See Wall's Critical Observations on the Old Testament, pp. 49, 50. We have also in this and the next section, two eminent facts to be observed, viz. the first example, that I remember in Josephus, of the onset of the Jews' enemies upon their country when their males were gone up to Jerusalem to one of their three sacred festivals; which, during the Theocracy, God had promised to preserve them from, Exod. xxxiv. 24. The second fact is this, the breach of the Sabbath by the seditious Jews in an offensive fight, contrary to the universal doctrine and practice of their nation in these ages, and even contrary to what they themselves afterward practised in the rest of this war. See the note on Antiq. B. XVI. ch. 2. sect. 4, Vol. II.

that rage which made them forget the religious observation [of the Sabbath] made them too hard for
their enemies in the fight: with such violence therefore did they fall upon the Romans, as to break into
their ranks, and to march through the midst of them,
making a great slaughter as they went, insomuch,
that unless the horsemen, and such part of the footmen as were not yet tired in the action, had wheeled
round, and succoured that part of the army which
was not yet broken, Cestius, with his whole army,
had been in danger: however, five hundred and fifteen
of the Romans were slain, of which number four
hundred were footmen, and the rest horsemen, while
the Jews lost only twenty-two, of whom the most
valiant were the kinsmen of Monobazus king of Adiabene, and their names were Monobazus and Kenedius;
and next to them were Niger of Perea, and Silas of
Babylon, who had deserted from king Agrippa to the
Jews; for they had formerly served in his army.
When the front of the Jewish army had been cut off,
the Jews retired into the city; but still Simon, the son
of Giora, fell upon the backs of the Romans, as they
were ascending up Beth-horon, and put the hindmost
of the army into disorder, and carried off many of
the beasts that carried the weapons of war, and led
them into the city. But as Cestius tarried there
three days, the Jews seized upon the elevated parts
of the city, and set watches at the entrances into the
city, and appeared openly resolved not to rest, when
once the Romans should begin to march.

3. And now when Agrippa observed that even
the affairs of the Romans were likely to be in danger,
while such an immense multitude of their enemies had
seized upon the mountains round about, he determined
to try what the Jews would agree to by words, as
thinking that he should either persuade them all to

desist from fighting, or, however, that he should cause the sober part of them to separate themselves from the opposite party. So he sent Borceus and Phebus, the persons of his party that were the best known to them, and promised them, that Cestius should give them his right hand, to secure them of the Romans' entire forgiveness of what they had done amiss, if they would throw away their arms, and come over to them; but the seditious, fearing lest the whole multitude, in hopes of security to themselves, should go over to Agrippa, resolved immediately to fall upon and kill the ambassadors: accordingly they slew Phebus before he said a word, but Borceus was only wounded, and so prevented his fate by flying away; and when the people were very angry at this, they had the seditious beaten with stones and clubs, and drove them before them into the city.

4. But now Cestius, observing that the disturbances that were begun among the Jews afforded him a proper opportunity to attack them, took his whole army along with him, and put the Jews to flight, and pursued them to Jerusalem. He then pitched his camp upon the elevation called *Scopus,* [or watch tower,] which was distant seven furlongs from the city; yet did not he assault them in three days' time, out of expectation that those within might perhaps yield a little; and in the meantime he sent out a great many of his soldiers into the neighbouring villages, to seize upon their corn. And on the fourth day, which was the thirtieth of the month Hyperbereteus [Tisri,] when he had put his army in array, he brought it into the city. Now for the people, they were kept under by the seditious; but the seditious themselves were greatly affrighted at the good order of the Romans, and retired from the suburbs, and retreated into the inner part of the city, and

into the temple. But when Cestius was come into the city, he set the part called *Bezetha,* which is called *Cenopolis,* [or the new city,] on fire; as he did also to the timber market: after which he came into the upper city, and pitched his camp over against the royal palace; and had he but at this very time attempted to get within the walls by force, he had won the city presently, and the war had been put an end to at once; but Tyrannius Priscus, the muster-master of the army, and a great number of the officers of the horse, had been corrupted by Florus, and diverted him from that his attempt; and that was the occasion that this war lasted so very long, and thereby the Jews were involved in such incurable calamities.

5. In the meantime many of the principal men of the city were persuaded by Ananus, the son of Jonathan, and invited Cestius into the city, and were about to open the gates for him; but he overlooked this offer, partly out of his anger at the Jews, and partly because he did not thoroughly believe they were in earnest; whence it was that he delayed the matter so long, that the seditious perceived the treachery, and threw Ananus and those of his party down from the wall, and pelting them with stones, drove them into their houses; but they stood themselves at proper distances in the towers; and threw their darts at those that were getting over the wall. Thus did the Romans make their attack against the wall for five days, but to no purpose; but on the next day, Cestius took a great many of his choicest men, and with them the archers, and attempted to break into the temple at the northern quarter of it: but the Jews beat them off from the cloisters, and repulsed them several times when they were gotten near to the wall, till at length the multitude of the darts cut them off, and made them retire; but the

first rank of the Romans rested their shields upon
the wall, and so did those that were behind them,
and the like did those that were still more backward,
and guarded themselves with what they call *Testudo,*
[the back of] a tortoise, upon which the darts that
were thrown fell, and slided off without doing them
any harm; so the soldiers undermined the wall, without being themselves hurt, and got all things ready
for setting fire to the gate of the temple.

6. And now it was that a horrible fear seized
upon the seditious, insomuch, that many of them ran
out of the city, as though it were to be taken immediately: but the people upon this took courage,
and where the wicked part of the city gave ground,
thither did they come, in order to set open the gates,
and to admit Cestius as their benefactor, who, had
he but continued the siege a little longer, had certainly taken the city; but it was, I suppose, owing
to the aversion God had already at the city, and the
sanctuary, that he was hindered from putting an end
to the war that very day.

7. It then happened that Cestius was not conscious
either how the besieged despaired of success, nor
how courageous the people were for him; and so
he recalled his soldiers from the place, and by despairing of any expectation of taking it without
having received any disgrace, he retired from the
city, without any reason in the world. But when
the robbers perceived this unexpected retreat of his,
they resumed their courage, and ran after the hinder
parts of his army, and destroyed a considerable number of both their horsemen and footmen: and now
Cestius lay all night at the camp which was at Scopus,
and as he went off farther next day, he thereby invited the enemy to follow him, who still fell upon the
hindmost, and destroyed them; they also fell upon

the flank on each side of the army, and threw darts
upon them obliquely, nor durst those that were hind
most turn back upon those who wounded them behind, as imagining that the multitude of those that
pursued them was immense; nor did they venture to
drive away those that pressed upon them on each
side, because they were heavy with their arms, and
were afraid of breaking their ranks to pieces, and
because they saw the Jews were light, and ready
for making incursions upon them. And this was
the reason why the Romans suffered greatly, without
being able to revenge themselves upon their enemies;
so they were galled all the way, and their ranks were
put into disorder, and those that were thus put out
of their ranks were slain; among whom were Priscus,
the commander of the sixth legion, and Longinus
the tribune, and Emilius Secundus, the commander
of a troop of horsemen. So it was not without difficulty that they got to Gabao, their former camp, and
that not without the loss of a great part of their
baggage. There it was that Cestius stayed two days,
and was in great distress to know what he should
do in these circumstances; but when, on the third
day, he saw a still much greater number of enemies,
and all the parts round about him full of Jews, he
understood that his delay was to his own detriment,
and that if he stayed any longer there, he should
have still more enemies upon him.

8. That therefore he might fly the faster, he gave
orders to cast away what might hinder his army's
march, so they killed the mules, and other creatures,
excepting those that carried their darts, and machines,
which they retained for their own use, and this principally because they were afraid lest the Jews should
seize upon them. He then made his army march
on as far as Beth-horon. Now the Jews did not so

much press upon them when they were in large open places, but when they were penned up in their descent through narrow passages, then did some of them get before, and hindered them from getting out of them, and others of them thrust the hindermost down into the lower places, and the whole multitude extended themselves over against the neck of the passage, and covered the Roman army with their darts. In which circumstances, as the footmen knew not how to defend themselves, so the danger pressed the horsemen still more, for they were so pelted, that they could not march along the road in their ranks, and the ascents were so high, that the cavalry were not able to march against the enemy; the precipices also, and valleys into which they frequently fell, and tumbled down, were such on each side of them, that there were neither place for their flight, nor any contrivance could be thought of for their defence; till the distress they were at last in was so great, that they betook themselves to lamentations, and to such mournful cries, as men use in the utmost despair; the joyful acclamations of the Jews also, as they encouraged one another, echoed the sounds back again, these last composing a noise of those that at once rejoiced, and were in a rage. Indeed, things were come to such a pass, that the Jews had almost taken Cestius' entire army prisoners, had not the night come on, when the Romans fled to Beth-horon, and the Jews seized upon all the places round about them, and watched for their coming out [in the morning.]

9. And then it was that Cestius, despairing of obtaining room for a public march, contrived how he might best run away; and when he had selected four hundred of the most courageous of his soldiers, he placed them at the strongest of their fortifications, and gave order, that when they went up to the morn-

ing guard, they should erect their ensigns, that the Jews might be made to believe that the entire army was there still, while he himself took the rest of his forces with him, and marched, without any noise, thirty furlongs. But when the Jews perceived, in the morning, that the camp was empty, they ran upon those four hundred who had deluded them, and immediately threw their darts at them, and slew them, and they pursued after Cestius. But he had already made use of a great part of the night in his flight, and still marched quicker when it was day Insomuch that the soldiers, through the astonishment and fear they were in, left behind them their engines for sieges, and for throwing of stones, and a great part of the instruments of war. So the Jews went on pursuing the Romans as far as Antipatris, after which, seeing they could not overtake them, they came back, and took the engines, and spoiled the dead bodies, and gathering their prey together, which the Romans had left behind them, came back running and singing to their metropolis. While they had themselves lost a few only, but had slain of the Romans five thousand and three hundred footmen, and three hundred and eighty horsemen. This defeat happened on the eighth day of the month Dius, [Marhesvan,] in the twelfth year of the reign of Nero.

CHAPTER XX.

Cestius sends ambassadors to Nero. The people of Damascus slay those Jews that lived with them. The people of Jerusalem, after they had [left off] pursuing Cestius, return to the city, and get things ready for its defence, and make a great many generals for their armies, and particularly Josephus, the writer of these books. Some account of his administration.

1. AFTER this calamity had befallen Cestius, many of the most eminent of the Jews swam away from the city, as from a ship when it was going to sink; Costobarus, therefore, and Saul, who were brethren, together with Philip, the son of Jacimus, who was the commander of king Agrippa's forces, ran away from the city, and went to Cestius. But then how Antipas, who had been besieged with them in the king's palace, would not fly away with them, was afterwards slain by the seditious, we shall relate hereafter. However, Cestius sent Saul and his friends, at their own desire, to Achaia, to Nero, to inform him of the great distress they were in, and to lay the blame of their kindling the war upon Florus, as hoping to alleviate his own danger, by provoking his indignation against Florus

2. In the meantime, the people of Damascus, when they were informed of the destruction of the Romans, set about the slaughter of those Jews that were among them; and as they had them already cooped up together in the place of public exercises, which they had done out of the suspicion they had

of them, they thought they should meet with no
difficulty in the attempt; yet did they distrust their
own wives, who were almost all of them addicted to
the Jewish religion; on which account it was, that
their greatest concern was, how they might conceal
these things from them; so they came upon the Jews,
and cut their throats, as being in a narrow place, in
number ten thousand, and all of them unarmed, and
this in one hour's time, without anybody to disturb
them.

3. But as to those who had pursued after Cestius,
when they were returned back to Jerusalem, they
overbore some of those that favoured the Romans
by violence, and some they persuaded [by entreaties]
to join with them, and got together in great numbers
in the temple, and appointed a great many generals
for the war; [1] Joseph also the son of Gorion, and
Ananus the high priest, were chosen as governors of
all affairs within the city, and with a particular charge
to repair the walls of the city; for they did not ordain
Eleazar the son of Simon to that office, although
he had gotten into his possession the prey they had
taken from the Romans, and the money they had
taken from Cestius, together with a great part of
the public treasures, because they saw he was of a
tyrannical temper, and that his followers were, in
their behaviour, like guards about him. However,
the want they were in of Eleazar's money, and the
subtle tricks used by him, brought all so about, that
the people were circumvented, and submitted themselves to his authority in all public affairs.

---

[1] From this name of Joseph the son of Gorion, or Gorion the son
of Joseph, as B. IV. ch. iii. sect. 9, Vol. IV., one of the governors of
Jerusalem, who was slain at the beginning of the tumults by the zealots,
B. IV. ch. vi. sect. 1, the much later Jewish author of a history of that
nation takes his title, and yet personates our true Josephus, the son of
Matthias: but the cheat is too gross to be put upon the learned world.

4. They also chose other generals for Idumea, Jesus, the son of Sepphias, one of the high priests, and Eleazar, the son of Ananias, the high priest; they also enjoined Niger, the then governor of [1] Idumea, who was of a family that belonged to Perea, beyond Jordan, and was thence called the *Peraite,* that he should be obedient to those forenamed commanders. Nor did they neglect the care of other parts of the country, but Joseph, the son of Simon, was sent as a general to Jericho, as was Manasseh to Perea, and John, the Essene, to the toparchy of Thamana; Lydda was also added to his portion, and Joppa, and Emmaus. But John, the son of Matthias, was made governor of the toparchies of Gophnitica, and Acrabattene, as was Josephus, the son of Matthias, of both the Galilees. Gamala also, which was the strongest city in those parts, was put under his command.

5. So every one of the other commanders administered the affairs of his portion with that alacrity and prudence they were masters of; but as to Josephus, when he came into Galilee, his first care was to gain the good-will of the people of that country, as sensible that he should thereby have in general good success, although he should fail in other points. And being conscious to himself that if he communicated part of his power to the great men, he should make them his fast friends; and that he should gain the same favour from the multitude, if he executed his commands by persons of their own country, and with whom they were well acquainted; he chose out seventy of the most prudent men, and those elders

---

[1] We may observe here, that the Idumeans, as having been proselytes of justice since the days of John Hyrcanus, during about 195 years, were now esteemed as part of the Jewish nation, and were provided with a Jewish commander accordingly. See the note upon Antiq. B. XIII. ch. ix. sect. 1, Vol. II.

in age, and appointed them to be rulers of all Galilee, as he chose seven judges in every city to hear the lesser quarrels; for as to the greater causes, and those wherein life and death were concerned, he enjoined they should be brought to him, and the seventy elders.

6. Josephus also, when he had settled these rules for determining causes by the law, with regard to the people's dealings one with another, betook himself to make provisions for their safety against external violence; and as he knew the Romans would fall upon Galilee, he built walls in proper places about Jatapata and Barsabee, and Selamis; and besides these about Caphareccho, and Japha, and Sigo, and what they call Mount Tabor; and Taricheæ, and Tiberias. Moreover, he built walls about the caves near the lake of Gennesar, which places lay in the Lower Galilee; the same he did to the places of Upper Galilee, as well as to the rock called *the Rock of the Achabari,* and to Seph, and Jamneh, and Meroth; and in Gaulanitis he fortified Seleucia, and Sogane, and Gamala; but as to those of Sepphoris, they were the only people to whom he gave leave to build their own walls, and this because he perceived they were rich and wealthy, and ready to go to war, without standing in need of any injunctions for that purpose. The case was the same with Gischala, which had a wall built about it by John the son of Levi himself, but with the consent of Josephus; but for the building of the rest of the fortresses, he laboured together with all the other builders, and was present to give all the necessary orders for that purpose. He also got together an army out of Galilee, of more than a hundred thousand young men, all of which he armed with the old weapons, which he had collected together, and prepared for them.

7. And when he had considered that the Roman power became invincible, chiefly by their readiness in obeying orders, and the constant exercise of their arms, he despaired of teaching these his men the use of their arms, which was to be obtained by experience, but observing that their readiness in obeying orders was owing to the multitude of their officers, he made his partitions in his army more after the Roman manner, and appointed a great many subalterns. He also distributed the soldiers into various classes, whom he put under captains of tens, and captains of hundreds, and then under captains of thousands; and besides these he had commanders of large bodies of men. He also taught them to give the signals one to another, and to call and recall the soldiers by the trumpets, how to expand the wings of an army, and make them wheel about, and when one wing hath had success, to turn again and assist those that were hard set, and to join in the defence of what had most suffered. He also continually instructed them in what concerned the courage of the soul, and the hardiness of the body; and above all he exercised them for war, by declaring to them distinctly the good order of the Romans, and that they were to fight with men who, both by the strength of their bodies, and courage of their souls, had conquered, in a manner, the whole habitable earth. He told them that he should make trial of the good order they would observe in war, even before it came to the battle, in case they would abstain from the crimes they used to indulge themselves in, such as theft, and robbery, and rapine, and from defrauding their own countrymen, and never to esteem the harm done to those that were so near of kin to them, to be any advantage to themselves; for that wars are then managed the best when the warriors preserve a good

conscience; but that such as are ill men in private
life, will not only have those for enemies who attack
them, but God himself also for their antagonist.

8. And thus did he continue to admonish them.
Now he chose for the war such an army as was
sufficient, i. e. sixty thousand footmen, and [1] two hundred and fifty horsemen: and besides these, on which
he put the greatest trust, there were about four
thousand five hundred mercenaries; he had also six
hundred men as guards of his body. Now the cities
easily maintained the rest of his army, excepting the
mercenaries, for every one of the cities enumerated
above, sent out half their men to the army, and retained the other half at home, in order to get provisions for them; insomuch that the one part went to
the war, and the other part to their work, and so
those that sent out their corn were paid for it by
those that were in arms, by that security which they
enjoyed from them.

CHAPTER XXI.

*Concerning John of Gischala. Josephus uses strata-
gems against the plots John laid against him; and
recovers certain cities which had revolted from him.*

1. Now as Josephus was thus engaged in the administration of the affairs of Galilee, there arose a
treacherous person, a man of Gischala, the son of
Levi, whose name was John. His character was that
of a very cunning, and very knavish person, beyond

---

[1] I should think that an army of 60,000 footmen should require many
more than 250 horsemen; and we find Josephus had more horsemen under
his command than 250 in his future history. I suppose the number of
the thousands is dropped in our present copies.

the ordinary rate of the other men of eminence there, and for wicked practices he had not his fellow anywhere. Poor he was at first, and for a long time his wants were a hinderance to him, in his wicked designs. He was a ready liar, and yet very sharp in gaining credit to his fictions; he thought it a point of virtue to delude people, and would delude even such as were the dearest to him. He was a hypocritical pretender to humanity, but where he had hopes of gain, he spared not the shedding of blood: his desires were ever carried to great things, and he encouraged his hopes from those mean wicked tricks which he was the author of. He had a peculiar knack at thieving; but in some time he got certain companions in his impudent practices; at first they were but few, but as he proceeded on in his evil course, they became still more and more numerous. He took care that none of his partners should be easily caught in their rogueries, but chose such out of the rest as had the strongest constitutions of body, and the greatest courage of soul, together with great skill in martial affairs; so he got together a band of four hundred men, who came principally out of the country of Tyre, and were vagabonds that had run away from its villages; and by the means of these he laid waste all Galilee, and irritated a considerable number, who were in great expectation of a war then suddenly to rise among them.

2. However, John's want of money had hitherto restrained him in his ambition after command, and in his attempts to advance himself. But when he saw that Josephus was highly pleased with the activity of his temper, he persuaded him, in the first place, to intrust him with the repairing of the walls of his native city [Gischala,] in which work he got a great deal of money from the rich citizens. He

after that contrived a very shrewd trick, and pretending that the Jews who dwelt in Syria were
obliged to make use of oil that was made by others
than those of their own nation, he desired leave of
Josephus to send oil to their borders: so he bought
four amphoræ with such Tyrian money as was of
the value of four Attic drachmæ, and sold every half
amphora at the same price. And as Galilee was
very fruitful in oil, and was peculiarly so at that time,
by sending away great quantities, and having the
sole privilege so to do, he gathered an immense sum
of money together, which money he immediately used
to the disadvantage of him who gave him that priv
ilege. And, as he supposed, that if he could once
overthrow Josephus, he should himself obtain the
government of Galilee, so he gave orders to the
robbers that were under his command, to be more
zealous in their thievish expeditions, that by the rise
of many that desired innovations in the country, he
might either catch their general in his snares, as he
came to the country's assistance, and then kill him;
or if he should overlook the robbers, he might accuse
him for his negligence to the people of the country.
He also spread abroad a report far and near, that
Josephus was delivering up the administration of
affairs to the Romans: and many such plots did he
lay, in order to ruin him.

3. Now at the same time that certain young
men of the village Dabaritta, who kept guard in the
great plain, laid snares for Ptolemy, who was
Agrippa's and Bernice's steward, and took from
him all that he had with him, among which things
there were a great many costly garments, and no
small number of silver cups, and six hundred pieces
of gold, yet were they not able to conceal what they
had stolen, but brought it all to Josephus, to Taricheæ.

Hereupon he blamed them for the violence they had offered to the king and queen, and deposited what they brought to him with Eneas, the most potent man of Tarichea, with an intention of sending the things back to the owners at a proper time; which act of Josephus' brought him into the greatest danger; for those that had stolen the things, had an indigna tion at him, both because they gained no share of it for themselves, and because they perceived before hand what was Josephus' intention, and that he would freely deliver up what had cost them so much pains to the king and queen. These ran away by night to their several villages, and declared to all men that Josephus was going to betray them: they also raised great disorders in all the neighbouring cities, insomuch that in the morning a hundred thousand armed men came running together; which multitude was crowded together in the hippodrome at Tarichea, and made a very peevish clamour against him; while some cried out, That "they should depose the traitor;" and others, That "they should burn him " Now John irritated a great many, as did also one Jesus the son of Sapphias, who was then governor of Tiberias. Then it was that Josephus' friends, and the guards of his body, were so affrighted at this violent assault of the multitude, that they all fled away but four; and as he was asleep, they awaked him, as the people were going to set fire to the house. And although those four that remained with him persuaded him to run away, he was neither surprised at his being himself deserted, nor at the great multitude that came against him, but leaped out to them with his clothes rent, and ashes sprinkled on his head, with his hands behind him, and his sword hanging at his neck. At this sight his friends, especially those of Tarichea, commiserated his condition; but those that

came out of the country, and those in their neighbourhood, to whom his government seemed burdensome,
reproached him, and bid him produce the money which
belonged to them all immediately, and to confess
the agreement he had made to betray them; for they
imagined from the habit in which he appeared, that
he would deny nothing of what they suspected concerning him, and that it was in order to obtain pardon,
that he had put himself entirely into so pitiable a
posture. But this humble appearance was only designed as preparatory to a stratagem of his, who
thereby contrived to set those that were so angry at
him at variance one with another, about the things
they were angry at. However, he promised he would
confess all: hereupon he was permitted to speak, when
he said, "I did neither intend to send this money
back to Agrippa, nor to gain it myself; for I did
never esteem one that was your enemy to be my
friend, nor did I look upon what would tend to your
disadvantage, to be my advantage. But, O you
people of Taricheæ, I saw that your city stood in
more need than others of fortifications for your security, and that it wanted money in order for the
building it a wall. I was also afraid lest the people
of Tiberias and other cities should lay a plot to
seize upon these spoils, and therefore it was that I
intended to retain this money privately, that I might
encompass you with a wall. But if this does not
please you, I will produce what was brought me, and
leave it to you to plunder it; but if I have conducted
myself so well as to please you, you may if you please
punish your benefactor."

4. Hereupon the people of Taricheæ loudly commended him, but those of Tiberias, with the rest of
the company, gave him hard names, and threatened
what they would do to him; so both sides left off

quarrelling with Josephus, and fell on quarrelling with one another. So he grew bold upon the dependence he had on his friends, which were the people of Taricheæ, and about forty thousand in number, and spoke more freely to the whole multitude, and reproached them greatly for their rashness, and told them, That "with this money he would build walls about Taricheæ and would put the other cities in a state of security also; for that they should not want money, if they would but agree for whose benefit it was to be procured, and would not suffer themselves to be irritated against him who procured it for them."

5. Hereupon the rest of the multitude that had been deluded retired; but yet so that they went away angry, and two thousand of them made an assault upon him in their armour; and as he was already gone to his own house, they stood without and threatened him. On which occasion Josephus again used a second stratagem to escape them; for he got upon the top of his house, and with his right hand desired them to be silent, and said to them, "I cannot tell what you would have, nor can hear what you say, for the confused noise you make: but he said, that he would comply with all their demands, in case they would but send some of their number in to him that might talk with him about it." And when the principal of them, with their leaders, heard this, they came into the house. He then drew them to the most retired part of the house, and shut the door of that hall where he put them, and then had them whipped till every one of their inward parts appeared naked. In the meantime the multitude stood round the house, and supposed that he had a long discourse with those that were gone in, about what they claimed of him. He had then the doors set open immediately;

and sent the men out all bloody, which so terribly
affrighted those that had before threatened him, that
they threw away their arms and ran away

6. But as for John, his envy grew greater [upon
this escape of Josephus,] and he framed a new plot
against him; he pretended to be sick, and by a letter
desired that Josephus would give him leave to use
the hot baths that were at Tiberias, for the recovery
of his health. Hereupon Josephus, who hitherto suspected nothing of John's plots against him, wrote to
the governors of the city, that they would provide
a lodging and necessaries for John; which favours,
when he had made use of, in two days' time he did
what he came about; some he corrupted with de-
lusive frauds, and others with money, and so persuaded them to revolt from Josephus. This Silas,
who was appointed guardian of the city by Josephus,
wrote to him immediately, and informed him of the
plot against him; which epistle when Josephus had
received, he marched with great diligence all night,
and came early in the morning to Tiberias; at which
time the rest of the multitude met him. But John,
who suspected that coming was not for his advantage,
sent however one of his friends, and pretended that
he was sick, and that being confined to his bed he
could not come to pay him his respects. But as soon
as Josephus had got the people of Tiberias together
in the Stadium, and tried to discourse with them about
the letters that he had received, John privately sent
some armed men, and gave them orders to slay him.
But when the people saw that the armed men were
about to draw their swords, they cried out, at which
cry Josephus turned himself about, and when he
saw that the swords were just at his throat, he marched
away in great haste to the sea shore, and left off
that speech which he was going to make to the people,

upon an elevation of six cubits high. He then seized on a ship which lay in the haven, and leaped into it, with two of his guards, and fled away into the midst of the lake.

7. But now the soldiers he had with him took up their arms immediately, and marched against the plotters: but Josephus was afraid lest a civil war should be raised by the. envy of a few men, and bring the city to ruin; so he sent some of his party to tell them, that they should do no more than provide for their own safety, that they should not kill anybody, nor accuse any for the occasion they had afforded [of a disorder.] Accordingly these men obeyed his orders, and were quiet; but the people of the neighbouring country, when they were informed of this plot, and of the plotter, they got together in great multitudes to oppose John. But he prevented their attempt, and fled away to Gischala, his native city, while the Galileans came running out of their several cities to Josephus; and as they were now become many ten thousands of armed men, they cried out that 'they were come against John, the common plotter against their interest, and would at the same time burn him, and that city which had received him. Hereupon Josephus told them that he took their good-will to him kindly, but still he restrained their fury, and intended to subdue his enemies by prudent conduct, rather than by slaying them; so he excepted those of every city which had joined in this revolt with John, by name, who had readily been showed him by these that came from every city, and caused public proclamation to be made, that he would seize upon the effects of those that did not forsake John within five days' time, and would burn both their houses and their families with fire. Whereupon three thousand of John's party left him immediately, who

came to Josephus, and threw their arms down at his feet. John then betook himself, together with his two thousand Syrian runagates, from open attempts, to more secret ways of treachery. Accordingly he privately sent messengers to Jerusalem, to accuse Josephus, as having too great power, and to let them know that he would soon come, as a tyrant, to their metropolis, unless they prevented him. This accusation the people were aware of beforehand, but had no regard to it However, some of the grandees, out of envy, and some of the rulers also, sent money to John privately, that he might be able to get together mercenary soldiers, in order to fight Josephus; they also made a decree of themselves, and this for recalling him from his government, yet did they not think that decree sufficient; so they sent withal two thousand five hundred armed men, and four persons of the highest rank amongst them: Joazar the son of Nomicus, and Ananias the son of Sadduk, as also Simon and Judas, the sons of Jonathan, all very able men in speaking, that these persons might withdraw the good-will of the people from Josephus. These had it in charge if he would voluntarily come away, they should permit him to [come and] give an account of his conduct, but if he obstinately insisted upon his continuing in his government, they should treat him as an enemy. Now Josephus' friends had sent him word that an army was coming against him, but they gave no notice beforehand what the reason of their coming was, that being only known among some secret councils of his enemies; and by this means it was that four cities revolted from him immediately, Sepphoris, and Gamala, and Gischala, and Tiberias. Yet did he recover these cities without war, and when he had routed those four commanders by stratagems, and had taken the most potent of their warriors, he sent them to Jerusalem; and the people [of Galilee] had great indignation at them, and were in a zealous disposition to slay, not only these forces, but those that sent them also, had not these forces prevented it by running away.

8. Now John was detained afterward within the walls of Gischala, by the fear he was in of Josephus; but within a few days Tiberias revolted again, the people within it inviting king Agrippa [to return to the exercise of his authority there.] And when he did not come at the time appointed; and when a few Roman horsemen appeared that day, they expelled Josephus out of the city. Now this revolt of theirs was presently known at Taricheæ, and as Josephus had sent out all the soldiers that were with him to gather corn, he knew not how either to march out alone against the revolters, or to stay where he was, because he was afraid the king's soldiers might prevent him if he tarried, and might get into the city: for he did not intend to do any thing on the next day, because it was the sabbath day, and would hinder his proceeding. So he contrived to circumvent the revolters by a stratagem; and in the first place he ordered the gates of Taricheæ to be shut, that nobody might go out and inform [those of Tiberias,] for whom it was intended, what stratagem he was about: he then got together all the ships that were upon the lake, which were found to be two hundred and thirty, and in each of them he put no more than four mariners. So he sailed to Tiberias with haste, and kept at such a distance from the city, that it was not easy for the people to see the vessels, and ordered that the empty vessels should float up and down there, while himself, who had but seven of his guards with him, and those unarmed also, went so near as to be seen; but when his adversaries, who were still re-

proaching him, saw him from the walls, they were so astonished that they supposed all the ships were full of armed men, and threw down their arms, and by signals of intercession they besought him to spare the city

9. Upon this Josephus threatened them terribly, and reproached them, that when they were the first that took up arms against the Romans, they should spend their force beforehand in civil dissensions, and do what their enemies desired above all things; and that besides they should endeavour so hastily to seize upon him who took care of their safety, and had not been ashamed to shut the gates of their city against him that built their walls; that, however, he would admit of any intercessors from them that might make some excuse for them, and with whom he would make such agreements as might be for the city's security. Hereupon ten of the most potent men of Tiberias came down to him presently, and when he had taken them into one of his vessels he ordered them to be carried a great way off from the city. He then commanded that fifty others of their senate, such as were men of the greatest eminence, should come to him, that they also might give him some security on their behalf. After which, under one new pretence or another, he called forth others, one after another, to make the leagues between them. He then gave order to the masters of those vessels which he had thus filled, to sail away immediately for Taricheæ, and to confine those men in the prison there; till at length he took all their senate, consisting of six hundred persons, and about two thousand of the populace, and carried them away to Taricheæ.

10. And when the rest of the people cried out, that it was one Clitus that was the chief author of this revolt, they desired him to spend his anger upon

him [only;] but Josephus, whose intention it was to
slay nobody, commanded one Levius, belonging to
his guards, to go out of the vessel in order to cut
off both Clitus' hands; yet was Levius afraid to go
out by himself alone, to such a large body of enemies,
and refused to go. Now Clitus saw that Josephus
was in a great passion in the ship, and ready to leap
out of it, in order to execute the punishment himself;
he begged therefore from the shore, that he would
leave him one of his hands, which Josephus agreed
to, upon condition that he would himself cut off the
other hand; accordingly, he drew his sword, and with
his right hand cut off his left, so great was the
fear he was in of Josephus himself. And thus
he took the people of Tiberias prisoners, and recovered the city again with empty ships [1] and seven
of his guard. Moreover, a few days afterward he
took Gischala, which had revolted with the people
of Sepphoris, and gave his soldiers leave to plunder
it; yet did he get all the plunder together, and restored it to the inhabitants, and the like he did to
the inhabitants of Sepphoris and Tiberias. For when
he had subdued those cities, he had a mind, by letting
them be plundered, to give them some good instruction, while at the same time he regained their good-
will, by restoring them their money again.

[1] I cannot but think this stratagem of Josephus' which is related both
here and in his life, sect. 32, 33, Vol. III. to be one of the finest that
ever was invented and executed by any warrior whatsoever.

CHAPTER XXII.

The Jews make all ready for the war. And Simon the son of Gioras falls to the plundering.

1. AND thus were the disturbances of Galilee quieted, when, upon their ceasing to prosecute their civil dissensions, they betook themselves to make preparations for the war with the Romans. Now in Jerusalem the high priest Ananus, and as many of the men of power as were not in the interest of the Romans, both repaired the walls, and made a great many warlike instruments, insomuch that in all parts of the city darts and all sorts of armour were upon the anvil. Although the multitude of the young men were engaged in exercises, without any regularity, and all places were full of tumultuous doings; but the moderate sort were exceedingly sad, and a great many there were who, out of the prospects they had of the calamities that were coming upon them, made great lamentations. There were also such omens observed as were understood to be forerunners of evils, by such as loved peace, but were by those that kindled the war interpreted so as to suit their own inclinations; and the very state of the city, even before the Romans came against it, was that of a place doomed to destruction. However, Ananus' concern was this, to lay aside, for a while, the preparations for the war, and to persuade the seditious to consult their own interest, and to restrain the madness of those that had the name of *zealots;* but their violence was too hard for him, and what end he came to we shall relate hereafter.

2. But as for the Acrabbenne toparchy, Simon,

the son of Gioras, got a great number of those that
were fond of innovations together, and betook himself to ravage the country; nor did he only harass
the rich men's houses, but tormented their bodies,
and appeared openly and beforehand to affect tyranny
in his government. And when an army was sent
against him by Ananus, and the other rulers, he and
his band retired to the robbers that were at Masada,
and stayed there, and plundered the country of
Idumea with them, till both Ananus and his other
adversaries were slain, and until the rulers of that
country were so afflicted with the multitude of those
that were slain, and with the continual ravage of
what they had, that they raised an army, and put
garrisons into the villages, to secure them from those
insults; and in this state were the affairs of Judea
at that time.

END OF VOLUME THIRD.

Date Due

CAT NO 23 233   PRINTED IN U S A

Made in the USA
Las Vegas, NV
03 October 2022